Feminist Theories of Crime

The Library of Essays in Theoretical Criminology

Series Editor: Stuart Henry

Feminist Theories of Crime

Edited by

Meda Chesney-Lind

University of Hawaii at Manoa, USA

and

Merry Morash

Michigan State University, USA

ASHGATE

Published by
Ashgate Publishing Limited
Wey Court East
Union Road
Farnham
Surrey GU9 7PT
England

Ashgate Publishing Company
Suite 420
101 Cherry Street
Burlington, VT 05401-4405
USA

www.ashgate.com

British Library Cataloguing in Publication Data
Feminist theories of crime. – (The library of essays in
   theoretical criminology)
   1. Feminist criminology. 2. Female offenders. 3. Abused
   women. 4. Women–Crimes against. 5. Sex discrimination in
   justice administration.
   I. Series II. Chesney-Lind, Meda. III. Morash, Merry, 1946–
   364'.082–dc22

Library of Congress Control Number: 2011921468

ISBN 9780754629719

Printed and bound in Great Britain by
TJ International Ltd, Padstow, Cornwall.

Contents

Acknowledgements

The editor and publishers wish to thank the following for permission to use copyright material.

American Society of Criminology for the essay: Lisa Maher and Kathleen Daly (1996), 'Women in the Street-Level Drug Economy: Continuity or Change?', *Criminology*, **34**, pp. 465–91.

Oxford University Press for the essays: Michele J. Burman, Susan A. Batchelor, and Jane A. Brown (2001), 'Researching Girls and Violence: Facing the Dilemmas of Fieldwork', *British Journal of Criminology*, **41**, pp. 443–59. Copyright © 2001 Centre for Crime and Justice Studies; Russell P. Dobash and R. Emerson Dobash (2004), 'Women's Violence to Men in Intimate Relationships: Working on a Puzzle', *British Journal of Criminology*, **44**, pp. 324–49. Copyright © 2004 Centre for Crime and Justice Studies; Karen Joe Laidler and Geoffrey Hunt (2001), 'Accomplishing Femininity among the Girls in the Gang', *British Journal of Criminology*, **41**, pp. 656–78. Copyright © 2001 Centre for Crime and Justice Studies.

Palgrave Macmillan for the essay: Julia Sudbury (2002), 'Celling Black Bodies: Black Women in the Global Prison Industrial Complex', *Feminist Review*, **70**, pp. 57–74. Copyright © Feminist Review.

Sage Publications for the essays: Elizabeth Comack (1999), 'Producing Feminist Knowledge: Lessons from Women in Trouble', *Theoretical Criminology*, **3**, pp. 287–306. Copyright © 1999 Sage Publications; Teela Sanders (2004), 'The Risks of Street Prostitution: Punters, Police and Protesters', *Urban Studies*, **41**, pp. 1703–17. Copyright © 2004 The Editors of Urban Studies; Elizabeth A. Stanko (2006), 'Theorizing about Violence: Observations from the Economic and Social Research Council's Violence Research Program', *Violence Against Women*, **12**, pp. 543–55. Copyright © 2006 Sage Publications; Hoan Bui and Merry Morash (2008), 'Immigration, Masculinity, and Intimate Partner Violence from the Standpoint of Domestic Violence Service Providers and Vietnamese-Origin Women', *Feminist Criminology*, **3**, pp. 191–215. Copyright © 2006 Sage Publications; Hillary Potter (2006), 'An Argument for Black Feminist Criminology: Understanding African American Women's Experiences with Intimate Partner Abuse Using an Integrated Approach', *Feminist Criminology*, **1**, pp. 106–24. Copyright © 2006 Sage Publications; Nikki Jones (2004), '"It's Not Where You Live, it's How You Live": How Young Women Negotiate Conflict and Violence in the Inner City', *Annals of the American Academy of Political and Social Science*, **595**, pp. 49–62. Copyright © 2004 Sage Publications; Yasmin Jiwani (2005), 'Walking a Tightrope: The Many Faces of Violence in the Lives of Racialized Immigrant Girls and Young Women', *Violence Against Women*, **11**, pp. 846–75. Copyright © 2005 Sage Publications; Edna Erez, Madelaine Adelman and Carol Gregory (2009), 'Intersections of Immigration and Domestic Violence: Voices of Battered Immigrant Women', *Feminist Criminology*, **4**, pp. 32–56. Copyright © 2009 Sage Publications; John M. Macdonald and Meda Chesney-Lind (2001), 'Gender Bias and Juvenile

Series Preface

Because of its pervasive nature in our mass mediated culture, many believe they are experts in understanding the reasons why offenders violate the law. Parents and schools come high on the public's list of who to blame for crime. Not far behind are governments and legal systems that are believed to be ineffective at deterring offenders – too many legal protections and too few serious sentences. Some learn how to behave inappropriately as children, while others are said to choose crime because of its apparent high reward/low cost opportunity structure. Yet others hang out with the wrong crowd, or live in the wrong neighborhood, or work for the wrong corporation, and may get their kicks from disobeying rules in the company of like-minded others. A few are seen as evil, insane or just plain stupid. While such popular representations of the causes of crime contain glimpses of the criminological reality, understanding why people commit crime is a much more complex matter. Indeed, for this reason the quest to establish the causes of crime has been one of the most elusive searches confronting humankind.

Since the mid-19th century, following the advent of Charles Darwin's *The Origin of Species*, those who sought scientific knowledge to understand crime abandoned philosophical speculation and economic reductionism. In its place they founded the multifaceted interdisciplinary field of criminology. Unlike criminal law and legal theory that explored the logic of prohibitions against offensive behavior, and in contrast to criminal justice that examined the nature and extent of societies' responses to crime through systems of courts, police and penology, criminology's central focus is the systematic examination of the nature, extent and causes of crime. Criminological theory as a subset of criminology, comprises the cluster of explanation seeking to identify the causes or etiology of crime. This *Library of Essays in Theoretical Criminology* is designed to capture the range and depth of the key theoretical perspectives on crime causation.

While there are numerous criminological theories, most can be clustered into 10 or 12 theoretical perspectives. Moreover, each of these broad theoretical frameworks is, itself, rooted in a major academic discipline. The most predominant disciplines influencing criminological theory include: economics, anthropology, biology, psychology, geography, sociology, politics, history, philosophy, as well as the more recent multi-disciplinary fields such as gender studies, critical race studies and postmodernist social theory.

Criminological theories are rarely discrete. Although they often emphasize a particular disciplinary field, they also draw on aspects of other disciplines to strengthen their explanatory power. Indeed, since 1989 a major development in criminological theory has been the emergence of explicitly integrative theoretical approaches (See Gregg Barak, *Integrative Criminology*; Ashgate, 1998). Integrative/interdisciplinary approaches bring together several theories into a comprehensive explanation, usually to address different levels of analysis; these range from the micro-individual and relational approaches common in biology and psychology, to the meso-level institutional explanations that feature in sociological analysis, to the macro-level geographical, political, cultural and historical approaches that deal with societal and global structures and patterns. Recent developments in criminological theory have seen an acceleration of this trend compared with that of single disciplinary explanations of crime (See Stuart Henry and Scott Lukas, *Recent Developments in Criminological Theory*; Ashgate, 2009).

Although there are now over 20 English-language criminological theory textbooks and numerous edited compilations, there is a need to make available to an international audience a series of books that brings together the best of the available theoretical contributions. The advantage of doing this as a series, rather than a single volume, is that the editors are able to mine the field for the most relevant essays that have influenced the present state of knowledge. Each contribution to the series thus contains many chapters, each on a different aspect of the same theoretical approach to crime causation.

In creating this series I have selected outstanding criminologists whose own theories are discussed as part of the literature and I have asked each of them to select a set of the best journal essays to represent the various facets of their theoretical framework. In doing so, I believe that you will receive the best selection of essays available together with an insightful and comparative overview placing each essay in the context of the history of ideas that comprises our search to better understand and explain crime and those who commit it.

STUART HENRY
Series Editor
School of Public Affairs
San Diego State University, USA

Introduction

Criminology was, at its inception, the study of male crime and largely male victimization, and theorizing about crime and justice followed much the same intellectual trajectory (see Deegan, 1990). Theories that were generated to explain 'delinquency' and 'crime' were actually theorizing male deviance and criminality with a specific focus of showcasing the utility of applying the scientific paradigm to the study of the distributions and causes of these crimes. This development came over the very pronounced objections of prominent women scholars of the time such as Jane Addams, who lamented the lack of concern for what we would today call social justice. In 1899, when she addressed the American Academy of Political and Social Science, Addams took the opportunity to reflect on the role of the social science of her day:

> As the college changed from teaching theology to teaching secular knowledge the test of its success should have shifted from the power to save men's [and women's] souls to the power to adjust them in healthful relations to nature and their fellow men [and women]. But the college failed to do this, and made the test of its success the mere collecting and dissemination of knowledge, elevating the means unto an end and falling in love with its own achievement. (Addams, 1899, pp. 339–40)

Almost a century later, another prominent woman scholar and activist, Jessie Bernard, would correctly identify one more important aspect of criminology's problematic legacy as an offshoot of the sociology done at the University of Chicago. She noted in 1973 that 'practically all sociology to date has been a sociology of the male world' (Bernard, 1973, p. 782). She went on to say that this myopic focus concerned her not so much because of its effects on the women in the field (although she was clearly concerned about that), but more importantly because of 'the costs of this bias to the discipline itself' (Bernard, 1973, p. 776).

Writing about the multiple schools of feminist thought embedded in numerous academic disciplines in the twenty-first century, past-president of the scholarly association Sociologists for Women in Society, Joey Sprague, reinforces a crucial point that is directly relevant to a core aspect of feminist criminology. She argues that there is a virtual consensus that across disciplines, feminist theory and research are characterized by a commitment to social justice. Echoing Jane Addams, she notes that 'understanding how things work is not enough – we need to take action to make the social world more equitable' (Sprague, 2005, p. 3). Expressed slightly differently, we, as feminist scholars shoulder many burdens, but perhaps the most daunting is the one articulated by a British researcher on sexualized violence, Liz Kelly: 'Feminist research investigates aspects of women's oppression while seeking at the same time to be a part of the struggle against it' (Kelly, 1990, p. 107). Feminist theorizing in criminology is ultimately about addressing the twin intellectual deficiencies – the failure to create and use knowledge to promote social justice and the exclusion of gender as a central focus of the discipline.

To recognize the unique contributions of feminist criminological theory, it is important to consider what is missed by other paradigms. Prior to the development of feminist criminology, theorists almost completely overlooked women's crime and they ignored, minimized and trivialized female victimization (Hughes, 2005). This neglect was certainly not justified by the actual scope of social control exerted over girls and women. In the United States, for example, research on the early history of separate justice systems for girls and boys showed that concern for girls' immoral conduct fuelled the so-called 'child-saving movement' which established a separate system of justice for youth and ended up incarcerating large numbers of girls for sexual offenses for many decades into the twentieth century (Chesney-Lind, 1973; Schlossman and Wallach, 1978; Odem, 1995).

When non-feminist theory did consider women, it considered them in relation to men, and discussions of these relations never included details of the horrific violence that women suffered at the hands of those men. As yet another example of the blind spots in criminological theory, even though boys and men have always committed the most crime, especially of a violent type or in the 'crimes of the powerful' category (see, for example, Daly, 1989; Schwartz, Steffensmeier and Feldmeyer, 2009; Steffensmeier, Schwartz, Zhong and Ackerman, 2005), criminologists by and large failed to address the gender gap. Feminist criminologists were also the first to recognize that many girls penetrated into the justice system after they had run away from a sexually abusive parent; they were then arrested for running away or for 'survival crime' and were then criminalized by the system (Chesney-Lind, 1989). This discovery stimulated much research on girls' and women's unique pathways into illegal activity and institutions of control (see, for example, Belknap and Holsinger, 2006; Davis, 2007, Holsinger, 2000; Van Voorhis, Wright, Salisbury and Bauman, 2010) and on the high prevalence of victimization among women offenders (Browne, Miller and Maguin, 1999; Moe, 2004; Richie, 1996). Another first for feminist criminologists was their connection of masculinity and gender arrangements to men's widespread perpetration of harm (see, for example, Anderson and Umberson, 2001; Messerschmidt, 1993). As shown by these examples, feminist criminologists challenged the masculinist bias in their field, and they continue to do so today. Given the growing significance of crime policy and the criminal justice system in an era of government investment and involvement in the 'penal state' – that is, 'governing through crime' (Simon, 2007) – and the resulting mass incarceration of women in many parts of the world (Carlen, 2002; Carlen and Tombs, 2006; Lee, 2007; Mauer, 1999), the feminist perspective on crime and crime policy in modern society is increasingly relevant and necessary.

Another limitation of much social science theory is its failure to explain the privilege and behaviour of powerful people and its complementary concentration on understanding people who lack power (Sprague, 2005, pp. 11–12). Feminist criminologists in particular need to be quite careful about 'studying down' – that is, focusing exclusively on the powerless – which can result in pathologizing crime victims or girls and women in conflict with the law rather than showing how oppressive gender arrangements lead to victimization and harsh punishment. Sprague (2005, p. 195) recommends a corrective in research, to 'work from the standpoint of the disadvantaged' and create knowledge that 'empowers' them.

Feminist Theory and Criminology

In a collection devoted to showcasing important contributions that feminist theory brings to any field, it is essential to describe the 'theory'. The inclusion of women in criminological research was catalysed by the second wave of the feminist movement in the late 1960s and early 1970s.[1] A first task of the earliest feminists was to direct attention to important areas neglected by prior scholarly literature. Adler's studies of women offenders and women addicted to drugs documented issues related to their children, their needs, inadequacies of the justice system, and their uniqueness from male offenders (Flynn, 1998). Adler's book, *Sisters in Crime* (1975), preceded several essays she wrote on women offenders as well as other scholars' research and critiques concerning the changing patterns of women's criminality. Also in 1975, Simon's book, *Women and Crime*, generated interest in women offenders. To explain their empirical findings about women, the justice system, and crime, Adler drew on the work of sociologist Durkheim, and Simon identified the women's movement as the key causal factor.

As might be expected, many feminist criminologists of this period brought the insights of other feminist theorists into their ground-breaking work and focused on women's oppression as a key cause of injustice and victimization. In the United States, Klein and Kress (1973) edited a classic special volume of *Issues in Criminology* on women and crime. The scope and significance of women's victimization was then explored in two very influential books: Brownmiller's exposure of the extent of rape in *Against our Will* (1975) and Martin's *Battered Wives* (1977). British feminists were early to spark the development of criminological theory with the appearance of Heidensohn's path-breaking paper, 'The Deviance of Women' in 1968 (also see Heidensohn, 1985) and Smart's *Women, Crime and Criminology* in 1976. Clearly, a signal event was the founding of the Women and Crime Division of the American Society of Criminology in 1982 (Rafter, 2000, p. 9).

Since the ground-breaking publications and events that began at the end of the 1960s, the exponential growth in feminist criminology makes it increasingly impossible to do justice to all its dimensions in one book. This collection, as a consequence, focuses on the challenges facing our important field in the new millennium. Contemporary criminologists who work from a feminist perspective continue to borrow heavily from the disciplines of women's studies, gender studies and feminist scholarship in other social sciences and fields of study. Often their insights come when they transgress criminology – that is, when they focus on concepts apart from crime, victimization and the justice system; these imported concepts shed light on the operation of gender as these operations pertain to the core interests of criminology (Cain, 1990). All of these disciplines that rely on feminist theory have different strands that vary in degrees of theoretical attention to race, class, ethnicity and other status markers that have their effect on social life and individuals in combination with gender. Yet, there are important key concepts, as well as epistemological and theoretical assumptions, which cut across the variants of feminist theory.

---

[1]　　The women's movement has traditionally been divided into two historic 'waves', despite the fact that work on the status of women can be dated well before the first of these events, and continued in a rather clear form after the first 'wave' had passed. Generally, however, the first 'wave' is recognized as starting with the Seneca Falls Convention in 1948, and the second 'wave' is dated to the publication of Betty Friedan's influential book, *The Feminine Mystique* in 1963.

Patriarchy Matters

While the dictionary defines feminism as simply 'the theory of the political, economic, and social equality of the sexes' (Merriam Webster, 2009), the terrain has been made much more complicated in the years that followed that 1895 definition. The sex/gender system (also referred to as gender organization and gender arrangements) stands as a central concept in feminist theory. The sex/gender system exists globally and in countries, cultures, regions, communities, organizations, families and other groups. It affects individuals by impacting on their identities, imposing gendered expectations on them, and prohibiting and sanctioning 'gender inappropriate' behaviour. Patriarchal sex/gender systems are characterized by men's exercise of power and control to oppress women (Hondagneu-Sotelo, 1994). The degree and the form of patriarchy vary by place and time and even for subgroups (for example, social class, racial, ethnic and age groups) sharing the same geography and period (Lerner, 1986; Lown, 1983; Pateman, 1988, 1989).

The sex/gender system typically functions as a system of social stratification in which both men and women, and the tasks performed by them, are valued differently – with men's assumed qualities and the work they do valued more highly (Conway, Pizzamiglio and Mount, 1996; Eagly, Wood and Diekman, 2000; Fiske, Cuddy, Glick and Xu, 2002; Gerber, 2009). One component of a sex/gender system is the social regulation of sexuality, in which particular forms of sexual expression are positively and negatively sanctioned (Renzetti and Curran, 1999, p. 3).

The feminist conceptualization of the sex/gender system contrasts sharply with representation of a person's biological sex category as an individual-level variable. In feminist theory, gender is not a variable nor is it an unchanging personal trait. A person's gender is constructed through actions and interactions to produce a form of 'masculinity' or 'femininity' that either reproduces or challenges common expectations for gender-appropriate behaviours (West and Zimmerman, 1987; see also West and Fenstermaker, 1995). The sex/gender system at the macro (or structural) level affects individuals by affording them access to influence and resources depending on their sex and gender. Thus, in order to begin to fully explain key phenomenon, such as the gender gap in crime, as well as the sometimes perplexing responses of the criminal justice system to girls and women as both victims and offenders, we must *theorize* gender in terms of identity and interactions at the individual level embedded in a broader macro-level system.

Feminist criminologists (for example, Hunnicutt, 2009; Ogle and Batton, 2000) struggle to keep attention focused on how different forms of patriarchy influence crime, victimization, the justice system and workers in that system. They document inequities and suffering introduced by patriarchal arrangements in order to protest and change them.

Schools of Feminist Criminological Theory

To best undertake feminist theoretical work that incorporates gender into thinking about crime and justice, criminologists must become familiar with the best work on the sex/gender system in contemporary society – which is to say, the major schools of modern and postmodern feminist theory. A number of writers describe in some detail various schools of feminist criminology, legal thought or social science (Britton, 2000; Chesney-Lind and Faith, 2001;

Daly, 1990; Daly and Chesney-Lind, 1988; Lorber, 1994; Messerschmidt, 1988; Ogle and Batton, 2009; Rafter and Natalizia, 1981; Tong, 1998). Here, we highlight selected differences to lay the groundwork for understanding the degree to which these various theoretical strands offer great promise to the field of criminology. These different theoretical strands informed the choices of essay for inclusion in this volume, since each essay selected not only tends to contribute to the field of criminology, but also demonstrates the utility of particular feminist perspectives to the discipline.

The best known of the early theoretical influences on criminology were the notions of *radical feminist theory, liberal feminist theory* and *socialist feminist theory. Radical feminism* stresses that patriarchal gender arrangements lead to men's efforts to control women's sexuality (and their reproductive capacity) often through violence and abuse (for example, rape and wife-battering). Men dominate women throughout society, and meaningful change requires the obliteration of gender differences in power and opportunities (Millett, 1970; Brownmiller, 1975). *Liberal feminism* suggests that gender oppression would be reduced or eliminated by altering the way in which girls and boys are socialized and by reforming laws and their implementation – for example, by eliminating bias in the sentencing of women and men and between racial groups (Bickle and Peterson, 1991; MacDonald and Chesney-Lind, Chapter 15, this volume). *Socialist feminism* made an important contribution to understanding that not just gender, but also class, results in oppression, so, for example, countries where women receive little education and hold low occupational status experience high levels of sexual violence against women and are characterized by women's tremendous fear of crime (see Borer, Chapter 23, this volume; also Martin, Vieraitis and Britto, 2006; Whaley, 2001; Yodanis, 2004). According to socialist feminists, since gender oppression takes on alternative forms and intensity depending on social class, reforms require change in the economic system (for example, a shift towards socialism), not just in the sex/gender system.

New schools of thought continue to appear on the feminist theoretical landscape and they, too, are of clear relevance to criminology. Each school has challenged both mainstream criminology and other feminist theory to more fully account for the complexity of how gender is connected to crime and justice. Although feminism, by definition, is grounded in women's experience, critical male and other scholars have increasingly adopted feminist perspectives in their own research on men and male behavior, as well as on women (Danner and Carmody, Chapter 9, this volume; Messerschmidt, 1993; Bui and Morash, Chapter 10, this volume; Schwartz and DeKeseredy, 1997). A focus on different masculinities encourages research on the links between the pressure to conform to particular aspects of manhood and male involvements in crime. Another example of a productive new direction, *multicultural feminism*, highlights how race, class, sexual orientation, age and myriad other differences intersect with gender to explain the nature of gender oppression (see Jiwani, Chapter 13, this volume; Laidler and Hunt, Chapter 7, this volume). *Black feminist theory* highlights the intersection of race and gender (Collins, 1990; Flavin, 1998; Potter, Chapter 11, this volume) as they affect crime, victimization and justice system processing. Recognitions of diversity are clearly vital to the study of women and crime or criminal justice (since girls and women of colour are overrepresented among those in American jails and prisons), and, for this reason, this literature is particularly relevant to feminist criminologists.[2]

---

[2] This same issue relates to differences between and among lesbians and heterosexual women.

Postmodern feminist theory analyses direct important attention on the role of professional and bureaucratic language (or 'discourse') in the domination of one group over another. This theory also focuses on the 'construction' of truth in such cultural outlets as the media, which, as we shall see in Chapters 9 and 21 of this volume, by Danner and Carmody and Websdale respectively, can play a very critical role in the public's perception of the crime 'problem'. Finally, *global feminism* introduces a world perspective by clarifying how economic and political conditions across First World, Third World, colonialist and colonized countries influence gender oppression (see Erez, Adelman and Gregory, Chapter 14, this volume).

All strains of feminism recognize the oppression of women, but they identify different causes of that oppression, and thus different ways of reducing and eliminating it. The question that readers of this collection can ask about each essay is whether the theoretical framework identifies a source for oppression that then suggests changes in gender arrangements as well as in class, race and other structures. Finally, what does the essay suggest about the necessary role for criminologists in promoting such changes?

Each of the essays in this volume considers the sex/gender system (or more specifically patriarchy) and its effect on crime and justice. Part I, on feminist epistemology, explores the dilemmas and offers solutions relevant to fruitful research on individuals in patriarchal systems, on the nature and impact of those systems, and on how to do research that not only exposes, but also improves, lives. Part II includes essays on patriarchy, crime and the justice system. Part III focuses on masculinities and femininities, thereby calling attention to gender as it exists at the micro level where people enact their version of being 'women' and 'men' or 'girls' and 'boys' in light of patriarchal norms and gender arrangements. The essays in Part IV complicate our understanding of patriarchy by showing the intersections of gender with race, class and immigration status. These same themes are evident in Part V which considers the criminal justice system's perpetuation of inequities and oppression due to gender, race, class and country. This fifth section provides critiques of the justice system that are grounded in feminist perspectives on social justice – notably, empowering the disadvantaged, and placing emphasis on restoring and healing human relationships, non-violence and community (Sprague, 2005; Daly and Stubbs, Chapter 22, this volume). Finally, Part VI explores the ways in which the various strands of feminist thinking might revise and re-envision how we respond to crime in the twenty-first century.

We do not attempt to categorize the essays according to the many strains of feminist theory, both within and outside of criminology. The separation of feminist theories into clear, distinct 'ideal types' (or labels) is fraught with difficulties,[3] given cross-fertilizations and the resultant hybrid theories.[4] In addition, very few feminist criminologists label themselves as to which kind of feminism they represent. However, exploring some major types of feminist theory, and illustrating their impact on the field of feminist criminology, will clearly show how vital these perspectives are to a criminology that includes girls and women. In selecting essays

---

[3]   Feminist typologies of feminisms began with the work of Alison Jaggar and colleagues in 1978 (Jaggar and Struhl, 1978), and typologies appeared in the appendices of essays on feminist criminological theory (cf. Daly and Chesney-Lind, 1988).

[4]   In 1991 two Canadian scholars stated: 'For the past twenty years, theoretical and militant debates and positions have co-existed, mutually influencing, interpenetrating, clashing, even contradicting each other in the discursive space occupied by women' (Descarries-Bélanger and Roy, 1991, p. 1).

for this volume (within the constraints of availability of literature in English and the need to limit ourselves to one volume) we have tried to provide exemplars of theory development that consider patriarchy but also take class and other 'intersections' into account, and recognize globalization as a force that impacts on women's status and quality of life worldwide. We have also tried to achieve some balance in focus on girls, males affected by gender arrangements, women in conflict with the law, gender-related victimization, and the justice system.

Feminist Epistemology

Although all sorts of research methods have been used to develop and improve feminist theory (Sprague, 2005), feminist criminologists have contributed some unique insights on 'how we know' about social life while also challenging masculinist science that renders the researcher invisible. A central idea cutting across the three essays in Part I is that the subjects of research can contribute crucial information about their experiences, and that these experiences must be considered in context to be understood. In their 2001 essay, 'Researching Girls and Violence: Facing the Dilemmas of Fieldwork' (Chapter 1), Michele Burman, Susan Batchelor and Jane Brown exemplify this point by writing specifically about the research methods they used as they sought to understand Scottish girls' experience of violence. Their methods reflect a common feminist understanding of how to do research on girls (and others) in a context marked by hierarchies of gender, class, age and sexuality. As shown by the title of their study, 'View from the Girls Project', they believe that theory should be grounded in the experiences of the people being studied. Thus, researchers must attempt to establish non-hierarchical relationships with those they study, and must think reflexively about how their own experiences shape data collection and interpretation (see also Flavin, 2001). Many feminists insist that research must be done collaboratively with subjects who can provide insight into the key questions to be asked and a credible interpretation of findings (Campbell, Adams and Wasco, 2009; Wahab, 2003).

The second essay on feminist epistemology is Elizabeth Comack's 'Producing Feminist Knowledge: Lessons from Women in Trouble' (Chapter 2). This essay, originally published in 1999, illustrates how, in an improvement on merely applying existing positivist methodologies to more studies of women, examining women's standpoints and postmodern feminism provide opportunities to carry out research that reinvents how knowledge is produced and increases the production of knowledge for women's benefit. Comack provides the concrete example of her study of women in a Canadian provincial jail. She considers the ways in which women in prison experience their lives – in particular, their own histories of abuse. She also describes efforts to communicate selected experiences to her, as 'researcher', and her efforts to understand, present and explain the women's standpoints in writings that challenge dominant understandings of women's oppressions.

In Chapter 3, 'Women's Violence to Men in Intimate Relationships: Working on a Puzzle', Russell and Emerson Dobash link the research issue of appropriate measures of intimate partner violence to the different policy implications that would result if violence is perpetuated equivalently by men and by women, as opposed to usually being directed by men against women. If men's violence often results as a response to women's violence, then conjoint family therapy is appropriate. However, adequate measurement requires adequate theoretical conceptualization of violence and its context (see also Dobash, Dobash, Wilson and Daly,

1992; Loseke, 1991; Melton and Belknap, 2003; Saunders, 2002). Thus, a measure of abuse cannot be just counts of several types of act, but must provide information on severity of injury, victim perceptions and attacker motivations. Guided by feminist theory, Dobash and Dobash collected qualitative and quantitative data from a sample of couples. Their findings justify public policies that emphasize men's violence against women as well as cautions against the practice of double arrests, in which police take couples into custody together.

A central tenet of feminist methodologies is that research methods must be up to the task of producing knowledge that shapes positive social change. Feminist criminologists often collaborate with, and carefully listen to, the people they study. In addition, they often collaborate with advocates to ensure that theoretical discoveries are translated into programme and policy action (Haviland, Frye and Rajah, 2008).

Patriarchy, Crime and Justice

A key contribution of radical feminist theory is the direction of our attention to how daily life reflects 'micro-inequities' stemming from the larger structure of patriarchy (Lorber, 1998, p. 66). Lisa Maher and Kathleen Daly present a clear example of this process at work in their 1996 essay, 'Women in the Street-Level Drug Economy: Continuity or Change?' (Chapter 4). The crack market in one neighbourhood at the beginning of the 1990s failed to provide women with new or equal work opportunities that opened up for men. Players in the drug market viewed women as weak and not 'bad enough' to hold the job of 'seller'. The drug-market economy restricted women to sporadic, low-level jobs selling sex or helping men who took the lead in the most lucrative criminal activities.

Teela Sanders' 2004 essay, 'The Risks of Street Prostitution: Punters, Police and Protesters (Chapter 5) also shows how several features of a patriarchy combine to impinge on women's daily lives. For women working as prostitutes, these features include violence by clients, overpolicing, and harassment by community protesters seeking to rid the streets of signs of prostitution. Sanders' essay exemplifies the simultaneous occurrences of being labelled 'criminal' and exposure to past and current victimization. Feminist theorists have discovered and, as illustrated by Sanders, continue to document the misleading practice of dichotomously categorizing women as 'victim' or 'offender'. Indeed, many girls and women are labelled both victims and offenders. Another contribution of Sanders' essay is the description of how women actively work to manage various risks within the constraints of punitive police and public policies that make it difficult for women to ensure safety for themselves or their clients.

In the last several decades feminists have exposed the disproportionate violence and resulting harm falling on girls and women in multiple contexts of a patriarchal power imbalance that favours men. Girls and women disproportionately suffer intimate partner violence, child sexual abuse, sexual assault and sexual harassment. To show the continued need for theory development on these issues, Elizabeth Stanko, in 'Theorizing about Violence: Observations from the Economic and Social Research Council's Violence Research Program' (Chapter 6) considers the relevance of gender to findings of government-funded research in Great Britain. Several recent studies sponsored by this programme showed that women continue to be overrepresented as victims and underrepresented as offenders in numerous types of violent encounter. Stanko identifies failures to adequately theorize violence against women. One failure is disinterest and lack of programme and policy attention to many known sorts of violence against women – for instance, violence documented in medical and social service records. Consistent with feminist epistemology, she also highlights the continued importance of victims', observers' and perpetrators' accounts of violence in revealing social norms that condone such harms.

Masculinities and Femininities

A key feminist contribution is the recognition that men have a gender: masculinity. Consideration of the impact of masculinity on the crime problem has often been rendered invisible because of male dominance. In essence, the feminist perspective calls attention to gender as something that is enacted in the context of patriarchal privilege, class privilege, and racism. The power of this perspective is clearly evident in Mona Danner's and Dianne Carmody's 2001 essay, 'Missing Gender in Cases of Infamous School Violence' (Chapter 9), which documents how the media accounts of school shootings completely missed the role of gender in these crimes that so horrified the American nation. Surveying newspaper coverage of school shootings in Littleton, Colorado, and Jonesboro, Arkansas, and five other communities, they note that while the media was obsessed with the story, all the stories rounded up all the 'usual suspects' – the general culture of violence, violent media, gangs, the access to guns, youth culture and so on – with virtually no realization that *all* the perpetrators were male and the victims were predominantly female.

Masculinity is also the central theme in Hoan Bui's and Merry Morash's work on domestic violence in immigrant communities ('Immigration, Masculinity, and Intimate Partner Violence from the Standpoint of Domestic Violence Service Providers and Vietnamese-Origin Women', Chapter 10). Here, Bui and Morash focus on the ways in which male violence is produced by the stresses that immigration places on men whose masculinity (and male privilege) have been threatened by the consequences of geographic (and social) mobility. The immigrant men they studied experienced dramatic downward mobility and gender role reversals because of the structure of the their new country's economy, with women frequently more readily able to find employment in the service economy. They note, in particular, that immigrant men found troubling ways to deal with this loss of masculinity; they employed displays of aggression, violence and jealousy – essentially using their physical dominance over women as a way of coping with their loss of status in other areas of life.

What about girls? Well, the story is about how girls, particularly girls involved in crime, negotiate feminine norms that tend to reward obedience to authority (particularly male authority), passivity and nurturance. Consider girls who are gang members. Despite the stereotype of gangs as hyper-masculine, girls are also present in gangs, and present in very significant numbers (one estimate is that that girls comprise roughly one-third of gang members; see Snyder and Sickmund, 2006). Exactly how do these girls negotiate what some might imagine as a quintessentially male space? Are they simply embracing a 'bad girl femininity' as aggressive, tough, crazy and violent gang members? In 'Accomplishing Femininity among the Girls in the Gang' (Chapter 7), Karen Laidler and Geoffrey Hunt do an outstanding job of documenting how African-American, Latina and Asian American girls negotiate not only dangerous neighbourhoods and risky peer groups (since most girls are in mixed-sex gangs), but also very complicated cultural notions of femininity. Contrary to the construction of the gang girl as 'a bad ass' (p. 148), Laidler and Hunt note that girls place a very high value on both 'respect' and 'respectability' They alternately challenge and embrace notions of traditional femininity through interactions with others in a range of settings, but always return to behaviours that involve 'defending one's reputation as respectable' (p. 149).

In 'Girls' Violence: Beyond Dangerous Masculinity' (Chapter 8) Katherine Irwin and Meda Chesney-Lind build on the insight that girls' and women's crime, even violent crime, is not well understood or explained by simply assuming that girls are mimicking their male counterparts and taking up a form of dangerous masculinity (the 'bad ass' perspective). Long dominant in criminology, these theories of 'violence' assume that female violence can be explained by the same factors that have long been studied to explain male violence, since these 'bad' women are seeking equality with men in the area of violence (and acting just like men). Irwin and Chesney-Lind also identify other approaches to female violence that stress not only its roots in female victimization in patriarchal society, but also the role of deteriorated neighbourhoods in producing a female version of the 'code of the streets' tough femininity, particularly for urban girls of colour. Building on these more recent constructions, the authors conclude that one must examine how the multiple systems of oppression (based on class, race and gender) interact in complex but co-equal ways to produce contexts in which girls' violence makes sense (often as a survival mechanism); gender must be understood as something one 'does' or doesn't do while negotiating more robust systems of race and class oppression.

Intersections

As discussed by Hillary Potter in Chapter 11, black feminist criminology recognizes race-related structural oppression, the influence of the black community and culture, intimate and familial relations affected by race, and the nature of women's identities as black, female, of a particular class and so on. Like multicultural feminist theory, it considers the intersections of gender with other status markers (notably race) as components of a person's identity and context. In 'An Argument for Black Feminist Criminology: Understanding African American Women's Experience with Intimate Partner Abuse Using an Integrated Approach' (Chapter 11), Potter examines the multifaceted influences of social structure, community, family and identity on black women's experience of battering, as well as their own and the justice system's response. In the same vein, Nikki Jones in her essay '"It's Not Where You Live, It's How You Live": How Young Women Negotiate Conflict and Violence in the Inner City' (Chapter 12) introduces the reader to her larger research agenda, which is to hear the voices of black girls who confront violence on a daily basis in their communities (see Jones, 2010). Providing an example of feminist theory that attends to identity, context, race and gender, Jones rejects placing the justice system at the centre of the girls' lives and assuming that justice system labelling is a meaningful descriptor for the girls. Instead, she builds theory based on the girls' experience of managing expectations for being 'good girls' in communities and schools that are marked by conflict.

Feminist theory makes a key contribution by identifying and naming often-ignored types of violence directed against women and girls. Also, taking a feminist approach to building theory by hearing from girls and observing their lives, Yasmin Jiwani in 'Walking a Tightrope: The Many Faces of Violence in the Lives of Racialized Immigrant Girls and Young Women' (Chapter 13) has designed a study in a way that minimizes power differences between the researcher and the 'researched'. The immigrant Canadian girls she studied named racism, often intertwined with sexism, as the most pervasive form of violence impacting on their lives. Racist incidents assaulted girls' identities and sometimes disrupted their identification with similarly situated immigrants and supportive family. Teachers, school administrators, dominant-group peers and more assimilated immigrant youth perpetrated or ignored these assaults.

There are an estimated 214 million international migrants worldwide, and 49 per cent of them are women (see International Organization for Migration, n.d.). For several reasons, migrant women are at high risk of sexual exploitation and violence perpetrated by intimate partners (Piper, 2003). For example, women's and their families' hopes that moving to a new country will open up better prospects for education and career than are available in countries of origin has made women's marriage migration attractive (Palriwala and Uberoi, 2008). Women who join men as 'picture brides' may barely, if at all, know the men they marry. They often find themselves vulnerable to abuse because they are isolated in a new country, unable to speak the local language and are unfamiliar with the justice system and sources of help. Alternatively, women may be lured to foreign countries to take jobs in which they are exploited or forced to work in the sex trades. These and other circumstances create new patterns of girls' and women's victimization and new challenges for justice system response. In a study of battered women in the United States, 'Intersections of Immigration and Domestic Violence: Voices of Battered Women', Edna Erez and her colleagues (Chapter 14) show how the intersection of immigration status with gender shapes women's understanding of violence and responses to it. Just as Yasmin Jiwani (Chapter 13) showed for immigrant girls in Canada, national origin affected marginalization and identity.

Feminist Assessments of the Criminal Justice Enterprise

Early feminist work on the pervasive institutionalized gender discrimination found in virtually all aspects of the criminal justice system was among the most powerful work done by feminist criminologists (see Chesney-Lind and Faith, 2001). Whether it was serving on juries, being able to attend law school or enter the field of policing, the liberal feminist analysis of how the systems of social control clearly policed girls' and women's sexuality with determination while simultaneously either blocking women entirely from whole fields (like law and policing) or restricting them to roles as 'their sisters' keepers' (Freedman, 1981; Martin and Jurik, 2007) was important work not only for the field of criminology, but also for society as a whole. Moreover, organizations are 'gendered', which means that distinctions between female and male, feminine and masculine, are connected to identities adopted by, and attributed to, people in the organization, and thus to the distribution of jobs and other resources in the organization (Acker, 1990).

One particularly rich example of a pattern of sex discrimination that has persisted to the present is the harsh sanctioning of girls for sexual behaviour that would be ignored in boys. In 'Gender Bias and Juvenile Justice' (Chapter 15) John MacDonald and Meda Chesney-Lind examine this pattern, using several decades of quantitative court data, and show that once a girl gets past the earliest stage of court decision-making she is more likely than her male counterpart to be sanctioned harshly, particularly for the offence of running away (which has long been a code word for a girl who is 'out of control' sexually). Importantly, the essay also highlights the fact that race and gender interact to doubly disadvantage girls of colour.

Complementing this quantitative approach to the documenting of discrimination are studies like that done by Emily Gaardner, Nancy Rodriques and Marjorie Zatz (Chapter 16) which explains how particular actors – in this case, probation officers – within the criminal justice system tend to view girls as more difficult and challenging to work with than boys. The authors start by saying that the shortage of programmes for girls substantially feeds into this, since the modern juvenile justice system is clearly a boy-centric system. That said, the probation officers often viewed girls in 'stereotypical' ways as having 'too many issues', being 'too needy' and 'manipulative'. They also tended to disbelieve the girls' accounts of sexual assault, be interested in monitoring their sexual behaviour, and were judgemental about the girls' and the mother's deportment. Ultimately, one can put the two studies together to see a system that judges and monitors girls in different and sexualized ways, resulting in the enforcement of gender norms as well as laws in ways that disadvantage girls. This finding builds on a long tradition of work, including studies in Great Britain (for example, Gelsthorpe, 1986, 1989), showing the manifestations of sexism in the justice system.

Feminist criminologists integrate their knowledge of patriarchy with postmodern concerns about the infusion of 'experts' whose discourses shape practices and protocol in justice system organizations so as to negatively impact girls and women. In courts of law, unfounded 'expert' witnesses' claims – that the typical battered woman suffers from 'battered women syndrome' – leads to the discrediting of many women who are not helpless in the face of abuse as Kathleen Ferraro documents in her 2003 essay, 'The Words Change, But the Melody Lingers' (Chapter 17). In the same vein, both Kelly Hannah-Moffat, in 'Moral Agent or Actuarial Subject: Risk and Canadian Women's Imprisonment' (Chapter 18) and Jill MacCorkle, in 'Embodied Surveillance and the Gendering of Punishment' (Chapter 19), theorize about the damaging effects for women of the use of expert-driven regimes developed for male prisoners to manage and control women in prison. The resulting female–male 'equality with a vengeance' (Chesney-Lind and Pollock-Byrne, 1995) occurs partly because gendered organizations transform women's needs – often caused by women's low socioeconomic status in society – into 'risks' that require increased controls (Hannah-Moffat, Chapter 18) at the same time that they focus prison staff on policing and punishing deviations from behaviour perceived to be appropriately 'feminine' (MacCorkle, Chapter 19).

In 'Celling Black Bodies: Black Women in the Global Prison Industrial Complex' (Chapter 20) Julia Sudbury provokes us to think about how patriarchy and capitalism cause the United States to promote the incarceration of black women in particular not only within, but also outside, its boundaries. There is no doubt that in the United States the 'war on drugs' morphed into a 'war against women', as women make up a growing proportion of those incarcerated, especially for non-violent, often drug-related offences (Chesney-Lind, 1996; Johnson, 2003). What is often overlooked, however, is the involvement of businesses and US government entities and politicians in promoting arrest, prosecution and incarceration of women worldwide. For instance, US pressure to criminalize people involved in the international drug trade and prostitution had the unanticipated effect of promoting the punishment of women whose only means of survival, economically or in face of pressures from criminal men, is to carry drugs or prostitute themselves (Kempadoo, 2005). Sudbury's essay shows the intertwining of US international policies, racial inequities and the prison industrial complex to produce widespread surges in women's incarceration.

Feminist Perspectives on the Law and on Justice

Postmodern feminism also directs attention to the 'construction' of truth in such cultural outlets as the media, which can play a very critical role in the public's perception of the crime 'problem'. It is this emphasis on culture and the production of knowledge, rather than on structure, that is a hallmark of postmodernism. Two decades of backlash journalism in the United States, which served up constructions of the crime problem that supported mass incarceration, are now coming under increasing scrutiny by feminist criminologists such as Neal Websdale who, in 'Predators: The Social Construction of "Stranger-Danger" in Washington State as a Form of Patriarchal Ideology' (Chapter 21), documents the impact of the passage of a law permitting 'indefinite civil commitment' of sexual predators. Ironically, as he notes, by excluding any intra-family violence, the law creates a discourse that sex crimes, rather than being routine, are 'dreadful, but rare' and require tough sanctions rather than 'social reform' (p. 483).

Social reform of the increasingly punitive penal regimes requires a different approach to law-breaking, which is precisely what Kathleen Daly and Julie Stubbs offer up in 'Feminist Engagement with Restorative Justice' (Chapter 22). The authors direct attention to feminist thinking about 'care' as opposed to 'justice' drawing on the work of Gilligan (1982) and noting that restorative justice clearly tracks with the feminist values of 'care' and the importance of relationships. They urge that feminists advance beyond the current punishment approach to crime, even for wife-battering, given the implications for even more incarceration, particularly of racial minorities, in responses that are punitively crafted.

Perhaps no place offers a greater test of the value of such a feminist approach than the sober assessment of the functioning of truth commissions in violent and war-torn South Africa, yet that is the locale where Tristan Borer applies feminist theory in 'Gendered War and Gendered Peace: Truth Commissions and Postconflict Gender Violence' (Chapter 23). Borer notes that these commissions were overwhelmed and unable to cope with the large numbers of women who came to them to report violations at the hands of men, often relatives. Commissioners were suddenly and powerfully confronted with the profound way in which traditional patriarchy routinely disadvantaged South African women, something that was not seen as part of their mandate in the seeking of 'truth'. Women's silence about sexual assault under apartheid was also noted and explained by the fact that many of the perpetrators were now in positions of authority in the new government, so sadly women's loyalty to the cause of the ANC, plus their fear of not being believed, silenced them. Again, the systems established to 'right' the scales of justice were androcentric and failed to anticipate the dimensions of women's burden under patriarchy before and after the easing of apartheid.

Concluding Thoughts

Returning to the beginning of this Introduction, what do feminism and feminist theory offer criminology? We hope that this collection illustrates that the feminist criminology of the twenty-first century is not a new criminological theory or even a distinct body of research. Instead, it is a rewriting and reimagining of the entire existing field of criminology from a distinctly feminist set of perspectives and values.

The essays in this volume present women as agents – not passive victims or pawns of a system that moves them to break the law or stay within its boundaries. Even though work, resources and gender expectations differ according to sex categories, all individuals have some capacity to shape their lives and act with agency (Lerner, 1986, p. 239). This recognition moves feminist theory away from the assumption that women are powerless in an overpowering system. Theorists/researchers sometimes ignore women's agency and focus only on their compliance with patriarchal constraints (Gallagher, 2007; MacLeod, 1991). Theorists included in this volume document that girls negotiating dangerous neighbourhoods must navigate between what Jones (2010) describes as 'good' and 'ghetto' messages about black femininity, but ultimately they can still be the victims of male violence. Even under extreme conditions, people struggle to assert their identities and affect their own lives. For instance, Bosworth and Carrabine (2001) detailed how women in prison, suffering from a profound loss of freedom, found a variety of ways to resist, cope with and survive the conditions of their endangerment. In the process, they made choices. These choices were constrained by structures – for example, capitalism and patriarchy. Also highlighting the importance of understanding both agency and constraints, and thereby seeing both self-direction and the effects of injustice and inequity, black feminist criminology pays attention to women's resistance to oppression while it documents the toll that oppression extracts.

Feminist theory calls attention to 'what's missing' (Sprague, 2005). In criminology what has traditionally been 'missing' from conversations about crime is the fact that the vast majority of serious violent crime is committed by men. The fact that for centuries (racially, economically, nationally) advantaged men have used systems of male privilege to access the criminal justice system in order to enforce male dominance has enormous relevance not only to feminist criminology, but also to the entire field. Feminist work additionally calls attention to male violence and also documents the ways in which masculinity itself could be seen as criminogenic.

Beyond the idea of gender, we contend, there is a continuing need to better theorize feminist notions of patriarchy. Borrowing from the work of feminist political scientists such as Walby (1990), which identified early on that liberal notions of 'public' and 'private' greatly disadvantaged women, we must begin to systematically think about the links between the observed patterns of women's victimization, women's offending and women's experience of the criminal justice system within the context of patriarchy.

We must also think about how feminist theorizing assists us in building a less violent and more just world, including systems of crime control that take us out of the penal regimes of the past century. Notions of reconciliation, truth-telling (that includes gender) and social responses to law-violating that heal rather than punish and incapacitate will not only better reduce crime, but also humanize the current dehumanizing systems of punitive juvenile courts and institutions, jails and prisons that oppress and destroy not only those held within them, but also those who are employed as guards and wardens.

Theory as a tool to fuel the disassembly and replacement of destructive processes in the name of crime control and prevention is long overdue in both the United States and all the countries that are tempted to emulate the penal regimes on which the United States has become so reliant. Does the new century offer any hopeful signs for such a conversion in theory? The very fact that progressive criminology, and particularly feminist criminology, has survived two decades of furious backlash politics gives us reason for hope. Beyond that, there is the vitality of our field. To do feminist criminology, this volume has posited, does not necessarily mean that one is restricted to what was once the standard trilogy: women as offenders, victims and workers in the criminal justice system. Instead, the whole field can fruitfully be rethought from a feminist perspective.

Furthermore, there is the feminist requirement that we act to improve the social world in which we have found ourselves. This means, of course, that we again confront the question: what constitutes feminism and being a feminist? Here, we would like to conclude with first-wave author and activist Rebecca West's wry, and as it turns out, timeless observation:

> I myself have never been able to find out what feminism is; I only know that people call me a feminist whenever I express sentiments that differentiate me from a doormat or a prostitute. (West and Marcus, 1982, p. 219)

Hopefully, we have persuaded our readers that rather than being an insult, feminism and feminist theory offer criminology incredible intellectual vitality and a recommitment to go beyond the 'collecting and disseminating of knowledge' to seeking a just, equitable and healthy world for all.

References

Acker, J. (1990), 'Hierarchies, Jobs, Bodies: A Theory of Gendered Organizations', *Gender and Society*, **4**(2), pp. 139–58.

Addams, J. (1899), 'A Function of the Social Settlement', *Annals of the Academy of Political and Social Science*, **13**(3), pp. 323–45.

Adler, F. (1975), *Sisters in Crime*, New York: McGraw Hill.

Anderson, K.L. and Umberson, D. (2001), 'Gendering Violence: Masculinity and Power in Men's Accounts of Domestic Violence', *Gender and Society*, **15**(3), pp. 358–80.

Belknap, J. and Holsinger, K. (2006), 'The Gendered Nature of Risk Factors for Delinquency', *Feminist Criminology*, **1**(1), pp. 48–71.

Bernard, J. (1973), 'My Four Revolutions: An Autobiographical History of the ASA', *The American Journal of Sociology*, **78**(4), pp. 773–91.

Bickle, G.S. and Peterson, R.D. (1991), 'The Impact of Gender-Based Family Roles in Criminal Sentencing', *Social Problems*, **38**(3), pp. 372–94.

Bosworth, M. and Carrabine, E. (2001), 'Reassessing Resistance: Race, Gender, and Sexuality in Prison', *Punishment and Society: The International Journal of Penology*, **3**(4), pp. 501–15.

Britton, D.M. (2000), 'Feminism in Criminology: Engendering the Outlaw', *Annals of the American Academy of Political and Social Science*, **771**(1), pp. 57–76.

Browne, A., Miller, B. and Maguin, E. (1999), 'Prevalence and Severity of Lifetime of Physical and Sexual Victimization among Incarcerated Women', *International Journal of Law and Psychiatry*, **22**(3–4), pp. 301–22.

Brownmiller, S. (1975), *Against Our Will: Men, Women, and Rape*, New York: Bantam.

Cain, M. (1990), 'Towards Transgression: New Directions in Feminist Criminology', *International Journal of the Sociology of Law*, **18**(1), pp. 1–18.

Campbell, R., Adams, A.E. and Wasco, S.M. (2009), 'Training Interviewers for Research on Sexual Violence: A Qualitative Study of Rape Survivors' Recommendations for Interview Practice', *Violence Against Women*, **15**(5), pp. 595–617.

Carlen, P. (2002), 'Controlling Measures: The Repackaging of Common Sense Opposition to Women's Imprisonment in England and Canada', *Criminal Justice*, **2**(2), pp. 155–72.

Carlen, P. and Tombs, J. (2006), 'Reconfigurations of Penalty: The Ongoing Case of the Women's Imprisonment and Reintegration Industries', *Theoretical Criminology*, **10**(3), pp. 337–60.

Chesney-Lind, M. (1973), 'Judicial Enforcement of the Female Sex Role: The Family Court and the Female Delinquent', *Issues in Criminology*, **8**(2), pp. 51–70.

Chesney-Lind, M. (1989), 'Girls' Crime and Woman's Place: Toward a Feminist Model of Female Delinquency', *Crime and Delinquency*, **35**(1), pp. 5–29.

Chesney-Lind, M. (1996.) 'Sentencing Women to Prison', in Race, Gender and Class in Criminology: The Intersection. Martin D. Schwartz and Dragan Milovanovic, (eds.) New York: Garland Press, pp. 127-140.

Chesney-Lind, M. and Faith, K. (2001), 'What about Feminism? Engendering Theory-Making in Criminology', in R. Paternoster and R. Bachman (eds), *Explaining Criminals and Crime: Essays in Contemporary Criminological Theory*, Los Angeles, CA: Roxbury Press, pp. 287–302.

Chesney-Lind, M. and Pollock-Byrne, J. (1995), 'Women's Prisons: Equality with a Vengeance', in J. Pollock-Byrne and A. Merlo (eds), *Women, Law and Social Control,*. Boston, MA: Allyn and Bacon, pp. 155–75.

Collins, P.H. (1990), *Black Feminist Thought: Knowledge, Consciousness, and the Politics of Empowerment*, Boston, MA: Unwin Hyman.

Conway, M., Pizzamiglio, M.T. and Mount, L. (1996), 'Status, Communality, and Agency: Implications for Stereotypes of Gender and Other Groups', *Journal of Personality and Social Psychology*, **71**(1), pp. 25–38.

Daly, K. (1989), 'Gender and Varieties of White-collar Crime', *Criminology*, **27**(4), pp. 769–94.

Daly, K. (1990), 'Reflections on Feminist Legal Thought', *Social Justice*, **17**(3): pp. 7–24.

Daly, K. and Chesney-Lind, M. (1988), 'Feminism and Criminology', *Justice Quarterly*, **5**(4), pp. 497–535.

Davis, C.P. (2007), 'At-risk Girls and Delinquency', *Crime and Delinquency*, **53**(3), pp. 408–35.

Deegan, M.J. (1990), *Jane Addams and the Men of the Chicago School*, New Brunswick, NJ: Transaction Books.

Descarries-Belanger, Francine & Shirley Roy. 1991. The Women's Movement and Its Currents of Thought: A Typological Essay. Ottawa, Ontario: Canadian. Research Institute for the Advancement of Women.

Dobash, R.P., Dobash, R.E., Wilson, M. and Daly, M. (1992), 'The Myth of Sexual Symmetry in Marital Violence', *Social Problems*, **39**(1) pp. 71–91.

Eagly, A.H., Wood, W. and Diekman, A.B. (2000), 'Social Role Theory of Sex Differences and Similarities: A Current Appraisal', in B. Eckes and H.M. Trautner (eds), *The Developmental Social Psychology of Gender*, Mahwah, NJ: Erlbaum, pp. 123–74.

Fiske, S.T., Cuddy, A.J.C., Glick, P. and Xu, J. (2002), 'A Model of (Often Mixed) Stereotype Content: Competence and Warmth Respectively Follow from Perceived Status and Competition', *Journal of Personality and Social Psychology*, **82**(6), pp. 878–902.

Flavin, J. (1998), *Cutting the Edge: Current Perspectives in Radical/critical Criminology and Criminal Justice*, Westport, CT: Praeger.

Flavin, J. (2001), 'Feminism for the Mainstream Criminologist', *Journal of Criminal Justice* **29**(4), pp. 271–85.

Flynn, E.E. (1998), 'Freda Adler: A Portrait of a Pioneer', *Women and Criminal Justice*, **10**(1), pp. 1–26.

Freedman, E.B. (1981), *Their Sisters' Keepers: Women's Prison Reform in America, 1830–1930*, Women and Culture Series, Ann Arbor: University of Michigan Press.

Friedan, B. (1963), *The Feminine Mystique*, London: Gollancz.

Gallagher, S.K. (2007), 'Agency, Resources, and Identity: Lower-Income Women's Experiences in Damascus', *Gender and Society*, **21**(2), pp. 227–49.

Gelsthorpe, L. (1986), 'Towards a Skeptical Look at Sexism', *International Journal of the Sociology of Law*, **14**(2), pp. 125–52.

Gelsthorpe, L. (1989), *Sexism and the Female Offender: An Organizational Analysis*, Aldershot: Gower.

Gerber, G.L. (2009), 'Status and the Gender Stereotyped Personality Traits: Toward an Integration', *Sex Roles*, **61**(5–6), pp. 297–316.

Gilligan, C. 1982. In a Different Voice: Psychological Theory and Women's. Development. Cambridge: Harvard University Press.

Haviland, M., Frye, V. and Rajah, V. (2008), 'Harnessing the Power of Advocacy Research Collaborations: Lessons from the Field', *Feminist Criminology*, **3**(4), pp. 247–75.

Heidensohn, F.M. (1968), 'The Deviance of Women: A Critique and Inquiry', *British Journal of Sociology*, **19**(2), pp. 160–75.

Heidensohn, F.M. (1985), *Women and Crime: The Life of the Female Offender*, New York: New York University Press.

Holsinger, K. (2000), 'Feminist Perspectives on Female Offending: Examining Real Girls' Lives', *Women and Criminal Justice*, **12**(1), pp. 23–51.

Hondagneu-Sotelo, P. (1994), *Gendered Transitions: Mexican Experiences of Immigration*, Berkeley: University of California Press.

Hughes, L.A. (2005), 'The Representation of Females in Criminological Research', *Women and Criminal Justice*, **16**(1–2), pp. 1–28.

Hunnicutt, G. (2009), 'Varieties of Patriarchy and Violence against Women: Resurrecting "Patriarchy" as a Theoretical Tool', *Violence Against Women*, **15**(5), pp. 553–73.

International Organization for Migration (n.d.), 'Facts & Figures', at: http://www.iom.int/jahia/Jahia/about-migration/facts-and-figures/lang/en.

Jaggar, A.M. and Struhl, P.R. (1978), *Feminist Frameworks*, New York: McGraw-Hill.

Jones, N. (2010), *Between Good and Ghetto: African American Girls and Inner City Violence*, New Brunswick, NJ : Rutgers University Press.

Johnson, P. (2003), *Inner Lives: Voices of African American Women in Prison*, New York: New York University Press.

Kelly, L. (1990)."Journeying in Reverse: possibilities and problems in feminist research on sexual violence. In L. Gelsthorpe and A. Morris (eds). Feminist Perspectives in Criminology. Milton Keynes: Open University Press.

Kempadoo, K. (ed.) (2005), *Trafficking and Prostitution Reconsidered: New Perspectives on Migration, Sex Work, and Human Rights*, Boulder, CO: Paradigm Publishers.

Klein, D. and Kress, J. (eds) (1973), 'Women, Crime and Criminology', *Issues in Criminology*, **8**(3).

Lee, M. (2007), 'Women's Imprisonment as a Mechanism of Migration Control in Hong Kong', *British Journal of Criminology*, **47**(6), pp. 847-60.

Lerner, G. (1986), *The Creation of Patriarchy*, New York: Oxford University Press.

Loseke, D.R. (1991), 'Reply to Murray Straus: Readings on "Discipline and Deviance"', *Social Problems*, **38**(2), pp. 133–54.

Lorber, J. (1994), *Paradoxes of Gender*, New Haven, CT: Yale University Press.

Lorber, J. (1998), G*ender Inequality, Feminist Theories and Politics*, Los Angeles, CA: Roxbury.

Lown, J. (1983), 'Not So Much a Factory, More a Form of Patriarchy: Gender and Class during Industrialisation', in E. Gamarnikow, D. Morgan, J. Purvis and D. Taylorson (eds), *Gender, Class and Work*, London: Heinemann, pp. 28–45.

MacLeod, A. (1991), *Accommodating Protest: Working Women, the New Veiling, and Change in Cairo*, New York: Columbia University Press.

Martin, D. (1977*), Battered Wives*, New York: Pocket Books.

Martin, K., Vieraitis, L.M. and Britto, S. (2006), 'Gender Equality and Women's Absolute Status – A Test of the Feminist Models of Rape', *Violence Against Women*, **12**(4), pp. 321–39.

Martin, S.E. and Jurik, N.C. (2007), *Doing Justice, Doing Gender: Women in Legal and Criminal Justice Occupations*, Thousand Oaks, CA: Sage.

Mauer, M. (1999), *Race to Incarcerate*, New York: The New Press.

Melton, H.C. and Belknap, J. (2003), 'He Hits, She Hits: Assessing Gender Differences and Similarities in Officially Reported Intimate Partner Violence', *Criminal Justice and Behavior*, **30**(3), pp. 328–48.

Merriam-Webster Dictionary at: http://www.merriam-webster.com/dictionary/feminist (accessed 31 March 2009).

Messerschmidt, J.W. (1988), 'From Marx to Bonger: Socialist Writings on Women, Gender, and Crime', *Sociological Inquiry*, **58**(4), pp. 378–92.

Messerschmidt, J. (1993), *Masculinities and Crime: Critique and Reconceptualization of Theory*, Lanham, MD: Rowman and Littlefield.

Millett, K. (1970), *Sexual Politics*, Garden City, NY: Doubleday.

Moe, A.M. (2004), 'Blurring the Boundaries: Women's Criminality in the Context of Abuse', *Women's Studies Quarterly*, **32**(3–4), pp. 116–38.

Odem, M. (1995), *Delinquent Daughters*, Chapel Hill: University of North Carolina Press.

Ogle, R.S. and Batton, C. (2009), 'Revisiting Patriarchy: Its Conceptualization and Operationalization in Criminology', *Critical Criminology*, **17**(3), pp. 159–82.

Palriwala, R. and Uberoi, P. (2008), *Marriage Migration and Gender: Women and Migration in Asia*, New Delhi: Sage Publications.

Pateman, C. (1988), *The Sexual Contract*, Stanford, CA: Stanford University Press.

Pateman, C. (1989), *The Disorder of Women: Democracy, Feminism, and Political Theory*, Stanford, CA: Stanford University Press.

Piper, N. (2003), 'Feminization of Labor Migration as Violence against Women: International, Regional, and Local Nongovernmental Organization Responses in Asia', *Violence Against Women*, **9**(6), pp. 723–45.

Rafter, N. H. (Ed.). (2000). Encyclopedia of Women and Crime. Phoenix, AZ: Oryx Press.

Rafter, N.H., and Natalizia, E.M. (1981), 'Marxist Feminism: Implications for Criminal Justice', *Crime and Delinquency*, **27**(1), pp. 81–98.

Renzetti, C. and Curran, D.J. (1999), *Women, Men and Society*, Boston, MA: Allyn and Bacon.

Richie, B. (1996), *Compelled to Crime: The Gender Entrapment of Battered Black Women*, New York: Routledge.

Saunders, D.G. (2002), 'Are Physical Assaults by Wives and Girlfriends a Major Social Problem?', *Violence Against Women*, **8**(12), pp. 1424–48.

Schlossman, S. and Wallach, S. (1978), 'The Crime of Precocious Sexuality: Female Juvenile Delinquency in the Progressive Era', *Harvard Educational Review*, **48**(1), pp. 65–94.

Schwartz, J., Steffensmeier, D.J. and Feldmeyer, B. (2009), 'Assessing Trends in Women's Violence via Data Triangulation: Arrests, Convictions, Incarcerations, and Victim Reports', *Social Problems*, **56**(3), pp. 494–525.

Schwartz, M.D. and DeKeseredy, W.S. (1997), *Sexual Assault on Campus*, Thousand Oaks, CA: Sage Publications.

Simon, R. (1975), *Women and Crime*, Lexington, MA: Lexington Books.

Simon, J. (2007), *Governing Through Crime*, Oxford: Oxford University Press.

Smart, C. (1976), *Women, Crime and Criminology: A Feminist Critique*, London: Routledge & Kegan Paul.

Snyder, H.N. and Sickmund, M. (2006), *Juvenile Offenders and Victims: 2006 National Report*, Washington, DC: Office of Juvenile Justice and Delinquency Prevention.

Sprague, J. (2005), *Feminist Methods for Critical Researchers: Bridging Differences*, Walnut Creek, CA: Altamira Press.

Steffensmeier, D., Schwartz, J., Zhong, H. and Ackerman, J. (2005), 'An Assessment of Recent Trends in Girls' Violence Using Diverse Longitudinal Sources: Is the Gender Gap Closing?', *Criminology*, **43**(2), pp. 355–405.

Sudbury, J. (ed.) (2005), *Global Lockdown: Race, Gender, and the Prison-Industrial Complex*, New York: Routledge.

Tong, R.P. (1998), *Feminist Thought: A More Comprehensive Introduction*, Boulder, CO: Westview Press.

Van Voorhis, P., Wright, E.M., Salisbury, E. and Bauman, A. (2010), 'Women's Risk Factors and Their Contributions to Existing Risk/Needs Assessment: The Current Status of a Gender-Responsive Supplement', *Criminal Justice and Behavior*, **37**(3), pp. 261–88.

Wahab, S. (2003), 'Creating Knowledge Collaboratively with Female Sex Workers: Insights from a Qualitative, Feminist, and Participatory Study', *Qualitative Inquiry*, **9**(4), pp. 625–42.

Walby, S. (1990). Theorizing patriarchy. Oxford: Basil Blackwell.

West, C. and Fenstermaker, S. (1995), 'Doing Difference', *Gender and Society*, **9**(1), pp. 8–37.

West, C. and Zimmerman, D.H. (1987), 'Doing Gender', *Gender and Society*, **1**(2), pp. 125–51.

West, R. and Marcus, J. (1982), *The Young Rebecca: Writings of Rebecca West*, selected and introduced by Jane Marcus Macmillan in association with Virago Press, London: Virago.

Whaley, R.B. (2001), 'The Paradoxical Relationship between Gender Inequality and Rape', *Gender and Society*, **15**(4), pp. 531–55.

Yodanis, C.L. (2004), 'Gender Inequality, Violence against Women, and Fear: A Cross-national Test of the Feminist Theory of Violence against Women'. *Journal of Interpersonal Violence*, **19**(6), pp. 655–75.

Part I
Feminist Epistemology

[1]

RESEARCHING GIRLS AND VIOLENCE

Facing the Dilemmas of Fieldwork

MICHELE J. BURMAN, SUSAN A. BATCHELOR and JANE A. BROWN*

This paper explores key methodological and analytical issues encountered in an exploratory study of teenage girls' views and experiences of violence, carried out in Scotland. Researching the ways in which girls conceptualize, experience and use violence raises a number of dilemmas due in part to the sensitive nature of the research topic, and the age and gender of those taking part. Drawing on feminist debates about objectivity, the role of the researcher, power relationships in the production of knowledge, and representation, this article highlights the difficulties of adapting such principles to the day-to-day practicalities of conducting empirical research on girls and violence. It shows how the research itself has been enhanced by having to engage with and work through this complexity.

'Violence' and violent behaviour have been conceptualized and researched from a variety of philosophical, sociological, psychological and moral perspectives (Domenach 1981). Although these perspectives inform the ways in which violence is portrayed, evaluated and responded to, there is a common recognition of the *gendered* patterning of violence. Extreme forms of violence, in particular, are definitively masculine. It is well established that males account for most violence, most homicides, most violent assaults, as well as most forms of violent victimization (Newburn and Stanko 1994).[1] Hence, violence is recognized as a problem and consequence of masculinity (Braithwaite and Daly 1994).

Violence perpetuated by females, on the other hand, is uncommon.[2] Whilst official statistics give the impression that the numbers of young women convicted of 'violence against the person' in England and Wales has grown over the previous ten years, the figure remains small. Numerically and statistically insignificant, female violence is easily dismissed as inconsequential compared to the problem of male violence. Not only are women involved in violence to a lesser extent, but they rarely participate in extreme forms.[3] When female violence does occur, it is commonly considered 'unfeminine', 'unnatural' and thereby pathological (Heidensohn 1985). The depiction of girls as the 'new lads' is most clearly seen in newspaper accounts of violent incidents involving young women (see, for example, Brinkworth and Burrell 1994; Coggan, 2000; Cohen 1994;

* Michele J. Burman, Susan A. Batchelor and Jane A. Brown. Department of Sociology and Anthropology, University of Glasgow. This project, 'A View From The Girls: Exploring Violence and Violent Behaviour', is funded by the Economic and Social Research Council (ESRC), Award No: L133251018. It is one of 20 projects operating under the ESRC's Violence Research Programme.

[1] In Scotland in 1998, convictions for non-sexual crimes of violence accounted for 5 per cent or less of persons with a charge proved for all age and sex groupings, with the highest percentage being for males aged under 21 (n=1,400), (Scottish Executive 1999). According to the 1996 Scottish Crime Survey, men were most likely to be victims of violent crime than women, with three per cent of males and two per cent of females reporting such crimes (MVA 1998).

[2] In 1998, females accounted for just 7.5 per cent of non-sexual crimes of violence in Scotland (Scottish Executive 1999).

[3] The female homicide rate is 10.07 and 9.25 per million population in Scotland and England respectively, compared to the male homicide rate in Scotland (28.84), and England (13.40) (Soothill *et al.* 1999).

Knowsley 1994; Mitchell, 2000) where such violence is presented as a new and growing problem.

Patterns of female invisibility have also been set by male-centred research investigations, as most empirical research and theoretical explanations of violence have focused on men and boys, and the experiences of women and girls have been largely ignored. Where theories of female delinquency and aggression have been put forward, these have tended to be constructed out of existing theories premised upon male experience.[4] With a few notable exceptions (Campbell 1981, 1984; Chesney-Lind 1993, 1997) there has been little examination of how violence might figure in the everyday consciousness of young women and how it might be mobilized in the ordinary settings of their daily lives. There is scarce information about young women's pathways into violence; the manner in which they are violent; how they use or 'manage' violence; how they deal with potentially violent encounters; and how they desist from using violence. The implications of this relative invisibility are far-reaching. Not only does it present problems for 'seeing' girls' violence, but it also means that we lack an informed theoretical and analytical vocabulary to investigate or conceptualize female violence that is not grounded in male behaviour.

In Britain, work on girls and violence is at an embryonic stage. Very few British research endeavours have directly addressed female violence or the role that violence plays in the lives of girls.[5] In North America, however, academic engagement with these issues is burgeoning (see for example, Baskin and Sommers 1993, 1998; Campbell 1990; Chesney-Lind and Shelden 1992; Chesney-Lind 1997). For the most part, this interest has centred on gang involvement and the experiences of girls who are struggling at the socio-economic and socio-cultural margins and who are mostly black or Hispanic.[6] Whilst this research provides a useful theoretical background against which an understanding of girls and violence can be developed, such work is based in a different socio-economic and cultural setting, and cannot be easily projected on to the British context.

The Background to 'A View from the Girls' Project

In our current work, we are attempting to investigate teenage girls' views and experiences of violence and violent behaviour, placing these within the context of their everyday lives. Following Chesney-Lind and her colleagues (1992, 1997) we believe that in order to comprehend girls' relationships to violence it is necessary to understand the social, material and gendered circumstances of their lives, how they live their lives and make sense of their actions, by drawing on their personal accounts. Unlike Chesney-Lind, our focus is not on marginalized gang members, but on girls drawn from a range of socio-economic and class backgrounds, living in a variety of locations across Scotland. For the most part, these girls are not in the juvenile justice system[7] or part of an identifiable gang. Although some of those we have encountered during the research could be described as

---

[4] Such as those with a biological base (e.g. Wilson and Herrnstein 1985), those which emphasize gender roles (e.g. Berger 1989; Hagan *et al.* 1985, 1987), and those which embrace the 'masculinization' thesis (e.g. Adler 1975).

[5] That said, there are signs that academic interest in the UK is growing. When we first began research in this area in 1997, we were unaware of any other similar work ongoing in Britain. Since then, however, girls' violence has begun to figure increasingly as a topic for research (e.g. Archer 1998; Hardy and Howitt 1998; Kendall 1999).

[6] With one exception (Artz 1998), white girls tend not to be included in such studies.

[7] The Children's Hearing System in Scotland.

such, ours is not specifically a study of 'violent girls'. It looks at the everyday understandings, conceptualizations and experiences of 'ordinary' girls. In exploring girls'
everyday experiences, this research differs from much of the North American research
which has taken a quantified view, seeking to understand violence in terms of sociological and psychological variables and factors (Artz 1998: 19). It also marks a departure
from mainstream criminological research on violence, where the preoccupation has
been with the *criminal* violence of the public not the private (Stanko 1994: 97) and much
of women's experience of violence has been rendered invisible.

In approaching the research, we utilized a range of methods including the collection
of field-notes, self-report questionnaires, small-group discussions and individual, in-
depth 'conversations'. Although we did not conduct participant observation with all of
the groups all of the time, our qualitative research encounters were rarely 'one-off'
meetings and some contact spanned over two years. The richness, length and intensity of
these research encounters allowed us to define the style of research as ethnographic.
Sometimes interaction with the young women took the form of quiet chats; sometimes it
was more social, involving eating and drinking and smoking and 'having a laugh'. At
other times, discussion was more formal and structured around particular issues. We
drew on a range of visual stimuli and, on occasion, deployed techniques such as vignettes
and imaginary scenarios in order to elicit conversation. Although we guided the
discussion from time to time and, to an extent, set some parameters for the conversation,
we took an early decision to try to move away from the mode of single direct questions
and answers which is often the mode of communication that arises in adult-young person
interactions. Instead, we chose to conduct open conversations with girls in order to
generate data which, we hoped, would move beyond that which we would be able
to accumulate through other means. Our intention was to be responsive to the concerns
of the girls, letting them talk their own way into, and about, what *they* considered
important.

Approximately 800 girls, aged 13–16 years, participated in one or more aspects of our
study, a small number of whom had been formally labelled as 'troublesome' or 'violent'
or 'at risk' by the education or juvenile justice system. We had a number of reasons for
focusing on this particular age range. It has been argued that it represents a crucial time
for the development of feminine identity (Hey 1997; Lees 1986). It is also a time when
girls are nearing transition to the adult world and when they are facing important
decisions about their futures, and when their social worlds, life chances and experiences
are characterized by 'risks' associated with that transition (Cartmel and Furlong 1997).
Perhaps most significantly, it is a time when girls learn how to take up their place in
hierarchies and regimes of structural power (Hey 1997) and occupy gendered subject
positions. The experience of 'being a girl' is intrinsically bound up with gender, class,
race, age and sexuality. These categories operate as organizing principles in girls' everyday lives, imposing limits and boundaries on acceptable and unacceptable behaviour,
and structuring opportunities. Additionally, and importantly, girls of this age have gone
through the process of acquiring knowledge about what society will or will not tolerate in
terms of unacceptable behaviour and what happens (or does not happen) when certain
rules are broken or norms infracted.

There were other more conventionally criminological reasons for focusing on this age
group. For both boys and girls this period is identified as an important time for the onset
of offending behaviour, drug use, truancy and running away from home (Graham and

Bowling 1995). Whilst Home Office figures show an increase in 14–17 year olds convicted of 'violence against the person', this is in contrast to a considerable decrease in the number of females aged 18–20 years involved in such offences.[8] There is also an increasing awareness that the young are at a relatively high risk of violence, particularly from those known to them. Crime surveys show that young people (aged 16–24) of both sexes experience disproportionately more violence than older people, and that females experience very different types of violence to males, with 30 per cent of incidents of violence against women (in all age groups) classed as domestic violence, compared to only 3 per cent of incidents against men.[9] Young women are also more fearful of violence (particularly sexual violence). In the 1996 Scottish Crime Survey approximately half of the respondents in the Young Person's sample said that they were 'very' or 'fairly' worried for each type of crime, with females being more likely to be worried about being a victim of any of the types of crime listed.[10]

Feminist Method and Girls' Experience

We characterize this work as 'feminist' on the basis of our epistemological positioning and the methodological decisions made in advance of commencing the study. We assume, as Ramazanoglu has put it (1989), that a key imperative of feminist research is to produce knowledge that provides 'understanding of [women's] experience as they understand it, interpretation of their experience in the light of feminist conceptions of gendered relationships, and a critical understanding of the research process' (1989: 435). Hence our theoretical framework was complemented by reflection on appropriate methods for researching girls and violence and concern for the ethics of our research practice.

Although there is a lack of consensus amongst feminist researchers about what exactly constitutes 'feminist methodology' (Gelsthorpe 1992), there is a common insistence that gender and power, and particularly the interplay of the two, are central to the research endeavour (Harding 1987). Moreover, feminists have turned attention to the fluctuating and fluid nature of power, and the need to attend to gender and power relations between researchers and the researched within the research process.[11] This attention has played out in a refusal to treat women as objects of research, and led to attempts to engage them as active subjects in all stages of the research process (Stanley and Wise 1990). Additionally (and relatedly), there is an emphasis on the significance of reflexivity on the part of the researcher. Feminist concerns with reflexivity stress the situating of

---

[8] According to the Home Office, due to the disproportionate increase in offending amongst younger (under 18), female offenders, the peak age of offending dropped from 18 in 1997 to 15 in 1998 ((1999) Cautions, Court Proceedings and Sentencing, E&W, 1998).

[9] Domestic violence is defined as those incidents involving partners, ex-partners, household members and other relatives (MVA 1998).

[10] Two out of three female respondents said that they were worried about being sexually assaulted, attacked in the street, mugged and robbed (MVA 1998).

[11] Whilst other critical methodological perspectives (e.g. Marxists, Critical Theorists), have offered similar criticisms of social science research (about the need for dialogue with research participants, ethical considerations, and reflexivity within the research process, for example), feminist perspectives remain distinctive in their insistence upon the centrality of gender *and* power. Other perspectives often ignore or marginalize gender; sometimes perpetuating gendered power relations within the research process.

the researcher and understanding her 'personal history' (or 'herstory'), her lived experience (including the relation of research to experience), as integral to the research process (Maynard 1994). Reflexivity also entails a consideration of the *effects* of the experience of fieldwork on the researcher.

These considerations have been particularly important in the context of our study, translating into a number of imperatives that structured our approach. These were: a commitment to ground the study in young women's experiences of violence, hearing their accounts and privileging their subjective views; framing the research as a collaborative exercise in an attempt to reject hierarchical relationships within the research process; and attempting to make explicit the reasoning procedures that we use in carrying out our research (Morris *et al.* 1998) in the recognition that we as researchers are a central part of the research process. A central objective was to try to produce a reflexive, feminist account of knowledge production, whereby we made visible the specific social and political context shaping our research engagement with epistemological, methodological and ethical issues, and also with the interpretation of the 'data' that we generate.

The imperatives structuring the research, coupled with the volatile and sensitive nature of the research topic (violence) and the age and gender of those taking part (teenage girls), together threw up methodological, analytical and ethical dilemmas and practical challenges that form the basis of discussion in the rest of this paper.

Framing the Research as a Collaborative Exercise

Research with young people raises particular ethical issues (see Alderson 1995) in addition to the demands of 'good research practice'. From preliminary work in this area, we were aware of the complexity and the sensitivity of the research topic and of the imbalance of power between the girls and ourselves.[12] Asking research participants about their views and experiences of violence necessarily entails the disclosure of potentially sensitive material. This has implications not only relating to the exploitation of participants' vulnerabilities for the sake of career advancement (Finch 1984: 80; Skeggs 1994: 81), but also in terms of the personal, emotional, psychological and social effects of disclosing painful or personal incidents. As researchers, we had the power to define the research situation, to steer the agenda along a certain course, to control the information we ourselves were prepared to disclose, and also to shape the production of the data (Holland and Ramazanoglu 1994).

Attempting to maintain non-hierarchical power relations and foster collaboration proved difficult on a number of levels. Social and legal rules position young people as minors with few decision-making powers, and so accessing girls under the age of 16 involved gaining consent from adult gatekeepers, such as parents and teachers. Gaining consent from girls themselves does not ensure certainty either, because of their marginalized social, political and economic position. As James *et al.* (1998) recognize, such vulnerabilities may put young people 'at risk' in the research relationship through their placing of 'too much' trust in the adult researcher (1998: 187).

---

[12] Burman *et al.* (1997), *Report to the Calouste Gulbenkian Foundation* (unpublished).

In participating in the research, most girls were entering unfamiliar territory, unsure of what was required of them, of what was entailed in 'research' and of each of our respective roles. Very few had encountered researchers before and, perhaps more significantly, rarely encountered adults who were interested in what they had to say. Consequently, initial contact was very important in setting the tone of the research encounter.[13] Obtaining informed consent required that we tell potential participants what involvement entailed; yet, this was in itself problematic. An important aim of the research was to unpick girls' own meanings and definitions, for example of what they considered 'counted' as violence, and where violence 'fitted' into their lives. Hence, while we needed to explain the research and why it was being done, this had to be achieved without pre-defining the 'problem' or leading girls to give the responses they thought we were anticipating.[14]

From the outset, we stressed our general concern with girls' lives, but also our particular interest in their views and experiences of violence. A significant (but unsurprising) consequence of our decision to 'come clean' about the research topic was that, practically, it became very difficult to overcome the assumption that we were solely interested in the 'problem of violence'. So pervasive and powerful are the associations of violence that it quickly became prioritized as the template for discussion. Girls very rapidly moved on to talking about violence, often offering deeply personal accounts of victimization or involvement in violence, without much preamble. We were surprised at the frequency with which many girls articulated a clear 'need' to talk about the many forms of behaviour they experienced as violence or abuse, its impact on their lives, and their feelings about being subjected to or using violence. In retrospect, we underestimated the centrality of violence and abuse (verbal, physical, emotional and sexual), and the fear of violence, to young peoples' lives.[15]

One means advanced by researchers to redress the balance of power between themselves and their research participants is through reciprocity (Golde 1970/1986). As Hammersley and Atkinson have noted, 'It is hard to expect 'honesty' and 'frankness' while never being frank and honest about oneself' (1995: 91). Throughout the course of the research, girls were curious about our personal biographies and asked specific questions about our personal lives ('Are you two best friends?' or 'Do you have children?') and our past violent experiences ('Were you ever bullied?' or 'Have you ever been in a fight?'). Whilst such exchanges can facilitate the generation of much useful and important 'data', they must be handled sensitively as investment of personal identity in the research relationship can be risky and exploitative. Generally, we did our best to respond to personal questions at the end of the interview, but this was not always possible (for example, where respondents left suddenly). A particular problem we faced was in deciding how much self-disclosure was appropriate or fruitful. Commitment to

---

[13] This involved an initial visit by two researchers to introduce the project and distribute consent information. The aim was to encourage involvement in the project, whilst providing girls with the chance to go away and think about whether or not they wished to take part.

[14] Brannen (1988), highlights the problems of whether and how to name the topic under investigation; whether or not to reveal all at the outset, and whether or not to set the boundaries of the research (1988: 553).

[15] More than half of the girls in the quantitative sample said they were worried about being sexually attacked (58 per cent), or bullied (50 per cent). The overwhelming majority (91 per cent), had suffered verbal abuse, whilst 41 per cent had experienced someone deliberately hitting, kicking or punching them. A massive 98.5 per cent had witnessed at first hand some form of interpersonal physical violence, and 70 per cent had witnessed five or more different violent acts.

reflexivity suggests that the researcher disclose what are often intensely personal experiences and private emotions. In practice, however, the sensitivity of the research topic, combined with our own feelings of vulnerability, meant that we sometimes felt reluctant about exposing aspects of our own intimate relations.[16]

Group discussions have been proposed as effective in defusing the balance of power between researcher and researched (Barbour and Kitzinger 1999). Such groups dilute the effect of adult-young person power relationships and afford the opportunity of generating data in a situation more closely resembling that of other contexts involving interaction with a peer group. But there are issues of power *within* young people's peer groups to consider (Green and Hart 1999), particularly where participants disclose private intimacies in front of peers with whom they 'have a life' beyond the research. For some girls the group setting provided valuable peer support, in that it allowed them to express their views in an atmosphere of trust and minimal embarrassment. As Kelly (1988) has noted, the process of discussing violence can sometimes lead to a reflexive review of the respondent's experience; disclosure can be a means through which participants' experiences are validated (Currie and MacLean 1997: 167). Many girls maintained that taking part in the research enabled them to reflect upon their experiences and gain better understanding of the role and impact of violence in their lives.

For other girls the group format proved inhibiting. Some were clearly distressed at the turn taken by discussions and we, as researchers, needed to be not only attuned to the possibility of such situations arising, but also equipped to make quick decisions when they occurred. What do you do, for example, if a participant looks like she is about to cry? Or if someone discloses information that is distressing, not only for themselves, but for the other girls present? Should you fill 'uncomfortable silences', or should you sit back and let the participants speak? Questions such as these raise further queries about the appropriate researcher response, for example whether it is better to refocus the discussion on to safer ground (and risk invalidating an individual's experience) or halt the proceedings altogether (thereby drawing attention to the individual girl). In some cases, leaving girls themselves to fill 'uncomfortable silences' can be very revealing—in terms of who says what—but in others it is not appropriate. And one can always explore individual girls' disclosures further in a different (individual interview) setting.

Whereas some researchers argue, on pragmatic grounds, for ethical guidelines to be used on a more or less discretionary basis (e.g. Punch 1986); others point to the way in which ethnography poses a contradiction between feminist ethics and methods (e.g. Holland and Ramazanoglu 1994). A key issue is the inherent tension set up between the aims of research (to 'elicit information') and ethical concerns (to 'protect' those taking part). Having given informed consent, participants should (in theory, anyway) be aware of the potential harm and consequences of disclosure, though it is still the responsibility of the researcher to renegotiate this consent *throughout* the research encounter and in doing so to minimize harm. Our agreed strategy was to allow girls themselves to define how far distressing experiences should be talked about (be this through verbal or non-verbal means). That said, there were instances when *we* felt the need to steer the

---

[16] Other researchers have written about their ambivalence about wanting to preserve their privacy while asking others to make public parts of their private experience (Mauthner 1998; Bell 1998).

conversation away from sensitive issues, particularly in the group discussions conducted in drop-in centres and youth cafes, where there was a lack of privacy and lots of comings and goings by others not part of the group.[17]

While issues of power and control were clearly crucial, it would be inaccurate to depict girls as completely powerless in the research setting. There were many ways in which girls challenged and contested our power as researchers, for example, by not turning up to pre-arranged meetings, walking out in the middle of interviews, disrupting discussions via interpersonal violence and resisting attempts to restore order. Girls often arrived with pre-arranged appointments (e.g. to meet friends, to go to the cinema, to go shopping), and in doing so set us clearly defined time limits for discussion. A few brought along friends and boyfriends who would sit in on the discussion but refused to take part. Throughout the research, girls challenged our preconceptions about violence and abuse (emphasizing, for example, the serious consequences of verbal abuse and/or disputes among friends, or the 'naturalness' and 'fun' of sibling aggression or physical games), making us reconsider our ideas and reassess our theoretical (and political) positions.

Provoking Violence?

In the research setting, girls' accounts and definitions of violence were the result of their interaction with us as researchers. Girls were oriented towards thinking and talking about violence in advance of each encounter and they told their stories—and acted out their behaviour—as a direct result of our interest and intervention. As 'skilled' researchers, we structured and controlled each encounter; sometimes (it seemed) bordering on the coercive in our pursuit of information. We implicitly challenged girls' views by asking further questions, for expansion of particular points, and requesting examples, using language ('And then what happened?') as well as our bodies (posturing, leaning forward) to show active interest. Viewed this way, there is little difference between encouraging violent talk and the generating of 'data'; the research encounter itself has the potential to resemble and reproduce violence.[18]

By saying to girls that we are taking their accounts and views of violence seriously, we run the risk of contributing violence by and between girls, within and out with the research setting. There were several incidents where talk of violence spilled out into the acting out of physical violence. In some cases, girls spontaneously began to demonstrate certain tactics and manoeuvres. Whilst for the most part these demonstrations were accompanied by much laughter, on a couple of occasions they spilled over into 'serious' fights, and reminded us of the need for ground rules. One particular incident—a fist fight between two 14 year olds, where one girl was pushed into a glass door and hurt quite badly—arose from our use of vignettes and role-playing activities. We abandoned the use of such material thereafter.

---

[17] Some discussions were held in girls' regular meeting places, usually informal settings where complete privacy was often impossible, with people playing pool or listening to music. In youth centres, we were often unable to secure a private room and discussions took place in an office or kitchen. This is a common problem in research. Maintaining confidentiality in such settings is a tricky issue.

[18] Of course, this observation must be balanced with the fact that the purpose of our research was to generate 'data' on girls' views and experiences of violence and violent behaviour. In other words, producing 'talk' about violence was part of the job.

Violence research has the ability to revive old antagonisms and stir up latent harms not only in the fieldwork setting, but also beyond (Renzetti and Lee 1993; Kelly 1988). One notable example took place in a residential home where, shortly after completing the self-report questionnaire, one girl had what staff there termed a 'violent outburst'. We heard her being dragged, literally kicking and screaming, by care staff back to her room. Such incidents raise ethical concerns about conducting research in such settings and underline the unpredictability of each research encounter. We have little idea, in advance, of the fragility of girls' friendships, their family backgrounds, personal histories, and the legacies of violence in their own lives. This information can sometimes be gleaned from youth workers or other key informants, but is of little use when new girls, with unknown alliances and festering conflicts, turn up to participate in the study.

Interpreting Data—Making Sense of Experience

In conducting this research, we were aware of the importance of remaining reflexive, recognizing that our own (personal and theoretical) assumptions and beliefs needed to be carefully dissected and explicated in terms of their effects on the research process. Research of this nature inevitably involves issues of the personal, the emotional, and the self. As Coffey articulates, 'The memory that is brought to bear is both uniquely biographical and collective. The personal experience of autobiographical memory is organised through socially shared resources' (1999: 127). Researchers approach research both as academics and as individuals with personal lived experiences. As women who were once girls we shifted between being researcher/observer/listener to participant, as aspects of girls' experiences resonated with our own.

Several writers are alert to the effects on researchers of doing sensitive research (see, for example, Kelly 1988; Brannen 1988; Moran-Ellis 1996). Reactions may, in part, be due to the emotional intensity of the stories narrated, but sometimes fieldwork stirs up emotional issues of one's own. The present study has thrown up a myriad of painful disclosures, including: domestic violence, self-harm, being bullied, attempted suicide, rape, torture, as well as mental, physical and sexual abuse. Many of the research conversations were emotionally draining and demanding and, even now, at the writing up stage, it is hard to get away from the impact of some of the stories presented. Relistening to the tapes and rereading transcripts bring the research encounter back to life, often in vivid detail, and can exacerbate the emotions originally experienced (Bourne 1998: 99). Working as a four-person team meant that we were lucky insofar as we were able to discuss emotionally disturbing material in a mutually supportive environment.[19] Each of us was privy to fieldwork experiences that were distressing and as a result we had a shared understanding of the emotions engendered.

Acknowledging the sheer intensity of the emotions involved in the study of violence is vital for researchers as it enables us to analyse reflexively the differences between the values of the self and those of the other (Stanko 1997). According to Stanley and Wise (1990), a duty of feminist research is to deal with women's subjectivity, and that includes the (often conflicting and contradictory) inter-subjectivities of researchers and

---

[19] This is a luxury often denied to PhD and other lone researchers working on the topic of violence.

participants. What we see often mirrors our own experience as girls as the girls encounter many of the things that we remember doing or experiencing. A danger is, of course, that we begin to attribute *our* own views and motivations to *their* experiences. In this context, issues of power and control are again crucial in shaping the production of data for interpretation. We need to ask ourselves: To what extent do we reconstruct girls' experiences according to a narrative that is comfortable to us as individuals? What silences do we reproduce?

A recurrent example of where we had to balance our own interpretation of events with those of our participants was in relation to girls' definitions of what 'counted' as violence. In our presence, girls often took part in what they described as 'play fighting' or 'royal rumbles'. This took the form of dead-arm punches, arm wrenching, hair tugs, sitting on and slapping one another—all of which were accompanied by much laughter. Girls explained this as 'not violent', as 'okay', or as 'just having a laugh'. However, we observed so-called 'playful' behaviour where equality amongst girls did not seem (to us) to be the case—as 'play' fighting escalated into kicking and punching, and certain girls seemed targeted as victims. Hence while we try to avoid making judgments according to our criteria (personal or academic) on the intensity of the 'violent' experiences related to us, the only basis we have for this is what girls say and even this can be disputed. Although we have tried not to be tied to preconceived frameworks, we necessarily come away from each research encounter with a view. There is no such thing as a 'neutral' account of violence. Physical violence is something about which we have strong normative views, and these can encroach on our interpretations.

As Morris *et al.* have acknowledged, 'The closer our subject area is to our own lives and experiences, the more we can expect our own beliefs to shape . . . the interpretations we generate' (1998: 222). An example of this occurred during the first phase of the research, when one of the researchers was conducting fieldwork at her previous secondary school. She became aware that a group of girls completing the questionnaire was taunting another pupil. Despite appearing visibly distressed, this girl assured the researcher that she was 'okay' and 'not bothered' who responded by asking the 'bullies' to stop making hurtful remarks—they said they were only 'having a laugh'—and telling the 'victim' that she could sit somewhere else. On writing up her field-notes, the researcher reflected that the fact of having had (what appeared to be) a very similar experience—being bullied by girls at the same school—had had a direct impact upon how she interpreted the incident. In other words, she drew on her own experiences as a girl to explain participants' behaviour (as bullying, hurtful), rather than listening to the their own views and understandings (as only a bit of fun, not upsetting).

Inter-subjectivities exist not only between the researcher and the researched, but also between different members of the research team. As individuals within a research team we each have different biographies (in terms of age, class, cultural background and research training and experience) and so experience the research process differently. In addition to impacting upon what we 'see' as individuals, our individual biographies and self-presentation make a difference to how we are perceived by 'gatekeepers' and those taking part in the study. Girls responded to each of us quite differently and so, on subsequent occasions, with the same groups of girls, each of us came away with a different impression. Whilst attention has been paid to the emotionality, experience and subjectivity of individual researchers, discussion of these issues where there are more than one researcher involved is relatively scarce (see Kelly *et al.* 1994). As the nature of data generated is contingent upon the individual carrying out the research, then individual researchers may provide disparate perspectives and understandings of the research process and the research data, depending upon their varying knowledges, experiences and backgrounds.

An example of this lack of 'fit', between what we conceptualize or prioritize as individual researchers, relates to our recollection of group discussions with young women. All of our group discussions were co-moderated. At the end of each session, the two researchers completed a proforma that recorded details about the group dynamics and key issues discussed (for example, age differences and growing out of violence, threatening spaces, appearance as a key feature of inclusion/exclusion). On occasions, there were differences between what different members of the research team noted as important. Sometimes there were also differences in what they *both* recalled and what was actually recorded on tape. This was more than just an inaccuracy caused through mishearing or recall difficulties—in some cases it was a fundamental misinterpretation of what girls had said. Whilst such inconsistencies can be partially accounted for by the different modes of recording data—one where verbal data is privileged (transcript of tape) and the other where visual and non-verbal forms are evident (where researcher is watching closely for girls' reactions, body-language, posturing etc. as they speak)—the crucial question remains. That is, how do we deal with competing accounts between different members of the research team, whilst simultaneously taking account of girls' experiences and subjectivity? One way of addressing this issue was to ensure that all qualitative data were coded by two researchers. This can be very time-consuming, although it did go some way towards dealing with inconsistencies. Wherever possible, we try to explain the grounds on which particular interpretations have been made, by making explicit the process of decision making that produces the interpretation and the logic of the method on which these decisions are made. In common with other feminist research endeavours (see Maynard and Purvis 1994) we acknowledge the complexity and potential contradiction, and recognize the possibility of silences and absences in the data. Yet our experience would suggest that differences could also be seen as a research strength, as they can foster a higher level of conceptual thinking than individuals working alone. This can be particularly enriching for the process of analysis (Barry *et al.* 1999).

Whereas collaborative research shares similar limitations of lone research, it also presents 'special opportunities for expanding and improving the ways in which [researchers] present their work' (May and Pattillo-McCoy 2000). Most notably, it can provide a richer description than individual endeavour alone, by highlighting perceptual inconsistencies and thereby recognizing the influence of researchers' personal and intellectual background(s) on the collection and recording of data. Of course, the difficulty is that most academic texts require at least some suggestion that the author is offering the 'truth' about the field he or she has studied. We need to be able to present a coherent report to our funding body, and avoid the danger of retreating into epistemological and moral relativism. Research accounts that refuse to downplay the perceptual inconsistencies of two or more researchers highlight that there is no one truth or reality. After all, as Miri Song (1998) has acknowledged, the presentation of a polished, linear account does not in itself enhance the validity of the information contained therein. Reflexive accounts that indicate awareness that they are ultimately subjective are surely more credible than those feigning objectivity.

Disclosure and Representation

A key dimension of our work is to chart commonalties in the ways in which violence is experienced and utilized by young women, against the recognition that their views and experiences are not homogenous and vary according to age, ethnicity, class and personal experiences. In grounding our study in the lives of our research participants, we follow the general feminist axiom that recognizes 'experience' as an essential category of everyday knowledge that structures life in important ways. It has been well argued that experience is a starting point for feminist knowledge (see, for example, Harding 1987; Stanley and Wise 1990) but that experiences remain insufficient in themselves (Ramazanoglu 1989). There are two problematic issues here: the range of girls' experiences and how we interpret them.

Accounts will vary according to where respondents are socially positioned, their memory, and the context of the telling, as well as their wish to talk. Many of the girls in our study had not previously had the opportunity to talk about violence or associated issues, or to think about violence in relation to themselves in the way in which it was raised in the research encounter (thinking about fights between siblings, for example). Similarly, not all girls had the same ability to verbalize their experiences; whilst some were able to give detailed accounts of violence in their lives, to speak in a clear and articulate way, and to express their ideas coherently, others were not. Some girls talk a 'violent talk'; they speak about their own violence—sometimes quite explicitly and graphically; and they also relay their experiences of violence—sexual, physical and emotional. This ability to 'speak violence' also varies across different groups of girls and much has to do with the setting and context in which the research takes place. In some settings, such as residential schools and secure units where the experience of violence is often part of the reason a girl is being 'looked after', girls can be very forthcoming. Girls in such circumstances often operate an informal sharing of experiences between themselves, in addition to more formal interactions with staff that address violence explicitly. On many occasions, girls spoke to us—and each other—about being 'battered', raped, physically and sexually abused by family members and acquaintances and about being violent themselves in words that were forthright, highly descriptive, and sometimes shocking. Other girls talked much more tentatively about violence; some used rhetorical devices in the 'telling' and others did not speak at all. In common with research on women's experiences of violence (Kelly 1988), we found that many girls did not identify or name their experiences as 'violent', and often minimized the harm done to, or by, them.

The second issue relates to the interpretation of girls' experience. There is no such thing as an authentic experience unmediated by interpretation. Stories, narratives, accounts do not remain unchanged, but are edited, rewritten, and interpreted away from the social relationships in which they occurred. Reaching conclusions in research is a social process and interpretation of data is always a 'political, contested and unstable activity' (Maynard and Purvis 1994: 7). 'Working up' of data into a sociological research account inevitably places greater emphasis upon different ways of knowing about social life.

In any research there is always a danger that the voices of particular groups or participants become selected out, misinterpreted or misunderstood and problems of interpretation and representation were particularly pertinent here. In particular, we had problems in trying to find the terminology to reflect adequately the range of views and experiences about which girls told us, and in interpreting the similarities in accounts as well as the differences. An informing premise of the research was to 'give voice' to the cross-section of girls and young women who took part, in order to allow a public representation of their personal and social lives and understandings and conceptualizations of violence. For marginalized (and private) voices to be heard and communicated as public knowledge there must be an engagement with the issue of interpretation. As highlighted above, young peoples' voices are particularly susceptible to being marginalized and girls, in particular, are a socially silenced group. Their voices are rarely heard and they wield little power in the public sphere. Whilst we do not wish to mute the voices of our research respondents, there is a delicate balance to be struck between 'giving them voice' and opening them up to the possibilities of misappropriation and subjugation.

In particular, we continue to grapple with what Renzetti and Lee (1993) call the 'politics of disclosure'. Out of all of the data that we have accumulated exactly what, and how much, should be disclosed, to whom, and how should this be done? What do we include and what do we leave out? Do we apply a degree of self-censorship to some aspects of the data and, if so, which? Should we intentionally omit some material and, if so, how can we justify including other material?[20] As researchers researching private lives, yet working within an academic discourse, we are essentially straddling two social worlds. During the fieldwork and analysis, we are immersed in the less visible, private, personal lived experiences of girls. In disseminating these experiences to academic and wider audiences we enter the public sphere. Ribbens (1998) describes this as being at the 'edges' of different social worlds. Being 'at the edges' results in an inherent tension between privileging girls' accounts, on the one hand, and representing these within an academic framework, on the other. We want to remain true to the forms of knowledge that we gain in such private, personal settings but as researchers we also need to serve an academic audience, and beyond.

From the outset of the study, we have been mindful of the need to try to think through the potential results of our work, as well as possible areas of controversy or contention, as a way of anticipating potential distortions and misinterpretations. Consequently, some early decisions were made with both our intended and potential audiences in mind. Inevitably this brought with it more dilemmas, and forced us to consider, at an early stage, who the research was 'for' (see Edwards and Ribbens 1998). Considering the competing needs of multiple audiences and the methods of dissemination required to meet these needs is a fruitful (if potentially daunting) way to focus the mind. Reminding ourselves about why we embarked on the study has been a useful strategy throughout the process of doing it. A main reason is that we decided that there is value in making the experiences of girls available to public audiences. This in itself raises many difficulties, some of which we cannot resolve, but only manage in a principled and reflexive way.

---

[20] In many ways, this mirrors our preoccupations with what and how much of ourselves we include/reveal throughout the research process.

Conclusion

As the discussion above will hopefully illustrate, whilst we anticipated a number of practical dilemmas and challenges we would likely be confronted with, we certainly did not anticipate the centrality and importance of such challenges (and the means to overcome them) to the overall progress of the research and the insight gained. Having to engage with the theoretical and practical problems that arise and work through the layers of complexity involved has undoubtedly enhanced our research. Notably, thinking reflexively about the research process has forced us to re-examine the role of the researcher(s) and how that has impacted upon the data collection process and the data generated. It reminds us that there is neither one truth nor one objective reality in social scientific enquiry. As a result we need to be able to make explicit both the nature of the dilemmas and challenges that we face, as well as the losses and the gains that result from each of our decisions.

REFERENCES

ADLER, R. (1975), *Sisters in Crime*. New York: McGraw Hill.

ALDERSON, P. (1995), *Listening to Children: Children, Ethics, and Social Research*. London: Barnardos.

ALLDRED, P. (1998), 'Ethnography and Discourse Analysis: Dilemmas in Representing the Voices of Children', in R. Edwards and J. Ribbens, *Feminist Dilemmas in Qualitative Research: Public Knowledge and Private Lives*. London: Sage.

ARCHER, D. (1998), 'Riot Girl and Raisin Girl: Femininity within the Female Gang—The Power of the Popular', in J. Vagg and T. Newburn, eds., *The British Criminology Conference: Selected Proceedings. Volume 1: Emerging Themes in Criminology*. Papers from the 1998 British Criminology Conference, Loughborough University.

ARTZ, S. (1998), *Sex, Power and the Violent School Girl*. Toronto: Trifolium Books.

BARBOUR, R. (1998), 'Engagement, Representation and Presentation in Research Practice', in R. Barbour and G. Huby, eds., *Meddling With Mythology: Aids and the Social Construction of Knowledge* Routledge: London.

BARBOUR, R. and HUBY, G. (1998), eds., *Meddling With Mythology : Aids and the Social Construction of Knowledge*. Routledge: London.

BARBOUR, R. and KITZINGER, J. (eds.) (1999), *Developing Focus Group Research: Politics Theory and Practice*. London: Sage.

BARRY, C. A. ET AL. (1999), 'Using Reflexivity to Optimise Teamwork', *Qualitative Research Health Research*, 9/1: 24–44.

BASKIN, D. and SOMMERS, I. (1993), 'Females' Initiation into Violent Street Crime', *Justice Quarterly*, 10/4: 559–81.

——(1998), *Casualties of Community Disorder: Women's Careers in Violent Crime*. Oxford: Westview Press.

BOURNE (1998), 'Researchers Experience Emotions Too', in R. Barbour and G. Huby, eds., *Meddling With Mythology: Aids and the Social Construction of Knowledge*. Routledge: London.

BRAITHWAITE, J. and DALY, K. (1994), 'Masculinities, Violence and Communitarian Control', in T. Newburn and E. Stanko, eds., *Just Boys Doing Business? Men, Masculinities and Crime*. London: Routledge.

BRANNEN, J. (1988), 'Research Note: The Study of Sensitive Subjects: Notes on Interviewing', *Sociological Review*, 36/3: 552–63.

BRINKWORTH, L. and BURRELL, I. (1994), 'Sugar 'n Spice . . . Not At All Nice', *Sunday Times*, 27 November.

BURMAN, M., TISDALL, K. and BROWN, J. (1997), unpublished report to the Calouste Gulbenkian Fundation.

CAMPBELL, A. (1981), *Girl Delinquents*. New York: St Martin's.

——(1984), *The Girls in the Gang*. Oxford: Basil Blackwell.

——(1990), 'Female Participation in Gangs', in C. R. Huff, ed., *Gangs in America*. Newbury Park, CA: Sage.

CARTMEL, F. and FURLONG, A. (1997), *Young People and Social Change: Individualisation and Risk in Late Modernity*. Buckingham: Open University Press.

CHESNEY-LIND, M. (1993), 'Girls, Gangs and Violence: Reinventing the Liberated Female Crook', *Humanity and Society*, 17: 321–44.

——(1997), *The Female Offender: Girls, Women and Crime*. Thousand Oaks: Sage.

CHESNEY-LIND, M. and SHELDEN, R. (1992), *Girls' Delinquency and Juvenile Justice*. Pacific Grove, CA: Brooks/Cole.

COFFEY, A. (1999), *The Ethnographic Self—Fieldwork and the Representation of Identity*. London: Sage.

COGGAN, A. (2000), 'Debt, Drugs and an Ordinary Girl Turned Murderer', *Daily Express*, 10 March.

COHEN, J. (1994), '"The Great Moll Reversal": Violent Crime by Women', *Sunday Times*, 20 February.

CURRIE, D. and MacLEAN, B. (1997), 'The Interview as a Gendered Encounter', in M. Schwartz, ed., *Researching Sexual Violence against Women: Methodological and Personal Perspectives*. London: Sage.

DOMENACH, J. M. (1981), *Violence and its Causes*. Paris: Unesco.

EDWARDS, R. and RIBBENS, J. (1998), 'Living on the Edges: Public Knowledge, Private Lives, Personal Experience', in R. Edwards and J. Ribbens, *Feminist Dilemmas in Qualitative Research: Public Knowledge and Private Lives*. London: Sage.

FINCH, J. (1984), '"It's Great Having Someone to Talk to"': The Ethics and Politics of Interviewing Women', in C. Bell and H. Roberts, eds., *Social Researching: Politics, Problems, Practice*. London: RKP.

GELSTHORPE, L. 'Response to Martyn Hammersley's Paper: "On Feminist Methodology"', *Sociology*, 26/2: 213–18.

GOLDE, P. (1970/1986), *Women in the Field: Anthropological Experiences*. Berkeley, CA: University of California Press.

GRAHAM, J. and BOWLING, B. (1995), *Young People and Crime*, Home Office Research Study 145. London: HMSO.

GREEN, J. and HART, L. (1999), 'The Impact of Context on Data', in R. Barbour and J. Kitzinger, eds., *Developing Focus Group Research: Politics Theory and Practice*. London: Sage.

HAGAN, J., GILLIS, A., and SIMPSON, J. (1985), 'The Class Structure of Delinquency: Toward a Power Control Theory of Common Delinquent Behaviour', *American Journal of Sociology*, 90: 1151–78.

HAGAN, J., SIMPSON, J., and GILLIS, A. (1987), 'Class in the Household: A Power-Control Theory of Gender and Delinquency', *American Journal of Sociology*, 92: 788–816.

HAMMERSLEY, M. and ATKINSON, P. (1995), *Ethnography: Principles in Practice*, 2d ed. London: Routledge.

HARDING, S. (1987), *Feminism and Methodology*. Milton Keynes: Open University Press.

458   BURMAN ET AL.

HARDY, A. and HOWITT, D. (1998), 'Fighting in Adolescent Females: A Test of Gendered Representation, Gendered Trait and Gender Role Conflict/Transition Theories', paper presented at Psychology Postgraduate Affairs Group Annual Conference, Derby.

HEIDENSOHN, F. (1985), *Gender and Crime*. London: Macmillan.

HEY, V. (1997), *The Company She Keeps: An Ethnography of Girls' Friendships*. Buckingham: Open University Press.

HOLLAND, J. and RAMAZANOGLU, C. (1994), 'Coming to Conclusions: Power and Interpretation in Researching Young Women's Sexuality', in M. Maynard and J. Purvis, eds., *Researching Women's Lives from a Feminist Perspective*. London: Taylor and Francis.

HOLLAND, J., RAMAZANOGLU, C., SCOTT, S., SHARPE, S. and THOMSON, R. (1994), 'Methodological Issues in Researching Young Women's Sexuality', in M. Burton, ed., *Challenge and Innovation: Methodological Advances in Social Research on HIV and AIDS*. London: Taylor Francis.

JAMES, A., JENKS, C. and PROUT, A. (1998), *Theorising Childhood*. London: Polity Press.

KELLY, L. (1988), *Surviving Sexual Violence*. Cambridge: Polity Press.

KELLY, L., BURTON, S. and REGAN, L. (1994), 'Researching Women's Lives or Studying Oppression', in M. Maynard and J. Purvis, eds., *Researching Women's Lives from a Feminist Perspective*. London: Taylor and Francis.

KENDALL, K. (1999), 'Victims of Girls' Violence', paper presented at the British Criminology Society Conference, Liverpool, July 1999.

KNOWSLEY, J. (1994), 'Earrings, Bracelets and Baseball Bats: Girl Gangs in Spotlight After Attack on Hurley', *Sunday Telegraph*, 27 November.

LEE, R. (1993), *Doing Research on Sensitive Topics*. London: Sage.

LEES, S. (1986), *Losing Out: Sexuality and Adolescent Girls*. London: Hutchinson.

MAUTHNER, M. (1998), 'Bringing Silent Voices into a Public Discourse: Researching Accounts of Sister Relationships', in R. Edwards and J. Ribbens, *Feminist Dilemmas in Qualitative Research: Public Knowledge and Private Lives*. London: Sage.

MAY, R. and PATILLO-McCOY, M. (2000), 'Do You See What I See? Examining a Collaborative Ethnography', *Qualitative Enquiry*, 6/1: 65–87. Sage.

MAYNARD, M. (1994), 'Methods, Practice and Epistemology: The Debate about Feminism and Research', in M. Maynard and J. Purvis, eds., *Researching Women's Lives from a Feminist Perspective*. London: Taylor and Francis.

——(1998), 'Feminists' Knowledge and Knowledge of Feminisms: Epistemology, Theory, Methodology and Method', in T. May and M. Williams, eds., *Knowing the Social World*. Buckingham: OUP.

MAYNARD, M. and PURVIS, J. (eds.) (1994), *Researching Women's Lives from a Feminist Perspective*. London: Taylor and Francis.

MITCHELL, V. (2000), 'What Turned This Innocent Young Schoolgirl into Murderer?', *Daily Mail*, 10 March.

MORAN-ELLIS, J. (1996), 'Close to Home: The Experience of Researching Child Sexual Abuse', in M. Hester, I. Kelly and J. Radford, eds., *Women, Violence and Male Power*. Open University Press.

MORRIS, K., WOODWARD, D. and PETERS, E. (1998), '"Whose Side Are You On?" Dilemmas in Conducting Feminist Ethnographic Research with Young Women', *International Journal Of Social Research Methodology*, 1/3: 217–30.

MVA CONSULTANCY (1998), *The 1996 Scottish Crime Survey: First Results*. Edinburgh: The Scottish Office.

NEWBURN, T. and STANKO, E. (eds.) (1994), *Just Boys Doing Business? Men, Masculinities and Crime*. London: Routledge.

POLK, K. (1994), 'Masculinity, Honour, and Confrontational Homicide', in T. Newburn and E. Stanko, eds., *Just Boys Doing Business? Men, Masculinities and Crime.* London: Routledge.

PUNCH, M. (1986), *The Politics and Ethics of Fieldwork.* London: Sage.

RAMAZANOGLU, C. (1989), 'Improving on Sociology: The Problems of Taking a Feminist Standpoint', *Sociology*, 23: 427–42.

RAVEN, C. (1995), 'Girl Crazy', *The Guardian*, 25 May.

RENZETTI, C. and LEE, R. (eds.) (1993), *Researching Sensitive Topics.* London: Sage.

SCOTTISH EXECUTIVE (1999), *Criminal Proceedings in the Scottish Courts, 1998*, CrJ/1999/8. Edinburgh: Scottish Executive.

SKEGGS, B. (1994), 'Situating the Production of Feminist Ethnography', in M. Maynard and J. Purvis, eds., *Researching Women's Lives from a Feminist Perspective.* London: Taylor and Francis.

SONG, M. (1998), 'Hearing Competing Voices: Sibling Research', in R. Edwards and J. Ribbens, *Feminist Dilemmas in Qualitative Research: Public Knowledge and Private Lives.* London: Sage.

SOOTHILL, K., FRANCIS, B., ACKERLEY, E. and COLLETT, S. (1999), *Homicide in Britain: A Comparative Study of Rates in Scotland and England & Wales.* Edinburgh: The Scottish Office.

STANKO, E. (1994), 'Dancing With Denial: Researching Women and Questioning Men', in M. Maynard and J. Purvis, eds., *Researching Women's Lives from a Feminist Perspective.* London: Taylor and Francis.

——(1997), '"I Second That Emotion" Reflections on Feminism, Emotionality, and Research on Sexual Violence', in M. D. Schwartz, ed., *Researching Violence against Women: Methodological and Personal Perspectives.* London: Sage.

STANLEY, L. and WISE, S. (1990), 'Method, Methodology and Epistemology in Feminist Research Processes', in L. Stanley, ed., *Feminist Praxis: Research, Theory and Epistemology in Feminist Sociology.* London: Routledge.

WILSON, J. and HERRNSTEIN, R. (1985), *Crime and Human Nature.* New York: Simon and Schuster.

[2]

Producing feminist knowledge:

Lessons from women in trouble

ELIZABETH COMACK

University of Manitoba, Winnipeg, Canada

Abstract _____

In responding to the androcentrism of mainstream epistemologies, feminists have confronted the broader issues around how we can produce knowledge which will be helpful to women. In particular, the work of standpoint feminists—while focusing our attention on creating knowledge 'for' women—has been subject to the critical gaze of postmodern writers like Carol Smart. This article endeavors to add another voice to these deliberations. Informed by the experience of doing research with women in prison, I propose that by problematizing the differing conceptions of 'standpoint,' specifically, the 'women's standpoint' and the 'feminist standpoint,' we can better address the issues raised by postmodernists.

Key Words _____

feminist epistemology • postmodern feminism • standpoint feminism • women in prison

Introduction

All social theories, including feminist accounts of social life, entail some theory of knowledge, and some theory of how we come to know social life. All feminists are concerned with how knowledge which is helpful to women can best be produced and with what such knowledge should be like. These are epistemological questions.

(Cain, 1993: 73)

288   *Theoretical Criminology 3(3)*

As Maureen Cain's words suggest, our work as feminists is made all the more challenging once we stop to ponder the epistemological questions which emerge from our efforts to produce knowledge which is 'on' and 'for' women. Nowhere is this more evident than in the area of feminist criminology. Over the past two decades, feminist criminologists have made great gains in highlighting the errors of omission within 'malestream' criminological thought and in carving out a new terrain on which to fashion a more women-centered criminology.[1] In the process, they have often taken their lead from feminist writers in other areas of academe. For feminists in both criminology and elsewhere, the task of producing feminist knowledge initially appeared to be a straightforward one. There was a broad consensus which emanated from the point that we knew what it was we were rejecting: the androcentrism of the traditional research enterprise. However, as feminists began to respond to this common problematic, cracks in the consensus began to appear. Sandra Harding (1986) describes three different epistemological positions which emerged: feminist empiricism, standpoint feminism, and postmodern feminism.

Feminist empiricism refers to the position that, although what passes for science has traditionally been the world as it is seen through the male gaze, a truly objective science is possible and can be achieved by 'stricter adherence to the existing methodological norms of scientific inquiry' (Harding, 1990: 91). In this respect, feminist empiricists, by and large, left the scientific enterprise intact and called for more studies 'on' women in order to fill the historical gap which had been created by the exclusion of women as research subjects. Standpoint feminists, on the other hand, focused their attention more directly on creating knowledge 'for' women, which brought to the foreground the relationship between knowledge and politics (Harding, 1993). In its initial formulations, the focus of standpoint feminism appeared to be one of articulating the basis on which feminist knowledge is produced. Harding (1987) describes both feminist empiricism and standpoint feminism as 'transitional epistemologies.'[2] In the eyes of the postmodernist, however, both remain firmly grounded on a modernist[3] terrain. Rather than a third stage or a synthesis of the other two positions, Carol Smart (1995: 45) suggests that feminist postmodernism 'starts in a different place and proceeds in other directions.' Accordingly, postmodern feminists eschew the search for Truth, the certainty of progress and the grand narratives characteristic of modernism. Instead, the focus is on 'deconstructing Truth and analysing the power effects that such claims to truth entail' (Smart, 1995: 45).

No doubt like many other feminist academics, I have been following these epistemological discussions in the literature with considerable interest. Within the area of feminist criminology, I have been especially interested in the contributions of Maureen Cain (1990a, 1990b) and Carol Smart (1990, 1995), particularly in terms of their respective elaborations of the standpoint feminist and postmodern feminist positions.[4] These interventions will be the focus of this article. My aim will be to add yet another voice to the deliberations. Before proceeding, however, some preliminary comments are in order.

First, my intention is to avoid what Liz Stanley and Sue Wise (1990: 46) refer to as the 'uncharitable academic three step' whereby one's position is advanced at the expense of a 'bad Other.' Indeed, what is most seductive about the discussions around feminist epistemology are the compelling insights which various writers have to offer. This has created a certain ambivalence around the inclination to choose sides between the standpoint and postmodern positions. In this regard, I concur with Harding (1990: 86), who sees such ambivalence as a positive force. The tensions between the scientific and postmodern agendas, she argues, are desirable ones as 'they reflect different, sometimes conflicting, legitimate political and theoretical needs of women today.'

Second, it is also worth mentioning (and here I am taking a lesson from the literature) that my reading of an author will be 'particular.' What follows is very much governed by my own interpretation of what I 'think' a writer is trying to say to me. As well, both my reading of—and my contribution to—these discussions comes from a specific place or locale (dare I say, standpoint?). This is not only a historical, geographical, and cultural location, but a theoretical and political one.

Finally, part of what contributes to the 'openness of meaning' of these discussions is the level of generality at which they are framed. For example, there is talk of 'standpoints,' 'subjectivities,' 'research subjects,' and 'researchers'—all of whom are dealt with in relatively non-explicit and faceless terms. To the extent that epistemologies form the backdrops out of which our work emerges, this is understandable. Nevertheless, as Smart (1995: 231) cautions, if we remain on the terrain of 'theories about theories,' 'we risk turning women into ideas or fictions which we then theorize about.' In order to introduce some specificity into the discussion, therefore, I will use as a reference point my own experience of doing research with women in prison. This project consumed much of my thoughts and energies over a five-year period. It began with a quantitative analysis of the responses of 727 women who had been admitted to a provincial jail (over a five-year period) to questions about their experiences of physical and sexual abuse. The main finding to emerge from this analysis was that 80 percent of the women reported histories of physical and sexual abuse (Comack, 1993). Wanting to move my understanding of this issue beyond the sterile terrain of numbers and percentages, I subsequently met with 24 women at the prison. These interviews formed the basis of a book, *Women in Trouble*, which was published in 1996.

During the time I spent with the women, with the transcripts of our meetings, and with my struggle to construct the book manuscript, I was very much cognizant of the cautions raised by postmodern feminists (around pre-given categories like 'offenses' and competing truths or alternative accounts), the prescriptions of standpoint feminism (for sharing a theoretically chosen site or standpoint and recovering women's voices) and the aims of feminist research generally (locating the researcher within the project and dealing with issues of power in the research process). Now that the work is completed, I am moved to reflect back on what was done and on what lessons this particular piece of work offers in terms of the broader epistemological questions that impinge upon the production of feminist knowledge.

Since *Women in Trouble* was very much informed by standpoint feminism, I will begin with a discussion of that approach. This will establish the groundwork for introducing the postmodern critique of standpoint epistemology offered by Smart. Following this, I will elaborate on how I have attempted to reconcile these two (seemingly) divergent positions.

Standpoint feminism

Standpoint feminism starts from the recognition that what has counted as knowledge in mainstream scientific inquiry 'originates in and is tested against only a certain limited and distorted kind of social experience' (Harding, 1990: 95). Typically, this has been the experience of Caucasian, upper-class men. Early standpoint feminists like Nancy Hartsock (1987) and Dorothy Smith (1987) sought to counter this tendency by asserting that the experiences of women provided the basis for more complete and less distorted knowledge claims than men's experiences. Women's subordinate position in society gives them access to two worlds: their own and that of the dominant group. And it was this 'double vision' that provided the basis for feminist knowledge.

In positing women's experience as 'epistemologically privileged' (Cain, 1990b: 126), these initial formulations were criticized for encouraging an essentialist notion of 'Woman' on which to ground feminist knowledge. Subsequent to such critiques, standpoint feminism underwent a process of revision. Rather than homogenizing 'Woman' as a universal category (as in *the* 'woman's standpoint' or 'female experience') later writers spoke of the need to account for diversity and difference, of women's 'multiple realities' and 'fractured identities.' Harding (1991), for instance, asserted that no 'woman's standpoint' existed; women's lives are necessarily multiple and contradictory. According to Cain (1990b: 129), 'there are as many knowledges as there are people. And it is to deal with precisely this point that the standpoint epistemologies have been developed.' Moreover, in claiming women's lives as the basis for its knowledge, standpoint feminism countered the empiricist notion of experience 'in which the individual subject's relationship to her world is taken to be direct and concrete, unmediated by the ways of making sense historically available to her' (Hennessy, 1993: 15).

At the same time, there was a clarification of the nature and aims of feminist knowledge. This centered on the recognition that women's experiences of their lives are not necessarily the same as feminist knowledge of women's lives (Harding, 1991: 10–11; Hennessy, 1993: 15). Rather, a feminist standpoint is a socially produced position, and developing feminist knowledge about women's lives is a political enterprise. This is in contrast to relativism, as the aim is not simply to add to the stock of existing knowledge, but to disrupt the limits of 'legitimate' knowledge. In short, feminist knowledge is, by definition, 'oppositional.'

According to Cain (1990b: 132), a standpoint is 'a site which its creator and occupier has agreed to occupy in order to produce a special kind of knowledge and practice of which he or she is aware in a special, theoretical way.' Following Harding (1991: 123), for a position to count as a feminist standpoint, it must begin in the 'objective location of women's lives.' The authority for the feminist standpoint lies not in the authentic rendition of women's lives, but in 'the subsequently articulated observations and theory about the rest of nature and social relations—observations and theory that start out from, that look at the world from the perspective of, women's lives' (Harding, 1991: 124). Cain argues that, in order to decide which site to speak from, we need to engage in theoretical reflexivity, which means 'thinking about oneself in terms of a theory and understanding the site one finds oneself in.' Theory is thus an essential ingredient of the identification of standpoints. 'It enables us to abstract from the myriad of differences between us without denying them, and to reunite around important sameness' (Cain, 1990b: 134).

For Harding, what she calls 'strong objectivity' provides the means for validating knowledge claims. By this she means bringing scientific observation to those background assumptions which are taken for granted as natural or unremarkable from the perspective of men's lives (Harding, 1991: 150). For Cain (1990b), the aim is to produce 'good quality knowledge,' the key to which is the self-consciousness with which it is produced. This is knowledge which is 'accountable'; the objective being 'to produce knowledge from a site that one has identified theoretically and agreed or chosen to occupy *for* those people whose standpoint one shares' (Cain, 1990b: 136).

While offering more sophisticated versions of standpoint epistemology, these more recent formulations have not escaped critical commentary. In her evaluation of standpointism, Carol Smart (1995) raises two main issues. The first is that, while these revised versions may answer the critics in the philosophical mode, 'standpointism does not have the vocabulary to accommodate the complex meanings now attributed to it. It therefore celebrates difference but speaks of homogeneity' (p. 207). Smart's second point is that 'standpointism is a means of preserving a method and politics more appropriate to modernity than it is to postmodernity' (p. 206).

In addressing the issues raised by Smart, I will suggest (at the risk of oversimplification) that her main difficulty with standpoint feminism boils down to the fact that 'it is dependent on a particular Marxist inspired

292   *Theoretical Criminology 3(3)*

analysis of social relations' (p. 212). As such, it is this aspect of her critique which will be the focus of my discussion. Further, I will suggest that there has been some confusion within the standpoint feminist literature. This confusion stems, in large part, from differing conceptions of 'standpoint' which appear, each having its own meaning and referent. On the one hand, there is the notion of 'women's standpoint' or women's experiences of their lives. On the other, there is the notion of the 'feminist standpoint' or the knowledge which is produced about women's experiences. By problem-atizing these differing conceptions—and the tensions between them—we can better address the kinds of issues raised by postmodern writers like Smart.

'Women's standpoint'

'Women's lives' constitutes the subject matter or the 'empirical point of reference prior to feminism' (Hennessy, 1993: 15). However, unlike the Cartesian subject who exists a priori, outside of culture, women's lives are not self-evident or unmediated. In resolving this issue, standpoint epistemology takes as its starting point the *'experiential subject.'* More specifically, it asserts that all women share a set of common experiences which derive from their oppression. 'Oppression' thus becomes the oper-ative word; it is the oppressive conditions of women's lives which provide the impetus for feminist politics. To speak of oppression or oppressive conditions in relation to women's experiences connotes social relationships based on a power dynamic. Moreover, it suggests that there is a patterned, systemic, or structural basis for that oppression.

Accordingly, standpoint feminists have understood the nature of wom-en's oppression in materialist terms. Women's material life activity—rooted in the sexual division of labour—provides the basis for an analysis of the 'ways women both participate in and oppose their own subordination' (Hartsock, 1987: 175). Whereas Marxist theory views oppression from the standpoint of the proletariat (thereby focusing on activities more character-istic of males in a capitalist society), standpoint feminists seek to make visible the 'phallocratic institutions and ideology which constitute the capitalist form of patriarchy' (p. 159) from the standpoint of the women located within that form of society. It is in this sense that standpoint feminism marks an attempt to give voice to the knowledge arising from the lives of women in patriarchal capitalist societies; knowledge which has been 'silenced or subordinated by, or excluded from, dominant discourses' (Cain, 1993: 74). In Cain's (1993: 89) terms, the role of the feminist researcher is to do a 'midwifery job' in relation to women's knowledge.

However, in Smart's view, approaching women's lives in this manner is highly problematic. By invoking a 'Marxist inspired analysis of social relations' to make sense of women's oppression, the standpoint feminist inevitably pre-figures the knowledge which emerges from her work. Categories like class, race, or gender are essentially *imposed* upon the subjects of the research, who may well not see themselves in those terms. For those included within the standpoint, it means that they have to choose between categories which are not of their own making. While writers like Cain recognize the 'fractured identities' of individuals, her way of resolving this issue of the identification of standpoints is through theoretical reflexivity: 'It is only when we try to think more theoretically that we can work out where the fractures that matter are and why and when they matter' (Cain, 1990b: 134). For Smart, such a response smacks of a:

> revised and disguised form of the discredited false consciousness argument. It suggests that those who analyse the world differently or according to different categories simply cannot see the whole picture which is only available to the theoretician who has followed the correct procedures of standpointism.
>
> (1995: 208)

Smart therefore suggests that, rather than reproducing categorical divisions between gender or race as if they were natural or pre-given, these traditional categorizations themselves need to be scrutinized.

Further to this, Smart asserts that the standpoint feminist's recourse to the existence of more specialized standpoints—as in the example of women in prison (Smart, 1995: 208)—does not resolve the problem, since the question remains: How do we deal with the various accounts that arise from the lives of even a relatively homogeneous group of women? Harding's solution, which is 'to apply rational standards to sorting less from more partial and distorted belief,' does not suffice, since 'rational standards' are themselves far from self-evident. Smart clarifies that she is not saying that 'any account will do or that all accounts are equally valid; we do need some way of distinguishing between them' (p. 209). Nevertheless, *she does not intimate what the criteria might be for doing so.* Perhaps we can get some clues from Smart's postmodern position.

In contrast to standpoint feminism's 'experiential subject,' postmodern feminism focuses on the '*discursively constructed subject*.' This emphasis on the discursive construction of the subject:

> shifts attention away from the idea of pre-given entities (for example, the criminal, the prostitute or the homosexual) towards an understanding of how such subjects come into being at certain historical moments. This entails a significant shift in perception away from the idea that people exist in an a priori state, waiting for institutions to act upon them, towards thinking about subjects who are being continually constituted and who also constitute themselves through language/discourse.
>
> (Smart, 1995: 8)

294   *Theoretical Criminology 3(3)*

Such a formulation has the benefit of further developing the notion that women's lives are never unmediated. It thereby directs our attention toward the task of deconstructing the discourses—including dominant ones—which inform understandings of experience. As Smart (1992) argues, such an approach also has the advantage of avoiding essentialism, since viewing dominant discourses as 'gendered' does not require us at the outset to have a fixed category or empirical referent of Woman. In analysing such discourses as 'gendering strategies,' we can turn our focus to 'those strategies which attempt to do the "fixing" of gender to rigid systems of meaning rather than falling into this practice ourselves' (p. 33).

Smart (1989, 1992) has demonstrated the power of discourse analysis when applied to law, particularly in terms of the ways in which legal discourse is productive of gender difference and identity. However, where postmodernism begins to 'stick' epistemologically is when the claim that 'subjects are discursively constructed' is used to approach an understanding of the lives of specific groups of women.

To elaborate, Cain (1990a: 7) makes the argument that discourses are 'only' one aspect of reality, not the whole of it. Postmodernism, by giving ontological primacy to discourse, imputes that it is 'impossible to "have" a relationship which is not expressible in, and ultimately constituted by, some discourse or other' (Cain, 1993: 75). Cain's concern here is with the 'extra-discursive'; that aspect of social existence which is literally 'outside' of discourse and thus cannot be grasped by a discourse analysis. While Cain's response is to assert the distinction between 'transitive' and 'intransitive' relations, what I take from her analysis is the need to grapple with this distinction between the 'discursive' and the 'extra (non-)discursive' as it applies to women's lives. In other words, there is something more than just discourses at work, and that something may not be captured in the 'discursively constructed subject.'

We would appear to be at an impasse here. Just as 'experience' alone is not a sufficient source for revealing a 'women's standpoint,' approaching women as 'discursively constructed subjects' may impose—from the out-set—an unwarranted partiality to our understanding of women's lives. But do we have to choose between the two? Or does a 'more complete' understanding of women's lives involve *both* the experiential and the discursive? I will argue for the latter position. This involves acknowledging that there are experiences which women encounter in their lives (the 'non-discursive') as well as women's ways of making sense of those experiences and their effects (the 'discursive'). This is not to revert to an empiricist stance, nor does it by necessity impose a dualism between 'thought' and 'experience.' Rather, it suggests that women's standpoint(s) will be very much informed by their social context (what happens in their day-to-day lives), their histories (what has happened to them in the past), and their culture (the modes of thought or discourses available to them). In this respect, like all knowledge, women's knowledge of their lives will be partial.

While recognition of the (inter)connections between the experiential and the discursive helps to clarify what it is that we need to grasp when approaching women's standpoint(s), what of Smart's critique of the categories used by standpoint feminists to uncover the 'conditions of women's oppression'? If one of the aims of feminist research is to produce knowledge 'on' women, then we need some guidance in terms of how to approach an understanding of women's lives. In this respect, postmodernism does not offer much advice. As Stanley and Wise (1990: 40) have observed, while postmodernism may 'work' at the level of theory, it 'offers few clues as to how a substantive feminist research process concerned with actual, living, breathing, thinking, theorising people should proceed at the level of methodology translated into method.' Granted, we need to heed Smart's warning about problematizing the categories we use to make sense of women's lives. Within sociology, '*all* categories are social constructions' (p. 40), and we should be continually aware of their contingent nature. However, it remains the case that *some* categories, of one sort or another, must be brought into play in our efforts to 'midwife' women's accounts of their lives.

Contrary to Smart, then, locating women's lives within the nexus of class, race, and gender relations does not, by definition, mean that such categories are taken as 'natural' or 'pre-given.' For one, to say that women share a set of *common* experiences which derive from their oppression does not mean that they share the *same* experiences (Stanley and Wise, 1990: 21–2). The diversity of those experiences and the women's understandings of them thus become subjects of investigation. For another, to focus on the ways in which the class, race, and gender dynamics of a given social order are 'worked out' in women's everyday lives is not necessarily to 'impose' such categories on the subjects. Class, race, and gender distinctions are *not* the invention of the standpoint theorist. They are already (and widely) used to define, to separate, and to categorize individuals (as in the 'fixing' of a particular order of which Smart, 1992 speaks). That subjects may well be familiar with such distinctions and the ways in which they impinge upon their lives should come as no surprise. The task of the feminist researcher, then, is to discover how those distinctions are experienced and made sense of by the women she meets.

These issues are brought into bold relief once one leaves the 'noisy sphere' of the epistemological plain (the 'theories about theories') and enters the terrain of feminist research practice. It is here where we come face to face with 'real women,' and with the practical matter which Smart (1995: 209) raises of 'how to deal with the various accounts that arise from the lives of even a relatively homogeneous group of women?' Using my experience of working with women in prison, I will address the issues relating to 'women's standpoint' on a more practical level. In particular, I will consider three aspects as they related to that work: the partiality of the knowledge produced; what it means to 'share' a standpoint; and the content of the standpoint which emerges.

296   *Theoretical Criminology 3(3)*

The standpoint of women in trouble

The 'relatively homogeneous group' which became the focus of my research comprised 24 women prisoners. As a group, the women were under-educated and un/underemployed. Twenty of the 24 women had grade 10 or less education. Four had never worked for wages. Of those who had, the jobs were mostly unskilled and low paid (chambermaid, waitress, factory worker, and the like). Many of the women have had to rely on social assistance. Nineteen of the 24 women described themselves as either Native or Metis. Two of the women described themselves as Mulatto and four as Caucasian. Twenty of the 24 women had borne children, some as many as eight kids. All of the women I spoke with reported experiencing abuse in their lives (although of differing forms and frequencies). Given their location inside the prison walls, all of the women had been officially designated as 'Criminal.'

Like other projects informed by a standpoint feminist approach, *Women in Trouble* was motivated by the desire to make visible the standpoint of these women, to hear their stories. As Cain (1990a: 8) advises, there is a need to find out '*who* are women, and how do they become who they are.' And as feminist criminologists in general have noted, the voices of women behind bars have for too long been silenced; it is time we began to listen to what they have to say.[5] Cain goes on to propose that feminist criminology 'must explore the *total* lives of women . . . or women's experiences of their *total* lives' (Cain, 1990a: 10, emphasis added). Nevertheless, it quickly became apparent to me how improbable this task was. Women's lives can never be fully grasped in their 'totality.' The knowledge being produced was 'partial,' and for a number of reasons.

For one, the partiality of the women's accounts stemmed from the sort of information about a woman's life I chose to elicit from her. Our discussions covered two main topics: whether the woman had any experiences (as a child, a teenager, or an adult) which she considered to be abusive, and the circumstances surrounding her conflicts with the law. Just as approaching the women from the category of 'Criminal Woman' would contribute to a false dualism between the 'criminal' and the 'law abiding,' focusing on women's abuse experiences runs the risk of imposing an artificial uni-dimensionality to their lives. Without this acknowledgement of partiality, there is a danger of seeing the women as embodying victimization. Quite the contrary, there is much more going on in a woman's life than can be captured in a master status of 'victim of abuse.' Yet, as became evident during our meetings, abuse has had a profound affect on who the women are and what they are trying to become.

For another, the women's accounts were partial in the sense that it was each woman's perspective that I was listening to, her telling of her life. Further to this, what gets told depends very much on what a woman was willing or able to disclose to me at the time. As one woman commented: 'I haven't told you everything.' Given the women's histories of institutional confinement and other formal interventions into their lives—of being more or less 'poked and prodded' by the experts—the expectation that they would be wary of my inquiries seemed reasonable. This is especially so given the personal and painful nature of the subject matter of our discussions. Given the silencing that occurs—not just in terms of not having the language to speak about abuse experiences, but the social censuring that exists around the very telling of stories of abuse—speaking out can be a dangerous activity. Even so, for many of the women I interviewed, the silence was being broken for the first time. As one woman told me: 'I haven't talked to anybody. Except you now. You're the first.'

Finally, partiality also becomes evident in the time-limited nature of our meetings. If we can never fully know even those with whom we spend a lifetime, how much can we expect to know from one encounter with a person? This leads me to the question of what it means to 'share' a standpoint.

The act of sharing a standpoint raises the issue of sameness and/or difference between the researcher and the subjects of the research. It is one thing to identify a group of women—like the women in prison—whose standpoint one wishes to understand. It is another to attempt 'to grasp a putting of oneself into another's shoes' (Cain, 1993: 88). In my meetings with the women at the prison, there was much that we could share during our discussions. For example, we talked of our children and our pregnancies. (Two of the women were pregnant at the time of our meeting.) We were also able to share both laughter and tears. However, the differences between us were more readily apparent than were the similarities. On a more immediate level, I had the freedom to leave the confines of the jail after each meeting. This meant, among other things, that my strategies for coping with the stress of those meetings were more varied than those of the women prisoners. On a broader level, the fact that I was of a different class and race than most of the women meant that my life experience was markedly different from theirs. In the course of our discussions, the disparities in our experiences became clear. Not having grown up in poverty, how was I to comprehend what it was like to go to school without breakfast each morning? Not having lived on an isolated reserve, how could I really know what a Native woman's life has been like? Not having been beaten daily by my partner or gang raped as a teenager, how could I possibly understand that which I have not (yet) experienced? As Helen Longino states in relation to the life situations of women in India: 'However much I and they inform ourselves about one another's life situations we can neither share nor escape our social locations unless we materially dismantle them, and even then we cannot escape our histories' (Longino, 1993: 211).

The women I spoke to were very much aware of the differences between us. This is one of the exchanges I had with a woman I called Jessica[6] (my words are bracketed):

You know what I see? It's like, when you, when you do something, you're in a dark spot, right? And there's a lot of dark spots around. Like you gotta see what I see. It's like [pause] it's like a dark spot. You know, it's not like you—you're going to the university, right? But I'm living, like I'm used to living under the ground? Do you understand? Like, I don't know how you'd put it. But there's a—I think maybe that what I see just backfires. That's why it happens to you, and that's why nobody doesn't care or listens.

(because of who you are, is that what you're saying?)

Like, um, [pause] yeah. Something like that, yeah.

(do you think that's true?)

That's what I see. That's what I, that's the way I see it. Like there's a, like you live on the, on the grounds and I live underneath them. And because like, uh, people respect you in a different way. People respect me in a different way, too. Do you understand?

(it's a different world.)

Yeah.

(we live in very different worlds.)

Yeah.

This excerpt is revealing for reasons other than Jessica's awareness of our different life experiences. While I was struggling to hear what she had to say, Jessica was engaged in the work of trying to get me to understand what her life was like, the way she 'sees' it. Her queries of 'Do you understand?' reflect her attempts to gauge my success in this endeavor. What this excerpt also reveals, then, is that the standpoint of the women in prison includes, not simply a *description* of experiences, but their *understandings*—their discursive constructions—of those experiences.

In these terms, the act of sharing a standpoint is not so much one of 'participating in' as it is one of 'listening to' and trying to 'hear' what the women are saying. This is hard work, and the results are never certain. Moreover, the act of sharing a standpoint goes beyond the relationship between the researcher and the subjects of the research. It involves a much wider audience. After all, the whole point in reproducing the women's knowledge of their lives is to make public that which has been subordinated or excluded. This means that, in the same way that the researcher does the work of listening to and hearing women's stories, so too does the consumer of the final product of the research (in this case, a book built around the women's stories).

In naming their experiences of abuse, the women I met with were involved in the act of breaking the silence around abuse, in 'speaking the unspeakable.' This is a political act on their part. It constitutes an important component of their standpoint. It also connotes one source of their authority in the research process. As Cain suggests, my role in that process is one of midwife. This too has a political purpose, as the aim is to use my position of privilege as an academic to make that knowledge visible, to put the women's words on paper. Giving women a voice, therefore, means quite literally sharing authority with them on the written page. This includes making it clear when they are speaking and giving their words space alongside mine. In the process, their accounts or stories—and the differences and similarities between them—become visible.

The standpoint of the women in prison is made up of their experiences, understandings, and analyses. I suggest that it is something different from a 'feminist standpoint,' the second meaning of 'standpoint' which emerges within the standpoint feminist literature. Just as the conception of 'women's standpoint' carries particular meanings and political implications, so too does the 'feminist standpoint.'

Feminist standpoint(s)

A feminist standpoint involves the production of knowledge 'about' and 'for' women. 'Knowledge about' refers to the idea that a feminist standpoint is one which is grounded in and emerges out of a women's standpoint. 'Knowledge for' refers to the idea that a feminist standpoint has a political purpose; it is intended to challenge the dominant understandings of women's oppression. To quote Harding:

> Feminist sciences and epistemologies should help to bring to consciousness less mystified understandings of women's and men's situations so that these understandings can energize and direct women and men to struggle on behalf of eliminating the subordination of women in all of its race, class, and cultural forms.
>
> (1990: 90)

For postmodernists like Smart, this is troublesome. For one, to the extent that a feminist standpoint is designed to produce 'less mystified understandings' about women, it is *prescriptive*. In this regard, Smart (1990: 82) interprets the aim of standpoint feminism to be the establishment of the feminist Truth, 'to impose a different unitary reality' than the 'falsely universalizing perspective of the master.' Postmodernism, in contrast, 'refers to subjugated knowledges, which tell different stories and have different specificities . . . Feminist knowledge, therefore, becomes part of a multiplicity of resistances.'

For another, to the extent that a feminist standpoint is linked to a political venture of 'energizing and directing the struggle,' it is *proscriptive*. For Smart, this implies a 'return to certainty': if the standpoint feminist produces 'good quality knowledge' then the lines of action to follow will be clear. In contrast, Smart argues that 'there can never be this kind of certain relationship between understanding (formed at a precise moment in time/space/culture) and *future* events . . . whether knowledge *works* or not is always contestable or open to interpretation' (1995: 210).

How should we interpret this critique? Harding has replied that while it is accurate to depict feminism as believing in the desirability and the possibility of social progress and that improved theories about ourselves and the world around us will contribute to that progress, this does not necessarily result in the imposition of a 'different unitary reality.' To a large degree, such an assertion assumes a symmetry between 'truth' and 'falsity.' Instead, feminist inquiry 'can aim to produce less partial and perverse representations without having to assert the absolute, complete, universal, or eternal adequacy of these representations' (Harding, 1990: 100).

In this respect, just as there is no one 'women's standpoint,' there is no one 'feminist standpoint.' The formulation of a particular feminist standpoint will involve the self-conscious articulation of the theory which informs it. According to Cain (1990b: 131), the role of theory is to 'map relationships, constructing concepts which constitute and specify patterns of articulation (many and diverse) and dis-connection between the relationships observed, identified and explored.' This suggests, then, that the role of the feminist researcher is something more than midwifing the women's standpoint. I maintain that an added aspect of her work is that which is analogous to role of 'quilt maker.'

It was when I was in the process of doing the research with the women in the prison that I realized how similar it was to quilt making.[7] Each of the women I spoke with has been involved in constructing her own quilt piece. This work has involved the naming of her abuse and her own analysis of the ways in which abuse is situated within her biography. My role in this project was like that of a co-ordinator. By sewing the pieces together, patterns became visible in the ways in which the women have been rebuilding their lives over and around the abuse. Thus, while the heart of *Women in Trouble* is the voices of the women in the prison—their standpoint—the structure and design of the work represent my attempt to come to know and to make sense of the lives of all of the women who contributed their pieces to the quilt.

This is the essence of the feminist standpoint which is contained in *Women in Trouble*. Having the benefit of listening to all of the women's stories, my aim was to draw out the (inter)connections between the women's abuse histories and their law violations. As a theoretically informed standpoint, it offers a particular lens through which the women's lives can be interpreted. Because it is displayed within the text in a more or less shareable discourse (in a theory), this feminist standpoint is open to the scrutiny of the reader. It is not intended to speak 'for' the women (they can do that themselves once given the space in the text). Neither is it intended as a 'general theory' which imposes a unity or speaks in a 'falsely universalizing voice.' To this extent, there is compatibility between Smart's view of feminist knowledge as part of a 'multiplicity of resistances' and feminist standpoint(s) as oppositional knowledge about and for women.

What, then, of the proscriptive nature of standpointism? To hold that social progress is 'desirable' is not to say that it will be 'inevitable.' Smart is right. There are no guarantees, and standpoint feminism 'does not *tell* you what to do in policy terms' (Smart, 1995: 210). To be fair to Cain, she too recognizes this when she says that 'we are not speaking of knowledge which is guaranteed to be right or, sadly, even successful. The successor science remains a science of uncertainties' (Cain, 1990b: 132). But while I agree with Smart on this point, it is not for the reasons she discusses.

This returns us to the key issue in Smart's appraisal of standpoint feminism: that it is 'dependent on a particular Marxist inspired analysis of social relations.' In Smart's reading, such an analysis is 'no longer an adequate theorization of the conditions of our existence. Our habitat is postmodern, so operating within a set of presumptions forged within modernism' is problematic (Smart, 1995: 211). The set of presumptions to which she refers involves: a state-centred model in which a unified state sets the agenda and against which we can (must?) campaign and organize; and modernist categories like class, race, or gender which are 'too cumbersome to accommodate fragmented sociality.' Following Bauman (1991), Smart suggests that 'sociology's focus should be on agency and the habitat in which agency operates.' Instead of thinking in terms of a state, 'we should recognize that rather than a single goal setting agency there are numerous agencies with different goals, none of which is powerful enough to override the others.' Instead of a grand narrative or totalizing theory, preference is for more specific, local or historical analyses. This does not mean, according to Smart, that poststructuralism[8] has to lose sight of the global, 'but it is never taken-for-granted nor is it presumed that everything inevitably operates to reproduce it or can be understood in terms of some derived purpose indelibly etched into the global scenario' (Smart, 1995: 7).

My difficulty here is that, in advancing her position, Smart appears to have set up a straw person in the form of a Marxism which is overly determined, structuralist, and functionalist. This state-centred model is one contested by Marxist and feminist theorists alike. Few feminists (at least of the socialist variety) would hold to the view of the state as *the* centre of power in society.[9] Many recognize (no doubt under the influence of postmodernism) that the different institutions and agencies within the state 'establish multiple discourses about power' (Eisenstein, 1989: 20) which reflect and reinforce the truth claims of the privileged. In Gramsci's (1971) terms, such discourses become 'hegemonic.' Nevertheless, they go on to assert that the state does more than establish multiple discourses about power. It is one site where power is concentrated and exercised. (Indeed, the women in prison know this better than most. They are living with the immediate effects of state intervention into their lives.)

To recognize that power is exercised within the state is not to commit to a politics which takes the state as its only or even primary focus. One of the benefits of standpoint feminism is that it directs our attention to the ways in which women themselves exercise power. This became clear in speaking with the women in prison. While 'abuse' connotes the taking of control away from the person who experiences it, the women I met with did not simply acquiesce. They found a variety of ways to resist, to cope with and to survive the conditions of their endangerment. In the process, they made choices. But those choices are never 'free' or 'open.' To this extent, their lives 'cannot be separated from the complex social structures shaping them' (Hennessy, 1993: 23).

Standpoint feminism provides one way of 'seeing' what the choices are which the women have made, and the systemic barriers they confront which limit those choices. Retaining the notion that structures (like capitalism and patriarchy) do exist, and that those structures contour and condition the power and the choices of individuals who move within them, does not confine us to the idea that everything inevitably operates to reproduce those structures or can be written off in terms of some derived purpose. Neither does it simply map out a program of action which we can follow to ameliorate oppressive conditions.

That there are no easy answers rang clear to me in my meetings with the women in prison, especially when one of the women declared: 'It's hopeless.' Eileen is a Native woman with five children who lives on an isolated reserve. When I asked about her abuse experiences, she responded: 'My husband beats me a lot.' The abuse started shortly after her first child was born, 12 years previously. When I asked her how often it happened, she replied, 'Every day.' Eileen has tried a variety of strategies for dealing with the abuse (seeking shelter, calling the police). In the last seven years, she has started to fight back. Every time she does, *she* is the one who ends up in court. When I met her, Eileen was serving an eight-month prison sentence for assaulting her husband. (He received 30 days.) Eileen is very concerned about her future. Her wish is '[t]hat everything will be okay. And he won't beat me up anymore. Or nothing like that.'

Once we begin to appreciate Eileen's situation, her sense of hopelessness becomes understandable. It also becomes questionable whether engaging the state or law to 'fix' things would 'make everything okay.' As Smart (1989) has demonstrated in her work, law has been nearly resolute in its inability to hear women's voices. While this does not mean that we should simply ignore law (its effects on women's lives are too invasive to ignore), we do need to be very cautious in approaching it. Nevertheless, while law may not be able to hear women's voices, *we* can. Part of the difficulty in our efforts to assess strategies is that we have only begun to listen to what women have to say. Perhaps we are simply not ready for answers yet.

Conclusion

This discussion has taken many twists and turns as I have worked my way through the epistemological questions which emerge in our endeavor to produce feminist knowledge. What becomes evident in this process is that, while standpoint feminism has helped to 'reframe the terrain on which epistemology can be done' (Longino, 1993: 212), it is—like other feminist epistemologies—'transitional' (Harding, 1987). As such, it should not be construed as a finished product but as an effort which informs an ongoing practical struggle (Cain, 1990b). For the standpoint feminist, a key component of that struggle is to give voice to knowledges which have been silenced. Nevertheless, I have argued that the work of the standpoint researcher is made clearer once we distinguish between the two meanings of 'standpoint.' On the one hand, the 'women's standpoint' is both experiential and discursive. It refers to women's knowledge about their lives, knowledge which is informed by their social context, their histories and their culture. In the process of midwifing this knowledge, our task is one of listening to—and trying to hear—what women have to say. The 'feminist standpoint,' on the other hand, is grounded in and emerges out of a women's standpoint. Like a quilt maker, the standpoint feminist engages in the work of drawing the pieces together, and in a theoretically informed and reflexive way. The result is neither the imposition of a 'different unitary reality' nor a 'return to certainty.'

As Smart informs us, we are indeed in a postmodern era. However, the epistemologies appropriate to addressing the needs of women 'are not exhausted by those theorists labelled as *postmodernist*' (Longino, 1993: 208). In the same way that the women in prison resist and challenge the conditions of their oppression, so too can feminist knowledge resist and challenge those conditions. In the process, new spaces open up and new possibilities emerge for broadening the choices available to women for resolving their troubles.

Notes

This is a revision of a paper presented at the 'Gender and the Colour of Law and Other Normative Systems' Workshop, International Institute for the Sociology of Law, Oñati, Spain, July 1997. The author would like to thank the participants of the workshop—especially our Chairperson, Marie-Andrée Bertrand—for their insights. She would also like to thank Piers Beirne for his work as editor as well as the journal's two anonymous reviewers for their helpful comments. As always, the shortcomings of the article are my own doing.

1. See, for example, Morris (1987); Naffine (1987, 1995); Daly and Chesney-Lind (1988); Gelsthorpe and Morris (1990); Rafter and Heidensohn (1995).
2. Similarly, Maureen Cain (1990b: 128) describes standpoint feminism as a 'successor science,' but notes that 'it might be helpful to escape the connotations of the term science and the clouds of meaning which it trails.'
3. Smart defines modernism as:

    a world view, a way of seeing and interpreting, a science which holds the promise that it can reveal the truth about human behaviour . . . Implicit in the modernist paradigm is the idea that there is progress . . . And because progress is presumed to be good and inevitable, science inevitably serves progress.

(1990: 74–5)

4. Feminist empiricism does not receive the same attention in the literature as standpoint or postmodern feminism. I attribute this to two reasons. First, feminist empiricism tended to predominate, at least in criminology, in the early stages of feminist criminology (the 1970s and early 1980s). It corresponded with the initial concern to make women more visible within the discipline. Second, because the issue of creating knowledge 'for' women is more implicit in feminist empiricism, it has not been as central in the ongoing debates around the production and status of knowledge. For these reasons, the focus of this article will be on the dialogue between standpoint and postmodern feminists.

5. See, for example, Carlen (1983, 1985); Adelberg and Currie (1987, 1991); Worrall (1990); Faith (1994).

6. In reproducing the women's stories, I used the names of women I know in their place. This seemed appropriate since these women could just as easily be the women with whom I share close relationships (my sisters, my daughter, my friends).

7. Some clarification is necessary here since, for some readers, quilt making may conjure up images of bourgeois Victorian ladies in their parlours. In contrast, the image I have in mind is of the quilt making which has historically been carried out by Canadian rural women as well as Aboriginal women (in the form of star blankets). Thanks to Anne Worrall for drawing this to my attention.

8. Smart (1995: 8) comments on the distinction between postmodernism and poststructuralism: 'Postmodernism is a critique of epistemology. It makes us rethink and reconsider the foundations of what we think we know. But poststructuralism is more intimately involved with the construction of local knowledge.' Smart's poststructualist position derives from the work of Michel Foucault and, especially in the present context, in Foucault's rejection of the Marxist conception of power and its general or 'totalizing' theory of capitalism.

9. See, for example, Boyd (1994); Snider (1994).

References

Adelberg, Ellen and Claudia Currie (eds) (1987) *Too Few to Count: Canadian Women in Conflict with the Law.* Vancouver: Press Gang.

Adelberg, Ellen and Claudia Currie (eds) (1991) *In Conflict with the Law: Women and the Canadian Justice System.* Vancouver: Press Gang.

Bauman, Zygmunt (1991) *Intimations of Postmodernity.* London: Routledge.

Boyd, Susan (1994) '(Re)Placing the State: Family, Law and Oppression,' *Canadian Journal of Law and Society* 9(1): 39–73.

Cain, Maureen (1990a) 'Towards Transgression: New Directions in Feminist Criminology,' *International Journal of the Sociology of Law* 18: 1–18.

Cain, Maureen (1990b) 'Realist Philosophy and Standpoint Epistemologies or Feminist Criminology as a Successor Science,' in Loraine Gelsthorpe and Allison Morris (eds) *Feminist Perspectives in Criminology*, pp. 124–40. Milton Keynes: Open University Press.

Cain, Maureen (1993) 'Foucault, Feminism and Feeling: What Foucault Can and Cannot Contribute to Feminist Epistemology,' in Caroline Ramazanoglu (ed.) *Up Against Foucault: Explorations of Some Tensions Between Foucault and Feminism*, pp. 73–96. London: Routledge.

Carlen, Pat (1983) *Women's Imprisonment*. London: Routledge & Keagan Paul.

Carlen, Pat (ed.) (1985) *Criminal Women*. Cambridge: Polity Press.

Comack, Elizabeth (1993) *Women Offenders' Experiences with Physical and Sexual Abuse: A Preliminary Report*. Criminology Research Centre: University of Manitoba.

Comack, Elizabeth (1996) *Women in Trouble: Connecting Women's Law Violations to Their Histories of Abuse*. Halifax: Fernwood Publishing.

Daly, Kathleen and Meda Chesney-Lind (1988) 'Feminism and Criminology,' *Justice Quarterly* 5(4): 101–43.

Eisenstein, Zillah R. (1989) *The Female Body and the Law*. Berkeley, CA: University of California Press.

Faith, Karlene (1994) *Unruly Women: The Politics of Confinement and Resistance*. Vancouver: Press Gang.

Gelsthorpe, Loraine and Allison Morris (eds) (1990) *Feminist Perspectives in Criminology*. Milton Keynes: Open University Press.

Gramsci, Antonio (1971) *Selections from the Prison Notebooks*. New York: International Publishers.

Harding, Sandra (1986) *The Science Question in Feminism*. Milton Keynes: Open University Press.

Harding, Sandra (1987) *Feminism and Methodology*. Milton Keynes: Open University Press.

Harding, Sandra (1990) 'Feminism, Science, and the Anti-Enlightenment Critiques,' in Linda J. Nicholson (ed.) *Feminism/Postmodernism*, pp. 83–106. London: Routledge.

Harding, Sandra (1991) *Whose Science? Whose Knowledge?* Ithaca, NY: Cornell University Press.

Harding, Sandra (1993) 'Rethinking Standpoint Epistemology: What is "Strong Objectivity"?,' in Linda Alcoff and Elizabeth Potter (eds) *Feminist Epistemologies*, pp. 49–82. London: Routledge.

Hartsock, Nancy (1987) 'The Feminist Standpoint: Developing a Ground for a Specifically Feminist Historical Materialism,' in Sandra Harding (ed.) *Feminism and Methodology*, pp. 157–80. Milton Keynes: Open University Press.

Hennessy, Rosemary (1993) 'Women's Lives/Feminist Knowledge: Feminist Standpoint as Ideology Critique,' *Hypatia* 8(1): 14–34.

Longino, Helen E. (1993) 'Feminist Standpoint Theory and the Problems of Knowledge,' *Signs* Autumn: 201–12.

Morris, Allison (1987) *Women, Crime and Criminal Justice.* London: Basil Blackwell.

Naffine, Ngaire (1987) *Female Crime: The Construction of Women in Criminology.* Sydney: Allen & Unwin.

Naffine, Ngaire (ed.) (1995) *Gender, Crime and Feminism.* Aldershot: Dartmouth.

Rafter, Nicole and Francis Heidensohn (eds) (1995) *International Feminist Perspectives in Criminology.* Buckingham: Open University Press.

Smart, Carol (1989) *Feminism and the Power of Law.* London: Routledge.

Smart, Carol (1990) 'Feminist Approaches to Criminology or Postmodern Woman Meets Atavistic Man,' in Loraine Gelsthorpe and Allison Morris (eds) *Feminist Perspectives in Criminology,* pp. 70–84. Milton Keynes: Open University Press.

Smart, Carol (1992) 'The Woman of Legal Discourse,' *Social and Legal Studies* 1(1): 29–44.

Smart, Carol (1995) *Law, Crime and Sexuality: Essays in Feminism.* London: Sage Publications.

Smith, Dorothy (1987) *The Everyday World as Problematic: A Feminist Sociology.* Toronto: University of Toronto Press.

Snider, Laureen (1994) 'Feminism, Punishment and the Potential of Empowerment,' *Canadian Journal of Law and Society* 9(1): 75–104.

Stanley, Liz and Sue Wise (1990) 'Method, Methodology and Epistemology in Feminist Research Processes,' in Liz Stanley (ed.) *Feminist Praxis: Research, Theory and Epistemology in Feminist Sociology,* pp. 20–60. London: Routledge.

Worrall, Anne (1990) *Offending Women: Female Lawbreakers and the Criminal Justice System.* London: Routledge.

ELIZABETH COMACK is an Associate Professor in Sociology at the University of Manitoba in Winnipeg, Canada. She has published in the areas of sociology and law and feminist criminology. Her recent works include *Women in Trouble* (1996) and an edited collection entitled *Locating Law: Race/Class/Gender Connections* (1999). Her current research is on women's violence.

[3]

WOMEN'S VIOLENCE TO MEN IN INTIMATE RELATIONSHIPS

Working on a Puzzle

RUSSELL P. DOBASH*[1] and R. EMERSON DOBASH*

Different notions among researchers about the nature of intimate partner violence have long been the subjects of popular and academic debate. Research findings are contradictory and point in two directions, with some revealing that women are as likely as men to perpetrate violence against an intimate partner (symmetry) and others showing that it is overwhelmingly men who perpetrate violence against women partners (asymmetry). The puzzle about who perpetrates intimate partner violence not only concerns researchers but also policy makers and community advocates who, in differing ways, have a stake in the answer to this question, since it shapes the focus of public concern, legislation, public policy and interventions for victims and offenders. The question of who are the most usual victims and perpetrators rests, to a large extent, on 'what counts' as violence. It is here that we begin to try to unravel the puzzle, by focusing on concept formation, definitions, forms of measurement, context, consequences and approaches to claim-making, in order better to understand how researchers have arrived at such apparently contradictory findings and claims. The question also turns on having more detailed knowledge about the nature, extent and consequences of women's violence, in order to consider the veracity of these contradictory findings. To date, there has been very little in-depth research about women's violence to male partners and it is difficult, if not impossible, to consider this debate without such knowledge. We present quantitative and qualitative findings from 190 interviews with 95 couples in which men and women reported separately upon their own violence and upon that of their partner. Men's and women's violence are compared. The findings suggest that intimate partner violence is primarily an asymmetrical problem of men's violence to women, and women's violence does not equate to men's in terms of frequency, severity, consequences and the victim's sense of safety and well-being. But why bother about the apparent contradictions in findings of research? For those making and implementing policies and expending public and private resources, the apparent contradiction about the very nature of this problem has real consequences for what might be done for those who are its victims and those who

* Russell P. Dobash is Professor of Criminology and Rebecca Emerson Dobash is Professor of Social Research at the University of Manchester. They have been researching violence against women since the 1970s and have co-authored several books, numerous government reports and scores of articles on the subject. Their books include *Violence against Wives* (1979), *The Imprisonment of Women* (1986), *Women Viewing Violence* (1992), *Women, Violence and Social Change* (1992), *Penal Theory and Penal Practice: Traditions and Innovations* (1994), *Gender and Crime* (1995), *Rethinking Violence Against Women* (1999) and *Changing Violent Men* (2000). They have won the World Congress of Victimology Award for Original Research and Publications in the area of Domestic Violence, the American Society of Criminology's Distinguished Book Award for Comparative Research and the August Vollmer Award. The main focus of their research is violence and the policies and interventions relating to it. Specific studies include the areas of violence against women; convicted child sex abusers; evaluation of criminal justice-based treatment programmes for violent men; bodybuilding, steroids and violence; men's and women's responses to televised violence and the first national study of Homicide in Britain. They have held research grants and/or fellowships from the Carnegie Foundation, the Rockefeller Foundation, the Fulbright Foundation, the Harry Frank Guggenheim Foundation, the Economic and Social Research Council, the Home Office, the Scottish Office and other government departments. They have served as research and policy advisors to various government agencies in Britain, Canada, United States, Australia and several European countries.

Contact: R. P. Dobash, Williamson Building, Oxford Road, University of Manchester, Manchester, M13 9PL, email Russell.Dobash@man.ac.uk.

[1] The Study was funded by The Scottish Office, now the Scottish Executive, and the Home Office. The research team included Russell Dobash and Rebecca Emerson Dobash (principal investigators) and Kate Cavanagh and Ruth Lewis (researchers).

are its perpetrators. Worldwide, legislators, policy makers and advocates have developed responses that conceive of the problem as primarily one of men's violence to women, and these findings provide support for such efforts and suggest that the current general direction of public policy and expenditure is appropriate.

Introduction

Violence against women by an intimate male partner is now recognized throughout most of the world as a significant social problem. It has been identified by many countries, the United Nations and the European Union as an issue of human rights (United Nations 1995; Kelly 1997; Journal of Violence against Women (JrVAW) 2001). In the past two decades, significant changes in policies and practices have occurred worldwide, but particularly in the United States, Britain, Canada and Australia (Dobash and Dobash 1979; 1992; Schechter 1982; Heise 1994; Stubbs 1994; Mullender 1996; JrVAW 2001; Schneider 2002). The majority of changes have been in the areas of community support, public policy, social services and civil and criminal law and law enforcement.

On a daily basis, police, hospital emergency services, social services and voluntary organizations struggle with questions about how best to help victims who seek assistance because of violent episodes. Their focus is on injuries, homelessness, dislocation of children from their homes and schools, emotional stress and a raft of other problems experienced by the women who seek assistance for themselves and their children. Almost all pragmatic interventions in the form of emergency services, programmes and other responses are primarily designed to deal with the serious problem of male violence against an intimate female partner, and not the obverse. For the most part, legislators, policy makers, legal and social service professionals and community advocates have dealt with the issue of 'domestic violence' as primarily a problem of men's violence against a woman partner. Across these organizations in countries throughout the world, the operating definition of the problem they confront is overwhelmingly one of male violence against a female partner. For them, violence against women is *the* problem and the one in need of urgent solution.

The pragmatic experience of most community advocates and professionals dealing with violence between intimates on a regular basis and the research findings of most social scientists studying this phenomenon agree that 'intimate partner violence' is overwhelmingly an issue of male violence against a female partner. However, the findings of some social scientist, particularly in the United States, appear to support the notion that the phenomenon is equally likely to be women's violence against a male partner, and some even claim that women are more likely than men to be violent to their intimate partner.

Thus, the question becomes one of who is likely to use violence against an intimate partner: men, women or both? At stake for researchers and others is how the problem is conceptualized (as men's violence against women, as women's violence against men, as equivalent and/or reciprocal violence by men and by women). Also at stake, although less so for researchers than for policy makers and practitioners in criminal justice and social services, is the nature of actions to be taken in search of a remedy to the problem as defined and identified. If one accepts the notion that there should be a relationship between the nature of any social issue and the form of policies and interventions seeking a solution, then this contradiction in definitions and findings about 'intimate partner violence' has serious implications for policy and intervention. That is, if the problem is one of men's violence against women (asymmetry), then the current policies and practices are apt. If the problem is one of the equivalence of violence perpetrated by men and by women (symmetry), then the direction of current policies and practices is inappropriate and needs to be fundamentally transformed.

Different notions among researchers about the nature of 'domestic violence' (asymmetrical or symmetrical) have long been the subjects of popular and academic debate. Within the area of research, contradictory findings constitute a puzzle. Working on this puzzle is the task of this paper. The question is whether men and women are equally likely to perpetrate violence in an intimate relationship or whether it is primarily men who do so. In order to address this, we will focus on concept formation, definitions, forms of measurement, context, consequences and approaches to claim-making in order better to understand how researchers arrived at such apparently contradictory findings and claims. We then examine in some detail the nature, severity and consequences of violence perpetrated by women against male partners, in order to consider more carefully the nature of the violence that forms the claim of symmetry of violence between women and men.

In order to examine women's violence, we present findings from a study that included 95 couples in which men and women reported separately upon the violence in their relationship. This included both men's violence against women partners and women's violence against male partners in terms of the nature, frequency, severity and physical and emotional consequences. A close examination of women's violence is especially important because there is a need to reflect on both men's and women's violent behaviour in order to consider the veracity of these contradictory findings. To date, there has been very little in-depth research about women's violence to male partners and it is difficult, if not impossible, to consider this debate without such knowledge. But why bother about the apparent contradictions in findings from research? For those making and implementing policies and expending public and private resources, the apparent contradiction about the very nature of this problem has real consequences for what might be done for those who are its victims and those who are its perpetrators.

Symmetry or Asymmetry in the Perpetration of Violence to an Intimate Partner?

Over the last three decades, knowledge about intimate partner violence or 'domestic violence' has grown exponentially. From the outset, there has been disagreement among researchers about definitions, methods and the resulting findings regarding the direction and impact of violence between men and women in intimate relationships. Elsewhere, we have characterized the two approaches to research as 'family violence' (FV) and 'violence against women' (VAW) (Dobash and Dobash 1992: 258–84). While these approaches are relatively distinct, there are elements that overlap and, thus, comparisons need to be treated as characterizations rather than absolutes.

Family violence research

Family violence (FV) researchers claim that intimate partner violence is symmetrical, with men and women equally likely to be the perpetrator of violence against an intimate partner. In attempting to establish the prevalence of violence in relationships, FV researchers have primarily relied on the measurement of discrete 'acts', e.g. 'slap' or 'punch', as the primary or sole source of data about the violence of individual respondents. Using this 'act-based' approach, FV researchers have variously claimed that intimate partner violence is 'symmetrical' and 'reciprocal' (each gives as good as they get), or that women perpetrate more violence and are more likely than men to use 'severe' violence against a male partner (Straus and Gelles 1990; Morse 1995; Moffitt, Robins and Caspi 2001). Some 'act-based' measurements include sexual violence and show that men are equally as likely to report sexual violence/abuse from their female partner as the obverse. In some surveys, men are more likely than women to report sexual victimization by their partner. One US study of University students found that 38 per cent of the men and 30 per cent of the women reported at least one incident of sexual coercion from an intimate partner of the opposite sex. Using a sexual chronicity scale, men reported more incidents than women (18.5 vs 11.8 incidents) (Straus, Hamby, Boney-McCoy and Sugarman 1996).

FV researcher's further suggest that women's violence to a male partner cannot be construed as 'self-defence' because they claim that women are equally likely to initiate violence (Stets and Straus 1990: 161), and because the 'individual characteristics' of women who use such violence parallel those of their violent male partner (Moffitt *et al.* 2001). With no consideration of the sequence of acts involved in a violent event and based on the notion of similar 'individual characteristics likely to predict abuse', FV researchers assume equivalence in men's and women's motivations and, in turn, the likelihood that the violence may have been used in self-defence (Moffitt *et al.* 2001: 25, n. 8). Further, this 'act-based' approach to the measurement of violence is usually based on the assumption that men and women can and do provide unbiased, reliable accounts of their own violent behaviour and that of their partner. Using this approach, reports of violence and injuries from men or women, from victims or perpetrators, about oneself or about one's partner are all treated as unproblematic and as a solid evidentiary basis for estimates of prevalence and the development of explanatory accounts (Morse 1995; Moffitt, Caspi, Krueger, Magdol, Margolin, Silva and Sydney 1997; Archer 1999).

Despite the claims of equal violence by men and by women, policy suggestions regarding women's violence are not generally offered. However, a prominent proponent of the 'symmetry' thesis has noted that 'assaults by women are a serious social problem', and suggests that '...assaults by wives are one of the many *causes* of wife beating [our emphasis]...' (Straus 1993: 78, 80). As such, it is the responsibility of 'wives' to refrain from physical attacks on their male abuser 'no matter what the provocation' (Straus 1993: 80). Furthermore, if women's 'assaults' cause more male violence, then public policy and practices should change accordingly, '...including public service announcements, police arrest policy, and treatment programmes for batterers' (Straus 1993: 80). According to this notion, ending male violence against women is at least partially dependent on women ending their violence against men. Stressing the supposed equivalent and reciprocal nature of men's and women's violence both as perpetrators and as victims, others propose conjoint, couple therapy in order to deal with this problem (Moffitt 2001: 27).

Violence against women research

VAW researchers claim that intimate partner violence is asymmetrical, with men more likely than women to perpetrate violence against an intimate partner. Historical and

contemporary evidence from many societies indicates that lethal and non-lethal intimate partner violence is overwhelmingly perpetrated by men against women (Dobash
and Dobash 1979; 1992; Pleck 1987; Gordon 1988; Daly and Wilson 1988; Levinson
1989; Dobash, Dobash, Wilson and Daly 1992; Wilson and Daly 1992, 1998; Kurz 1993;
Bourgois 1995; Nazroo 1995; Descola 1996; Dobash *et al.*, 2004). For example, when
men and women are asked to report on victimization throughout their lifetime (ever
prevalence), women report at least two to four times more violence than men, and
women are much more likely to report chronic levels of abuse (Gaquin 1977/78;
Schwartz 1987; Sacco and Johnson 1990; Bachman and Saltzman 1995; Tjaden and
Thoennes 1998; Mirrless-Black 1999). Direct measures of the consequences of violent
acts suggest that women are much more likely than men to report physical injuries and
emotional and psychological effects (e.g. depression, anxiety and fear) as a result of
men's violence toward them (Schwartz 1987; Campbell 1998; Dobash and Dobash
2001). Ironically, FV researchers acknowledge that women are six to ten times more
likely than men to sustain serious injuries as a consequence of violent acts by their partner (Straus 1993; Gelles 1997: 93) but some, nonetheless, continue to claim that
women are more likely than men to perpetrate violence, including 'severe' violence,
against an intimate partner. What might this mean?

VAW researchers stress that in order to understand this violence, it should be studied
within the wider context of ongoing violent events and intimate relationships. Violent
events should also be studied within the context of actions and intentions associated
with the event and its aftermath. Purely 'act-based' approaches rarely consider contextual issues that promote fuller understandings and more adequate explanations of such
events. When one considers the violent event in the context of an intimate relationship,
evidence suggests that men's physical and sexual violence against women is often associated with a 'constellation of abuse' that includes a variety of additional intimidating,
aggressive and controlling acts (Pence and Paymar 1993; Dobash *et al.* 2000; Gondolf
2002). Physical and sexual acts of violence and the wider 'constellation of abuse' may
result in physical injuries as well as other related emotional and/or economic consequences for victims as men seek to control and regulate the lives of women partners
(Browne, Salomon, Bassuk 1999; Campbell 1999; Lloyd and Taluc 1999; MacMillan and
Gartner 1999). Such consequences and the wider 'constellation of abuse' are not evident in reports about women's violence against male partners.

Researchers who study the whole violent event, rather than a list of 'acts' that may have
occurred across many such events, find that women's violence (lethal and non-lethal) is
often associated with self-defence and/or retaliation against a male partner. This frequently occurs after years of physical abuse from the male partner (Berk, Berk, Loseke and
Rauma 1983; Browne 1987; Daly and Wilson 1988; Browne, Williams and Dutton 1999).
Professionals who work with male abusers also find that the violence women direct at male
partners usually, though not always, occurs in a context of ongoing violence and aggression by men directed at women (Saunders 1988; Pence and Paymar 1993; Miller 2001).

Defining, Measuring and Reporting Intimate Partner Violence and Abuse

The debates in this arena are often highly political but here we wish, instead, to focus
on methodological issues in order to consider the 'puzzle' of how the FV and VAW
approaches to research have resulted in such different findings. We begin with the

assumption that theoretical and methodological approaches to research (including concepts, definitions and measurement) shape the nature of what is studied and the findings produced, which, in turn, inform policies and practices (Dobash and Dobash 1990a; 1990b). We consider the different approaches of FV research and VAW research to the issues of how violence is conceptualized and measured, and how findings are reported, followed by a close examination of the violence perpetrated by women. These form important keys to the puzzle. This, in turn, is used to consider what conclusions might be drawn about the similarities and differences between violence perpetrated by women and that perpetrated by men.

Measuring and reporting violence and abuse

The attempt to bring rigor, precision, clarity and understanding to the study of the social world is both necessary and worthy. It is not, however, an easy or straightforward task, as the complex and 'messy' nature of everyday life is distilled into various measures or assessments that are meant to represent or 'stand-in' for the complexity of life. Both FV research and VAW research attempt to do this, but the breadth and depth of what is studied vary with each approach. VAW research is wider in scope and has more depth and detail in what is studied, while FV research is narrow in scope, depth and detail. VAW research examines violent 'acts', violent 'events' and the context and consequences in which they occur, while FV research focuses almost exclusively on distinct 'acts'.

In the 'act-based' approach, the attempt to bring rigor and statistical precision relies almost exclusively on the use of lists of items intended to measure conflict, violence and other forms of abuse. These lists are then translated into scales and scale scores are then used to assess individuals as 'violent' or 'non-violent'. Finally, the scores may be used to estimate the proportion of violent men and women in the specific study and to generalize to the wider population. The most widely used and widely criticized example of such a list is the Conflict Tactic Scales (CTS) (Straus 1980; Straus and Gelles 1990).

For scientific purposes, lists or scales intended to assess social problems must be valid and reliable, and the CTS has been shown to have a certain degree of reliability (Archer 1999). However, critics have been particularly concerned about its external or theoretical validity (Szinovacz 1983; Browning and Dutton 1986; Margolin 1987; Dobash *et al.* 1992; Kurz 1993; Dobash, Dobash, Cavanagh and Lewis 1998). Critics note that the meaning of certain 'acts' in the CTS is highly variable and the outcome of specific 'acts' is almost impossible to discern from the 'act' itself. For example, in one version of the CTS, men and women were asked whether they had ever 'thrown an object at your partner' or 'hit or tried to hit your partner with something' (Moffitt *et al.* 1997: 51). It can readily be seen that throwing a lamp at a partner is very different from throwing a pillow, and that actually hitting a partner is very different from 'trying to hit' a partner. Importantly, the exact nature and consequences of any 'act' cannot be assessed solely through the knowledge that it occurred. Yet, the 'act-based' approach must invariably equate the physical impact/consequences of a 'slap' delivered by a slight, 5 ft 4 inch woman with the 'slap' of a heavily built man of 6 ft 2 inches. In addition, motivations and intentions cannot be assumed from the 'act'; instead, they must be assessed directly. For example, a woman may 'try to hit' her partner in the context of his holding her at arms length after he has inflicted a serious punch to her face. Her intentions may be self-defence, retaliation or something else.

A narrow 'act-based' approach makes it nearly impossible to consider the context, wider consequences and intentions associated with violent acts or the meanings and consequences of such acts for victims and for perpetrators. It could be argued that it is not necessary to understand the context of the violent acts of men and of women in order to compare the prevalence of each. However, the entire edifice of the FV approach to comparing the violent 'acts' of men with those of women is built on the assumptions that the 'acts' of men and women are equivalent and that the context in which they occur and their meaning for the victim and the perpetrator are not relevant. We shall return to these issues when reporting the findings about women's violence.

An additional problem with 'act-based' measures is that the usual scoring methods are such that it is only necessary for a man or a woman to indicate that they have committed *one single 'act'* on the list in order to be defined as 'violent'. This means that those who have perpetrated *several violent 'acts'* (no matter how serious) and those who have reported committing only one act (no matter how trivial) are both defined as 'violent'. This approach also treats very different acts in a similar manner. For example, the woman who admits that she 'tried to hit her partner' is equated with the man who reports 'beating up' his partner—both have perpetrated an act of violence against their intimate partner. Using the conventional scoring method, both the man and the woman are deemed to be violent; thus, it is concluded that there is 'symmetry' in the perpetration of violence by the woman and the man; both behaved in a similar fashion; both are defined as 'violent'. One outcome of this approach is the reporting of extremely high levels of violence and abuse. For example, using this method, a study conducted in a small New Zealand city found that 75 per cent of the 'couples' reported at least one such act, with a mean score of 2.0 acts of physical abuse perpetrated by men and a slightly higher score of 2.1 acts of violence perpetrated by women (Moffitt *et al.* 2001: 13).

It seems reasonable to ask if this approach distorts the reality of intimate partner violence and/or if the consumers of such findings bring to the reading an understanding of 'violence' that is somehow at variance with the 'acts' involved in the scores reported for men and those for women. The number of acts perpetrated may be similar for men and women, but are the acts themselves also similar? For example, if the authors were to provide greater specification of the *nature* of the 'acts' composing the scores for men and those for women, might they look different in *character* even though they remain similar in number? That is, we might find that the average woman perpetrated 2.1 acts of physical abuse composed of one slap to the face and one punch to the arm and the average man perpetrated 2.0 acts of physical abuse involving one punch to the face and one kick to the stomach. While the number of 'acts' may be similar, their nature (not to mention possible consequences) is vastly different. Based on the number of 'acts', a conclusion of 'symmetry' might be made, but clear specification of the nature of such acts would lead to a conclusion of 'asymmetry'.

Similar definitional problems occur when researchers attempt to investigate other behaviours that are defined as 'abuse', e.g. when a list of discrete acts defined as 'psychological' or 'emotional abuse' is used to assess the 'victimization' of men and women. As with the assessment of 'violence', the term 'abuse' occurs in an abstracted and generalized fashion, making it impossible to know whether the perpetrator and/or the 'victim' considered such acts as abusive. This is a serious problem. For example, one item on a 'psychological abuse' scale is 'made threats to leave'. Using this scale, it was reported that 44.3 per cent of women and 35.9 per cent of men made 'threats to leave' and, as such, were defined as having 'abused' their partner in this way (Moffitt *et al.* 1997: 51). We suggest that it may be impossible to define such an act as 'abusive' and that it would certainly not be possible to do so without knowledge of the context in which it occurs. Women who experience frequent violence from an intimate partner often 'threaten to leave'. Does this constitute the woman's abuse of her violent male partner? It seems reasonable to ask how this act can be defined as 'abusive'.

Another problem is the conflation of 'violence' (physical and sexual acts) with other non-violent acts of 'abuse' (shouting, name calling, etc.). The conflation problem occurs at several stages: when defining the phenomenon to be studied, when measuring 'acts' and when reporting the findings. The two things are collapsed into a single category, variously called 'violence' or 'abuse', and these terms are often used interchangeably, even after the author may have introduced them separately. A common problem is to introduce the single topic of 'violence', discuss the two issues of 'violence' (slapping, punching) and 'abuse' (threatening to leave, name-calling, etc.) and then report the combined findings under a single label of 'violence' or 'abuse'. This problem occurs in both the FV approach and the VAW approach (e.g. Dekeserady 2000) and can lead to confusion and/or to misleading findings. For example, researchers may conclude that women are just as violent as men when what may, in fact, be under discussion is men's *'acts' of physical and sexual violence* and women's *'acts' of arguing or shouting.*

This is not to claim that women never engage in acts of physical violence, but here the problem is one of conflating verbal 'acts' with 'physical/sexual acts' and referring to all of them as 'violence'. In other words, the problem is one of definitions about what 'counts' as violence—'physical/sexual acts' and/or 'verbal acts'—at the point when the data are collected and then at the point at which the findings are reported. At the first point of data collection or measurement, the information gathered may in fact be about a variety of physical and sexual 'acts', as well as various verbal 'acts' but, at the final point of presenting findings, all of these differences are collapsed into one category or concept of 'violence', 'abuse' or 'aggression'. This is also not to imply that non-violent acts of 'abuse' are not problematic or consequential but, rather, that these acts and their consequences should be clearly differentiated, examined and reported in their own right.

Conceptualizing Violence and Abuse

Within both the FV and VAW approaches, researchers sometimes fail to articulate the complex nature of intimate partner violence as they build their concepts and the tools used to measure it. Many of the 'act-based' approaches are so highly operational that the specification of what counts as intimate partner abuse and/or violence is restricted simply to the lists of acts used to gather data. Theoretical definitions and concepts play almost no role in the approach in which 'violence' is no more or less than what is measured using the list of 'acts'. Even when issues beyond the 'acts', such as the intent to do harm, are included in the definition of 'violence', these are rarely if ever measured (Gelles and Straus 1979; Gelles 2000: 785–6).[2] Such an operationalist approach to the meaning of concepts has a long history in the physical and social sciences, although its

---

[2] In the Canadian Violence Against Women Study, Johnson added the notion of 'intention to do harm' to several of the items on the modified CTS (Johnson and Sacco 1995).

serious limitations have been exposed from the outset (Bridgman 1927; Lundberg 1942; Adler 1947). In order to generate more adequate explanatory accounts, concepts need to be embedded in explicit theoretical frameworks. In so doing, definitions and the meaning of concepts such as 'violence' and 'abuse' are made more explicit. In short, in order to research any social issue and the policies and interventions associated with it, it is necessary adequately to define and specify the problem itself.

Social scientists and philosophers have long suggested that an understanding of the social world would advance through a careful consideration of the role of concepts and their development in social research. Lazarsfeld (1967) suggested several stages in the development of concepts: articulate an initial imagery of the concept; specify the 'dimensions' associated with the concept and divide it into its constituent parts; translate the various parts into observable indicators that can be measured empirically; and combine the empirical indicators into indices or scale scores. Through this process, researchers can specify the significant properties of the phenomenon to be studied. Lazarsfeld also suggested that researchers should begin with 'real life situations'—not abstract, artificial experiments—and that concepts must be nested within an overarching theoretical framework in order to be meaningful for empirical research: 'In scientific inquiry, concept formation and theory formation must go hand in hand' (Hempel 1966: 97). A purely 'act-based' approach to the study of intimate partner violence pays scant attention to the initial steps in the process of concept formation, rarely offering characterizations or definitions that specify the constituent elements of 'violence' and/ or 'abuse', and rarely locating these terms in an explanatory framework. Because the 'acts-based' approach is highly operational, the 'acts' that are measured are stripped of theoretical and social meanings and, as such, provide an inadequate basis for describing or explaining the violent acts of men and women.

Claims of 'symmetry' in the perpetration of violence by women and men, and of 'equivalence' of the violence itself, rest almost solely on the operational procedures associated with the 'act-based' approach. On the other hand, 'asymmetry' in the perpetration of violence by men and women, and 'non-equivalence' in the violence itself, emerge from research using a concept specific (Dobash and Dobash 1983) approach to definitions, concepts and measurement of violence. Let us consider the puzzle of 'symmetry' and 'equivalence' by focusing primarily on the violence of women against an intimate male partner. We begin by considering the importance of studying couples, and then proceed to our own study.

Intimate Partner Violence: Studies of Couples

When attempting to study men's and women's accounts of 'shared' experiences, it is useful to study those who have shared such experiences. An important method of investigating the potentially conflicting accounts of intimate partner violence is to compare the reports of couples—accounts of victims and perpetrators, i.e. parties to the same events. There is a long history of studying couples in order to consider the lives that men and women lead within intimate relationships and families, and to reflect on the different ways in which they report and evaluate their 'common' experiences. The focus has often been on household tasks and attitudes and the findings often show divergence between men and women about some of the most common aspects of the world they occupy together (for a review, see Szinovacz 1983). One might expect to find even more divergence between the accounts of men and women about the far more contentious issue of violence.

Research using couples generally shows that men and women often disagree about the occurrence of violence in relationships (see, e.g. Szinovacz 1983; Jouriles and O'Leary 1985; Browning and Dutton 1986; Edleson and Brygger 1986; Margolin 1987; Cantos, Nazroo 1995; Moffitt *et al.* 1997; Dobash *et al.* 1998; Archer 1999; Schafer, Caetano and Clarke 2002). So how do we understand these differences? More expansive information about the context of violent 'events' and their meanings to those involved help make sense of the differences between men's and women's accounts and move toward a fuller understanding of the dynamics of such events and relationships.

In an extensive review of the literature, Margolin (1987) concluded that there was little overall agreement between couples about men's and women's violence, and that women are more likely than men to acknowledge their own violence. Women were also more likely to experience considerably more violence and women's initiation of violence was often appropriately defined as 'protective reactive' responses—a term initially used by Gelles (1997). She noted that 'Spouses may have different definitions and thresholds as to what they view as violent, may ascribe self-serving labels and interpretations to behaviours, or, simply falsify reports' (Margolin 1987: 77). One significant finding of Margolin's own research was that it was impossible to make sense of her results without a consideration of the meanings attached to the violence of men and women. She noted that, 'While CTS items appear behaviourally specific, their meanings are open to question' (Margolin 1987: 82). As an example of this problem, she cites a couple that reported kicking each other—clearly an act of violence—yet, in her subsequent in-depth interviews, she discovered that this was a playful activity that they engaged in when in bed. She concluded that assessments of violence should include a consideration of the severity of injuries, the perceptions of the victims and the intentions of the attackers: 'A woman's hardest punches, which might be laughed at by her husband, would count as "husband abuse" based on actions alone' (Margolin 1987: 83).

A study of intimate partner violence reported by couples

In order to consider the claims of equivalence in the perpetration of violence by men and by women, we present findings from in-depth interviews with couples that were part of a larger study of criminal justice intervention in intimate partner violence (Dobash *et al.* 2000). The wider study included a sample of 122 men and 134 women, drawn from cases dealt with in two different courts. The sample used here is based on 190 interviews with 95 men and 95 women.[3] In-depth interviews were conducted separately with men and women. A context-specific method was used[4] and both quantitative and qualitative data were gathered. While men's violence was the main focus of the study, women's violence and aggression were also examined. Using the quantitative and qualitative data from the interviews, we examined the prevalence and incidents of men's violence and women's violence, the detailed nature of the physical and sexual acts involved, and of the injuries inflicted. Focusing on women's violence, we consider the nature of women's violence, of men's reactions and the issue of self-defence. Little is known

---

[3] Studies of couples where violence is involved usually have relatively small samples because of issues of access, cooperation of both parties, safety and the like; they range in size from 30 to 360 (Browning and Dutton 1986; Cantos *et al.* 1994; Jouriles and O'Leary 1985; Margolin 1987; Moffitt *et al.* 2001; Nazroo 1995; Szinovacz 1983).

[4] For further delineation of the context-specific approach, see Dobash and Dobash 1979; 1983; Dobash *et al.* 2000.

about the specific nature and context of women's violence and yet this is essential if the claim of equivalence between men and women is to be assessed.

All the men in the study had been convicted of an act involving violence against their partner and, as such, constitute a criminal justice sample of male perpetrators. Some researchers argue that individuals involved with criminal justice may be reluctant to discuss their 'illegal' acts; we did not find this. It may be that once such acts have been made public, men and women partners are able to discuss them with a researcher, provided they receive the usual guarantees of confidentiality and anonymity. Certainly, offenders may be reticent to report violent criminal acts if reporting rules require researchers and professionals to report heretofore undisclosed criminal acts (this usually occurs in cases of physical and/or sexual violence against children). This was not the case in the jurisdictions included in this study and we had no such problems. It should be noted that while the focus of this paper is on women's violence to a male partner, the sample is drawn from men who have used violence against a woman partner. As such, women's violence is being examined in the context of men's violence. While it might be useful to study only women who have been arrested for using non-lethal violence against a male partner, this is such a rare occurrence that it would be difficult to obtain an adequate sample.[5] As such, women's violence within the context of a sample of male abusers may be the most realistic approach to sampling, given that the focus is on violent behaviour and not domestic conflicts, disagreements, arguments, name calling and the sort of 'aggressive' behaviour often measured using the CTS and, in turn, defined as violence. As with all samples, this one has its limitations, but this sample has allowed us to open a window on the existing body of knowledge by providing intensive and extensive knowledge about intimate partner violence from both men and women partners, who discussed at length and in great detail their own violence and that of their partner.

In using only couples, we focus on violent events where both parties were present. The main concern is to consider men's accounts and women's accounts of violent 'acts', 'events', injuries and consequences, as well as their contexts, meanings and interpretations.[6] Both quantitative and qualitative results are presented. 'Violence' is conceptualized as malevolent physical or sexual 'acts', used in a purposive manner and intended to inflict physical and/or psychological harm. Such acts usually, although not always, have harmful consequences for the victim, particularly physical injuries. In addition, the wider 'constellation of abuse' includes acts that are not physical per se but are meant to frighten, intimidate and coerce. Intimidating and coercive 'acts' are measured and/or assessed separately and reported separately from physical/sexual 'acts', in order that they are not conflated. It should be stressed that coercive and intimidating acts may have important and negative consequences for victims but, as discussed earlier, it is important that they are not collapsed into one category and referred to as though there is no difference between them.

[5] Of the 933 court cases of 'domestic violence' from which the present sample was drawn, there were only three cases of women charged with using violence against a male partner.

[6] When reporting findings from couples, it is important to disaggregate the reports of men from those of women. In their sample of 360 young couples, Moffitt *et al.* (2001: 13, 20) identified and reported upon 28 couples whom they defined as 'clinical', i.e. reached levels of partner abuse that 'resulted in injury (sprains, bruises, cuts, knocked-out, loss of consciousness, broken bones, loose teeth), medical treatment, and police and/or court conviction'. The findings are presented in such a way that it is impossible to know who (man or woman) required medical treatment, sought refuge or was arrested or convicted. This information is essential in order to assess the nature and consequences of violence perpetrated by men and by women within these relationships.

Men's and Women's Perpetration of Violence and Injuries to an Intimate Partner

Violent events: couples' reports of men's violence

The couples were asked how often the man had been violent to the woman during the previous year. It was difficult for respondents to give a precise number of *violent events*, particularly if there had been many such events. As such, respondents were asked to indicate how many events occurred in a usual month and this was used to arrive at an annual estimate. As shown in Table 1, men generally reported perpetrating significantly fewer violent events against their woman partner than were reported by the women themselves. Of the sample, no direct physical violence was reported in the interviews by 21.1 per cent of women and 30.5 per cent of men.[7] Of those reporting violence in the interviews, 47.4 per cent of women and 55.8 per cent of men reported one to four violent events, 17.9 per cent of women and 9.5 per cent of men reported five to nine violent events, and 13.7 per cent of women and 4.2 per cent of men reported ten or more incidents of violence perpetrated by the man.

Couples' reports of women's violence

The couples were also asked how often the woman had been violent to the man during the year prior to the interview (Table 1). Most had little difficulty in giving a precise number of violent events, because the number of incidents perpetrated by women against men was usually few or none. Just under half of the men and women agreed that there had been *no* physical violence perpetrated by the woman against the man (46.3 per cent of women and 40.0 per cent of men reported *NO* violence by the woman). Of those reporting violence by the woman: 44.2 per cent of women and 50.6 per cent of men reported one to four events; 4.2 per cent of women and 7.4 per cent of men reported five to nine events; and 5.3 per cent of women and 2.1 per cent of men reported ten or more events perpetrated by the woman.

TABLE 1   *Men's and women's reports of violent incidents against their partner*

	Men's violence to women***		Women's violence to men (ns)	
	Men %	Women %	Men %	Women %
No violence	30.5	21.1	40.0	46.3
1–4 events	55.8	47.4	50.6	44.2
5–9 events	9.5	17.9	7.4	4.2
10+ events	4.2	13.7	2.1	5.3

Note: asterisks identify statistically significant chi-square results.
n = 95 couples.
*, p < 0.05; **, p < 0.01; ***, p < 0.001.

---

[7] All the men had been arrested for an offence that involved an incident of violence against the woman or damage of domestic property in the context of domestic conflict. Of the entire sample, 80% of the men were arrested and convicted for assault and 20% were convicted of offences involving breach of the peace, damage to property and threatening behaviour.

Frequent violence: five or more violent events within one year

A comparison of the general pattern of men's and women's reporting of the violence perpetrated by each provides some striking differences (Table 1). First, there is significant discordance between men's and women's reports of men's violence. Of particular note is the discrepancy in the reports of 'frequent' violence during a one-year period (combining the two categories of five to nine and ten or more incidents in Table 1). About one-third (31.6 per cent) of the women reported five or more incidents perpetrated by their male partner, while only 13.7 per cent of the men agreed that they had perpetrated this number of incidents. By contrast, men's and women's reports of women's violence were more congruent, including those about violence in general and about 'frequent' violence. Nearly identical proportions of men (9.3 per cent) and women (9.5 per cent) reported that women perpetrated five or more incidents during the one-year period. It should be noted that although the men in this sample had perpetrated a considerable amount of violence in these relationship, just under half of the women (46 per cent) and the men (40 per cent) reported that women had not used violence during the year preceding the interview.

Violent 'acts'

The couples were also asked to specify the different types of violent 'acts' that made up the physical or sexual violence within these 'events'. Both men and women reported a much wider range of violent physical and sexual 'acts' committed by men against women than vice versa. For the purposes of comparing men's violence and women's violence, we include only those physical 'acts' committed by both men and women. While this allows for direct comparisons of men's and women's violence, it omits some of the 'high-end' violence that was perpetrated only by men against women, including sexual assault. We include ten comparisons of physical 'acts' perpetrated by men and women against their partner.

Several general patterns can be seen in Table 2. First, whether reported by men or by women and whether the differences between them are great or small, many more men perpetrate every type of violent or threatening 'acts' than do women. Secondly, sometimes a larger percentage of women than men report their own violence (e.g. slap, push–shove and kick body), while men never report more of their own violence than is reported by their female partners. Thirdly, some 'acts' are perpetrated by a large percentage of men but are rarely perpetrated by women (e.g. choke, damage property and threaten to hit). Fourthly, men and women tend to agree more about women's violence than about men's violence. The rarity of women's 'threats to hit' men would seem to be indicative of an absence of the overall 'constellation of abuse' so familiar in men's abusive behaviour.

While not shown in Table 2, many men perpetrated these 'acts' on a *frequent* basis; women did not do so (Dobash *et al.* 2000). In addition to the 'acts' listed in Table 2, as noted above, other 'acts' have not been included here because both men and women agree that while men perpetrated such acts, they were never perpetrated by women (e.g. forced sex, kick face, etc.). For example, about 40 per cent of women reported that their male partner had 'demanded sex' from them and nearly 20 per cent indicated that their partner had 'forced' them to have sex on at least one occasion. By comparison, far fewer men reported having committed such acts against their woman

TABLE 2   *Intimate partner violence: a comparison of couples' reports of violent or threatening 'acts' perpetrated by men against women and women against men*

'Acts'	Men's violence to women		Women's violence to men	
	Men's reports %	Women's reports %	Men's reports %	Women's reports %
Damage property	80.0	87.4 (ns)	4.2	1.1 (ns)
Threaten to hit	69.5	84.2 (ns)	5.3	3.2 (ns)
Throw something to 'hit'	68.4	81.1*	26.3	25.3 (ns)
Push–shove	94.7	96.8 (ns)	10.5	20.0 (ns)^
Slap	82.1	88.4 (ns)	20.0	29.5 (ns)^
Scratch	62.1	76.8 (ns)	16.8	10.5 (ns)
Punch	68.4	88.4*	31.6	31.6 (ns)
Kick body	54.7	78.9***	17.9	23.2 (ns)^
Use object as weapon	37.9	60.0**	16.8	15.8 (ns)
Choke	48.4	66.3***	1.1	1.1 (ns)

Note: asterisks identify statistically significant chi-square results.
^, a higher proportion of self-reports than partner's reports.
n = 95 couples.
*, p < 0.05; **, p < 0.01; ***, p < 0.001.

partner, with about 15 per cent saying that they had 'demanded sex' and about 3 per cent saying that they had 'forced sex' on their woman partner. None of the men or women in the study reported sexual coercion or violence perpetrated by women.

Couples' reports of injuries inflicted by men and women on partners

Several general patterns about injuries can be seen in Table 3 that show both concordance and discordance in the reports of men and women. First, regardless of who is reporting, it can be seen that many more men inflict every type of injury against women than do women against men. Secondly, some injuries are inflicted by a fair percentage of men but by very few women (e.g. split lip, fractured teeth/bones, black-out/unconscious). Thirdly, a considerable percentage of men and of women

TABLE 3   *A comparison of couples' reports of injuries inflicted by men against women partners and by women against male partners*

Injuries	Men's injuries to women		Women's injuries to men	
	Men's reports %	Women's reports %	Men's reports %	Women's reports %
Bruise	87.4	96.8 (ns)	12.6	13.7 (ns)^
Black eye	57.9	76.8**	9.5	4.2 (ns)
Cut body	18.9	45.3***	11.6	8.4 (ns)
Cut/scratch face	36.8	53.7***	26.3	27.4 (ns)^
Split lip	31.6	61.1***	3.2	2.1 (ns)
Fracture teeth/bones	21.1	42.1***	5.3	1.1 (ns)
Black-out/unconscious	13.7	33.7***	2.1	1.1 (ns)

Note: asterisks identify statistically significant chi-square results.
^, a higher proportion of self-reports than partner's reports.
n = 95 couples.
*, p < 0.05; **, p < 0.01; ***, p < 0.001.

report that men inflict bruises and black eyes on women but both report that women rarely do the same to men. Overall, the couples agree that the *injuries inflicted by women upon men* are less frequent and less severe. By contrast, the couples disagree about the *injuries inflicted by men upon women*, with men reporting less of their own violence to their partner, while women report more of men's violence. In short, men and women tend to agree about the low level of injuries inflicted by women upon men but differ about the frequency and severity of injuries inflicted by men upon women.

In addition to the injuries shown in Table 3, others have not been included because they were only inflicted by men upon women but not the obverse (e.g. miscarriage, 5 per cent; vomiting, 57 per cent). As reported elsewhere, these data also show that while many men inflicted injuries on a frequent basis, women rarely did so (Dobash *et al.* 2000: 188–9). The greater levels of agreement between men and women about injuries inflicted by women may be because women commit far less violence and inflict far fewer injuries and, as such, each event and each injury may be more memorable to both parties.

Perceived seriousness of men's and women's violence

Women and men were also asked about their perceptions of the seriousness of their partner's violence to them. As shown in Table 4, the overall pattern is one in which men and women generally agree that *men's violence* is 'serious' or 'very serious' and that *women's violence* is 'not serious' or 'slightly serious'. The vast majority of both women (82.0 per cent) and men (66.1 per cent) describe men's violence as either 'serious' or 'very serious', whereas only 36.0 per cent of women and 28.5 per cent of men describe women's violence similarly.

Contextualizing Women's Violence against Male Partners

Evidence from this study provides information about the prevalence of violence and injuries among couples and the perceived seriousness of men's and women's violence.

TABLE 4   *A comparison of couples' reports of the seriousness of violence by men against women and women against men*

Seriousness	Men's violence to woman partner*		Women's violence to male partner (ns)	
	Men's reports (n = 92) %	Women's reports (n = 92) %	Men's reports (n = 56) %	Women's reports (n = 50) %
Not serious	10.5	5.0	55.4	40.0
Slightly serious	23.4	13.0	16.1	24.0^
Serious	38.4	36.0	23.2	32.0^
Very serious	27.7	46.0	5.3	4.0
	100%	100%	100%	100%

Note: asterisks identify statistically significant chi-square results.
The ns vary because, in many of the relationships, there was no violence by the woman.
^, a higher proportion of self-reports than partner's reports.
*, p < 0.05; **, p < 0.01; ***, p < 0.001.

While the main pattern is one of men's violence to women, nonetheless the evidence suggests that some women do commit violence against male partners. Here, we examine women's violence by considering more fully its nature, context and consequences, as well as how men and women view women's violence. In order to do this, we use qualitative evidence from the in-depth interviews, which were tape-recorded and analysed using QSR Nud.ist software. The qualitative findings presented below corroborate the quantitative findings presented above. The qualitative findings reveal the nature of the differences between men's and women's violence and provide insight into the meanings each attaches to it.

Nature of women's violence

The findings presented in Tables 1–4 suggest that while women do not generally use serious, consequential violence or perpetrate violence on a frequent basis, men and women report that a few women do use serious violence against their male partner. During the lengthy interviews in which violent events were discussed in detail, women were usually more willing to speak at length about their own violence than were men. The following comments illustrate this violence.

How serious would you say your violence was? Well I suppose the fact that I stabbed him made it pretty serious. I was arrested for attempted murder but, I mean, he gets arrested for a 'domestic' and I get arrested for 'attempted murder'. It was dropped to 'assault', right enough, and I got eighteen months probation. (woman.1082)

That time he had cracked my cheekbone, I went for him with a knife. After he done it [abused her], I just went for him. (woman.1160)

Reports of *serious* violence by women were not the norm, as shown in the reports of injuries in Table 3 and the evaluation of seriousness in Table 4. Accordingly, the majority of men's and women's reports show a restricted range of 'acts' and types of injuries perpetrated by women, as revealed in the comments of both men and women.

Have you ever been violent to him? Oh, I've kind of thrown things, and things like that, but no punching and kicking or that kind of thing. (woman.1041)

Well, apart from throwing that cup, which I don't see as being violent because I got it worse that time. (woman.1064)

How many times has [she] been violent to you? Four or five times. *What usually leads up to this?* An argument over something or other and [she] lashes out but, as I say, she throws—it could be just a wet cloth or she'll punch me in the chest or something like that or hit me with the strap of her handbag but it's never, very rarely, sore. *Have you ever had any injuries?* Except for her scratching me, that's the only real injury I've had. She's never bruised me. (man.056)

Does she ever resort to violence? Yes. *What would she do?* Throw a cup, break the hi-fi. (man.055)

Men's reactions to women's violence against them

Men and women reacted very differently to the violence they experienced. In order to understand better men's reactions to women's violence, it is important to set them in the context of women's reactions to men's violence. The 95 women indicated that they reacted to the violence perpetrated against them in ways that illustrate the impact and importance of these events in their lives. Here, we report only a few. Most women said they were usually 'frightened' (79 per cent), felt 'helpless' (60 per cent), 'alone' (65 per cent) and 'trapped' (57 per cent). They felt 'abused' (65 per cent) but were also 'bitter' (82 per cent) and 'angry' (80 per cent).

Men's reactions to women's violence against them usually did not reflect the negative consequences similar to those reported by women. Of the men who described their response to the violence of their woman partner, the largest proportion said they were 'not bothered' (26 per cent), followed by those who felt that the woman was 'justified' (20 per cent) and those who 'ridiculed her' (17 per cent) or were 'impressed' (3 per cent) that she had managed to respond. Others felt 'angry' (14 per cent) or 'surprised' (6 per cent) and there were a variety of 'other' reactions (8 per cent). Only a few of the men felt 'victimized' (6 per cent).

Men often described women's violence toward them as insignificant:

Has her violence toward you been serious? No, never. *Not at all?* No. (man.123)

Do you feel concerned about her violent behaviour? No, not really. (man.116)

Men sometimes viewed women's violent/aggressive acts as comical or ludicrous.

Like we've had an argument and I've had the clothes flung at me and a cup smashed over my head. You know, she does that to me and I end up laughing and it makes her worse. (man.036)

Who hit first? Me likely. *And what did you think about her being violent to you?* I just laughed, probably laughing and joking about it. She trying to hit me? Like, trying to hurt me? [incredulous] (man.058)

What would you do or say [when she hit you]? If she hit us, I would say, 'is that the best you can do?' She'd hit me again and I'd say something like, 'Oh [Betty], for God's sake, just pack it in'. *So, you'd make fun of her?* I would just laugh at her, you know, just laugh at her [saying] 'you're mental'! (man.055)

And what would you do [when he hit you]? I don't know, probably try to hit him. *How serious would you be?* Very serious. *Does he take it seriously?* Most times he just laughs at me and that makes it worse. (woman.1055)

Some men found it impossible to contemplate women's violence. It was only men who could and should use violence, not women.

What do you think about her being violent to you? Well, I think she's not got the right to do that. I'm a man, she's a woman! (man.008)

He says it's degrading to him to have a woman lift her hand to him. (woman.1082)

Has [she] ever been violent to you? No, because she's a woman, I'm a man. Basically, my wife's 98lbs. (man.041)

A few men even expressed a form of 'admiration' of the woman's violent reaction to their abuse. For them, the violence seemed to be the only meaningful expression of her objections to his violence toward her. While women repeatedly expressed their rejection of and anger about his violence to her, for some men these actions were 'invisible' or inconsequential. Women may have reacted in these ways for many years; it was only when she acted 'like a man' that he appeared to notice her objections. Ironically, the woman's response to the man's repeated abuse might serve to expurgate his guilt.

How do you feel about the violence? Good. *How's that?* The fact that she's getting her aggression back out on me what I used to do to her. (man.038)

It did me good. I was quite pleased she did it because I knew she was starting to stand up for herself. (man.089)

Both the quantitative and qualitative evidence suggest that men's reactions to and interpretations of the violence they experienced differ from those expressed by women about men's violence. The fear, bewilderment and helplessness expressed by the women were not apparent in the responses of the men. Unlike the women, few of the men reacted to the violence in ways that suggested it had seriously affected their sense of well-being or the routines of their daily life. Rather, in those relationships in which women's violence occurred, men were often unconcerned and viewed it as relatively inconsequential and of no lasting effect. Although a few men were affected in a negative fashion and did experience serious injuries, this was not the norm for most of the men in the study.

Self-Defence

The issue of self-defence in intimate partner violence has been a subject of considerable debate. As recognized in law, the concept of self-defence and its corollary, provocation, incorporate contextual and situational elements (Polk 1997). In order to define an act as 'self-defence', it is necessary to consider the context in which the 'act' occurred, including the interaction between the individuals involved. These elements are essential in the application of the term 'self-defence'. It is inappropriate, as has been done in some research, to infer 'self-defence' or lack thereof from simple, static information, such as the 'personal characteristics' of the individuals involved and/or who acted first (Moffitt *et al.* 2001: 25; Stets and Strauss 1990: 161).

In this study, men and women were asked about the use of violence in 'self-defence'. The responses are highly gendered and illustrate the complexity of this issue. Men generally did not use the term 'self-defence' to describe their violence toward women. When discussing the violent event that led to their arrest and conviction, only six of the 95 men indicated that they hit their partner because 'she hit him first', but even they did not describe this as 'self-defence'. By contrast, women often used the term 'self-defence' or 'self-protection' to describe their violence to men.

Men and women were asked whether women's use of violence was 'always' in self-defence. Focusing only on responses from individuals where women had used violence, 75 per cent of these women said their violence was 'always' in self-defence and 54 per cent of men agreed. The different terms used by respondents to describe what might be seen as 'reactions' in response to particular 'acts' of violence (e.g. raise an arm to deflect a blow, push against the chest in order to facilitate running from the room to escape further blows, etc.) raise questions about how such acts might be defined by the men and women involved, as well as by researchers. Are these acts of 'self-protection' and/or 'self-defence', or acts of 'violence'? Acts of 'self-protection' might include such things as 'putting one's arms up to deflect an oncoming blow', while an act of 'self-defence' might include the 'return of a blow'. Surely, these are not acts of malevolent violence. This is a complex issue, as reflected in some of the comments made by men and women about women's violence.

Was she ever violent when you were arguing? No, not really. She would usually try and protect herself. (man.089)

What did you usually try to do? I tried to hold my hands up. *To protect yourself?* Yes, and when he used to punch me, I used to try and grab his hands or just hold his hands, and he'd be kicking me. He would just come up and kick me but I would try to put out my hand to stop him from kicking me. I was trying to defend myself really, which I never done before. (woman.1064)

Did [she] ever try to stop you being violent to her? She'd pick up something, like a glass for instance and warn me. She's kicked me out of the house and I couldn't get back in because of the [my] violence. (man.041)

These quotes demonstrate some of the complications of this issue. In the literature, it is often implied that women's reactions to men's violence do not include elements of retaliation and/or revenge. In this study, it was clear that women did at times respond to their abusive male partner out of 'reactive anger' about a specific attack against her or as a result of the cumulative effect of many attacks over a prolonged period of abuse.

Have you ever been violent to him? Only sort of in self-defence. *So you have retaliated if you have been hurt?* Yes. *Have you ever hurt him in any way or has he been bruised as a result of what you have done?* The first time it happened, I picked up a shoe and smacked him across the face with it and his nose went a bit 'squifff' for a while, but then things went back to normal [him hitting her]. (woman.1081)

He's hurt me a good few times but I've always been able to fight back, except for the last time. One night I told him if he didn't stop hitting me I'd pick something up and hit him with it, and I did. I picked up an empty juice bottle and hit him with it. But it was the only way I could get him to stop. And he was going to get me charged for hitting him...and I said to the policeman 'Oh, that's fine, go ahead, charge me. But what about what he's done to me? That doesn't matter because I defended myself?' And the policeman, said, 'Right, we'll separate you for the night'. (woman.1066)

Women's use of violence, whether in self-protection, self-defence or retaliation, sometimes resulted in an escalation of the man's violence toward her.

Have you ever been violent to him? A couple of times I've sort of slapped him back, but I mean I don't get anywhere so I didn't bother. *When you've slapped him back, how did he respond?* I get it all the more, that's why I don't bother. (woman.1126)

Did that [trying to protect yourself] reduce it [the violence]? No, it didn't reduce it. It made things a bit worse actually because it made him hit harder just in case I tried to hit back. If he was going to hurt me, he made sure that it was bad enough that I wouldn't be able to get up. I mean, there's not much I can do with broken fingers or there's not much you can do when you're being stoated [bounced] off a wall. (woman.1064)

How did he respond to your violence? I think the fact that I tried defending myself made him ten times worse. (woman.1066)

Conclusions and Implications for Legislation, Policies and Interventions

We began with a 'puzzle' about contradictory research findings concerning the violence of men and women against an intimate partner. Research findings are contradictory, suggesting, on the one hand, *symmetry*, with men and women equally likely to perpetrate violence against an intimate partner, and, on the other hand, *asymmetry*, with men the primary perpetrators of violence against women partners. These contradictory research findings not only have implications for academic research but also for policies and interventions. This adds importance to the task of trying to unravel the puzzle of how researchers arrived at such contradictory findings. In order to do this, we considered how this 'violence' is conceptualized, defined, measured and reported. We suggest that FV research that uses a narrow, 'act-based' approach to the definition and measurement of violence is more likely to find 'symmetry' or equivalence of 'violence' between men and women. This is because it conflates acts of violence and aggression and does not examine the context, consequences, motivations, intentions and reactions associated with the overall violent 'event' or the relationships in which the violence occurs. The more comprehensive methodology used in VAW research provides additional data about the problem, including a more detailed look at the violence itself, as well as inclusion of factors such as context, consequences and intentions. This approach provides a wider base of relevant knowledge about the violence and illustrates important differences between men and women in the perpetration of violence, as well as its consequences. Findings from this more comprehensive methodology support the notion that *serious* intimate partner violence is asymmetrical, with men usually violent to women.

In those cases where women had used violence against their male partner, the findings reported here suggest that women's violence differs from that perpetrated by men in terms of nature, frequency, intention, intensity, physical injury and emotional impact. All of the women in this study had been the victims of repeated physical violence from their male partner, often over many years. Despite this, just over half had used any form of violence against their abuser, none had used sexual violence and only a few had used serious or injurious violence. Of the women who had used violence, the consequences in terms of emotional impact were usually inconsequential; the consequences in terms of injuries were usually, though not always, less severe; the violence often, though not always, occurred in the context of 'self-defence' or 'self-protection'; and women's violence was usually, although not always, rated by both partners as 'not serious'. In addition, women did not use intimidating or coercive forms of controlling behaviour associated with the 'constellation of abuse'. Men who were the recipients of women's violence usually reported that it was 'inconsequential', did not negatively affect their sense of well-being and safety, and these men rarely, if ever, sought protection from the authorities. These findings regarding the nature and consequences of women's violence make it impossible to construe the violence of men and women as either equivalent or reciprocal.

Men's and women's reports about their own violence and the violence of their partner reveal that they tend to agree about the nature, frequency and impact of the violence perpetrated by women but disagree about men's violence. With respect to women's violence, there is considerable concordance between men and women in reporting that women do not usually perpetrate violence. When women do use violence, men and women agree that it is generally infrequent, is rarely 'serious', results in few, if any, injuries and has few, if any, negative consequences for men. By contrast, there is considerable discordance between men's and women's reports about men's violence. Men and women disagree about the nature, frequency and impact of violence perpetrated by men—women report more and men report less. Curiously, while men never report more of their own violence than that reported by women partners, women sometimes do. These results correspond to findings from other research (Szinovacz 1983; Margolin 1987).

What are the policy implications of these findings? These findings indicate that the problem of intimate partner violence is primarily one of men's violence to women partners and not the obverse. A recent review of existing policies on domestic violence in England and Wales includes a comprehensive list of 'detailed recommendations on key policy areas' (Harwin 2000). The general principles underlying a national strategy should include: promoting the protection of women and children at risk of violence; prevention through public awareness, education and the law; and the provision of effective services. The 'framework for action' includes a host of specific recommendations across a broad spectrum, including: specialist refuge and advocacy services, civil law, criminal law, law enforcement, divorce and court proceedings, child protection services, social services, welfare benefits and related issues, housing, immigration laws and education (Harwin 2000: 382–91). These efforts are overwhelmingly directed at the problem of men's violence to women.

The findings reported here are in line with this overall orientation to policy. They support the general trend of policies and interventions relating to intimate partner violence that are almost wholly designed to deal with the serious problem of men's violence directed at women (Dobash 2003). While any and all conflict and negative encounters between couples is regrettable, policies and interventions, particularly those of criminal justice, are not developed to provide wide-scale responses to such encounters; nor are public resources spent upon them. This is not to say that conflicts, heated arguments, name-calling or a one-off push or shove are unimportant but, rather, that great care must be taken in the definition and measurement of any such behaviour before it is labelled as 'violence' and before public policies and interventions are directed at it (Gordon 2000: 750).[8]

Even so, what about the perennial question of women's violence to male partners? If such violence occurs with the same frequency and ferocity as men's violence and has a similar impact on the victims, then responding to the needs of male victims should be identical to those for women victims. Accordingly, laws, social services, health care, education and the like would all need to expend similar resources in assisting the equal numbers of male victims of violence to escape to shelters where they might be safe, to obtain protection orders so that they might be safe, and to access public housing for themselves and their children in order that they might be safe. A follow-up study of men who identified themselves as victims of domestic violence in the Scottish Crime Survey 2000 was conducted in order to examine the nature and veracity of these reports and to consider the need for services for such 'abused' men (Gadd, Farrall, Dallimore and Lombard 2002). The findings revealed that one-quarter of the men had not experienced violence from their partner but had misunderstood the meaning of the term 'domestic violence' and were referring, instead, to crimes in the domestic dwelling (e.g. non-domestic assaults

---

[8] This is also supported by survey research that shows that respondents do not define as 'violence' minor, infrequent or moderate acts as reported on the CTS (Hamby, Poindexter and Gray-Little 1996).

and property crimes). The follow-up showed that some of the men were also assailants and very few defined themselves as 'victims'. Of those men who did experience some form of violence from their female partner, they were less likely than women to be repeat victims, to have been seriously injured and to report feeling fearful in their own home. Based on these findings, the researchers concluded that there was no need for a special agency or refuge provision for men (Gadd, Farrall, Dallimore and Lombard 2002). In the United States, more women are being brought into the criminal justice system because of 'domestic violence', primarily because of dual arrests of both the man and the woman (Miller 2001). This may suggest the occurrence of violence by both women and men and the need for victim services for both. However, a closer examination of these cases suggested that the majority of the women were rarely the 'primary' perpetrator, were often the victims of violence from their male partner, and that men's and women's need for services were rarely equivalent (Hamberger and Poternte 1994; Miller 2001).

If women's violence is not equivalent to that of men and does not require identical policies and interventions, then how do we conceive of women's violence and what is to be done by way of intervention and prevention? According to the findings of this and other research, when women's violence against a male partner does occur, it is usually, although not always, in the context of men's violence to the woman (Swan and Snow 2002). However, as already stated, this violence is rarely identical or truly reciprocal. The type and level of violence, the nature and number of injuries, the perceived seriousness of the violence and the sense of safety and well-being are not the same for men and women. For the most part, women's violence is reactive and self-protective and is often in self-defence.

As mentioned earlier, it has been suggested that one strategy for reducing intimate partner violence is to propose that woman never use violence against a male partner, regardless of the circumstances, because this may result in the escalation of the man's violence against the woman (Straus 1993). It is neither possible nor reasonable to make 'fixed' recommendations about the nature of how any woman should respond to violence against her, because it is impossible to know the relevant circumstances within a given event or relationship. It would be similar to recommending in advance that a woman who is being raped should never 'fight back' or 'always fight back'. Perhaps a more positive strategy for preventing or reducing women's violence, and one in keeping with the findings of this study, is to eliminate men's violence against women partners.

Reductions in the rates of homicide in the United States over the last two decades reflect on several aspects of this issue: women's serious violence, fighting back in the context of violence from the male partner and relevant interventions for the victim and the perpetrator. In the United States, as elsewhere, much of the lethal violence committed by women against men occurs in the context of ongoing physical abuse by the man (Browne 1987; Wilson and Daly 1992). In the United States, there has been a significant reduction in homicides among intimate partners, particularly the killing of African-American men by their women partners. Evidence suggests that this reduction in intimate partner homicides is related to more effective responses to abusers and improved social and legal services for abused women. These provide women with supports and escape routes so that they are less likely to respond to men's violence in this most extreme fashion (Browne and Williams 1989; 1993; Browne, Williams and Dutton 1999). As such, policies and interventions aimed at eliminating men's violent abuse of women, along with services for women victims, may be important contributors to the reduction in homicides where women use lethal violence against a male partner against a backdrop of ongoing violence against her.

Finally, what is to be done about the very small number of women who may *initiate* severe, persistent, repeat physical and sexual violence against a male partner in a context of no violence from the man? We have yet to see any evidence that would enable us to consider this issue. Identification of this putative group would require the same kind of intensive studies that have been done on men's violence, using both qualitative and quantitative data to provide a holistic picture of the violence and the context, consequences, motives and intentions associated with it. What is required is research methods that provide a more adequate representation of this violence and the contexts in which it occurs, rather than conceptual and operationalist abstractions that are once removed from such real-life events. Even if this were to be found, all extant evidence would predict that the numbers would be very small. As such, priority should continue to be given to policies that seek to effectively intervene to end violence against women in intimate relationships.

References

ADLER, F. (1947), 'Operational Definitions in Sociology', *American Journal of Sociology*, 52: 438–44.

ARCHER, J. (1999), 'Assessment of the Reliability of the Conflict Tactics Scales: A Meta-Analytic Review', *Journal of Interpersonal Violence*, 14: 1263–89.

BACHMAN, R. and SALTZMAN, L. E. (1995), *Violence against Women: Estimates from the Redesigned Survey*. Special Report of the Bureau of Justice Statistics. Washington, DC: US Department of Justice.

BERK, R., BERK, S. F., LOSEKE, D. R. and RAUMA, D. (1983), 'Mutual Combat and Other Family Myths', in D. Finkelhor, R. J. Gelles, G. T. Hotaling and M. A. Straus, eds., *The Dark Side of Families: Current Family Violence Research*. Sage: Newbury Park.

BOURGOIS, P. (1995), *In Search of Respect: Selling Crack in El Barrio*. New York: Cambridge University Press.

BRIDGMAN, P. (1927), *The Logic of Modern Physics*. New York: Macmillan.

BROWNE, A. (1987), *When Battered Women Kill*. New York: Free Press.

BROWNE, A., SALOMON, A. and BASSUK, S. S. (1999), 'The Impact of Recent Partner Violence on Poor Women's Capacity to Maintain Work', *Violence Against Women*, 5/4: 393–426.

BROWNE, A. and WILLIAMS, K. R. (1989), 'Exploring the Effect of Resource Availability and the Likelihood of Female-Perpetrated Homicide', *Law and Society Review* 23: 75–94.

BROWNE, A. and WILLIAMS, K. R. (1993), 'Gender, Intimacy, and Lethal violence: Trends from 1976 through 1987', *Gender and Society*, 7: 78–98.

BROWNE, A., WILLIAMS, K. R. and DUTTON, D. G. (1999), 'Homicide between Intimate Partners: A 20-Year Review', in M. D. Smith and M. A. Zahn, eds, *Homicide: A Sourcebook of Social Research*. Thousand Oaks: Sage. pp. 149–64.

BROWNING, J. and DUTTON, D. G. (1986), 'Assessment of Wife Assault with the Conflict Tactics Scale: Using Couple Data to Quantify the Differential Reporting Effect', *Journal of Marriage and the Family*, 48: 375–9.

CAMPBELL, J. C. (1998) 'Making the Health Care System an Empowerment Zone for Battered Women', in J. C. Campbell, ed., *Empowering Survivors of Abuse: Health Care for Battered Women and Their Children*. Thousand Oaks: Sage. pp. 3–22.

CAMPBELL, J. C. (1999), 'Forced Sex and Intimate Partner Violence', *Violence Against Women*, 5: 1017–35.

CANTOS, A. L., NEIDIG, P. H. and O'LEARY, K. D. (1994), Injuries to Women and Men in a Treatment Programme for Domestic Violence', *Journal of Family Violence*, 9: 113–24.

DALY, M. and WILSON, M. (1988), *Homicide*. New York: Aldine De Gruyter.

DEKESERADY, W. S. (2000), 'Current Controversies on Defining Nonlethal Violence against Women in Intimate Heterosexual Relationships', *Violence Against Women*, 6(7): 728–46.

DESCOLA, P. (1996), *The Spears of Twilight: Life and Death in the Amazon Jungle* (translated by J. Lloyd). Glasgow: Harper-Collins.

DOBASH, R. E. (2003), 'Domestic Violence: Arrest, Prosecution and Reducing Violence', *Crime and Public Policy* 2(2): 313–18.

DOBASH, R. E. and DOBASH, R. P. (1979), *Violence against Wives*. New York: The Free Press.

DOBASH, R. P. and DOBASH, R. E. (1983), 'The Context Specific Approach', in D. Finkelhor *et al.*, eds., *The Dark Side of Families*. Beverly Hills: Sage.

DOBASH, R. E. and DOBASH, R. P. (1990a), 'How Theoretical Definitions and Perspectives Affect Research and Policy', in D. M. Besharov, ed., *Family Violence: Research and Public Policy Issues*. Washington, DC: The AEI Press. pp. 108–29.

DOBASH, R. P. and DOBASH, R. E. (1990b), 'How Research Makes a Difference to Policy and Practice', in D. M. Besharov, ed., *Family Violence: Research and Public Policy Issues*. Washington, DC: The AEI Press. pp. 185–204.

DOBASH, R. E. and DOBASH, R. P. (1992), *Women, Violence and Social Change*. London and New York: Routledge.

DOBASH, R. P. and DOBASH, R. E. (2001), 'Violence against Women: A Review of Recent Anglo–American Research, *Journal of Conflict and Violence Research*, 3: 5–22.

DOBASH, R. P., DOBASH, R. E., CAVANAGH, K. and LEWIS, R. (1998), 'Separate and Intersecting Realities: A Comparison of Men's and Women's Accounts of Violence Against Women', *Violence Against Women*, 4: 382–414.

DOBASH, R. P., DOBASH, R. E., CAVANAGH, K. and LEWIS, R. (2000), *Changing Violent Men*. Thousand Oaks, CA: Sage.

DOBASH, R. E., DOBASH, R. P., CAVANAGH, K. and LEWIS, R. (2004), 'Not an Ordinary Killer—Just an Ordinary Guy: When Men Murder an Intimate Woman Partner', *Violence Against Women* (forthcoming).

DOBASH, R. P., DOBASH, R. E., WILSON, M. and DALY, M. (1992), 'The Myth of Sexual Symmetry in Marital Violence', *Social Problems*, 39: 71–91.

EDLESON, J. and BRYGGER, M. P. (1986), 'Gender Differences in Reporting of Battering Incidents', *Family Relations*, 35: 377–82.

GADD, D., FARRALL, S., DALLIMORE, D. and LOMBARD, N. (2002), *Domestic Abuse against Men in Scotland*. Edinburgh: Scottish Executive.

GAQUIN, D. A. (1977/78), 'Spouse Abuse: Data from the National Crime Survey', *Victimology*, 2: 632–43.

GELLES, R. and STRAUS, M. (1979), 'Determinants of Violence in the Family: Toward a Theoretical Integration', in W. R. Burr, R. Hill, F. I. Nye and I. L. Reiss, eds., *Contemporary Theories About the Family*. Volume 1. New York: Free Press. pp. 549–81.

GELLES, R. J. (1997), *Intimate Violence in Families*. 3rd edition. Thousand Oaks, CA: Sage.

GELLES, R. J. (2000), 'Estimating the Incidence and Prevalence of Violence against Women', *Violence Against Women*, 6(7): 784–804.

GONDOLF, E. Batterer Intervention Systems Safe. Berely Hills CA.

GORDON, L. (1988), *Heroes of Their Own Lives: The Politics and History of Family Violence: Boston 1880–1960*. New York: Viking.

GORDON, M. (2000), 'Definitional Issues in Violence against Women: Surveillance and Research from a Violence Research Perspective', *Violence Against Women*, 6(7): 747–83.

HAMBERGER, L. K. and POTENTE. (1994), 'Counseling heterosexual women arrested for domestic violence: Implication for theory and practice', *Violence And Victims*, 9: 125–37.

HAMBY, S. L., POINDEXTER, V. C. and GRAY-LITTLE, B. (1996), 'Four Measures of Partner Violence: Construct Similarity and Classification Differences', *Journal of Marriage and the Family*, 58: 127–39.

HARWIN, N. (2000), 'Families without Fear: Women's Aid Agenda for Action on Domestic Violence', Appendix 1, in J. Hanmer and C. Itzin, eds., (with S. Quaid and D. Wigglesworth), *Home Truths About Domestic Violence*. London: Routledge.

HEISE, L. L. (with PITANGUY, J. and Germain, A.) (1994), *Violence against Women: The Hidden Health Burden*. World Bank Discussion Papers. Washington, DC: World Bank.

HEMPEL, C. G. (1966) Philosophy of Natural Science. New York: Prentice-Hall, NY.

JOHNSON, H. and SACCO, V. (1995), 'Researching Violence against Women: Statistics Canada's National Survey', *Canadian Journal of Criminology*, 37(3): 281–304.

JOURILES, E. N. and O'LEARY, K. D. (1985), 'Interspousal Reliability of Reports of Marital Violence', *Journal of Consulting and Clinical Psychology*, 53: 419–21.

KELLY, L. (1997), *Final Report of the Activities of the EG-S-VL Plan of Action for Combating Violence against Women*. Strausbourg, France: Council of Europe.

KURZ, D. (1993), 'Physical Assaults by Husbands: A Major Social Problem', in R. J. Gelles and D. R. Loseke, eds., *Current Controversies on Family Violence*. Newbury Park, CA: Sage. pp. 88–103.

LAZARSFELD, P. F. (1967), 'Concept Formation and Measurement in the Behavioral Sciences: Some Historical Observations', in G. J. Dinenzo, ed., *Concepts, Theory and Explanation in the Behavioral Sciences*. New York: Random House.

LEVINSON, D. (1989), *Family Violence in Cross-Cultural Perspectives*. Newbury Park, CA: Sage.

LLOYD, S. and TALUC, N. (1999), 'The Effects of Male Violence on Female Employment', *Violence Against Women*, 5(4): 370–92.

LUNDBERG, G. A. (1942), 'Operational Definitions in the Social Sciences', *American Journal of Sociology*, 47: 735.

MACMILLAN, R. and GARTNER, R. (1999), 'When She Brings Home the Bacon: Labor-Force Participation and the Risk of Spousal Violence against Women', *Journal of Marriage and the Family*, 61: 947–58.

MARGOLIN, G. (1987), 'The Multiple Forms of Aggressiveness between Marital Partners: How Do We Identify Them?', *Journal of Marital and Family Therapy*, 13: 77–84.

MILLER, S. (2001), 'The Paradox of Women Arrested for Domestic Violence: Criminal Justice Professionals and Service Providers Respond', *Violence Against Women*, 7: 1339–76.

MIRRLEES-BLACK, C. (1999), *Domestic Violence: Findings from a New British Crime Survey Self-Completion Questionnaire, A Research, Development and Statistics Directorate Report*. London: Home Office.

MOFFITT, T. E., CASPI, A., KRUEGER, R. F., MAGDOL, L., MARGOLIN, G., SILVA, P. A. and SYDNEY, R. (1997), 'Do Partners Agree about Abuse in their Relationship? A Psychometric Evaluation of Interpartner Agreement', *Psychological Assessment*, 9: 47–56.

MOFFITT, T. E., KRUEGER, R. F., CASPI, A. and FAGAN, J. (2000), 'Partner Abuse and General Crime: How Are They the Same? How Are They Different?', *Criminology*, 38: 199–232.

MOFFITT, T. E., Robins, Caspi. (2001), 'A Couples Analysis of Partner Abuse with Implications for Abuse-Prevention Policy', *Criminology and Public Policy*, 1: 5–36.

MORSE, B. J. (1995), 'Beyond the Conflict Tactics Scale: Assessing Gender Differences in Partner Violence', *Violence and Victims*, 10: 251–72.

MULLENDER, A. (1996), *Rethinking Domestic Violence: The Social Work and Probation Response*. London: Routledge.

NAZROO, J. (1995), 'Uncovering Gender Differences in the Use of Marital Violence: The Effect of Methodology', *Sociology*, 29: 475–94.

PENCE, E. and PAYMAR, M. (1993), *Education Groups for Men who Batter*. New York: Springer.

PLECK, E. (1987), *Domestic Tyranny*. Oxford: Oxford University Press.

POLK, K. (1997) 'A Reexamination of the Concept of Victim-Precipitated Homicide', *Homicide Studies*, 1: 141–68.

UNITED NATIONS (1995), *Platform for Action*. Report of the Fourth World Conference on Women, Beijing, September (UN Publication, E96.IV.13). New York: United Nations.

SACCO, V. F. and JOHNSON, H. (1990), *Patterns of Criminal Victimization in Canada*. Ottawa: Statistics Canada.

SAUNDERS, D. G. (1988), 'Wife Abuse, Husband Abuse, or Mutual Combat?', in K. Yllo and M. Bograd, eds., *Feminist Perspectives on Wife Abuse*. Beverly Hills, CA: Sage.

SCHAFER, J., CAETANO, R. and CLARKE, C. L. (2002), 'Agreement about Violence in U.S. Couples', *Journal of Interpersonal Violence*, 17(4): 457–70.

SCHECHTER, S. (1982), *Women and Male Violence: The Visions and Struggles of the Battered Women's Movement*. Boston: South End Press.

SCHNEIDER, E. (2002), 'The Law and Violence against Women in the Family at Century's End: The US Experience', in S. N. Katz, J. Eekelaar and M. Maclean, eds, *Cross Currents: Family Law and Policy in the US and England*. Oxford: Oxford University Press. pp. 471–94.

SCHWARTZ, M. D. (1987), 'Gender and Injury in Marital Assault', *Sociological Focus*, 20: 61–75.

STETS, J. E. and STRAUS, M. A. (1990), 'Gender Differences in Reporting Marital Violence and its Medical and Psychological Consequences', in M. A. Straus and R. J. Gelles, eds., *Physical Violence in American Families*. New Brunswick: Transaction Publishers. pp. 151–66.

STRAUS, M. A. (1980), 'Measuring Intrafamily Conflict and Violence: The Conflict Tactics Scales', *Journal of Marriage and the Family*, 41: 75–88.

STRAUS, M. A. (1993), 'Physical Assaults by Wives: A Major Social Problem', in R. J. Gelles and D. R. Loseke, eds, *Current Controversies on Family Violence*. Newbury Park, CA: Sage. pp. 67–88.

STRAUS, M. A. and GELLES, R. J., eds., (1990), *Physical Violence in American Families*. New Brunswick, NJ: Transaction Publishers.

STRAUS, M. A., HAMBY, S. L., BONEY-MCCOY, S. and SUGARMAN, D. B. (1996), 'The Revised Conflict Tactics Scales (CTS2)', *Journal of Family Issues*, 7(3): 283–316.

STUBBS, J., ed. (1994), *Women, Male Violence and the Law*. Sydney: The Institute of Criminology.

SWAN, S. C. and SNOW, O. L. (2002), 'A Typology of Womens Use of Violence in Intimate Relationships', *Violence Against Women* 8(3): 286–319.

SZINOVACZ, M. E. (1983), 'Using Couple Data as a Methodological Tool: The Case of Marital Violence', *Journal of Marriage and the Family*, 45: 633–44.

TAJEDA, P. and THOENNES, N. (1998), *Prevalence, Incidence, and Consequences of Violence against Women: Findings From the National Violence Against Women Survey*. Research in Brief. National Institute of Justice, Center for Disease Control Prevention. Washington, DC: US Department of Justice.

Violence Against Women (Journal of) (2001). Special issue: 'European Perspectives on Violence Against Women', 7(7): 727–850.

WILSON, M. and DALY, M. (1992), 'Who Kills Whom in Spouse Killings? On the Exceptional Sex Ratio of Spousal Homicides in the United States', *Criminology*, 30: 189–215.

WILSON, M. and DALY, M. (1998), 'Lethal and Nonlethal Violence against Wives and the Evolutionary Psychology of Male Sexual Proprietariness', in R. E. Dobash and R. P. Dobash, eds, *Rethinking Violence against Women*. Thousand Oaks, CA: Sage. pp. 199–230.

Part II
Patriarchy, Crime and Justice

[4]

WOMEN IN THE STREET-LEVEL DRUG ECONOMY: CONTINUITY OR CHANGE?*

LISA MAHER
The University of New South Wales, Sydney

KATHLEEN DALY
Griffith University, Brisbane

Images of women in the contemporary drug economy are highly mixed. Most scholars emphasize change in women's roles, some emphasize continuity, and others suggest that both change and continuity are evident. At issue is whether an increased share of women were involved in selling and higher-level distribution roles in the crack cocaine markets of the late 1980s and early 1990s, compared to the heroin markets of the 1960s and 1970s. We present the results of an ethnographic study of women drug users conducted during 1989-92 in a New York City neighborhood. Contrary to those who suggest that crack cocaine markets have provided "new opportunities" for women, we find that such opportunities were realized by men. At the same time, the conditions of street-level sex work, which has traditionally provided women drug users with a relatively stable source of income, have deteriorated.

Images of women in the contemporary drug economy are highly mixed. Most scholars emphasize *change* in women's roles in U.S. drug markets of 1960-1985, organized primarily around heroin, compared to women's roles in more recent drug markets with the advent of crack cocaine (e.g., Baskin et al., 1993; Bourgois, 1989; Dunlap and Johnson, 1992; Inciardi et al., 1993; Mieczkowski, 1994; C. Taylor, 1993). Some emphasize *continuity* from previous decades (Adler, 1985; Koester and Schwartz, 1993; Maher and Curtis, 1992). Others suggest that both change and continuity are evident, with women inhabiting "two social worlds" (Fagan, 1994:212): one of increased participation in, and the other of continued restriction by, male-dominated street and drug networks.

One should expect, on the one hand, to see variation in women's positions in the drug economy. Research on drug markets in New York City (Bourgois, 1995; Curtis and Sviridoff, 1994; Hamid, 1990, 1992; Johnson et

* The research on which this article is based was supported by the award of a Dissertation Fellowship from the Harry Frank Guggenheim Foundation. We are indebted to the women who participated in the study, to Richard Curtis and Ansley Hamid for their many contributions to the research, and to the reviewers for helpful comments on earlier drafts of this manuscript.

466   MAHER AND DALY

al., 1985, 1992; Williams, 1989), Miami (Inciardi et al., 1993), Washington, D.C. (Reuter et al., 1990), Detroit (Mieczkowski, 1986, 1990; C. Taylor, 1990), Chicago (Padilla, 1992), Milwaukee (Hagedorn, 1994), Los Angeles, and the West Coast (Adler, 1985; Morgan and Joe, 1994; Skolnick, 1989; Waldorf et al., 1991) reveals differences in the racial and ethnic composition of participants and who controls markets, the kinds of drugs sold, how markets are organized, and participants' responses to law enforcement. Such differences are likely to affect women's positions and specific roles.

At the same time, the varied characterizations of women's roles reflect differences in the theoretical assumptions and methodological approaches taken by scholars. For example, women's increasing presence in the drug economies of the late 1980s and early 1990s is said to reflect (1) emancipation from their traditional household responsibilities (Bourgois, 1989; Bourgois and Dunlap, 1993), (2) an extension of their traditional household responsibilities (Wilson, 1993), and (3) the existence of "new opportunities" in street-level drug markets (Mieczkowski, 1994), especially with increased rates of incarceration of minority group men (Baskin et al., 1993). These explanations reveal different assumptions about changes (or not) in the gendered structure of drug markets and about the links (or not) between women's participation in crime and their domestic responsibilities.

Data sources and methods also affect the quality and content of the inferences drawn. Some have analyzed Uniform Crime Report (UCR) arrest data (e.g., Wilson, 1993), others have interviewed women arrested on drug charges or through snowball samples (e.g., Baskin et al., 1993; Fagan, 1994; Inciardi et al., 1993; C. Taylor, 1993), and a handful have conducted ethnographies of particular neighborhoods (e.g., Bourgois, 1989; Maher and Curtis, 1992). While interview-based studies may offer an empirical advantage over the inferences that can be drawn from UCR arrest data, the one-time interview may not elicit complete or reliable information about the changing contexts of women's income generation in the informal economy.

This article presents the results of an ethnographic study of women drug users conducted during 1989-1992 in a New York City neighborhood. We assess whether women's involvement in U.S. drug markets of the mid-1980s onward reflects change, continuity, or a combination of change and continuity from patterns in previous decades. We find that contrary to the conclusions of Baskin et al. (1993), Fagan (1994), Inciardi et al. (1993), Mieczkowski (1994), and C. Taylor (1993), crack cocaine markets have not necessarily provided "new opportunities" for women, nor should such markets be viewed as "equal opportunity employers" (Bourgois, 1989; Wilson, 1993). Our study suggests that recent drug markets continue to be

WOMEN IN THE DRUG ECONOMY 467

monopolized by men and to offer few opportunities for stable income generation for women. While women's *presence* on the street and in low-level auxiliary roles may have increased, we find that their *participation* as substantive labor in the drug-selling marketplace has not.

WOMEN IN THE DRUG ECONOMY

DRUG MARKETS OF THE 1960s TO THE MID-1980s

Prior to the advent of crack cocaine in the mid-1980s, research on women in the drug economy used one or more of four elements to explain women's restricted roles in selling and distributing drugs:[1] intimate relationships with men, the availability of alternative options for income generation, restrictions on discretionary time, and institutionalized sexism in the underworld.

Female heroin users were often characterized as needing a man to support their consumption (e.g., File, 1976; File et al., 1974; Hser et al., 1987; Smithberg and Westermeyer, 1985; Sutter, 1966). They were also described as being "led" into crime by individual men (Covington, 1985; Pettiway, 1987), although this may apply more to white than minority group women (Anglin and Hser, 1987; Pettiway, 1987). The typical pattern was of low-status roles in which participation was short-lived, sporadic, and mediated by intimate relationships with men (Adler, 1985; Rosenbaum, 1981). Alternative sources of income generation, such as prostitution and shoplifting, may have been preferable to female drug users, especially heroin users (File, 1976; Goldstein, 1979; Hunt, 1990; Inciardi and Pottieger, 1986; James, 1976; Rosenbaum, 1981). Some suggest, in addition, that women's household and childcare responsibilities may have limited their full participation in the drug economy (e.g., Rosenbaum, 1981; A. Taylor, 1993; see also Wilson, 1993).

Women's peripheral roles in male-dominated drug selling networks (Auld et al., 1986; Goldstein, 1979; Rosenbaum, 1981) can also be explained by "institutionalized sexism" in the "underworld" (Steffensmeier, 1983; Steffensmeier and Terry, 1986; see also Box, 1983). Steffensmeier (1983:1013-1015) argues that male lawbreakers prefer to "work, associate, and do business with other men" (homosocial reproduction); they view women as lacking the physical and mental attributes considered essential to working in an uncertain and violent context (sex-typing and task environment of crime). In the drug economy, in particular, women are thought to be unsuitable for higher-level distribution roles because of

---

1. *Selling* refers to the direct exchange of drugs for cash; *distributing* refers to low-level distribution roles that do not involve direct sales but provide assistance to sellers.

an inability to manage male workers through threatened violence (Waterston, 1993:114).

CRACK COCAINE MARKETS OF THE MID-1980s ONWARD

Women have been depicted as more active participants in selling and distributing drugs in the crack cocaine economy of the late 1980s compared to previous drug eras. While some find that women's roles continue to be mediated by relationships with men (Koester and Schwartz, 1993; Murphy et al., 1991) and that women remain at the bottom of the drug market hierarchy (Maher and Curtis, 1992), others suggest that there has been decisive change. Specifically, it is argued that "drug business" crimes (that is, street-level drug sales) generate a higher share of women's income than in the past, with a concomitant decrease in prostitution-generated income (Inciardi et al., 1993). More generally, it is argued that the crack-propelled expansion of drug markets has provided "new opportunities" for women.

The "new opportunities" argument is made by the majority of those in the field (see, e.g., Baskin et al., 1993; Bourgois, 1989; Bourgois and Dunlap, 1993; Fagan, 1994; Inciardi et al., 1993; Mieczkowski, 1994). It takes two forms: a general claim that women's emancipation in the wider society is evident in "all aspects of inner-city street life" (Bourgois, 1989:643-644) and a more restricted claim that the weakening of male-dominated street networks and market processes has made it possible for women to enter the drug economy. For example, in his study of New York City women, Fagan (1994:210) concludes that

> while women were consigned secondary, gender-specific roles in . . . [drug] businesses in the past, the size and seemingly frantic activity of the current drug markets has made possible for women new ways to participate in street networks. Their involvement in drug selling at high income levels defies the gendered norms and roles of the past, where drug dealing was an incidental income source often mediated by domestic partnerships . . . the expansion of drug markets in the cocaine economy has provided new ways for women to escape their limited roles, statuses and incomes in previous eras.

While two-thirds of the women in Fagan's (1994) sample did not sell drugs and while most who sold drugs acted alone (p. 197), Fagan was struck by "the emergence of women sellers earning high incomes and avoiding prostitution" (p. 211). He concluded that "two social worlds" of continuity and change characterized women's participation in drug markets. One difficulty in assessing this claim is that no estimate is given of the proportion of women who were earning high incomes from drug business, avoiding prostitution, and "def[ying] the gendered norms and roles of the past."

WOMEN IN THE DRUG ECONOMY 469

Fagan's research offers a good comparison to our study. He draws from interviews with 311 women, the majority of whom were drug users or sellers, in two New York City neighborhoods (Washington Heights and Central Harlem in northern Manhattan). The interviews were conducted during the late 1980s; the sample included women with police arrest records, in residential treatment programs, and those who had not been arrested. The women in our sample lived just a few miles away in Bushwick, a Brooklyn neighborhood. Very few of the Bushwick women were active dealers, and virtually all supported themselves by prostitution. Whereas Fagan sees two worlds of continuity and change, we see just one of continuity. Before describing that social world, we sketch the study site and the methods used in gathering the data.

RESEARCH SITE AND METHODS

RESEARCH SITE

Bushwick, the principal study site, has been described as hosting "the most notorious drug bazaar in Brooklyn and one of the toughest in New York City" (New York Times, October 1, 1992:A1). Historically home to large numbers of European Jews, by the 1960s Bushwick was dominated by working-class Italians. Since the late 1960s, the area has become the home of low-income Latino populations, predominantly Puerto Ricans, although Dominicans and Columbians have begun to move in. In 1960 the population was 89% white, 6% black, and 5% Hispanic. By 1990 it was 5% white, 25% black, and 65% Hispanic (Bureau of the Census, 1990). In 1990 Bushwick was Brooklyn's poorest neighborhood with a median household income of $16,287; unemployment was twice the citywide rate; and more than half of all families and two-thirds of all children lived under the official poverty line (Bureau of the Census, 1990).

Between 1988 and 1992 drug distribution in Bushwick was intensely competitive; there were constant confrontations over "turf" as organizations strove to establish control over markets. Like many drug markets in New York City (see, e.g., Curtis and Sviridoff, 1994; Waterston, 1993), Bushwick was highly structured and ethnically segmented. The market, largely closed to outsiders, was dominated by Dominicans with networks organized by kin and pseudo-kin relations.[2]

FIELDWORK METHODS

Preliminary fieldwork began in the fall of 1989 when the senior author

---

2. At one level, language served as a marker of identity; "outsiders" were those who were not "Spanish," with country of origin often less salient than an ability to speak Spanish or "Spanglish." However, the distribution of opportunities for income generation also involved finely calibrated notions of ethnicity.

established a field presence in several Brooklyn neighborhoods (Williamsburg, East Flatbush, and Bushwick). By fall 1990 observations and interviews were intensified in Bushwick because it hosted the busiest street-level drug market in Brooklyn and had an active prostitution stroll. As fieldwork progressed, it became apparent that the initial plan of conducting interviews with a large number of women crack users was not, by itself, going to yield a complete picture. For example, few women initially admitted that they performed oral sex for less than $20, and none admitted to participating in sex-for-crack trades.

By the end of December 1991, interviews had been conducted with 211 active women crack users in Williamsburg, East Flatbush, and Bushwick. These were tape recorded and ranged from 20 minutes to 3 hours; they took place in a variety of settings, including private or semiprivate locations (e.g., apartments, shooting galleries, abandoned buildings, cars) and public locales (e.g., restaurants, parks, subways, and public toilets).[3] From January to March 1992, a preliminary data sort was made of the interview and observational material. From that process, 45 women were identified for whom there were repeated observations and interview material. Contact with these women was intimate and extensive; the number of tape-recorded interviews for each woman ranged from 3 to 15. Unless otherwise noted, the research findings reported here are based on this smaller group of 45 Bushwick women.

PROFILE OF THE BUSHWICK WOMEN

The Bushwick women consisted of 20 Latinas (18 Puerto Ricans and 2 Dominicans), 16 African-Americans, and 9 European-Americans; their ages ranged from 19 to 41 years, with a mean of 28 years. At the time of the first interview, all the women used smokable cocaine (or crack), although only 31% used it exclusively; most (69%) had used heroin or powder cocaine prior to using crack. The women's average drug use history was 10.5 years (using the mean as the measure); heroin and powder cocaine initiates had a mean of about 12 years and the smokable cocaine initiates, about 6 years.

Most women (84%) were born in the New York City area, and more than half were born in Brooklyn. About one-quarter were raised in households with both parents present, and over one-third (38%) grew up

---

3. Each woman was given $10 or the equivalent (e.g., cash, food, clothing, cigarettes, makeup, subway tokens, or a combination) for the initial tape-recorded interview. However, field observations and many of the repeat interviews were conducted on the basis of relations of reciprocity that did not involve direct or immediate benefit to those interviewed. While this research focused on women's lives, interviews and observations were also undertaken with the women's female kin, male partners, and children.

WOMEN IN THE DRUG ECONOMY   471

in a household in which they were subjected to physical abuse. Most (84%) had not completed high school, and 55% had no experience of formal-sector work. A high proportion were homeless (91%), alternating between the street and short-term accommodations in shelters, apartments of friends, and homes of elderly men (see also Maher et al., 1996). Most women were mothers (80%); the 36 mothers had given birth to 96 children, whose ages ranged from newborns to 26 years. Few of the mothers (9%) had their children living with them during the study period. Fourteen women (31%) had tested positive for HIV, and an additional five women believed that they were HIV positive; but most women said they did not know their serostatus. By the end of the study period, two women had stopped using illicit drugs, and five had died: two from HIV-related illnesses and three from homicide.

These 45 women represent the range of ages, racial-ethnic backgrounds, life experiences, and histories of crack-using women among the larger group of Brooklyn women interviewed. We are cognizant, however, of the limits of using ethnographic research in one area to generalize to other areas. For example, there is a somewhat higher proportion of Latinas (44%) in our sample than in Fagan's (1994:225) sample in Central Harlem (23%) and Washington Heights (33%). A higher share of the Bushwick women had not completed high school, had no experience in the formal labor force, and were homeless.

STRUCTURE OF NEW YORK CITY CRACK MARKETS

Street-level crack markets have frequently been characterized as unregulated markets of freelancers engaged in individual entrepreneurial activity (Hunt, 1990; Reuter et al., 1990). Some evidence suggests, however, that once demand has been established, the freelance model may be superseded by a more structured system of distribution. When the crack epidemic was at its peak in New York City during the late 1980s, Bushwick (like other neighborhoods) hosted highly structured street-level drug markets with pooled interdependence, vertical differentiation, and a formal, multi-tiered system of organization and control with defined employer-employee relationships (Curtis and Maher, in press; Johnson et al., 1990, 1992). This model is similar to the "runner system" used in heroin distribution (see Mieczkowski, 1986).

In selling crack cocaine, drug business "owners" employ several "crew bosses," "lieutenants," or "managers," who work shifts to ensure an efficient organization of street-level distribution. Managers (as they were known in Brooklyn) act as conduits between owners and lower-level employees. They are responsible for organizing and delivering supplies and collecting revenues. Managers exercise considerable autonomy in the hiring, firing, and payment of workers; they are responsible for labor force discipline and the resolution of workplace grievances and disputes. Next down the hierarchy are the street-level sellers, who perform retailing tasks having little discretion. Sellers are located in a fixed space or "spot" and are assisted by those below them in the hierarchy: lower-level operatives acting as "runners," "look-outs," "steerers," "touts," "holders," and "enforcers." Runners "continuously supply the sellers," look-outs "warn of impending dangers," steerers and touts "advertise and solicit customers," holders "handle drugs or money but not both," and enforcers "maintain order and intervene in case of trouble" (Johnson et al., 1992:61-64).

In New York City in the early 1990s, it was estimated that 150,000 people were involved in selling or helping to sell crack cocaine on any given day (Williams, 1992:10). Crack sales and distribution became a major source of income for the city's drug users (Hamid, 1990, 1991; Johnson et al., 1994). How, then, did the Bushwick women fit into this drug market structure? We examine women's involvement in a range of drug business activities.

SELLING AND DISTRIBUTING DRUGS

During the entire three years of fieldwork, including the interviews with the larger group of over 200 women, we did not discover any woman who was a business owner, and just one worked as a manager. The highly structured nature of the market in Bushwick, coupled with its kin-based organization, militated against personal or intimate sexual relationships between female drug users and higher-level male operatives. To the limited extent that they participated in drug selling, women were overwhelmingly concentrated at the lowest levels. They were almost always used as temporary workers when men were arrested or refused to work, or when it was "hot" because of police presence. Table 1 shows how the 45 women were involved in Bushwick's drug economy.

Of the 19 women (42%) who had some involvement, the most common role was that of informal steerer or tout. This meant that they recommended a particular brand of heroin to newcomers to the neighborhood in return for "change," usually a dollar or so. These newcomers were usually white men, who may have felt more comfortable approaching women with requests for such information. In turn, the women's perceptions of "white boyz" enabled them to use the situation to their advantage. Although they only used crack, Yolanda, a 38-year-old Latina, and Boy, a 26-year-old African-American woman, engaged in this practice of "tipping" heroin consumers.

> They come up to me. Before they come and buy dope and anything, they ask me what dope is good. I ain't done no dope, but I'm a professional player. . . . They would come to me, they would pay me,

WOMEN IN THE DRUG ECONOMY   473

Table 1.   Bushwick Women's Roles in the Drug Economy,
           1989–92

	N	%
No Role	26	58
Had Some Role	19	42
	45	100

Of the 19 women with roles in the drug economy during the three-year study period, the following shows what they did. Because most women (*N* = 13) had more than one role, the total sums to greater than 19.

Selling and Distributing Roles
Owner	0
Manager	0
Regular Seller	0
Irregular Seller	7
Runner	0
Look-out	0
Steerer or Tout	9
Holder	0
Enforcer	0

Selling/Renting Paraphernalia
Works Sellers	4
Stem Renters	6

Running a Gallery	3
Copping Drugs for Others	14

Other Drug Business Hustles
Street Doc	1

NOTE: While we have tried to be precise, we should note that it can be difficult to characterize women's roles—not only because drug markets are fluid and shifting but also because some women had varied mixes of roles over time.

they would come "What's good out here?" I would tell them, "Where's a dollar," and that's how I use to make my money. Everyday somebody would come, "Here's a dollar, here's two dollars." (Yolanda) [What other kinds of things?] Bumming up change. [There ain't many people down here with change.] Just the white guys. They give you more faster than your own kind. [You go cop for them?] No, just for change. You tell them what's good on [the] dope side. Tell them anything, I don't do dope, but I'll tell them anything.

474   MAHER AND DALY

> Yeah, it's kicking live man. They buy it. Boom! I got my dollar, bye.
> (Boy)

Within the local drug economy, the availability of labor strongly determines women's participation in street-level distribution roles. Labor supply fluctuates with extramarket forces, such as product availability and police intervention. One consequence of police activity in Bushwick during the study period was a recurring, if temporary, shortage of male workers. Such labor market gaps promoted instability: The replacement of "trusted" sellers (i.e., Latinos) with "untrustworthy" drug users (i.e., women and non-Latinos) eroded the social and kinship ties that had previously served to reduce violence in drug-related disputes (see also Curtis and Sviridoff, 1994).

Early in the fieldwork period (during 1989 and early 1990), both men and women perceived that more women were being offered opportunities to work as street-level sellers than in the past. Such opportunities, it turned out, were often part of a calculated risk-minimization strategy on the part of owners and managers. As Princess, a 32-year-old African-American woman observed, some owners thought that women were less likely to be noticed, searched, or arrested by police:

> Nine times out of ten when the po-leece roll up it's gonna [be] men.
> And they're not allowed to search a woman, but they have some that
> will. But if they don' do it, they'll call for a female officer. By the
> time she gets there, (laughs) if you know how to move around, you
> better get it off you, unless you jus' want to go to jail. [So you think it
> works out better for the owners to have women working for them?]
> Yeah, to use women all the time.

As the fieldwork progressed and the neighborhood became more intensively policed, this view became less tenable. Latisha, a 32-year-old African-American woman, reported that the police became more aggressive in searching women:

> [You see some women dealing a little bit you know.] Yeah, but they
> starting to go. Now these cop around here starting to unzip girls'
> pants and go in their panties. It was, it's not like it was before. You
> could stick the drugs in your panties 'cause you're a female. Now
> that's garbage.

Thus, when initially faced with a shortage of regular male labor and large numbers of women seeking low-level selling positions, some managers appear to have adopted the opportunistic use of women to avoid detection and disruption of their businesses. How frequent this practice was is uncertain; we do know that it was short-lived (see also Curtis and Sviridoff, 1994:164).

In previous years (the late 1970s and early 1980s), several Bushwick

WOMEN IN THE DRUG ECONOMY   475

women had sold drugs in their roles as wives or girlfriends of distributors, but this was no longer the case. During the three-year study period only 12 women (27%) were involved in selling and distributing roles. Of this group of 12, only 7 were able to secure low-level selling positions on an irregular basis. Connie, a 25-year-old Latina, was typical of this small group, and in the following quotation she describes her unstable position within the organization she worked for:

> I'm currently working for White Top [crack]. They have a five bundle limit. It might take me an hour or two to sell that, or sometimes as quick as half an hour. I got to ask if I can work. They say yes or no.

Typically the managers said no to women's requests to work. Unlike many male street-level sellers who worked on a regular basis for this organization and were given "shifts" (generally lasting eight hours), Connie had to work off-hours (during daylight hours), which were often riskier and less financially rewarding. Temporary workers were usually given a "bundle limit" (one bundle contains 24 vials), which ensured that they could work only for short periods of time. As Cherrie, a 22-year-old Latina, said,

> The last time I sold it was Blue Tops [crack]. That was a week ago. [What, they asked you or you asked them to work?] Oh, they ask me, I say I want to work. [How come they asked you?] I don't know. They didn't have nobody to work because it was too hot out there. They was too full of cops.

Similarly, although Princess was well-known to the owners and managers of White Top crack, had worked for them many times in the past year, and had "proved" herself by having never once "stepped off" with either drugs or money, she was only given sporadic employment. She reported,

> Sometime you can't [sell]. Sometime you can. That's why it's good to save money also. So when you don't get work. [How come they wouldn't give you work on some days?] Because of some favor that someone might've done or y'know, jus' . . . [It's not like they're trying to punish you?] No, but they will do that y'know. Somebody go and tell them something, "Oh, this one's doin' this to the bags or this one's doin' this to the bottles." OK, well they check the bags and they don' see nothin' wrong, but they came to look at it so they're pissed off so they'll take it away from you, y'know.

VIOLENCE AND RELATIONSHIPS

In addition to being vulnerable to arrest and street robbery, street-level sellers who use drugs constantly grapple with the urge to consume the product and to abscond with the drugs and/or the money. Retaliation by employers toward users who "mess up the money" (Johnson et al.,

476   MAHER AND DALY

1985:174) was widely perceived to be swift and certain. Rachel, a 35-year-old European-American woman, said,

> Those Dominicans, if you step off with one piece of it, you're gonna get hurt. They don't play. They are sick people.

The prospect of violent retaliation may deter women from selling drugs. Boy, a 26-year-old African-American woman, put it this way:

> I don' like their [the managers'] attitude, like if you come up short, dey take it out on you . . . I don' sell no crack or dope for dese niggers. Because dey is crazy. Say for instance you short ten dollars, niggers come across you wit bats and shit. It's not worth it, you could lose your life. If dey say you are short, you could lose you life. Even if you were not short and dey say you is short, whatever dey say is gonna go, so you are fucked all the way around.

However, considerable uncertainty surrounds the likelihood that physical punishment will be meted out. This uncertainty can be seen in the comments by Princess, who had a long but sporadic history of street-level sales before and after the advent of crack:

> It's not worth it. Number one, it's not enough. Come on, run away, and then *maybe* then these people want to heavily beat the shit out of you. And then they *may* hit you in the wrong place with the bat and *maybe* kill you (emphasis added).

Such disciplinary practices resemble a complex interplay between "patronage" and "mercy," which features in relations of dependence (Hay, 1975). The unpredictability of punishment may work as a more effective form of control than actual punishment itself. In Bushwick, the actuality of violent retaliation for sellers who "messed up" was further mediated by gender and ethnicity. In this Latino- (mainly Dominican) controlled market, the common perception was that men, and black men especially, were more likely than Latinas to be punished for "stepping off." Rachel described what happened after an African-American man had been badly beaten:

> [What happened to him. I mean he stepped off with a package, right?] Yeah, but everybody has at one time or another. But it's also because he's a black and not a Puerto Rican, and he can't, you know, smooze his way back in like, you know, Mildred steps off with every other package, and so does, you know, Yolanda, they all do. But they're Spanish. And they're girls. So, you know, they can smooze their way back in. You know, a guy who's black and ugly, you know, so they don't want to hear about it.

Relationships in the drug economy are fueled by contradictory expectations. On the one hand, attributes such as trust and reliability are frequently espoused as important to drug-selling organizations. On the other

WOMEN IN THE DRUG ECONOMY   477

hand, ethnographic informants often refer to the lack of trust and solidarity among organization members. This lack of trust is evident in the constant "scams" sellers and managers pull on each other and the ever-present threat of violence in owner-manager-seller relations.

STRATEGIES OF PROTECTION AND "BEING BAD"

Women who work the streets to sell or buy drugs are subject to constant harassment and are regularly victimized. The Bushwick women employed several strategies to protect themselves. One of the most important was the adoption of a "badass" (Katz, 1988), "crazy," or "gangsta bitch" stance or attitude, of which having a "bad mouth" was an integral part. As Latisha was fond of saying, "My heart pumps no Kool Aid. I don't even drink the shit." Or as Boy put it,

> Ac' petite, dey treat you petite. I mean you ac' soft, like when you dress dainty and shit ta come over here an' sit onna fuckin' corner. Onna corner an' smoke an you dressed to da teeth, you know, you soft. Right then and there you the center of the crowd, y'know what I'm sayin'? Now put a dainty one and put me, she looks soft. Dey look at me like "don't fuck wid dat bitch, she looks hard." Don' mess wit me caus I look hard y'know . . . Dey don't fuck wit me out here. Dey think I'm crazy.

Acting bad and "being bad" are not the same. Although many Bushwick women presented themselves as "bad" or "crazy," this projection was a street persona and a necessary survival strategy (see also Spalter-Roth, 1988). Despite the external manifestation of aggression, a posture and rhetoric of toughness, and the preemptive use of aggression (Campbell, 1993), women were widely perceived (by men and women alike) as less likely to have the attributes associated with successful managers and street-level sellers. These included the requisite "street cred" and a "rep" for having "heart" or "juice"—masculine qualities associated with toughness and the capacity for violence (Bourgois, 1989; Steffensmeier, 1983; Waterston, 1993). Women's abilities to "talk tough" or "act bad" were apparently not enough to inspire employer confidence. Prospective drug business employers wanted those capable of actually "being bad" (Bourgois, 1989:632). Because female drug users were perceived as unreliable, untrustworthy, and unable to deploy violence and terror effectively, would-be female sellers were at a disadvantage.

SELLING DRUG PARAPHERNALIA

In Bushwick the sale of drug paraphernalia such as crack stems and pipes was controlled by the bodegas, or corner stores, whereas syringes or "works" were the province of the street. Men dominated both markets although women were sometimes employed as part-time "works" sellers. Men who regularly sold "sealed" (i.e., new) works had suppliers (typically men who worked in local hospitals) from whom they purchased units called "ten packs" (10 syringes). The benefits of selling syringes were twofold: The penalties were less severe than those for selling drugs, and the rate of return was higher compared to the street-level sale of heroin or crack.[4]

The women who sold works were less likely than their male counterparts to have procured them "commercially." More often they "happened across" a supply of works through a family member or social contact who was a diabetic. Women were also more likely to sell works for others or to sell "used works." Rosa, a 31-year-old Latina, described in detail the dangerous practice of collecting used works strewn around the neighborhood. While she often stored them and later exchanged them for new works from the volunteer needle exchange (which was illegal at the time), Rosa would sometimes select the works she deemed in good condition, "clean" them with bleach and water, and resell them.

Although crack stems and pipes were available from neighborhood bodegas at minimal cost, some smokers chose not to carry stems. These users, almost exclusively men, were from outside the neighborhood. Their reluctance to carry drug paraphernalia provided the women with an additional source of income, usually in the form of a "hit," in exchange for the use of their stem. Sometimes these men were "dates," but more often they were "men on a mission" in the neighborhood or the "working men" who came to the area on Friday and Saturday nights to get high. As Boy put it,

> I be there on the block an' I got my stem and my lighter. I see them cop and I be askin' "yo, you need a stem, you need a light?" People say "yeah man," so they give me a piece.

An additional benefit for those women who rented their stems was the build up of crack residues in the stems. Many users savored this resin, which they allowed to accumulate before periodically digging it out with "scrapers" fashioned from the metal ribs of discarded umbrellas.

Some women also sold condoms, another form of drug-related paraphernalia in Bushwick. Although condoms were sold at bodegas, usually for $1 each, many of the women obtained free condoms from outreach health workers. Sometimes they sold them at a reduced price (usually 25

---

4. Street-level drug sellers typically made $1 on a $10 bag of heroin and 50 cents on a $5 vial of crack. Syringe sellers made at least $1.50 per unit, depending on the purchase price and the sale price.

cents) to other sex workers, "white boyz," and young men from the neighborhood. Ironically, these same women would then have to purchase condoms at the bodegas when they had "smoked up" all their condoms.

RUNNING SHOOTING GALLERIES

A wide range of physical locations were used for drug consumption in Bushwick. Although these sites were referred to generically as "galleries" by drug users and others in the neighborhood, they differed from the traditional heroin shooting gallery in several respects.[5] Bushwick's "galleries" were dominated by men because they had the economic resources or physical prowess to maintain control. Control was also achieved by exploiting women drug users with housing leases. Such women were particularly vulnerable, as the following quotation from Carol, a 40-year-old African-American woman, shows:

> I had my own apartment, myself and my daughter. I started selling crack. From my house. [For who?] Some Jamaican. [How did you get hooked up with that?] Through my boyfriend. They wanted to sell from my apartment. They were supposed to pay me something like $150 a week rent, and then something off the profits. They used to, you know, fuck up the money, like not give me the money. Eventually I went through a whole lot of different dealers. Eventually I stopped payin' my rent because I wanted to get a transfer out of there to get away from everything 'cause soon as one group of crack dealers would get out, another group would come along. [So how long did that go on for?] About four years. Then I lost my apartment, and I sat out in the street.

The few women who were able to maintain successful galleries operated with or under the control of a man or group of men. Cherrie's short-lived effort to set up a gallery in an abandoned burned-out building on "Crack Row" is illustrative. Within two weeks of establishing the gallery (the principal patrons of which were women), Cherrie was forced out of business by the police. The two weeks were marked by constant harassment, confiscation of drugs and property, damage to an already fragile physical plant, physical assaults, and the repeated forced dispersal of gallery occupants. Within a month, two men had established a new gallery on the same site, which, more than a year later, was thriving.

Such differential policing toward male- and female-operated galleries is

---

5. While consumption settings in Bushwick more closely resembled heroin shooting galleries (see, e.g., Des Jarlais et al., 1986; Murphy and Waldorf, 1991) than crack houses (see, e.g., Inciardi et al., 1993; Williams, 1992), many sites combined elements of both and most provided for polydrug (heroin and crack) consumption (for further details see Maher, in press).

explicable in light of the larger picture of law enforcement in low-income urban communities, where the primary function is not so much to enforce the law but rather to regulate illegal activities (Whyte, 1943:138). Field observations suggest that the reason the police did not interfere as much with activities in the men's gallery was that they assumed that men were better able than women to control the gallery and to minimize problems of violence and disorder.

Other factors contributed to women's disadvantage in operating galleries, crack houses, and other consumption sites. Male drug users were better placed economically than the women in the sample, most of whom were homeless and without a means of legitimate economic support. When women did have an apartment or physical site, this made them a vulnerable target either for exploitation by male users or dealers (as in Carol's case) or for harassment by the police (as in Cherrie's). Even when a woman claimed to be in control of a physical location, field observations confirmed that she was not. Thus, in Bushwick, the presence of a man was a prerequisite to the successful operation of drug-consumption sites. The only choice for those women in a position to operate galleries or crack houses was between the "devils they knew" and those they did not.

COPPING DRUGS

Many Bushwick women supplemented their income by "copping" drugs for others. They almost always copped for men, typically white men. At times these men were dates, but often they were users who feared being caught and wanted someone else to take that risk. As Rachel explained,

> I charge them, just what they want to buy they have to pay me. If they want twenty dollars they have to give me twenty dollars worth on the top because I'm risking my free time. I could get busted copping. They have to pay me the same way, if not, they can go cop. Most of them can't because they don't know the people.

Those who cop drugs for others perform an important service for the drug market because as Biernacki (1979:539) suggests in connection with heroin, "they help to minimize the possibility of infiltration by undercover agents and decrease the chance of a dealer's arrest." In Bushwick the copping role attracted few men; it was regarded by both men and women as a low-status peripheral hustle. Most women saw the female-dominated nature of the job to be part of the parallel sex market in the neighborhood. Outsiders could readily approach women to buy drugs under the guise of buying sex. As Rosa recounted,

> You would [be] surprise. They'd be ahm, be people very important, white people like lawyer, doctors that comes and get off, you'd be surprised. Iss like I got two lawyer, they give me money to go, to go

and cop. And they stay down over there parking . . . . [How do you meet them?] Well down the stroll one time they stop and say you know, "You look like a nice girl though, you know, you wanna make some money fast?" I say, how? So they say you know, "Look out for me." First time they give me like you know, twenty dollars, you know. They see I came back, next time they give me thirty. Like that you know. I have been copping for them like over six months already.

Sometimes this function was performed in conjunction with sex work, as Latisha's comment illustrates,

He's a cop. He's takin' a chance. He is petrified. Will not get out his car . . . But he never gets less than nine bags [of powder cocaine]. [And he sends you to get it?] And he wants a blow job, right, okay. You know what he's givin' you, a half a bag of blue (blue bag cocaine). That's for you goin' to cop, and for the blow job. That's [worth] two dollars and fifty . . . I can go to jail [for him]. I'm a piece of shit.

Women also felt that, given the reputation of the neighborhood as very "thirsty" (that is, as having a "thirst" or craving for crack), male outsiders were more likely to trust women, especially white women, to purchase drugs on their behalf. Often this trust was misplaced. The combination of naive, inexperienced "white boyz" and experienced "street smart" women produced opportunities for additional income by, for example, simply taking the "cop" money. This was a calculated risk and sometimes things went wrong. A safer practice was to inflate the purchase price of the drugs and to pocket the difference. Rosa explained this particular scam,

He think it a ten dollar bag, but issa five dollar. But at least I don't be rippin' him off there completely. [But you're taking the risk for him.] Exactly. Sometime he give me a hunert dollars, so I making fifty, right? But sometime he don't get paid, he got no second money, eh. I cop then when I come back the car, he say, "Dear I cannot give you nothin' today," you know. But I still like I say, I gettin' something from him because he think it a ten dollar bag.

Similar scams involved the woman's returning to the client with neither drugs nor money, claiming that she had been ripped off or, less often, shortchanging the client by tapping the vials (removing some crack) or adulterating the drugs (cutting powder cocaine or heroin with other substances). These scams reveal the diversity of women's roles as copping agents and their ingenuity in making the most of limited opportunities.[6]

---

6. By their own accounts, women took greater risks in order to generate income than they had in the past. More generally, the incidence of risky behavior increased as

482   MAHER AND DALY

OTHER DRUG BUSINESS HUSTLES

The practice of injecting intravenous drug users (IDUs) who are unable
to inject themselves, because they are inexperienced or have deep or collapsed veins, has been documented by others (e.g., Johnson et al., 1985;
Murphy and Waldorf, 1991). Those performing this role are sometimes
referred to as "street docs" (Murphy and Waldorf, 1991:16-17). In
Bushwick, men typically specialized in this practice. For example, Sam, a
Latino injector in his late thirties, lived in one of the makeshift huts or
"condos" on a busy street near the main heroin copping area. Those who
were in a hurry to consume or who had nowhere else to go would use
Sam's place to "get off." Sam had a reputation as a good "hitter" and
injected several women in the sample on a regular basis. He provided this
service for a few dollars or, more often, a "taste" of whatever substance
was being injected.

Only one woman in the sample, Latisha, capitalized on her reputation as
a good "hitter" by playing the street doc role. Latisha had a regular
arrangement with a young street thug named Crime, notorious for victimizing the women, who had only recently commenced intravenous heroin use and was unable to "hit" himself. While women IDUs were likely
to have the requisite level of skill, they were less likely than men to be able
to capitalize on it because they did not control an established consumption
setting.

DISCUSSION

A major dimension of drug economies, both past and present, is the
"human qualities" believed necessary for the performance of various roles.
Opportunities for income generation are defined, in part, by who has the
necessary qualities or traits and who does not. These traits, whether
grounded in cultural perceptions of biology and physiology (e.g., strength
and capacity for violence), mental states (e.g., courage and aggressiveness), or kinship (e.g., loyalty and trustworthiness), are primarily differentiated along the lines of gender and race-ethnicity. In this study, we found
that women were thought to be not as "strong" as men and that men,
particularly black men and Latinos, were thought to be more "bad" and
capable of "being bad." The gendered displays of violence that men incorporate into their work routines not only cement their solidarity as men,
but also reinscribe these traits as masculine (Messerschmidt, 1993). As a
consequence, men are able to justify the exclusion of women from more
lucrative "men's work" in the informal economy. All the elements of

---

conditions in the neighborhood and the adjacent street-level sex market deteriorated
(Maher and Curtis, 1992; see also Curtis et al., 1995).

underworld sexism identified by Steffensmeier (1983)—homosocial reproduction, sex-typing, and the qualities required in a violent task environment—featured prominently in Bushwick's street-level drug economy.

The significance of gender-based capacities and the symbolism used to
convey them was evident in the women's use of instrumental aggression.
Boy's discussion of how to "dress for success" on the streets reveals that
power dressing is "dressing like a man" or "dressing down." It is anything
but "dressing dainty." Both on the street and in the boardroom, it appears
that a combination of clothing and attitude makes the woman (Kanter,
1981, citing Hennig, 1970). In the drug business, conveying the message
"don't mess with me" is integral to maintaining a reputation for "crazi-
ness," which the women perceived as affording them some measure of
protection.

The Bushwick women's experiences within a highly gender-stratified
labor market provide a counter to the romantic notion of the informal
drug economy as an "equal opportunity employer" (Bourgois, 1989:630).
Their experiences contradict the conventional wisdom, shaped by studies
of the labor market experiences of minority group men (e.g., Anderson,
1990; Bourgois, 1989, 1995; Hagedorn, 1994; Padilla, 1992; C. Taylor, 1990;
Williams, 1989), that the drug economy acts as a compensatory mechanism, offering paid employment that is not available in the formal labor
force. While in theory the built-in supervision and task differentiation of
the business model, which characterized drug distribution in Bushwick,
should have provided opportunities to both men and women (Johnson et
al., 1992), our findings suggest that sellers were overwhelmingly men.
Thus, the "new opportunities" said to have emerged with the crack-propelled expansion of drug markets from the mid-1980s onward were not
"empty slots" waiting to be filled by those with the requisite skill. Rather,
they were slots requiring certain masculine qualities and capacities.

CONTINUITY OR CHANGE?

Those scholars who emphasize change in women's roles in the drug
economy with the advent of crack cocaine are correct to point out the
possibilities that an expanded drug economy might have offered women.
Where they err, we think, is in claiming that such "new opportunities"
were in fact made available to a significant proportion of women.
Granted, there were temporary opportunities for women to participate in
street-level drug distribution, but they were irregular and short-lived and
did not alter male employers' perceptions of women as unreliable, untrustworthy, and incapable of demonstrating an effective capacity for violence.

The only consistently available option for women's income generation
was sex work. However, the conditions of street-level sex work have been

adversely affected by shifts in social and economic relations produced by widespread crack consumption in low-income neighborhoods like Bushwick. The market became flooded with novice sex workers, the going rates for sexual transactions decreased, and "deviant" sexual expectations by dates increased, as did the levels of violence and victimization (Maher and Curtis, 1992). Ironically, the sting in the tail of the recent crack-fueled expansion of street-level drug markets has been a substantial reduction in the earning capacities of street-level sex workers.

Of the four elements that have been used to explain women's restricted involvement in drug economies of the past, we see evidence of change in two: a diminishing of women's access to drug-selling roles through boyfriends or husbands, especially when drug markets are highly structured and kin based, and decreased economic returns for street-level sex work. Because few Bushwick women had stable households or cared for children, we cannot comment on changes (if any) in discretionary time. Underworld institutionalized sexism was the most powerful element shaping the Bushwick women's experiences in the drug economy; it inhibited their access to drug business work roles and effectively foreclosed their ability to participate as higher-level distributors. For that most crucial element, we find no change from previous decades.

How can we reconcile our findings with those of researchers who say that the crack cocaine economy has facilitated "new opportunities" for women or "new ways for women to escape their limited roles, statuses, and incomes [compared to] previous eras" (Fagan, 1994:210)? One answer is that study samples differ: Compared to Fagan's sample, for example, our sample of Bushwick women contained a somewhat higher share of Latinas, whose economic circumstances were more marginal than those of the women in Central Harlem and Washington Heights. It is also possible that Latino-controlled drug markets are more restrictive of women's participation than, say, those controlled by African-Americans. Those who have studied drug use and dealing in Puerto Rican (Glick, 1990) and Chicano (Moore, 1990) communities suggest that "deviant women" may be less tolerated and more ostracized than their male counterparts. For Bushwick, it would be difficult to disentangle the joint influences of a male-dominated and Dominican-controlled drug market on women's participation. While seven women (16%) engaged in street-level sales during the study period, all women—whether Latina, African-American, or European-American—were denied access to higher levels of the drug business.

We lack research on how racial-ethnic relations structure women's participation in drug markets. Fagan's (1994:200-202) comparison of Central Harlem and Washington Heights indicates that a lower proportion of women in Central Harlem (28%) than in Washington Heights (44%)

WOMEN IN THE DRUG ECONOMY 485

reported being involved in drug selling; similar proportions (about 16%) were involved in group selling, however. While Fagan noted that drug markets in Washington Heights were Latino-controlled, he did not discuss the organization or ethnic composition of drug markets in Central Harlem. His study would appear to challenge any clear links between "Latino culture"—or the Latina share of women studied—and greater restrictions on women's roles compared to other racial-ethnic groups.

While disparate images of women in the drug economy may result from differences in study samples (including racial-ethnic variation in drug market organization, neighborhood-level variation, and when the study was conducted), a researcher's methods and theories are also crucial. For methods, virtually all U.S. studies of women drug users have employed one-time interviews. The ethnographic approach used in this study reveals that in the absence of a temporal frame and observational data, interviews may provide an incomplete and inaccurate picture. For example, in initial interviews with the larger group of Brookyn women, we found that when women were asked about sources of income, it was more socially desirable for them to say that it came from drug selling or other kinds of crime than from crack-related prostitution (Maher, in press). The one-time interview also misses the changing and fluid nature of relations in the informal economy. For example, for a short period there was a perception in Bushwick that "new opportunities" existed for women to sell crack. That perception faded as it became clear that managers and owners were "using" women to evade the constraints imposed on them by law enforcement and police search practices. Ethnographic approaches can offer a more dynamic contexualized picture of women's lawbreaking. While such approaches are relatively numerous in the study of adolescent and adult men in the United States (e.g., Anderson, 1990; Bourgois, 1989; Sullivan, 1989), they are rarely utilized in the study of women and girls.

For theory, women lawbreakers are rarely studied as members of social networks or as participants in collective or group-based activity (see also Steffensmeier and Terry, 1986). Nor have women been viewed as economic actors in illegal markets governed by occupational norms and workplace cultures (Maher, 1996). Those making a general claim about "women's emancipation" in the current drug economy ignore the obdurateness of a gender-stratified labor market and associated beliefs and practices that maintain it. Those making the more restricted claim that male-dominated street networks and market processes have weakened, thus allowing entry points for women, need to offer proof for that claim. We would expect to see variation in women's roles, and we would not say that Bushwick represents the general case. However, assertions of women's changing and improved position in the drug economy have not

486   MAHER AND DALY

been well proved. Nor are they grounded in theories of how work, including illegal work, is conditioned by relations of gender, race-ethnicity, and sexuality (see, e.g., Daly, 1993; Game and Pringle, 1983; Kanter, 1977; Messerschmidt, 1993; Simpson and Elis, 1995).

Our findings suggest that the advent of crack cocaine and the concomitant expansion of the drug economy cannot be viewed as emancipatory for women drug users. To the extent that "new opportunities" in drug distribution and sales were realized in Bushwick and the wider Brooklyn sample, they were realized by men. Women were confined to an increasingly harsh economic periphery. Not only did the promised opportunities fail to materialize, but the expanding crack market served to deteriorate the conditions of street-level sex work, a labor market which has historically provided a relatively stable source of income for women drug users.

REFERENCES

Adler, Patricia A.
   1985   Wheeling and Dealing: An Ethnography of an Upper-Level Drug
           Dealing and Smuggling Community. New York: Columbia University
           Press.

Anderson, Elijah
   1990   Streetwise: Race, Class and Change in an Urban Community. Chicago:
           University of Chicago Press.

Anglin, M. Douglas and Yih-Ing Hser
   1987   Addicted women and crime. Criminology 25:359-397.

Auld, John, Nicholas Dorn, and Nigel South
   1986   Irregular work, irregular pleasures: Heroin in the 1980s. In Roger
           Matthews and Jock Young (eds.), Confronting Crime. London: Sage.

Baskin, Deborah, Ira Sommers, and Jeffrey Fagan
   1993   The political economy of violent female street crime. Fordham Urban
           Law Journal 20:401-407.

Biernacki, Patrick
   1979   Junkie work, "hustles," and social status among heroin addicts. Journal of
           Drug Issues 9:535-549.

Bourgois, Philippe
   1989   In search of Horatio Alger: Culture and ideology in the crack economy.
           Contemporary Drug Problems 16:619-649.
   1995   In Search of Respect: Selling Crack in El Barrio. New York: Cambridge
           University Press.

Bourgois, Philippe and Eloise Dunlap
   1993   Exorcising sex-for-crack: An ethnographic perspective from Harlem. In
           Mitchell S. Ratner (eds.), Crack Pipe as Pimp: An Ethnographic
           Investigation of Sex-for-Crack Exchanges. New York: Lexington Books.

Box, Steven
   1983   Power, Crime and Mystification. London: Tavistock.

WOMEN IN THE DRUG ECONOMY   487

Bureau of the Census
  1990   Brooklyn in Touch. Washington, D.C.: U.S. Government Printing Office.

Campbell, Anne
  1993   Out of Control: Men, Women, and Aggression. London: Pandora.

Covington, Jeanette
  1985   Gender differences in criminality among heroin users. Journal of
            Research in Crime and Delinquency 22:329-354.

Curtis, Richard and Lisa Maher
  in press Highly structured crack markets in the southside of Williamsburg,
            Brooklyn. In Jeffrey Fagan (ed.), The Ecology of Crime and Drug Use in
            Inner Cities. New York: Social Science Research Council.

Curtis, Richard and Michelle Sviridoff
  1994   The social organization of street-level drug markets and its impact on the
            displacement effect. In Robert P. McNamara (ed.), Crime Displacement:
            The Other Side of Prevention. East Rockaway, N.Y.: Cummings and
            Hathaway.

Curtis, Richard, Samuel R. Friedman, Alan Neaigus, Benny Jose, Marjorie Goldstein,
  and Gilbert Ildefonso
  1995   Street-level drug markets: Network structure and HIV risk. Social
            Networks 17:229-249.

Daly, Kathleen
  1993   Class-race-gender: Sloganeering in search of meaning. Social Justice
            20:56-71.

Des Jarlais, Don C., Samuel R. Friedman, and David Strug
  1986   AIDS and needle sharing within the IV drug use subculture. In Douglas
            A. Feldman and Thomas M. Johnson (eds.), The Social Dimensions of
            AIDS: Methods and Theory. New York: Praeger.

Dunlap, Eloise and Bruce D. Johnson
  1992   Who they are and what they do: Female crack dealers in New York City.
            Paper presented at the Annual Meeting of the American Society of
            Criminology, New Orleans, November.

Fagan, Jeffrey
  1994   Women and drugs revisited: Female participation in the cocaine econ-
            omy. Journal of Drug Issues 24:179-225.

File, Karen N.
  1976   Sex roles and street roles. International Journal of the Addictions 11:263-
            268.

File, Karen N., Thomas W. McCahill, and Leonard D. Savitz
  1974   Narcotics involvement and female criminality. Addictive Diseases: An
            International Journal 1:177-188.

Game, Ann and Rosemary Pringle
  1983   Gender at Work. Sydney: George Allen and Unwin.

Goldstein, Paul J.
  1979   Prostitution and Drugs. Lexington, Mass.: Lexington Books.

488   MAHER AND DALY

Glick, Ronald
    1990   Survival, income, and status: Drug dealing in the Chicago Puerto Rican
            community. In Ronald Glick and Joan Moore (eds.), Drugs in Hispanic
            Communities. New Brunswick, N.J.: Rutgers University Press.

Hagedorn, John M.
    1994   Homeboys, dope fiends, legits, and new jacks. Criminology 32:197-219.

Hamid, Ansley
    1990   The political economy of crack-related violence. Contemporary Drug
            Problems 17:31-78.
    1991   From ganja to crack: Caribbean participation in the underground
            economy in Brooklyn, 1976-1986. Part 2, Establishment of the cocaine
            (and crack) economy. International Journal of the Addictions 26:729-738.
    1992   The developmental cycle of a drug epidemic: The cocaine smoking
            epidemic of 1981-1991. Journal of Psychoactive Drugs 24:337-348.

Hay, Douglas
    1975   Property, authority, and the criminal law. In Douglas Hay, Peter
            Linebaugh, John G. Rule, Edward Palmer Thompson, and Cal Winslow
            (eds.), Albion's Fatal Tree. London: Allen Lane.

Hennig, Margaret
    1970   Career Development for Women Executives. Ph.D. dissertation, Harvard
            University, Cambridge, Mass.

Hser, Yih-Ing, M. Douglas Anglin, and Mary W. Booth
    1987   Sex differences in addict careers. Part 3, Addiction. American Journal of
            Drug and Alcohol Abuse 13:231-251.

Hunt, Dana
    1990   Drugs and consensual crimes: Drug dealing and prostitution. In Michael
            Tonry and James Q. Wilson (eds.), Drugs and Crime. Crime and Justice,
            Vol. 13. Chicago: University of Chicago Press.

Inciardi, James A. and Anne E. Pottieger
    1986   Drug use and crime among two cohorts of women narcotics users: An
            empirical assessment. Journal of Drug Issues 16:91-106.

Inciardi, James A., Dorothy Lockwood, and Anne E. Pottieger
    1993   Women and Crack Cocaine. New York: Macmillan.

James, Jennifer
    1976   Prostitution and addiction: An interdisciplinary approach. Addictive
            Diseases: An International Journal 2:601-618.

Johnson, Bruce D., Paul J. Goldstein, Edward Preble, James Schmeidler, Douglas S.
Lipton, Barry Spunt, and Thomas Miller
    1985   Taking Care of Business: The Economics of Crime by Heroin Abusers.
            Lexington, Mass.: Lexington Books.

Johnson, Bruce D., Terry Williams, Kojo Dei, and Harry Sanabria
    1990   Drug abuse and the inner city: Impact on hard drug users and the
            community. In Michael Tonry and James Q. Wilson (eds.), Drugs and
            Crime. Crime and Justice, Vol. 13. Chicago: University of Chicago Press.

Johnson, Bruce D., Ansley Hamid, and Harry Sanabria
    1992   Emerging models of crack distribution. In Thomas M. Mieczkowski (ed.),
            Drugs and Crime: A Reader. Boston: Allyn & Bacon.

WOMEN IN THE DRUG ECONOMY 489

Johnson, Bruce D., Mangai Natarajan, Eloise Dunlap, and Elsayed Elmoghazy
   1994   Crack abusers and noncrack abusers: Profiles of drug use, drug sales, and
          nondrug criminality. Journal of Drug Issues 24:117-141.

Kanter, Rosabeth Moss
   1977   Men and Women of the Corporation. New York: Basic Books.
   1981   Women and the structure of organizations: Explorations in theory and
          behavior. In Oscar Grusky and George A. Miller (eds.), The Sociology of
          Organizations: Basic Studies. 2d ed. New York: The Free Press.

Katz, Jack
   1988   Seductions of Crime: Moral and Sensual Attractions of Doing Evil. New
          York: Basic Books.

Koester, Stephen and Judith Schwartz
   1993   Crack, gangs, sex, and powerlessness: A view from Denver. In Mitchell
          S. Ratner (ed.), Crack Pipe as Pimp: An Ethnographic Investigation of
          Sex-for-Crack Exchanges. New York: Lexington Books.

Maher, Lisa
   in press Making it at the Margins: Gender, Race and Work in a Street-Level
          Drug Economy. Oxford: Oxford University Press.
   1996   Hidden in the light: Discrimination and occupational norms among crack
          using street-level sexworkers. Journal of Drug Issues 26(1):145-175.

Maher, Lisa and Richard Curtis
   1992   Women on the edge of crime: Crack cocaine and the changing contexts
          of street-level sex work in New York City. Crime, Law, and Social
          Change 18:221-258.

Maher, Lisa, Eloise Dunlap, Bruce D. Johnson, and Ansley Hamid
   1996   Gender, power and alternative living arrangements in the inner-city crack
          culture. Journal of Research in Crime and delinquency 33:181-205.

Messerschmidt, James D.
   1993   Masculinities and Crime. Lanham, Md.: Rowman and Littlefield.

Mieczkowski, Thomas
   1986   Geeking up and throwing down: Heroin street life in Detroit. Criminol-
          ogy 24:645-666.
   1990   Crack dealing on the street: An exploration of the YBI hypothesis and
          the Detroit crack trade. Paper presented at the Annual Meeting of the
          American Society of Criminology, Baltimore, November.
   1994   The experiences of women who sell crack: Some descriptive data from
          the Detroit crack ethnography project. Journal of Drug Issues 24:227-248.

Moore, Joan W.
   1990   Mexican American women addicts: The influence of family background.
          In Ronald Glick and Joan Moore (eds.), Drugs in Hispanic Communities.
          New Brunswick, N.J.: Rutgers University Press.

Morgan, Patricia and Karen Joe
   1994   Uncharted terrains: Contexts of experience among women in the illicit
          drug economy. Paper presented at the Women and Drugs National
          Conference, Sydney, November.

490   MAHER AND DALY

Murphy, Sheigla and Dan Waldorf
    1991   Kickin' down to the street doc: Shooting galleries in the San Francisco
            Bay area. Contemporary Drug Problems 18:9-29.

Murphy, Sheigla, Dan Waldorf, and Craig Reinarman
    1991   Drifting into dealing: Becoming a cocaine seller. Qualitative Sociology
            13:321-343.

Padilla, Felix M.
    1992   The Gang as an American Enterprise. New Brunswick, N.J.: Rutgers
            University Press.

Pettiway, Leon E.
    1987   Participation in crime partnerships by female drug users: The effects of
            domestic arrangements, drug use, and criminal involvement. Criminology
            25:741-766.

Reuter, Peter, Robert MacCoun, and Patrick Murphy
    1990   Money from Crime: A Study of the Economics of Drug Dealing in
            Washington, D.C. Santa Monica, Calif.: Rand Corporation.

Rosenbaum, Marsha
    1981   Women on Heroin. New Brunswick, N.J.: Rutgers University Press.

Simpson, Sally S. and Lori Elis
    1995   Doing gender: Sorting out the caste and crime conundrum. Criminology
            33:47-81.

Skolnick, Jerome H.
    1989   The Social Structure of Street Drug Dealing. Report to the State of
            California Bureau of Criminal Statistics and Special Services. Sacra-
            mento: State of California Executive Office.

Smithberg, Nathan and Joseph Westermeyer
    1985   White dragon pearl syndrome: A female pattern of drug dependence.
            American Journal of Drug and Alcohol Abuse 11:199-207.

Spalter-Roth, Roberta M.
    1988   The sexual political economy of street vending in Washington, D.C. In
            Gracia Clark (ed.), Traders Versus the State: Anthropological
            Approaches to Unofficial Economies. Boulder, Colo.: Westview Press.

Steffensmeier, Darrell
    1983   Organization properties and sex-segregation in the underworld: Building
            a sociological theory of sex differences in crime. Social Forces 61:1010-
            1032.

Steffensmeier, Darrell J. and Robert M. Terry
    1986   Institutional sexism in the underworld: A view from the inside.
            Sociological Inquiry 56:304-323.

Sullivan, Mercer L.
    1989   Getting Paid: Youth Crime and Work in the Inner City. Ithaca, N.Y.:
            Cornell University Press.

Sutter, A. G.
    1966   The world of the righteous dope fiend. Issues in Criminology 2:177-222.

Taylor, Avril
    1993   Women Drug Users: An Ethnography of a Female Injecting Community.
            Oxford: Clarendon Press.

Taylor, Carl S.
    1990   Dangerous Society. East Lansing: Michigan State University Press.
    1993   Girls, Gangs, Women and Drugs. East Lansing: Michigan State Univer-
            sity Press.

Waldorf, Dan, Craig Reinarman, and Sheigla Murphy
    1991   Cocaine Changes: The Experience of Using and Quitting. Philadelphia,
            Pa.: Temple University Press.

Waterston, Alisse
    1993   Street Addicts in the Political Economy. Philadelphia, Pa.: Temple
            University Press.

Whyte, William Foote
    1943   Street Corner Society. Chicago: University of Chicago Press.

Williams, Terry
    1989   The Cocaine Kids. Reading, Mass.: Addison-Wesley.
    1992   Crackhouse: Notes from the End of the Line. New York: Addison-
            Wesley.

Wilson, Nancy Koser
    1993   Stealing and dealing: The drug war and gendered criminal opportunity.
            In Concetta C. Culliver (ed.), Female Criminality: The State of the Art.
            New York: Garland Publishing.

Lisa Maher is a Research Fellow in the National Drug and Alcohol Research Centre at the University of New South Wales in Sydney. Her research interests include gender, culture and informal sector markets. She has published several articles on women, crime, and drug use, and her book, *Making it at the Margins: Gender, Race and Work in a Street-level Drug Economy*, will be published by Oxford University Press in 1997.

Kathleen Daly is Associate Professor of Justice Administration at Griffith University (Brisbane). She has written on how gender and race structure patterns of lawbreaking and criminal court sentencing, responses to violence against women, media and crime, and the relationship of feminist theory to criminology, law, and justice. Her book, *Gender, Crime, and Punishment*, received the 1995 Hindelang award.

[5]

The Risks of Street Prostitution: Punters, Police and Protesters

Teela Sanders

[Paper first received, September 2003; in final form, February 2004]

Summary. For female street sex workers in Britain, selling sex means managing risks. Violence from male clients, harassment from community protesters and criminalisation through overpolicing are daily hazards on the street. Using qualitative data and extensive field observations of the street market in Birmingham, UK, it is argued in this paper that street sex workers do not passively accept these risks but, instead, manage occupational hazards by manipulating, separating, controlling and resisting urban spaces. Women actively use space to inform their collective and individual working practices to minimise harm and maximise profits. However, the findings conclude that sites of street prostitution are made increasingly dangerous for women through punitive policing policies, conservative heterosexual discourses and a lack of realistic prostitution policy that addresses the central issues relating to commercial sex.

Introduction

The nature of street prostitution has been well documented in the UK and world-wide (Benson and Matthews, 1995; Hoigard and Finstad, 1992; May *et al.*, 1999; McKeganey and Barnard, 1996; Raphael and Shapiro, 2004; Williamson and Cluse-Tolar, 2002). These empirical findings have mainly concentrated on characteristics of the women involved in the street markets and visible harms such as violence, drug use and sexual health. The relationships between space, risk and prostitution have been made by scholars who have merged an analysis of geographical space with the dynamics of the social context in which women sell sex, in particular sociological discourses of sexuality and space (Duncan, 1996; Hubbard, 1999; Hubbard and Sanders, 2003; Larsen, 1992; Lowman, 2000; Porter and Bonilla, 2000; Sharpe, 1998).

This paper adds to the growing realisation that the space in which prostitution is advertised, negotiated and administered (Ashworth *et al.*, 1988) is an integral part of why and how prostitution happens in certain streets of cities and towns. The paper identifies how the geographical space that women rely on to make money is not a haphazard or neutral locale in the urban landscape. Using the case study of Birmingham, I identify how the place of street prostitution is often highly politicised by competing interests such as community protesters, services that advocate for sex workers, and law enforcement agencies and the sex workers. Sites of prostitution are the target of resources from public services, especially the growth of multiagency

Teela Sanders is in the School of Sociology and Social Policy, University of Leeds, Leeds, LS2 9JT, UK. Fax: 0113 233 4415. E-mail: t.l.m.sanders@leeds.ac.uk. Special thanks to Martin Smith and Phil Hubbard for introducing the relevance of geography to my work. Alan Collins has shown great encouragement and the two reviewers from Urban Studies have been helpful with their critical direction. It goes without saying that the women who shared their lives are ultimately to be thanked. The outreach workers who relentlessly take services to the streets in politically hostile circumstances showed me how persistence and commitment can make a difference partnerships and forums created to consider and act upon what has historically been considered a 'spoiled identity' (Pile, 1996), associated with 'drugs, diseases, dysfunctional families and danger' (Boynton, 1996).

Secondly, this paper clarifies the types of occupational hazards involved in street prostitution by dividing risks into three main categories: violence from male clients, issues relating to policing and community protesters. Thirdly, findings from the case study advance the literature on survival techniques or 'strategies of resistance' by illustrating how street sex workers manage these risks through calculated tactics that manipulate, manage and reinterpret space to their own advantage. Street workers constantly assess the levels of risk from punters, police and protesters in the urban market before engaging in commercial transactions. This paper makes a fourth contribution to the literature that is established by arguing that despite sex workers' active reactions to the risks they face evidence suggests that the policing and regulation of the sites of street prostitution increases the prevalence of danger for individual women. The urban site of prostitution is the target of punitive policing policies, intense community actions sanctioned by the state that victimise and criminalise street workers rather than address the issues that make commercial sex dangerous.

Risk, Relationships and the Realities of Sex Work

Understanding the relationship between sex workers' responses to occupational hazards and the site of prostitution in the urban landscape can be contextualised within wider theories of risk. Mary Douglas (1992), in her essay *Risk and Danger*, analyses voluntary risk-taking in a society where the reality of danger has been overlooked by the perception of risk. Douglas argues that taking risks is not irrational or a trait of a skewed personality but is understood as a character flaw because of the culturally biased model of risk perception in modern industrial society. Douglas (1992, p. 41) claims that risk-averse cul-

ture has vanquished the risk-seeking culture and that this bias should be corrected in order to understand risk as a choice in society. Douglas (1992, p. 102) proposes that the self is risk-taking or risk-averse according to the relationship between the person and others in the community.[1]

In prostitution, the consequences of risk are different across markets because "different categories of women have different risk profiles ... they have different degrees of control over their exposure to these risks" (Gysels *et al.*, 2002, p. 190). The risk of violence from pimps and dealers is not the same for those who work indoors as it is for street workers (May *et al.*, 1999). Douglas (1992) argues for a contextual approach to understanding risk from qualitative work that explores cultural, individual and interactional aspects. Responses to danger should not be quantitatively categorised or marked as 'rational' or 'irrational' according to our judgements, but we should try to make sense of different communities' dispositions towards authority and boundaries. Staying close to the sex workers' words and retelling their experiences avoids making judgements but tries to locate their dilemmas and decision-making in their own realities. If we are to understand how others interpret their social environments in deciding what is too risky and what is worth the risk, their reactions to the space in which they face the dilemma is an integral part of understanding risk in society. Individuals do not simply engage in risk-taking or risk-averse behaviour as a result of predisposed traits or irrational responses. Sex workers react to their surroundings and, through a complex process of assessing their own biography, skills and experience, decide whether to take or avoid risks.

The public nature of the street market makes this site of commercial sex significantly vulnerable and exposed. The commodification of an essentially private act in the public realm challenges acceptable mores about the expression of sexuality and the place of sexual behaviour. Sibley (1995) explains how spatial and social boundaries are part of the process that excludes and controls groups who do not conform to dominant ideologies and practices. It has been argued that isolating and separating those who are created as 'others' takes place in the urban city through policies and practices. Sexual minorities have been documented as a group that have been 'other-ed' through a spatial as well as social process of seclusion (Skeggs, 1999; Duncan, 1996). The historical case of street prostitution in Birmingham is an example of the continuation of 'othering' in the urban city where sex workers are depicted as a social threat to moral and familiar cohesion (Hubbard, 1998a). As a consequence, women are shifted from one location to another, in an attempt to remove them from the 'safe spaces' to the margins. The dislocation of sex workers from certain spaces interacts with the processes of risk-aversion and risk-taking. As Douglas states, if risk is specifically about the relationships individuals have with those in the community and not necessarily a reflection between their character, it is the interaction between social groups that must be the focus of any understanding of risk-taking. This paper examines the relationships between sex workers and both their physical geographical environment and the social environment and relationships which determine their position in the risk dilemma.

The Hazards of Prostitution in a Public Space

It has been well documented how street sex workers endure working conditions that stigmatise, criminalise and pose threats of physical, emotional and psychological harm (Hoigard and Finstad, 1992; O'Neill, 2001; Phoenix, 1999; Sterk, 2000). The occupational hazards open to street sex workers can be divided between the public and the private manifestations of risk. In public, women fear violence from clients and other people on the street, arrest from the police with the increasing possibility of imprisonment and further harassment from community protesters. In private, the

stigmatisation and marginalisation as a result of working in prostitution are as equally stressful as women constantly fear that their friends, family or partner could discover their money-making activities. Although there is no time in this paper to consider fully the private dynamics of risk, the implications of the public risks are inevitably expressed in the private domain (see Sanders, forthcoming).

The prevalence of violence within prostitution has been well established in Britain (Barnard, 1993, Day and Ward 2001, Sanders, 2001) and world-wide.[2] The street market is increasingly vulnerable to violence and robbery. From a study across three cities in Britain, Church *et al.*, (2001) found that 81 per cent (93) of street workers had experienced violence from clients, compared with 48 per cent (60) who worked indoors. Benson (1998) found that 98 per cent (49) of street prostitutes experienced some form of violence at work, while Kinnell (1992) reported that 75 interviewees experienced 211 violent incidents during their careers. However, the perpetration of violence against sex workers is not predictable because "occupational studies of, and service for, prostitutes cannot be confined to the risks posed directly by exchanges with customers" (Day and Ward, 2001, p. 230). Other empirical findings demonstrate the high likelihood of street workers experiencing violence from other working women, predatory men involved in prostitution, the general public (Benson, 1998) and severe physical harm from boyfriend/pimps (May *et al.*, 2000, p. 18).

In addition, sex workers experience intimidation and harassment from the communities where they work and sometimes live. Several cities in Britain have experienced a clash between community groups and the sex work community (Leeds, Bradford and Bristol are described in Hubbard, 1998a; Liverpool and London are described by Campbell *et al.*, 1996). In Birmingham, street prostitution co-exists, albeit uncomfortably, alongside those who claim the same physical space as their community, territory or 'back-yard'. Over the past decade, Birmingham has experienced community campaigns against street prostitution that have been highly organised and intensively resourced.

Community action groups have several legitimate issues to raise about the implications of commercial sex advertised, negotiated and often delivered in the same spaces as those in which they live. Benson and Matthews (2000, p. 247) describe how residents complain about litter (particularly used condoms), noise and extra traffic from kerb-crawlers, while Hubbard (1998a, p. 272) explains how Birmingham residents felt that prostitution made their areas unsafe by attracting unscrupulous people, increasing drug-related crime and street robberies. The presence of men who cruise the streets looking to purchase sex has also caused problems for other women in the neighbourhood as they are inappropriately approached (see Brooks-Gordon and Gelsthorpe, 2003). These incidents invariably happen where children are present. However, while these concerns are real, the actions of protesters can also be understood as a public display of aggressive masculinity against a group of women that are understood as 'deviant others' and scapegoated for urban degeneration and wider political, economic and social change (Hubbard, 1999). Larsen (1992, p. 187) evaluates the anti-prostitution community groups in four Canadian cities and notes that there is a socioeconomic class bias regarding who is given powers to control street prostitution.

In addition to community policing, street sex workers are under constant pressure to avoid the police and the processes of criminalisation that pose severe risks to their livelihood. Although there is no law against two consenting adults swapping sex for cash or commodities, under the Street Offences Act, 1959, loitering and soliciting in a public place for the purpose of prostitution are illegal. As a response to complaints by local residents, the police are involved in a considerable amount of controlling and regulating street prostitution. Locally, there are several joint initiatives between the police

and residents to monitor, track, record and report information about individual workers and their activities. Multiagency policing of prostitution has taken on a punitive agenda in response to changes in the law under the Crime and Disorder Act, 1998, that introduced Anti-social Behaviour Orders (hereafter, ASBOs) to be used against those who cause 'alarm, distress and harassment' to communities. Strengthened in their applicability under the Police Reform Act, 2002, ASBOs place geographical exclusion zones on women who are considered to be a persistent nuisance in an area. More seriously, if an ASBO is breached, women face up to five years' imprisonment. These more recent developments are rapidly changing the nature of risk in the street market, the practice of commercial sex and the organisation of street markets.

The Study

This paper draws on a 10-month ethnographic study of the sex industry in Birmingham, UK, during 2000–2001. Observations were made in both the street and indoor sex markets including saunas, working premises and escort agencies. Fifty interviews were conducted with sex workers and a further five interviews with women who owned or organised sex establishments. Fifteen interviewees had experience of working on the street and five currently remained in this market. The number of street workers formally interviewed is small due to the specific problems of accessing a group of women who live chaotic lives, on different timeframes, often with serious drug addictions and sometimes with a boyfriend-pimp (see Faugier and Sargeant, 1996; Maher, 2000; and Miller, 1995, for further details of the difficulties accessing this group). At least 20 other women agreed in principle to be formally interviewed, but in reality women either forgot the time and meeting-place, were too concerned with 'punting and scoring' or were agitated, depressed or had no time to talk to a researcher. The 15 interviews (which lasted between 45 minutes and 7 hours) were transcribed verbatim and analysed on the computer package Atlas.ti.

The interview data are strongly supported by over 400 hours of observations of the street market where informal conversations took place with many other street workers. Similar to other research (Porter and Bonilla, 2000; McKeganey and Barnard, 1996), this access was facilitated through a sexual health project that operates an outreach service specifically for women in prostitution. I was able to accompany the outreach workers on their nightly patrols of the street in their specialist equipped van, supplying condoms, needle syringes and hot chocolate to women on the street. This privileged position meant that I was privy to many incidents amongst the street sex work community that enabled me to piece together a picture of the types of risks that women faced. For instance, on several occasions I saw women arrested by police as they walked the beat, were hailing taxis to get a ride home or were approached when they were chatting with non-prostitute women in the neighbourhood. I saw groups of middle-class, middle-aged men and women protesting by congregating on street corners, communicating on two-way radios, taking down notes and even photographing women. Male vigilantes were also observed shouting verbal abuse to street workers, intimidating them with their physical presence and dogs. On one occasion, a mob of approximately 20 men chased a lone woman out of a particular neighbourhood because they assumed she was loitering for business. As Porter and Bonilla (2000, p. 106) note from their research methods, observing and interviewing sex workers in their working environment has specific advantages for the outsider as the contexts of the women's lives and activities inform and enrich the data collected.

Sex workers used the private 'women only' space in the van as their safe haven on the beat. Sometimes, the mobile unit really was a safe place to hide, seek protection and assistance. On six occasions, women came into the van after clients, pimps or dealers had attacked them. Equally, the van was a space where women could openly be themselves, free from the fear that they would be judged, recorded or condemned. At times, the van was a 'hot house' of gossip, laughter and information-sharing. Women would also share their latest encounters with 'dodgy punters', up-to-date reports on policing activity, or the whereabouts of the residents. This enabled me to witness first-hand the effective and speedy communication network that women use to pass on crucial information (such as description of men, cars and registration numbers) to keep themselves safe and stay out of danger.

Half way through the fieldwork, the sexual health project obtained a 'drop-in' centre in the neighbourhood where the women worked. This was open between 7pm and 11pm before the mobile outreach service began. Women would use the facility to discuss issues with the various drug specialists, community nurses, sexual health practitioners, housing officers and domestic violence workers who were present. More informally, the drop-in was a place where the women, like in any work environment, shared a communal space to have a chat over coffee, exchange working tips, talk about their day, their children and family. Also it was a place where women sought emotional refuge: women were often in dire conditions from heroin and crack withdrawal, rock-bottom from having children removed by state authorities, in the aftermath of abortions and miscarriages, homeless and excluded from family, clinging onto life, using prostitution to survive.

Over the period, I built up strong relationships with women, especially those who I saw several times a week. Ethnography is a powerful tool for accessing women's lives and, although "it is a messy business" (Maher, 2000, p. 232) it enables a process of representation of those who often have little voice. Questions may be asked about the representativeness of this case study due to the small numbers and the purposive nature of the sample selection. However, Maher (2000, p. 29) criticises the emphasis on representativeness because it "obscures what the anomalous or the marginal can reveal about the centre ... and perhaps most of all, strate-gies of resistance". The street sex market I observed and the women I spoke with were a snapshot of other similar markets across Britain and perhaps other Western countries. This can be said with conviction because the sex workers, many of whom had worked in several cities, and experts representing na-tional networks, confirmed that my findings were reflective of other street markets. The accounts and evidence in this paper are taken from this ethnographic process and it is a truthful account of my observations and the women's stories.

As Figure 1 identifies, the location of this research was the city of Birmingham, the UK's second-largest city. The location of street prostitution at the time of the fieldwork was a square mile of residential streets in Edgbaston, south of the city. It consists of a number of tree-lined streets, less than two miles from the city centre and adjacent to one of the main entertainment strips (hotels, conference centres, casinos, restaurants, bars, lap dancing clubs) running into the city. The location has a reservoir and a park where sex workers sometimes take their clients. Edg-baston is an affluent, leafy suburb, with Vic-torian period houses and a high proportion of home-ownership. The residents are mainly White, middle-class professionals or retired, older people. Due to house prices and the increasing number of students (the university is within one mile) this is changing as large houses become multioccupancy dwellings for students and those on welfare benefits and low wages. However, Edgbaston still remains a haven amidst areas of increased poverty, high-rise social housing and social exclusion.

This area can be contrasted to the previous location of street prostitution throughout the 1990s. Balsall Heath is only two miles south of Edgbaston and is markedly different in population. Balsall Heath has been home to South Asian immigrants for the past 50 years and has a strong community with mosques and many Asian businesses and shops. How-ever, similar to Edgbaston, there is a large park and a central road that runs to the city

centre. The original community action group 'Streetwatch' campaigned relentlessly to re-move prostitution from the windows and streets of Balsall Heath. Traffic-calming measures, urban regeneration and a degree of vigilantism eventually moved prostitution to the neighbouring district of Edgbaston. Al-though the boundaries of the commercial area are in constant flux as women move their working territory in response to local politics and dynamics, Edgbaston is still the predominant place for trading sex.

Rationality, Strategy and Public Space

This section explores the direct responses sex workers create, implement and share to resist some of the occupational hazards of the ur-ban market-place. Women use space strategi-cally to avoid physical violence, arrest, criminalisation and harassment. The debates of agency and victimhood within prostitution have set out the complex parameters of whether a woman can consent to sell access to her body parts or whether all forms of prostitution are exploitative (for reviews, see Gulcur and Ilkkaracan, 2002; Kesler, 2002; O'Connell Davidson, 2002). However, my research and this paper argue that although women may not rationally decide to enter prostitution, their responses to the daily haz-ards they face are often calculated strategies of resistance. In this sense, the space on which women rely to advertise, negotiate and supply commercial sex is strategically used to their advantage in order to make cash and minimise chances of harm. This section builds on the arguments presented by Hub-bard (1999, pp. 180–209) that flesh out how resistance is underpinned by intentionality. Powerless groups such as sex workers "re-work and divert these spaces to create an alternative meaning of space—a space that has its own morality, rhythms and rituals which are often invisible to outsiders" (Hub-bard, 1999, p. 183).

Managing Physical Harm

During the period 1989–2002, sex workers in

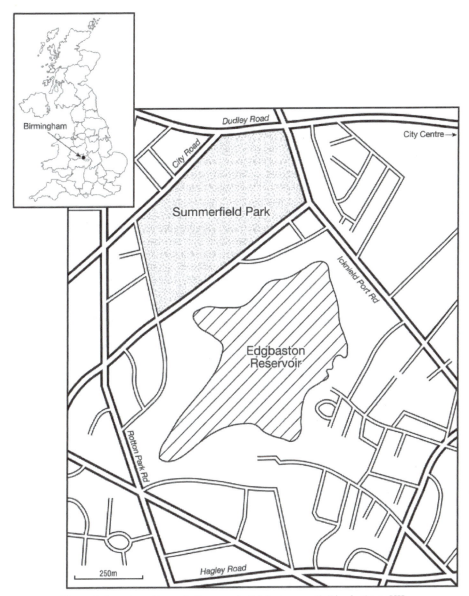

Figure 1. Location of prostitution area in Edgbaston, south Birmingham, UK.

Birmingham, the majority of whom worked on the street, reported over 400 separate incidents of physical or sexual attacks by clients to a local health organisation. Of the street workers I spoke with, those who had not been attacked were in the minority. In all, 15 women retold their experiences of multiple violence from clients: 7 had been raped; 14 had been physically beaten; 5 had been robbed at knife-point; 3 had been confined against their will or kidnapped; a further 3 had been robbed at gun-point; and 2 had been drugged by a client.

Violence, as an occupational hazard, has varying consequences for the women. Some decide that prostitution is too dangerous and leave all together, or leave the street for a safer working environment. Debbie explains how violence prompted her to work from a private rented flat

> I worked on the streets in 1993 and there was a girl killed by a punter. I knew her really well. I was only speaking to her a couple of hours before she was killed. I thought no, I better come off these streets (Debbie, 28, worked on the street for 4 years).[3]

Others learn quickly by their mistakes and change their working practices to reduce the risks of violence

> When I went out there to begin with I just used to get into any car, with two or three men and never used to check or anything. I got into quite a lot of trouble doing that ... I was raped and kidnapped and had to spend time in hospital (Nicky, 22, worked in different sectors for 5 years).

The strategies that women devise to protect themselves mean that in the majority of transactions women are not attacked, raped or robbed. Controlling the environment is a tactic sex workers use to prevent attacks and to ensure that sexual negotiations and transactions occur without incident. Sex workers said that the stages of the commercial transaction where they feel most vulnerable were during the negotiations with a client in his car and when engaged in the sexual activity. In response, women do not haphazardly go about 'doing business' without thinking about the safety issues. The geographical location of the commercial sex act is a crucial aspect of the precautions, deterrent and protection strategies that sex workers create and implement to keep themselves safe. Women have clear plans regarding the location of each stage of the transaction and stringently apply their working rules

> You never go where they want you to go, you always take them to somewhere that you know is safe. Never let them take you to another town as they will kidnap you ... Never go with two men ... always check that there is no-one hiding in the back ... don't get into vans (Melissa, 25, worked on the street for 7 years).

All of the respondents insisted the client drove to a predetermined location for the service: "If they want to take me to their spot then no way, I have been taken to their spots before and left stranded, and I have not had a clue where I am" (Nicky, 22, worked in different sectors for 5 years). If women are familiar with the physical lay-out of the area then they have more chance of escaping or calling for help. Women try to work away from dead-end roads or cul-de-sacs that may prevent their escape but instead work close enough to residential houses that may be called upon for assistance.

On the street, sex workers construct working practices that rely on technology as a deterrent to a client who may intend to harm or rob. Annie explains how she chooses the location for administering the sexual service with care and will only provide sexual services in public areas where CCTV is in operation

> I always take them to places where there are cameras. I don't normally point them out unless they are going to start to be funny then I will say to them that there are cameras out there and it is all being filmed and if they don't want business then to drop me off. I normally take them to the hospital, as it is all camera-ed there (Annie, 22, worked on the street for 4 years).

All of the street workers that I met carried some form of implement that could be used as a weapon in case they were attacked. Knives, blades, CS spray and lighters were said to be the best forms of weapons. One woman hid a metal bar in the bushes where she took her clients and had used it on several occasions to beat off attackers. As previously reported by other studies (Dunhill,

1989, p. 205; McKeganey and Barnard, 1996), to keep track of the client, street workers note car registration numbers: "One girl will take the registration number of the car ... Where I worked we all stuck together on the beat which was like a little community" (Katrina, 32, reflecting on street experiences). Sometimes this is done so that the client can see their vehicle is being recorded. Often women would inform friends and boyfriends where they take clients in case they did not return when expected.

As a reaction to the increasing levels of violence, drug-related crimes and policing, it was becoming increasingly popular to combine working on the street with working from indoor locations: "Before I was out there every day but I have cut it down and work from the phones" (Nicky, 22, worked in different sectors for 5 years). Two routes of mobility were noted amongst street workers: either women continued to use the streets to attract clients but performed the service at an indoor location (hired flat, home, hotel, client's home); or they found permanent work indoors (often a rented establishment with others), only venturing onto the street to attract new clients or when business was quiet. This can be understood as a positive displacement of prostitution from the street to indoor locations which are generally safer and tolerated by law enforcers.

Avoiding Protesters

Hubbard (1997) describes the policing of prostitution as a spatial process that perpetuates the marginal status of those involved. At a local level, the community politics of direct action against prostitution in Birmingham over the past decade have determined official responses. During the mid 1990s, the South Asian community of Balsall Heath initiated direct action tactics (nightly patrols, pickets, media campaigns and car registration recording scheme) to remove prostitution from its streets. Many of the sex workers contacted in this fieldwork remembered the pressure from the vigilantes

If ever I went out and the vigilantes were out or the media I would just go back home ... half of the vigilantes were hypocrites because they were punters themselves. Well a few times they would try and push you about. A mate of mine, they would batter her with sticks and things and they were always giving verbal abuse. Or you maybe crossing the road and they would put their foot down on the car and you would have to run (Sally, 34 years old, worked on the street for 10 years).

As a direct result of displacement due to intense community action and state policing, sex workers moved their site of work to another area, one mile from the old district. This prompted the revival of the original Streetwatch action group under new management. The membership of mainly South Asian males was replaced by White, middle-class, older professional males who rapidly won the support of politicians, local counsellors, law enforcement agencies and the city council. Intense patrolling of the main streets was reinstated on a nightly basis. The police I interviewed described close partnerships with the Streetwatch community group who acted as informers, monitors and direct surveillance. One Inspector commented: "We work as a team with members of Streetwatch, who have their own patrols monitoring the area and logging car registration numbers, which are then passed on to us" (*Birmingham Evening Mail*, 8 May 1998, p. 43). Indeed the police created a special 'hot line' telephone service so that protesters could inform the police of individuals' activities. The police and local authority had jointly funded a specially equipped vehicle for use by the Streetwatch group to patrol the area. This van was fitted with holding cells.

During my observations and discussion with street workers, the intimidation and direct harassment of the women were noted. Protesters followed individual women to their homes, took photographs, repeatedly quizzed women about their intentions on the street (What were they doing? Where were they going? Who were they going to visit?).

Annie felt particularly harassed by the Street-watch members as she lived and worked in the same area

> I will be walking up the road with my daughter and they will stop me. I say to them at night when I am on my own and I am dressed in mini skirts then they have got a right to stop me but not at 3 o'clock in the afternoon, with my baby in the push chair with about 6 carrier bags. I mean am I really doing business in that state? They still stop me (Annie, 22, worked the street for 4 years).

The direct action tactics employed by the protesters impinged on the women's personal space as much as it did on their commercial activities. Sex workers found it difficult to maintain any sense of privacy as the public nature of their work led to intrusion and interference. Nevertheless, methods of monitoring, observing and sharing information used by the protesters informed the sex workers' strategies for resisting state and community control

> I work in the day time to avoid the vigilantes. They are normally in the Streetwatch van, and when I see them coming round I jump into the bushes until they have gone. They usually drive round a set route and you know if they drive one way that you have got 15 minutes until they come back. You either walk the opposite way or you get a client and move off. The best thing to do is find out which way they are going and walk the opposite way and then get a customer as quickly as possible. Then I am away with the customer for 20 minutes and then they have not seen me as I have been in a car (Annie, 22, worked on the street for four years).

Women perceptively recreated tactics that were used to survey and control their behaviours to inform when and how they conducted business. A calculated cost and benefit analysis was performed to determine whether the likelihood of harassment was greater than attracting clients. Often, if the risk was too high, they would abandon their

plans. Instead, they would wait until later, move to another town, or simply get the often desperately needed cash through another acquisitive crime. Benson and Matthews (2000, p. 249) suggest that geographical mobility is common amongst street workers as a reaction to policing methods, leading to what one police officer in their study described as 'national displacement'. As discussed below, often the displacement is more than geographical but to other forms of crime.

Managing Policing

Avoiding the police was a daily hazard for most street workers. Of the 15 participants who had worked on the street, 8 women had between 1 and 5 prosecutions for prostitution-related offences. Several other women contacted in this study had received between 20 and 30 arrests within a year, incurring fines impossible to pay unless they increased prostitution activities or other acquisitive crimes. In the fieldwork site, 2 police officers were designated specifically for street prostitution. Birmingham City Council has recently set a legal precedent by issuing 19 women whom they consider to be persistent offenders with ASBOs, prohibiting them from entering certain geographical areas.[4] Other street workers in London have reported up to 217 arrests over a 3-year period (personal communication). Inconsistent policing practices and arbitrary 'crackdowns' mean that women have no clear sense of what is acceptable and work under the fear of arrest

> Last Friday night, the police were everywhere. I got pulled because I was on warrant and they called it up and I had given them his name [boyfriend's surname] and they checked and let me go ... So in the end I thought it was not worth working so I walked off up the road to get a taxi planning to go home. Got in the taxi and got nicked by vice. They would not even accept that I was going home, they had me for loitering. They said the taxi wasn't

prebooked. Different coppers from earlier, but they said they watched me walk up the road, but if they had they would have seen me get out of the first police car. Then the copper started to push me and I went mad at him. They took me to the police station and I refused to give details because I was on warrant ... So I was locked up in the cell and I was there for hours and hours ... Couple of hours later they let me go and I was out back at work (Steph, 20 years old, worked in different sectors for 3 years).

Apart from arrest and criminalisation, sex workers were concerned about the effect of police presence on their ability to make money. The presence of police patrol cars in the area where women advertise is an obvious deterrent for those who are looking to buy sex. The reduction in potential custom has repercussions on working practices and the safety of women. Respondents report that, before the continual police presence, at least half of their clientele each night were regular customers. During the fieldwork, this drastically changed as Nicky recounts: "You know once they [police and residents] are there you are not going to be getting into any car as the clients won't stop for you as they don't want their reg taken". With increased policing, women are taking even less time to assess the client. Often, when a car slows down, the woman will jump in within seconds to move off the street and away from police attention (Barnard, 1993). O'Kane (2002) also found that new powers for arresting kerb-crawlers put sex workers' lives in danger.

Despite vehement complaints about police activities, the same women saw no reason to be hostile to officers who arrested them: "If you run from the vice ... they get you straight away. So the rules are you don't run from the vice you just have to come in" (Katrina, 32, reflecting on street experiences). Some workers discussed the importance of showing compliance and co-operation to the police, sometimes developing effective working relationships with

individual officers: "They are sweet the police, if you are sweet with them then they will be sweet back" (Lucy, 19, worked on the street for 1 year). These relationships were often a trade-off for lenient treatment in exchange for information about other, more serious crimes.

The Consequences of Controlling Space

From these empirical findings several points can be raised. First, the way in which police and protesters control the sites of street prostitution has significant implications for the way in which the street market is organised and for the safety of individual women. Secondly, solutions sought through community safety policing result in the geographical displacement of prostitution at both local and national levels. Thirdly, local policies that focus on the 'disorder' in relation to the presence of prostitution inevitably criminalise individuals rather than tackling the issues associated with making the sex market safer for those who sell and buy commercial sex. These contributions will be discussed in turn.

The implications of intense policing activities and persistent protesters mean that women have to adapt their working practices to avoid harassment and arrest. Increasingly, because of the pressures to move off the beat and not be seen with a client, sex workers are not making preliminary checks when a man approaches. This is dangerous, as it does not allow time for women to think and check any dangerous signs or what type of client the man is. In the car, when there is time to assess the client, it can often be too late. During the fieldwork, there was a notable change in the working patterns of sex workers. In direct response to the presence of protesters, women arrive on the streets much later (around midnight) and work into the dawn. Many of the women who have costly heroin and crack cocaine addictions avoid the streets by staying in crack houses in between attracting customers. Women who continue to use the streets to advertise are working in increasingly dangerous places, away from the safety of the public streets. This change in working hours and practices avoids the police and protesters but at the same time increases their exposure to danger from clients, pimps and dealers.

Another effect of intense policing is that there is less stability within the organisation of sex markets: "Everyday arrests, imprisonment, fines and police raids led women to move within the industry to minimise their risks" (Day and Ward, 2001, p. 230). Mobility has taken two forms. Street workers are moving between different geographical areas in order to avoid becoming known as 'a prostitute' by law enforcement agencies. This means that women work several beats in one night in order to reach their cash targets and avoid arrest. Secondly, the movement between street and indoor markets is becoming increasingly fluid as women rent premises or only rely on the streets for advertising. Mobility away from the street market could potentially reduce the risk of violence as the indoor environments tend to be safer. However, there is a strong likelihood that pushing sex markets further into an illegal and illicit economy only ostracises some of the most vulnerable women in society. Encouraging women to hide their involvement in prostitution creates difficulties for health care and support agencies to make relationships with individuals, preventing any chance of accessing drug rehabilitation.

The policing practices that have been adopted as solutions to street prostitution are essentially community safety strategies. This style of policing is written into the Crime and Disorder Act, 1998, as a form of crime prevention in urban areas. This has been criticised because "intensive policing may also produce harmful forms of social displacement" (Maher and Dixon, 1999, p. 503). Displacement of prostitution happens in terms of relocating the activity to other geographical areas which essentially only "shuffles crime from one area to the next but never reduces it" (Pease, 2003, p. 956). In terms of prostitution, 'crime shuffling' can at best dissuade women from earning cash through commercial sex but through acquisitive crimes such

as shoplifting, forgery and selling drugs. The community safety policies' focus on removing the 'problem' in neighbourhoods, rather than finding wider solutions to tackle the underlying causes of the crimes. The most effect displacement policy can achieve is the reduction in criminal inclination, because high-profile policing may persuade new or novice sex workers to work indoors or use other localities. Arresting and prosecuting women or using ASBOs to prohibit women from certain areas only targets individuals and does nothing to find effective solutions to the place of prostitution in the city. Serving deterrents that are costly and difficult to police on women who are usually heavily entrenched in prostitution and street-related activities is neither offering a way out for women, nor addressing issues raised by the community. As individuals are removed, others will take their place because the factors that determine women's involvement in the street sex economy—namely, drug addiction and coercive male relationships—are not the centre of any cohesive policy approach.

Instead, the focus of urban prostitution policies is on the 'disorder' and 'nuisance' that are associated with this visible illicit sex economy. The nuclei of prostitution policy are on the dangers created to others in the community and the impact of punitive policies on the vulnerability levels of sex workers is not taken into consideration. Hubbard (1998b, p. 56) suggests that the "ordering (and representation) of urban space plays a crucial role in producing and reproducing gender, sex and bodily identities". In urban spaces, territory is marked out for those who can legitimately and safely use space, while groups who are outside the mainstream are confined, or at least attempts are made to confine them, to hidden shadows, away from a legitimate place in public and their rights to full citizenship. Pratt and Hanson (1994, p. 25) echo a similar point: "social boundaries are constructed and maintained through geographical ones that mark off distinctive ways of life". Indeed, society is concerned with regulating the type of sex and the types of sexual identity that are tolerated in public. The ways in which sex workers experience the street can be understood through wider issues of how space is used to reinforce the social conditioning of gender norms (Duncan, 1996). Although this paper has argued that sex workers create resistance strategies to manage occupational risks, doing business is increasingly dangerous because of community safety policies and policing practices. If the sites of prostitution are being increasingly reduced while at the same time made the target of surveillance and scrutiny then sex workers are given little option but to take risks. Remembering Douglas' emphasis on the need to understand the dilemma of risk-taking and risk-aversion from the individual's interaction with the community, there seems little reason in dividing those who have vested interests in the same streets. Work by O'Neill and Campbell (2001) demonstrates how sex workers and community residents can come together through community arts projects and research initiatives to establish ways to introduce effective urban policy that is neither punitive, moralistic nor biased. Until the implications of these so-called solutions are fully realised, the prostitute and the punter will continue furtively to use the city streets to match need with desire, while the police and protester chase them from one place to the other.

Notes

1. Douglas demonstrates this by an example of the homosexual man who is advised by his doctor to stem certain practices because of the dangers. The man's refusal to act on the advice because he enjoys the risky lifestyle is not a weakness of understanding or irrational behaviour, but a preference (Douglas, 1992, p. 103). Rhodes (1997, p. 215) explains this further with the example of unprotected sex with partners who are known to be HIV-positive can be understood as 'situated rationality' or 'informed-choice making'.

2. The prevalence of violence in prostitution is reported in the US (James, 1974; Maher, 2000, pp. 155–159; Miller, 1997; Silbert and Pines, 1985), Canada (Lowman, 2000), Europe (Hoigard and Finstad, 1992; Mansson

and Hedin, 1999), South America (Downe, 1999; Nencel, 2001) and South Africa (Wojcicki and Malala, 2001).

3. All names have been changed to protect anonymity but the rest of the details are factually correct.

4. These civil actions were taken at the beginning of 2003 and a reliable source indicates that at least half of the women who were served these civil actions remain working the streets.

References

ASHWORTH, G., WHITE, P. and WINCHESTER, H. (1988) The red light district in the west European city: a neglected aspect of the urban landscape, *Geoforum*, 19, pp. 201–212.

BARNARD, M. (1993) Violence and vulnerability: conditions of work for street using prostitutes, *Sociology of Health and Illness*, 15, pp. 5–14.

BENSON, C. (1998) *Violence against female prostitutes*. Department of Social Sciences, Loughborough University.

BENSON, C. and MATTHEWS, R. (1995) *National Vice Squad survey*. School of Sociology and Social Policy, Middlesex University.

BENSON, C. and MATTHEWS, R. (2000) Police and prostitution: vice squads in Britain, in: R. WEITZER (Ed.) *Sex for Sale*, pp. 245–264. London: Routledge.

BOYNTON, P. (1996) *Beauty, envy, disease and danger: stereotypes of women in pornography*. Paper presented at '*Issues in Pornography*' Conference, University of West England.

BROOKS-GORDON, B. and GELSTHORPE, L. (2003) Prostitutes' clients, Ken Livingstone and a new trojan horse, *The Howard Journal*, 42, pp. 437–451.

CAMPBELL, R., COLEMAN, S. and TORKINGTON, P. (1996) *Street prostitution in inner city Liverpool*. Liverpool Hope University College.

CHURCH, S., HENDERSON, M., BARNARD, M. and HART, G. (2001) Violence by clients towards female prostitutes in different work settings: questionnaire survey, *British Medical Journal*, 322, pp. 524–525.

DAY, S. and WARD, H. (2001) Violence towards female prostitutes, *British Medical Journal*, 323, p. 230.

DOUGLAS, M. (1992) *Risk and Danger: Essays in Cultural Theory*. London: Routledge.

DOWNE, P. (1999) Laughing when it hurts: humour and violence in the lives of Costa Rican prostitutes, *Women's Studies International Forum*, 22, pp. 63–78.

DUNCAN, N. (1996) Renegotiating gender and sexuality in public and private spaces, in: N. DUNCAN (Ed.) *Bodyspace*, pp. 127–145. London: Routledge.

DUNHILL, C. (1989) Working relations, in: C. DUNHILL (Ed.) *The Boys In Blue*, pp. 205–208. London: Virago.

FAUGIER, J. and SARGEANT, M. (1996) Boyfriends, pimps and clients, in: G. SCAMBLER and A. SCAMBLER (Eds) *Rethinking Prostitution*, 121–136. London: Routledge.

GULCUR, L. and ILKKARACAN, P. (2002) The 'Natasha' experience: migrant sex workers from the former Soviet Union and eastern Europe in Turkey, *Women's Studies International Forum*, 25, pp. 411–421.

GYSELS, M., POOL, R. and NSALUSIBA, B. (2002) Women who sell sex in a Ugandan trading town: life histories, survival strategies and risk, *Social Science and Medicine*, 54, pp. 179–192.

HOIGARD, C. and FINSTAD, L. (1992) *Backstreets: Prostitution, Money and Love*. Cambridge: Polity.

HUBBARD, P. (1997) Red-light districts and toleration zones: geographies of female street prostitution in England and Wales, *Area*, 29, pp. 129–140.

HUBBARD, P. (1998a) Community action and the displacement of street prostitution: evidence from British cities, *Geoforum*, 29, pp. 269–286.

HUBBARD, P. (1998b) Sexuality, immorality and the city: red light districts and the marginalisation of female street prostitutes, *Gender Place and Culture*, 5, pp. 55–72.

HUBBARD, H. (1999) *Sex and the City: Geographies of Prostitution in the Urban West*. Aldershot: Ashgate.

HUBBARD, P. and SANDERS, T. (2003) Making space for sex work: female street prostitution and the production of urban space, *International Journal of Urban and Regional Research*, 27, pp. 73–87.

JAMES, J. (1974) Motivation for entrance into prostitution, in: L. CRITHES (Ed.) *The Female Offender*, pp. 177–205. London: Heath.

KESLER, K. (2002) Is a feminist stance in support of prostitution possible? An exploration of current trends, *Sexualities*, 5, pp. 219–235.

KINNELL, H. (1992) *Wolverhampton sex workers survey*. Birmingham: Safe Project, Birmingham Health Authority.

LARSEN, E. (1992) The politics of prostitution control: interest group politics in four Canadian cities, *International Journal of Urban and Regional Research*, 16, pp. 169–189.

LOWMAN, J. (2000) Violence and the outlaw status of (street) prostitution in Canada, *Violence Against Women*, 6, pp. 987–1011.

MAHER, L. (2000) *Sexed Work: Gender, Race and Resistance in a Brooklyn Drug Market*. Oxford: Oxford University Press.

MAHER, L. and DIXON, D. (1999) Policing and public health, *British Journal of Criminology*, 39, pp. 488–512.

MANSSON, S. A. and HEDIN, U. (1999) Breaking the Matthew effect: on women Leaving prostitution, *International Journal of Social Welfare*, 8, pp. 67–77.

MAY, T., EDMUNDS, M. and HOUGH, M. (1999) *Street business: the links between sex and drug markets*. Police Research Series Paper 118. London: Home Office.

MAY, T., HAROCOPOS, A. and HOUGH, M. (2000) *For love or money: pimps and the management of sex work*. Police Research Series Paper 134. London: Home Office.

MCKEGANEY, N. and BARNARD, M. (1996) *Sex Work on the Streets*. Buckingham: Open University Press.

MILLER, J. (1995) Gender and power on the streets, *Journal of Contemporary Ethnography*, 24(4), pp. 427–451.

MILLER, J. (1997) Researching violence against street prostitutes, in: M. SCHWARTZ (Ed.) *Researching Sexual Violence Against Women*, pp. 144–156. London: Sage.

NENCEL, L. (2001) *Ethnography and Prostitution in Peru*. London: Pluto Press.

O'CONNELL DAVIDSON, J. 2002. The rights and wrongs of prostitution, *Hypatia*, 17, pp. 84–98.

O'KANE, M. (2002) Prostitution: the Channel 4 survey (http:www.channel4.com/news/microsites/D/Dispatches/prostitution/survey.html).

O'NEILL, M. (2001) *Prostitution and Feminism*. London: Polity Press.

O'NEILL, M. and R. CAMPBELL. (2001) *Working together to create change*. Walsall Consultation Research, Staffordshire University & Liverpool Hope University.

PEASE, K. (2003) Crime reduction, in: M. MAGUIRE, R. MORGAN and R. REINER (Eds) *Oxford Handbook of Criminology*, pp. 948–979. Oxford: Oxford University Press.

PHOENIX, J. (1999) *Making Sense of Prostitution*. London: Macmillan.

PILE, S. (1996) *The Body and the City*. London: Routledge.

PORTER, J. and BONILLA, L. (2000) Drug use, HIV and the ecology of street prostitution, in: R. WEITZER (Ed.) *Sex for Sale*, pp. 103–121. London: Routledge.

PRATT, G. and HANSON, S. (1994) Geography and the construction of difference, *Gender, Place and Culture*, 1, pp. 5–29.

RAPHAEL, J. and SHAPIRO, D. (2004) Violence in indoor and outdoor prostitution venues, *Violence Against Women*, 10, pp. 126–139.

RHODES, T. (1997) Risk theory in epidemic times: sex, drugs and the social organisation of 'risk behaviour', *Sociology of Health and Illness*, 19, pp. 208–227.

SANDERS, T. (2001) Female street sex workers,

sexual violence and protection strategies, *Journal of Sexual Aggression,* 7, pp. 5–18.

SANDERS, T. (forthcoming) *Sex Work: A Risky Business.* Cullompton: Willan.

SHARPE, K. (1998) *Red Light, Blue Light: Prostitutes, Punters and the Police.* Aldershot: Ashgate.

SIBLEY, D. (1995) *Geographies of Exclusion: Society and Difference in the West.* London: Routledge.

SILBERT, A. and PINES, M. (1985) Sexual abuse as an antecedent of prostitution, *Child Abuse and Neglect,* 5, pp. 407–411.

SKEGGS, B. (1999) Matter out of place: visibility and sexualisation in leisure spaces, *Journal of Leisure Studies Association,* 18, pp. 213–232.

STERK, C. (2000) *Tricking and Tripping: Prostitution in the Era of AIDS.* New York: Social Change Press.

WILLIAMSON, C. and CLUSE-TOLAR, T. (2002) Pimp-controlled prostitution: still an integral part of street life, *Violence Against Women,* 8, pp. 1074–1092.

WOJCICKI, J. and MALALA, J. (2001) Condom use, power and HIV/AIDS risk: sex-workers bargain for survival in Hillbrow/Joubert Park/Berea, Johannesburg, *Social Science and Medicine,* 53, pp. 99–121.

[6]

Theorizing About Violence

Observations From the Economic and Social Research Council's Violence Research Program

Elizabeth A. Stanko
Royal Holloway, University of London

The director of the Economic and Social Research Council Violence Research Program (VRP) in the United Kingdom discusses and debates the impacts of the program in the context of contemporary ideas about violence and current U.K. policy and practice in the field. The projects in the program included 2 historical studies and 18 contemporary studies of violence in the home, schools, prisons, neighborhoods, leisure establishments, massage parlors, and on the street. For example, studies focusing on the nighttime economy in U.K. cities, on paramilitary punishment beatings in Northern Ireland, and on violence experienced and perpetrated by girls are discussed here. Five projects addressed gendered violence, and three addressed domestic violence specifically. Lessons from the VRP are drawn out in this article in a personal account. These lessons include the fact that violence is not hidden, that the meanings of violence are gendered, and that people's accounts of violence matter.

Keywords: *gender; synergies; violence research program*

In the United Kingdom, the government-sponsored Economic and Social Research Council (ESRC) is the premier funding body for social science research. During 5 years (1997 to 2002), the ESRC sponsored a research program on violence. Twenty projects, selected from 241 proposals, were funded, exploring diverse topics such as domestic violence in pregnancy, violence in prisons, paramilitary punishment beatings in Northern Ireland, violence within schools and children's homes, and others.[1] Interdisciplinary in its scope, the Violence Research Program (VRP) aimed to learn about violence to the person. The studies focused on examining violence in particular arenas—homes, schools, prisons, neighborhoods, leisure establishments, massage parlors, and on the street, and two historical projects brought a perspective that challenged our contemporary assumptions about how we understood and accounted for violence. Despite this diversity, however, there were many synergies in the findings. The lessons mapped across the projects were taken to policy makers, academics, activists, and practitioners for debate, discussion, and challenge to current practice.

Of special relevance is the way gender—as a way of grounding our theorizing—intersects the study of violence, and, of course, there are many lessons from the VRP to assist our thinking about violence of and to men. My expertise as director of the program drew from my own experience as a commentator on violence against women for more than 25 years. I also drew on this expertise to assist me to draw lessons common across projects exploring very different forms of violence. I was later invited to put some of these lessons from the VRP into practice by the London Metropolitan Police, and in doing so I tested out my own presumptions about thinking about violence. In September 2000, for instance, I conducted the first U.K. nationwide day count of domestic violence within four organizations (Stanko, 2001). From 2001 to 2002, I directed an action research project within the metropolitan police examining ways of using the police crime records on hate crime and domestic violence as strategic information for innovation in police practice (Stanko et al., 2003). This practical work taught me about the advantages of using perspectives on violence against women to think more creatively across all forms of violence. (I enjoyed this work so much I have now left academic life to work full-time with the metropolitan police.)

This article seeks to draw out a few of the synergies to share with those who work on the problem of violence against women in the United Kingdom, the United States, and internationally. The program awarded five of its 20 projects specifically to studies of violence against women: three exploring domestic violence, one examining violence against prostitutes, and one focusing on girls' experiences of violence. But virtually all the studies—particularly the work on homicide, violence against professionals working in the community, violence in the leisure industry, and violence in residential homes, neighborhoods, and schools—have relevant findings that can be linked to our thinking about violence and gender, and by extension violence against women. Taken as a whole, the VRP's findings demonstrate the significance of why we need to take gender seriously. The more we know about the relationships between victim and perpetrator and between both these parties and the institutions with which each (and often both) interact, the better able we are to challenge so many forms of violence against women.

The Study of Violence and the Study of Violence Against Women

Twenty-five years ago, when I began my work on violence, along with most criminologists and police officials I assumed that only strangers committed "real" violence. It was my PhD thesis research that forced me to rethink this criminological axiom.[2] During my work in the New York district attorney's office (Stanko, 1981 to 1982), I learned that much of the violence that comes to the attention of the criminal justice arena involves parties who are known to each other. In the mid-1970s, domestic violence (a term I had not yet heard) was not the kind of violence that prosecutors often took seriously. I still remember the district attorney saying about a woman who had been shot in the head by her boyfriend, "If she dies we have manslaughter, if she lives and is a vegetable, we have assault in the first degree, and if she recovers she will probably drop the charges." This quote haunts me to this day. It is one that I have returned to time and time again to understand professionals' and institutions' responses to violence.

Understanding violence requires one to develop a cognitive map for contextualizing "what happened." The landscape is tightly woven around social identities, social meanings, and social context. It is virtually impossible, I would argue, to separate the social and legal meaning of an incident from its wider social, political, and economic context. Statute on criminal harm occasionally specifies such context (excluding the legal definition of rape from those parties who are legally married, e.g., move). But usually, the context of violence provides a powerful grounding for establishing its meanings.

The VRP projects consistently affirmed the significance of context—for theorizing, for practice, for policy. How "seriously" we as a society respond to an incident of violence varies by the situation within which it takes place. The study of punishment beatings in Belfast, Northern Ireland, for example, used the statement of politicians that the peace agreement had led to "an acceptable level of violence." The researchers were challenging this "acceptable" level because it denied the impact of such beatings on its victims. The assumptions about the social context of the politics of the "peace agreement," the collective tolerance of a population embedded in such politics, and expectations that witness intimidation was so rife that frontline youth or social workers had to constantly manage people's anxieties about punishment beatings combined to influence the way in which communities in Northern Ireland understood this form of torture (see Knox & Monaghan, 2003). That punishment beatings became a part of the political debate in some ways glossed over the devastating effects on individuals. Articulating the tension over levels of tolerance that perhaps tacitly associated punishment beatings with peace was necessary to challenge this form of violence, the researchers argued.

Another of the VRP projects explored bouncers in the nighttime economy. The researchers revealed—based on their extensive ethnographic work—that bouncers were hired to be intimidating and to use, if necessary, violence to maintain order in pubs and clubs. The mostly male victims who might have come to police attention because they were beaten up or injured in a nightclub or pub failed to substantiate reports of violence. Few of these incidents found their way through the criminal justice system (Winslow, Hobbs, Lister, & Hadfield, 2003). The men's reluctance to substantiate allegations of pub violence sounds strikingly similar to those of battered women or women sexually assaulted: "It was my fault"; "it was just a fight"; "I was drunk"; or the police failed to take the details in a way that led to a criminal investigation. These are but a few of the justifications for failing to prosecute criminal injuries arising from pub and club violence.

The VRP studies underscored the observation that social context is highly relevant to the way in which violence is defined as criminal harm or as harmful by perpetrator, victim, criminal justice official, and society at large. In many respects, the feminist challenge to criminological theorizing revolved around the demand to recognize how familiarity is a central feature of criminal violence to women. Indeed, familiarity facilitates discourses for minimizing the harm of violence—for women as well as for men. Remember the words of the prosecutor I cited earlier. So much of the feminist work on domestic and sexual violence articulates the ways familiarity disables a language of criminal harm. Battered women speak of damaging relationships, of their reluctance to separate children from a dangerous father, of their family and kin ties to a man who is violent. Women's use of a discourse of self-blame has not diminished during the 25 years I've been working in this field. Just sit around the kitchen of any refuge or battered women's shelter today. Our feminist theorizing has been able to capture this discourse and others, a tribute largely to the antiviolence work of feminists and other activists who insisted that we deal with "the ordinary and the everyday" violence in women's lives.

I'd like to focus here on three broad points to illustrate the collective lessons from the VRP and how I think these could be reflected in the debate in the field of violence against women. The first is the truism linked to much of the work on violence against women: Violence is hidden. I question whether it is useful to insist on thinking about violence as if it is largely hidden. In doing so, we render invisible what we do see and know about. The second lesson addresses the link between gender and the meaning of violence. What does knowing gendered perspectives tell us about violence—and women? And finally, I would like to return to the importance of using women's ordinary voices in accounts and accounting for violence. We had to learn to hear ordinary women about ordinary violence. Now we sometimes listen to what they say. But all too often, in so many areas around the world, we still do not listen enough or effectively. If we did, perhaps we would challenge violence against women—and all violence—more effectively.

Lesson 1: Violence Is Not Hidden

In the closing months of the VRP, I hosted five regional seminars on the findings from the program. Inevitably—as it happened—one of the first questions asked about the program was about the hidden nature of violence. People seemed more interested not in what the researchers found but in what part of the phenomenon—violence—remained out of frame. Audience after audience asked the researchers first about aspects of the work that was still "unknown," hidden. For whatever reason, the audience wanted to talk about findings about violence as if the researchers' work was not a form of documentation and analysis of violence. Where did these questions come from? Perhaps people now accept the findings of the late 1970s and early 1980s that clearly demonstrated that much violence is often hidden from official view. Early feminist work exposed the commonness of sexual abuse and physical assault among populations of women. Such exposure relied heavily on examining women's experiences through social science surveys, typically modelled after crime victim surveys.

As study after study reveals, little of violence against women comes to the attention of criminal justice officials. People's acceptance, however, of the hidden nature of violence has left a gap in our ability to challenge the current state of responses to violence when it *is* reported to any official agency. What are the implications of not acting on what we do indeed know? Official documentation—from police records to social services files—are not explored for what kind of action leads to successful or helpful interventions. Moreover, we virtually ignore the information about violence held by family and friends—often the first port of call for advice and assistance following violence.

Records of social service departments in the United Kingdom, rehousing requests for those seeking safe refuge, episodes recorded by schools, medical histories, and records from prisons, residential homes, and even the police are rife with documented incidents of violence. Yet, we seem to take "hidden" violence more seriously, almost to the extent that we accept that recorded incidents are a distortion of the hidden and thus less relevant to our understanding of violence. Instead, we should view documentation as giving insight into what does come to be recorded so that we can begin to interrogate what such records tell us or what the participants tell us about why, when, and where violence (that is known to officials) happens. When we study the public records, we can hold officials to account for addressing in a holistic way the violence they do know about from their *own* information. We should be asking how those who come to the attention of officials will be supported, helped, or provided with competent, sympathetic treatment. And we should have a way of documenting why such support did not lead to a successful intervention. We need to know *why* official knowledge about violence is not often translated into action that supports, helps, or furthers policy to reduce violence and to make people's lives following violence better.

In Britain, our ability to interrogate our official records for the lessons about violence lags behind the study of violence gleaned from victim surveys and qualitative research with survivors. One opportunity to use routine medical care and records came in the study in the VRP of the relationship between domestic violence and pregnancy (see Bacchus, Mezey, & Bewley, 2003, 2006 [this issue]). Along with capturing an estimate of the prevalence of domestic violence, the study demonstrated the difficulties in changing the practice and the culture of medical care to include systematic understanding about domestic violence. Midwives were trained and supported to ask what were considered to be highly sensitive questions about violence and its history in women's lives. Yet, many of the midwives felt uncomfortable. And the chaos of the institution's records was revealed. Women's medical records were lost or otherwise incomplete, preventing medical practitioners from seeing important clinical information about patients. The researchers also documented how some women did attend antenatal clinics in a distressed state, needing immediate support and advice about domestic violence. But few health staff could cope with this interruption to their normal routine of administering antenatal care. Advice and support was and still is not readily available throughout the National Health Service.

Domestic violence has an impact on the work of clinical staff, but it is not well managed, not considered a routine part of "doing medicine." Recognizing that domestic violence must be addressed as part and parcel of clinical care might ease the resistance of the midwives to incorporating screening and monitoring questions into their normal antenatal practices. As such, domestic violence comes to light in the course of standard medical care for pregnant women. It is not, as such, hidden. Worse, it is treated as not relevant to the medical care of pregnant women. The more we ask direct questions about domestic violence in pregnancy, and record it as part of the medical record, the more domestic violence becomes known as a potential danger to pregnant women and their unborn children. Making the known visible, rather than "discovering" hidden violence, should change practice and reduce violence.

But visibility does not always change practice and policy. Another VRP project exposed high levels of violence to some groups of women. For these women, violence is a very part of their working lives. Women who sell sex experience very high rates of men's violence. The study by Hart and Barnard (2003) found that nearly two out of three female prostitutes had experiences of serious violence in their lives. One in three of the 240 working women who completed questionnaires reported at least one instance of violence in the previous six months. Of the women reporting violence, nearly one in two reported being slapped, kicked, or punched. In fact, violence is much more of a problem and leads to more injurious consequences for the women than sexual diseases. The project sought to examine the differences in the kinds and levels of violence women who sell sex on the streets or in massage parlors experience. Street-working prostitutes experienced higher rates of violence and were most likely to report violence to police. Yet, many of the outreach projects for women selling sex in the United Kingdom focus on women's sexual health and aim specifically to prevent the risk of infection of sexually transmitted diseases. Similar to the care of pregnant women, health care for street-working women should also link up with the need for advice and support around violence as an essential part of services to working women. The high proportion of street-working women who encounter violence is known to police, to the women themselves, to other health and social service providers. Indeed, working women incorporate violence avoidance into the very way they "do sex work"—sex acts incorporate self-protection (see Hart & Barnard, 2003). Planning to avoid violence becomes the routine for many women who sell sex. And as a result, much of the violence perpetrated by the clients goes unchallenged because its avoidance is part of better working practices. Treating violence *as routine* is mistakenly understood as treating violence as hidden.

We must find a way of documenting good and helpful intervention rather than continuously documenting "hidden" violence against women. Research on domestic violence in the United Kingdom suggests that family and friends are told about abuse by more than half of the women answering surveys. So too, we find other public service professionals come into contact with sexually and physically abused women on a regular basis. Indeed, U.K. studies suggest that women tell their family doctors about domestic violence as often as they tell police. Moreover, we might further speculate that next to help with the care of children, women most often use public service contacts to minimize the impact of violence. What amazes me—in a country such as the United Kingdom that values its public services—is that we do not know the impact of the need for services triggered by violence. We do not properly document the best practice that delivers the best outcomes for the safety of women and children—despite what must be a volume of information throughout our public service records. If we treat violence as hidden, we even fail to interrogate the impact of "revealing" violence on public service provision itself—even though we know it must be a substantial contribution to why women seek the advice and support of public services.

What I learned about the study of hidden violence from the VRP is that there is record after record of violence in so many places, especially in public services. Why do we insist on speaking about the hidden when we can be documenting and challenging what we do see in a more comprehensive and systematic way? Perhaps it is because we accept the premise that violence is hidden in official records because we naturalize the relationship between gender and violence—and its different forms. For example, it is misleading in social policy terms to fail to think about the relationship between masculinities, leisure, and violence when speculating about how to reduce the copresence of alcohol with violence in many public records. Any visit to a casualty department in a hospital on a Friday or Saturday evening would demand that policy makers, hospital administrators, and staff ask questions about the way leisure, gender, and violence coexist with such regular frequency and causing such regular damage. The complexities of addressing ways of minimizing the harm of these important features of some forms of violence would take us away from the hospital casualty department and into the very way the leisure industry has changed in the past few years. This change dovetails alongside wider social developments in young people's social lives (more money for public socializing), town center planning (less choice to socialize outside of places where alcohol is sold cheaply), and policing a large number of very drunken young men and women. Although only one of the constellation of factors, ignoring gender in any analysis of violence contributes to hiding its impacts.

Lesson 2: The Meanings of Violence Are Gendered

The debate—is violence gendered?—rages across academic and popular discussions about men's violence to women. The undercurrent—some have even labelled it a backlash against feminism—is the assertion that men's experiences of physical and sexual violence are the same as women's in the domestic setting. Some argue—with great vitriol at times—that as a result of this presumed symmetry, there should be no special attention paid to violence against women. What is at the heart of this debate about the symmetry of violence, I suggest, is the denial of gender as adding anything special to our thinking about violence, including that in the domestic settings.

Why is it so important that I argue here that gender is a feature of what we know about the way violence affects people's lives? Gender is more than being male or female. It is a system of reference, a psychological and social grounding in community. It might be absurd to suggest such a simplistic précis of gender in this journal titled *Violence Against Women*, but the debate is one that many of this journal's readers have engaged with—as students, as activists, as policy makers, as feminists. What many of the projects from the VRP showed was that at the very least, *gender matters*—to those who experience violence, to the way it is understood by others, and to the way institutions are capable of addressing the complex web of social relations that must be in place to support the victim and to challenge and support the offenders (to stop hurting others), and to insist that other people and institutions play their part in supporting the transformation of gendering that leads to harm.

A good example of my argument can be found in the study by Michele Burman and her colleagues (Burman, Brown, & Batchelor, 2003) of girls' experiences of violence in Scotland. This study attracted much attention from journalists throughout the 5 years of VRP. Journalists' questions were indicative of what they argued were common public assumptions about girls and violence: (a) girls who commit violence were very bad or very mad; (b) violence was understandable "when committed by men"; (c) our sense of societal equilibrium is linked with never being afraid of the stilettos walking behind you. Burman and her colleagues were insistent on opening the inquiry in a way that listened to what girls had to say about violence. The journalists were searching for evidence of changing cultural norms for girls that have (somehow until now) managed to contain its "unwomanly" forms. These forms, I would suggest, are most transparent when we examine girls' violence. Although violence has always been part of girls' and women's lives (we "understand" that women are victims, for instance), the violence of women has been condemned, vilified as indiscretions beyond the imagination of womanhood itself. Throughout the history of criminology as a discipline, women's law breaking (and especially the use of violence) has been portrayed as out of character for normal women (see Klein, 1973). What this project exposed is the fact that we as a society are still firmly entrenched in thinking about girls' violence as unnatural.

Girls, this study showed, manage the violence in their lives. Burman and her colleagues challenged the notions that violence is hidden from girls' lives. The study found that 98.5% of the girls had witnessed firsthand some form of fighting. Nearly two out of three of the girls knew someone who had been physically hurt or injured by violence. Two in five of the girls experienced someone deliberately hitting, punching, or kicking them. The journalists concluded that far from naming violence as a part of girls lives to be managed, the findings exposed an aspect of gender that must be changing. Girls, the journalists speculated, were becoming "more violent."

The heart of the debate in theorizing about violence is theorizing about difference—and thinking about how differences maintain so many of the boundaries between privilege and degradation. The intersection of such major features of one's being—gender, class, sexuality, race, age, and so forth—and the way in which social privilege is awarded, challenged, denied, or assumed is the core substance of sociological and economic debate. It is at the heart of whether violence is "naturalized" or "condemned." Social and economic privilege becomes the medium to make visible or invisible the impact of violence. We do not need to see the suffering of the excluded. Indeed, we do not want to see the suffering of the excluded. Worse, we make conscious decisions about what suffering is visible. Often, there is an attempt to turn its meaning into something else (defiance, resentment, self-harm, and so forth).

What difference does gender make in theorizing about violence? The projects of the VRP demonstrated time and time again the salience of gender to the meanings of violence. Gender—whether one is male or female (or even has the knowledge of both, as in the case of transsexuals)—is core to the way inmates, schoolchildren, young residents of residential homes, and users of public space for leisure (to name only a few) speak about their lives vis-à-vis violence and safety. People understand the impact of violence, the way they are treated, as "just a part of their daily lives." They also understand whether those in a position of power to mediate or to minimize the violence will do so or will stay silent. The mechanisms of silence are so embedded in the texture of social and economic privilege. Gender thrives within this fluidity of privilege and exclusion. This does not mean that all women or all men have the same relationship to privilege and exclusion. Gender, quite simply, still matters and influences the way we speak, conceptualize, and challenge violence. To lose sight and insight by ignoring how gender matters impoverishes any analyses of violence.

Nearly all acts of violence are either witnessed directly or known about by third parties, the VRP study of bystander intervention found (Levine, Reicher, Cassidy, & Harrison, 2002). The responses of bystanders are crucial in determining whether violence thrives or subsides. Moreover, the behavior of bystanders depends upon how they understand their social relationships with the three parties to violent events: fellow bystanders, the victim, and the perpetrator. Where bystanders perceive themselves to be a part of a common group, the behavior of others will influence what they do. Where bystanders perceive themselves and the victim of aggression to be a part of a common group, they are more likely to intervene and support the victim. Promoting intervention against violent crime depends upon developing a broader sense of group membership so that others are protected as part of a common in-group.

Many of us are bystanders. Our access to witnessing violence is also often gendered. We know now that most women who are battered tell someone, usually a friend or a relative. If battering persists, gets worse over time, and becomes potentially lethal, we also know that many people know about the woman's situation. The accumulated research on violence against women, moreover, gives us plenty of information about the nature of violence in the home—the patterns of desistence, the patterns of escalation, the patterns of denial, the patterns of escape, the patterns of challenge, and so forth. Social policy defines the boundaries of state responsibility or state responsiveness to social and criminal harm. In the United States, with the virtual demise of any welfare-based social and economic cushion, the debate revolves primarily around the parameters of the legal responses to physical and sexual violence. In many other countries in the West, the resources of social policy include escape routes that may be facilitated by other social benefits, such as access to social housing and public and child benefits.

Gender still matters in criminal harm—for men as well as for women. By and large men hurt other men and are often the perpetrators of women's and children's abuse. Women—when they are the perpetrators—also hurt women, children, and men, but at rates significantly different to those of men. We learn this when we listen to the voices—of the carers, of the victims, of the perpetrators. The VRP demonstrated clearly the importance of these voices to the study of violence, and it is to the importance of voice that I now turn.

Lesson 3: People's Accounts Matter

Researchers who participated in the VRP spoke to a wide range of people and examined a host of official and unofficial documents during their studies. The voices of those many people who provided our researchers with data were central to our discussions. Our internal debates often returned to trying to come up with a definition of what violence means, justifying one position or another through the voices of those many research participants. Despite an assumed, almost self-evident core, as I have suggested elsewhere (Stanko, 2003), violence as a term is ambiguous and its usage is in many ways molded by different people, as well as by different social scientists, describing a whole range of events, feelings, and harm. What violence means is and will always be fluid. It is this fluidity that provides the space for disrupting violence, altering its impact on people's lives and on the way in which we give meaning to it in society at large.

As an interdisciplinary social science program on violence, the VRP reflected the actions and accounts of a great many different kinds of people analyzed through many different lenses. One thread running through the various projects is how many of those affected by violence understood the unspoken and unwritten rules of engagement. People give us accounts of these unspoken rules. For example, there is a great deal of concern about rises in assaults within prison. The VRP's study of prison violence, for instance, found that most prisoners who became involved in violent incidents did not want to fight. The inmates reported that they did so because "they saw no other option" (Edgar, O'Donnell, & Martin, 2002). The researchers found that in every incident they studied, there was an identifiable conflict between the parties involved. The conflict might have been imagined by one party—conflict does not always have to be mutual or mutually understood. (Why would we expect a woman to understand why a man would hit her because the dinner was late?) But the use of force to resolve the conflict was not mindless. One or more of the parties could always explain why the incident had occurred. Nor was the target of the violence random. In very few cases were the parties completely unknown to each other. The researchers conclude that the focus on violence in prisons is often through the lens of how best to contain the violent person. The researchers criticize such thinking for missing a key to the prevention of prison violence—the possible reluctance of one party to fight. As Edgar and his colleagues (2002) argue, it is critical to explore why—not just who, and how—not just how often—fights and assaults occur. Simply, most fights in prison are assumed to fit within the rules of engagement. Prison governors presumed that inmates settle their disputes inevitably by fighting. Only the accounts of people enable us to articulate how the conflict is understood (or not) by the parties themselves. How else are we going to confront the rules of engagement?

Challenging the rules of engagement can flow from the way in which victims, perpetrators, prison guards, and others account for the violence that happens around them. The many projects of the VRP found creative ways of giving voice to different ways of viewing violence. Children living in residential care in England, for instance, provided graphic explanations on the use of violence, the way it is (or was) legitimized in their lived environments, and how violence was endemic in negotiating their way through life (at such a young age; Renold & Barter, 2003). For the majority of the young people interviewed by these researchers, fighting back was treated as a form of social justice.

Accounts offered by racist offenders also brought the perspectives of the "harmers" into debates about the "harmed" (Ray, Smith, & Wastell, 2003b). What was important about the findings of this study interviewing violent offenders included the way they said they did not act in a racist way when they attacked their victims. These offenders shared many assumptions about race with other members of their communities. In many respects, these largely young men were not more racist than some of their friends and neighbors, they were more violent. Not unlike the perpetrators of punishment beatings in Northern Ireland, the seeds of the legitimacy of acts of violence are clearly present in many communities.

Women's accounts of domestic and sexual violence stress the continuity in processes for legitimizing the harm that befalls them. Often wrapped in discourses of heterosexuality, intimacy, and psychological perversity, much violence against women finds its legitimacy in wider social and community relations. Accounts of violence—whether women describing a battering, rape, sexual harassment, or other forms of gendered bullying—are accounts of gendered social relations. Much of the work on violence against women relies on women to tell their stories—and that these stories reflect patterns of the denial of harm and the legitimacy of "hurting the one you love." Women are still told—and still feel—that sexual assault is her fault, and that battering would stop if she were a good wife. Accounts matter, and so it still matters how carefully we as researchers are able to hear what people are saying. Careful analysis of the voices—of victims, offenders, carers—coupled with the documentation of what happened enables us to hear the way in which we as society continue to condone violence through the common discourses people use to explain what happened. To challenge both its legitimation and its direct harm to individuals, we must understand these discourses as well.

Concluding Thoughts

What I found most useful, as a resource from which to draw common threads from an eclectic program of research, was my own research and activist experience and my work on violence against women. The various projects displayed ways in which violence can be made invisible, and the process of denial could be documented. Violence is visible, but the way in which politicians, practitioners, and the public see it often distorts its forms, its impact, its features. As a consequence, different forms of violence are explored separately, as if these phenomena are unique. What is often missing from a general understanding of violence is asking what can be learned from the struggles feminists have waged for decades now against sexual and physical assault. Similarly, those working on racist violence, violence in prisons, violent ethnic conflict, and war all have insight to contribute to the way we can challenge violence against women as well. These lessons from the struggles of feminists and others to challenge violence, I fear, continue to be isolated from each other as knowledge about violence. We need to find a way to bring these dialogues closer together.

The politics of gender equality remain contested ground (and I do not underestimate how much this stifles cooperation). So too do the debates about the politics of hatred, ethnicity, and, these days, fundamentalism and Western imperialism, and how these dovetail with the research and activism on violence against women. But there is always more to learn, to share, and to take back to our communities that daily confront violence. I have offered three synergies from the findings of the VRP: that violence can be studied from its visible features, that gender matters in theorizing and analyzing violence, and that the accounts of people help expose the rules of engagement for violence. These common threads give clues to how we should rethink our theory and our practices to minimize the harm of violence.

Notes

1. For a full list of the projects, see www.rhul.ac.uk/sociopolitical-science/vrp/realhome.htm
2. Readers interested in my philosophy on criminology, see Stanko (1998).

References

Bacchus, L., Mezey G., & Bewley, S. (2003). Researching domestic violence in a maternity setting: Problems and pitfalls. In R. Lee & E. A. Stanko (Eds.), *Researching violence* (pp. 192-216). London: Routledge.

Bacchus, L., Mezey G., & Bewley, S. (2006). A qualitative exploration of the nature of domestic violence in pregnancy. *Violence Against Women, 12,* 588-604.

Burman, M., Brown, J., & Batchelor, S. (2003). "Taking it to heart": Girls and the meaning of violence. In R. Lee & E. A. Stanko (Eds.), *Researching violence* (pp. 71-89). London: Routledge.

Edgar, K., O'Donnell, I., & Martin, C. (2002). *Prison violence: The dynamics of conflict, fear and power.* Devon, UK: Willan.

Hart, G., & Barnard, M. (2003). Jump on top, get the job done: Strategies employed by female prostitutes to reduce the risk of client violence. In E. A. Stanko (Ed.), *The meanings of violence* (pp. 32-48). London: Routledge.

Klein, D. (1973). The etiology of female crime: A review of the literature. *Issues in Criminology, 8*(3), 3-30.

Knox, C., & Monaghan, R. (2003). Fear of reprisal: Researching intra-communal violence in Northern Ireland and South Africa. In R. Lee & E.A. Stanko (Eds.), *Researching violence* (pp. 157-176). London: Routledge.

Levine, M., Reicher, S., Cassidy, C., & Harrison, K. (2002). Promoting intervention against violent crime: A social identity approach. *Findings from the ESRC Violence Research Programme.* Swindon, UK: Economic and Social Research Council.

Ray, L., Smith, D., & Wastell, L. (2003a). Racist violence from a probation service perspective: Now you see it, now you don't. In R. Lee & E. A. Stanko (Eds.), *Researching violence* (pp. 217-231). London: Routledge.

Ray, L., Smith, D. and Wastell, L. (2003b). Understanding racist violence. In E. A. Stanko (Ed.), *The meanings of violence* (pp. 112-129). London: Routledge.

Renold, E., & Barter, C. (2003). Hi I'm Ramon and I run this place: Challenging the normalization of violence in children's homes from young people's perspectives. In E. A. Stanko (Ed.), *The meanings of violence* (pp. 90-111). London: Routledge.

Stanko, E. A. (1981-1982). The impact of victim assessment on prosecutors' screening decisions: The case of the New York County district attorney's office. *Law & Society Review, 16*(2), 225-240.

Stanko, E. A. (1998). Making the invisible visible in criminology: A personal journey. In S. Holdaway & P. Rock (Eds.), *Thinking about criminology* (pp. 35-54). London: UCL Press.

Stanko, E. A. (2001). The day to count: Reflections on a methodology to raise awareness about the impact of domestic violence in the UK. *Criminal Justice, 1*(2) 215-226.

Stanko, E. A. (2003). Introduction. In E. A. Stanko (Ed.), *The meanings of violence* (pp. 1-13). London: Routledge.

Stanko, E. A., Kielinger, V., Paterson, S., Richards, L., Crisp, D., & Marsland, L. (2003). Grounded crime prevention: Responding to and understanding hate crime. In H. Kury & J. Obergfell-Fuchs (Eds.), *Crime prevention: New approaches* (pp. 123-154). Mainz, Germany: Heisser Ring.

Winlow, S., Hobbs, D., Lister, S., & Hadfield, P. (2003). Bouncers and the social context of violence: Masculinity, class and violence in the night-time economy. In E. A. Stanko (Ed.), *The meanings of violence* (pp. 165-183). London: Routledge.

Elizabeth A. Stanko is Senior Advisor, Strategic Analysis, Strategy, Modernization and Performance Directorate, in the London Metropolitan Police, United Kingdom. She is also a visiting professor of Criminology at Royal Holloway, University of London.

Part III
Masculinities and Femininities

[7]

ACCOMPLISHING FEMININITY AMONG THE GIRLS IN THE GANG

KAREN JOE LAIDLER and GEOFFREY HUNT*

Sociologists and criminologists in America have had a longstanding interest in youth gangs dating back to the pioneering work of Frederick Thrasher through to the subcultural theories of the 1960s–1970s to the present. Until recently, the primary focus was on the role of male gang members. In contrast, discussions about young women's involvement in gangs, with a few notable exceptions, have been typically shallow and sexist. In this paper we examine the meanings, expressions and paradoxes of femininity as they are understood and experienced by Latina, African American and Asian-Pacific American female gang members. The analysis, based on in-depth interviews with 141 gang members, is part of a long-term study (1990–present) of youth gangs in the San Francisco Bay Area.

Approximately 2 million American adolescents are involved in serious criminal offences (Inciardi et al. 1993). Because of this high prevalence rate for serious delinquency, criminal justice officials and researchers have shifted their attention from the 'typical' delinquent or what Inciardi et al. (1993) have called the 'garden variety' delinquent to that of the serious delinquent (Horowitz 1990). As a result of this shift in attention, interest in youth gangs has also occurred. This came about partly because of the belief that serious delinquents are more likely to be found in youth gangs and partly because of the perceived relationship between gangs, drugs and violence. The development of the drug trade in the 1980s signalled a transformation from the idea of gangs as 'transitory adolescent social networks to nascent criminal organizations' (Fagan 1990: 183).

Official estimates of the number of youth involved in gangs have increased dramatically over the past decade. Currently, over 90 per cent of the nation's largest cities report youth gang problems, an increase of about half since 1983, and police estimates now put the number of gangs at 4,881 and the number of gang members at approximately 249,324 (Curry et al. 1992). As a result, although the study of gangs is not new (the first major work was done by Thrasher in 1927) public concern about the involvement of young people in gang activity, and the perceived violence associated with this lifestyle, has soared.

Part of this concern about the increase in gangs has focused on the participation of women in gangs. While some researchers argue that girl gang membership is increasing, others have been more cautious, believing that participation has remained relatively stable over time. Estimates of girl gang membership today range from 10 to 30 per cent of all gang members (Campbell 1984; Chesney-Lind 1993; Curry et al. 1994; Esbensen and Huizinga 1993; Fagan 1990; Klein 1995; Moore 1991). These estimates, based on

* Respectively, Associate Professor, Sociology, University of Hong Kong; and Senior Scientist Institute for Scientific Analysis, Alameda, CA. Collection of data for this article was made possible by funding from the National Institute on Alcohol Abuse and Alcoholism (R01-AA10819), administered by Susan Martin, PhD.

self-reports and community recognition (e.g. police, schools, youth agencies), include young women involved in all girl gangs and mixed (male and female) gangs.

There is little doubt that in recent years female gang participation has generated much public concern and media attention in the US, in large part because they are presumed to be rebelling against traditional notions of femininity. They are typically characterized as becoming more like their male counterparts: wild, hedonistic, irrational, amoral and violent (see Chesney-Lind 1993). Women's magazines like *Harper's Bazaar* try to illustrate vividly that these 'bad girls' have crossed the gender divide with photographs of girl gang members aiming guns with one hand, and throwing hand signs with the other hand (O'Malley 1993). Book length journalistic accounts provide similar impressions (Sikes 1997).

Yet are these young women defiantly challenging traditional gender roles? Although research on female gangs is relatively limited (compared to males), a number of perspectives have emerged. Traditional accounts (Cloward and Ohlin 1960; Cohen 1955; Miller 1958; Thrasher 1927) of female gang involvement have downplayed and minimized the role and motivations of girl gang members. They are portrayed in stereotypical ways from personal property to sexual chattel to maladjusted tomboys (see extended review in Joe and Chesney-Lind 1995). A more recent study continues to advance this male-centred view (Sanchez-Jankowski 1991). In essence, these accounts view the involvement of girls in gangs in relation to their sexuality. Their sexuality then serves as the basis for their identity as 'bad girls'. Other recent views offer a contrasting view, very similar to those in the media, of girl gang members seizing the streets, gaining independence from, and almost competing with, their male counterparts (Fleisher 1998; Taylor 1993). These contrasting accounts share, and at the same time suffer, from a one-sided, male-focused perspective, and fail to locate the situational context of being young, female, of colour, and poor.

How then do female gang members understand and accomplish femininity? How do they interpret their involvement in delinquency and violence? We explore these questions by first examining recent discussions about masculinity and 'bad girl' femininity on the streets. We then begin our analysis by looking at the different ways in which femininity is constructed within the family among a group of girl gang members. We then turn to examine how girls renegotiate and manage the paradoxes of femininity on the streets and at home.

Bad Girls and Femininity

Masculinities and crime has become the subject of much criminological interests and research in the last several years (Bourgois 1996; Collison 1996; Connell 1987; Jefferson 1996; Katz 1988; Messerschmidt 1986, 1993, 1997; Newburn and Stanko 1994). This new direction in the study of crime stems from wider discussions in the social sciences and arts on masculinities, and calls from within the discipline to 'take men seriously', particularly as the 'crisis of masculinity' heightens in post-modern society (Jefferson 1996). At a general level, this new orientation is trying to reconcile longstanding epistemological debates about the relationship (and dialectics) of social structure and interaction. In doing so, it locates acts of manliness within the broader economic and social class context, and at the same time, leaves room for human agency and interaction. Essentially masculinities and crime studies examine 'varieties of real men' in relation to their differential access to power and resources, and how these different groups of men construct and negotiate with similarly situated others, the meaning of manliness (Messerschmidt 1997; Newburn and Stanko 1994). Messerschmidt (1993, 1997), in particular, suggests that the social structure situates young men in relation to similar others so that collectively they experience the world from a specific position and differentially construct cultural ideas of hegemonic masculinity, namely, dominance, control and independence (Joe and Chesney-Lind 1995).

Young males in gangs provide the example, par excellence, as they embody all of the problems of power in contemporary society: violence, guns, drugs, poverty, unemployment, decay of community life, and educational malaise. Young minority male gang members living in marginalized communities, have little access to masculine status in the economy and in education like their white middle and working class counterparts (Bourgois 1996; Joe and Chesney-Lind 1995; Messerschmidt 1997). This collectively experienced denial of access to 'legitimate' masculine status creates an arena for exaggerated public and private forms of aggressive masculinity. 'Street elite posturing' (Katz 1988) among male gang members with dramatized displays of toughness accounts for one cultural form of public aggressiveness. Male gang members' constant and aggressive pursuit of 'respect' represents another way to construct and affirm manliness in an alienated environment. Gang intimidation and violence are more than simply an expression of the competitive struggle in communities with little to offer, but rather, a vehicle for a meaningful identity and status. Gang banging then is a gender resource for young minority gang members to express their masculinity (Joe and Chesney-Lind 1995; Messerschmidt 1997). At the immediate level of interaction, then, the street is a battleground and theatre for young marginalized minority males to define, shape and do gender (Connell 1987).

This same level of theoretical interest has yet to be extended to women and crime, and raises a fundamental question for 'doing gender' and 'doing difference': if crime is a resource for expressing masculinity, how then are we to understand the experiences of women and their involvement in delinquency and crime? As Daly asks, 'would the claim that crime is a "resource for doing femininity"—for women and girls to "create differences from men and boys or to separate from all that is masculine"—have any cultural resonance?' (1997: 37).

Messerschmidt (1997) argued critically that the general tendency in criminological investigations has been to focus exclusively on differences in men's and women's crime, and as a result, women are conceptualized in masculine terms when they engage in 'typically' masculine crimes like violence. Therefore, we must look at both the similarities and differences between their involvement in crime to determine when crime is not a resource for doing masculinity.[1] From this vantage point, girls' participation in gangs offers an avenue for challenging and testing normative gender roles or what Connell (1987) calls, 'emphasized femininity'.

---

[1] Joe and Chesney-Lind's (1995) and Moore's (1991) analyses of gangs in Hawaii and East Los Angeles respectively, juxtapose female and male experiences in gang activity and highlight how gender is accomplished in gangs.

Partaking in the specific social situation of the gang, girls use the resources available to construct not masculinity but a specific type of femininity and notwithstanding, challenge notions of gender as merely difference (Messerschmidt 1997: 69).

Drawing from the limited but rich ethnographic studies on female gangs, Messerschmidt contends that female gang violence and displays of toughness are 'resources' for establishing a particular notion of femininity, that of the 'bad girl'. This street reputation and status translate as power for girls who operate within the patriarchal power structure of the gangs, the streets, and society. At the same time, girl gang members embrace and engage in some forms of 'culturally appropriate' femininity (1997: 83). Most ethnographic studies on female gangs, for example, find that gang girls concentrate on 'feminine activities' such as appearance and endless sessions of talking. Many also find themselves in typically gendered lower and working class jobs like janitorial services, babysitting and clerical work, and hold unrealistic feminine aspirations like rock singers and professional modelling (Campbell 1990; Joe and Chesney-Lind 1995).

These ethnographic studies further suggest that these two specific cultural forms of femininity frequently conflict with each other. Studies on Latina homegirls illustrate this point. Quicker (1983), Harris (1988) and Moore (1991) find some Chicana gang members adopt a 'macho' homegirl image, but in rejecting the Latino cultural norms of being a woman (i.e. wife and mother), male gang members and community residents view the girls as 'tramps' and not the type to marry. A significant focus for inquiry then is how girl gang members constantly negotiate a distinctive sense of femininity in different interactional settings within both their ethnic culture and delinquent subculture.

Research on African American girls also underscores the importance of focusing on cultural and ethnic differences across girl gang groups. Fishman (1988) and Lauderback et al. (1992) indicate that the adoption of a bad girl identity with exaggerated displays of toughness have less to do with rejecting or testing cultural gender norms and more to do with adopting 'greater flexibility in their roles' as they are expected to defend themselves against male violence (Fishman 1988: 15). At the same time, these female gang members are preoccupied with their responsibilities as young mothers including income generating strategies (e.g. drug dealing) and community activism (improving quality of life in their neighbourhoods; making the streets safe for their children) (Venkatesh 1998). Joe Laidler and Hunt (1997) show that African American female gang members are more likely to perceive the group as a source of autonomy, independence and empowerment from men than Latina gang girls, who are organized in relation to their male counterparts.

This article builds on these ethnographic studies and recent discussions on 'bad girl' femininity. It is specifically concerned with uncovering the meaning, expression and paradoxes of femininity as it is understood and experienced by Latina, African American and Asian-Pacific American female gang members. The analytical framework is based on several assumptions. The normative expectations of young women to be feminine and to be a teenager are often at odds. Generally, adolescence is a time for challenging authority, rebelling, seeking recognition among peers, independence; attributes that are associated with masculinity. Femininity, by contrast, starts early on in a girl's life, and is associated with passiveness, obedience, dependency, innocence, chastity and maturity. As Hudson (1984) has noted, 'adolescence is subversive of femininity; young girls' attempts to be accepted as "young women" are always liable to be undermined (subverted) by perceptions of them as childish, immature or any other of the other terms by which we define the status "adolescent"' (p. 32). McRobbie (1981) shows that English working class teenage girls respond to their contradictory position of being perceived as 'children' and expectations and fears of entering womanhood by forming tight knit groups. These peer groups are not oppositional, but rather a cultural form of resistance which offers an exclusive and private space for girls to define for themselves, 'what is feminine'. Membership in female gangs then operates in a similar fashion. Moreover, these conflicting normative standards constantly confront girl gang members in their interactions with family, their male counterparts and their homegirls and become the basis for evaluating themselves and other girls' femininity.

At the same time, it is important to underscore that notions of femininity are not fixed, but ever changing, depending on the situational context (Messerschmidt 1997). 'Being feminine' does not automatically change but is negotiated in the specific social contexts with interactions with other people. These notions may be contradictory in some settings, but are nevertheless seen as an accommodation to the setting. These interactions and negotiated definitions of femininity occur within the race, class and patriarchal constraints of a larger social structure. Young women's location within the social structure simultaneously affects their interactions and their notions of being feminine. This analysis heeds other recent critiques of Messerschmidt's recent work as being more structure than action oriented in his supporting evidence (see Jefferson 1996 for a fuller discussion), and examines not only how girl gang members reproduce normative gender expectations, but also how they resist and devise alternative forms of femininity. These alternative forms include but are not restricted to the 'bad girl'. The following discussion then, begins to tease out the construction and negotiation of femininity, particularly in relation to respectability among girl gang members in their interactions with family, homeboys and boyfriends, and homegirls and other young women.

Research Methods

The data for this analysis are drawn from a long-term, comparative qualitative study of ethnic gangs in the San Francisco Bay Area that began in 1991 and continues to the present. From 1991 to 1993, we conducted face to face interviews with over 600 self-identified male and female gang members (see Joe 1993; Waldorf 1993). The 65 female gang members interviewed were from seven different groups, and were located using the snowball sampling approach (Biernacki and Waldorf 1981). This sampling strategy relied on respondents referring members of their group or other groups to be interviewed. The same technique was used in our second study that extended our comparative research to Southeast Asian gangs in the same locale. In this effort, we interviewed 91 male and 19 female Southeast Asian gang members during 1993 through 1994. At present, we are engaged in a third study that revisits and explores other contemporary gang issues among males and females in the San Francisco Bay Area. We have included 57 of the female interviews from the current study for this analysis. From the three studies then, we will be drawing on a total sample size of 141 interviews with female gang members.

The in-depth interview involved a two-step process in which the interviewee first answered a series of questions from a quantitative schedule. The second step entailed a tape-recorded session, and members reflected on questions from a semi-structured guide about their gang experiences. This combined approach of a qualitative and close-ended questionnaire provided an opportunity to focus on the group's histories, organization and activities, personal demographics, alcohol and drug use, individual history and involvement with the group, and prior contact with the criminal justice system. We also asked the young women about power relations and gender expectations within the group, with the various males in their lives and with their families.

From the three studies, we recruited and trained five female and four male fieldworkers to conduct the female interviews. All of the fieldworkers were familiar with the gang scene in their communities, having either been directly involved in the street scene or as community workers (e.g. youth workers, public housing liaison). Given their role within the community, they had no difficulties in establishing rapport and trust with the girls. The interviews were conducted in a variety of settings ranging from the respondent's or peer's residence, parks, youth centres and coffee shops. The interview with the African American and Samoan girls were conducted in English. The Latinas and Vietnamese women were interviewed in English or their native language (or a combination), depending on their preference. The fieldworkers assisted in translating the Spanish and Vietnamese interviews. Interviews lasted from 90 minutes to three hours. We gave a 50-dollar honorarium in recognition of their participation and time.

Profile

The 141 young women in this study are current members of one of 44 different gangs.

Table 1 offers an overview of their personal characteristics. The 17 African American women belong to one of six groups. Unlike any of the other ethnic groups, four of the African American female gangs are organized as 'independent', without any affiliation or ties to any male group. The other two gangs are part of a larger 'mixed' group which includes females, but comparatively more male members. The African American women in the sample were older than the females of other ethnic gangs with a median age of 23 years (age range of 14 to 27). The members of the 'independent' groups had known each other since childhood, having grown up in the same neighbourhood. All of the African American women lived in or nearby public housing estates, and described their neighbourhoods as dangerous areas for themselves and their children. These are areas where 'people are outside smoking, getting high, drunk, loud and violent' [HG009], and more generally 'people look nasty. The streets are black, they stink. There's so much garbage. People look all dried up, they walking dead' [HG016]. Drug sales and prostitution are plainly visible on the streets in the afternoons, with activity heightening in the evening.

All of the African American women came from extremely marginalized backgrounds. Although slightly over 50 per cent of them reported that they lived principally with their mother and father until their mid-teen years, one of the parents, usually the father, often left home for months at a time due to alcohol and drugs. The majority of the girls stated that their fathers were either unskilled labourers or unemployed (data not shown). Over one-third of them lived only with their mother, and had had very limited or no contact at all with their fathers. Their mothers tended to be either working in the service sector or unemployed. Several of the girls reported that they had either cut off or limited their

TABLE 1   *Personal characteristics of girls in the gang*

	African American (N = 17)		Latina (N = 98)		Asian American (N = 26)		Total (N = 141)	
Age (median)	23 years		18 years		18 years		18 years	
Place of birth								
California	16	95.0%	57	59.0%	7	26.9%	80	56.7%
Other US	1	5.0%	3	3.1%	0	0.0%	4	2.8%
Mexico/Latina America	0	0.0%	38	38.8%	0	0.0%	38	27.0%
Vietnam	0	0.0%	0	0.0%	19	73.1%	19	13.5%
Domestic unit prior to 16 years of age								
Mother and father	9	52.9%	28	28.6%	16	61.5%	53	37.6%
Mother and stepfather	0	0.0%	5	5.1%	0	0.0%	5	3.5%
Mother only	6	35.3%	47	47.9%	3	11.5%	56	39.7%
Father only	0	0.0%	4	4.1%	3	11.5%	7	5.0%
Other relative	2	11.8%	9	9.2%	2	7.7%	13	9.2%
Other	0	0.0%	5	5.1%	0	0.0%	5	3.5%
Unknown	0	0.0%	0	0.0%	2	7.7%	2	1.4%
Education completed								
9th grade or less	4	23.5%	41	41.8%	6	23.1%	51	36.2%
10th grade	4	23.5%	16	16.3%	6	23.1%	26	18.4%
11th grade	6	35.3%	21	21.4%	9	34.6%	36	25.5%
12th grade	3	17.6%	16	16.3%	3	11.5%	22	15.6%
Junior College	0	0.0%	4	4.1%	0	0.0%	4	2.8%
Unknown	0	0.0%	0	0.0%	2	7.7%	2	1.4%
Employed full or part time	0	0.0%	29	29.6%	4	15.4%	33	23.4%
If employed, type of work								
Skilled	0	0.0%	6	20.7%	2	50.0%	8	24.2%
Service industry	0	0.0%	16	55.2%	1	25.0%	17	51.5%
Child care	0	0.0%	5	17.2%	0	0.0%	5	15.2%
Unskilled	0	0.0%	2	6.9%	1	25.0%	3	9.1%
Primary source of income								
Job	0	0.0%	24	24.5%	4	15.4%	28	19.8%
Family/friends	1	5.9%	39	39.8%	19	73.1%	59	41.8%
Public assistance	6	35.3%	16	16.3%	0	0.0%	22	15.6%
Hustles	7	41.2%	4	4.1%	3	11.5%	14	9.9%
Combination	3	17.6%	15	15.3%	0	0.0%	18	12.8%
Marital status								
Single	12	70.6%	76	77.6%	24	92.3%	112	79.4%
Living with partner	3	17.6%	14	14.3%	1	3.8%	18	12.8%
Married	1	5.9%	7	7.1%	1	3.8%	9	6.4%
Separated	1	5.9%	1	1.0%	0	0.0%	2	1.4%
Number of children								
None	3	17.6%	56	57.1%	24	92.3%	83	58.9%
One	7	41.2%	20	20.4%	1	3.8%	28	19.8%
Two	3	17.6%	13	13.3%	0	0.0%	16	11.3%
Three or more	4	23.5%	2	2.0%	0	0.0%	6	4.3%
Pregnant	0	0.0%	7	7.1%	1	3.8%	8	5.7%
Number of children residing with you								
None	1	5.9%	4	4.1%	0	0.0%	5	3.6%
One	7	41.2%	19	19.4%	1	3.8%	27	19.1%
Two	3	17.6%	10	10.2%	0	0.0%	13	9.2%
Three or more	3	17.6%	2	2.9%	0	0.0%	5	3.5%
Not applicable	3	17.6%	63	64.3%	25	96.2%	91	64.5%

contact with their mothers who were addicted to crack or heroin. Only 18 per cent of the girls had completed high school, and none of them reported any legitimate employment. The girls relied principally on hustling (drug sales and shoplifting) and public assistance to support themselves and their children.

Among the other ethnic groups, the majority of the young women belong to an 'auxiliary' group to a male gang. All of the Latina and 17 of the Asian-Pacific American girls belong to one of these groups that consider themselves 'separate but equal' to their male counterparts. The median age of the Latinas is 18 years of age with a range of 14 to 32. The Latinas come from more diverse communities and backgrounds than the African American girls. Among Latinas, half of them live in a highly congested and dense area in the city where the shops and residents are predominantly of Hispanic origins. Residential units vary with two major housing projects on either end of the community, transient motels used principally for short-term housing, prostitution and drugs, small apartment complexes, flats and single family homes. Most of the girls came to know each other from having a relative in the group or living on the same street or same public housing project. Gang alliances and rivalries were partly based on territory and ethnicity within the Latina community in San Francisco. The other half of the respondents live in a neighbouring city to San Francisco, which is experiencing an urban sprawl. Therefore, unlike their city counterparts, they did not live in a highly congested area, but instead lived in apartments and houses scattered throughout the city. Nearly 40 per cent of the Latinas were born in Mexico or Latin America, and immigrated with at least one parent. Almost 30 per cent of the girls lived with their mother and father. Nearly half of the girls indicated that they lived principally with their mothers, and several indicated that their fathers had either left the family or returned to their native land. When fathers were present, they were skilled, semi-skilled or unskilled labourers. Most mothers worked in the service sector or in unskilled positions. Among the 98 Latinas, approximately one-third reported that at least one of their parents had problems with alcohol or drugs.

Despite the median age of the Latinas, over 78 per cent had not completed high school. Forty per cent of them relied principally on their family and friends for money, and another 25 per cent supported themselves from employment, usually in the service industry. Over three-fourths of the girls were single. Forty-two per cent either had children or were about to give birth. Most of the girls reported that their children lived with them.

The median age of the Asian American females was similar to the Latinas at 18 years of age with a range of 15 to 21. The majority of Asian American girls were Chinese, Chinese Vietnamese and Vietnamese, and had immigrated from Vietnam. The girls came from different neighbourhoods, primarily working class houses and flats. Members came to know each other primarily through school or friends. Over 60 per cent of them live with both parents. The respondents' fathers work in small businesses and semi-skilled jobs, and their mothers work in the small business or in semi-skilled or service industry jobs. Most of the girls were still attending school, and relied principally on their family and friends for money. Only one was living with her partner and was pregnant.

Four Samoan girls were from one group with approximately 15 to 20 members. Members came to know each other through living in the same housing project or through a relative. The respondents' families were lower working class with fathers working in semi-skilled and unskilled labouring jobs and mothers in unskilled and service industry jobs. All the Samoan girls were still enrolled and attending high school.

Most relied on their families for money, but the eldest girl was married with one child, employed in the service sector, and dealt crack with her husband to supplement their income.

The female gang members in this study are similar to the girls reported in other research (Campbell 1984; Chesney-Lind and Hagedorn 1999; Fishman 1988; Harris 1988; Joe and Chesney-Lind 1995; Moore and Hagedorn 1996). They are young women of colour, from families that are either completely marginalized or barely surviving, and living in typically dense and congested neighbourhoods. They live in communities with limited employment prospects and few incentives to stay in school.

The Structure of Accomplishing Femininity

Much of recent gang research, and more generally, street life ethnographies have underscored the importance of 'respect' among inner city young minority men. In this masculine context, 'respect' demands deference to, and at the same time, commands status, power and authority in an environment with few legitimate avenues (e.g. employment, education) to attain a sense of esteem and importance for oneself and among one's peers. The 'pursuit of respect' (Bourgois 1996) and consequently affirmation of masculinity for young minority males is expressed through exaggerated demonstrations of bravado, fearlessness and aggressiveness with others on the street.

According to Messerschmidt, female gang members, like their male counterparts, constantly seek 'respect' from similarly situated others as a way of demonstrating and affirming power and status in a highly marginalized and patriarchal environment. While we recognize that female gang members operate in a male dominated environment, and may sometimes engage in what may be perceived as 'aggressive' masculine behaviours, it may have less to do with adopting the 'style' of their homeboys, and more to do with other contextual factors. Importantly, our respondents' interactions, evaluations of others and self definitions suggest that respect is highly gendered, and holds a very different meaning for females compared to males. For females, the notion of 'respect' should not be solely understood in masculine street terms of power and control. Among the young women in our study, respect is associated with the pursuit of respectability, one important dimension of 'being feminine'.

Respect has a lot to do with the way she presents herself. The way she acts around guys and girls at all times. She isn't a ho [whore], she's not all desperate with the drugs. She acts like a woman. Some girls kick back and don't have respect for the guys. Some homegirls [gang girls] see each other, and they start cussing [at each other and at the guys], 'fucking bitch this, fucking that, fucking asshole'. It starts getting ugly, and he'll hit her. Better calm down. They [those homegirls] got no respect for themselves. [F24]

Nearly all of the girls described respect(ability) in these highly gendered and normative terms regardless of their ethnic and cultural background. As the girls remind us, respectability involves both appearance and conduct. Her clothing, hairstyle, make-up, and stride signify her status as a reputable young woman. Yet her subtleness, restraint, and regard for others are also critical to distinguishing her from others. Skeggs (1997) notes the importance of appearance, conduct and distancing in her recent ethnography of the lives of Northwest working class women. She argues that respectability is a class signifier for differentiating those who are legitimate from those who are not. It is a distancing mechanism to identify the 'other'. And perhaps most importantly, 'respectability is usually the concern of those who are not seen to have it . . . It would not be of concern here, if the working classes had not consistently been classified as dangerous, polluting, threatening . . . pathological and without respect. It would not be something to desire, to prove and to achieve, if it had not been seen to be a property of "others", those who were valued and legitimated' (1997: 1). Still respectability in its normative form is not 'blindly accepted', women may express ambivalence, dis-identify or resist and devise alternatives (Skeggs 1997).

As the girls in this study suggest, the meaning of 'respectability' goes beyond the middle class notions of the term in other ways. Given their embeddedness in street life culture, and for some, at a very early age, respectability also means being aware and being able to stand up for oneself.

R: A homegirl has to have a mean head on her shoulders. She has to be responsible or respectable.

I: How do you do that?

R: Keep your head up and watch over the moves of others. You can't let nobody get you or you will be got.

The young women in this study, as we will see below, are well aware that to be entirely feminine and to be respectable in their highly marginalized communities is unrealistic and dangerous. Respect(ability) requires a sense of strength and independence. As Skeggs succinctly points out, 'to be completely feminine for most women would be almost impossible: it would be to be without agency, to be a sign of powerlessness' (1997: 102). And as she notes, the women in her study devise different forms of femininity, some of which are an expression of cultural resistance. Similarly then, among the young women in this study, respectability is negotiated and continually challenged in a number of interactional settings.

Interactions with family

There are a range of experiences and expectations among the girls in their family relationships. Regardless of the strength of their parental ties, all the girls believed that it is the family, particularly mothers, who should set the expectations and boundaries for them as girls and young women. In this normative context, it is the mother who they define as the primary caregiver and nurturer in their family. It is the mother who they look to for shelter, care, affection, support, discipline, guidance and structure. As Gina states, 'I got respect for mothers when they *care* for their children' [F38]. Because many respondents' fathers were absent (periodically or permanently), their mothers worked long hours. In these cases, the girls indicated that they or their elder sisters assumed the parental role, babysitting and caring for the younger ones in the family, preparing meals, and cleaning house. This assumption of the motherly role from early adolescence is consistent with other studies on female gang members (Fishman 1988; Joe and Chesney-Lind 1995).

In light of the girls' highly gendered expectations within their own family, some girls describe themselves as coming from a 'traditional' background whereby the mother and father 'expect me to be perfect. To do well in school. To avoid trouble' [F12]. Notably, several Latina and Asian immigrant girls consider themselves very 'traditional' in their appearance, conduct and aspirations, and take great pride in distinguishing themselves from their American born counterparts. By the same token, they rationalize some of their 'unconventional' activities as part of accomplishing femininity.

Rachel, a 22-year-old Mexican homegirl reports that she came to America when she was 12 years of age. Her father brought the family to California after labouring for three years here and believing he could provide them with a better life. She considers herself 'more like a Mexican girl' than the girls here. She holds traditional ideas about life events like the quincinera and weddings when a girl wears 'white' and has a large party for the family and friends. 'Girls from here just run away or don't bother' [F22]. She holds a great deal of respect for her parents who she states are always loving and giving her guidance. Although she has moved out on her own, she still retains a close relationship to them, and tries to live up to their expectations as a young woman and as a daughter. 'When I go to my mom's, I always help her clean house, take care of my niece. Help her to cook, do stuff around the house and take her to the store' [F22]. Her parents don't like the idea that she 'hangs around with trouble'. She has only had two boyfriends whom she has slept with because 'she is not that *kind* of girl'. She rationalizes her use of crystal methamphetamines as a way of losing weight and becoming attractive. 'I started using it because I had this boyfriend. He always used to tell me, You're too fat, you're ugly, nobody's gonna like you. So I started using it, knowing that you get skinny, I only use it now, you know, to lose weight' [F22].

Likewise, other Latina, Vietnamese, Samoan and Filipino girls find their families extremely traditional and conservative in their expectations of them as girls. The Vietnamese girls complain of the double standards and excessive controls they face as girls. Janet describes the differences in treatment between her brother and herself:

My family still holds Vietnamese traditions. Like they want me to come home after school, cook dinner, clean up the house, Can't go out, just got study. And that is it. No going out. Once in awhile but that is it. Your curfew is 9:00. No boys, they don't want you talking, you are too young for boys. They don't want you to get in love with boys, they might influence you and then you might drop out of school . . . My brother could go out all the time. After he got arrested, my parents try to watch out for us more, but the more they tell us what to do, we disobey them more. We lie to them . . . I mean I know better not to. [617]

Cindy, a 16-year old, echoes this view:

Like see parents, they don't understand that what it's like for guys, they think guys can't get pregnant so they get to go out all the time and they don't care. But when a girl goes out they think we're gonna come home pregnant. That is a big discrimination. Like we are all the same. We can't go out because they think girls are suppose to stay home, cook, clean and guys can just go out and have fun. That isn't right. [610]

All of the Vietnamese girls note that their parents were particularly strict with them throughout their early childhood and teen years. The girls contend that the imposition of curfews and restrictions are not solely to keep them out of trouble, but more importantly, to preserve them and therefore, their 'reputation'. The young women expressed a similar view to this 18-year old, 'Like the Vietnamese, they always think like, they care most about their reputation. Americans don't. In Vietnamese custom, they don't let girls in their teens date or go with boyfriends or even go out' [605]. In this case, her reputation refers to the preservation of her chastity and sexual innocence. But other Vietnamese respondents add that it is also the preservation of her innocence more generally; she should stay out of trouble at school and with the law. In terms of her parents, her reputation as a 'good girl' is an indicator of their reputation as 'good parents'. Some girls devise ways to 'please' their parents by maintaining the image of the 'good girl', and still engage in more 'liberating' experiences. For example, Susan reports that she brings home friends who are 'good girls' (e.g. dress conservatively, get straight As, and don't go out with boys) to make a good impression on her parents, but goes out to meet her homegirls in the gang to party and 'look for trouble' [614].

Paradoxically, despite our Vietnamese and a few of the Latina respondents' complaints of traditionalism and cultural gaps, many evaluate themselves in the gendered terms of their parents. They describe their transition from a 'good girl' to a 'bad girl', and believe that they are a disappointment to themselves and their families. This transition typically began in school as this 18-year-old Vietnamese woman notes:

Before I was always like a hard working student because my parents expected me to get good grades and also their friends would think that they had good kids who went to school everyday. They wanted their children to give them a good reputation. And I did get good grades and they were proud. But as I got into the peer pressure and the influence of my friends, I started cutting school. I was a very good student and a very good kid but from these influences, I am getting badder every day . . . I get into fights a lot. I don't stay home a lot no more. I know my parents always worry. [605]

While these young women complain about parental control, other gang girls describe almost a complete absence of parental expectations or controls. Approximately three-fourths of the African American young women and over one-half of the Latinas are critical of one or both parents. Most often, they vocalize their lack of respect for their fathers who rarely or sporadically surface, have drug or alcohol problems and/or are violent toward their mothers or them. Several young women judge their own mothers in relation to conventional standards of respectability and more generally, femininity.

I got along with my mom until I was a teenager. Till I could think my own thing and be my own person. She turned into an alcoholic. That's why I don't drink. I don't want to be like her. She used to beat me a lot. I can't stand her. She's a whore. She just don't get paid for her services. I tell her Ma ya know . . . make some extra money on the side. "Don't talk to me that way I'm your mother." I say so . . . your degrading yourself why can't I degrade you? She's had some awful dudes. I remember one guy came home drunk and beat her up and I went in there and bit his leg. Then when he threw me it was a big old oak dresser and she went nuts. He and she used to do coke. They'd try to play it off . . . oh no holier than though righteous bitch. I don't understand your coke addiction. Yeah mom you're stupid, you ain't never done nothing . . . But my dad he's old fashion. I can't live with him either. He believes a woman should be in the house cooking. Cleaning and having dinner ready by the time he gets home from work. Man I couldn't do that. No friends, no life nothing. [F9]

A few gang girls are not only angered by their mothers' drug use and associated problems (e.g. violence, money), but also, their mothers' inability to fulfil their roles and duties as parents. These girls have little respect for their mothers who they point out abandoned them early on for a life on the streets. To these girls, their mothers are everything they do not want to be.

Gang girls respond in different ways to what they perceived as their mothers' defiance toward and violation of conventional expectations of femininity and motherhood. African American respondents tend to completely sever ties to their mothers if they have problems with drugs. Their drug using mothers are perceived as adding another layer of risk to their current life at home and on the street. Latinas rarely cut off all ties, but instead either restricted their contact with their 'problematic' mothers or stand by their mothers, becoming the caregiver.

Although our respondents have quite diverse interactions within their families, they tend to develop conventional notions about gender roles, and in particular, what it means to be a woman and to be a mother. She is someone who is 'respectable'. She does not sleep around and she does not get heavily involved in drugs and alcohol. She looks after her family, providing care and affection. Importantly, they evaluate their own mothers, and sometimes themselves, in relation to this traditional good girl versus bad girl dichotomy. Some of our respondents acquire these expectations from an early age as they assume a parental role when their mothers are busy working or coping with family violence or drug problems. Many respondents who are from immigrant families develop strategies for fulfilling familial expectations of them as 'good girls'. Outside the family arena, however, the girls, in their interactions with other females and males, try to negotiate a balance between 'being respectable', 'being an adolescent' and 'being on the street'.

Interactions with homegirls and other women

There are two distinct arenas of interaction with other women in which girl gang members find themselves negotiating femininity. One arena involves the interaction they have among themselves. The second arena of interaction entails homegirls' encounters with other women outside of their group. In both arenas, the girls have very distinct notions and expectations of other female members' appearance and conduct that are clearly tied to their sexual reputation.

Don't be a flirt or anything, cause then you have no respect, you're supposed to stick by your old man. [F8]

Some girls are respected. Some girls are treated like hos. It depends on how you act . . . how many guys you slept with. [F012]

To get respect out on the street you should like not get all fucked up with all kinds of guys and do stupid things in front of guys . . . or going out with your friends and her getting into a fight and you causing it but running away and leaving her there. Make sure you can control your drugs and if you drink, just don't get too fucked up. Don't make a fool of yourself. [F23].

At times, they can be more judgmental regarding other girls' respectability than their male counterparts. Excessive drinking and drugging are defined as disreputable because like flirting and sleeping around, a young woman is likely to get out of control and become sexually promiscuous. This evaluative stance among homegirls is not surprising as others have noted that 'what is most significant about the stigma attached to sexual reputation is that young women police each other . . . Such policing has material effects in constricting young women's . . . expression of her sexuality and her freedom of action—her independence' (Lees 1997: 35). As in Lees' study of English girls (1997), we find gang girls spending a great deal of energy 'bitching' or casting doubt on others' reputations. This cross-cultural process operates not only as a mechanism of social control, but also of distancing and confirming one's own reputation.

Louisa, a 19-year-old Latina, vividly recalls why her group of girls broke off from their former set but continues to see the same problem with the younger members of her current gang. As she sees it, the 'problem' is the sexual promiscuity of other members, which reflects poorly on the respectable girls in the group (like her). *Their* conduct gives them a 'bad name', and gives rise to sexual harassment.

We use to belong to the Down Town Nortenas. They have guys and girls. Then we broke off from the girls, calling them the Down Town Max cause the girls were just real slutty, real hos, and it was like all the girls that respect themselves, that demand respect. We started our own group . . . These younger girls are out there being slutty with this guy and that guy, it makes everybody look bad, you know? Couple of the girls are real loose with their bodies and when we're kicking it with the guys, they start looking at us like . . . and we go NO HONEY . . . don't even think of me like that. Then they get all pissed off . . . and they say, well your homegirl . . . Just cause she does, doesn't mean that's me. [F009]

Hey (1997) also finds that bitching serves as a significant cultural practice for white working class English girls in their attempts at 'othering'. Othering or distancing carries enormous 'incentives', providing the means for claiming moral superiority, or more specifically, respectability over 'bad girls'. In this way, othering reinforces one's own identity and investments in femininity. In relation to the immediate group, othering strengthens the solidarity of members and at the same time, increases the conflict and competition with more peripheral members of the group and outsiders.

Despite the energy invested in 'the way a girl presents herself . . . the way she acts around other girls and guys' [F24], these young women are also confronted with the expectations and pressures of adolescence which often run counter to their efforts to be 'respectable'. This contradiction is clearest in the girls' desires to 'party', or more specifically, to drink and use drugs as noted above. Some of the Latinas and Asian-Pacific American females tend to avoid drinking and using drugs altogether, believing that these behaviours put themselves at risk of being branded by other homegirls and homeboys as being a 'druggie' or a drunk. Moreover, drinking and drugging are associated with promiscuity if a girl parties primarily with only homeboys. This 18-year-old Latina describes the setting:

I don't drink. There's a lot of girls who kick back, but they all get drunk and they be with all the guys in there so they wouldn't have no respect for them. I wouldn't let them disrespect me or tell me what to do. [F36]

Yet, with only a few exceptions, our respondents admitted that they had both experimented, and often regularly used alcohol and drugs (principally marijuana, but also *pingas* and crack cocaine). While a few of the homegirls reported drinking or using drugs in the presence of other homeboys and homegirls with little worry about others' perceptions, most of the respondents devised ways to drink or use drugs and maintain their respectability. The most common practice among Latinas and Asian-Pacific American homegirls involves 'safe partying' whereby the girls watch each others' back while drinking and drugging and at the same time, avoiding risky situations.

Like the drug use. It's all individual. I mean you ain't gonna go get high and drunk with some guy you just met you know. You gotta have your friends there to make sure you all take care of each other. We're not supposed to be using Pingas cause some girls ran into some problems, they got raped. [F39]

You gotta be open with them. If you think they're doing something stupid, don't be afraid to tell them. Tell them how it is. Make sure you're there for them all the time . . . Like you want to party. Somebody is gonna care for you so once they see you getting a bit too drunk and a guy comes around and tries to like try something with you. They won't let him. They'll be like, well you know she's wasted, you can't be talking to her right now. [F39]

Respondents rationalize the use of these strategies as a way to circumvent what they perceive to be the 'double standard' for young women. This suggests that the girls actively negotiate a distinctive sense of femininity, one that embraces normative notions of femininity, but also accommodates to the curiosities and pressures of a male oriented-adolescent culture.

Over half of the African American young women, and approximately one-fourth of the Latinas try to restrict heavy drinking or drugging as much as possible to private settings with only other homegirls. In this way, they do not risk negative evaluations from their male peers. Moreover, this partying with 'just the girls' provides freedom and privacy to explore issues of adolescence and femininity unhindered from male 'protection' and control. This private setting, usually at one of the girl's home or apartment, offers a venue for discovery, sharing and support.

One 17-year-old Latina recalls her first drinking session with her homegirls. They enjoyed themselves in this setting so much that it eventually became a regular custom for them to get together on their own to 'unload'.

The first time I drank, I drank with my homegirls at my house in the backyard and we were just drinking Millers. We got drunk. Fried. We had fun and then we started crying. So we went upstairs and went to bed. We were crying about whatever we was talking about. Now we pitch in, go to one of the girl's house, and kick back to drink. If you stay on the street, you'll get picked up. [F23]

Although girl gang members tend to provide each other with some degree of 'freedom' to party, they place distinct boundaries on what constitutes respectable behaviour. When a young woman (regardless of whether she is a member or an outsider living in the same neighbourhood) crosses the line from partying to chasing a high, female gang members define her in ways similar to male gang members. She is the antithesis of a respectable woman. Her drug use is not only out of control and 'unfeminine', but also ruins her sexual reputation because she is perceived to do 'anything' for a high. Many African American and Latina respondents refer to this 'type of girl' in sexualized terms like 'drug sluts', and 'hubba hoes', and rationalize their lack of empathy in this way: 'I can't respect a female that don't respect herself'. [G608]

Our earlier research also shows that female drug sellers hold similar moralistic views of women who have crossed over to become 'drug fiends' (Lauderback et al. 1992; Joe Laidler and Hunt 1997). Importantly, female drug sellers describe their own involvement in dealing as a vehicle for surviving (Joe Laidler and Hunt 1997; Venkatesh 1998). According to Dunlap and her colleagues' case study (1994), Rachel, a female crack dealer and user in New York was able to sustain an independent and successful business without resorting to violence and adopted ways to maintain her respectability to counter the image of her as a 'bad person'. Nevertheless, as Dunlap, Johnson and Manwar have pointed out (1994) women dealers as well as users are typically perceived as having crossed the boundaries of femininity and are stigmatized as 'whores' (1994: 7).

Given the girls' preoccupation with respectability, how then do we explain girl gang members' aggressive posturing and violence among girl gang members? How do we account for this paradox between their aspirations of 'being a young woman' and 'being bad'? At one level, female gang members' 'in your face' aggressive posturing is an attempt to 'look bad', (as opposed to 'being bad'), and is part of an overall protective strategy to the dangers of a highly masculinized street environment (Campbell 1984; Maher 1997). The girls' participation in violence is an expression of youth resistance as well as a power struggle among a group who are constrained by their race, class and gender (Messerschimdt 1997). As the young women in this study overwhelmingly agreed, fighting brings status and honour in a bleak and limiting environment. At another level, however, their participation in violence is also one of the few available resources for defending their reputation as a 'decent' girl and confirming to others that they are 'nobody's fool'. Respondents indicate that one of the major reasons for female on female violence is due to the 'slutty' behaviour of others.

Q: What is the most violent incident you've been involved in?

A: When I hit this girl over the head with a bat. She had screwed my dude. I walked in on them. After that, that bitch got up, went outside. That bitch slipped up one day, and I busted her on the head with the bat. [HG16]

These types of violent incidents usually occur after the girls have been drinking among themselves. Respondents indicate that drinking loosens them up, and provides courage for confronting other females who disrespect them by coming on to their boyfriends and partners. Janine, a 20-year-old Filipina, recalls the last serious incident arising when she and her homegirl were on their front steps drinking:

This was one of them days that I happened to be getting drunk and my homegirl was too. And we was sitting there, and I accidentally slipped, 'Oh, I seen that bitch with your man'. She was like, 'What? Well, why didn't you tell me this before?' I didn't know what to do. I'm drunk and just telling all. She had just got up and she just went out . . . She dropped her little cup with some E & J, and just stepped up to the girl. And that girl wasn't going out like no punk. She said, 'I'm fucking your man, so what?' And my homegirl she just dipped off into her ass. [HG011]

Leticia, a 20-year-old African American woman, describes her most recent fight was with a woman from her neighbourhood who sold her a gold ring that turned her finger green. She found the fight unsettling principally because it occurred when she was dressed up and situated in a party setting.

R: My cousin said they was rolling around. But you see I wasn't really trippin' because I was on the corner with my uncles and aunties getting drunk and high. I was chillin'. I wasn't in no kind of fightin' clothes. I was in some heels and a good dress and had my nails and hair done.

I: Where were you coming from?

R: It was one of them days. I thought I would be cute for the guys outside. They come up behind my back talking about, 'Where is my money or my ring at?' I says, 'Excuse me? You better get out of my face with that'. She was helluva taller than me . . . I am little short stubby. So I had to duck. And just had to catch and just knocked her down. And then two hos came up and started jumpin' me on my back. It was one on one at first until the two girls came and got on me. They almost stabbed me until my uncle came. (HG23)

As gang girls move out of the family arena and into the domain of their female peers, it becomes clear that they construct a distinctive sense of femininity. For them, femininity is, on the one hand, tied to conventional middle class notions of respectability whereby young women do not openly draw attention to themselves in appearance and conduct. Sexual reputation is at the core of their definition of female respect(ability). Public displays of 'bad girl' behaviour are condemned through 'othering' or 'distancing'. On the other hand, gang girls would hardly accept total submission to normative notions of femininity. Being a young woman does not mean sacrificing exploration and independence. Hanging out and kicking back on the streets are an expression of this independence. However, gang girls also devise methods and rationales for engaging in behaviour more typically associated with their male counterparts on the streets like drinking and drugging. Importantly, however, the girls are always aware of the male gaze to the extent that they demarcate how far 'respectable' behaviour can be pushed, and vigilantly police themselves.

Interactions with homeboys and lovers

It is in the girls' interactions with homeboys and lovers that they become fully aware of the power of the male view. Accordingly, the girls quickly learn that the males in their lives have a number of general assumptions about and categories of women, all of which can be understood in sexualized terms. Tomboys dress, act and are treated like one of the guys. They are counted on when there are fights. Bitches hang around, but are not taken seriously, as they are loud, overly aggressive and bring unwanted attention. Sluts are only around to be passed around. They 'ask for it', by getting loaded, drinking too much and flirting. 'Good girls' are the antithesis of the slut. They know how to have fun but is always in check and in control.

In light of the girls' awareness of these definitions, and their own sense of femininity, how do gang girls understand their own relationships with homeboys and lovers? Our respondents uniformly agree that the men in their lives have certain conventional expectations of them. Natalie, a 24-year-old African American girl in an independent group succinctly summarizes this common view: 'He just want me to *act like a woman*' (her emphasis) [604]. The girls are very clear on what the men define as 'acting like a woman'. One of her defining features is domestic. Many of the girls in the auxiliary groups complain that they are constantly cleaning and cooking when they hang out with the homeboys at somebody's house, when they are partying, and when they have barbecues and picnics at the park. The girls' reaction to these expectations varies with some accepting this 'feminine duty', and others completely rejecting and confronting the males with the 'chores'.

In several of the African American and some of the Latina girls' relationships with their lovers, however, there are additional expectations. As Tanya, a 23-year-old African American girl, makes clear, she is in a very strained and contradictory position. Her 'nigger' (her words) boyfriend not only expects her to fulfil the traditional domestic duties of a housewife, but he also demands that she bring in her share of the household income. When she doesn't comply with both of these roles, he often resorts to violence.

He wants me to do everything for him. He wants me to cook his dinner, wash his clothes and shit, and he slaps me around when I don't do it . . . Because I didn't have his dinner ready when he came from outside selling his dope. And I didn't have his tennis shoes, wasn't white enough one time, so he beat me up . . . He is mean to me at times. He wants to control me. I go out to make money for my kids and he wants my money so he can invest it in his dope and get more dope. I am like what if somebody takes it off him, where is my money. It is gone. He wants me to be just down for him and do whatever he wants. He wants me to sell dope for him. But I don't. I sell it for myself to make money for my kids. [G607]

Tanya, and others in similar situations to her, indicate that they try to fulfil the domestic duties for their boyfriends or lovers, but are unwilling to be 'duped' into giving their income, usually from drug dealing or shoplifting, to them. She works for herself and her children. As indicated earlier, the gang girl's negotiated definition of femininity is based partly on normative notions of the 'good woman' but also, because of her marginalized position, is grounded in notions of autonomy and self-reliance.

According to the girls, homeboys and lovers hold other traditional expectations of them. In particular, they should act within the confines of 'appropriate respectable behaviour'. The list of 'don'ts' include not to flirt with men, not to sleep with men other than your boyfriend, not to take drugs or too much alcohol, and not to be loud and foul-mouthed especially in the presence of 'others'.

The guys say is isn't right for one of the homegirls to be looking like *that* in front of people. You know we have parties. It isn't right or we look like sluts out there. [F12]

In their interactions with homeboys, the girls realize that this is a double standard to which they are held accountable. They also recognize the power associated with their homeboys' expectations. The consequence of completely defying or resisting these expectations is to categorized as a 'bitch' or 'slut'. In the girls' interactions with her boyfriend, however, the consequences can be more severe, involving violence. Jenny, a 19-year-old African American woman, describes the fear she feels from her boyfriend's obsessive concern with her 'being a woman'.

I am afraid to look at other men because he is so jealous . . . He has a violent streak in him. He wants me to be passive all the time. He likes to speak for me, he likes to tell me what I should wear and how to act when I am out on the street with him. I don't like it, because I have my own personality. But if I try to say I don't like it, he wants to hit me. He thinks that it is his way of showing affection to me. We do fight, over me wanting to go out there and sell my dope. He wants me to give my dope to him. He gets jumped by the police and ends up in jail, and there goes the money for me and my son that I have to take care of. He pushes me around. Bitch you ain't shit, Bitch you can't go out. I am all kind of bitches but then I am supposed to be his woman. [G608]

Homegirls also recognize that homeboys and lovers constantly preach and regulate their behaviour in large part to protect their own image and status, that is, they don't want to be associated in any meaningful way with 'bad girls'. 'Bad girls' are simply for fun. But reputable girls don't make them out as fools. It is his image that is to be protected as 'master' rather than 'fool'.

Q: Are there any things that homeboys expect the women to do in the gang?

A: To watch out for themselves and not be just with any guy. Don't be with guy after guy after guy cause they don't like their homegirls to be talked about. And not to do any drugs. Doing drugs to make a fool out of yourself, they don't want cause they don't want people talking. [F23]

On partying, some girls, as noted above, try to avoid using or putting themselves at risk when partying with homeboys. Several respondents noted that not only did heavy partying put their reputation with the guys at risk, but it also presented dangers in terms of unwanted sexual advances and sometimes resulted in sexual assault. While some homeboys try to take advantage of the homegirls when they are high, many girls report that the males took a protective and paternalistic attitude. Some girls interpret this paternalistic attitude as distinctively chauvinistic and took pride in resisting the homeboys' attempts to control them. Linda, a 24-year-old Chicana who reports moderately high levels of alcohol and marijuana use, reasons this way:

> Yeah, the guys try to control us. They say, 'Hey girl, you know, slow it down'. But then, you know you don't like any guy telling a woman what to do, of course. So we just speed it up. Then that's when you start drinking faster and they're telling you this and that, and you don't like a guy to be telling you nothing while your drinking. And then you know conflicts start. Sometimes the guys even slap the girls to calm them down because everybody is all drunk and stupid. [F45]

Some of the Asian American homegirls also resist what they perceive to be homeboys' attempts at controlling them—in both their appearance and conduct. This 15-year-old Vietnamese girl notes the differences between her and some of the older girls. From her point of view, the older girls look more feminine, but are really to be admired for their ability to fight and defend themselves.

> They [the guys] don't like it when we [the homegirls] dress like a guy with the baggy clothes. They will want us to wear dresses. They do! They go, 'You got to act more like girls'. We are all like a family. And then they tell us to act like a girl. Me and my best friend, we dress like a guy, talk like a guy, and they tell us talk and dress like a girl okay. We never dress like a girl. The older girls dress like 'girls'. You know how, like fancy and stuff that is how they dress. But they can fight too. [603]

It appears then that homegirls' definition of respectability involves both the adoption and rejection of some of the conventional roles of 'being a woman'. Yet it is important to point out that the girls' believe that autonomy and independence in their relationships with others, particularly males, are crucial to being respectable. According to several young women, independence means 'not being pushed around', 'having my opinions heard and counted', and 'standing up for what I believe in'. As Tanya and Jenny suggest, it also means 'taking care of business (to make money) so that we don't have to rely on anyone'. They have experienced too many disappointments with family and lovers.

Based on their interactions with homeboys, but particularly with lovers, the girls develop their own notions of men and masculinity as well. In their eyes, a man has to have respect for her as a woman and as an individual.

> I don't like guys that don't have respect for girls. I wouldn't want to be with a guy that thinks of a woman that's less than a man is so he had to respect me. [F19]

> We are looking for working men basically. Men that want to work and are going to be responsible. Like if they get us pregnant we want them to stay with us. We are looking for men that want to marry us hopefully one day. Whereas the men that we are left with are the street niggers that wear gold rings, wears gerry curls. You see, I am just with him because that is the environment that I am in, and I am trying to get out of this environment. I would like to have a man. Not no nigger that wants to beat me and makes me make money all the time and give it to him. I want somebody you know that cares about me and loves me, and loves my kids and helps me raise them, and give them a good family. [G07]

Despite these aspirations of finding a 'decent man' of someone who is 'nice', and has a job, many homegirls believe that this is only a dream as they do not have the resources to get out of their neighbourhoods to find a legitimate job nor meet a decent man.

Discussion/Conclusion

Good girls go to heaven but bad girls go everywhere. (Wurtzel 1998: 8)

The idea of the Madonna versus the whore has a long history, and has served the ranks of the middle class well as a method of 'distancing' the disreputable woman (that is, those from the working and lower classes). This patriarchal contrast of the 'good girl/bad girl' continues through the present, and permeates all social classes. As we have shown here, it serves as an 'othering' mechanism even among young marginalized women of colour.

The popular view of the gang girl today is someone who is essentially 'a bad ass'. She is similar to her male counterpart: aggressive, tough, crazy and violent. Yet as we have tried to show in this article, the young women in this study are situated in and must accommodate to the constraints of their structural position in society as well as on the streets. They are female, adolescents and young adults, of colour, poor, living under stressful family conditions and trying to negotiate a sense of identity, including what it means to be feminine. In other words, they *are affected by and affect* their structural position in society.

Our analysis has examined the girls' construction of femininity as they interact with family, other girls and young women, and with the males in their lives. A persistent theme throughout the analysis is the value the girls place on respect(ability). In all three interactional arenas we have looked at, their 'reputation' is one of the most salient markers of their identity as a young woman to the point that they would resort to violence to defend their status and honour. In their interactions with family, they expect their mothers and to some extent themselves to fulfil the normative roles of being female. Our respondents' experience a range with some parent(s) taking a traditional and controlling approach towards their daughters while other parent(s) have abandoned their daughters. Despite this variation, it is clear that the girls' evaluate their mothers' femininity and hold certain expectations about her respectability. In the girls' interactions with each other, they also construct distinct notions of femininity and respectability, and devise methods for resisting and exploring adolescence. As Hey (1997) rightly points out, female relationships are clearly structured in terms of patriarchal assumptions. Among the gang girls themselves, bitching, self-policing, and 'hidden' partying are clear indicators of the significance and ever-presence of the male gaze. The physical presence of males is not essential to the power and control they yield over females (Hey 1997). When homeboys and lovers are present, the girls are clearly aware of the importance of 'acting like a woman', but also define how far they are willing to do this, and refuse to give up their autonomy as individuals. For gang girls, respect(ability) in all three settings, means not only having a 'clean sexual reputation' but it also means being independent. The importance of independence must be underscored. In a recent historical analysis of court records, Davies (1999) found that despite the strong pressures of Victorian respectability in the middle and working classes, female 'scuttlers' in Manchester and Salford were relatively independent as they generated income from factory jobs and experienced some degree of freedom as they transitioned to adulthood and marriage. Given their presence on the streets and their sense of independence, these young working class women sometimes settled disputes and insults through physical fights in public.

What is the meaning then of gang girls' displays of 'toughness' or what Messerschmidt calls, 'bad girl femininity'? Their aggressive posturing is popularly perceived as an attempt to 'become macho' like their male counterparts. As Miller's study (1998) shows, however, young women are clearly aware of the gendered nature of the streets, and their robbery strategies take this into account as they target other women who are less likely to fight back, manipulate men by appearing sexually available, or working with male partners. Their own perceptions of their involvement in the violent crime of robbery varies with some adopting a masculine identity and others contending that they are not criminal. Our respondents' experiences suggest that there are a number of reasons for 'acting bad' and for engaging in violence. To some extent, 'looking bad' (as opposed to 'being bad') is a protective strategy to the patriarchal environment at home and on the street. It is also a defence mechanism for coping with their 'emotional vulnerability and perpetual disappointment' (Hey 1997: 97). It is also a form of resistance to informal controls on their attempts to explore adolescence and femininity, and for demonstrating a sense of power in an environment that provides them with little status. In this connection, gang girl violence is also one of the very few resources for defending one's reputation as respectable. This is not to say that some gang girls may engage in violence for other reasons.

Middle class girls, by comparison, have a range of resources for exploring femininity and defending a reputation. When middle class girls come together, they are popularly known by adults and their peers as cliques and friendship groups (as compared to lower working class girls who are seen as gang girls). It is in the clique that middle class girls negotiate femininity and adolescence. 'Being nice' as opposed to 'being bossy' means demonstrating 'reliability, reciprocity, commitment, confidentiality, trust and sharing' (Hey 1997: 65). Middle class girls do draw on 'othering' or 'bitching' as a mechanism for demarcating others, but given their broader resources, they also invest a great deal of energy in exclusionary acts such as guilt and isolation, subtle but obvious displays of in versus out, and selective invitations to social activities and outings (Hey 1997).

This analysis has tried to demonstrate that the notion of the 'bad girl' is a complex one, riddled with questions of not only gender, but also class and ethnicity. Contrary to the idea that gang girls constantly engage in the construction of a 'bad ass' image, we suggest that the accomplishment of femininity occurs through interaction with others and is based in large part, but not exclusively, on acting and being respect(able).

References

Biernacki, P. and Waldorf, D. (1981), 'Snowball Sampling: Problems and Techniques of Chain Referral Sampling', *Sociological Methods and Research*, 10: 141–63.
Bourgois, P. (1996), 'In Search of Masculinity', *British Journal of Criminology*, 36/3: 412–27.
Campbell, A. (1984), *The Girls in the Gang*. Oxford: Basil Blackwell.
——(1990), 'Female Participation in Gangs', in C. R. Huff, ed., *Gangs in America*. 163–82. Newbury Park, CA: Sage.
——(1993), *Men, Women and Aggression*, New York: Basic Books.
Campbell, A. and Muncer, S. (1989), 'Them and Us: A Comparison of the Cultural Context of American Gangs and British Subcultures', *Deviant Behavior*, 10: 271–88.
Chesney-Lind, M. (1993), 'Girls, Gangs and Violence: Anatomy of a Backlash', *Humanity and Society*, 17: 321–44.
Chesney-Lind, M. and Hagedorn, J., eds. (1999), *Female Gangs in America*. Chicago: Lake View Press.

CLOWARD, R. and OHLIN, L. (1960), *Delinquency and Opportunity: A Theory of Delinquent Gangs*. New York: Free Press.

COHEN, A. (1955), *Delinquent Boys: The Culture of the Gang*. Glencoe, IL: Free Press.

COLLISON, M. (1996), 'In Search of the High Life', *British Journal of Criminology*, 36/3: 428–44.

CONNELL, R. (1987), *Gender and Power*. Stanford, CA: Stanford University Press.

CURRY, G. D., BOX, R., BALL, R., and STONE, D. (1992), *National Assessment of Law Enforcement Anti-Gang Information Resources*, draft 1992, Final Report. West Virginia University: National Assessment Survey.

CURRY, G. D., BALL, R. and FOX, R. (1994), *Gang Crime and Law Enforcement Record Keeping*. Washington, DC: National Institute of Justice.

DALY, K. (1997), 'Different Ways of Conceptualizing Sex/Gender in Feminist Theory and Their Implications for Criminology', *Theoretical Criminology*, 1: 25–51.

DAVIES, A. (1999), 'These Viragoes are No Less Cruel than the Lads: Young Women, Gangs and Violence in Late Manchester and Salford', *British Journal of Criminology*, 39/1: 72–89.

DUNLAP, E., JOHNSON, B. and MANWAR, A. (1994), 'A Successful Female Crack Dealer: Case Study of a Deviant Career', *Deviant Behavior*, 15: 1–25.

ESBENSEN, F. and HUIZINGA, D. (1993), 'Gangs, Drugs and Delinquency in a Survey of Urban Youth', *Criminology*, 31: 565–89.

FAGAN, J. (1990), 'Social Processes of Delinquency and Drug Use Among Urban Gangs', in C. R. Huff, ed., *Gangs in America*, 183–222. Newbury Park, CA: Sage.

FISHMAN, L. (1988), *The Vice Queens: An Ethnographic Study of Black Female Gang Behavior*, paper presented at the Annual Meeting of the American Society of Criminology, Chicago (November).

FLEISHER, M. (1998), *Dead End Kids: Gang Girls and the Boys They Know*. Madison: University of Wisconsin.

HARRIS, M. (1988), *Cholas: Latino Girls and Gangs*. New York: AMS Press.

HEY, V. (1997), *The Company She Keeps*. Buckingham: Open University.

HOROWITZ, R. (1990), 'Sociological Perspectives on Gangs: Conflicting Definitions and Concepts', in C. R. Huff, ed., *Gangs in America*, 37–54. Newbury Park, CA: Sage.

HUDSON, B. (1984), 'Femininity and Adolescence', in A. McRobbie and M. Nava, eds., *Gender and Generation*, 31–53. London: MacMillan.

INCIARDI, J., HOROWITZ, R. and POTTIEGER, A. E. (1993), *Street Kids, Street Drugs, Street Crime: An Examination of Drug Use and Serious Delinquency in America*. Belmont: Wadsworth Publishing.

JEFFERSON, T. (1996), 'Introduction to Special Issue on Masculinities and Crime', *British Journal of Criminology*, 36/3: 337–47.

JOE, K. (1993), 'Getting in the Gang: Methodological Issues in Studying Ethnic Gangs', in M. De La Rosa and J. Adrados, eds., 234–57. *Drug Abuse Among Minority Youth: Methodological Issues and Recent Research Advances*, National Institute on Drug Abuse Research Monograph Series 130. Washington, DC: US Government Printing Office.

JOE, K. and CHESNEY-LIND, M. (1995), 'Just Every Mother's Angel: An Analysis of Gender and Ethnic Variations in Youth Gang Membership', *Gender and Society*, 9/4: 408–31.

JOE LAIDLER, K. and HUNT, G. (1997), 'Violence and Social Organization in Female Gangs', *Social Justice*, 24/4: 148–69.

KATZ, J. (1988), *Seductions of Crime*. NY: Basic Books.

KLEIN, M. (1995), *The American Street Gang: Its Nature, Prevalence and Control*. New York: Oxford University.

LAUDERBACK, D., HANSEN, J. and WALDORF, D. (1992), 'Sisters are Doin' It For Themselves: A Black Female Gang in San Francisco', *The Gang Journal*, 1: 57–72.

LEES, S. (1997), *Ruling Passions*. Buckingham: Open University.

MAHER, L. (1997), *Sexed Work: Gender, Race, and Resistance in a Brooklyn Drug Market*. New York: Oxford University Press.

MCROBBIE, A. (1981), *Feminism and Youth Culture: From Jackie to Just Seventeen*. London: MacMillan.

MESSERSCHMIDT, J. (1987), *Capitalism, Patriarchy and Crime Toward a Socialist Feminist Criminology*. Totowa, NJ: Rowman and Littlefield.

——(1993), *Masculinities and Crime: Critique and Conceptualization of Theory*. Lanham, MD: Rowman and Littlefield.

——(1997), *Crime as Structured Action: Gender, Race, Class and Crime in the Making*. Thousand Oaks: Sage.

MILLER, J. (1998), 'Up It Up: Gender and the Accomplishment of Street Robbery', *Criminology*, 36/1: 37–66.

MILLER, W. (1958), 'Lower Class Culture as a Generating Milieu of Gang Delinquency', *Journal of Social Issues*, 3: 5–19.

MOORE, J. (1991), *Going Down to the Barrio: Homeboys and Homegirls in Change*. Philadelphia: Temple University.

MOORE, J. and HAGEDORN, J., eds., (1996), 'What Happens to Girls in the Gang?', in C. R. Huff, ed., *Gangs In America*, 2nd ed., 205–18. Thousand Oaks: Sage.

NEWBURN, T. and STANKO, E., eds. (1994), *Just Boys Doing Business*. London: Routledge.

O'MALLEY, S. (1993), 'Girlz N the Hood', *Harper's Bazaar*, October, 238–43, 272, 281, 284.

QUICKER, J. (1983), *Homegirls*. San Pedro, CA: International Universities Press.

SANCHEZ-JANKOWSKI, M. (1991), *Islands in the Street*. Berkeley: University of California.

SIKES, G. (1997), *8 Ball Chicks: A Year in the Violent World of Girl Gangsters*. New York: Anchor.

SKEGGS, B. (1997), *Formations of Class and Gender: Becoming Respectable*. London: Sage.

TAYLOR, C. (1993), *Girls, Gangs, Women and Drugs*. East Lansing, MI: Michigan State University Press.

THRASHER, F. (1927), *The Gang*. Chicago: University of Chicago.

VENKATESH, S. A., (1998), 'Gender and Outlaw Capitalism: A Historical Account of the Black Sisters of the United "Girl Gang"', *Signs*, 23/3: 681–709.

WALDORF, D. (1993), *Final Report of the Crack Sales, Gangs and Violence Study to the National Institute on Drug Abuse*. Alameda, CA: Institute for Scientific Analysis.

WURTZEL, B. (1998), *Bitches: In Praise of Difficult Women*. NY: Anchor.

[8]

Girls' Violence: Beyond Dangerous Masculinity

Katherine Irwin[1]* and Meda Chesney-Lind[2]

[1] Department of Sociology and [2] Women's Studies Program, University of Hawai'i at Mānoa

Abstract

In this article, we review criminological perspectives of girls' violence. To do this, we first look at the 20th-century tendency to view violent girls as being the same as violent boys or as taking up dangerous types of masculinity. Second, we consider the contemporary ways that researchers have tried to move beyond male-centered and masculinized explanations of female violence. Noting potential problems with current perspectives, we argue that researchers need to address the contexts surrounding female offending, which includes understanding the effects and nature of gender, race, and class inequalities and how they (singly and in combination) predict popular representations and treatment of violent girls. We conclude by cautioning contemporary researchers to avoid returning to andro-centric perspectives of girls' physical aggression. Not only are such perspectives logically problematic, they are also consequential. In particular, they have facilitated the masculinization and punishment of poor or working-class girls of color who are filling US detention centers and juvenile prisons in ever increasing numbers.

Violent girls: Don't believe the hype

The turn of the century was characterized by a startling criminological development. The long-standing gender gap in youth violence appeared to be swiftly closing.[1] The buzz about the increasing dangerousness of girlhood started when arrest data from the 1990s revealed dramatic growth in girls' arrest rates for violent crimes in comparison to boys' rates, which appeared to be either leveling off or dropping. For example, between 1986 and 1995, girls' arrests for violence increased by 124% while boys' increased by 60% (Federal Bureau of Investigation 1996). By 1999, boys' violence arrests seemed to slow down (decreasing 10% between 1990 and 1999) whereas girls' arrest rates continued to climb (by nearly 40% during this same period) (Federal Bureau of Investigation 2000).

We now know that the evidence for girls' increasing violence was not being found in other measures designed to track girls' behavior. Generally speaking, when criminologists study crime trends, there are three data sources available: arrest, self-report, and victimization data. At the same

838   Girls' Violence: Beyond Dangerous Masculinity

time that girls were being arrested for violence more frequently, a variety of data sources indicated that girls were not self-reporting more violence (see Centers for Disease Control and Prevention 1992–2006; Chesney-Lind and Belknap 2004; Huizinga 1997). In addition, girls' violence was also not increasing according to the national victimization studies (Steffensmeier et al. 2005). Because the upsurge in girls' violence appeared only in the arrest data, and not in the two other sources, it seemed likely that the rising arrest rates for girls' violence had more to do with the changes in police practices than dramatic changes in girls' behaviors. Explaining this trend, Chesney-Lind (2001) noted that there has always been, and will always be, violent girls. During some epochs, violent girls are ignored and trivialized. During other eras, however, girls' violence is 'rediscovered' and hyped. At the dawn of the 21st century, girls' violence has been rediscovered in ways that have spurred new theory making about girls' violence. These perspectives, we contend, are consequential since we think that at least some of them have encouraged a broader policing of girls in a variety of contexts.

Although increases in girls' arrest rates tracked changes in police practices rather than changes in girls' violence, the idea that girls were becoming equally as violent as boys became a media staple. Newspaper articles announced that 'girls are moving into the world of violence that once belonged to boys' (Ford 1998), that '... in a new twist on equality, girls' crime resembles boys" (Guido 1998), and that 'there are more girls in gangs, more girls in the drug trade, more girls carrying guns and knives, more girls in trouble' (Lee 1991, A1). It is important to note that the images of violent girls in the media accounts were primarily girls of color, often pictured brandishing weapons or even peering over the barrel of a gun. Popular trade books such as Prothrow-Stith and Spivak's (2005) *Sugar and Spice and No Longer Nice* and Garbarino's (2006) *See Jane Hit* endorsed the media message that girls were growing more violent. As a result of increasing popular culture attention, girls' violence also prompted a growing number of academics to think seriously about the topic.

Given the importance of this topic, we feel that it is a good time to take stock of what we know about girls' violence and identify some trends in the contemporary academic literature. In this paper, we identify several ways that criminologists have thought about girls and violence. We start with the historic tendency to explain girls' violence through the same lens used to examine boys' violence. We link this pattern to theories suggesting that violent girls are escaping their femininity by taking on the traits of their male counterparts. We also trace how the old and newer 'masculinization' assumptions have shaped juvenile justice practice. Looking at several contemporary treatments of girls' violence that attempt to depart from masculinization perspectives, we offer a view of girls' violence that accounts for gender inequalities and girls' agency in ways that do not describe violent girls in terms of male offending.

Are girls the same as or different from boys? The emergence of masculinized perspectives of violent girls

Since Lombroso (1894), criminological thinking about female offending has been plagued by a series of questions and limitations. One question is whether female crime can be explained using the same theories that explain male crime. In other words, are female offenders the same as or are they different from male offenders? Authors have used several terms to capture this historic criminological theme. For example, Daly and Chesney-Lind (1988, 508) argue that 'theories of gender and crime can be built in several ways ... Some are focusing on what we have called the generalizability problem, while others are interested in what we have termed the gender ratio problem.' Generalizability refers to the quest to find theories that account equally for male and female offending. The gender ratio problem describes scholarship focused on the 'gap' or difference between male and female offending. Miller (2001, 199) suggests that the 'gender ratio' and 'generalizability' problem fits within a larger 'gender differences' and 'gender similarities' framework and argues that the '... the former tends to essentialize differences between women and men, fails to account for similarities in their experiences, and also overlooks important differences between women ... On the other hand, the "gender similarities" approach often results in a failure to be attentive to the importance of gender.'

There are several versions of gender similarities and gender differences perspectives in the criminology literature. Universal theories of crime, for example, have focused on neighborhood, family, school, or peer contexts. These fit within the gender similarities perspective as they attempt to explain crime causation across gender lines. Interestingly, while aiming for universality, several of the seminal criminological theories were developed using data with boys and men and then were generalized to include girls and women (see Hirschi 1969). There are also a variety of gender difference perspectives, which focus on biology, psychology, everyday interactions, and structural constraints. One enduring problem is that gender differences tend to be interpreted as gender deficiencies, with girls and women being viewed as sick, pathological, victimized, or powerless (see Pollak 1961).

Despite some consensus among feminist criminologists that gender 'similarities/differences' or gender 'generalizability/ratio' constructions are inherently limited, this dichotomous framework continues to drive how female offenders are theorized, constructed by the media, and treated within institutions. An example of the persistence of the similarities or differences framework can be seen in the emergence and popularity of the masculinization hypothesis. The masculinization perspective suggests that female offenders, especially violent girls, abandon their femininity and take on the masculine traits of their male counterparts. At its core, masculinization is a gender similarities perspective because it assumes that the same forces that propel men into violence will increasingly produce

840   Girls' Violence: Beyond Dangerous Masculinity

violence in girls and women once they are freed from the constraints of their gender. In fact, masculine theories of female violence reinforce the historic problem with universal theories of crime. They imply that contemporary theories of violence (and crime, more broadly) need not attend to gender, but can simply 'add women and stir'. Since girls and women are now acting more like boys and men and gaining access to traditionally male settings, the theories will work to explain girls' behavior.

The masculinization hypothesis has emerged as a dominant perspective of violent girls in theory, the media, and criminal justice practice. At a time when punishment, retribution, and law and order dominate criminal justice philosophy and practice, viewing violent girls as 'masculine' and equally as dangerous as violent boys places girls in a precarious position within the justice system. In the following, we trace the origins of this hypothesis in criminological theories.

Sisters are doing it for themselves

The masculinization perspective became explicit in criminological work developed in the 1970s, at the same time as the rekindling of the women's rights movement. Adler's (1975) *Sisters in Crime* and Simon's (1975) *Women and Crime* comprise the classic statements at the time and crystallize public anxieties about a looming 'darker side' of women's emancipation (Adler 1975, 3). One common idea between these works is that women's emancipation allows women and girls to enter and gain equal footing in masculine domains. Freed from the protective constraints of traditional femininity and liberated from institutionalized inequalities blocking women from entrance into masculine worlds that confer prestige and wealth, many imagine that emancipated girls and women are free to become just as violent as boys and men in contexts that valorize danger, risk-taking, and crime.

The media were quick to pounce on the bad news about feminism. Often, these articles included law enforcement officers describing the new offenders along with pictures showcasing such notorious characters as Leslie Van Houten (convicted murderer and Charles Manson follower), Friederike Krabbe (kidnapper and member of the Red Army Faction terrorist organization), and even Patricia Hearst (who joined forces with the urban guerrilla warfare group, the Symbionese Liberation Army, who kidnapped her). In each case, the idea that women were entering masculine and violent worlds of serial killing, radical guerrilla warfare, and terrorism fueled the media's fascination with the dark side of women's equality.

Street liberation perspectives

In the 1980s, women's liberation theories of crime coupled with emerging perspectives of urban disadvantage to produce another installment of masculinization theories. Regarding a contemporary focus on urban strains and inner-city disadvantage, scholars examined increasingly dire circumstances in US inner cities since the 1980s. Wilson (1996, 1987) focuses on the out-migration of industrial jobs from American urban centers. Wacquant (2001) looks at a 'deadly' combination of US institutionalized racism and neoliberal politics. Blumstein (1995) focuses on the emergence of new drug markets and the ensuing violence surrounding a new, underground industry. Combined these forces have turned poor urban neighborhoods into what some called 'hyper ghettos' that are wrought with unemployment, violence, and a growth of underground opportunities (see Venkatesh 2006). Researchers chronicled the effects of these shifts on masculinity and violence (Anderson 1999; Bourgois 1996). Anderson (1999) notes that these overarching conditions limit avenues to middle-class, white respectability for inner-city African Americans. As a result, some African American boys grow up craving status so much that they participate in an alternate avenue to respect: a violent and masculine 'code of the streets'. Similarly, Bourgois (1996) traces the effects of US colonialism in Puerto Rico and Puerto Rican immigration patterns to the alienation experienced by El Barrio residents. He notes that larger conditions leave second-generation, inner-city Puerto Rican men with few avenues to attain 'respeto', or the respect traditionally and ideally afforded to patriarchs. Violence becomes a rationalized response among these structurally 'vulnerable' men.

Offering what might be called a street liberation perspective, some explain women's and girls' inner-city experiences using the same theoretical framework to explain men's hypermasculinity and violence. In a series of articles and a subsequent book, Baskin and Sommers, in particular, examined African American girls and women in New York (Baskin et al. 1993; Sommers and Baskin 1992, 1993), and argue that 'violent offending rates of black females parallel [those] of white males' (Sommers and Baskin 1992, 191). The central argument cutting across their studies is that the socioeconomic situation in the inner city, specifically as it is affected by the drug trade, creates 'new dynamics of crime where gender is a far less salient factor' (Baskin et al. 1993, 417). The street liberation thesis, in fact, turns the 'emancipation' hypothesis on its head. Now, it is not presumed that economic gain promoted 'equality' in crime, rather economic marginalization and racism cause women to move out of their 'traditional' roles and into dangerous and masculine criminal worlds.

It is notable that this latest masculinization image of female offenders specifically pictures urban women of color, where the earlier masculinization manifestation featured theories (and media stories) showcasing white women. Similar to the previous masculinization theory, though, this perspective also gained considerable media attention, particularly when coupled with dramatic increases in girls' arrests for violent offenses. This time around, though, the media showcased girls of color, often in gang attire, peering menacingly over the barrels of guns (Chesney-Lind and Irwin 2008).

Contemporary perspectives of girls' violence

In the past decade, girls' violence has become an increasingly key topic in criminology, given the rising violence arrest rates for girls. Consequently, new versions of gender similarities and gender differences perspectives have emerged, with some researchers attempting to bridge the divide between these dichotomies. We argue that in an era when the masculinization perspective dominates, theorists must be mindful that their theories about girls have consequences. These theories are, in fact, used to understand the 'criminal' behavior of girls as well as to craft criminal justice responses. To construct a non-masculinized theory of girls' violence, we take a look at contemporary perspectives of female violence, including those that look at patriarchy and gender inequalities, girls' attempts to be 'one of the guys', and girls' participation in a violent code of the streets.

Patriarchy and gendered inequalities

As we noted earlier, there are problems with constructing girls as being different from boys. One problem is that gender differences are often pathologized; this is especially true in individualistic biological and psychological theories. Gender differences in individualistic theories, as we have previously noted, are often located in girls' sick or weak biological or psychological makeup. Conversely, gender difference perspectives focusing on social structures tend to locate sickness and pathology in institutions and social systems. Although not perfect, such perspectives promise to locate problems outside individual girls and offer a critical gaze at larger social forces.

In the early 2000s, several scholars examined the role of patriarchy and gender inequality in girls' violence. Artz's (1998), Brown's (2003), and Morash and Chesney-Lind's (2006) work have been particularly influential in building a framework. A major premise of their work is that girls' violence is framed within a patriarchal context, meaning that gender inequalities, such as male domination (especially physical domination), lack of equal opportunities for women and girls, and pervasive control over girls and women (especially over their bodies and sexuality), are central and reoccurring themes in girls' violence. For example, Artz (1998) found that violent schoolgirls in Canada reported significantly greater rates of victimization and abuse than their nonviolent counterparts. Patterns for sexual abuse were even starker; roughly one out of four violent girls had been sexually abused compared to one in ten of nonviolent girls (Artz 1998). The idea that girls' physical and sexual victimization marks their trajectory toward violence is not new. Campbell (1984), as one example, also highlights the ways that gendered victimization frames girls' violence.

A new twist in patriarchy and gender inequality perspectives in the last decade has been to see girls' violence toward other girls as a form of horizontal violence – violence expressed toward members of the same group or other oppressed groups. Borrowing concepts from Freire (1970), Artz (1998), Brown (2003), and Morash and Chesney-Lind (2006) note that pervasive gender inequalities make it difficult, if not impossible, for girls to express anger and aggression (physical or indirect) toward boys and men, without, of course, dire consequences. Instead, girls take out their legitimate anger on other powerless girls (often with boys as the audience).

Emancipation and street liberation theorists contend that violent girls reject feminine norms and break into male dominant worlds. In contrast, the horizontal violence thesis views female violence as a result of vast and ever-present gender inequalities. In fact, empirical research on female violence suggests that offenders are, ironically, often quite committed to the 'ideology of familial patriarchy ... [that] supports the abuse of women who violate the ideals of male power and control over women' (DeKeseredy 2000, 46). Artz (1998) builds on that point by suggesting that violent girls more often than not 'buy-in' to traditional beliefs and 'police' other girls' behaviors, thus serving to preserve the status quo, including their own continued oppression. Artz et al. (2000, 31) also note this in their study of girls in custody in British Columbia, Canada. The researchers found that the majority of girls were male-focused, expressed hostility to other girls, and wanted very much to have boyfriends – always making sure that they had at least one, both in and out of jail. Vividly chronicling a 'no-win' situation for girls, the researchers note the many ways that horizontal violence set up girls to be targets. The power hierarchies among girls meant that girls could be targeted if they were 'too pretty' and thus risked becoming the center of boys' attention. Alternately, 'ugly' or 'dirty' girls (those designated as sluts) were also targets for girl-to-girl victimization because they 'deserved' to be beaten for their unappealing looks and for their gender-norm-violating behaviors.

Although powerful in moving beyond identifying essential differences between boys and girls, patriarchal interpretations of female violence have been critiqued. Miller (2001), for example, argues that gender difference theories focusing on gender inequality risk overemphasizing girls' and women's victimization and powerlessness. Her particular concern is that these perspectives place an 'overemphasis on women's gendered victimization – and with it, the accentuation of gender differences ...' In addition to portraying women and girls as 'hapless victims' without agency or culpability for their crimes, Miller suggests that gender difference perspectives tend to ignore other 'broader motives and rewards for involvement in crime'.

844   Girls' Violence: Beyond Dangerous Masculinity

Beyond victimization: Violent girls as 'one of the guys'

Miller (2001) explains girls' offending in ways that take gender into account, while not overemphasizing gender differences. In essence, she articulates how gang girls and boys are the same as well as different. Based on research with female gang members in Columbus and St. Louis, Miller does acknowledge gender differences and that gender shapes much of girls' gang experiences. For example, girls, compared with boys, experienced more family victimization, and girls rarely occupied gang leadership positions, carried guns, or dealt drugs. In addition, pervasive beliefs of girls as 'soft' meant that they were not expected to fully engage in gang conflicts. Miller also notes girls' victimization in the gang. Some girls were 'sexed into the gang', announcing double standards in initiation practices. The stereotype of girls as 'weak' made girls seem easy targets, and girls were often punished for behaving in 'sexually inappropriate ways'.

While there were clear gender inequalities and pervasive victimization of girls (in and out of the gang), Miller argues against 'overemphasizing' these aspects of gang life. She offers two reasons not to overemphasize gender differences. First, she argues that gender's 'significance is variable' and depends on context. Thus, perspectives focusing on gender differences fail to offer a complete or whole picture of girls' lives in the gang and the reasons for their criminal participation. Second, Miller suggests that there are broader motives and processes than gender differences that shape both girls' and boys' experiences. Regarding this point, she notes that gender inequalities play a role, but girls' decisions '... are also patterned in important ways by larger dynamics within gangs such as group processes shaping notions of threat and respect' (p. 11). In addition, violence and crime allowed both girls and boys to 'be down' for their gangs and friends, retaliate against past transgressions, and protect gang territory. The most troubling similarity between girls and boys, to Miller, was the fact that gang girls, along with boys, perpetuated gender stereotypes of girls and women and applied double standards to girls' behavior. She argues that 'identifying with dominant beliefs about women while rejecting such images for themselves allowed many young women to construct themselves as "one of the guys" ... this allowed them to draw particular advantages from their gangs that were less available in other social spaces' (p. 198).

While Miller argues that patriarchy and gender inequality theories overemphasize gender differences, we believe that the 'one of the guys' thesis minimizes gender inequalities. For example, by suggesting that gender is variable and that its salience ranges by context, Miller imagines gender as being a flexible dynamic that comes to the fore in some contexts, and fades into the background during others. In addition to being flexible and ranging in salience, gendered processes such as victimization, sexual double standards, and lack of leadership roles are seen as particular to girls. On the other hand, 'other forces' such as '... group processes shaping notions of threat and respect and the normative responses to such phenomena' are seen as broad and large gang motivations that boys and girls share (Miller 2001, 11).

We have some concerns about how gender and gender inequalities are positioned in the 'one of the guys' thesis. First, we question perspectives of female offending in which gender and gender inequalities are considered variable, while other forces are considered fixed and universally salient. We wonder if there is a way to view gender as equally 'fixed' and universal as other forces and inequalities. In our vision, gender is not less broad, or less universally relevant, than other experiences, inequalities, and systems of oppression. Second, we argue that gender inequalities, in addition to being broad and large, are also something that girls and boys share. After all, respect, status, retaliation, alienation, anger, and frustration are linked intimately to gender hierarchies, as well as to class and race oppression.

Arguing that gender's relevance is variable implies that girls' need for gender-specific services and interventions is also 'variable'. Similarly, emphasizing that girls and boys share 'broader' motives for crime than gender suggests that girls and boys will respond equally to interventions that target large and non-gender-specific criminal motivations. In our contemporary era of just deserts punishments, such a scheme promises gender parity with a vengeance. Because this vision downplays gender differences and plays up gender similarities, the need to focus on girls' and boys' shared culpability for crime will trump the need to attend to girls' victimization, unique needs, and circumstances. This is unfortunate.

Girls' code of the streets: Considering race, class, and gender

Jones (2004) and Ness (2004) also offer an image of girls' violence that attempts to bridge the 'similarities and differences' divide. Ness (2004) and Jones (2004) focus on low-income, inner-city girls of color and note that boys and girls participate in a violent 'code of the streets' (Anderson 1999) in parallel ways. Ness states that girls in distressed communities, similar to boys, find violence to be a 'source of pleasure, self-esteem, and cultural capital' (Ness 2004, 33). Ness further argues that violent girls in her study 'are not viewed as defying feminine norms ...' when they '... enjoy physically dominating others and take pleasure in inflicting pain and emerging victorious' (p. 45). In Ness's and Jones's work, violence is a means for girls to achieve powerful femininities and boys to achieve powerful masculinities within contexts where adolescents have a profound sense of being 'closed out of white, middle-class America and abandoned by the failing institutions meant to serve them' (Ness 2004, 36).

By arguing that violence is a means of achieving resilient femininities in distressed communities, Ness and Jones push past the street liberation thesis offered by Baskin and Sommers. Instead of suggesting that urban realities make gender norms irrelevant, Ness and Jones argue that femininity remains central to women's and girls' lives and, more specifically, femininity can be altered to respond to race and economic inequalities. For example, Ness (2004, 37) argues that low-income, Hispanic and African American girls 'selectively appropriate' middle-class and white femininity norms (which eschew violence) and place them 'alongside values that more closely fit their lives'. Jones makes a similar argument when she outlines that being known as a good fighter is the most 'reliable social resource' available to girls in disadvantaged urban environments. Therefore, violent girls recraft, remake, and resolve femininities to attend to the contexts around them.

Similar to our concern with Miller's thesis, we wonder if there is a way to imagine gender as equally fixed as other inequalities and systems of oppression. In the girls' code-of-the-streets thesis, femininity is perceived as 'flexible' and 'variable' while other 'larger' and 'broader' forces, such as race and class inequalities, are imagined as fixed and central. Jones and Ness argue that gender is crafted and fashioned to attend to the class and race circumstances pressing down on boys and girls. Therefore, just as Miller, Ness and Jones imagine that boys and girls are equal in being left out of middle-class, white society. What makes them different, in this scheme, is how they craft and fashion their gender to attend to larger circumstances.

The media's fascination with the urban girl of color and her violence call for careful attention to how gender, class, and race inequalities play out in violence theories. At a time when popular representations of girls' violence reinforce the idea that girls are giving up their femininity and becoming just as violent as boys, we wonder what stereotypes might unintentionally emerge from viewing violent girls participating in a feminine 'code of the streets'. Our ultimate concern is that we will replace one set of problematic stereotypes with another. We specifically anticipate that at a time when violent men, especially working-class and poor young men of color, are seen as potentially violent and 'dangerously masculine', arguing that girls are the same as and different from boys will translate into a 'dangerously feminine' stereotype. Dangerously feminine girls are likely to be denied services attending to their unique circumstances. Such girls are also likely to be the targets of a punitive justice paradigm originally designed to combat male violence.

Context matters in girls' violence

Our primary concern with contemporary theories of girls' violence, especially efforts to get beyond the similarities/differences divide, is that they tend to push gender processes and inequalities to the sidelines, while foregrounding race, class, neighborhood, and peer processes. As we have noted, gender and gender inequalities are viewed as variable in salience, unique to girls, flexible, and less broad than 'other' criminal motivations shared by girls and boys.

Building on the work detailed above, we argue that looking at the context of girls' violence allows us to combine key insights from gender similarities and gender differences perspectives in ways that do not marginalize gender inequalities. To do this, we must understand gender as a fixed component of a sex/gender system that organizes every context in which girls and boys grow up. In addition, we must acknowledge that gender is also flexible, negotiated, and achieved variously in different contexts, as West and Zimmerman (1987) articulate.

Acknowledging the fixed, broad, and pervasive aspects of gender means identifying a sex/gender system. The sex/gender system is one in which men have greater power than women, male power over girls and women can be expressed through physical and sexual domination, and girls and women lack the same opportunities afforded to boys and men. Girls' victimization in the family, among peers, and at school is a product of a universal sex/gender system. Similarly, school, neighborhood, and peer cultures that devalue and demoralize girls and women, while celebrating boys and men, are products of persistent inequalities in a sex/gender system. Understanding the context of girls' lives means understanding how girls grow up in a world where they are trivialized and sexualized and rewarded for being attractive to and dependent on boys. It also means understanding how girls are placed in direct competition with other girls for male approval and affirmation (Brown and Gilligan 1992; Orenstein 1994; Pipher 1994).

The sex/gender system in which girls and boys grow up has consequences for all adolescents. Large-scale gender inequalities, thus, are not simply something that girls share with girls or something located within and among girls. In contexts in which class and race inequalities make men vulnerable, the sex/gender system gives men an outlet to express power. It is not surprising that in such contexts women and girls become targets for men's and boys' attempts to assert control. By acknowledging that gender inequalities shape every context in which girls and boys grow up, we are not denying that adolescents are vulnerable to other inequalities, such as poverty and racism. We contend, though, that to fully understand community distress, disadvantage, or disorganization, scholars must understand that gender is one among many inequalities complicating childhood and adolescence.

Taking context into account also means understanding that gender is a flexible force that can be appropriated and shaped to fit complex realities. Here, as West and Zimmerman (1987) acknowledge, gender is an ongoing achievement. There are aspects of gender, therefore, that can be flexible, dynamic, and differentially constructed to attend to varying contexts. The flexibility of gender constructions in multiple contexts allows girls the chance to construct a sense of femininity in multiple ways, even, as Miller (2001, 198) notes, in ways that allow girls to identify '... with dominant beliefs about women.' Morash and Chesney-Lind (2006) extend this idea by noting that girls' violence is multifaceted and multidimensional. Girls are violent to express anger at past victimization, defend themselves, or prevent future victimization. Violent girls also act out the pervasive gendered victimization around them. At the same time, girls are violent to express strength, power, and resilience. Girls' aggression can send a strong 'don't mess with me' signal to others. Violence, therefore, can be reactionary and proactive, instrumental and expressive, protective and retaliatory, rational and irrational. Girls' violence can result from pro-violence rationalizations, motives, and rewards received from friends, boyfriends, or family members. It can signal all the ways that girls are 'down for' their friends or their gang. On the other hand, some girls turn to violence to rebel against a preponderance of messages that violence is wrong, unfeminine, and relationally destructive. Here, girls' violence does not express how they are 'down for their friends' but to rebel against all the messages informing them that violence is unladylike. In this complex vision, the violent motivations that girls share with girls are not any less broad, variable, or salient than the motivations that girls share with boys.

Our emphasis on fixed as well as flexible aspects of gender and the need to understand that gender inequalities are equally as broad as other systems of oppression, comprises our effort to get beyond male-centered and masculinized perspectives. Specifically, we outline that there are fixed and universal gender inequalities that cut across all contexts (i.e., the sex/gender system) in which girls and boys grow up. These are large-scale, broad, and central, rather than marginal, concerns that need to be addressed when looking at adolescent violence. In addition, we also note that there are flexible and dynamic ways that gender is enacted in particular contexts (i.e., gender as achieved statuses). Above, we have argued that understanding the context of girls' violence will result in perspectives of girls as vulnerable within a sex/gender system as well as resilient in crafting strategies to maximize their power and self-protection in particular contexts. A complex analysis of the context of girls' violence, however, is not complete unless we also examine the policies and practices crafted in response to violent girls.

Masculinization and the jailing of girls

Gender similarities perspectives of girls' violence, particularly those articulated in the emancipation and street liberation perspectives, are problematic in many ways, not the least of which is that girls who are assumed to be 'like' their 'dangerous' male counterparts can be punished as if they were male. We are concerned that contemporary theories of girls' violence that marginalize the significance of gender inequalities behind 'larger' criminal motivations that girls and boys share also risk continuing a problematic trend in criminal justice practice. One of the historic challenges, in our opinion, is that girls' unique circumstances are trivialized or ignored when girls are assumed to be like boys or when gender inequalities are assumed to be less important than and outside of broader criminal motivations.

In short, universal images of delinquency tend to support the notion that violent girls do not need gender-specific responses because their violence is caused by the same forces that cause boys' violence; then, by extension, the same programs that have been shown to be effective in curbing violence in boys will automatically work for girls. In other words, the dominant perception coming out of universal perspectives of delinquency is that it is okay to ignore girls or to give them the same services provided to boys.

One historic by-product of the universal and male-centered theories of delinquency is the masculinization of delinquency prevention and intervention services and the glaring lack of services for girls. In 1975, a Law Enforcement Assistance Administration report noted that only 5% of federally funded juvenile projects targeted girls and that girls received only 6% of local juvenile justice funds (Female Offender Resource Center 1977, 34). Twenty years later, the lack of services for girls remained a problem. A 1996 Girls Incorporated study, for example, found that only 2 out of 26 of the Office of Juvenile Justice and Delinquency Prevention's promising programs were programs designed for girls, at a time when girls accounted for almost a third of all juvenile arrests (Federal Bureau of Investigation 2006). Even more ironic was the fact that there was one program identified to serve incarcerated teen fathers, while there was no program identified for incarcerated teen mothers (Girls Incorporated 1996). Reports from San Francisco (Siegal 1995), Washington, DC (Viner, personal communication, October 21, 2003), and Ohio (Holsinger et al. 1999), to name a few, corroborated this same trend. Delinquent girls continued to be 'out of sight, out of mind'. As Schaffner et al. (1996) note in their California detention study, detained girls tended to be overlooked and forgotten. The result was that they remained in detention, on average, far longer than boys, despite being charged with far less serious offenses. For example, 6% of boys were detained for more than 7 days, while 60% of girls were detained that long.

The invisibility of girl delinquency theories, particularly theories that explain the complexity of girls' violence, means they often receive interventions designed for boys. This can clearly be seen in the youth violence prevention field. The theories that underlie the 'best practices' for violence prevention programs draw from 'universal' theories of delinquency, and, thus, girls are rarely ever assumed to need unique prevention approaches. In the world of detained and incarcerated youths, the idea that girls and boys are the same has often meant that girls receive programs and services that were designed for boys, such as outdoor sports and recreation activities. This trend continues, although research has found that these 'male-centered' programs given to girls are not only inappropriate for girls but are limited compared with what boys receive (Kersten 1989; Mann 1984).

Finally, the masculine violent girl stereotype makes the punishment of girls much more politically palatable. Sadly, public awareness of the masculine girl delinquent, particularly the urban girl, appeared at the same time as a peak in rampant public fears about 'superpredator' violent juveniles (see DiIulio 1995) and a national 'get tough on crime' criminal justice agenda. In the adult offending population, public fears about violent offenders have discouraged a response to crime that includes service provision and rehabilitation and moved toward a punishment-oriented system that relies on lengthy incarceration (see Garland 2001). A concomitant effect in the juvenile justice system has been what Chesney-Lind and Belknap (2004) call up-criming (criminalizing minor offenses) and re-labeling status offenses such as running away and incorrigibility as violent offenses such as assault or abuse of a family member.

The available statistics regarding girls in the juvenile justice system illustrate the effect of contemporary punitive policies on girls' lives. Since the 1980s, increases in girls' court referrals, detentions, and commitments have outpaced increases for boys. From 1985 to 2002, girls' juvenile court cases increased by 92%, while boys' court cases increased by 29% (Snyder and Sickmund 2006). Detention and commitment figures also showed steep increases in girls' incarceration for the first time since the de-institutionalization trends of the 1970s. From 1991 to 2003, the detention and commitment of girls increased by 98% and 88%, respectively, while boys' detention rate rose by 29% and their commitment rate rose by 23% (Snyder and Sickmund 2006). Looking closely at the nature of girls' court, detention, and commitment cases reveals a consistent story. Since the 1980s, girls have been increasingly entering the juvenile justice system for 'violent' or person offense, even though self and victim reports continue to show no actual increases in girls' violence. Astonishingly, the most recent data show a larger proportion of girls than boys in court for 'person' offenses; in 2002, 26% of female referrals but only 23% of male referrals to court were for 'person' offenses (Snynder and Sickmund 2006, 162).

In this paper, we have focused on one problematic turn in justice policy and practice; namely, how viewing girls as the same as boys facilitated the emergence of an era in which punishing girls as if they were boys became a politically acceptable project. In fact, the construction of youth, particularly girls of color, as hyperviolent, makes the dramatic increases we have seen in the detention and incarceration of girls, particularly girls of color, less controversial.

Conclusion

In this discussion, we have focused on two problematic developments in the girls' violence literature. The first is the persistence of the 'similarities/ differences' problem in female offending theories. The similarities/differences problem captures the tendency of theories to explain how girls and women are either the 'same as' or 'different from' men or boys. The second problematic trend is the rise (and popularity) of a particularly troubling trend in gender similarities theories; namely, the proliferation of the masculinization hypothesis in criminological theory and popular culture. Since the 1960s and 1970s, female offenders have been described as being liberated from femininity and allowed to break into masculine criminal worlds. We also noted the recent media enthusiasm for such an explanation. Recall, though, that there is scant evidence that girls are actually committing more violence; indeed, most of the evidence that exists is to the contrary. There is, though, very strong evidence that certain women, particularly girls of color, are being constructed by the press and popular culture as dangerously masculine and violent. The function of such a construction is clear: to create a social and political climate that supports increasing imprisonment for these groups of girls and women. There is also the larger cultural message to all women that if they seek political and social equality with men, they risk losing the positive aspects of womanhood and developing some of the worst attributes of masculinity.

Given these two problems with theory development (i.e., the 'similarities/ differences' problem and the masculinization thesis), we examined contemporary girls' violence scholarship. We looked at three developments, including theories of patriarchy and girls' violence, perspectives of gang girls as 'one of the guys', and works looking at girls' participation in a violent street code. We note that patriarchy and gender inequalities perspectives have been critiqued for overemphasizing girls' oppression and victimization, and proliferating images of girls as hapless and powerless victims. We feel that perspectives offered to get beyond girls' victimization, however, have minimized the role of gender inequalities. Our concern about theory construction is important given the dominance of the masculinization perspective in popular culture and criminal justice. We argue that how theorists attend to gender similarities and differences is consequential to how girls will be treated. Our concern is that logical imprecision will continue or exacerbate the troubling trend of viewing girls as dangerously masculine.

To construct a satisfying theory that does not overemphasize victimization or marginalize gender oppression, we offer a perspective of the context of girls' violence. We argue that there are both fixed and broad aspects of gender (i.e., a sex/gender system) that influence boys and girls. In addition, there are flexible components of gender. In the fixed sex/gender system, gender inequalities provide overarching and broad motivations for crime and violence among girls and boys in ways that generally grant power and control to boys at the expense of girls. Within the flexible and achieved components of gender, girls and boys are able to 'fashion' their gender in various ways to fit and respond to larger contexts, including racism, classism, sexism, ageism, heterosexism, and ableism. Here, gender inequalities are not moved to the sidelines of theories and are one among many constraints that all youth confront and that make youth vulnerable. In addition, viewing gender as flexible accounts for differences among girls in various contexts. By placing gender inequalities back in the center of theories about how girls are the same as well as different from boys, we have an opportunity to view violent girls as deserving of interventions that attend to overarching and broad gender inequalities.

Our final contribution in this paper is to note that theories about girls' violence are consequential. Put plainly, our assumptions about violent girls' natures tend to predict the available services for and punishments leveled against girls. Because what we think about girls translates into how we control girls, we are particularly interested in examining ways that contemporary theorists attempt to move beyond the view that violent girls are essentially the same as boys. Clearly, we need more nuanced studies of the expression of aggression and violence in women and girls, and we need to divorce such studies from rigid conceptualizations of masculinity and femininity as individual attributes. Finally, male and female violence has to be understood from within the social context of patriarchy, as well as within systems of race privilege, heterosexism, and class privilege.

Short Biography

Katherine Irwin's research areas include juvenile delinquency, deviance, drug use, violence, youth culture, gender and crime, research methods, and delinquency prevention. In addition to recently co-authoring (with Meda Chesney-Lind) *Beyond Bad Girls: Gender, Violence and Hype* (Routledge 2007), she has authored and co-authored papers in such journals as *Qualitative Sociology*, *Symbolic Interaction*, *Youth Violence and Juvenile Justice*, *Youth and Society*, *Critical Criminology*, *Sociological Perspectives*, and *Sociological Forum*. She holds a BA in Sociology from Smith College and a PhD in Sociology from the University of Colorado, Boulder, and is currently an Associate Professor of Sociology at the University of Hawai'i at Mānoa. She is also a principal investigator for the Asian and Pacific Islander Youth Violence Prevention Center at the John A. Burns School of Medicine, University of Hawai'i at Mānoa.

Meda Chesney-Lind is Professor of Women's Studies at the University of Hawai'i at Mānoa. Her books include *Girls, Delinquency and Juvenile Justice* (Wadsworth 1992) and *The Female Offender: Girls, Women and Crime*

(Sage 1997). Her most recent book (co-authored with Katherine Irwin) is *Beyond Bad Girls: Gender, Violence and Hype* (Routledge 2007). She has received numerous awards for her research on girls' and women's crime as well as her advocacy for criminalized girls and women. From the Academy of Criminal Justice Sciences she received the Bruce Smith Sr. Award and has received the Donald Cressey Award from the National Council on Crime and Delinquency. Within the American Society of Criminology, she has received the Women and Crime Division's Distinguished Scholar Award, the Division of Critical Criminology's Major Achievement Award, and the Herbert Block Award for service to the society and the profession. In 1996, she was named a fellow of the American Society of Criminology.

Notes

* Correspondence address: Department of Sociology, University of Hawai'i at Mānoa, Saunders Hall 247, Honolulu, HI 96822, USA. Email: kirwin@hawaii.edu

[1] Although violence is a broad category with numerous definitions, throughout this paper we describe violence in terms of categories used within the Uniform Crime Reports and self-report studies. When discussing overall violent arrest rates, violence includes aggravated assault, forcible rape, robbery, and homicide. Other assaults are also included in Uniform Crime Reports statistics, but are not measured within the violent crime index. Self-report studies include behaviors such as getting into a fight.

References

Adler, Freda 1975. *Sisters in Crime: The Rise of the New Female Criminal*. New York, NY: McGraw-Hill.
Anderson, Elijah 1999. *Code of the Street: Decency, Violence, and the Moral Life of the Inner City*. New York, NY: Norton.
Artz, Sibylle 1998. *Sex, Power, and the Violent School Girl*. Toronto, ON: Trifolium Books.
Artz, Sibylle, Monica Blais and Diana Nicholson 2000. *Developing Girls' Custody Units*. Unpublished report.
Baskin, Deborah, Ira B. Sommers and Jefferey Fagan 1993. 'Females' Initiation into Violent Street Crime.' *Justice Quarterly* **10**: 559–81.
Blumstein, Alfred 1995. 'Youth Violence, Guns, and the Illicit-drug Industry.' *Journal of Criminal Law & Criminology* **86**: 10–34.
Bourgois, Philippe 1996. 'In Search of Masculinity: Violence, Respect and Sexuality among Puerto Rican Crack Dealers in East Harlem.' *British Journal of Criminology* **36**: 412–427.
Brown, Lyn Mikel 2003. *Girlfighting*. New York, NY: New York University Press.
Brown, Lyn Mikel and Carol Gilligan 1992. *Meeting at the Crossroads: Women's Psychology and Girls' Development*. New York, NY: Ballantine.
Campbell, Anne 1984. *The Girls in the Gang*. London, UK: Basil Blackwell.
Centers for Disease Control and Prevention 1992–2006. *Youth Risk Behavior Surveillance – United States, 1991–2001*, CDC Surveillance Summaries. Atlanta, GA: Centers for Disease Control and Prevention, US Department of Health and Human Services.
Chesney-Lind, Meda 2001. 'Are Girls Closing the Gender Gap in Violence?' *Criminal Justice* **16**: 18–23.
Chesney-Lind, Meda and Katherine Irwin 2008. *Beyond Bad Girls: Gender, Violence, and Hype*. New York, NY: Routledge.
Chesney-Lind, Meda and Joanne Belknap 2004. 'Trends in Delinquent Girls' Aggression and

854   Girls' Violence: Beyond Dangerous Masculinity

Violent Behavior: A Review of the Evidence.' Pp. 203–22 in *Aggression, Antisocial Behavior and Violence among Girls: A Developmental Perspective*, edited by Martha Putallaz and Karen L. Bierman. New York, NY: Guilford Press.

Daly, Katheen and Chesney-Lind Meda 1988. 'Feminism and Criminology.' *Justice Quarterly* **5**: 497–548.

DeKeseredy, Walter 2000. *Women, Crime and the Canadian Criminal Justice System*. Cincinnati, OH: Anderson.

DiIulio, John J. 1995. 'The Coming of the Super-Predators.' *The Weekly Standard* November 27, 23.

Federal Bureau of Investigation 1996. *Crime in the United States 1995*. Washington, DC: Government Printing Office.

Federal Bureau of Investigation 2000. *Crime in the United States 1999*. Washington, DC: Government Printing Office.

Federal Bureau of Investigation 2006. *Crime in the United States 1999*. Washington, DC: Government Printing Office.

Female Offender Resource Center 1977. *Little Sisters and the Law*. Washington, DC: American Bar Association.

Ford, Royal 1998. 'The Razor's Edge.' *Boston Globe Magazine* **13** (May 24), 22–8.

Freire, Paulo 1970/1993. *Pedagogy of the Oppressed*. Translated by Myra Bergman Ramos. New York, NY: Continuum.

Garbarino, James 2006. *See Jane Hit: Why Girls Are Growing More Violent and What We Can Do About It*. New York, NY: Penguin Press.

Garland, David 2001. *The Culture of Control: Crime and Social Order in Contemporary Society*. Chicago, IL: University of Chicago Press.

Girls Incorporated 1996. *Prevention and Parity: Girls in Juvenile Justice*. Indianapolis, IN: Girls Incorporated National Resource Center.

Guido, Michelle 1998. 'In a New Twist on Equality, Girls' Crimes Resemble Boys'.' *San Jose Mercury* June 4, 1B–4B .

Hirschi, Travis 1969. *Causes of Delinquency*. Berkeley, CA: University of California Press.

Holsinger, Kristi, Joanne Belknap and Jennifer L. Sutherland 1999. *Assessing the Gender Specific Program and Service Needs for Adolescent Females in the Juvenile Justice System*. Columbus, OH: A Report to the Office of Criminal Justice Services.

Huizinga, David 1997. *Over-Time Changes in Delinquency and Drug Use: The 1970's to the 1990's*. Unpublished report. Washington, DC: Office of Juvenile Justice and Delinquency Prevention.

Jones, Nikki 2004. '"It's Not Where You Live, It's How You Live": How Young Women Negotiate Conflict and Violence in the Inner City.' Pp. 49–62 in *Being Here and Being There: Fieldwork Encounters and Ethnographic Discoveries: Annals of the American Academy of Political and Social Science*, edited by Elijah Anderson, Scott N. Brooks, Raymond Gunn and Nikki Jones. Thousand Oaks, CA: Sage.

Kersten, Joachim 1989. 'The Institutional Control of Girls and Boys.' Pp. 129–44 in *Growing Up Good: Policing the Behavior of the Girls in Europe*, edited by Maureen Cain. London, UK: Sage.

Lee, Felicia R. 1991. 'For Gold Earrings and Protection, More Girls Take the Road to Violence.' *New York Times* November 25, A1.

Lombroso, Cesare 1894. *The Female Offender*. London, UK: Fisher Unwin.

Mann, Coramae Richey 1984. *Female Crime and Delinquency*. Tuscaloosa, AL: University of Alabama Press.

Miller, Jody 2001. *One of the Guys: Girls, Gangs, and Gender*. New York, NY: Oxford University

Morash, Merry and Meda Chesney-Lind 2006. *Girls Violence in Context*, Office of Juvenile Justice and Delinquency Prevention Girls Study Group Volume, edited by Margaret Zahn. Philadelphia, PA: Temple University Press.

Ness, Cindy D. 2004. 'Why Girls Fight: Female Youth Violence in the Inner City.' Pp. 32–48 in *Being Here and Being There: Fieldwork Encounters and Ethnographic Discoveries: Annals of the American Academy of Political and Social Science*, edited by Elijah Anderson, Scott N. Brooks, Raymond Gunn and Nikki Jones. Thousand Oaks, CA: Sage.

Orenstein, Peggy 1994. *Schoolgirls: Young Women, Self-Esteem and the Confidence Gap*. New York, NY: Anchor.

Pipher, Mary B. 1994. *Reviving Ophelia: Saving the Selves of Adolescent Girls*. New York, NY: Ballantine.

Pollak, Otto 1961. *The Criminality of Women*. New York, NY: A.S. Barnes and Company.

Prothrow-Stith, Deborah and Howard R. Spivak 2005. *Sugar and Spice and No Longer Nice: How We Can Stop Girls' Violence*. San Francisco, CA: Jossey-Bass.

Schaffner, Laurie, Shelly Schick, Andrea D. Shorter and Nancy S. Frappier 1996. *Out of Sight, Out of Mind: The Plight of Girls in the San Francisco Juvenile Justice System*. San Francisco, CA: Center for Juvenile and Criminal Justice.

Siegal, Nina 1995. 'Where the Girls Are.' *San Francisco Bay Guardian* October 4, 19–20.

Simon, Rita James 1975. *Women and Crime*. Lexington, MA: Lexington Books.

Snyder, Howard N. and Melissa Sickmund 2006. *Juvenile Offenders and Victims: 2006 National Report* (NCJ 178257). Washington, DC: U.S. Department of Justice, Office of Justice Programs, Office of Juvenile Justice and Delinquency Prevention.

Sommers, Ira and Deborah Baskin 1992. 'Sex, Race, Age, and Violent Offending.' *Violence and Victims* **7**: 191–201.

Sommers, Ira and Deborah Baskin 1993. 'The Situational Context of Violent Female Offending.' *Journal of Research in Crime and Delinquency* **30**: 136–162.

Steffensmeier, Darrell, Schwartz Jennifer, Hua Zhong and Jeff Ackerman 2005. 'An Assessment of Recent Trends in Girls' Violence Using Diverse Longitudinal Sources: Is the Gender Gap Closing?' *Criminology* **43**: 355–406.

Venkatesh, Sudhir Alladi 2006. *Off the Books: The Underground Economy of the Urban Poor*. Cambridge, MA: Harvard University Press.

Viner, Elana 2003. Personal communication with the second author (Chesney-Lind on October 21).

Wacquant, Loic 2001. 'Deadly Symbiosis: When Ghetto and Prison Meet and Mesh.' *Punishment and Society* **3**: 95–134.

West, Candace and Don H. Zimmerman 1987. 'Doing Gender.' *Gender & Society* **1**: 125–51.

Wilson, William J. 1987. *The Truly Disadvantaged: The Inner City, the Underclass, and Public Policy*. Chicago, IL: University of Chicago Press.

Wilson, William J. 1996. *When Work Disappears: The World of the New Urban Poor*. New York, NY: Alfred A. Knopf.

[9]

MISSING GENDER IN CASES OF INFAMOUS SCHOOL VIOLENCE: INVESTIGATING RESEARCH AND MEDIA EXPLANATIONS*

MONA J.E. DANNER**

DIANNE CYR CARMODY***

Old Dominion University

The shootings at Columbine and Jonesboro, along with multiple shootings at five other schools, captured the nation's attention and received widespread media coverage. Utilizing a feminist perspective that addresses masculinity, we explore research and major newspaper coverage of infamous school violence to determine how extensively gender is considered as a contributing factor. Results indicate that data sources on violent deaths at school miss the gendered nature of the violence. Similarly, media coverage of the seven cases under study discount the role of masculinities, bullying, and male violence against girls and women, and few of the policy recommendations address these concerns. The relative absence of attention to the gendered nature of school violence encourages incomplete explanations and ineffective policies.

* The authors gratefully acknowledge suggestions for improvement of this manuscript, received from the editor and three anonymous reviewers. We also thank LeKeshia Washington and Elizabeth Barnes for their assistance in data collection. An earlier version of this paper was presented at the 1998 annual meetings of the American Society of Criminology, held in Washington, DC. Address correspondence to the authors at the Department of Sociology and Criminal Justice, Old Dominion University, Norfolk, VA 23529; e-mail MDanner@odu.edu; DCarmody@odu.edu.

** Mona J.E. Danner is an associate professor of sociology and criminal justice at Old Dominion University. Her interests are in criminal justice and social inequality (gender, race/ethnicity, class, nation), and women globally. Her research on the effects on women of crime control policies ("Three Strikes and It's *Women* Who Are Out: The Hidden Consequences for Women of Criminal Justice Policy Reforms") is a chapter in *Crime Control and Women: Feminist Implications of Criminal Justice Policy* (edited by Susan L. Miller; Sage, 1998). Professor Danner is a recipient of the New Scholar Award from the Division on Women and Crime of the American Society of Criminology.

*** Dianne Cyr Carmody is an assistant professor of sociology and criminal justice at Old Dominion University. Her research focuses on the criminal victimization of women and children and on the media coverage of crime. Professor Carmody has published several articles and book chapters on sexual assault, domestic violence, and related topics.

88   GENDER AND SCHOOL VIOLENCE

The April 1999 shootings at Columbine High School in Littleton, Colorado and the March 1998 shootings at a Jonesboro, Arkansas middle school were among seven cases of multiple shootings by students in U.S. schools that received widespread media coverage over a 19-month period. These seven shootings—in Pearl, Mississippi; West Paducah, Kentucky; Stamps, Arkansas; Jonesboro, Arkansas; Fayetteville, Tennessee; Littleton, Colorado; and Conyers, Georgia—involved nine perpetrators and resulted in 24 deaths and injuries to 58 persons. Columbine and Jonesboro in particular received significant media attention because of the large number of victims, the use of high-powered weapons, and the clothing worn by the assailants. Columbine stood out because of the audaciousness of the direct attack, the trench coats worn by the assailants, and the affluent suburban location. Jonesboro was memorable because of its status as the site of the first dramatic assault, the youth of the offenders and nearly all of the victims, the ambush style of attack, the offenders' camouflage clothing, and the rural southern location.

In addition to reporting the details of the shootings, newspaper journalists attempted to answer the questions that occupied many minds: "Why? Why this shooting? Why this rash of shootings in schools?" Experts, politicians, and parents indicted the general culture of violence in the United States, a southern culture of violence, media violence in the news and entertainment industries, a generation of kids out of control, gangs, individual psychopathology, family problems, and guns.

Only a very few commentators paid attention to one of the most striking features of the shootings: the gendered nature of the violence. A sex-specific count reveals that these seven shootings, by nine male students, resulted in the deaths of 13 female and nine male students as well as one female and one male teacher, and injuries to 32 female and 24 male students and two female teachers. Statistically, 100 percent of the offenders were male and 59 percent of the victims were female.

During the initial days following the attack in Jonesboro, we were struck by what we perceived as a lack of attention to gender by the media in general and by expert commentators in particular, especially because the earliest reports linked the incident to a girl's rejection of one of the boys. These observations motivated the present project, which is designed to explore the following question: To what extent, if any, is gender implicated in the explanations and proposed policy responses found in the scholarly literature and media reports surrounding cases of infamous school violence? We introduce the concept of "infamous school violence" to refer to violent acts in schools that generate widespread media attention.

To address the question, we first present feminist theory as the analytical framework that guides the investigation. We then review the literature on school violence, especially regarding violent deaths at school. The literature review reveals that the two primary data sources on school-associated deaths completely miss the gendered nature of the violence in their investigations and reports. After discussing relevant research on media coverage of crime, we describe our content analysis of major newspaper coverage of seven cases of infamous school violence. Finally, we discuss the implications of these findings.

THE CONTRIBUTIONS OF A FEMINIST THEORETICAL ANALYSIS

A feminist theoretical perspective guides our research. Feminist theory is "a women-centered description and explanation of human experience and the social world" (Danner 1991:51); thus feminist researchers place women at the center of inquiry. Where the issue initially appears to be gender-neutral, as in discussions of "school violence," feminists ask "Where are women and girls?" and "Where is a gender-aware investigation or interpretation of the phenomenon?" The questions arise because of our awareness that gender matters.

Feminists understand that along with race/ethnicity and social class, "gender is a central organizing principle for contemporary life" (Caulfield and Wonders 1994:215). Feminists assume that "gender is not a natural fact but a complex social, historical, and cultural product," and that "gender and gender relations order social life and social institutions in fundamental ways" that result in "constructs of masculinity and femininity (that) are not symmetrical but are based on an organizing principle of men's superiority and social and political-economic dominance over women" (Daly and Chesney-Lind 1988:504). "Gender" refers to the socially constructed meanings attached to "sex," the biological differences between females and males which produce visible secondary sex characteristics. Because biological sex remains relatively constant while societal meanings of femaleness/femininity and maleness/masculinity vary across historical time and geographical space, biology cannot be a sufficient explanation for gender inequality. Close attention to "sex" — as in counting the male and female offenders and victims and making disproportionate numbers a research problem — implies close attention to "gender," especially when such attention has not been given previously.

Further, all social institutions, including those associated with intellectual inquiry and the pursuit of knowledge, are gendered in that they "reflect men's views of the natural and social world" (Daly and Chesney-Lind 1988:504). Because men's views and experiences have been assumed to be the norm, feminist placement of women and gender at the center of inquiry challenges the social and intellectual world, including the criminological discipline. Eigenberg, Mullins, and Scarborough (1994:45) note that this challenge comes in the form of two questions: "First, are gender and the effects of gender socialization examined in this study or theoretical discussion? And second, would the answer to this research question be the same if gender was included in the analysis?"

By highlighting gender, feminists "make women visible and interrogate and deconstruct the manner in which women do appear" (Danner 1998:3); feminists also make men and masculinity visible. As a discipline, criminology has largely maintained an unquestioned male-centered orientation and has ignored or denigrated feminist insights. The relatively small proportion of females in arrest rates remains the primary explanation for this lack of attention to gender. Yet it is exactly this overrepresentation of men and boys in crime and violence that demands investigation: Why is masculinity so criminogenic? A gender-aware investigation of school violence focuses attention on boys, who are the great majority of offenders, as gendered beings — that is, as males who move through the world exploring, asserting, and defending their masculinity.

"The idealized form of masculinity in a given historical setting" is hegemonic masculinity (Messerschmidt 1993:82; also see Connell 1987, 1995). In the contemporary United States, hegemonic masculinity remains defined as different and separate from, in opposition and superior to, femininity. Boys become "real men" or "normal men" through active heterosexuality, homophobia, physical strength and aggression, the objectification and control of females, and the willingness to use violence to achieve one's goals or protect one's interests (Connell 1987, 1995; Messerschmidt 1993). Yet "boys will be boys' differently, depending upon their position in social structures and, therefore, upon their access to power and resources"; thus a variety of masculinities exists (Messerschmidt 1993:87-88). Subordinated masculinities are those which are identified as less masculine, in part because they approach femininity, resist hegemonic masculinity, or are subordinate as the result of race/ethnicity or class. This category includes boys and men who are identified as "faggots," "geeks," "nerds," "brains," "wimps," "mama's boys," "sissies," "pushovers," "fatties," or "freaks."

Hegemonic masculinity does not cause violence, but male violence, force, harassment, and bullying are resources for "doing" masculinity: that is, for "creating differences between girls and boys and women and men" (West and Zimmerman 1987:137) by engaging in behaviors that assert one's manliness, whether the acts are directed toward females or other males. As noted by Braithwaite and Daly (1998:152), the gendered pattern of violence implicates multiple masculinities. "Men's violence toward men involves a masculinity of status competition and bravado among peers. . . . Men's rape and assault of women reflect a masculinity of domination, control, humiliation, and degradation of women." When directed toward other males, violent behavior may represent dominance bonding among members of a group's elite, such as a high school's "jocks," or retaliation against the elite by males who have been victims of bullying. In essence, bullying by high-status males is a challenge to the victim's masculinity, which in turn "may motivate social action toward masculine resources. . .that correct the subordinating social situation" (Messerschmidt 2000:13).

Stanko and Hobdell (1993:43) document that male victims of assault "view their victimization through a male frame." The assault victims they interviewed reported feeling weak, helpless, vulnerable, and less manly as result of the attacks. They also reported being angry, and they prepared themselves for future attacks both psychologically and physically by arming themselves; these strategies were a resource for reclaiming their sense of safety and security as well as their manliness. Similarly, school violence by boys may be a response to masculinity challenges and therefore a resource for accomplishing masculinity. This may be particularly true when violence is perpetrated by low-status boys.

We have already provided a sex-specific count of assailants and victims in seven cases of infamous school violence. This count alone clearly demonstrates that such violence is not gender-neutral; females accounted for 59 percent of the victims (what some would argue is a relatively even distribution), but 100 percent of the offenders were male. If school violence were not gendered, sex-specific counts of assailants as well as victims should be proportionate to the population. The fact that they are not, in combination with insights acquired from a feminist theoretical framework that problematizes masculinity, suggests that "the gendered nature of school violence" has several implications. First, one sex (in this case, males) is represented disproportionately among assailants and/or victims. Second, when violence is perpetrated by low-status males against high-status males or random victims, it suggests a response to masculinity challenges such as bullying. Third, when violence is perpetrated by either high- or low-status males against current, former or desired girlfriends or random females, it is an assertion of masculine superiority in the subordination of female autonomy. Working on this theoretical foundation, we examine the popular explanations and proposed policy responses found in the scholarly literature and media reports surrounding cases of infamous school violence.

REVIEW OF THE LITERATURE

School Violence

"School violence" refers to violence that occurs in or around K-12 schools. Elliott, Hamburg, and Williams define school violence as

> . . .the threat or use of physical force with the intention of causing physical injury, damage, or intimidation of another person. . .this includes homicide, aggravated assault, armed robbery, and forcible rape. . . . It also includes shoving, punching, hitting, and throwing objects when the intent is to harm or intimidate another human being. Verbal and psychological abuse are not included. . . (1998:13)

This definition provides the framework for most of the literature and for the most comprehensive data resource on school violence, *Indicators of School Crime and Safety, 1998* and *1999* (Kaufman et al. 1998; Kaufman et al. 1999). Produced by the U.S. Departments of Education and Justice by order of President Clinton after the December 1997 shootings in West Paducah, Kentucky, *Indicators* is a compilation of data from various sources including (among others) the National Crime Victimization Survey (NCVS), the 1989 and 1995 School Crime Supplement to the NCVS, and the Monitoring the Future study.

Indicators of School Crime and Safety, 1999 reported more than 1.05 million violent victimizations (serious violent crimes and simple assaults) at school experienced by students ages 12 to 18 in 1997, a rate of 40 violent victimizations per 1,000 students. Only 201,800 of these were serious violent crimes (rape, sexual assault, robbery, aggravated assault), a rate of eight per 1,000 students; most of the violent victimizations were simple assaults (Kaufman et al. 1999:45). Elliott et al. (1998:4-5) described the violence experienced by young people in the 1990s as an "epidemic" of lethal, random violence that was more likely to occur in places formerly regarded as safe, such as schools. In reality, however, violent victimization at school actually declined every year from 1992 to 1997 (Kaufman et al. 1999:45). In fact, schools have been relatively safe places for children and teens: there they are at far less risk of death and injury than in their own homes or neighborhoods (Donohue, Schiraldi, and Ziedenberg 1998; Kaufman et al. 1999).

Few students fear violent victimization at school. Only 9 percent of students in 1995 said that sometimes or most of the time they feared being attacked or harmed at school (Kaufman et al. 1999:71). Although boys were more at risk of violent victimization than girls, girls reported more fear of attack or harm at school or traveling to or from school (Kaufman et al. 1999:71).

Gangs are a particular concern in school violence research, and appear to be prevalent in schools. In 1995, 28 percent of students reported that street gangs were present at their school, nearly double the 15 percent reported in 1989 (Kaufman et al. 1999:32). Students who reported being the victims of any violent crime at school, knowing a student who brought a gun to school, or seeing a student with a gun at school also were more likely to report the presence of street gangs at school (Kaufman et al. 1999:19). The 1995 School Crime Supplement to the NCVS asked students specifically whether gangs had been involved in school violence, drug sales, or bringing guns to school, but analyses of those responses have not been published. Thus we know that students identified gangs in their schools, but we do not know the extent of gang involvement in, or responsibility for, violent victimizations.

Bullying is a more frequent problem for students in school than violent criminal victimization. Estimates of the extent of bullying vary widely, depending on the definition employed. The National Household Education Survey defined bullying as behaviors that "treat other persons abusively or affect others by means of force or coercion" (Kaufman et al. 1999:153). Eight percent of students in 1993 reported that they had been bullied at school during the year, one-half million more than had reported violent victimization in that year (Kaufman et al. 1999:53, 42). A broader definition of bullying, also called peer child abuse, includes "name calling, fistfights, purposeful ostracism, extortion, character assassination, libel, repeated physical attacks, and sexual harassment" (Arnette and Walsleben 1998:3). The *1999 Annual Report on School Safety* (U.S. Department of Education and U.S. Department of Justice 1999:10) reported that approximately 15 percent of 11-, 13-, and 15-year-olds "had been bullied because of their religion or race," and "over 30 percent. . .had been bullied by sexual jokes, comments, or gestures directed at them."

Limbar and Nation's (1998:4) summary of school case studies reveals a greater prevalence of bullying than those found in national surveys. According to one study, 25 percent of grade 4 to 6 students in the rural south "had been bullied with some regularity within the past 3 months." Another study in small midwestern junior and senior high schools reported that 77 percent of students had been bullied at some point in their school years. When bullying involves physical contact, it reaches at least the level of simple assault, but the extent to which students identify this as a crime remains unclear.

Research indicates that boys and girls experience bullying differently (Farrington 1993). Boys are more likely than girls both to bully and to be bullied. Bullying behavior decreases significantly with age for girls, but less so for boys. In addition, boys and girls bully differently. Boys are more likely than girls to engage in direct physical bullying, although most bullying by boys is verbal or nonphysical harassment. Girls generally use "more subtle and indirect ways of harassment such as slandering, spreading of rumors, and manipulation of friendship relationships" (Olweus 1993:19). Finally, boys overwhelmingly are bullied by other boys, whereas most girls are bullied by boys or by both boys and girls (Olweus 1993:19; also see Farrington 1993).

Most scholarly explanations of school violence point to social structural/ecological and situational perspectives (Anderson 1998; Fagan and Wilkinson 1998a; Gottfredson and Gottfredson 1985; Welsh 2000). Unsafe schools are usually surrounded by socially disorganized communities with high rates of poverty, single-parent households, and limited economic and educational opportunities. In addition, the climate in the school matters: negative perceptions of rule clarity and fairness, respect for the principal, cooperation between teachers and administrators, and school attachment are correlated with school violence. Finally, "situational approaches view violent events as interactions involving the confluence of motivations, perceptions, technology (in this case, weapons), the social control attributes of the immediate setting, and the ascribed meaning and status attached to the violent act" (Fagan and Wilkinson 1998b:128; also see Luckenbill 1977; Luckenbill and Doyle 1989). In short, socially disorganized communities and negative school climates combine to make violence seem an acceptable or even necessary act in interpersonal interactions.

To address problems of school violence, the U.S. Departments of Education (DOE), Health and Human Services (HHS), and Justice (DOJ) have long funded a variety of prevention and intervention programs; DARE and the Safe and Drug-Free Schools Program are well-known examples. Such programs include training in conflict resolution, building social skills, anger control, mentoring, after-school activities, programs designed to help students talk about victimization without identifying the talk as tattling, and zero tolerance for violence and bullying (Arnette and Walsleben 1998; OJJDP 1999).

The Safe Schools/Healthy Students Initiative is the most recent multiyear, multimillion-dollar government funding opportunity. The Initiative's goal is to promote "healthy childhood development and prevent violence and alcohol and drug abuse" through coordinated and comprehensive "educational, mental health, social service, law enforcement, and juvenile justice system services" (U.S. Department of Education and U.S. Department of Justice 1999:11). The Initiative was announced in direct response to school shootings that involved multiple fatalities: 54 grants were awarded in 1999.

School Violence Resulting in Death: The Data

Data about school violence resulting in death comes primarily from two sources: a study conducted by the Centers for Disease Control and Prevention (CDC) published in the *Journal of the American Medical Association* (Kachur et al. 1996) and information collected by and maintained on the website of the National School Safety Center (1998, 2000). Although both serve as important resources for information about school violence resulting in death, their gender-neutral tone camouflages important realities about the gendered quality of such violence.

The CDC researchers worked with the National School Safety Center to identify 105 instances of school-associated violent deaths from 1992 to 1994: 85 homicides and 20 suicides (Kachur et al. 1996). The definition employed in the study focused on location: violent deaths on the campus, on the way to campus, or while the victim was attending or traveling to or from an official school event. Sixty percent of the deaths occurred in urban communities, followed by suburban (30.5 percent) and rural locations (9.5 percent). Deaths were more likely to occur in secondary (70.5 percent) than in elementary schools, and to be caused by firearms (77 percent). Only 65 percent of the deaths occurred on campus; the rest occurred off campus on streets or sidewalks, in vehicles, or on private property.

Because the definition focused on the location of incidents, victims included staff members, nonstudents, and nonstaff members as well as students. Most victims (72 percent) were students at the time of death; these included a higher proportion of homicide victims (74 percent) than of suicide victims (65 percent). Given that most victims were students, it is not surprising that most (77 percent) were under age 20, although this was true for more victims of homicide (80 percent) than of suicide (65 percent). Males were the most frequent victims of death at school: 83 percent of the total cases, 81 percent of homicides, and 90 percent of suicides. The researchers identified nine possible motives for the deaths. Interpersonal disputes that did not involve romantic relationships were the most common motive (33 percent), followed by gang-related activities (31 percent). Disputes over romantic relationships were the fifth most frequently cited motive, accounting for just 11 percent of cases.

The authors called the study the "first systematic review of school-associated homicides and suicides across the country," and stated that they were interested primarily in estimating the risk of violent death in schools and in identifying common features of the cases (Kachur et al. 1996:1729). They relied heavily on descriptive statistics and, to a far lesser extent, matched-pairs analysis. In matched-pairs analysis they identified the ratio of discordant pairs for the 79 homicides for which data on both victims and primary offenders were available. One of the variables was "male," but the authors' comment about the ratio of discordant pairs on this variable obscured the importance of gender: "[V]ictims were less likely than primary offenders to have been male" (Kachur et al. 1996:1732).

The information presented must be scrutinized very closely in order to reveal the gendered nature of the violence. Such scrutiny reveals that males were the victims in 81 percent of the cases, but in only 3 percent of those cases was the offender a female. In sharp contrast, the offender was male in 100 percent of the cases in which a female was murdered. From the data contained in the article, it is impossible to determine other relevant details of these homicides, such as students' status, age, or motive. On the basis of what we know about violence against women (Bachman 1994), however, it is possible that many of these female homicides involving male offenders were related to romantic disputes, and that some of the male suicides in the study followed the killing of a female. In fact, at least 10 percent of the 40 deaths occurring at schools in 1997-1998 fit this profile exactly (Donohue et al. 1998). It is unremarkable, given the statistics on violent crime in general, that males were overrepresented as offenders and that all murdered females were the victims of males; even so, these facts are made invisible by the continual use of the gender-neutral term "students."

The National School Safety Center worked with the CDC on the Kachur et al. (1996) study and features it prominently on its web page. The Center still maintains a count of school-associated deaths, based on newspaper reports, and has recorded 261 such deaths since 1992; 76 of these have occurred since the beginning of the 1997-1998 school year (National School Safety Center 2000).

The current list of motives for all cases in the data set excludes "disputes over romantic relationships" and identifies these simply as "interpersonal disputes," thereby disguising the gendered nature of this type of violence.

School Violence Resulting in Death: Policy Responses

The seeming rash of school shootings resulting in death during 1997-1999 frightened parents and politicians, who responded with a call for hearings, studies, and policy recommendations. After the December 1997 shootings in West Paducah, President Clinton ordered the Departments of Justice and Education to produce an annual report on school violence ("Clinton Orders" 1997; Radio Address 1997). The House of Representatives held a hearing after the Jonesboro shootings. Although gun availability and gun control were among the most frequently cited and hotly contested explanations in the media, these issues did not appear in official policy recommendations nor in school practices. The Justice Policy Institute (Donohue et al. 1998) noted four primary responses by politicians: ending after-school programs,[1] assigning police officers to schools, imposing expulsions and suspensions in cases of threats of violence, and trying juveniles as adults. *Indicators of School Crime and Safety, 1998* (National Center for Education Statistics 1998), occasioned by President Clinton's order, reported that the most common school practices and policies related to safety include zero tolerance policies toward serious student offenses, especially for possession of firearms; various security measures such as requiring visitors to sign in and restricting students from leaving school for lunch; and formal school violence prevention or reduction programs. Schools rarely reported having police regularly on the premises.

The Justice Policy Institute's report, *School House Hype* (Donohue et al. 1998), correctly identified much of the response to the shootings as a moral panic. The Institute's review of data from Kachur et al. (1996), the National School Safety Center, and other reports focused on the fact that violent deaths at school are extraordinarily rare, despite the 1997-1998 shootings, especially when compared with other risks of violence that youths face, such as death from family violence. In addition, Donohue et al. (1998:6-7) pointed out that at least four of the multiple deaths at schools during 1997-1998 were murder-suicides not involving students, in which a male killed a female over a romantic relationship. They

---

[1] The governor of Virginia proposed eliminating after-school programs after a nonfatal shooting in Richmond (as cited in Donohue et al. 1998:13). He later submitted legislation that would allow students to possess weapons on school grounds during hunting season (Hardy and Schapiro 1999).

proposed three policies aimed at reducing the violence facing children: expanding after-hours programs in schools, restricting mass gun sales, and encouraging the media to provide the correct context in cases of school violence.

We cannot overemphasize the significance of the failure of the Kachur et al. (1996) study to recognize the salience of gender: the great majority of assailants were male, and all of the deaths of girls and women occurred at the hands of males. The findings occupied important places on the National School Safety Center's (1998) website, in the Justice Policy Institute's report (Donohue et al. 1998), and in Congressional testimony. In addition, this study still is the only data source about deaths due to violence at schools cited in three recently released government reports: *Indicators of School Crime and Safety, 1998* (Kaufman et al. 1998), the Office of Juvenile Justice and Delinquency Prevention's *Combating Fear and Restoring Safety in School* (Arnette and Walsleben 1998), and the *1998 Annual Report on School Safety* (U.S. Departments of Education and Justice 1998).

The consequences of ignoring the gendered quality of the violence are revealed in the policy recommendations contained in these sources. Only the *1998 Annual Report on School Safety* mentions gender-based violence, and only in the context of model programs for improving school safety. Six percent of the 47 model programs identified deal with sexual harassment or sexual violence; another 6 percent address bullying. None of the 54 Safe Schools/Healthy Student Initiative grants described in the *1999 Annual Report on School Safety* (U.S. Departments of Education and Justice 1999) mention sexual harassment or dating violence; only two mention bullying. None of the recommendations in any publication address the fact that most females killed in school-associated violence are murdered by males. The factors associated with doing masculinity thus are not recognized as factors contributing to at least some of the violence in schools.

Although such reports influence our understanding of school violence, common sense and research tell us that public opinion and policy recommendations are also influenced by the media. The impact of the media has been documented in a variety of studies. Forst and Blomquist (1991) traced an increase in social concern about the plight of missing children to the increase in media attention to the topic. This led to increased political pressure to respond to the problem. In a similar vein, Fishman (1978) illustrated the role of the media in creating a perceived "crime wave" by emphasizing crimes against the elderly in New York City in 1976. Politicians responded to public concerns by allocating additional staff members to special police squads and introducing legislation. Although it would be simplistic to argue that the relationship between public policy and media coverage of events is direct and clear, the media certainly provide us with the frames of reference for perceiving our world (Surrette 1992). For this reason it is critical to explore the media images of crime and infamous school violence.

Media Coverage of Crime and Violence

Many journalists underestimate their role in the social construction of events, but routine practices of the media result in repetitive patterns in the coverage of crime. Warr (1982:187) argued that media distortions in crime coverage are due to the "overemphasis on violent crime, the creation of artificial crime waves, the use of crime news as 'filler,' misleading reports of crime statistics, and police control of crime news." It is important to examine repetitive media images of crime for several reasons. First, as researchers note, public attitudes about crime are affected by the media; greater exposure to mass media sources may result in inaccurate beliefs about crime (Cavender and Bond-Maupin 1993; Graber 1980; Surrette 1998). Public surveys have shown that up to 95 percent of the general population cite the mass media as their primary source of information on crime (Tunnell 1992). In addition, some researchers argue that heavy media exposure is linked to heightened fear of crime (Altheide 1997; Glassner 1999; Graber 1980); others question this connection, however, especially in the case of print media (Chiricos, Eschholz, and Gertz 1997; Gomme 1986; Liska and Baccaglini 1990). Public opinion polls following the Jonesboro and Columbine shootings reflected parents' fear for their children's safety at school (Gillespie 2000). Most respondents also believed it was likely that a school shooting could occur in their community (Saad 1999). The media clearly devote an inordinate amount of attention to murder (Chermak 1995; Meyers 1997); researchers have suggested that this emphasis shapes policies on crime and justice as well as attitudes in the general public (Surrette 1998).

Some journalists present themselves as impartial and objective reporters of reality (Beckett 1997; Tuchman 1972), but research suggests that journalists' presentation of the news reflects a clear selection bias (Condit 1989; McAdam, McCarthy and Zald 1988; Tuchman 1978). Journalists follow clear rules for event selection: drama, titillation, personal focus, and simplification determine newsworthiness (Caringella-MacDonald and Humphries 1998). An event is considered newsworthy if it is unusual or strange (Chermak 1995; Liska and Baccaglini 1990). Journalists also organize stories around typifications that support existing images

100   GENDER AND SCHOOL VIOLENCE

and assumptions (Hall 1977; Tuchman 1974, 1978). These typifications provide ready-made scripts that support race and gender stereotypes (Chermak 1995; Meyers 1997).

On the basis of the concepts of newsworthiness and typifications, the school shooting cases had clear news value. In the United States, journalists report fairly routinely on violent crimes, but the school shooting cases were sensational because of their variation on this theme. It is not especially newsworthy when certain children are murdered (witness the relative lack of coverage of homicides of most inner-city children), but it is unusual for 10-year-olds to shoot their classmates on school property in rural areas. These cases violated cultural beliefs concerning children's capacity for lethal violence and schools as safe havens.

In addition, those shootings which involved male offenders and female victims fit easily into the popular typification of male aggression and female victimization (Meyers 1997). They could be scripted easily and were consistent with popular gender stereotypes, making them attractive to journalists. Thus they reinforced popular cultural beliefs about male violence and female victimization (Caringella-MacDonald 1998; Carmody 1998; Madriz 1997).

The 1989 massacre of 14 women in Montreal demonstrates the failure of the media to recognize gender-based violence as such. On December 6, a man entered a classroom in a science and engineering building at the École Polytechnique, ordered the men and the women to go to separate sides of the room, and announced "The women here are a bunch of feminists." He allowed the men to leave the room and then shot and killed seven women. After walking through the building and killing seven more women, he killed himself (Bertrand 1991:3). In a suicide letter the gunman wrote that he undertook these actions "for political reasons" aimed at "the feminists who have always ruined [his] life" (Bertrand 1991:24). The gunman's letter indicted women engaged in nontraditional work and ended with a list of 19 prominent women who also would have died that day but for "the lack of time." Media coverage and commentary on the massacre by law enforcement, politicians, and pundits ignored the gunman's own statements, constructed him as a madman, and denied feminists' calls for the recognition of the gender-based nature of the act (Caputi and Russell 1992; Juteau and Laurin-Frenette 1991; Radford 1992; Rosenberg 1996).

In the present analysis, we examine newspaper coverage of seven infamous school shootings. Although we suspect that the media may tend to ignore or minimize the role of gender in these cases, it is important to explore the most popular media frames or themes in these articles and to subject our suspicions to scientific investigation. Research suggests that media coverage of crime influences the audience's perceptions of crime and affects criminal justice policy; therefore it is imperative that we examine these issues in the current analysis.

THE SAMPLE OF CASES

We initially identified the sample of infamous school violence cases included here in media accounts of the Jonesboro shootings (Bragg 1998). We then expanded it to include additional incidents that occurred in the 1997-1999 school years.

Not all acts of violence within schools receive national media exposure. Thus it is not the violence per se that causes a case to be labeled "infamous," but the media attention given to the incident; generally, but not always, these acts involve multiple shootings resulting in at least one death. But not even all multiple shootings are newsworthy. For instance, the media account that we used initially to identify the cases for analysis mentioned a case in Norwalk, California. In late October 1997, a 21-year-old male shot and killed his 16-year-old former girlfriend and himself at John Glenn High School (Bragg 1998). Yet in our database search we found no articles specifically covering the Norwalk shooting; retrievals using terms connected with the Norwalk case yielded articles about other cases and mentioned Norwalk only in passing. This relative lack of media attention disqualifies Norwalk as "infamous," and we did not include it in the analysis. Other cases also could have been included: In 1998, school shootings occurred in Edinboro, Pennsylvania, Pomona, California, and Springfield, Oregon, among other places. When we undertook data collection, however, the search engine did not bring them up.

In the present analysis we examine newspaper coverage of infamous school shootings. We chose newspapers rather than television or radio reports for two reasons. First, newspapers are searched easily via a variety of indexes; radio and television stories are far more difficult to trace and collect. Second, newspaper stories often serve as the foundation for radio, television, and magazine news about crime (Meyers 1997). As Ericson, Baranek, and Chan (1991:43-46) observe, "[B]roadcast journalists use newspaper reports verbatim, as background detail that they cite without attribution, for matching stories suitable to their medium, and as second day leads, that. . .further the story through a different angle, or at least a different twist." For these reasons, we chose newspapers as the data source for our content analysis. Table 1 contains information about the sample of cases.

102   GENDER AND SCHOOL VIOLENCE

Table 1.   Seven Cases of Infamous School Violence

Pearl, MS	On October 1, 1997, a 16-year-old boy used a butcher knife to kill his mother at home. Then he drove to school, where he shot and killed his ex-girlfriend and her best female friend, and wounded four other girls and three boys (Edsall 1997).
West Paducah, KY	On December 1, 1997, shots fired into a prayer circle at a high school by a 14-year-old boy killed three girls and wounded three other girls and two boys (Braun and Pasternak 1997).
Stamps, AR	On December 15, 1997, a 14-year-old boy shot two girls outside their rural high school (Watts 1999).
Jonesboro, AR	The March 24, 1998 shootings by two boys age 11 and 13 resulted in the deaths of four girls and one female teacher and the injuries of 12 girls, one boy, and another female teacher (Schwartz 1998).
Fayetteville, TN	On May 19, 1998, an 18-year-old male shot and killed another male student in the school parking lot. The two had argued over a girlfriend (Watts 1999).
Littleton, CO	On April 20, 1999, two young men used semiautomatic weapons and bombs to kill four female and eight male classmates, a male teacher, and themselves. They also wounded eight female and 14 male students and one female teacher (Watts 1999).
Conyers, GA	On May 20, 1999, a 15-year-old male armed with two guns walked into the commons area of Heritage High School and opened fire, wounding two female and four male students (Firestone 1999).

METHODOLOGY

We identified and downloaded print articles using the on-line Lexis-Nexis search engine. The media sources we searched were *The Washington Post, The Los Angeles Times, The New York Times,* and wire services (United Press International, AAP Newsfeed, and Associated Press). Lexis-Nexis is the premier search engine but it covers only major newspapers (newspapers of record). Thus it does not include other print media sources or local newspapers, any of which might have offered alternative accounts of the shootings.

The search, conducted between April 15, 1998 and December 1999, focused on the cases of infamous school violence listed in Table 1. The offenders' names and city locations served as key search terms; we also used "school violence" as a search term, but this yielded only articles already retrieved. Articles published within two weeks of the event were included in the analysis.

Content analysis of all articles focused on the identification of dominant frames or explanations offered for the crimes; we coded up to five explanations for each article. A frame is a "(schema) of interpretation that allows its user to locate, perceive, identify, and label a seemingly infinite number of concrete occurrences" (Goffman 1974:21). Thus frames are "unifying concepts" (Gamson 1988) used to organize information. Frames frequently assign blame or causality for the event under discussion (Snow and Benford 1992). In this analysis, we were interested in how each crime was "framed" in the news article: that is, what explanations were offered to explain the event. We also coded the gender and occupation or profession of the source associated with the frame.

Our search yielded a total of 230 articles: 33 on Jonesboro, 15 on Pearl, 16 on Conyers, 134 on Littleton, 21 on West Paducah, seven on Fayetteville, and four on Stamps. From an initial reading of the articles, we identified dominant themes. We then constructed operational definitions of these themes to produce the frames we utilized. Each article was coded by two independent coders using the frames as shown in Table 2. Intercoder reliability was 84 percent. For each article, up to five frames could be identified. For purposes of this study, the frame was the unit of analysis ($N = 489$).

FINDINGS

As Table 3 shows, the most frequent explanation for the shootings was "response to bullying" (19.6 percent of all frames). This frame captures explanations that described the offenders' violence as a response to being "picked on" or bullied by fellow students. Journalists frequently described the school social environment as an emotionally painful place, where the offenders were the target of taunting and mean-spirited jokes at the hands of more popular students. In this context, the shootings were portrayed as the expression of pent-up rage and frustration.

The second most frequent frame concerned guns (15.7 percent). Here we counted explanations that focused on the easy availability of weapons, the modeling of gun use by relatives, or the widespread cultural approval of guns. This frame was especially prominent in media coverage of the shootings in Jonesboro and Conyers.

The "defies explanation/psychopathology" frame also appeared frequently, accounting for 14.9 percent of the total. To qualify for this category, the explanation had either to specifically state that the offender was mentally ill or to suggest that there was "no rational explanation" for the violence, thus implying that only an "irrational" person would engage in such behavior. This frame appeared in the newspaper coverage of all the shootings under study except the Stamps case.

In some cases (12.5 percent of the frames), the offender warned of the impending violence, either verbally or in writing. The failure of parents and of school and law enforcement officials to recognize these threats and respond appropriately was captured by the

Table 2.   Operational Definitions of Frames Used in Content Analysis of Newspaper Articles on Infamous School Violence Cases

Frame	Operational Definition
Response to Bullying	This frame reflects explanations that linked the violence to the offenders' experience of bullying victimization.
Guns	This frame includes explanations focusing on the easy availability of guns to minors, the modeling of gun use by offenders' relatives, and also the cultural values that support gun use.
Defies Explanation/ Psychopathology	In some articles, offenders were described as "crazy" or "mentally ill." Frequently these explanations were combined with statements such as, "There is no rational explanation for this."
Threats Not Taken Seriously	In several cases, the offenders warned others about the impending attack. Some offered verbal warnings; others posted Internet messages threatening violence.
Retaliation Against Girlfriend	In some articles, the violence was specifically linked to a recent breakup with a girlfriend. In some cases, the violence was focused on a current or former girlfriend.
Media Violence	This frame emphasizes the role of violence in television, movies, video games, and the Internet in an effort to explain the shootings.
Lack of Parental Involvement	Some articles focused on parents' failure to monitor their children. They asked, "How could the parents not know?" and suggested that the offenders' parents should be held accountable.
Kids out of Control	This frame focuses on the "moral decline" of youths as a whole, or emphasizes the lack of societal control over the young.
Child Abuse	The child abuse frame focuses on past physical, sexual, and/or emotional abuse of the offender(s) as an explanation for the violence.
Lack of Religion/ Satanism	This frame focuses on the absence of traditional religious values in the lives of the offender(s). It also includes those who link the violence to the work of Satan.
Drugs	The "drugs" frame focuses on the role of drug abuse on the offenders' behavior.
Gangs	The "gangs" frame explains offenders' actions by linking them to identification with, or membership in, a gang.
Violent Culture	This frame places the school shootings in the larger cultural context of violence. Some connected the shootings to a culture that supports the use of violence in a variety of settings; others emphasized a subculture of violence limited to southern states.
Lack of School Security	Some articles focused on preventive efforts and noted that the shootings might have been avoided if school security efforts had been increased. Metal detectors, searches of backpacks and lockers, and security officers were mentioned.

"threats not taken seriously" frame. This frame appeared frequently in the media coverage of the shootings in West Paducah.

"Retaliation against girlfriend" also was a popular frame, but only in the media coverage of three cases: Jonesboro, Pearl, and

Table 3. Distribution of Frames Among Cases of Infamous School Violence (N = 489)

Frame	Jonesboro, AR n = 111 Col% (N)	Pearl MS n = 35 Col% (N)	Conyers, GA n = 36 Col% (N)	Littleton, CO n = 267 Col% (N)	W.Paducah, KY n = 30 Col% (N)	Fayetteville, TN n = 8 Col% (N)	Stamps, AR n = 2 Col% (N)	Total n = 489 Row% Row (N)
Bullying	1.0 (1)	31.4 (11)	2.8 (1)	25.5 (68)	23.3 (7)	75.0 (6)	100 (2)	19.6 (96)
Guns	23.4 (26)	— (0)	30.5 (11)	13.9 (37)	10.0 (3)	— (0)	— (0)	15.7 (77)
Defies Exp./ Psychopath	15.0 (17)	17.1 (6)	16.7 (6)	14.6 (39)	13.3 (4)	12.5 (1)	— (0)	14.9 (73)
Threats Not Taken Seriously	11.7 (13)	— (0)	16.7 (6)	13.1 (35)	20.0 (6)	12.5 (1)	— (0)	12.5 (61)
Retaliation Against Girlfriend	18.9 (21)	25.7 (9)	30.5 (11)	.4 (1)	— (0)	— (0)	— (0)	8.6 (42)
Media Violence	1.0 (1)	— (0)	— (0)	11.2 (30)	26.7 (8)	— (0)	— (0)	8.0 (39)
Lack of Parental Involvement	3.6 (4)	— (0)	2.8 (1)	10.9 (29)	— (0)	— (0)	— (0)	7.0 (34)
Gangs	4.5 (5)	14.3 (5)	— (0)	2.6 (7)	— (0)	— (0)	— (0)	3.5 (17)
Violent Culture	4.5 (5)	— (0)	— (0)	3.7 (10)	— (0)	— (0)	— (0)	3.1 (15)
Lack of Religion	1.0 (1)	11.4 (4)	— (0)	2.2 (6)	3.3 (1)	— (0)	— (0)	2.5 (12)
Kids out of Control	7.2 (8)	— (0)	— (0)	.4 (1)	— (0)	— (0)	— (0)	1.8 (9)
Child Abuse	7.2 (8)	— (0)	— (0)	.4 (1)	— (0)	— (0)	— (0)	1.8 (9)
Drugs	— (0)	— (0)	— (0)	1.0 (3)	— (0)	— (0)	— (0)	.6 (3)
Lack of School Security	1.0 (1)	— (0)	— (0)	— (0)	3.3 (1)	— (0)	— (0)	.4 (2)
	100 (111)	100 (35)	99.9 (36)	99.9 (267)	99.9 (30)	99.9 (8)	100 (2)	100 (489)

Conyers. Just 8.6 percent of all frames studied focused on this aspect of the violence. Approximately the same amount of attention was received by "media violence" (8 percent) and "lack of parental involvement" (7 percent).

Table 4 links the gender and occupation of the sources with the most popular frames where source data were reported (*N* = 317). For all frames, the sources were primarily male. The largest proportion of female sources (23.1 percent) was associated with the "retaliation against girlfriend" frame.

Sources were divided into seven major categories. The first category, "schoolmate," includes fellow students, some of whom were shooting victims or witnesses to the attacks. Sources in this category were linked to more than half (53.5 percent) of the "response to bullying" frames, 56.4 percent of the "threats not taken seriously" frames, and 62.8 percent of the "retaliation against girlfriend" frames.

Law enforcement officials also were popular with the journalists, and were linked to 17.4 percent of the frames in which sources were identified. These "police" sources typically offered statements

106   GENDER AND SCHOOL VIOLENCE

Table 4. Occupation of Sources Associated with Popular Media Frames in Cases of Infamous School Violence (N = 317)

Frame	Gender % Female	Schoolmate Col % / Row % / (N)			Community Col % / Row % / (N)			Professional Col % / Row % / (N)			Govt.Official Col % / Row % / (N)			Academic Col % / Row % / (N)			Police Col % / Row % / (N)			Offender Col % / Row % / (N)		
Bullying (N = 71)	16.6	34.2	53.5	(38)	7.4	5.6	(4)	23.1	8.5	(6)	6.5	4.2	(3)	13.3	2.8	(2)	20.0	15.5	(11)	70.0	9.9	(7)
Guns (N = 2)	17.3	6.3	13.5	(7)	25.9	26.9	(14)	15.4	7.7	(4)	32.6	28.8	(15)	20.0	5.8	(3)	16.4	17.3	(9)	—	—	(0)
Defies Exp./ Psychopath (N = 63)	18.5	10.8	19.0	(12)	29.6	25.3	(16)	42.3	17.5	(11)	23.9	17.5	(11)	6.7	1.6	(1)	20.0	17.5	(11)	10.0	1.6	(1)
Threats Not Taken Seriously (N = 55)	20.0	27.9	56.4	(31)	20.3	20.0	(11)	7.7	3.6	(2)	2.2	1.8	(1)	6.7	1.8	(1)	14.5	14.5	(8)	10.0	1.8	(1)
Retaliation Against Girlfriend (N = 35)	23.1	19.8	62.8	(22)	5.6	8.6	(3)	3.8	2.9	(1)	4.3	5.7	(2)	13.3	5.7	(2)	7.3	11.4	(4)	10.0	2.9	(1)
Media Violence (N = 17)	4.3	.9	5.9	(1)	3.7	11.8	(2)	3.8	5.9	(1)	17.4	47.0	(8)	6.7	5.9	(1)	7.3	23.5	(4)	—	—	(0)
Lack of Parental Involvement (N = 24)	14.3	—	—	(0)	7.4	16.7	(4)	3.8	4.2	(1)	13.0	25.0	(6)	33.3	20.1	(5)	14.5	33.3	(8)	—	—	(0)
Totals		35.0		(111)	17.0		(54)	8.2		(26)	14.5		(46)	4.7		(15)	17.4		(55)	3.2		(10)

supporting the "response to bullying" and "defies explanation/psychopathology" frames. The next category, "community," includes neighbors, community leaders, and relatives of victims and offenders (17 percent). These individuals may have been associated with offenders and/or victims, but were not involved directly with the shooting. In this group, the "defies explanation/psychopathology," "guns," and "threats not taken seriously" frames were most popular. Government officials and attorneys also were quoted in the articles we studied (14.5 percent). Although most of their explanations qualified for the "guns" frame, many of their statements also supported "defies explanation/psychopathology."

The category "professionals" included members of social service and medical professions, as well as clergy and school officials (8.2 percent of frames with sources identified). The most popular frame linked to this group was "defies explanation/psychopathology." Academics, mostly psychology faculty, were the source in only about 5 percent of the frames. They offered a variety of explanations for the violence, most frequently linked to the "lack of parental involvement" and "guns" frames. Finally, 3.2 percent of the frames were linked to the offenders themselves. In 70 percent of these, the offender's explanation fell into the "response to bullying" frame.

DISCUSSION AND CONCLUSIONS

We began this research by asking "To what extent, if any, is gender implicated in the explanations and proposed policy responses found in the scholarly literature and media reports surrounding cases of infamous school violence?" Schools are important institutions for doing gender, especially for constructing and reproducing hegemonic masculinity in at least two forms: male dominance over females and dominance by high-status males over low-status males (Connell 1996; Lesko 2000). In our content analysis of major newspaper coverage of seven cases of infamous school violence, we found that gender-aware explanations surfaced when appropriate to the case, and were as common as explanations focusing on guns or individual psychopathology.

Those closest to the suspects and victims in the incidents—their classmates—were most likely to report that the violence was a response to bullying or a retaliation against a girlfriend in those cases where this was a likely explanation; they recognized the interpersonal and gendered dynamics behind the attacks. In contrast, "experts" such as academics, professionals, and law enforcement officials rarely identified the violence in this manner. Experts most frequently emphasized individual psychopathology or gun control. In the current study, law enforcement personnel were among the most frequently cited sources. This finding is consistent with earlier research showing that journalists tend to turn to criminal justice professionals first, and to academics last (Surrette 1998; Welch, Fenwick, and Roberts 1997).

Our findings suggest that the persons closest to the violence (e.g., schoolmates, victims) explain it most frequently in terms of bullying or retaliation against a girlfriend. As journalists turn to other sources such as professionals and academics, the explanations tend to focus on other issues such as gun control or individual psychopathology. Media coverage of the Jonesboro case illustrates this phenomenon. All five people killed and 13 of the 14 wounded were female. According to early reports citing classmate sources, one of the offenders was upset because a female student did not want to be his girlfriend; both boys frequently were teased by other students. In addition, within two days of the shootings, the ABC Television newsmagazine, *PrimeTime*, aired an interview with the grandfather of one of the suspects, who said "They [the victims] were selected because of their sex, or who they (were). It was not a random shooting" ("Ambush" 1998:1).

The following morning, National Public Radio's *Morning Edition* broadcast a report examining possible motives for the Arkansas shootings ("Motives" 1998). The story focused on a portion of the U.S. Education Secretary's testimony to a Congressional committee during the previous day, along with interviews with two criminologists and a sociologist. The Education Secretary stated, "[O]ur culture seems to glorify violence. . .from television to movies to comic books to video games." The academics mentioned "a culture of violence in the south," "firearms," "watching violence," "breakdown of the family," "ready availability of guns," "upbringing," "the movies," "the absence of parents," and "various subcultures." None of these experts commented on the gendered nature of the Jonesboro shootings, suggested that violence is a means for asserting one's masculinity, or implicated violence against women and girls in any way.

The Columbine shootings contain a similar story. The group of outcast students known as the "Trench Coat Mafia" were so named by the school's male athletes. The athletes and other popular, high-status boys also taunted the group by calling them "faggots," "geeks," "nerds," and "Goths." They were pushed into lockers. Rocks and mashed potatoes were thrown at them (Cart 1999; Denver 1999). After the shootings, one athlete justified the teasing, stating that the group's members were "different" and "weird" (Wilgoren 1999). In their diaries and videos, the offenders spoke of the jocks as their enemies because of the bullying they had endured. In this case, both groups of male students were "doing masculinity." The popular male students used bullying to assert their hegemonic masculinity; in response to such challenges, the assailants finally used violence, another tool of masculinity.

The media coverage of school shooting cases illustrates an interesting and troubling pattern. The current cases were newsworthy because they offered a variation on the rather routine theme of crime and violence: they involved white children in the safety of their own rural or suburban school. Although they fit neatly into the conceptual frame of "killer kids," the offenders were unusual enough to attract and hold media attention. The gendered quality of the violence, however, was not emphasized in the media coverage of the cases. The fact that young boys were shooting young girls or were shooting randomly after months of being bullied by boys was rarely noticed, especially by experts, and was never presented as an issue of gendered violence. Instead it was framed as evidence of an individual aberration, used to further the agendas of gun control advocates or supporters of media censorship, or discounted because it was most likely to be identified by students, who were viewed as non-experts.

Individual psychopathology emerged as one of the most popular explanations for school violence, and was offered frequently during the initial media coverage of the cases. Sources were attempting to explain violent behaviors that defied explanation; to argue that the offenders were "crazy" apparently was a somewhat comforting response. This emphasis on individual responsibility is a standard frame for crime news (Barlow, Barlow, and Chiricos 1995; Cavender and Mulcahy 1998). It shifts the focus away from larger cultural and structural issues associated with hegemonic masculinity—female subordination and male status hierarchy—and depicts the crime as an isolated event not requiring individual or societal changes.

Female subordination remains a key aspect of hegemonic masculinity. More than two decades of research on domestic violence suggests that the factors which encourage violence against wives also increase the risk of violence against girlfriends (Dobash et al. 1992). Studies have established that sexual harassment and dating violence are widespread among junior and senior high school students and that females are more likely to be the victims of severe forms of physical and sexual abuse in dating relationships (Eder 1995; Levy 1998; Makepeace 1981; Roscoe and Callahan 1985). Stein (1995) argues that teasing and bullying are the antecedents of sexual harassment in schools. Most studies of teens' use of violence, however, indicate that teens minimize its seriousness.

Gamache (1998) observes that such attitudes are reinforced by an inconsistent and ineffective criminal justice response to bullying and dating violence. In addition, parents, teachers, school officials, and even Supreme Court justices support a "boys will be boys" attitude. In *Davis v. Monroe County Board of Education*, the 5-4 majority held that school boards may be held liable under federal law for ignoring the "severe, pervasive and objectively offensive" sexual harassment of one student by another. The Georgia school board had refused to take any action in the case of a 10-year-old girl who was sexually harassed so severely by a fifth-grade boy that her high grades had declined and she had written a suicide note. In his dissenting opinion, Justice Kennedy equated sexual harassment with "the routine problems of adolescence" and described schools as places "where teenage romantic relationships and dating are a part of everyday life. . .a teenager's romantic overtures to a classmate (even when persistent and unwelcome) are an inescapable part of adolescence." Apparently the minority did not find it problematic that some students' access to education was denied because "children's social development (is) rife with inappropriate behavior by children who are just learning to interact with their peers." The problem of gendered violence and the failure to take it seriously pervade our society; it is time to realize that they also permeate our schools.

Again we point to the significance of the failure, by Kachur et al. (1996) and the National School Safety Center (1998, 2000), to recognize the magnitude of gender in school associated deaths. Their error is compounded because it is cited again and again by the Center's staff, government officials, and other experts. By missing the gendered nature of violence in their analyses, these investigators render violence against women and girls invisible. They also miss the crucial role of male bullying in the Columbine tragedy; in their update to the school violence death count, the motive for Columbine is listed as "hate crime" rather than as "response to bullying" (National School Safety Center 2000). In addition, much of the criminological literature on school violence in general hardly notices educational research on bullying, sexual harassment, and the effects of doing masculinity at school (Connell 1989, 1996; Eder 1995; Lesko 2000; Stein 1995).

The consequences of ignoring the gendered quality of this violence are revealed in the policy recommendations made by experts, politicians, and parents, and reported in the media. Few of the recommendations addressed the fact that violence occurs as a response to bullying by boys who are subordinated in the school structure, and that most females killed in school-associated violence were murdered by males. Even the recommendations by the Justice Policy Institute (Donohue et al. 1998) failed to deal with these facts, although they noted correctly that some of the multiple deaths at schools were related to male violence against girls and women. Thus the factors associated with being "a real man" are not recognized as contributing to much of the school violence resulting in death.

Consequently the experts' failures are manifested in the media. Despite our findings that most of the research and media explanations are gender-blind, the current research and the sex-specific count demonstrate clearly that infamous school violence is not gender-neutral. The relative absence of expert and media attention to the social construction of gender encourages incomplete explanations of school violence, and therefore fosters ineffective policy recommendations. Existing research links sexual harassment and dating violence to other forms of violence against women, and connects bullying to male violence; yet the "experts" failed to emphasize these connections when approached by the media. By offering instead a virtual "laundry list" of explanations, they missed the opportunity to direct media attention toward gender-based violence.

School violence victimizing girls and low-status boys reflects the larger societal problems of hegemonic masculinity, violence against women, homophobia, and rejection of difference. Until researchers make these connections clear, the media coverage of these events will remain skewed, and public policy aimed at increasing school safety will fail to protect the lives of all students.

REFERENCES

Altheide, D.L. 1997. "The News Media, the Problem Frame, and the Production of Fear." *Sociological Quarterly* 38:647-68.

"Ambush in Arkansas: Interview with Andrew Golden's Grandfather." 1998. *Prime-Time*, broadcast March 25, ABC News. Retrieved March 29, 1998 (http://www.abcnews.com/onair/ptl/html_files/transcripts/ptl0325a.html).

Anderson, D.C. 1998. "Curriculum, Culture, and Community: The Challenge of School Violence." Pp. 317-63 in *Youth Violence*, edited by M. Tonry and M.H. Moore. Chicago, IL: University of Chicago Press.

Arnette, J.L. and M.C. Walsleben. 1998. *Combating Fear and Restoring Safety in Schools*. Washington, DC: U.S. Department of Justice.

Bachman, R. 1994. *Violence Against Women: A National Crime Victimization Survey Report*. Washington, DC: U.S. Department of Justice.

Barlow, M.H., D.E. Barlow, and T. Chiricos. 1995. "Mobilizing Support for Social Control in a Declining Economy: Exploring Ideologies of Crime Within Crime News." *Crime and Delinquency* 41:191-204.

Beckett, K. 1997. *Making Crime Pay: Law and Order in American Politics*. New York: Oxford University Press.

Bertrand, M. 1991. "Feminists Targeted for Murder: Montreal 1989. Introduction: The Facts." *Feminist Issues* 11(2):3-4,23-24.

Bragg, R. 1998. "5 are Killed at School; Boys, 11 and 13, are Held." *New York Times*, March 25, p. A1.

Braithwaite, J. and K. Daly. 1998. "Masculinities, Violence and Communitarian Control." Pp. 151-80 in *Crime Control and Women: Feminist Implications of Criminal Justice Policy*, edited by S.L. Miller. Thousand Oaks, CA: Sage.

Braun, S. and J. Pasternak. 1997. "Student Opens Fire on Prayer Group, Kills 3." *Los Angeles Times*, December 2, p. A1.

Caputi, J. and D.E.H. Russell. 1992. "Femicide: Sexist Terrorism Against Women." Pp. 13-21 in *Femicide: The Politics of Woman Killing*, edited by J. Radford and D.E.H. Russell. New York: Twayne.

Caringella-MacDonald, S. 1998. "The Relative Visibility of Rape Cases in National Popular Magazines." *Violence Against Women* 4(1):62-80.

Caringella-MacDonald, S. and D. Humphries. 1998. "Guest Editor's Introduction." *Violence Against Women* 4(1):3-9.

Carmody, D.C. 1998. "Mixed Messages: Images of Domestic Violence on 'Reality' Television." Pp. 159-74 in *Entertaining Crime: Television and Reality Programs*, edited by M. Fishman and G. Cavender. New York: Aldine.

Cart, J. 1999. "Tragedy in Colorado Recalling the Slain and Their Slayers: Contrasting Pictures Emerge of Youths Who Erupted in Violence." *Los Angeles Times*, April 22, p. A2.

Caulfield, S. and N. Wonders. 1994. "Gender and Justice: Feminist Contributions to Criminology." Pp. 213-29 in *Varieties of Criminology: Readings From a Dynamic Discipline*, edited by G. Barak. Westport, CT: Praeger.

Cavender, G. and L. Bond-Maupin. 1993. "Fear and Loathing on Reality Television: An Analysis of 'America's Most Wanted' and 'Unsolved Mysteries.'" *Sociological Inquiry* 63:305-17.

Cavender, G. and A. Mulcahy. 1998. "Trial by Fire: Media Constructions of Corporate Deviance." *Justice Quarterly* 15:697-717.

Chermak, S.M. 1995. *Victims in the News: Crime and the American News Media*. Boulder, CO: Westview.

112   GENDER AND SCHOOL VIOLENCE

Chiricos, T., S. Eschholz, and M. Gertz. 1997. "Crime, News and Fear of Crime: Toward an Identification of Audience Effects." *Social Problems* 44:342-57.

"Clinton Orders a Survey of School Violence." 1997. *New York Times,* December 7, p. 40.

Condit, C.M. 1989. "The Rhetorical Limits of Polysemy." *Critical Studies in Mass Communication* 6:103-22.

Connell, R.W. 1987. *Gender and Power: Society, the Person and Sexual Politics.* Stanford, CA: Stanford University Press.

———. 1989. "Cool Guys, Swots and Wimps: The Interplay of Masculinity and Education." *Oxford Review of Education* 15:291-303.

———. 1995. *Masculinities.* Berkeley, CA: University of California Press.

———. 1996. "Teaching the Boys: New Research on Masculinity, and Gender Strategies for Schools." *Teachers College Record* 98:206-35.

Daly, K. and M. Chesney-Lind. 1988. "Feminism and Criminology." *Justice Quarterly* 5:497-538.

Danner, M.J.E. 1991. "Socialist Feminism: A Brief Introduction." Pp. 51-54 in *New Directions in Critical Criminology,* edited by B.D. MacLean and D. Milovanovic. Vancouver: Collective Press.

———. 1998. "Three Strikes and It's *Women* Who Are Out: The Hidden Consequences for Women of Criminal Justice Policy Reforms." Pp. 1-14 in *Crime Control and Women: Feminist Implications of Criminal Justice Policy,* edited by S.L. Miller. Thousand Oaks, CA: Sage.

Denver, S.G. 1999. "Trench Coat Mafia Teen Describes School Life Filled With Taunts, Abuse." *Denver Post,* April 24, p. A1.

Dobash, R.P., R.E. Dobash, M. Wilson, and M. Daly. 1992. "The Myth of Sexual Symmetry in Marital Violence." *Social Problems* (39):71-91.

Donohue, E., V. Schiraldi, and J. Ziedenberg. 1998. *School House Hype: School Shootings and the Real Risks Kids Face in America.* Washington, DC: Justice Policy Institute, Center on Juvenile and Criminal Justice.

Eder, D. 1995. *School Talk: Gender and Adolescent Culture.* New Brunswick, NJ: Rutgers University Press.

Edsall, T.B. 1997. "Mississippi Boy Held in School Killing Spree: Teenager Is Also Accused In Mother's Stabbing Death." *Washington Post,* October 2, p. A3.

Eigenberg, H., J.L. Mullings, and K.E. Scarborough. 1994. "Feminism, Gender and Criminology." Pp. 41-83 in *Multicultural Perspectives in Criminal Justice and Criminology,* edited by J.E. Hendricks and B. Byers. Springfield, IL: Thomas.

Elliott, D.S., B. Hamburg, and K.R. Williams. 1998. "Violence in American Schools: An Overview." Pp. 3-28 in *Violence in American Schools: A New Perspective,* edited by D.S. Elliott, B. Hamburg, and K.R. Williams. New York: Cambridge University Press.

Ericson, R.V., P.M. Baranek, and J.B.L. Chan. 1991. *Representing Order: Crime, Law, and Justice in the News Media.* Toronto: University of Toronto Press.

Fagan, J. and D.L. Wilkinson. 1998a. "Social Contexts and Functions of Adolescent Violence." Pp. 55-93 in *Violence in American Schools: A New Perspective,* edited by D.S. Elliott, B. Hamburg, and K.R. Williams. New York: Cambridge University Press.

———. 1998b. "Guns, Youth Violence and Social Identity in Inner Cities." Pp. 105-88 in *Youth Violence,* edited by M. Tonry and M.H. Moore. Chicago, IL: University of Chicago Press.

Farrington, D. 1993. "Understanding and Preventing Bullying." Pp. 381-458 in *Crime and Justice: A Review of Research,* Vol. 17, edited by M. Tonry. Chicago, IL: University of Chicago Press.

Firestone, D. 1999. "Guns and Schools: An Affinity for Weapons, but No Sign of Anger." *New York Times,* May 20, p. 22.

Fishman, M. 1978. "Crime Waves as Ideology." *Social Problems* 25:531-43.

Forst, B.E. and M. Blomquist. 1991. *Missing Children: Rhetoric and Reality.* New York: Lexington Books.

Gamache, D. 1998. "Domination and Control: The Social Context of Dating Violence." Pp. 69-83 in *Dating Violence: Young Women in Danger,* edited by B. Levy. Seattle, WA: Seal Press.

Gamson, W.A. 1988. "Political Discourse and Collective Action." *International Social Movement Research* 1:219-44.

Glassner, B. 1999. *The Culture of Fear: Why Americans Are Afraid of the Wrong Things.* New York: Basic Books.

Gillespie, M. 2000. "School Violence Still a Worry for American Parents." Gallup Organization poll release, September 7, 1999. Retrieved May 9, 2000 (http://www.gallup.com/poll/releases/pr990907.asp).

Goffman, E. 1974. *Frame Analysis*. Cambridge, MA: Harvard University Press.

Gomme, I. 1986. "Fear of Crime Mounting Among Canadians: A Multivariate Analysis." *Journal of Criminal Justice* 14:249-58.

Gottfredson, G.D. and D.C. Gottfredson. 1985. *Victimization in Schools*. New York: Plenum.

Graber, D. 1980. *Crime News and the Public*. New York: Praeger.

Hall, S. 1977. "Culture, the Media and the 'Ideological' Effect." Pp. 315-48 in *Mass Communication and Society*, edited by J. Curran, M. Gureevitch, and J. Woollacott. Beverly Hills, CA: Sage.

Hardy, M. and J.E. Schapiro. 1999. "Tuition Break Extension Requested/Gilmore Proposes Cuts to Run to 2004." *Richmond Times-Dispatch*, March 31. Retrieved April 7, 1999 (http://gatewayva.com/rtd/dailynews/virginiaarch/gilmor31.shtml).

Juteau, D. and N. Laurin-Frenette. 1991. "A Sociology of Horror." *Feminist Issues* 11(2):15-23.

Kachur, S.P., G.M. Stennies, K.E. Powell, W. Modzeleski, R. Stephens, R. Murphy, M. Kresnow, D. Sleet, and R. Lowry. 1996. "School-Associated Violent Deaths in the United States, 1992 to 1994." *Journal of the American Medical Association* 275:1729-33.

Kaufman, P., X. Chen, S.P. Choy, K.A. Chandler, C.D. Chapman, M.R. Rand, and C. Ringel. 1998. *Indicators of School Crime and Safety, 1998*. Washington, DC: U.S. Department of Education and U.S. Department of Justice.

Kaufman, P., X. Chen, S.P. Choy, S.A. Ruddy, A.K. Miller, K.A. Chandler, C.D. Chapman, M.R. Rand, and P. Klaus. 1999. *Indicators of School Crime and Safety, 1999*. Washington, DC: U.S. Department of Education and U.S. Department of Justice.

Lesko, N., ed. 2000. *Masculinities at School*. Thousand Oaks, CA: Sage.

Levy, B., ed. 1998. *Dating Violence: Young Women in Danger*. Seattle, WA: Seal Press.

Limbar, S.P. and M.M. Nation. 1998. "Bullying Among Children and Youth." Pp. 3-4 in *Combating Fear and Restoring Safety in Schools*, edited by J.L. Arnette and M.C. Walsleben. Washington, DC: Office of Juvenile Justice and Delinquency Prevention.

Liska, A. and W. Baccaglini. 1990. "Feeling Safe by Comparison: Crime in the Newspapers." *Social Problems* 37:360-74.

Luckenbill, D.F. 1977. "Homicide as a Situated Transaction." *Social Problems* 25:176-86.

Luckenbill, D.F. and D.P. Doyle. 1989. "Structural Position and Violence: Developing a Cultural Explanation." *Criminology* 27:419-36.

Madriz, E. 1997. *Nothing Bad Happens to Good Girls: Fear of Crime in Women's Lives*. Berkeley, CA: University of California Press.

Makepeace, J.M. 1981. "Courtship Violence Among College Students." *Family Relations* 30:97-102.

McAdam, D., J.D. McCarthy, and M.N. Zald. 1988. "Social Movements." Pp. 695-737 in *Handbook of Sociology*, edited by N.J. Smelser. Newbury Park, CA: Sage.

Messerschmidt, J.W. 1993. *Masculinities and Crime: Critique and Reconceptualization of Theory*. Lanham, MD: Rowman & Littlefield.

———. 2000. *Nine Lives: Adolescent Masculinities, the Body, and Violence*. Boulder, CO: Westview.

Meyers, M. 1997. *News Coverage of Violence Against Women: Engendering Blame*. Newbury Park, CA: Sage.

"Motives for Arkansas Shooting." 1998. *Morning Edition* (broadcast March 26). Washington, DC: National Public Radio, Inc.

National Center for Education Statistics (NCES). 1998. *Indicators of School Crime and Safety, 1998*. Retrieved November 4, 1998 (http://nces.ed.gov/pubs98/safety).

National School Safety Center. 1998. "Latest News." Retrieved October 5, 1998 (http://www.nssc1.org/latenews.htm).

National School Safety Center. 2000. *The National School Safety Center's Report on School Associated Violent Deaths*. Retrieved March 6, 2000 (http://www.nssc1.org/home.htm).

114   GENDER AND SCHOOL VIOLENCE

Office of Juvenile Justice and Delinquency Prevention (OJJDP). 1999. "Combating School Violence: OJJDP Talking Points." Retrieved March 3, 2000 (http://ojjdp. ncjrs.org/about/spchsprng99.html).

Olweus, D. 1993. *Bullying at School: What We Know and What We Can Do.* Oxford: Blackwell.

Radford, J. 1992. "Introduction." Pp. 3-12 in *Femicide: The Politics of Woman Killing,* edited by J. Radford and D. Russell. New York: Twayne.

Radio Address by the President to the Nation. 1997. Retrieved July 17, 1998 (http://www.pub.whitehouse.gov).

Roscoe, B. and J.E. Callahan. 1985. "Dating Violence Among High School Students." *Psychology* 23(1):53-59.

Rosenberg, S. 1996. "Intersecting Memories: Bearing Witness to the 1989 Massacres of Women in Montreal." *Hypatia* 11(4):119-29.

Saad, L. 1999. "Public Views Littleton Tragedy As Sign Of Deeper Problems in Country." Gallup Organization poll release, April 23, 1999. Retrieved May 9, 2000 (http://www.gallup.com/poll/releases/pr990423.asp).

Schwartz, J. 1998. "Boys' Ambush at Ark. School Leaves 5 Dead; Suspects Are 11 and 13; 11 Wounded in Rampage." *Washington Post,* March 25, p. A1.

Snow, D.A. and R.D. Benford. 1992. "Master Frames and Cycles of Protest." Pp. 133-55 in *Frontiers in Social Movement Theory,* edited by A.D. Morris and C.M. Mueller. New Haven, CT: Yale University Press.

Stanko, E.A. and K. Hobdell. 1993. "Assault on Men: Masculinity and Male Victimization." *British Journal of Criminology* 33:400-15.

Stein, N. 1995. "Sexual Harassment in School: The Public Performance of Gendered Violence." *Harvard Educational Review* 65:145-62.

Surette, R. 1992. *Media, Crime and Criminal Justice: Images and Realities.* Pacific Grove, CA: Brooks/Cole.

————. 1998. *Media, Crime and Criminal Justice: Images and Realities.* 2nd ed. Belmont, CA: West/Wadsworth.

Tuchman, G. 1972. "Objectivity as Strategic Ritual: An Examination of Newsmen's Notions of Objectivity." *American Journal of Sociology* 77:660-70.

————. 1974. "Making News by Doing Work: Routinizing the Unexpected." *American Journal of Sociology* 79:110-31.

————. 1978. *Making News: A Study in the Construction of Reality.* New York: Free Press.

Tunnell, K. 1992. "Film at Eleven: Recent Developments in the Commodification of Crime." *Sociological Spectrum* 12:292-313.

U.S. Department of Education and U.S. Department of Justice. 1998. *1998 Annual Report on School Safety.* Washington, DC: U.S. Department of Education and U.S. Department of Justice.

————. 1999. *1999 Annual Report on School Safety.* Washington, DC: U.S. Department of Education and U.S. Department of Justice.

Warr, M. 1982. "The Accuracy of Beliefs About Crime: Further Evidence." *Criminology* 20:185-204.

Watts, J.C. 1999. *Talking Points: Chronological History of School Shootings.* Retrieved May 25, 1999 (http://hillsource.house.gov/Issuefocus/TalkingPoints/TP106).

Welch, M., M. Fenwick, and M. Roberts. 1997. "Primary Definitions of Crime and Moral Panic: A Content Analysis of Experts' Quotes in Feature Newspaper Articles on Crime." *Journal of Research in Crime and Delinquency* 34:474-94.

Welsh, W.N. 2000. "The Effects of School Climate on School Disorder." *Annals of the American Academy of Political and Social Science* 567:88-107.

West, C. and D.H. Zimmerman. 1987. "Doing Gender." *Gender and Society* 1:125-51.

Wilgoren, J. 1999. "School Rampage/Parents, Friends, Classmates Paint Different Picture of 'Mafia' Group/They Say Trench-Coat Clique Sought Own Place." *Houston Chronicle,* April 25, p. A3.

CASE CITED

Davis v. Monroe County Bd. Of Educ. 000 U.S. 97-843 (1999)

[10]

Immigration, Masculinity, and Intimate Partner Violence From the Standpoint of Domestic Violence Service Providers and Vietnamese-Origin Women

Hoan Bui
University of Tennessee, Knoxville
Merry Morash
Michigan State University

Data from in-depth interviews with Vietnamese immigrant women residing in the United States and both interviews and a focus group with service providers for abused Vietnamese immigrants suggest a complex relationship among job market context, changing norms about appropriate feminine behavior, immigration adaptation, masculinity, and men's violence against intimate partners. During immigration resettlement, men's economic status can worsen, there can be gender role reversals, and men can feel a profound loss of power and social status. Aggression is one way to overcome the perceived loss of one form of masculine identity through a symbolic reassertion of power and privilege as it is constructed in Vietnamese culture and reinforced by aspects of U.S. culture. These dynamics suggest that interventions into domestic violence require not only increasing economic opportunities for immigrants to reduce adaptation stress but also changing gender relations that do not reproduce the belief in male supremacy and men's control of women as part of masculine identity.

Keywords: *domestic violence; immigration resettlement; masculinity; Vietnamese; intimate partner violence; service providers; gender identity; hegemonic masculinity*

Gender identity, perceptions of oneself as appropriately masculine or feminine, is important in explaining how a person behaves. Individuals construct or actualize their gender identities through their actions, though certain contexts and structural inequalities can limit their means to do so. Messerschmidt's (1986, 1993) work in particular has emphasized that for lower-class men, who are often men of color, lack of work opportunities makes it impossible to establish power through earnings, providing for the family, and other traditional means. To accomplish their masculinity, some men with limited resources resort to violence to achieve masculine ideals of control and power.

In the United States, a dominant form of contemporary masculinity, called "hegemonic" masculinity, associates manhood with power achieved through sexual domination over women, the exclusion of women from decision making, the control of other men, and the provision of goods and food for families and communities (Connell, 1995, 2005; Kaufman, 1994; Kersten, 1996). Common culturally scripted feminine traits are complementary and include submissiveness, passivity, and nurturance; the role of women is to be supportive of and subordinate to male partners (Boonzaier & de La Rey, 2003), and this version of femininity supports and affirms hegemonic masculinity. However, the institutional class, race, and ethnic structures in the United States limit opportunities for some minority men to exercise power in the public realm (Abraham, 2000). Thus, for some men, violence is one means of constructing a hegemonic form of masculinity (Jasinski, 2001).

There has been some limited research in very diverse settings on how men who feel a loss of power and status accomplish their masculinity through violence against women. According to Hampton, Oliver, and Maggarian (2003), the economic underdevelopment of African American men has historically been a source of their anger and frustration. The phrase "frustrated masculinity syndrome" describes how some African American men use violence against their wives and children in response to racial prejudice and institutional barriers to actualizing their manhood (p. 539). A study of domestic violence among African Americans suggests that disparity indicated by wives' higher level of education and occupational status can translate into marital tension and husbands' subsequent violence (Nash, 2005). Similarly, research on domestic violence in Vietnam found that husbands with lower resources or status than their wives were most likely to engage in abusive behavior (Luke, Schuler, Bui, Pham, & Tran, 2007). In a sub-Saharan region of Africa, some men respond to women's joining the paid labor force and their own unemployment by publicly beating them. The underlying reason was that to remain as heads of households, men wanted to control household income and avoid doing household labor (Bank, 1994). A survey of more than 8,000 Canadian women similarly revealed that women's risk for physical abuse, jealous oversight, and denied access to money were highest when they were employed and their partners were unemployed (Macmillan & Gartner, 1999, p. 956). When sexual assault (both in and outside of marital relationships) is considered, if women have become more equal to men, they are more at risk because some men who feel that their identity is threatened force sex to assert a powerful sense of self (Messerschmidt, 1986, 1993; Schwartz & DeKeseredy, 1997; Scully & Marolla, 1985; Whaley, 2001). These studies indicate threats to men's dominance in the family and their perceptions of inability to "be masculine" have led to sexual and other physical violence against women in many different contexts (Jewkes, Levin, & Penn-Kakana, 2002; Whaley, 2001; Yick, 2001).

Circumstances of immigration can intensify men's violence against partners. Song and Moon (1998), for example, found that for South Korean immigrants to the United States, men felt that their absolute dominance in the family was threat-ened because they could not find well-paying jobs; their wives had to work to pro-vide adequate family income, and working wives challenged the assignment of all household and child-rearing tasks to women. The authors concluded that "under these circumstances, the Korean American men, in an attempt to prove their mas-culinity, may follow the old pattern of harassing and punishing a 'disobedient wife' through physical violence" (p. 169). Bourgois (1996) described the situa-tion of Puerto Ricans whose immigrant fathers could not find jobs in the United States and, therefore, asserted their power through violence against women. Many boys in the Puerto Rican neighborhood grew to see masculine dignity as the capacity to engage in interpersonal violence and sexual domination. In a study of domestic violence in Mexican-origin families, Morash, Bui, and Santiago (2000) found that families with abusive men were characterized by immigration-induced role changes that caused men's loss of family and social status. In a final example that is especially pertinent to the present research, Bui (2002) found that domes-tic violence among Vietnamese immigrants occurred within the context of gender role reversal and men's downward mobility following immigration to the United States.

The studies cited above establish a framework for the examination of hegemonic masculinity, men's actualization of their gender identity in the immigration context, and intimate partner violence for Vietnamese immigrant couples in the United States. Immigrant men's lack of language skills, discriminatory hiring requirements that employees have U.S. work experience and certifications, and racial and ethnic prejudice are barriers to obtaining employment commensurate with education and training (Abraham, 2000; Gold, 1992). Consequently, even educated and skilled immigrant men find themselves relegated to subordinate positions in the workplace (Abraham, 2000). In contrast, immigrant women often enjoy increased economic opportunity and tolerance of their work outside of the home (Gold, 1992; Kibria, 1993). The result can be a narrowing of the gap in economic standing between men and women or even reversal of men's better economic standing in relation to their partners' economic situation. This article reports on the perceptions of Vietnamese immigrant women and the professionals who provide them with domestic violence services. The focus is on perceptions of the dynamics of work activity and status change in relationship to intimate partner violence. This research also considers insights into other reasons for violence, notably jealousy and the practice of send-ing remittances to relatives in the home country. Because the construction of women, men, femininity, and masculinity is a part of the dynamic leading to abuse and because these concepts emerge as the crystallization of the particular ways in which meanings are invoked in local spaces (Rydstrom & Drummond, 2004), an examination of the construction of masculinity in Vietnamese culture is important to understanding intimate partner violence by Vietnamese immigrant men.

Masculinity in Vietnamese Culture

Accomplishing masculinity is associated with three areas of social action: procreation, protection, and provision of goods and food for families and communities (Kersten, 1996). Gender practices relevant to these areas do not occur in a vacuum but are influenced by the gender ideals that have been accepted as normal and proper, social structural constraints, and the construction of personal history up to a specific time and place (Messerschmidt, 1993). Thus, gender identities are influenced by and reproduce and support religious beliefs, cultures, and labor arrangements (Connell, 1987).

Religious beliefs have had the most powerful influence in the formation of Vietnamese society. Despite the introduction of Christianity into Vietnam in the 16th century, the religious traditions of Buddhism, Confucianism, and Taoism formed the core of the Vietnamese religious-cultural tradition (Gold, 1992). Of the three religions, Confucianism and Taoism exerted the greatest impact on gender relations in Vietnamese society. Confucianism, which has been practiced in Vietnam for hundreds of years, remains central to the organization of Vietnamese society and is a major influence on dominant forms of gender identity. Under Confucianism, men's superior status is embedded across kinship and political, legal, and economic institutions and is reflected in various traditional ideals and practices (Kibria, 1993; C. Tran, 1997). Patriarchal family systems and the practices of patrilineal ancestor worship lead to a preference for male progeny and reify men's ability to reproduce sons (Rydstrom, 2004). Thus, male celibacy is an unacceptable form of filial impiety. Confucian teachings enable the husband to formalize his position as the "superior" by assuming the features of mandarin and teacher who is responsible for commanding, guiding, teaching, nurturing, and protecting the "inferior" wife and child (O'Harrow, 1995).

In traditional Vietnamese society, men were expected to work outside the home and serve the community, and without the community, they had no raison d'etre (T. Tran, 1959). In contrast, Vietnamese women were completely absent from all political and leadership positions, because only men could be heads of towns and family groups (Kibria, 1993). Women were expected to follow the principle of "three obediences": Women should obey and submit to their fathers when young, to their husbands when married, and to their oldest son when widowed (Nguyen, 1987). In addition, a model woman should possess the "four virtues," which include good working habits, attractive appearance, polite speech, and exemplary conduct. The dominant position of the husband is also evident in ancient laws that sanctioned wife beating and allowed a man to repudiate his wife on several grounds, such as childlessness, lasciviousness, refusal to serve and obey parents-in-law, jealousy, or incurable diseases (Ta, 1981). The idealized image of a "good woman" has been used to create a double standard for judging sexual conduct. Embedded in the four virtues is the unwritten rule that women must "retain their purity" before marriage (C. Tran,

1997), but men's sexual prowess is positively valued. Traditionally, Vietnamese men were allowed to be sexually promiscuous before and within marriage, and men's common, open, and frequent affairs with multiple women were viewed as a demonstration of manly prowess and superiority. In fact, traditional legal codes sanctioned polygamy, which was held as a mark of affluence and prestige and was usually practiced by wealthy men (Kibria, 1993). The double standard for sexual conduct is reflected in the popular old saying *"Trai nam the bay thiep, gai chinh chuyen mot chong"* (A man could have five wives and seven concubines, but a woman should have one husband) (Bui, 2004, p. 22).

Taoism stresses the idea of harmony between human beings and the universe (Nguyen, 1987). Under this view, male and female bodies and characters are associated with two main nature forces, yin and yang (Rydstrom, 2003). The belief in the dominant forces of yin and yang has influenced the constructions of Vietnamese masculinity and femininity. Female characters are associated with yin, representing water, cold, passivity, responsiveness, and inferiority. Male characters are connected to yang, representing fire, heat, activity, stimulation, and superiority (Rydstrom, 2003). Under the combined influence of Confucianism and Taoism, men's violence and aggressiveness are considered natural. With inferior status, women are expected to comply with their husbands' wishes and endure their "hot" tempers (Rydstrom, 2003, pp. 684-685). Besides religious traditions, a long history of war promoted the association of Vietnamese masculinity with military experience. In general, military training promotes constructions of masculinity that embody dominance, violence, control, and heroism (Adelman, 2003; Connell, 2005). More specifically, the image of warrior men as heroes who sacrificed for the nation appears in numerous Vietnamese folklores, war stories, and classic and contemporary literature (e.g., see Huynh Sanh Thong, 2001; Phan Huy Ich, 1986; Vo Phien, 1999).

Wars, urbanization, and contacts with Western cultures during both French colonization and the Vietnam War altered the basic structure of the Vietnamese traditional family. Men's deaths and absences from home made it difficult to maintain the expected ancient family traditions and practices. Women who were left alone to support themselves, children, and elderly relatives became family providers and caretakers involved in social and economic activities (Bui, 2004). These factors led to some elevation of women's position in the family and society, although practices of male superiority remained (Le Thi Quy, 1996; Le Thi, 1996; Luke et al., 2007). Although the three obediences and four virtues are no longer embraced in contemporary Vietnam, women are expected to conform to an inferior status and socially constructed femininity, and when they do not , they often encounter cultural acceptance of the idea that it is a man's right to punish his wife (Rydstrom, 2003). Recent research on domestic violence in Vietnam suggests that men's violent behavior against their wives continues to be largely accepted as a normal response of the head of the family to women's inappropriate behavior, disobedience, or disrespect (Rydstrom, 2003; Vu, Vu, Nguyen, & Clement, 2000).

Vietnamese immigrants often transport ideologies of male superiority and elements of traditional versions of masculinity that are rooted in long-standing Confucian beliefs (Bui, 2004; Gold, 1992). Coming from a country where notions about masculinities, femininities, and gender arrangements were already changing, Vietnamese immigrants to the United States enter a context characterized by a greater variety of culturally supported gender identities, a changed array of employment opportunities for both women and men, and problems related to language and adaptation. How do men's notions about masculinity, as women see them expressed through words and actions, and the resources available to accomplish masculinity explain violence against partners? This is the central question of the research described in this article.

Research Method

A qualitative method is required to capture the complexity of situational, cultural, and structural factors associated with the construction of masculinity and the experience of intimate partner abuse. Thus, the present study involves analysis of extensive interview data collected from Vietnamese immigrant women living in different areas of the United States and from service providers who worked with abused Vietnamese immigrant women in those locations. Information from different sources and geographic areas was used to establish the validity of findings, though it is recognized that the standpoints considered do not include those of the men who are women's husbands and partners.

Sample and Data

Data were combined from two research projects that both authors of this article were involved with and which shared several key topic areas. The first project focused on factors contributing to domestic violence and abused women's help-seeking behavior. Project participants were 129 Vietnamese immigrant women recruited in an East Coast northern metropolitan area and a focus group with 10 service providers, including domestic violence advocates, social workers, counselors, a Vietnamese police liaison, and one legal counsel.[1] The second project focused on the intervention experiences of abused Vietnamese immigrant women. Participants were 34 women recruited in different locations in the East Coast, the Midwest, the West Coast, and the South, and 3 service providers drawn from these geographic areas. These combined data sets resulted in a sample of 13 service providers and 155 Vietnamese immigrant women who were married to or had an intimate relationship with a Vietnamese immigrant man.[2]

The sample included a large number of women who had experienced abuse and some participants from the same communities who had not experienced abuse to provide for some comparisons between the two groups. The two projects shared the same recruitment criteria and techniques for the women interviewed. The majority of women (98 women or 63%) were identified through referrals from social services and domestic violence advocacy agencies (Texas and East Coast metropolitan), a health care center that provided counseling services to domestic violence victims (East Coast metropolitan), and three civic organizations serving immigrant populations (East Coast metropolitan and California). The sample was increased and diversified through snowball sampling to include an additional 49 women (32%). Finally, 7 women (5%) responded to requests for participants during one Vietnamese radio talk show in Texas and another in California.[3]

In-depth interviews were conducted in 2000 and 2001 by one of the authors and trained interviewers who were bilingual professionals or adult university students from the immigrant community. The two projects shared a major part of the interview instrument, which included closed-ended and open-ended questions designed to obtain information about demographic characteristics, family backgrounds, immigration history, experiences with resettlement, family relationships, and experiences of abuse. All study participants elected to be interviewed in Vietnamese. Most interviews (150) were conducted face-to-face; 5 interviews were conducted via telephone at the request of the participants. Interviews typically took from 2 to 4 hours and often required multiple sessions. Most of the women received an incentive worth $40 for participating in the interview.[4] In addition, interviews with 3 Vietnamese-origin service providers in two locations of the study (Texas and California) and a focus group with 10 service providers in the East Coast metropolitan area were conducted. All interviews with the women were recorded in writing in Vietnamese; most service provider interviews and the focus group were recorded in writing in English. The Vietnamese interview transcripts were translated into English by one of the authors (Bui) who is a Vietnamese immigrant. There were some Vietnamese terms and idioms that could not be translated into English without losing the original meanings, so both Vietnamese and English versions of the interview transcripts were used for data analysis. All quotes from the women who were interviewed are translations from the Vietnamese version of the transcript.[5]

A software program for qualitative analysis (QSR N5) was used for data coding. Both authors reviewed coding results to confirm or question patterns in the data. Any discrepancies were resolved through discussion.

Characteristics of Women Participants and Their Husbands/Intimate Partners

The women participants had diverse demographic characteristics and immigration experiences (see Table 1). Their ages ranged from 21 to 69, with a median of 40 years. They had come to the United States in different ways and under different circumstances. Thirty-six percent of the women participants escaped Vietnam and arrived in a third country before being admitted to the United States; 24% were dependents of husbands who had been political detainees in Vietnam and, therefore, were allowed to resettle in the United States with their husbands[6]; 8% were sponsored by their husbands with U.S. immigration; 13% were sponsored by their relatives; 19% came to the United States through a special program that allowed the resettlement of Vietnamese Amerasians in the United States.[7] Most of the women emigrated as adults; 25% came to the United States when they were older than 40. Only 10% arrived in the United States when they were younger than 18. By the time of the interview, the women had spent from 1 to 26 years in the United States, with a median of 8 years. Thirty-five percent of the women were U.S. citizens; 52% were permanent residents, and 13% were legal aliens. The proportion of women participants who had U.S. citizenship was somewhat lower than the 44% who were citizens in the general Vietnamese American population (U.S. Census Bureau, 2003). The women participants also tended to have low levels of U.S. education. Although 41% of the women had a high school education or higher in Vietnam, only 21% completed a high school education, had some college education, or had a college degree in the United States. In addition, 35% of the women did not attend school in the United States, and 37% only attended ESL (English as a second language) classes. A few other women (3%) had received vocational training. Twenty-nine percent of the women considered their English (reading and speaking) as good or excellent, 43% said they had problems with English, and 28% reported that they had no ability to speak and read English at all. According to U.S. Census 2000 (U.S. Census Bureau, 2003), 31% of Vietnamese Americans aged 5 or older who lived in "non-English-at-home" households spoke English very well, and 54% of Vietnamese Americans aged 25 or older had completed a high school education or more. These statistics indicate that compared to the general Vietnamese American population, women participants had a similar level of English proficiency but a lower level of education. Otherwise, women participants were not different from the general Vietnamese American population in labor force participation. The percentage of women participants who reported that they worked (56%) was very similar to the proportion of employed women in the general Vietnamese American population (56.4%) (U.S. Census Bureau, 2003). Most employed participants worked in manual-labor jobs.

The women participants provided information about their partners' demographic characteristics and immigration experiences. The age of the women's partners ranged from 25 to 72 years, and the median was 43.5 years. About one half of the men (49.5%) were evacuated or escaped Vietnam and arrived in a third country before they were allowed to resettle in the United States. About one quarter of them (26%) came directly to the United States because they had been political detainees in Vietnam and, therefore, were allowed to resettle in the United States. A small number of the women's partners (7%) came to the United States under the sponsorship of their relatives. Finally, less than one fifth of the men (16.5%) arrived in the

Table 1
Demographic Characteristics of Women Participants and Their Partners

	Women Participants *n* (%)	Partners *n* (%)
Age (at the time of interview)		
Range	21-69 years	25-72 years
Median	40 years	43.5 years
Age (at the time arrived in the United States)		
Younger than 18	16 (10%)	11 (7%)
18-39	100 (65%)	96 (62%)
Older than 40	39 (25%)	48 (31%)
Types of immigration to the United States		
Evacuated or escaped Vietnam	56 (36%)	77 (49.5%)
Dependents of husbands	37 (24%)	N/A
As former political detainees	N/A	40 (26%)
Sponsored by husbands	13 (8%)	N/A
Sponsored by other relatives	20 (13%)	11 (7%)
Amerasian program	29 (19%)	26 (16.5%)
Time in the United States		
Range	1-26 years	2-25 years
Median	8 years	10 years
Legal status		
U.S. citizens	54 (35%)	70 (45%)
Permanent residents	81 (52%)	67 (43%)
Legal aliens	20 (13%)	18 (12%)
Education and training in Vietnam*		
High school and higher	64 (41%)	87 (56%)
Less than high school	85 (55%)	65 (42%)
No education	6 (4%)	—
Education and training in the United States*		
High school or higher	33 (21%)	47 (30%)
ESL class only	57 (37%)	67 (43%)
Vocational training only	5 (3%)	—
No education	53 (35%)	26 (17%)
English proficiency		
Very good	45 (29%)	62 (40%)
Some problems	67 (43%)	70 (45%)
No ability at all	43 (28%)	23 (15%)
Employment		
Employed	87 (56%)	115 (74%)
Not employed	68 (44%)	40 (26%)
Experience with abuse		
Verbal abuse	116 (75%)	N/A
Physical abuse	97 (63%)	N/A
Sexual abuse	72 (46%)	N/A

Note: The numbers do not add to 100% due to missing information. ESL = English as a second language; N/A = not available.

United States under a program created to resettle Vietnamese Amerasians, although some of them were not Amerasians but relatives of Amerasians.[8] Most partners had come to the United States as adults, and almost one third (31%) came when they were older than 40; only 7% arrived in the United States when they were younger than 18. The men had been in the United States from 2 to 25 years, with a median of 10 years. Forty-five percent of the men had U.S. citizenship; 43% were permanent residents, and 12% were legal aliens.[9]

Women participants indicated that their husbands/partners had low levels of U.S. education and lacked English skills. Fifty-six percent of the partners had at least a high school education in Vietnam, but only 30% had at least a high school education in the United States. In addition, 17% percent of the men had never attended school in the United States, and 43% had only attended English classes. More than one third of the women participants (40%) said that their husbands'/partners' English skills were good; 45% said that their husbands/partners had problems with English, and 15% said that their husbands/partners had no ability to speak or read English at all. Seventy-four percent of the women reported that their husbands/partners worked, and 62% reported that their husbands/partners worked in manual labor, semiskilled labor, or clerical jobs. The proportion of employed men in the general Vietnamese American population was 70% (U.S. Census Bureau, 2003). In sum, compared to Vietnamese-origin men in the U.S. population, the women's partners had lower levels of education but about the same English proficiency, citizenship status, and labor force participation. The descriptive statistics suggest that the study participants would include couples with men who work in jobs with less status than their prior work in Vietnam or who are unemployed and women who are in the workforce and potentially doing as well or better than their partners. Thus, the sample is useful for an examination and expansion of some of the dynamics of abuse identified in the literature review.

Findings

Analysis of women's responses to closed-ended questions identified three forms of abuse that women experienced before and after immigration. The forms are physical (twisting arms or hair, pushing and shoving, kicking, punching and hitting, choking or strangling, slamming against the wall, beating up, grabbing, slapping, threatening to hit or throwing something, burning or scalding, and using or threatening to use a gun or knife), sexual (insisting on having sex, forcing her to have sex; forcing her to have sex in the way she did not want to, and using threats to have sex), and verbal (swearing, calling names or calling her ugly, destroying her belonging, shouting or yelling at her, accusing her of being sexually unfaithful, and calling her stupid or crazy in front of others). The present study focused on women's experience with abuse in the United States. Three fourths of the sample (75% or 116 women) reported verbal abuse, two thirds of the sample (63% or 97 women) reported physical abuse, and almost half of the sample (46% or 72 women) reported sexual abuse (see Table 1). Virtually all of the 97 women who experienced physical abuse also experienced verbal abuse. In addition, 57 women (37%) experienced both physical abuse and sexual abuse.

Men's Downward Mobility, Masculinity, and Gender Role Reversals

Prior research has established that Vietnamese resettlement in the United States changed Vietnamese family dynamics by reducing men's economic and social status and by increasing women's opportunities (Gold, 1992; Kibria, 1993). Men's loss of status is particularly acute among former Vietnamese military officers who have skills that are not marketable in the United States and, therefore, have to hold jobs at lower levels in the occupational structure. It is not uncommon for former colonels, captains, and lieutenants to work in manual, temporary, low-status jobs (e.g., janitor, factory assembler, warehouse stoker, and security guard; Gold, 1992). Those who worked as professionals in Vietnam but could not update their professional credentials in the United States often hold jobs at the levels of technician, secretary, clerk, and manual laborer. Vietnamese immigrant men's downward mobility is often accompanied by a role reversal and a shift of power in the family (Gold, 1992). When a man's salary is not sufficient to meet the high cost of living, his wife has to work to contribute to the family economy. Different from patterns in Vietnam, the economic contributions of Vietnamese immigrant women to the family budget have risen higher relative to or even more than those of Vietnamese immigrant men (Kibria, 1993). Women could make more money than men because unskilled female-oriented jobs, such as housecleaning and hotel and food services, were more available than unskilled male-oriented jobs (Gold, 1992). In addition, Vietnamese immigrant women have been willing to work in menial jobs to provide food and clothes for everyone in the household, because they were traditionally charged with responsibility for taking care of household "internal affairs" (Bui, 2004, p. 24). Men, in contrast, have been more concerned with their social status and often tried to find high-status jobs that were less available for new immigrants (Gold, 1992). It is not uncommon for Vietnamese immigrant women to work two jobs, while their husbands hold a part-time job or are unemployed (Bui, 2002). In these cases, women's relative financial contribution to the family shifts the couple's roles, with the wife becoming the primary wage earner. Studies of non-Vietnamese samples have shown that men who do not have financial and job-status resources to confirm typical constructions of masculinity tend to react with displays of toughness, bravado, cool pose, or hombre (Connell, 1987; Hondagneu-Sotelo & Messner, 1997). The reaction may be more extreme among men who had military experience because of their past training and actual experience with violence as well as the (lost) meaning of militarized masculinity associated with physical strength, superiority and heroism (Adelman, 2003).

Data from the focus group of service providers in the East Coast metropolitan area confirmed the loss of economic power among Vietnamese men. One service provider said, "[Vietnamese immigrant] men have lost power after immigrating to the U.S. Many felt bad because they lacked language and occupational skills and could not support their families." This view was shared by most focus group participants. Analysis of women's responses to both closed- and open-ended questions showed that men's employment and occupation status was associated with violence against their intimate partners. Quantitative data indicated that women with unemployed intimate partners were more likely than women with employed intimate partners to report physical abuse (60% and 50%, respectively), sexual abuse (50% and 40%, respectively), and verbal abuse (85% and 70%, respectively).[10] In addition, women whose partners worked in manual jobs were more likely than women whose partners worked as professionals or technicians to report physical abuse (55% and 33%, respectively), sexual abuse (45% and 25%, respectively), and verbal abuse (75% and 60%, respectively). In addition, women whose partners were former political detainees were more likely than other women to report physical abuse (62% and 55%, respectively) and verbal abuse (90% and 70%, respectively). Most of these political detainees had been military officers in the South Vietnamese government.

The stories of Tuyen, Tam, and Ly illustrate the connections of men's lack of job status and subsequent role reversal to family violence. Tuyen was evacuated from Vietnam in 1975, when her husband was in Europe serving as a diplomat for the South Vietnam government. He joined her several months later in the United States. Tuyen talked about her husband's resettlement experience and his violence as follows:

> We first arrived in [New England] where my husband got a job in a lumberyard as a laborer (lumberjack). Vietnamese have a small body, and he couldn't keep up with his American coworkers. He had to stand all day, endure the cold, and he couldn't take it. I encouraged him to find work elsewhere. He looked for [professional] jobs in Washington, D.C.; Virginia; and New York City, but he couldn't find any. So I went to [an East Coast area] and got a job as a seamstress. I worked while my husband stayed home watching the children. Later, my husband got a typing job. Then, he worked as a clerk for the city's human resource department. . . . He often came home tired and angry, and he began arguing. He was always worried about making money and providing enough for our children. . . . In Vietnam, he was a nice man, but he became violent here. When we argued, he hit me. He just hit me. . . . Every time he saw me, he would yell, swear, put me down, hit my head, or kick me. One time, he took up a knife and said that he would kill me if I didn't believe in him.

Ly, who came with her husband to the United States under the sponsorship of his sister, described a similar pattern in the development of violence. She and her husband had finished high school in Vietnam, where they ran a small business. When they arrived in the United States, their relatives advised both to attend English and vocational training classes. Ly followed the advice and even took college courses at night while working during the day. With her English skills and her ability to adapt quickly to life in the United States, Ly became successful as a salesperson, while her husband worked as a courtesy clerk for an advertising company that provided advertising services for Ly's employer. Ly reported that her husband changed greatly since the couple came to the United States; he had a hot temper and became violent and jealous.

> When we were in Vietnam, we rarely argued. Since we came to the United States, he seemed to lose his temper and became violent. He would slap me or pull my hair when I argued against him. He beat me because he wanted to teach me a lesson. He felt that because I made more money than him, I became arrogant and disrespectful.

Tam and her husband, who had been a military officer, escaped Vietnam and were allowed to resettle in the United States. They owned a restaurant. A few years later, her husband was robbed and shot, and his health deteriorated so much that he could no longer run the business. After the business was closed, Tam attended vocational training and became a home-care nurse, and her husband worked as an electronics assembler. She made more money than he did, and her earnings covered most of the household expenses. She believed that her husband's inability to support the family made him angry, distressed, controlling, and jealous:

> After the accident, he changed a lot. He would become angry easily, and when he was angry, he destroyed things in the house. He made the house like hell. . . . I thought after we sold the business, he felt bad because I made more [money] than he did. He often said that he felt useless because he couldn't support the family. . . . He also wanted to control the [family] money and would get angry if he thought that I had secretly sent money to my family in Vietnam.

The narratives of women participants show how the erosion of men's status, the inversion of the traditional gender order in Vietnamese families, men's perceived loss of parental authority over children, humiliating conditions of working in menial jobs, and status inconsistency can cause distress and provoke hostility, resentment, and violence among Vietnamese immigrant men. When elements of masculinity become unachievable, some immigrant men take this as a challenge to their role and experience a crisis in their identity. In this situation, violence can be used to compensate for a perceived loss of masculine identity and as a symbolic reassertion of male power and privilege (Boonzaier & de La Rey, 2003).

Men's Sexual Jealousy

As already described, in Vietnamese traditional culture, masculinity was associated with men's sexual promiscuity and control over women's sexuality and was supported by a construction of femininity that emphasized women's virginity and purity. Changes in living conditions that affect Vietnamese traditional norms of gendered behavior and women's changing status within the context of immigration and adaptation are major factors in men's sexual jealousy and related violence (Bui, 2002). Sexual jealousy among Vietnamese immigrant men is often based on their perception that, contrary to the Vietnamese norm for feminine behavior, women in the United States have many opportunities to socialize with men outside the family circle and have more freedom to engage in intimate relationships (Bui, 2002). A man's perception that his wife or partner is unfaithful is not only a serious challenge to his patriarchal authority but also can feed a fear that she will choose another man whom she views as more "manly" (Messerschmidt, 1993). Vietnamese men in the United States may be more likely than men in Vietnam to feel sexually jealous. They may feel threatened by the stereotype in American society that Asian men are weak and nonmasculine and Asian women are feminine and adorable (Lin, Tazuma, & Masuda, 1979). In addition, Vietnamese immigrant men may feel threatened by their perception that "American" men have superior economic power and thus are more attractive to Vietnamese immigrant women (Bui, 2002).

In the present study, men's sexual jealousy was a fairly common theme in the conversations with service providers and the narratives by women who experienced abuse. A Vietnamese-origin social worker (Trinh) made this observation about sexual jealousy among Vietnamese immigrants in the United States:

> In Vietnam, married women were often worried about their husbands' disloyalty because most married men had girlfriends, mistresses, or concubines at some point in their marriages. In the U.S., [Vietnamese] men have become very jealous, and they are usually worried about their wives or partners leaving them to go with American men. Their concerns are unfounded because not many [Vietnamese] women are married to American men. However, many [Vietnamese] men have become paranoid because they think that they are less attractive than their American counterparts and that [Vietnamese] women have more freedom to engage in intimate relationships in the U.S. than they did in Vietnam.

More than one third of women who experienced abuse (40%) told stories about their partners' sexual jealousy. Comments by these women suggest an association between men's jealousy and men's related feelings about their inability to control their wives' and partners' sexual involvements when these women obtained education or other means of access to independent interactions with other men. Thu-Le's husband was a high ranking government official in South Vietnam but had no job in the United States. Her story suggests that her husband's extreme jealousy and fears that she would leave him led to his abusive behavior.

> He was very jealous, and he often physically and sexually abused me out of his jealousy. He threatened to kill me. . . . [H]e said he would hire someone to kill me if I left him. He didn't want me to go to school in the U.S. . . . I was not allowed to keep money. He kept all money [from welfare]. When he was angry with me, he hit me in my face. . . . He broke

my nose several times. One time, I had to be hospitalized for 3 days and had eight stitches [on my face]. He also forced me to have sex when I didn't want to. If I refused, he would beat me. . . . I felt so stressed and depressed that I became mentally ill.

Yen-Vy and her husband, both Amerasians with very limited education and English proficiency, were not working at the time of the study. According to Yen-Vy, her husband thought that she lacked sexual restraints because she was Amerasian (mixed race). Sharing the viewpoint of the Vietnamese social worker cited above, Yen-Vy said that her husband was worried about losing her because women had more opportunities to have relationships with men in American society than in Vietnam, and she attributed her husband's abusive behavior to his jealousy. She explained,

He was always jealous, and he often beat me when he saw me talking with other men. . . . He said that I made his life harder because I was Amerasian, and he wanted me to admit that I had cheated on him.

The already described abusive behavior associated with a woman's higher occupational status and greater financial success relative to her partner's can be intertwined with jealousy to produce violence. Interviews with service providers indicated that some men attempted to repress their wives' educational and career development or made their wives become totally dependent by prohibiting them from working in the paid labor force. This practice suggests that men might prohibit women from working outside the home, because men felt such work would enable and require women to abandon lifestyle restrictions associated with feminine identities that complement hegemonic masculinity. Ly, whose experience with domestic violence was noted in a previous section, said that her husband, who worked as a courtesy clerk, became very jealous when she was successful in her real estate business. He did not like her sales career, which necessitated her attention to her appearance, flexible work hours, and socializing with customers, including men. She described how her husband tried to reimpose restrictions and, when she would not agree, criticized her very self and attacked her physically for not living up to prescribed femininity.

My husband tried to control my work schedule, and he wanted me to be home at 5 or 6 in the afternoon, but my job required me to go out often, even outside business hours. When he could not control my schedule, he became suspicious and jealous. When I talked back to him because of his unreasonable jealousy, he slapped me or pulled my hair. He frequently accused me [of] lacking respect for him, losing chastity, and becoming arrogant. He often told me that he would kill me if he caught me dating other men.

Women's narratives indicated that factory and restaurant jobs, which require working at night, and hotel service jobs, such as cleaning and being a chambermaid, often aroused suspicions among Vietnamese immigrant men who rigidly adhered to norms of women's restricted activity outside the home. Historically, in Vietnam, there have been prohibitions against women going out alone at night, and hotels have been seen as unsuitable workplaces for women because of possible prostitution activities. These ideas might lead many men, like the husbands of Tam and Xuan, to be suspicious and jealous of working partners. Tam, whose experience with her husband's abusive behavior following his loss of status in the family has been discussed, worked as a home-care nurse. She explained that her husband was suspicious about her sexual integrity because her job demanded that she work into the evening and she had several American male clients.

> He was angry every time I returned home from work at night. He would approach my car and check to see if there was something unusual and asked many questions. When he was not satisfied with my responses, he would become angry and begin destroying things in the house.

Xuan's husband, a former captain in the South Vietnamese military force, could not attain a comparable status in the United States. She reported that he had rigid gender-norm expectations but could not live up to them because he was unable to support the family. Unable to find a full-time job that was not manual labor, he worked part-time. Xuan had two hotel chambermaid jobs and made enough money to support the family of six (Xuan, her husband, and four children). Xuan's story suggests that her husband's inability to support the family and his disapproval of her jobs were transformed into jealousy that led to family conflicts and his violence. Xuan revealed these dynamics:

> We got married in Vietnam, but I had never seen him become so jealous; only after we came to the U.S. I was almost 50 years old, but he usually thought that I acted like a 20-year-old girl, trying to get other men. I was working at two hotels downtown, but he did not like it. He told me to change jobs many times because in his view, only prostitutes worked in hotels. . . . He got mad, and he called me [a] whore when I brought home good money from [customers'] tips. Then, he started scrutinizing the way I dressed. He even prohibited me from wearing makeup and certain kinds of clothing. When I disregarded his unreasonable demands, he beat me and even threatened to kill me.

Other women participants who worked in settings with opportunities to socialize with men outside the family circle also experienced abuse that they attributed to their husbands' sexual jealousy. Particularly, when their husbands asked them to have sex but they refused, their husbands often verbally abused them by accusing them of having relationships with men at work or sexually and physically abused them.

Vietnamese immigrant men's sexual jealousy may also be facilitated by their own working conditions. Hue's situation illustrated how men's job requirements to be away from home at night could spark sexual jealousy, related controls, and violence. Her husband, who was 6 years older than she was and came to the United States several years earlier, felt strongly about women's role. Because he earned enough to support the family, he asked Hue to stay home and take care of the couple's son. According to Hue, her husband worked the night shift, and he often beat her because he worried that she had contact with other American men in the apartment complex while he was at work. Hue explained,

> He was very jealous. He worked the night shift, and when he came home the following morning, he often looked around to check whether someone had come to visit me during his absence. He checked on me all the time. He would ask me if someone had come the night before, and he would check food in the refrigerator to see if someone had come and eaten with me. . . . For the last incident, he came home from work in the morning, and he talked with our 4-year-old son. Because he suspected that someone had visited me last night, he began yelling at me. We had an argument. At some point, he put a knife to my neck, threatening to cut my throat. When I got loose from him, I called the police.

Stories told by women participants indicated that the realities of the local job market, which were shaped by the intersection of immigrant status and gender, have contributed to men's decreased status and their lower economic status relative to their partners. These stories suggest that the realities of couples' work lives have created conditions that have aggravated men's feeling about a lack of control over their partners' activities and jealousy that these activities included sex with other men. In the United States, where women are expected to have interactions outside the home and in the labor market available to immigrant couples, men who felt they should fully control their partners appeared to often check on them, verbally accuse them of failing to be idealized "females," and use violence as a punishment, as a warning, or out of anger and frustration.

Men's Downward Mobility and Remittances to Relatives "Back Home"

Inability to achieve social status in the United States can lead to men's seeking respect and status in the community of origin by sending remittances. International remittances not only improve the quality of life for family members (Thai, 2006), but they also provide emotional benefits for the senders, allowing them to maintain social ties (Lillard & Willis, 1997; Thai, 2006; Wucker, 2004) and claim social worth in the community of origin (Thai, 2006). For immigrant men who experience downward mobility as well as social and cultural isolation, these social ties provide an important sense of self-worth, respect, and recognition in the community of origin (Thai, 2006). They allow immigrant men to actualize a familiar masculine identity "long distance." However, remittances can lead to economic neglect and hardship for women and children in the United States, and when women contest men's tendencies to send remittances too often, the result can be arguing and physical abuse.

Indeed, an examination of women's accounts of their abuse indicates that remittances were a major source of family conflicts that led to men's violence. Less than half of the women participants (43%) reported that they had sent money to relatives in Vietnam; more than half of the women (56%) reported that their partners had sent money to Vietnam. One third of the women (36% or 56 women) reported that remittances caused conflicts in their families, either because their partners did not allow them (21% or 32 women) or they did not allow their partners to send them (2.5% or 4 women), or they did not agree with the remittances their partners had sent (13% or 20 women). Couples disagreed over the amount, frequency, and recipients of remittances. Although it was common for Vietnamese immigrants to send remittances, women tended not to make remittances a priority over their financial needs in the United States when the recipients were not their parents and siblings. They wanted to help relatives in Vietnam, but they also wanted to save money for their children in the United States and for their retirement. In some situations, men sent remittances more often, even when their wives felt they did not make enough money to support their families in the United States.

Violence by men against their partners often followed family conflicts resulting from disagreement on remittances. Most of the women who were not allowed to send money (80% of 32 women), two thirds of the women who disagreed with the remittances their husbands had sent (65% of 20 women), and all women who did not allow their partners to send remittances (4 women) experienced physical abuse by their husbands. The experiences of Nhung, Tram, and Lan showed the relationship between family conflicts over remittances, men's efforts to control, and men's violence against their intimate partners.

Nhung's husband had been a high-ranking officer in the South Vietnamese government and after the Vietnam War, he spent many years in a reeducation camp under the communist regime. On release, he worked as a carpenter in Vietnam. In the United States, both Nhung and her husband received public assistance. Feeling that their income from public assistance was barely enough to help them maintain a frugal lifestyle, Nhung did not want to send remittances too often. When she discovered that her husband, who kept the family money, had sent remittances to his parents and siblings in Vietnam more often than she expected, she confronted him. Nhung explained the resulting violence,

> He kept the [family] money, and he used that money to send remittance to his parents and sibling in Vietnam, but he hid it from me. That caused conflict between us, and he beat me when I argued against him.

Lan and Tram described a similar pattern. Lan said,

> We often had conflicts because of money. He wanted to send money to his family and friends in Vietnam, and I didn't agree. It is not because I didn't want to help other family members and friends, but I didn't want him to send too much. I need to save money for my family here and my old age.

Tram reported that her husband sent most of his earnings from work to his family in Vietnam and did not save any for the family in the United States.

> Because we were on welfare, he couldn't get a real job. He worked under the table for cash in construction. He paid the rent with his welfare money. My disability check paid for all other expenses. He controlled all money from his work and sent most of his earnings to his family in Vietnam; he kept the rest for his gambling and drinking. When I asked him to save some for the family, he disagreed. He said it was his money because he worked for it. He always went out. He liked to hang out with his friends, drinking and gambling. When he lost money on gambling, he threatened to beat me up if I didn't give him the money he needed.

Tram's story suggests that her husband maintained status not only by sending remittances but by engaging in "masculine" pursuits of drinking and gambling with other men in the local Vietnamese community. These activities might mark him as a man with the resources for these leisure activities and give him local status at the same time that remittances might give him status with his relatives in Vietnam.

Analysis of interview transcripts showed that both men and women wanted to help their families of origin to fulfill their filial piety; however, men more often considered their families of origin a priority, especially when family resources were limited. Interviews with service providers in the East Coast area indicated that some men even prohibited their wives or partners from sending money to help relatives back in Vietnam. This practice appears to be consistent with the cultural belief that the husband's family is "inside lineage" and more important than the wife's family, which is considered as "outside lineage (Rydstrom, 2002, p. 361). Disagreements could lead to verbal fights and men's use of violence to take control, as illustrated by the experiences of two women, Diep and Quy.

> He hit me to make me shut up when he wanted to send more money to his family in Vietnam. He only sent money to his family but not my family. (Diep)
>
> We did not have enough money, and we often argued about sending money to the families on both sides in Vietnam. Because he did not allow me to send money to my family in Vietnam, I did not agree with his sending money to his family. He often criticized me for not working to make money. Our disagreements and verbal fights often ended up in his beating me. (Quy)

Women's narratives revealed that remittances sent to men's ex-wives, ex-girlfriends, and children from extramarital relationships were another source of family disputes leading to men's violence. Vietnamese cultural norms that support men's sexual privileges combined with the family instability specific to the history of Vietnam have facilitated men's multiple relationships. In Vietnam, family separations caused by the war, unprepared evacuation after the fall of Saigon, and clandestine escapes afterward increased opportunities for extramarital relationships among

Vietnamese men. Thus, many men secretly had extramarital affairs that produced children prior to migration, in some cases when their wives had emigrated before them. Members of resulting unofficial families were often left behind in Vietnam. Other men left wives and children in Vietnam and established new families in the United States. Unsatisfied with a lack of status in both the family and society, some men may strive to fulfill the masculine ideal by continuing to provide for another family in Vietnam. Violence could be used against women who wanted to protect financial resources for the family in the United States. Khanh provided an example of this situation:

> The reason for my family problem was money. We had problems whenever he didn't give me the full amount of money from his paycheck. I thought that he probably had sent money to his own son in Vietnam. He wanted me not to talk about money, but I couldn't stop because I need the money for my daughter and myself.

Another woman, Cuc, described a similar situation. Her husband had an extra-marital relationship with a woman who was left behind in Vietnam with two sons. Because their income from public assistance was low, Cuc's husband wanted to send money only to his ex-wife and children in Vietnam and prohibited her from sending money to her parents. During arguments about remittances, Cuc's husband typically used force in an attempt to maintain his authority and control of the family financial resources. Thuy was in a somewhat different situation. Her cohabiting partner had a wife and two children in Vietnam. His desire to control the family money and send remittances to his wife and children in Vietnam was a source of conflicts leading to his use of violence against her.

Conclusion

The present analysis can be criticized because it did not directly ask men how they saw their ideal selves "as men" or how they felt about actualizing these ideals. Instead, it relied on identifying descriptions of men's actions based on insights of women and professionals about men's statements and actions in relation to the construction of masculinity. The decision to rely on women's perceptions was based, in part, on concern for their safety; the men were not in any programs that could mitigate the risk of violence precipitated by the interviews. Because men's views were omitted from the analysis, findings from the study should be considered as suggestive. In addition, due the nature of the purposive sample, the generalizability of the study findings is limited. Future research might take a more direct approach and try to assess the degree to which a Vietnamese version of hegemonic masculinity characterized the men who were violent, or it might focus on immigrant men who had different versions of masculinity and, therefore, were not violent in the face of labor market constraints and women's changing gender norms and practices. Nonetheless, the research described in this article has provided a rare look at the standpoint of Vietnamese immigrant women affected by intimate partner violence as they explain incidents of and reasons for that violence. The accounts, views, and insights of such women are largely absent from the literature. Domestic violence is considered a highly private matter in Vietnamese culture, and because of language and cultural differences, immigrants and their communities often are inaccessible to researchers.

Analysis of material from the standpoints of both service providers and Vietnamese women suggests the connections of gender role norms and specific, gender-related job opportunities in immigrants' new homeland with men's resources and strategies for accomplishing masculinity, including the use of violence against an intimate partner. At least three key factors can lead up to violence. One is men's downward movement in social and economic status, often accompanied by women's upward movement, resulting in women's insistence or capacity to take on roles previously associated with traditional (hegemonic) forms of masculinity (e.g., family provider) and to avoid actions that were part of supportive femininity. The result can be men's use of violence to protest and reinforce their dominant positions in the family. Another factor is men's fear; women's work outside the home and the perceived loss of control over women's sexual exclusivity can result in intrusive efforts to oversee and control women's activities and can culminate in conflict and violence. Finally, remittances to relatives and additional partners and children in Vietnam allow men to demonstrate their masculinity long distance, and when their U.S.-based partners protest these expenditures, men can use violence to stop their interference and assert their control over this resource and the potential status it could bring from people in Vietnam.

Findings from the study suggest that men's use of violence against an intimate partner is consistent with masculine identity that is defined in terms of power, authority, sexual prowess, and ability to control women. Although a general construct of hegemonic masculinity is important for understanding men's behavior, an integrated framework of gender, race, ethnicity, class, and culture is required for understanding domestic violence among immigrants. Domestic violence occurs in the family, where important elements of power dynamics and gender meanings are constructed and where gender ideology is put into practice; however, family dynamics cannot be understood in isolation from the society at large because of the interactions of social structures and culture. Immigration adaptation can change gender dynamics in immigrant families and exert an important impact on masculinity manifestation, as indicated by the present study and prior research (Morash et al., 2000). Men who are unable to adapt to new economic situations and challenges to traditional norms for appropriate femininity and masculinity often experience a loss of economic power and social status. Men's lack of economic power can also facilitate sexual jealousy, which is often motivated by men's fear of losing their partners and not being able to realize the man's role of heading the household and producing sons to carry on the family line, which is an important aspect of Vietnamese traditional masculine identity. Men's downward mobility often clashes with women's new economic roles and elevated status after immigration and their increased activity and freedom outside the home (Gold, 1992). Unable to live up to the idealized hegemonic masculine identity in the new society, some men feel powerless and depressed. Although Vietnamese immigrant women have experienced an increase in economic power, many still expect men to be able to provide for the family (Bui, 2002; Kibria, 1993). Thus, men who experience an economic downturn often feel it is difficult to find and keep a partner in the United States (Thai, 2005). Violence against women can be used to overcome the perceived loss of power and feeling of inferiority, to boost self-esteem, and to reassert authority.

Understanding men's violence against women as a way of accomplishing a form of masculinity has an important implication for social policies and program interventions. In a patriarchal society, the social and cultural constructions of masculinity and femininity not only reinforce gender inequality and give men as a group the power to control and dominate women, but idealized masculinity also causes problems for men. The construction of masculinity through physical strength, the use of force, and the control of women leaves violence against women a resource for manifesting gender identity when other means are unavailable (Messerschmidt, 1993). Men who fail to live up to an idealized masculinity associated with power and authority due to their social locations in the hierarchy of race, class, immigration status, ethnicity, and gender can feel the pain of an inability to actualize masculine identity. Service providers and community education efforts need to directly address the meaning that men attach to remittances, the roots of their jealousy, and their losses to be most effective in preventing or stopping violence. Improving employment opportunities for immigrant men can increase men's economic power and reduce economic stress among men by helping them achieve masculine identity, but it does not eliminate the belief in men's control over women. Thus, long-term efforts of resettlement programs, community-based education and social services, and interventions into domestic violence require an emphasis not only on job preparation and the job market for men but also on gender equality. Crucially important for combating domestic violence is the elimination of the belief in male supremacy and men's control of women as part of masculine identity.

Notes

1. The study of domestic violence among Vietnamese immigrants in the East Coast area was supported by a grant from the National Science Foundation (1999-2003).

2. Eight women whose intimate partners were not of Vietnamese origin were not included in the present analysis. It should be noted that study participants were recruited from areas with high concentrations of Vietnamese immigrants, so women outside such areas are not represented.

3. One of the authors served as a guest speaker on two radio talk shows in Vietnamese communities and invited women in the audience to participate in the study.

4. Women who requested telephone interviews agreed not to receive the incentive because they did not want to disclose their mailing addresses.

5. To protect the confidentiality of the respondents, all names used in this article are pseudonyms.

6. The term *political detainee* is used to indicate a person who was a military officer or a high-ranking official in the South Vietnamese government and was detained in a reeducation camp under the communist regime.

7. The term *Vietnamese Amerasian* is used to indicate a person whose mother is Vietnamese and whose father is an American who served in the American mission in Vietnam. On December 22, 1987, the United States Congress passed into law the Amerasian Homecoming Act, allowing Vietnamese Amerasians who were born between 1962 and 1976 in Vietnam to enter the United State with their families with full refugee benefits.

8. Information is missing on one man's immigration experience.

9. Information about legal status was missing for one man.

10. We did not conduct tests of significance because the study used a purposive sample; thus, the assumption of a random sample cannot be met.

References

Abraham, M. (2000). *Speaking the unspeakable*. Philadelphia: Temple University Press.

Adelman, M. (2003). The military, militarism, and the militarization of domestic violence. *Violence Against Women, 9*, 1118-1152.

Bank, L. (1994). Angry men and working women: Gender, violence and economic change in Qwaqua in the 1980s. *African Studies, 53*, 89–114.

Boonzaier, F., & de La Rey, C. (2003). "He's a man, and I'm a woman": Cultural constructions of masculinity and femininity in South African women's narratives of violence. *Violence Against Women, 9*, 1005-1029.

Bourgois, P. (1996). In search of masculinity: Violence, respect, and sexuality among Puerto Rican crack dealers in East Harlem. *British Journal of Criminology, 36*, 412-427.

Bui, H. (2002). The immigration context of wife abuse: A case of Vietnamese immigrants in the U.S. In Roslyn Muraskin (Ed.), *It's a crime: Women and justice* (3rd ed., pp. 394-410). Upper Saddle River, NJ: Prentice Hall.

Bui, H. (2004). *In the adopted land: Abused immigrant women and the criminal justice system*. Westport, CT: Greenwood.

Connell, R. W. (1987). *Gender and power: Society, the person and sexual politics*. Stanford, CA: Stanford University Press.

Connell, R. W. (1995). *Masculinities*. Oxford, UK: Polity.

Connell, R. W. (2005). *Masculinities*. Berkeley: University of California Press.

Gold, S. (1992). *Refugee communities*. Newbury Park, CA: Sage.

Hampton, R., Oliver, W., & Maggarian, L. (2003). Domestic violence in African American community: An analysis of social and structural factors. *Violence Against Women, 9*, 533-541.

Hondagneu-Sotelo, P., & Messner, M. (1997). Gender display and men's power: The "new man" and the Mexican immigrant man. In M. B. Zinn, P. Hondagneu-Sotelo, & M. Messner (Eds.), *Through the prism of difference: Readings on sex and gender* (pp. 58-69). Needham Heights, MA: Allyn & Bacon.

Huynh Sanh Thong. (Ed.). (2001). *An anthology of Vietnamese poems: From the eleventh through the twentieth centuries* (Huynh Sanh Thong, Trans.). New Haven, CT: Yale University Press.

Jasinski, J. L. (2001). Theoretical explanations for violence against women. In C. M. Renzetti, J. L. Edleson, & R. K. Bergen (Eds.), *Sourcebook on violence against women* (pp. 5-21). Thousand Oaks, CA: Sage.

Jewkes, R., Levin, J., & Penn-Kakana, L. (2002). Risk factors for domestic violence: Findings from a South African cross-sectional study. *Social Science and Medicine, 55*, 1603-1617.

214　Feminist Criminology

Kaufman, M. (1994). Men, feminism, and men's contradictory experiences of power. In H. Brod & M. Kaufman (Eds.), *Theorizing masculinities* (pp. 142-163). Thousand Oaks, CA: Sage.

Kersten, J. (1996). Culture, masculinities, and violence against women. *British Journal of Criminology, 36,* 381, 395.

Kibria, N. (1993). *Family tightrope: The changing lives of Vietnamese Americans.* Princeton, NJ: Princeton University Press.

Le Thi. (1996). Women, marriage, family, and gender equality. In K. Barry (Eds.), *Vietnam's women in transition* (pp. 61-73). New York: St Martin's.

Le Thi Quy. (1996). Domestic violence in Vietnam and efforts to curb it. In K. Barry (Ed.), *Vietnam's women in transition* (pp. 263-247). New York: St Martin's.

Lillard, L., & Willis, R. J. (1997). Motives for intergenerational transfers: Evidence from Malaysia. *Demography, 34,* 115-134.

Lin, K., Tazuma, L., & Masuda, M. (1979). Adaptation problems of Vietnamese refugees. *Archives of General Psychiatry, 36,* 955-961.

Luke, N., Schuler, S. R., Bui, M. T., Pham, T. V., & Tran, M. H. (2007). Exploring couple attributes and attitudes and marital violence in Vietnam. *Violence Against Women, 13,* 5-27.

Macmillan, R., & Gartner, R. (1999). When she brings home the bacon: Labor-force participation and the risk of spousal violence against women. *Journal of Marriage and the Family, 61,* 947-958.

Messerschmidt, J. (1993). *Masculinities and crime.* Lanham, MD: Rowman & Littlefield.

Morash, M., Bui, H., & Santiago, A. (2000). Cultural-specific gender ideology and wife abuse in Mexican-descent families [Special issue]. *International Review of Victimology, 7,* 67-91.

Messerschmidt, J. W. (1986). Capitalism, patriarchy, and crime: Toward a socialist feminist criminology. Totowa, NJ: Rowman & Littlefield.

Nash, S. T. (2005). Through Black eyes: African American women's constructions of their experiences of intimate male partner violence. *Violence Against Women, 11,* 1420-1440.

Nguyen, L. (1987). Cross-cultural adjustment of Vietnamese in the United States. In L. B. Truong (Ed.), *Borrowings and adaptations in Vietnamese culture* (pp. 1-21). Manoa: University of Hawaii.

O'Harrow, S. (1995). Vietnamese women and Confucianism: Creating spaces from patriarchy. In W. J. Karim (Ed.), *"Male" and "female" in developing Southeast Asia* (pp. 161-180). Washington, DC: Berg.

Phan Huy Ich. (1986). *The song of a soldier's wife* (Huynh Sanh Thong, Trans., Ed.). New Haven, CT: Yale University Press.

Rydstrom, H. (2002). Sexed bodies, gendered bodies: Children and the body in Vietnam. *Women's Studies International Forum, 25,* 359-372.

Rydstrom, H. (2003). Encountering "hot" anger: Domestic violence in contemporary Vietnam. *Violence Against Women, 9,* 676-697.

Rydstrom, H. (2004). Female and male "characters": Images of identification and self-identification for rural Vietnamese children and adolescents. In H. Rydstrom & L. Drummond (Eds.), *Gender practices in contemporary Vietnam* (pp. 75-95). Singapore: University of Singapore Press.

Rydstrom, H., & Drummond, L. (2004). Introduction. In H. Rydstrom & L. Drummond (Eds.), *Gender practices in contemporary Vietnam* (pp. 1-25). Singapore: University of Singapore Press.

Schwartz, M. D., & DeKeseredy, W. S. (1997). *Sexual assault on the college campus: The role of male peer support.* Thousand Oaks, CA: Sage.

Scully, D., & Marolla, J. (1985). Riding the bull at Gilley's: Convicted rapists describe the rewards of rape. *Social Problems, 32*(3), 251-263.

Song, Y. I., & Moon, A. (1998). The domestic violence against women in Korean immigrant families: Cultural, psychological, and socioeconomic perspectives. In Y. I. Song & A. Moon (Eds.), *Korean American women: From tradition to modern feminism* (pp. 161-174). Westport, CT: Praeger.

Ta, T. V. (1981). The status of women in traditional Vietnam: A comparison of the Code of the Le Dynasty (1428-1788) with the Chinese Codes. *Journal of Asian History, 15,* 97-145.

Thai, H. C. (2005). Globalization as a gender strategy: Respectability, masculinity, and convertibility across the Vietnamese Diaspora. In R. P. Appelbaum & W. I. Robinson (Eds.), *Critical globalization studies* (pp. 76-92). New York: Routledge.

Thai, H. C. (2006). Money and masculinity among low wage Vietnamese immigrants in transnational families. *International Journal of Sociology of the Family, 32*, 247-271.

Tran, C. (1997). *Domestic violence among Vietnamese refugee women: Prevalence, abuse characteristics, psychiatric symptoms, and psychological factors.* Unpublished dissertation, Boston University.

Tran, T. (1959). *Vietnam.* New York: Frederick A. Praeger.

U.S. Census Bureau. (2003). *We the people: Asians in the United States.* Washington, DC: Author.

Vo Phien. (1999). *Van Hoc Viet Nam* (Vietnamese literatures, in Vietnamese). Westminster, CA: Van Nghe.

Vu, L. M., Vu, H. T., Nguyen, M. H., & Clement, J. (2000). *Gender-based violence: The case of Vietnam.* Washington, DC: World Bank.

Whaley, R. B. (2001). The paradoxical relationship between gender inequality and rape: Toward a refined theory. *Gender & Society, 15*, 531-555.

Wucker, M. (2004). Remittances: The perpetual migration machine. *World Policy Journal, 21*, 37-46.

Yick, A. G. (2001). Feminist theory and status inconstancy theory: Application to domestic violence in Chinese immigrant families. *Violence Against Women, 7*, 545-562.

Hoan Bui is an associate professor in the Department of Sociology, University of Tennessee, Knoxville. Her research particularly focuses on the influence of immigration resettlement on the constructions of masculinity and femininity and women's experiences of and responses to intimate partner violence. Her research has been published in *Violence Against Women, Women and Criminal Justice, International Review of Victimology,* and *Journal of Ethnicity and Criminal Justice.* She is the author of *In the Adopted Land: Abused Immigrant Women and the Criminal Justice System* (Greenwood, 2004).

Merry Morash is a professor at the School of Criminal Justice, Michigan State University, East Lansing. She is the author of *Understanding Gender, Crime and Justice* (Sage, 2006). Areas of research include policewomen, domestic violence in immigrant groups, sexual assault in prisons, juvenile delinquency, and women on probation and parole. Her research has been conducted in both the United States and South Korea. She is the director of the Michigan Community Policing Institute and the Michigan Victim Assistance Academy, which provides education for individuals who work with crime victims.

Part IV
Intersections

[11]

An Argument for Black Feminist Criminology

Understanding African American Women's Experiences With Intimate Partner Abuse Using an Integrated Approach

Hillary Potter
University of Colorado at Boulder

This article draws on existing feminist theoretical concepts to develop a Black feminist criminology (BFC), using intimate partner abuse against African American women to examine this pioneering approach. BFC expands on feminist criminology and is grounded firmly in Black feminist theory and critical race feminist theory. BFC recognizes a significant connection between intimate partner abuse against women and structural, cultural, and familial influences. It is argued that BFC aids in a more precise explanation of how Black women experience and respond to intimate partner abuse and how the crime-processing system responds to battered Black women.

Keywords: *Black feminist criminology; African American women; domestic violence*

Just as there are many types of feminisms and feminists, it undoubtedly follows that there are adaptations on feminist criminology and no single feminist criminology can exist (Britton, 2000; Daly & Chesney-Lind, 1988; Flavin, 1998). The impetus for proposing a Black feminist criminology (BFC) is supported by Britton's (2000) argument that traditional feminist criminology still has much work to accomplish in theorizing from intersecting identities as opposed to placing emphasis on a solitary component—such as considering gender but not race—at the forefront of and central to an analysis. Flavin (1998) expressly promoted a BFC that focuses on the specific experiences of Black individuals in the crime-processing system.[1] Although feminist criminology has its roots in mainstream feminist theories (Britton, 2000; Daly & Chesney-Lind, 1988),[2] the approach presented in this article, BFC, is grounded in Black feminist theory and critical race feminist theory (CRFT). To begin to understand and fully conceptualize BFC, this article considers intimate partner abuse against African American[3] women as an illustration of its ability to explain this transgression.

Author's Note: The author especially wishes to thank Dr. Joanne Belknap and the anonymous reviewers for their extensive comments and support in drafting this article.

Feminist criminology has aided in a notably improved understanding of gender variations in criminal activity and victimization and of the crime-processing system's dealings with female and male victims and offenders. Feminist criminology has significantly expanded the foci within the field of criminology beyond simply exploring female criminal offending and female offenders to also examining violent acts against girls and women (Britton, 2000). Although gender is certainly important and crucial to considering women's (and men's) involvement in crime either as victims or as offenders, for Black women, and arguably for all women, other inequities must be considered principal, not peripheral, to the analysis of women. This includes incorporating key factors such as race and/or ethnicity, sexuality, and economic status into any examination. Daly (1997) argued that considering how gender, race, and class distinctions intersect is absolutely necessary in criminology. Because traditional feminist criminology is built on mainstream feminism, which historically placed issues of race as secondary to gender (hooks, 2000; Lewis, 1977), it is reasoned here that starting at Black feminist theory and CRFT to investigate and explain the source of and reactions to crime among African Americans will be sure to explicitly take into account Black women's positions in society, in their communities, and in their familial and intimate relationships. This proposition does not serve to devalue the remarkable work resulting from the establishment of feminist criminology or the concepts purported by and examined under this rubric. Instead, BFC extends beyond traditional feminist criminology to view African American women (and conceivably, other women of color) from their multiple marginalized and dominated positions in society, culture, community, and families. Although the example provided here to tender a Black feminist criminological theory is on one form of victimization of African American women, it has been well documented in feminist criminology analyses that there is often a clear correlation and/or pathway between women's victimization and any ultimate criminal behavior (Belknap, 2001; Britton, 2000; Chesney-Lind & Pasko, 2004; Richie, 1996). As such, using intimate partner abuse against African American women as an illustration provides us with an example that may be applied beyond Black women's experiences with victimization into other encounters with crime and the crime-processing system.

As is demonstrated here, BFC can advance future theorizing, research, and policy making regarding battered Black women. At the outset, this article presents an historical overview of the attention given to the issue of intimate partner abuse by feminist activists and the problems with examining African American women's encounters with domestic abuse using theory based on White women's experiences. A comprehensive description of BFC is then provided and followed by the Black feminist and critical race feminist concepts on which it is constructed. Support for a BFC is demonstrated by evaluating African American women's experiences with and responses to intimate partner abuse and the crime-processing system's intervention in domestic violence incidents involving Black women under this model. Presented throughout this application are previous assessments on battered Black women in the works of some Black and critical race feminists. As with any new theoretical proposal, criticism of the concept is to be expected. Therefore, anticipated criticisms and potential limitations are addressed.

Historical Development of Feminist Advocacy Against Intimate Partner Abuse

An increased awareness of the problem of intimate partner abuse against women has occurred only during the past few decades. Until the 1970s, concern, advocacy, and protection for battered women by the general public and officials of the crime-processing system were tremendously lacking (Belknap, 2001; Tierney, 1982). Historians had sporadically recorded attempts of various individuals who raised public concern for these victims. However, these endeavors were largely unsuccessful until the 1970s. During this decade, there was an accelerating trend toward the criminalization of domestic violence perpetrators and an increase in the assistance afforded battered women. Feminist organizations began to highlight intimate partner violence against women as a social problem needing to be remedied (Schechter, 1982), and books written by battered women and their advocates began to appear with fervor (Belknap & Potter, 2006). In 1973, the United States saw one of its first shelters to assist wives battered by their alcoholic husbands at the Rainbow Retreat in Phoenix, Arizona (Tierney, 1982), and since this time, shelters have rapidly appeared across the country (Belknap, 2001). In addition to establishing places to harbor battered women and their children away from their male batterers, law enforcement and court intervention agents began to address woman battering more seriously with the enactment and increased enforcement of laws and sanctions relating to intimate abuse (Tierney, 1982). In 1994, President Bill Clinton signed into law the landmark Violence Against Women Act to combat violence against women by providing assistance to criminal processing agents (e.g., training), support for battered women's shelters and a national telephone "hotline," and funding for research on violence against women. The act was renewed in 2000 and provided financial support in excess of US$3 billion for 5 years. The second reauthorization of the Act was passed by both the U.S. Senate and the House of Representatives and was signed into law by President Bush in January 2006.

Along with the diligent labor of feminist activists, the battered women's movement was further assisted in its development and awareness efforts by the media's attention to the movement (Tierney, 1982). Through the mid-1970s, some popular magazines considered domestic violence to be acts of rioting and terrorism, but by the end of the decade, the term became equivalent with *wife abuse* (Tierney, 1982) and other forms of family-related interpersonal violence (Belknap, 2001). Indeed, between 1987 and 1997, the media representations of domestic violence as a serious issue were instrumental in decreasing the public's tolerance of wife abuse during this decade (Johnson & Sigler, 2000).

Although intimate partner violence has experienced increased attention by the public, researchers, and the crime-processing system, abuse among intimate partners as a social problem is still not receiving the level of attention it deserves from criminal processing agents (Erez & Belknap, 1998) and health professionals (Belknap, 2001; Rodriguez, Bauer, McLoughlin, & Grumbach, 1999). For instance, there is fairly recent evidence that police officers still respond leniently to male batterers (Fyfe, Klinger, & Flavin, 1997). That is, men who abuse their female intimate partners are arrested less often than other violent offenders. In addition, battered women's shelters continue to suffer from poor financial support and the inability to house every woman and child in need of and requesting sanctuary from their abusers (Belknap, 2001). As indicated by a survey conducted by the Center for the Advancement of Women (2003), a sizeable number of women deem that intimate partner violence warrants continued attention. In fact, the report indicates that 92% of the women surveyed believed that domestic violence and sexual assault should be the top priority for the women's movement. Violence against women as a main concern was succeeded by the following priorities: equal pay for equal work (90%), child care (85%), reducing drug and alcohol addiction among women (72%), and keeping abortion legal (41%). This finding underlies the need that much more work is needed to improve the lives of battered women and to better address the unwarranted behavior of batterers.

It is unmistakable that with the identification of domestic violence as a social problem approximately three decades ago came an unprecedented amount of research and activism surrounding the plight of battered women. In both the research and responses to intimate partner abuse, however, cultural, racial, and ethnic distinctions among women victims of intimate partner abuse have not been afforded equal levels of consideration (Bograd, 1999; Richie, 1996, 2000). Much of the extant research and policies regard all battered women as victims with similar life experiences (Richie, 2000; C. West, 2005); yet African American women and other women of color typically have life experiences distinct from White women. The research in the 1970s was conducted with predominately White samples and a failure to take into account how the surveys and findings might be problematic in reference to victims and offenders of color. It is regrettable that more recent investigations continue to follow this precedent. Stated alternatively, using research designed to study battered White women may not adequately explain how African American women experience and respond to intimate partner abuse. It is notable that Black women encounter the serious ramifications of racism in addition to sexism, and findings indicate they are the victims of intimate partner violence at higher rates than their White counterparts (Gelles & Straus, 1988; Hampton & Gelles, 1994; Rennison & Welchans, 2000). Basing investigations on theories that do not defer to the unique experiences of Black women may be erroneous and impractical to these women because of their prospects of encountering both racism and sexism within U.S. society.

BFC and Its Origins

The Tenets of BFC

BFC incorporates the tenets of interconnected identities, interconnected social forces, and distinct circumstances to better theorize, conduct research, and inform policy regarding criminal behavior and victimization among African Americans. (This concept may also have applicability with other groups of color and possibly with White women.) The interconnected identities to be considered among African American individuals include race and/or ethnicity, gender, sexuality, class status, national origin, and religion. Certainly, this is not a comprehensive list, as this precept allows for other identities to be included dependent on how an individual self-identifies. In U.S. society's stratified composition, occurrences of inequity are often experienced because of the spectrum of diversity within each identity and the intolerance and ignorance among some members of society. As such, various identities will be deemed of less value than others. This devaluation affects how certain individuals maneuver through life, including how they respond to events and opportunities with which they are confronted. Starting from this advantage point can help us begin to improve our explanations for the experiences of battered Black women's (a) entry into abusive relationships, (b) response to their abusers, and (c) use of systemic resources to aid in withdrawing from the relationships.

These interconnected identities are greatly shaped by larger social forces. That is, groups of individuals and society at large produce and perpetuate conflict, competition, and differences in merit between the members of society. It is not battered Black women's identities that exclusively form their perceptions and reactions but the treatment of these identities filtered down from (a) the impact of the social structure through (b) the community or culture and to (c) familial and intimate exchanges. Nevertheless, this does not necessitate a linear association in every case; instead, it serves to demonstrate and argue that a patriarchal, paternalistic, and racialized social structure affects all other institutions and interactions in society. Black women's reactions to abuse are affected by their "place" in society because of their intersecting identities. Being at the least valued end of the spectrum for both race and gender places these women in a peculiar position not faced by Black men or White women (although Black men and White women are indeed challenged with their relative and respective dominating forces). In a similar manner, other women of color, such as Latinas, Native American women, Asian American women, and immigrant women of color, can easily be placed alongside Black women in this analysis.

Last, the characteristic of "battered woman" or "criminal offender" should not be considered an element of the identities of women victims or offenders. Being abused or having committed criminal acts are situations which women encounter or in which women become implicated, not those that are endemic of their identity. Of course, this is not to diminish the seriousness of women being victimized or of criminality among women; instead, it is to emphasize that the individuals themselves rarely recognize these characteristics as central to their identity (see Potter, 2004, for an analysis of how battered Black women do not identify as victims or survivors and how abuse is a temporary setback and an additional act of oppression in their lives). Furthermore, incorporating these distinct circumstances into Black women's identity risks pathologizing Black women victims or offenders by making these events appear normal or expected among Black women.

Black Feminist and Critical Race Feminist Origins of BFC

BFC addresses concerns in the lives of Black women that are categorized into four themes: (a) social structural oppression, (b) the Black community and culture, (c) intimate and familial relations, and (d) the Black woman as an individual. As outlined above, the first three themes are components of interconnected social forces, whereas the fourth theme considers the interconnected identities of the Black woman as affected by the societal influences. The tenets of BFC are cultivated from Black feminist theory and CRFT. In general, Black feminist theory is the theoretical perspective that places the lived experiences of Black women, including any forms of resistance to their situations, at the focal point of the analysis. It considers Black women as individuals encompassing numerous and interwoven identities. The standpoint is that Black women are frequently oppressed within both the Black community (by Black men) and society at large based on their subordinated statuses within each of these spheres and that research on Black women should be conducted based on this perspective. Although the sexist oppression in the Black community may not appear as obvious as that in larger society, and presents itself in a different form, it undeniably exists. CRFT is similar to Black feminist theory in that it also considers women of color as individuals with multiple intersecting identities where one does not eclipse another. Specifically, however, CRFT has been used to consider the devalued position of women of color in greater society as their status relates to the legal field.

Unlike many White women who enjoyed the "feminist lifestyle" because it provided them the opportunity to meet and bond with other women, Black women have always had a sense of sisterhood (hooks, 2000). Although it is often assumed that Black women did not participate in the development of feminist ideology and the practice of gender equality, it is evident that Black women have indeed been involved in liberation efforts. By reading the works of women who considered themselves to be Black feminists, or were identified as such by others, Black women have a lengthy and valiant history in the liberation movement (Guy-Sheftall, 1995; King, 1988). Their struggles can be traced back to the 1600s when African women who were captured and enslaved in the so-called New World endured multiple forms of oppression by their slave masters (Fishman, 2003; Guy-Sheftall, 1995). Many of these women made attempts to defend themselves against the inhumane treatment. Recent survey research demonstrates that Black women, even more so than White women, are discontented with women's situation in society and are in want of changes in the social world that benefit women. According to Jones and Shorter-Gooden (2003), a Gallup poll conducted in June 2002 finds that 48% of Black women affirmed they were dissatisfied with the treatment of women within society as compared to 26% of White women.

Mainstream feminist theory places gender as the primary consideration in women's liberation efforts (hooks, 2000). Black women have expressed difficulty in identifying with mainstream feminist theory because of its focus on this single aspect of womanhood and because the lives and concerns of White middle-class women were placed at the forefront of the liberation efforts (Collins, 2000). Black women regularly convey that they deal not only with issues of gender inequality but with racial inequality as well (Crenshaw, 1994). It is this status, Crenshaw (1994) argued, that relegates women of color to an invisible class and pulls these women's loyalties in two directions, that is, feeling the need to either choose between being loyal to feminist ideas or being loyal to their racial or ethnic community. Patricia Hill Collins (2000), Black feminist author of

Black Feminist Thought: Knowledge, Consciousness, and the Politics of Empowerment, distinguished Black women's experiences from those of other groups of women and also considered Black women's lives as individuals:

> On the one hand, all African-American women face similar challenges that result from living in a society that historically and routinely derogates women of African descent. Despite the fact that U.S. Black women face common challenges, this neither means that individual African-American women have all had the same experiences nor that we agree on the significance of our varying experiences. Thus, on the other hand, despite the common challenges confronting U.S. Black women as a group, diverse responses to these core themes characterize U.S. Black women's group knowledge or standpoint. (p. 25)

This collective, yet individualized, aspect of Black women's lives is an important aspect in Black feminism and when considering Black women.

Used in conjunction with Black feminist theory, CRFT is a valuable approach for studies of crime and African American women because it provides a specific application to issues of women of color involved in the crime-processing system as victims, offenders, or both. Just as with many Black feminists, most critical race feminists have not involved themselves in the mainstream feminist movement but admit that they make use of certain themes of mainstream feminism in the social sciences (Wing, 2003). Developed in the 1990s, CRFT is based in the tradition of Black feminist theory, critical legal studies, and critical race theory (Wing, 1997). People of color, White women, and others were initially attracted to critical legal studies because it challenged laws related to oppression based on race and gender (Wing, 2003). Those credited with developing critical race theory reported disillusionment with critical legal studies' exclusion of the personal and intellectual viewpoints from scholars of color and White women scholars. Accordingly, critical race theory places more focus on the role of racism and a racist and classist society in the construction of realities among people of color. Although deemed as a move toward the inclusion of all people in the analysis of social interaction and social justice, many women of color continued to feel gender was not often introduced as a concern within critical race theory discourse and consequently, CRFT was born (Wing, 1997). According to Wing (1997), CRFT, like Black feminist theory, is grounded in "antiessentialism" and intersectionality. Antiessentialism asserts that there is more than one essential voice of women.[4] Battered Black women's experience with the crime-processing system and its agents can suitably be analyzed by incorporating a CRFT viewpoint into BFC.

In summation, numerous Black feminist and critical race feminist scholars have addressed the "intersecting oppressions" of Black women. In the classic article "Double Jeopardy: To Be Black and Female," Frances Beale (1970/1995), journalist and civil rights activist, wrote of the burden of the Black woman's disadvantaged status based on gender, race, and class. Gordon's (1987) analysis identified these three conditions as Black women's "trilogy of oppression" and stated that Black women are often confronted with determining which form of oppression is most important. King (1988) advocated for the term *multiple jeopardy* to describe Black women's oppression, given that Black women often undergo even more forms of subjugation and that these categories of oppression affect Black women simultaneously (also see Cleaver, 1997; Collins, 2000; Gordon, 1987; Guy-Sheftall, 1995; Hull, Bell Scott, & Smith, 1982; Smith, 1983; Terrelonge, 1984; Wing, 1997, 2003). Wing (2003), who used the term *multiplicative identity* to capture the identity of women of color, argued that "women of color are not merely White women *plus* color or men of color *plus* gender. Instead, their identities must be multiplied together to create a holistic One when analyzing the nature of the discrimination against them" (p. 7).

Although there is increased acceptance of a variety of feminist theories, hooks (2000) has continued to question whether contemporary White women understand that their perspectives may not be indicative of all women's realities and that their views may still be racist and classist. In referring to the issues raised regarding Anita Hill's reports of sexual harassment during the U.S. Senate hearings for Clarence Thomas's confirmation to the U.S. Supreme Court, McKay (1993) wrote that White women feminists "forgot that for Black women, issues of gender are always connected to race. . . . Black women cannot choose between their commitment to feminism and the struggle with their men for racial justice" (p. 276). Crenshaw (1994) echoed this sentiment by maintaining that modern discussions on feminism and antiracism have disregarded how racism and sexism are interwoven and "because of their intersectional identity as both women *and* people of color within discourses that are shaped to respond to one *or* the other, the interests and experiences of women of color are frequently marginalized within both" (p. 94). Collins's (2000) theoretical approach can be applied to how investigations on the lives of battered Black women should be conducted, as evident when she established that Black feminist theory is positioned within the "matrix of domination," as opposed to being dissociated from sociostructural truths.

Intimate partner abuse has been considered by many Black feminist scholars, even if only in a portion of their work (see Collins, 2000; Cole & Guy-Sheftall, 2003; hooks, 1981a, 1981b, 1989, 2000, 2004; Richie, 1996, 2000); and although still in its youthful stage, CRFT has been specifically applied to domestic violence in the lives of women of color (see Allard, 1991; Ammons, 1995; Coker, 2003; Crenshaw, 1994; Kupenda, 1998; Rivera, 1997, 2003; Valencia-Weber & Zuni, 2003). Considering issues of both multiplicative identity and intimate partner violence, Richie (2003) argued, "We now have data that supports [*sic*] the existence of racial and ethnic differences in rates but a theoretical orientation and public policy that can't accommodate or make sense of this new understanding" (p. 203). Using Black feminist theory and CRFT as foundations in considering the issues with intimate partner abuse against African American women, as well as considering their involvement in criminal behavior, will assist in addressing this limitation and contribute to the development of BFC.

Understanding Intimate Partner Abuse in the Lives of Black Women Using BFC

As established above, the four themes considered within BFC include social structural oppression, interactions within the Black community, intimate and familial relations, and the Black woman as an individual, all operating under the premise that these segments are interconnected. Each of these themes is addressed in detail here, specifically examining how BFC can assist with formulating analyses of African American women's encounters with intimate partner abuse. Use of this framework allows the connection between woman battering and structural, cultural, and familial restraints to be made.

Social Structural Oppression

Under the theme of social structural oppression, matters of institutional racism, damaging stereotypical images, sexism, and classism are routinely addressed by Black feminists and critical race feminists and incorporated for analysis. Included in the examination is the limited access to adequate education and employment as consequences of racism, sexism, and classism. As education and employment deficiencies have been found to be common among battered women (Rennison & Welchans, 2000), this area of focus by BFC considers the impact of these shortcomings on battered Black women's lives. Even for Black women who are able to attain advanced levels of education and high-status employment positions, it is unlikely they reached these junctures in their careers without facing blatant or covert racist and sexist attitudes, behaviors, and policies (see Collins, 1998; Jones & Shorter-Gooden, 2003). As a result, the sociostructural stressors of even middle- or upper-class battered Black women and how they may respond to intimate partner abuse must be assessed from this standpoint.

Concerns external to remaining in abusive relationships because of poor financial status must be considered with all battered Black women, particularly battered Black women belonging to higher socioeconomic statuses. Stigmatizing constraints forcing battered Black women to remain in abusive settings could include their resistance to engendering the controlling stereotypical image of the single, Black matriarch (Collins, 2000). Based on socially constructed perceptions of Black women, BFC scrutinizes how stereotypical images of these women affect the ways in which others respond to them. Poor responses by social services professionals and crime-processing agents to Black women's interpersonal victimization crises can be considered under the auspices of this framework. Social services used by domestic violence victims in their process of leaving abusive relationships include medical assistance, battered women's shelters, and therapeutic agents. It is regrettable that African American women are often reluctant to seek assistance via these opportunities (Crenshaw, 1994; Potter, 2004; Short et al., 2000). The barriers to using these sources may be in relation to not only the short supply of battered women's shelters and therapeutic resources in Black communities (Asbury, 1987; Sullivan & Rumptz, 1994) or known to the Black community but also the ability and lack of trust in those working in the helping professions who are not able to deliver adequate culturally competent services to African American women who have suffered abuse from their intimate partners (Ammons, 1995; Sharma, 2001; Williams & Tubbs, 2002).

The criminal processing system also has not been swift to aid battered Black women (Ammons, 1995; Robinson & Chandek, 2000), and battered women of color report distrust in using the formal criminal processing system to assist with their exodus from abusive relationships (Bennett, Goodman, & Dutton, 1999; Richie, 1996; Weis, 2001). A history of poor relations between criminal processing agencies (and their representatives) and communities of color can account for these misgivings (Brice-Baker, 1994). Even with higher law enforcement reporting rates than battered White women (Bachman & Coker, 1995; Rennison & Welchans, 2000), Black women victims still express reservations with trusting authorities in the criminal processing system. Reservations about using the crime-processing system are also said to transpire because speaking out about intimate partner violence can involve the risk of generating racial shame (Ammons, 1995; Kupenda, 1998; C. West, 2005; T. West, 1999), and Black women may be viewed as traitors to their race for adding more African American men to the system's offender population (Brice-Baker, 1994; Richie, 1996; Sorenson, 1996).[5]

A focus by BFC on this documented history of poor systemic responses allows for an examination of the way in which professionals working with battered Black women may rely on stereotypical (thus, often inaccurate) assumptions of Black women when making decisions about how to respond to them. An example of the harm of cultural insensitivity and typecasting is found in this author's in-depth interviews with a diverse sample of battered Black women (see Potter, 2004). For many of the participants, assuming the role of the Strong Black Woman, as well as being perceived as a Strong Black Woman, had policy implications for battered women's shelter and counseling services. The women who capitalized on using shelters and therapy to assist them with terminating the abusive relationships were often singled out because of their distinguishing experiences with abuse and as Black women. When the participants' experiences with intimate partner abuse were pointed out by the other clients, it tended to be done for the purposes of placing battering and abuse in a hierarchical sequence and served as a perverse source of competition for the other battered women. When the participants were singled out by counselors, it was for the seemingly innocuous purposes of benefiting the battered Black women, to highlight how they are stronger than the other women (i.e., the White women) and strong enough to get out of the relationships. Even if these assertions by other battered women and service providers were true, they often served as a detriment to battered Black women's inclination to leave abusive relationships. Undervaluing battered Black women's violent encounters because they are not in abusive relationships as long as White women or because their injuries are not (or do not appear to be) as severe as other women's essentially justifies battering to a certain degree. Furthermore, it perpetuates battered Black women's impression that they do not need to seek alternative or supplemental assistance to their familial and personal resources.

Black Community and Black Culture

The second theme addressed by BFC, the interactions within the Black community, is based on the cultural distinctions of African Americans. The nature of relationships among Blacks is a topic scrupulously discussed by critical race and Black feminists. These discussions often include the impact of historical experiences of African Americans in the United States. Some specific subjects addressed by Black feminists (although not an exhaustive list) include issues of Black women's and Black men's roles in the Black community, the occurrence of violence within the Black community, and the role of spirituality and the Black church as a staple institution in the Black community. Such a concentration allows for each of these features to be considered in how it affects Black women's encounters with domestic abuse. For instance, if indeed Black women's role in the Black community is one of an egalitarian and independent nature, how are issues of a batterer's power and control behaviors (i.e., typical qualities among batterers) displayed in relationships among Black couples? By scrutinizing the characteristics of batterers' abusive behaviors and the motivations for battered Black women to remain in abusive relationships, a sufficient explanation can be formed to demonstrate the method in which these men are still able to assert some level of power and control over the women. Again, recent qualitative research determines that battered Black women remain in abusive relationships more so out of fear of being without companionship, being without a father or father figure for minor children, and being stigmatized as yet another single Black mother than fear of further and more perilous battering incidents or of financial independence (Potter, 2004). Such fears are certainly inherent in Black women's distinctive experiences within U.S. society and the Black community and, thus, can be better understood from a BFC viewpoint.

The role of religion and spirituality must be strongly regarded when considering African American women's experiences with abuse. The substantial impact of religious practice and spirituality in the lives of battered Black women has been solidly established (Bell & Mattis, 2000; Potter, in press; T. West, 1999). Although battered Black women rely heavily on religion and/or spirituality, a number of clergy members have not always demonstrated the support that is expected of them by battered Black women parishioners (Potter, in press). To be sure, BFC considers the essential institutions and practices in any investigation of African Americans, crime, and violence, particularly in how they relate to preventing, controlling, or the perpetration of offending behaviors.

Familial and Intimate Relations

The intimate and familial relationships theme is the third area on which BFC concentrates. The family of origin and generational characteristics of the Black family is one of the foci here, including the embeddedness in othermothers[6] and family members outside of the immediate family unit (i.e., extended family). By considering family embeddedness as a major focal point among African Americans in an analysis of battered Black women's help-seeking behaviors, a more thorough assessment of their dependency on this custom as a resource, as opposed to relying on systemic resources, can be made. This same embeddedness can demonstrate how abuse in the family of origin and among other close family members can be a detrimental and compounding factor on the victims.

Intimate relationships of Black women and their roles within these relationships, including interracial and/or lesbian couples, are essential elements of BFC, particularly as they function in and are affected by the larger societal composition. Research on interracial battering relationships is particularly lacking, but this cross-cultural dynamic would be well served by study under the auspices of BFC in determining how the various lived experiences of the members of interracial couples may affect the relationship circumstances differently. Lesbian battering relationships among Black women can be examined from the compounding element of sexuality, especially in how this component of Black lesbians' identity is viewed by others and how the quality of the relationship is consequently affected. Lesbian relationships among Black women gained more attention within Black feminist theory when lesbian Black feminists expressed their dissatisfaction with the lack of attention heterosexual Black feminists gave lesbianism and homophobia in the Black community. As a result, Black feminists fastidiously include same-gender intimate relationships in their analyses. The implications for Black women who identify as both lesbian and battered clearly require future research (Robinson, 2003) and would prosper under a BFC investigation that necessarily considers intersectionality.

Black Woman as Individual

Last, the theme of Black women as individuals is afforded considerable examination in BFC. Although examined as an individual, the life of the Black woman is strongly connected to her location, status, and role in the social structure, the Black community, and interpersonal relationships. Within this category, issues such as mental health, sexual health, and sexuality are addressed. Inclusion of this precept allows a personal yet comprehensive view of battered Black women.

Consequently, battered Black women's personal strategies for dealing with the abuse can be analyzed under this notion. These strategies include how a battered Black woman may frame the effects of the abuse. As established, Black women face many forms of oppression, and this subjugation will undoubtedly affect a Black woman's mental fitness. It is clear that being abused by an intimate partner serves only to deteriorate a Black woman's mental health beyond the injury of the bias bestowed on countless African American women on a daily basis.

Another strategy exercised by battered women includes the use of physical force against batterers. The propensity of Black women to physically strike back against their intimate abusers has been determined to be at greater rates than battered White women's retaliation (Hampton, Gelles, & Harrop, 1989; Joseph, 1997; C. West & Rose, 2000). Although it is seen as a personal tactic among many battered Black women, considering their self-defense strategies through BFC would allow for the introduction of structural and cultural influences to be considered to begin to explain this phenomenon (see Potter, 2004, for an extended analysis on this topic).

Response to Anticipated Criticism

Although evidence has been presented to support the use of BFC to better understand domestic abuse and African American women, some criticism of this approach can be foreseen. To start, this theoretical contribution may be viewed as being too limiting because the examination expounded here is grounded in Black and critical race theories and focuses on Black women specifically. The claim might be made that this approach does not serve an overarching benefit to responding to and preventing intimate partner abuse. A rejoinder to this potential criticism would rationalize that because Black women are estimated to be victims of abuse at higher rates than White women, it is imperative that we make greater efforts to understand and determine how to address this concern. As Black women are also overrepresented in areas of the crime-processing system as offenders (e.g., arrests, incarceration; Belknap, 2001; Britton, 2000), a new approach for comprehending this trend should be welcomed as well. For both victim and offender status among Black women, starting at a place where Black women's historically and contemporarily situated place in society is strongly embraced will afford a more comprehensive understanding of a group disproportionately implicated in offending and victimization. Ignoring distinctions in identity and experiences based on that identity serves only to perpetuate indifference toward Black women and their plight.

BFC may also be critiqued as pathologizing Black women. By placing focus on Black women's distinctive standpoint, it may be seen as deeming Black women's victimization and criminality as something normal and endemic to their personality or genetic traits. Although there is a history within communities of color to not want to reveal the injurious behavior taking place between members of these communities—oftentimes for fear of upholding criminal stereotypes—it is imperative that more attention be given to the abuses subjected on women of color (see C. West, 2005). Exposing these concerns via a BFC demonstrates that the instances of crime and violence in the Black community are not because of a so-called acceptance of such behavior and illuminates the compelling effects of structural influences. In turn, this approach helps explain the prevalence of intimate partner abuse, how Black women experience such abuse, and the reactions by the criminal processing system and its representatives.

A third anticipated criticism of BFC is that by examining Black women as a group, it will be assumed all Black women have the same experiences. Although Black women in U.S. society indeed encounter similar circumstances, there are numerous gradations and variations in their lived experiences. As addressed above, Black feminist theory (see Collins, 2000) and as follows, BFC, consider Black women from their collective and their individual experiences simultaneously. Stories communicated by battered Black women result in similar trends that will aid in improving culturally competent services available to Black women. As with all battered women, their individual circumstances must always be considered in conjunction with the shared experiences of these women.

The specifying of a theory that seems to consider only Black females actually opens the field to considering gender, race, and class analyses of criminality, crime victimization, and observation of the crime-processing system. BFC highlights the need to consider intersectionality of individual identities in all crime-related concerns. Certain individuals in society are more privileged than others and social structure influences culture, families, and the individual; thus, it stands to reason that individuals other than Black women and Black men are affected by their positions in society.

As established at the outset, there can be many variations on feminist criminology. It is quite possible that there may be variations on BFC as well. Even so, this concept provides a solid starting point for placing Black women victims of intimate partner abuse at the center of analysis. As such, even if another BFC theoretical proposition leads in a different direction than that presented here, at least Black women's (and Black men's) interlocking identities will be considered central, as opposed to tangential or not at all, in relative investigations. Although there exists the potential for disapproving reactions to a BFC, such an approach to understanding abuse in African American women's intimate relationships is more desirable than disadvantageous.

Conclusion

Approaching issues of Black women and crime from the Black feminist and critical race feminist standpoints provides an extension to feminist criminology, which can aptly be titled *Black feminist criminology*. With increased attention given to women of color, violence, and nontraditional theoretical approaches (e.g., feminist), there is still a need to examine the experiences of "marginalized" women victims of violent crime from a combined gendered and racialized standpoint. Collins (2000) discussed at length the place of Black women scholars in the theory, research, and activism process. She argued that the continued development of Black feminist thought is imperative to the social theory discipline. This does not preclude those who are not Black women from participating in the advancement of Black feminist thought but instead, places Black women's intellectual and activist work on Black women at the forefront of theoretical hypothesizing and investigation. It is from this stance that examinations of the lives and experiences of Black women victims and offenders should be investigated. This article provides an analysis of how approaching intimate partner abuse against African American women from this position may offer a more comprehensive appraisal of their experiences with and responses to their victimization. Considering the historical experiences of Black women in the United States, which have been couched in multiple forms of domination, the approach advanced in this article is based on a fresh standpoint that regards how African American women's lives may position them to encounter intimate partner abuse differently than women of other races and ethnicities (especially in comparison to White women).

The argument expounded here by no intention undervalues the important and noble work done by original feminist criminology and its adherents. It is the advent, subsistence, and practice of feminist criminology that makes the concept insisted on here obtainable because of feminist criminology's position that although women and girl victims and offenders have parallel life circumstances, there are variations among them based on cultural, racial, and other distinctions. Indeed, mainstream feminist theory and feminist criminology allow for a more suitable assessment of women and criminal victimization than traditional male-centered criminology, but BFC necessarily provides for Black women's multiple and interconnected identity and their position in U.S. society to be considered as a central element of any analysis. This is an appropriate theory to apply when evaluating and attempting to understand intimate partner abuse against African American women, their responses to this maltreatment, and the responses to these women by official and unofficial outlets. Black feminist theory stresses that the Black woman encompasses many components that frame her identity. These elements include the general categories of race, ethnicity, gender, class, nationality, and sexuality. Moreover, the Black woman is not one or the other at different times and places in her life but all components at all times. BFC deems that being oppressed and discriminated against based on any or all of these parts of the Black woman's identity can occur at the structural/societal level, within the Black community, and within interpersonal relationships.

Although the example presented in this article involves intimate partner abuse against African American women, BFC can also sufficiently assess African American women's paths into criminal offending. Many Black women, regardless of offending status, are victims of differential treatment because of their subjugated racial status. As previous feminist criminology research has discovered that most female offenders have histories of childhood abuse victimizations (Belknap, 2001; Chesney-Lind & Pasko, 2004), BFC will be sure to substantiate that Black women and girl offenders likely have similar backgrounds of being treated negatively because of their intertwined identity of gender, race, sexuality, class, and so forth. Accordingly, an analysis of African American girls' and women's lives under the rubric of BFC will consider their offending from an intersecting identities perspective using, at the least, a racialized, gendered, and classed assessment.

Just as feminist criminology has afforded a more inclusive understanding of girls' and women's experiences with offending and victimization, BFC reaches beyond feminist criminology to the specific concern with African American women's distinctive position and history of domination in U.S. society that has continued on— although in varying and changing forms—to the present day. BFC focuses on African American women's devalued societal position. BFC enables the domestic violence researcher to analyze the data with the assumption that sociostructural, cultural, and familial factors affect Black women's experiences with intimate partner abuse. Scrutinizing structural, cultural, and familial dynamics aids in critically addressing the effectiveness of formal and informal regulation of partner violence against African American women. BFC may also do well in explaining the onset of and responses to abuse and crime in the lives of other women of color, White women, and even marginalized men. Hence, it is not implausible to extend a Black feminist criminological approach to understanding crime and violence in the lives of African Americans.

Notes

1. Consistent with Belknap (2001), in this article the term *processing* is used in place of *justice* when referring to law enforcement agencies and agents, court systems and their representatives, and sanctions for individuals convicted as criminal offenders. *Justice* implies that victims and offenders are treated justly and

equally within the "criminal justice system," however, this is not always true, particularly with African American women.

2. In this article, *mainstream* feminism or feminist theory are those efforts made toward gender equality by groups of predominantly White women feminists. The choice in the use of the term *mainstream* relates to the considerable attention—both negative and positive—given to the efforts of these women, as opposed to that afforded smaller, marginalized groups of feminists.

3. Throughout this article, *African American* and *Black* will be used interchangeably to describe U.S. citizens of Black African descent. Although there are instances where *Black* will not be capitalized, it is done so only in direct quotes of others who do not capitalize the term. There is no set standard for whether the term is to be capitalized when referring to race.

4. Collins (2000) defined *essentialism* as the "belief that individuals or groups have inherent, unchanging characteristics rooted in biology or a self-contained culture that explain their status" (p. 299).

5. It is interesting that this author's investigation of battered Black women determined that none of the respondents were deterred from contacting the police because of the concern of criminalizing another Black male. For those who did not call the police, their reasons centered on other factors, such as maintaining a resident father for their children.

6. *Othermother* refers to a woman in the Black community who shares the responsibility of mothering children with biological mothers and may or may not be related by blood or marriage (see Collins, 2000; Troester, 1984).

References

Allard, S. A. (1991). Rethinking battered woman syndrome: A Black feminist perspective. *UCLA Women's Law Journal, 1,* 191-207.

Ammons, L. L. (1995). Mules, madonnas, babies, bath water, racial imagery, and stereotypes: The African-American woman and the battered woman syndrome. *Wisconsin Law Review, 5,* 1003-1080.

Asbury, J. (1987). African-American women in violent relationships: An exploration of cultural differences. In R. L. Hampton (Ed.), *Violence in the Black family: Correlates and consequences* (pp. 89-105). Lexington, MA: Lexington Books.

Bachman, R., & Coker, A. L. (1995). Police involvement in domestic violence: The interactive effects of victim injury, offender's history of violence, and race. *Violence and Victims, 10,* 91-106.

Beale, F. (1995). Double jeopardy: To be Black and female. In B. Guy-Sheftall (Ed.), *Words of fire: An anthology of African-American feminist thought* (pp. 146-155). New York: New Press. (Original work published 1970)

Belknap, J. (2001). *The invisible woman: Gender, crime, and justice* (2nd ed.). Belmont, CA: Wadsworth.

Belknap, J., & Potter, H. (2006). Intimate partner abuse. In C. M. Renzetti, L. Goodstein, & S. L. Miller (Eds.), *Women, crime, and criminal justice: Original feminist readings* (2nd ed., pp. 172-188). Los Angeles: Roxbury.

Bell, C. C., & Mattis, J. (2000). The importance of cultural competence in ministering to African American victims of domestic violence. *Violence Against Women, 6,* 515-532.

Bennett, L., Goodman, L., & Dutton, M. A. (1999). Systemic obstacles to the criminal prosecution of a battering partner. *Journal of Interpersonal Violence, 14,* 761-772.

Bograd, M. (1999). Strengthening domestic violence theories: Intersections of race, class, sexual orientation, and gender. *Journal of Marital and Family Therapy, 25,* 275-289.

Brice-Baker, J. (1994). Domestic violence in African-American and African-Caribbean families. *Journal of Social Distress and Homeless, 3,* 23-38.

Britton, D. M. (2000). Feminism in criminology: Engendering the outlaw. *The Annals of the American Academy of Political and Social Science, 571*(1), 57-76.

Center for the Advancement of Women. (2003). *Progress and perils: New agenda for women.* Retrieved March 21, 2004, from http://www.advancewomen.org/womens_research/progress&perils.pdf

Chesney-Lind, M., & Pasko, L. (2004). *The female offender: Girls, women, and crime* (2nd ed.). Thousand Oaks, CA: Sage.

122   Feminist Criminology

Cleaver, K. N. (1997). Racism, civil rights, and feminism. In A. K. Wing (Ed.), *Critical race feminism: A reader* (pp. 35-43). New York: New York University Press.

Coker, D. (2003). Enhancing autonomy for battered women: Lessons from Navajo peacemaking. In A. K. Wing (Ed.), *Critical race feminism: A reader* (2nd ed., pp. 287-297). New York: New York University Press.

Cole, J. B., & Guy-Sheftall, B. (2003). *Gender talk: The struggle for women's equality in African American communities.* New York: Ballantine.

Collins, P. H. (1998). *Fighting words: Black women and the search for justice.* Minneapolis: University of Minnesota Press.

Collins, P. H. (2000). *Black feminist thought: Knowledge, consciousness, and the politics of empowerment* (2nd ed.). New York: Routledge.

Crenshaw, K. W. (1994). Mapping the margins: Intersectionality, identity politics, and violence against women of color. In M. A. Fineman & R. Mykitiuk (Eds.), *The public nature of private violence: The discovery of domestic abuse* (pp. 93-118). New York: Routledge.

Daly, K. (1997). Different ways of conceptualizing sex/gender in feminist theory and their implications for criminology. *Theoretical Criminology, 1*(1), 25-51.

Daly, K., & Chesney-Lind, M. (1988). Feminism and criminology. *Justice Quarterly, 5*(4), 499-535.

Erez, E., & Belknap, J. (1998). In their own words: Battered women's assessment of the criminal processing system's responses. *Violence and Victims, 13*, 251-268.

Fishman, L. T. (2003). "Mule-headed slave women refusing to take foolishness from anybody": A prelude to future accommodation, resistance, and criminality. In R. Muraskin (Ed.), *It's a crime: Woman and justice* (3rd ed., pp. 30-49). Upper Saddle River, NJ: Prentice Hall.

Flavin, J. (1998). Razing the wall: A feminist critique of sentencing theory, research, and policy. In J. I. Ross (Ed.), *Cutting the edge: Current perspectives in radical/critical criminology and criminal justice* (pp. 145-164). Westport, CT: Praeger.

Fyfe, J. J., Klinger, D. A., & Flavin, J. (1997). Differential police treatment of male-on-female spousal violence. *Criminology, 35*, 455-473.

Gelles, R. J., & Straus, M. A. (1988). *Intimate violence.* New York: Simon & Schuster.

Gordon, V. V. (1987). *Black women, feminism and Black liberation: Which way?* Chicago: Third World Press.

Guy-Sheftall, B. (Ed.). (1995). *Words of fire: An anthology of African-American feminist thought.* New York: New Press.

Hampton, R. L., & Gelles, R. J. (1994). Violence toward Black women in a nationally representative sample of Black families. *Journal of Comparative Family Studies, 25*, 105-119.

Hampton, R. L., Gelles, R. J., & Harrop, J. W. (1989). Is violence in Black families increasing? A comparison of 1975 and 1985 national survey rates. *Journal of Marriage and Family, 51*, 969-980.

hooks, b. (1981a). *Ain't I a woman: Black women and feminism.* Boston: South End.

hooks, b. (1981b). *Feminist theory: From margin to center.* Boston: South End.

hooks, b. (1989). *Talking back: Thinking feminist, thinking Black.* Boston: South End.

hooks, b. (2000). *Feminist theory: From margin to center* (2nd ed.). Boston: South End.

hooks, b. (2004). *The will to change: Men, masculinity, and love.* New York: Atria.

Hull, G. T., Bell Scott, P., & Smith, B. (Eds.). (1982). *All the women are White, all the Blacks are men, but some of us are brave: Black women's studies.* New York: Feminist Press.

Johnson, I. M., & Sigler, R. T. (2000). Public perceptions: The stability of the public's endorsements of the definition and criminalization of the abuse of women. *Journal of Criminal Justice, 28*, 165-179.

Jones, C., & Shorter-Gooden, K. (2003). *Shifting: The double lives of Black women in America.* New York: HarperCollins.

Joseph, J. (1997). Woman battering: A comparative analysis of Black and White women. In G. K. Kantor & J. L. Jasinski (Eds.), *Out of darkness: Contemporary perspectives on family violence* (pp. 161-169). Thousand Oaks, CA: Sage.

King, D. K. (1988). Multiple jeopardy, multiple consciousness: The context of Black feminist ideology. *Signs: Journal of Women in Culture and Society, 14*, 42-72.

Kupenda, A. M. (1998). Law, life, and literature: A critical reflection of life and literature to illuminate how laws of domestic violence, race, and class bind Black women. *Howard Law Journal, 42*, 1-26.

Lewis, D. K. (1977). A response to inequality: Black women, racism, and sexism. *Signs: Journal of Women in Culture and Society, 3*, 339-361.

McKay, N. Y. (1993). Acknowledging differences: Can women find unity through diversity? In S. M. James & A. P. A. Busia (Eds.), *Theorizing Black feminisms: The visionary pragmatism of Black women* (pp. 267-282). New York: Routledge.

Potter, H. (2004). *Intimate partner violence against African American women: The effects of social structure and Black culture on patterns of abuse.* Unpublished doctoral dissertation, University of Colorado–Boulder.

Potter, H. (in press). Battered Black women's use of religious services and spirituality for assistance in leaving abusive relationships. *Violence Against Women.*

Rennison, C. M., & Welchans, S. (2000). *Intimate partner violence.* Washington, DC: U.S. Department of Justice, Bureau of Justice Statistics.

Richie, B. E. (1996). *Compelled to crime: The gender entrapment of battered Black women.* New York: Routledge.

Richie, B. E. (2000). A Black feminist reflection on the antiviolence movement. *Signs: Journal of Women in Culture and Society, 25*, 1133-1137.

Richie, B. E. (2003). Gender entrapment and African-American women: An analysis of race, ethnicity, gender, and intimate violence. In D. F. Hawkins (Ed.), *Violent crime: Assessing race and ethnic differences* (pp. 198-210). New York: Cambridge University Press.

Rivera, J. (1997). Domestic violence against Latinas by Latino males: An analysis of race, national origin, and gender differentials. In A. K. Wing (Ed.), *Critical race feminism: A reader* (pp. 259-266). New York: New York University Press.

Rivera, J. (2003). Availability of domestic violence services for Latina survivors in New York State: Preliminary report. In A. K. Wing (Ed.), *Critical race feminism: A reader* (2nd ed., pp. 270-277). New York: New York University Press.

Robinson, A. (2003). "There's a stranger in this house": African American lesbians and domestic violence. In C. M. West (Ed.), *Violence in the lives of Black women: Battered, Black, and blue* (pp. 125-132). Binghamton, NY: Haworth.

Robinson, A. L., & Chandek, M. S. (2000). Differential police response to Black battered women. *Women and Criminal Justice, 12*(2/3), 29-61.

Rodriguez, M. A., Bauer, H. M., McLoughlin, E., & Grumbach, K. (1999). Screening and intervention for intimate partner abuse: Practices and attitudes of primary care physicians. *Journal of the American Medical Association, 28*, 468-474.

Schechter, S. (1982). *Women and male violence: The visions and struggles of the battered women's movement.* Boston: South End.

Sharma, A. (2001). Healing the wounds of domestic violence: Improving the effectiveness of feminist therapeutic interventions with immigrant and racially visible women who have been abused. *Violence Against Women, 7*, 1405-1428.

Short, L. M., McMahon, P. M., Chervin, D. D., Shelley, G. A., Lezin, N., Sloop, K. S., et al. (2000). Survivors' identification of protective factors and early warning signs for intimate partner violence. *Violence Against Women, 6*, 272-285.

Smith, B. (Ed.). (1983). *Home girls: A Black feminist anthology.* New York: Kitchen Table: Women of Color Press.

Sorenson, S. B. (1996). Violence against women: Examining ethnic differences and commonalities. *Evaluation Review, 20*, 123-145.

Sullivan, C. M., & Rumptz, M. H. (1994). Adjustment and needs of African-American women who utilized a domestic violence shelter. *Violence and Victims, 9*, 275-286.

Terrelonge, P. (1984). Feminist consciousness and Black women. In J. Freeman (Ed.), *Women: a feminist perspective* (3rd ed., pp. 557-567). Palo Alto, CA: Mayfield.

Tierney, K. J. (1982). The battered women movement and the creation of the wife beating problem. *Social Problems, 29*, 207-220.

124   Feminist Criminology

Troester, R. R. (1984). Turbulence and tenderness: Mothers, daughters, and "othermothers" in Paule Marshall's *Brown Girl, Brownstones. Sage: A Scholarly Journal on Black Women, 1*(2), 13-16.

Valencia-Weber, G., & Zuni, C. P. (2003). Domestic violence and tribal protection of indigenous women in the United States. In A. K. Wing (Ed.), *Critical race feminism: A reader* (2nd ed., pp. 278-286). New York: New York University Press.

Violence Against Women Act of 2005, Pub. L. No. 109-162 (2006).

Weis, L. (2001). Race, gender, and critique: African-American women, White women, and domestic violence in the 1980s and 1990s. *Signs: Journal of Women in Culture and Society, 27*, 139-169.

West, C. M. (2005). Domestic violence in ethnically and racially diverse families: The "political gag order" has been lifted. In N. J. Sokoloff (Ed.), *Domestic violence at the margins: Readings on race, class, gender, and culture* (pp. 157-173). Piscataway, NJ: Rutgers University Press.

West, C. M., & Rose, S. (2000). Dating aggression among low income African American youth: An examination of gender differences and antagonistic beliefs. *Violence Against Women, 6*, 470-494.

West, T. C. (1999). *Wounds of the spirit: Black women, violence, and resistance ethics.* New York: New York University Press.

Williams, O. J., & Tubbs, C. Y. (2002). *Community insights on domestic violence among African Americans: Conversations about domestic violence and other issues affecting their community.* St. Paul, MN: Institute on Domestic Violence in the African American Community.

Wing, A. K. (Ed.). (1997). *Critical race feminism: A reader.* New York: New York University Press.

Wing, A. K. (Ed.). (2003). *Critical race feminism: A reader* (2nd ed.). New York: New York University Press.

Hillary Potter is an assistant professor of sociology at the University of Colorado at Boulder, where she also received her doctorate in 2004. Her research and teaching concentrate on the intersections of race, gender, class, and crime. She is currently conducting research under this realm on intimate partner violence and the crime-related aftermath of Hurricane Katrina.

[12]

To navigate inner-city neighborhoods, young women, though reluctant at times, are often encouraged to become known as able fighters for their own protection. Among peers, one's reputation, once established, is an important social resource. The following narratives illustrate how two young women negotiate the context of violence they confront in their everyday lives.

Keywords: violence; youth; urban ethnography; violence in women; female offenders

"It's Not Where You Live, It's How You Live": How Young Women Negotiate Conflict and Violence in the Inner City

By
NIKKI JONES

S everal years ago, I was invited to work as an ethnographer for a city-hospital-based violence-intervention project—the Violence Reduction Program (VRP). The project serves youth aged twelve to twenty-four who present in the hospital's emergency room as a result of an intentionally violent incident, excluding domestic violence and child abuse. All of the young women and men in the project are purposely drawn from neighborhoods in the south, west, and southwest sections of a large northeastern city. Many of these neighborhoods are, as a consequence of patterns of racial segregation within the city, predominantly African American, and in turn, almost the entire population of young women and men in the violence-intervention project are African American youth.

Known drug markets operate within many of the neighborhoods, and residents can often quickly recall stories of violence associated with the salience of the neighborhood drug economy. While there is often a visible police presence in the neighborhood, many residents are reluctant to believe that the police are there to protect them.[1] Large orange "condemned" signs announcing that houses are being reclaimed by the city serve as visible markers of distress on individual blocks. On many of these blocks, trash accumulates in empty lots where aban-

Nikki Jones earned her Ph.D. in sociology and criminology at the University of Pennsylvania. She is an assistant professor at the University of California, Santa Barbara.

doned homes once stood. Seasonal signs of poverty and distress are less obvious: some homes are warmed by small box heaters on the coldest winter days and cooled with simple box fans during the hottest summer months. Additional signs of distress include what parents and students often refer to as "out of control" neighborhood schools. School counselors, who will often insist that there are "good kids" in the school, will also occasionally use war analogies to describe their day-to-day attempts to counsel youth. It is inside these schools and within these neighborhoods that young women and men are most likely to experience the violent incidents that lead to emergency-room visits—and their subsequent entrance into the violence-intervention project.[2]

Once they enroll in the violence-intervention project, a random sample of youth is assigned to receive intervention from a team of transitional counselors who, over the course of several months, visit the young people in their homes, offer referrals, and provide mentoring in an attempt to reduce the risk of subsequent violence. My primary role as a researcher was to qualitatively document this intervention process. My curiosity quickly extended beyond the process of intervention and into the lived experience of the young people who came through the hospital doors. I became especially interested in the experiences of young women and girls in the project.

In service of my curiosity, I began to ask the team of transitional counselors about girls and young women very early in the research process. On one of my very first days, I sat down and had a conversation with Tracey. She is an African American woman who was, at that time, twenty years old and a recent graduate of the same public city high school that some of the youth she now counseled attended. Tracey still lives in one of the inner-city neighborhoods included in the VRP's target area; she could even walk to some home visits. During this conversation, which took place in one of the hospital's conference rooms, I asked Tracey whether there were girls in the project. She said that there were. In fact, at that time, her entire caseload was made up of girls. Most of the girls, she told me, entered the emergency room with cuts or bruises from fights at school. The following is an excerpt from that conversation:

> "What are they fighting about?" I asked.
> "About being disrespected—that's about it," she replied.
> "Being disrespected?"
> "Yeah."
> "So how's that look? What does that mean?" I asked.
> "I don't know . . . they're always saying, like, 'nobody talks to me like that' and all. And I'm like, 'yeah, but would you rather die over something somebody said?'"
> "Do they see death as a real risk?" I asked her.
> "No, no. They just see getting beat up and getting laughed at, that's all. And I try to tell them that life is too short to just do stupid stuff. You can't argue over dumb stuff. I don't expect you to go to school and not fight anymore because that would just be too unreal. I was like, 'but time will tell.' I don't know. I don't know. I don't know. Just crazy. I'm like okay, ya'll were fighting because she said your sneakers were ugly—okay . . . and [*laughs*] where does the argument start at?"

"Do they answer you? Do they tell you where the argument starts?"
"Yeah, they were, like, she said my sneakers were ugly, and I said this, and then she said
   this, and next thing you know this girl said this and we just all started fighting."

This early conversation with Tracey (and similar conversations during the
course of the project) struck me for several reasons. First, descriptions of fights like
the ones Tracey described are most commonly associated with fights between boys
in inner-city high schools and neighborhoods. The social impetus for such violence
has been described in detail in Elijah Anderson's ethnography of "the moral code of
inner-city life." Specifically, in *Code of the Street*, Anderson (1999) defines "the
code" as a set of "informal rules of behavior organized around a desperate search
for respect that governs public social relations, especially violence among so many
residents [of the inner-city], particularly young men and women" (p. 10). Anderson
highlights especially the relationship between masculinity, respect, and the use of
violence, writing that "many inner-city young men in particular crave respect to
such a degree that they will risk their lives to attain and maintain it" (p. 75). While
Anderson's work emphasizes the relationship between masculinity and the code,
Tracey's claim that young women are fighting "about being disrespected—that's
about it" suggests that the code (i.e., the relationship between respect and violence
in the inner city) is not necessarily gender specific. Furthermore, Tracey's admission, "I don't expect you to go to school and not fight anymore because that would
just be too unreal," suggested to me that "girl fights" in this setting are not an anom-
aly but rather a real daily possibility. Girls and young women can and do fight.[3] As I
continued to develop this project, I began to consider the following questions:
What is the context of violence in the lives of young women in the inner city? How
do young women negotiate conflict and violence? What are the consequences of
these processes of negotiation?

To respond to this guiding set of research questions, I relied on my work with the
VRP, which introduced me to scores of young women and men who were injured
and who, in some cases, had injured others during violent incidents. I spent my first
year and a half in the field riding along on home visits with intervention counselors.[4] After I spent a year and a half observing home visits, informally interviewing
both young women and men injured in violent incidents and transitional counselors, I began to conduct one-on-one, in-depth interviews with young women and
men in the project. Some of these young people I was meeting for the first time,
while others I had met during the course of the previous year. In addition to these
interviews and visits, all of which took place in the neighborhoods and homes of the
young people in the project, I engaged in extended conversations with grandmothers, mothers, sisters, brothers, cousins, and friends of the young people. I also systematically observed interactions in the spaces and places that were significant (as
revealed during this initial period of fieldwork) in the lives of these young people.
These spaces included trolley cars and buses, a neighborhood high school nick-
named "the Prison on the Hill," the city's family and criminal court, and various
correctional facilities in the area.[5]

Girls Fight

Through this multilayered fieldwork experience, I have come to find, first, that girls do fight. Girls are not isolated from many forms of violence that men also experience in the inner-city setting. Furthermore, within the inner-city setting, girls, like their male counterparts, realize through observation and experience that violence is a potential tool to mediate the physical vulnerability they may experience in their everyday lives. Some young women, equipped with a history of fighting and winning, are invested in developing and maintaining a reputation as a

[A reputation as a "fighter"] is an important social resource because it can provide young women with a sense of security and confidence with which they can navigate their neighborhoods and school environments.

"fighter." This reputation is an important social resource because it can provide young women with a sense of security and confidence with which they can navigate their neighborhoods and school environments. Other young women, who are less invested in an identity as a fighter, will find ways to negotiate their way out of potential conflicts, with varying degrees of success. The following narratives, the first belonging to Terrie, a self-identified "violent person," and the second to Danielle, a young woman who has fought but is not a fighter, highlight the context in which young women negotiate potential conflicts and violence. In addition, these narratives demonstrate the various strategies young women consider and select to negotiate the neighborhood and school setting. Ultimately, these narratives illustrate young women's instrumental use of violence in the inner-city setting.

"Ain't I a Violent Person?": Terrie's Story

Terrie is seventeen years old and was just completing her junior year at a local public high school when we first met. She stands about 5 feet 8 inches and weighs about 165 pounds. She lives in an older row home with members of her immediate and extended family including her mother, her mother's fiancée, her Uncle Slim, and a collection of real and adopted sisters. Terrie has not seen her biological father, who is currently serving time in one of the state's prisons, in years. However, the man she terms her "real" father (her mother's ex-boyfriend), who Terrie believes "chose" to be her father (a lineage that she defines as far more significant), remains a stable presence in her life. During the day, Terrie is charged with taking care of her little sisters. Terrie's mother, who Terrie says is like her best friend, works two jobs and is home just two nights of the week. In addition to the role of caretaker that Terrie occupies within the home, she is often seen as a counselor for most of the younger kids in the neighborhood, who often come to her with questions and concerns.

Terrie's neighborhood is only blocks from the invisible yet well-known "cut-off point" that extends around the university area where I began most of my days in the field. A somewhat integrated neighborhood populated with working-class African American families and university students is bounded by a walking bridge that crosses over a set of regional railroad tracks. Quite literally on the other side of the tracks is Terrie's neighborhood, populated by a mix of residents whose income levels range from little to none to steady; often, the homes these residents inhabit share a wall with abandoned or condemned houses. Drug dealers, teenagers, and grandmothers share the space within the neighborhood boundary. At the end of the block is a house that is a center for a variety of illegal hustles, including drug selling and arbitrary violence. On the opposite end of Terrie's block is a corner that is a center of open-air drug trafficking and thus the locus of much of the violent activity that occurs in the neighborhood. Terrie can quickly recall several young men who have been shot on the corner in recent years, including her own cousin. She explains to me that whenever she walks by the corner all the guys say "Hi" to her. "See," she explains, "they all know me."

A Violent Person?

Everybody knows Terrie because, after living in the neighborhood for fifteen years, she has built a reputation as what she defines as a "violent person." As Terrie explains to me over a series of conversations, the fights she gets into serve in some way to protect this reputation and the authority and respect that enable her to navigate the neighborhood and school setting. The stage for her fights is often the public high school. Terrie explains to me in detail the fight that landed her in the emergency room.

She tells me that it was early one morning when she was approached by her cousin who informed her that another young woman was "stepping to her"—instigating a potential physical conflict. Terrie's cousin believed that she would likely end up in a physical battle with this young woman unless someone intervened, and this is why she came to Terrie.

Terrie tracked down the young woman who was "stepping" to her cousin, talked to her, and they agreed, Terrie says, to "squash it." Terrie explained very simply that if the young woman stepped to Terrie's cousin, she would have to step to Terrie. At this moment, the argument ended, according to Terrie, on the strength of her intervention. Later in the day, however, Terrie's cousin came back to her and told her that this young woman had stepped to her again. Terrie recognized this as a direct violation of the agreement she had reached with this young woman earlier in the day. It was, Terrie explains, "supposed to be squashed." According to Terrie, such a flagrant violation of their agreement had become a public sign of disrespect toward her. Terrie was essentially being "called out" and would now have to choose a response. She chose to publicly challenge the young woman.

Terrie catches up with the young woman in the hallway; they are surrounded by other young people who tend to gather at the scene of any potential fight. As Terrie turns to say something to a friend of hers, Terrie's cousin spots the young woman doing what young women do when they are preparing for a fight: she has taken off her wig and wrapped a scarf around her head to prevent the hair pulling that sometimes happens during the course of a fair one gone wild. "She's about to hit you!" someone calls out from the crowd. Recognizing that she will soon be at a disadvantage if she does not strike first, Terrie turns around and punches the young woman in the face. As additional punches are thrown the young woman bites down on Terrie's hand. Terrie grabs the young woman's head with her other hand and uses her body weight to bang the other woman's head into a vending machine until the blood from the woman's face is spilling into the open wound on Terrie's hand. School security guards finally reach the center of the fight and break it up. Terrie is quickly suspended and goes home more concerned about how she is going to deal with her mother's response to her suspension than her obviously injured hand. Terrie continues to ignore the gash on her hand until it has doubled in size as the result of an infection. Terrie finally visits the emergency room and has her infected wound cleaned and stitched back together.

Trading on Violence

Terrie gets something other than an infected wound from this fight. First, she has taken on a challenger and won in front of an audience. Her reputation as a fighter, as someone not to be bothered, is left intact. She is still a violent person. And she can now go on doing the things she does, walking the halls in school or the streets in her neighborhood, as someone whom "everybody knows" and respects. She can also continue to do the other things she does at her high school, including attending her advanced-placement classes. Terrie attended a course for gifted students at a local university over the summer, and she is now making plans to attend college. She plans to be the first in her family to graduate from high school and go to college.[6]

Terrie's use of violence to facilitate her mobility through both her neighborhood and her school is just one of the ways that Terrie can trade on her prowess and the reputation that is associated with it. Terrie can also trade on her reputation as a fighter in other ways; for example, she can come to the aid of people she sees as vulnerable. A year after the fight described in the previous section, Terrie stumbles upon the following scene: two young women are stopped in the hallway facing another young woman, most likely a very frightened freshman. It is clear to Terrie that the two girls are about to "roll on" (attack without much prior notice) this young woman, which, according to Terrie, "just wasn't fair." So Terrie steps in and asks what is going on. The young women says, "Well, I think she has a big mouth." Terrie responds that maybe *she* has a big mouth. Then she makes clear to the young women that this freshman is her "cousin," and she "doesn't want anyone to mess with her."[7] The two young women walk off in a huff, the freshman is relieved, and Terrie feels good about herself. Since this showdown, Terrie's newly minted cousin, acutely aware of the protection she received from her association with

---

[By intervening in a potential conflict], Terrie has tested and validated her reputation once again without having to actually fight.

Terrie, has repeatedly thanked Terrie for coming to her aid. She also continues to trade on this association as she makes her own way through the school. Terrie explains that whenever she sees her "cousin" in the crowded halls of the high school she yells out, "Hey Terrie!" loud enough for everyone to hear. Terrie laughs as she tells me this story. Terrie always says "Hi" back but, she confides, "still has no idea what that little girl's name is."

Ultimately, the girl's name does not matter. The purpose of Terrie's intervention is really twofold. First, Terrie clearly derives a sense of power and self-confidence from intervening in an unfair situation and making it right simply on the strength of her own reputation. Perhaps most important, however, Terrie has tested and validated her reputation once again without having to actually fight and thus has avoided the threat of suspension or expulsion, which allows her to continue her other activities in the school, including continuing to pursue her goal of graduating and going to college.[8]

"It's Not Where You Live"

The strategies used by young women to negotiate conflict and violence are illuminated by examining not only the stories of those with well-established reputations as fighters, such as Terrie, but also of those who have not established such reputations. One example of such a person is Danielle, who would rather do anything but fight. She is a slim, brown-skinned young woman who recently graduated from one of the city's public high schools. While in high school, she was on the track team and performed well enough in her classes to enroll in a small, predominantly white university hours outside of the city, one that by her own account, is worlds away from her inner-city home. While she enjoyed her experience with college life, Danielle left school in the middle of her freshman year, after discovering that she was several weeks pregnant. Her baby's father, Jimmy, attended the same university on a partial athletic scholarship, but he too dropped out and returned to the inner-city neighborhood across town from Danielle's. Jimmy calls and visits Danielle often, and while Danielle is excited about "making a family," as Jimmy often promises, she has also had to confront her regret about being "back here" in the project apartment where she grew up. "When I left," she tells me, "I didn't plan on coming back except for holidays and stuff like that."

Danielle now spends most of her days in the eleventh-floor apartment she shares with her mother and two brothers, one nine and the other an eleven-month-old. Danielle's grandmother and grandfather live several floors below, and Danielle visits often. This family unit, along with her Christian faith, provides Danielle with a relatively stable support system that she often uses to insulate herself from various forms of conflict. While much of Danielle's time is spent imagining what life will be like when her baby arrives, our series of conversations about life in the projects and her direct and indirect experiences with violence highlighted for me the complicated backdrop of violence that informs the everyday lives of young women who grow up in distressed inner-city neighborhoods.

Violence as the Backdrop of Everyday Life

During our first visit, I ask Danielle how she likes living in the projects.

> "It could be better," she responded, "without the drugs and all, the violence that go on, like cops and stuff and the fire alarms be going off in the middle of the night, like 3:00 or 4:00 in the morning, because some kid pulled the alarm. . . . And, you know, crackheads that be in the building and stuff like that knock on your door asking for stuff. . . . It could be better."

The projects where Danielle lives, like many housing projects around the country, are now in transition. These changes, which redistribute complex residents to different areas in the city, have tangibly affected the environment in Danielle's home, as residents from the northside projects, the eastside projects, and Danielle's complex are required to share space after years of conflict. As a result, Danielle tells me, there have been a lot more fights in the complex this past summer.

Danielle's most personal and still most memorable experience with violence occurred during her early teen years when she was dating Jamal, a young man who she inadvertently learned was also a local drug dealer after greeting him with a hug and finding a gun tucked in his waistband. Danielle became quite upset when she found the gun and began to yell at Jamal, who asked her to just let him explain. Jamal went on to explain his strained relationship with his mother, how Danielle was the first woman to ever express love for him, and how she was the first woman that he ever cared about.

Against her better judgment, Danielle continued to date Jamal and, while doing so, encouraged him to make some changes. For example, she got him to constrain his selling to less hard drugs—"weed," for example—instead of crack. Still, dating a drug dealer, Danielle confides, was difficult and included restraints on their mobility within the neighborhood. She explains what this was like: "it was hard, like, we couldn't go anywhere, to the movies or anything because he was selling and you never knew when someone who was looking for him would find him." While visiting her boyfriend on the block one day, Danielle quickly learned that dating a drug dealer was not just potentially dangerous but actually dangerous. The following is an excerpt from my conversation with Danielle:

> Well, one day I wanted to go see him on the block. I wanted to see him because I hadn't seen him in a few days and my cousin was with me and she wanted to see her boyfriend, too. But Jamal told me never to come to the corner when he was working. But my cousin and I went to see them and we walked up to him and my cousin's boyfriend. The next thing I remember is this black car with tinted windows pulling up to the corner. As I'm talking to my boyfriend and she is talking to her boyfriend the next thing I see is a gun pointed at my cousin's head. I'm like frozen. The guy with the gun is asking my cousin's boyfriend where his $700 is. He keeps saying, "Where my money!" After, like, forever, my boyfriend reaches into his pocket and pulls out a thick wad, *thick*, he pulls out $900 and gives it to the guy. He's like, "Here it is and here's an extra $200. Just take it."

Danielle tells me that the guy with the gun took the money, got back into the black car, and pulled away. After the young men left the corner, Danielle's cousin collapsed and Danielle attempted to revive her and regain her own composure. While some young women are undoubtedly attracted by the lifestyle that some drug dealers can afford, for women like Danielle, the risk of danger associated with dating a drug dealer is not worth the energy or the effort. For Danielle, the experience described above was enough for her to refuse to date Jamal or any other drug dealer in the future. Her constraint on this particular type of social relationship is just one of the ways she chooses to negotiate a potentially violent setting.

"It's How You Live"

While Danielle agrees that much of project life is characterized, fairly or unfairly, by the types of experiences I have described, she is also able to reflect positively on how she has lived out her own life within this context; "I'm blessed," she tells me, "I really am." She continues, "Some people will use living in the projects as an excuse but not me. It's not where you live, it's how you live." It is to a certain degree how Danielle lived that helped her to make it through almost her entire nineteen years without a fight. Danielle was particularly adept at mediating potential fights in school before they reached the point of a fistfight or worse.

Danielle is able to identify at least three strategies that she used to negotiate potential conflicts in the school setting. First, Danielle was careful in the way she presented herself. For example, she did not exhibit a demeanor that indicated "she had a point to prove," as some young women do, and in fact, Danielle did not feel like she did have a point to prove or a reputation as a fighter that she needed to protect. Second, because Danielle had no point to prove, she did not feel compelled to meet every challenge with a challenge—that is, every bump with a bump. When a potential conflict did arise, Danielle was quick to activate her networks of authority. Danielle sums up these two strategies when I ask her how she avoided getting into a fight:

> Not saying nothing. If people, like, call me names or push me or something I just brush it off. Something like that. Or go to someone, like, I talk to a teacher. I was always talking to a teacher [*laughs*]. I'm scared, I'm a punk [*laughs*]. Little punk.

Danielle also tried to talk out potential conflicts before they escalated into a public battle. For example, she once approached a young woman who had been "talking about her" after school, away from the eyes of an audience. Cutting through the tough front this young woman presented, Danielle simply explained to her "you don't even know me." The two talked briefly, and the next day, the young woman told her friends that Danielle was "okay." And that was it.

Despite the energy Danielle exerted to avoid potential conflicts each day, she did end up in a fight once. One of the common ways that young women who are not fighters get involved in fights is through their "loyalty links." The strength of these loyalty links is often designated by the given status of a young woman's relationship to other young women. At least two status positions exist: "friend" indicates a strong link and "associate" indicates a weaker link. It is commonly assumed that young women should fight for a friend but are not necessarily required to fight for an associate. So one of the ways that young women insulate themselves from potential conflicts is by limiting the strength of their social relationships with other young women.

Loyalty Links

Danielle explains to me how her loyalty link to her best friend resulted in her being in her first and only fight in nineteen years. She tells me that a group of girls had been threatening her best friend who, at the time, lived with Danielle and her family in their project apartment. This group of girls repeatedly threatened to "get" her best friend after school. Danielle was very concerned about this because, as she explains, "It's my best friend and I don't want nobody to hurt her." As Danielle and her friend began to walk home from the high school to the projects, the group of young women followed, making it clear that they wanted to fight. During the walk, the young women continued to test Danielle and her friend. Danielle explains,

> And we were walking and they were following her, calling her names, telling her that you better watch your back "B" or fight me now, just sayin' stuff. So we got in front of [the local hospital] and I said, "Katrina, drop your bags," 'cause they're behind me and they're coming closer, and I dropped my bags. Just to make sure that nobody not tryin' to jump her.

Even though Danielle had never been in a fight before, she was aware of how to handle such a situation. She explains that you cannot keep walking with your back turned or you might get "jumped." Danielle had also done what many young

One of the ways that young women insulate themselves from potential conflicts is by limiting the strength of their social relationships with other young women.

women do when a fight is imminent; she called ahead to her mother who then met them halfway home. When Danielle's mom arrived on the scene, she was prepared to do her part to make sure that the fight did not get out of hand, despite the fact that she was several months pregnant. Danielle continues,

> So my mom was there and everything like that. And Katrina got into the street—and this was something—they was about to swing and fight each other. And I, my mom was there and I was there, so we can make sure that nobody don't interfere with their fight. You know, make sure it's not a blood bath or nothing like that, you know, make sure . . . 'cause sometimes you got to fight, not fight, but get into that type battle to let them know that I'm not scared of you and you can't keep harassing me thinking that it's okay.

Once Katrina and the young woman she squared off with began to fight, Danielle was quickly moved from being a bystander to a participant when another young woman punched her in the face. Danielle explains,

> I was there, like, just watching everything and then before I knew it I got snuck. . . . I got, somebody came and pulled my hair and hit me in the eye. So I'm, [I] can't see. I'm like, "what's going on?" I'm tripping over the curb, fallin' on the ground, hit my back on the curb and everything like that and I'm on the ground and I'm getting like this girl beat-

> ing on me and stuff and I'm, like, "who is this?" I couldn't really see 'cause my eye got
> hit and I'm trying to see who this is and me and her fighting and everything.

Danielle eventually regained her composure and moved from receiving punches
to landing some punches herself:

> So I flip her over and I finally get my sight back and we fighting because she hittin' me, I'm
> hittin' her and everything. Then she get up and I run after her 'cause I'm real angry. I
> want to like hurt this girl because she hit me for no reason. So I go up to her [and] me
> and her fightin' and then they ran . . . and we was, like, "Come back and finish! Don't
> run now because you getting your butt kicked!" So they left and we got in the car and
> came home. My eye was black. I was seeing stars [*laughs*].

While this fight did not convert Danielle into a fighter, she does confide in me
that she felt good when she went to school the next day. She felt confident that she
could handle herself. She was not, after all, "a punk." Since this fight, Danielle's
best friend has moved down South with her family. Danielle did not have any additional problems with the young women she fought. She has continued to engage in
strategies to negotiate conflict before it can escalate. For example, when she ran
into the girls, she would make an attempt to avoid walking by them or speaking
directly to them.

If not for her loyalty link to her best friend, Danielle may have made it through
her entire high school career, as some young women undoubtedly do, without ever
getting into a fight. If that would have happened, however, it would be a result not
of luck or even because Danielle is "blessed" but, as is demonstrated above, of her
investment in negotiating potential threats of interpersonal conflict before they
reach the point of a violent battle. In her neighborhood, Danielle restricted her
social network to a few friends and a tight-knit family who had a strong relationship
with the church. At home, Danielle chose to spend most of her time in her apartment, to avoid being involved in her neighbor's "petty" arguments that could
quickly escalate into fights. In school, Danielle sought to address perceived conflicts by talking with other young women or, when that was not a sufficient remedy,
by seeking the help of other authority figures whom she could trust. Danielle's only
direct involvement in a fight stemmed from her strong allegiance to Katrina, her
best friend. Not willing to let someone "just hurt her," Danielle realized that the
two of them would have to meet the challenge presented by the group of young
women who were following them home. She realized this herself, she prepared for
it, and when she had to, she fought.

Conclusion

In distressed inner-city neighborhoods young women like Danielle and Terrie
come of age against a backdrop of real and potential violence. This remains true
despite the decline of the types of violence that characterized the nation's inner cities during the late 1980s and early 1990s. Often, young women in distressed inner-

city neighborhoods are encouraged to both be and become known as able fighters for their own protection. The utility of such a reputation is demonstrated in Terrie's narrative. A self-identified violent person, Terrie is known and respected by both the drug dealers and the grandmothers on her block. Being known in this way allows Terrie a certain degree of security and mobility in her neighborhood and school setting. To maintain this reputation and its benefits, Terrie must at times fight, and she does so when necessary. Young women without a known reputation as an able fighter must still account for the violence that exists beneath the surface of everyday life. As demonstrated in Danielle's narrative, while she is not a fighter, she still exerts quite a bit of energy negotiating potential conflicts with a remarkable degree of success. The narratives of Terrie and Danielle, and other young women like them, encourage us to reconsider current conversations about "violent girls" that tend to pathologize young (predominantly African American) women who use violence while ignoring the structural and cultural context within which young women negotiate conflict and violence and the variety of strategies they use to do so. For young women in distressed inner-city neighborhoods, being able to fight and being known as a fighter are at times the most reliable social resources available to them in their everyday lives.

Notes

1. In my own fieldwork, I have found much support for this theme, which Elijah Anderson explores in detail in *Code of the Street* (1999). Regarding the relationship between the police and many inner-city residents, Anderson writes, "The police, for instance, are most often viewed as representing the dominant white society and not caring to protect inner-city residents." See also "Going Straight: The Story of a Young Inner-city Ex-convict" (Anderson 2001, 136).

2. See Massey and Denton's *American Apartheid* (1994) for a discussion of the consequences of concentrated poverty. For a discussion of how the interaction of "structure" and "culture" influence crime and victimization in distressed inner-city neighborhoods, see Lauritsen and Sampson's "Minorities, Crime, and Criminal Justice" (1998, 65-70) and Sampson and Wilson's "Toward a Theory of Race, Crime, and Urban Inequality" (1995).

3. My own fieldwork suggests that despite the decline in the violence that characterized the inner city in the late 1980s and early 1990s, many young men and women still rely on the "code of the street" as a useful framework in which to consider potential threats of violence and its consequences. This research complements the work of Anderson by examining how *young women* experience the threat of violence and, in turn, work "the code" to mediate those threats.

4. During this time, I developed a close relationship with two women who grew up in the same inner-city neighborhoods where they now worked for the Violence Reduction Program: Stephanie, who was the intervention team coordinator, and Tracey, the intervention counselor I described earlier who evolved into a "key informant" in the field.

5. Anderson defines a staging area as "hangouts where a wide mix of people gather for various reasons. It is here that campaigns for respect are most often waged" (Anderson 1999, 77). During visits to the homes of young women and men in the project, fostered initially by Tracey, and then in my own observations of public transportation scenes during key times of the day, I discovered the trolley as an additional staging area for youth of high school age.

6. It is important to note that while the use of violence can ensure a degree of respect, freedom, and protection, for some young women like Terrie and those she deems worthy, this same reputation is essentially meaningless in the face of other threats young women face, particularly the threat of sexual assault. For example, during a visit to her boyfriend's neighborhood, Terrie took a walk to the corner store. After she entered

the store, the owner proceeded to lock the front door, trapping Terrie inside. But he was then interrupted by a customer knocking on the locked glass door. When he returned to the front door and unlocked it, Terrie slipped out. She was clearly shaken by the experience but eventually calmed herself down enough to talk with her boyfriend about what she considered a potential sexual assault. She told me that her boyfriend wanted to go to the store to "see" this man, but Terrie forbade him to do so. "If I wanted someone to shoot him," she explained to me, "I'd get my brothers." This brief example demonstrates that despite Terrie's physical strength and her strong reputation as a fighter, she is less capable of challenging certain forms of violence. I pursue this theme in greater detail in my dissertation *Girls Fight: Understanding the Context of Violence in the Lives of African American Inner City Girls*.

7. The adoption of fictive kin has been discussed in classic ethnographic studies including Elijah Anderson's *A Place on the Corner* (1976).

8. One would be incorrect to conclude that Terrie is essentially a violent person. Erving Goffman's discussion of the presentation of self in everyday life is helpful in considering the role of the self to the "performance" in which Terrie is so deeply invested (Goffman 1959). Goffman writes, "A correctly staged and performed scene leads the audience to impute a self to a performed character, but this imputation—this self—*is a product of a scene that comes off, and is not a cause of it*. The self, then, as a performed character is not an organic thing that has a specific location, whose fundamental fate is to be born, to mature and to die; it is a dramatic effect arising diffusely from a scene that is presented, and the characteristic issue, the crucial concern, is whether it will be credited or discredited" (Goffman 1959, 253; emphasis added). Goffman's explanation encourages us to consider the present analysis not as a study of violent girls per se but rather as a study of how young women and girls use violence to mediate potential threats of violence in their everyday lives.

References

Anderson, Elijah. 1976. *A place on the corner*. Chicago: University of Chicago Press.

———. 1999. *Code of the street: Decency, violence and the moral life of the inner city*. New York: W.W. Norton.

———. 2001. Going straight: The story of a young inner-city ex-convict. *Punishment and Society* 3 (1): 135-52.

Goffman, E. 1959. *The presentation of self in everyday life*. New York: Doubleday.

Lauritsen, Janet L., and Robert J. Sampson. 1998. Minorities, crime, and criminal justice. In *The handbook of crime and punishment*, edited by Michael Tonry. Oxford: Oxford University Press.

Massey, D. S., and N. A. Denton 1994. *American apartheid: Segregation and the making of the underclass*. Cambridge, MA: Harvard University Press.

Sampson, Robert J., and William Julius Wilson. 1995. Toward a theory of race, crime, and urban inequality. In *Crime and inequality*, edited by John Hagan and Ruth Peterson. Palo Alto, CA: Stanford University Press.

[13]

Walking a Tightrope

The Many Faces of Violence in the Lives
of Racialized Immigrant Girls and Young Women

YASMIN JIWANI

Concordia University

This article explores a hidden yet pervasive form of violence that marks the lives of young women from racialized immigrant communities in western Canada. It argues for an intersectional analysis that takes into consideration their heightened vulnerability to systemic and institutional forms of violence. Situated at the intersections of race, class, gender, and age, these young women walk a tightrope between the violence of racism they experience from the host and/or dominant society and the pressures to conform imposed from within their communities. Challenging previous culturalist explanations, the article suggests that racism constitutes a significant form of structural violence experienced by these young women.

Keywords: *intersectional violence; racialized girls; racism; victimization*

> Our societal definition of violence must include the direct results of poor medical care, economic inferiority, oppressive legislation, and cultural invisibility. By broadening our definition of violence, we combat the minimalization of our experiences as women of color by the dominant culture. We must name the violence, or we will not be able to address it.
>
> —Carraway, 1991, p. 1302

Carraway's quote foregrounds the violence of racism that is experienced by people of color living in White settler societies (Razack, 2002). Yet, in the dominant discourses, racism is not readily

AUTHOR'S NOTE: Funding for this research was made possible by support from a grant from Social Sciences and Humanities Research Council of Canada (#829-1999-1002) and the Status of Women Canada. I would like to acknowledge the assistance of Helene Berman, Nancy Janovicek, Linnet Fawcett, Holly Wagg, and the constructive comments I received from the anonymous reviewers.

acknowledged or recognized as a form of systemic, institutional, and daily violence. This article focuses on racism as a hidden yet pervasive form of violence that marks and influences the lives of young women from immigrant communities in Canada who are racialized. Drawing from interviews and focus groups with young women of color living in western Canada, this article explores the everyday incidents of violence they experience and highlights the different ways in which racism and sexism intersect and influence their lives. In the first section, I provide a statistical profile of immigrant girls and young women in Canada who are racialized and contextualize contemporary debates surrounding their lived realities in Western societies. I problematize the notion of culture as an explanatory framework through which to understand the realities of girls who are racialized and, in so doing, challenge the concept of so-called cultural conflicts that has been so predominant in the literature in this area. In the following sections, I bring together the voices of the young women who participated in the current study to illustrate the ways in which racism and sexism intersect in their lives, and to highlight the multiple ways in which they experience the violence of racism.

BACKGROUND AND RELEVANCE

In 1996, 24.3% of the visible minority population in Canada was younger than age 15 years, and the majority of these youths were immigrants (Kobayshi, Moore, & Rosenberg, 1998). One of every 10 immigrants is a female younger than age 15 years. In the metropolitan centers of Vancouver, Toronto, and Montreal, Canadian statistics indicate that *visible minorities* (official government terminology for racialized groups) constitute anywhere from one fourth to one third of the city's total population. The increasing size of this population combined with widespread sensational media coverage of several cases concerning violence among and against girls who are racialized has served to direct public attention to, and provoke academic scrutiny of, the factors influencing the lives of these girls and young women and the role played by various institutions such as the schools in exacerbating or dismantling the barriers they face (Bourne, McCoy, & Smith, 1998; Jiwani, 1999; Wideen & Bernard, 1999). Furthermore, and from a policy perspective, the heightened focus on girls and young women has been motivated by the *Beijing Declaration and Platform for Action* (1995) and Canada's commitment to the latter (see for instance, Berman & Jiwani, 2002; Russell, 1996).

A review of the literature reveals a paucity of Canadian studies examining the realities and experiences of girls from immigrant and refugee families who are racialized (Jiwani, 1998). In general, studies concerning young women from immigrant and racialized backgrounds in other countries have tended to focus on issues of cultural difference and culture conflict (Drury, 1991; Jabbra, 1983; Kim, 1980; Rosenthal, Ranieri, & Klimidis, 1996). In part, this preoccupation with culture may have to do with a reluctance to address the issue of race given the moot biological validity of the latter. Furthermore, the focus on culture as a site of identity formation and struggle can be understood within the context of the sociological literature on migration in terms of its emphasis on the processes of immigrant settlement through assimilation, acculturation, and the like. Hence, the questions shaping the dominant discourse in migration studies have more to do with assessing ethnic identity in terms of its constructed nature versus its primordial character (Geertz, 1963; Isaacs, 1975; Keyes, 1981; Lyman & Douglas, 1973).

Undoubtedly, migration has a significant impact on the transition processes of young immigrant women who are racialized. These transition processes are not only marked by adjustment and settlement within a new milieu but are also often accompanied by the transition from girlhood to young womanhood. Dislocation resulting from migration can be highly traumatic—even more so when that migration is enforced as opposed to voluntary. There is a sense of grief as one leaves what is familiar, euphoria as one experiences relief and novelty from being in a new situation, disillusionment as the reality of uprooting sets in, and finally a sense of settlement that comes with integration or adaptation to the new space (Beiser, 1998). This cycle of grief, euphoria, disillusionment, and settlement is not peculiar to young women; it is a cycle that most immigrants and refugees experience as a result of dislocation. However, that sense of dislocation is more pronounced when the individuals involved are marked by physical and cultural differences, in other words, when they are racialized. It influences the cycle resulting in adjustment, and it continues to affect individuals in terms of their social and economic mobility, not to mention their acceptance by and integration into the milieu to which they have relocated. As the Working Group on Girls notes in its report (Friedman with Cook, 1995), immigrant and refugee girls experience higher rates of violence not only because of dislocation and racism but also the sexism they experience within their own communities and within the external society. Caught between two cultures, where their own is devalued and constructed as inferior, and where the cultural scripts in both worlds encode patriarchal values, these girls face a tremendous struggle in trying to fit in and often suffer intense rejection and backlash as a result of their failure to do so.

As noted above, dominant frameworks for understanding the lives and realities of girls of color tend to focus on cultural differences (Jiwani, 1992). Narayan (1997) has argued that within these paradigms culture becomes the terrain on which colonial binaries are constructed. With regard to girls who are immigrants and refugees, and more particularly girls of color, the tendency has been to understand their lives through the prism of so-called cultural conflict. Here *conflict* is used to explain the dissonance and dissatisfaction that girls experience in dealing with the supposedly contradictory and opposing normative structures of the dominant "host" society on one hand, and their own cultural communities on the other (Basit, 1997; Hutnik, 1986; Miller, 1995; Mogg, 1991; Onder, 1996; Rosenthal et al., 1996). Deeper questions regarding this conflict's underpinnings or why it exists in the first place are rarely examined in terms of the structural relations of power that inhere in the dominant, host society—that is, the subordination of minority groups vis-à-vis the hegemonic power of the dominant society. Studies have demonstrated how girls who are racialized are inferiorized and how they internalize dominant values that embody a rejection of the self and their cultural communities (Bourne et al., 1998; Handa, 1997; Matthews, 1997). This rejection varies and is compounded by strategies of negotiation wherein girls try to fit in to the normative standards imposed on them by the wider society while simultaneously adhering to the culturally prescribed standards of their own communities.

In her study of South Asian girls in Canada, for instance, Handa (1997) demonstrated how the girls' lives are shaped by these competing discourses. On one hand, they have to deal with

850 VIOLENCE AGAINST WOMEN / July 2005

the pressures of assimilation in the context of school, employ-ment, and acceptance in the wider society. On the other hand, as signifiers of culture by their families and communities,[1] there is an emphasis on protecting them from the Westernizing influence of the dominant society and ensuring their conformity to and main-tenance of cultural traditions. Western traditions are perceived as weakening the moral fabric of community life. Yet, to belong and gain a sense of acceptance, the girls have to engage with the domi-nant Western norms and mores in the public domain of their lives. This is the site of the "cultural" conflict. However, Handa (1997) has problematized the notion of culture that is couched within the conflict paradigm, arguing against the way in which culture is perceived to be static and "frozen" in the latter, rather than dynamic and relational.

The discourse of cultural racism and cultural violence marks the lives of girls and young women who are immigrants. How-ever, cultural racism and cultural violence are predicated on the gendered and racialized context of girls and young women who are immigrants and refugees. Racism becomes culturalized by virtue of its use of culture as the signifier of inferiorized difference (Gilroy, 1987; Hall, 1990). Cultural norms and traditions that are perceived to be different and negatively valued become the vehi-cles through which the hierarchy of preference and privilege are communicated and sustained. Violence is similarly culturalized because it is understood as stemming from a cultural conflict, rather than a structural inequality (Razack, 1998). In other words, violence is perceived to be an inherent feature of the racialized culture and a sign of its failure to adapt and/or assimilate to the dominant, Western context.

This is not to suggest that gender-based violence does not occur within racialized, immigrant communities. Rather, my argument here is to underline the ways in which dominant and legitimized frameworks of analysis are themselves often situated in a stand-point that perceives racialized communities as the so-called other. For instance, violence against young women is widespread in the dominant society. In Canada, adolescent wives between ages 15 and 19 years are 3 times more likely to be murdered compared to wives who are older (Canadian Centre for Justice Statistics, 1994). Canadian girls are victims in 84% of reported cases of sexual abuse, in 60% of reported cases of physical abuse, and in 52% of reported cases of neglect (Thomlinson, Stephens, Cunes, Grinnell, & Krysik, 1991). A survey of secondary school students in British Columbia revealed that an average of 32% of girls and 15% of boys have experienced a history of physical and/or sexual abuse. It has been found that girls are likely to be sexually abused in their teen years between ages 11 and 14, and boys between ages 4 and 6. Research also suggests that 94% to 100% of the abusers are men in cases of child sexual abuse involving girls, with men also accounting for 85% of the perpetrators in cases of child sexual abuse involving boys (Duffy & Momirov, 1997).

Despite this reality, the intersecting influences of age and gender are rarely treated as factors contributing to vulnerability to violence. Instead, age and gender tend to be coupled as problematic signifiers of increasing girl-on-girl or youth violence (Faith & Jiwani, 2002; Schissel, 1997). Racialization complicates the situation of girls of color as it adds yet another dimension of risk. Through racialization—a "process or situation wherein the idea of 'race' is introduced to define and give meaning to some particular populations, its characteristics and actions" (Miles, 1989, p. 246)—physical differences become signified with particular valuations and connotations. Those who are racialized are often the targets of racism, an institutional and everyday practice of othering based on perceived physical and cultural differences. The othering resulting from gendered socialization combined with the othering resulting from racialization heightens the complex and intersecting forms of violence that girls and young women of color experience.

The culturalist argument, for want of a better term, tends to locate the cause and type of violence, along with the response to the violence, within a primordial interpretation of culture and cultural identity. Within this framework, women who are immigrants are considered to be high risk because of their location at the intersection of two cultures (Meleis, 1991). Likewise, Mexican American men who batter will be seen as having a more so-called traditional cultural orientation (Champion, 1996). The same argument has been advanced with regard to Korean men who batter (Choi, 1997; Rhee, 1977), and South Asian women who remain in abusive relationships (Dasgupta & Warrier, 1996; Huisman, 1996). Perilla, Bakeman, and Norris (1994) attributed the gendered nature of violence in Latino communities to cultural scripts such as *marianismo* and *machismo*. In their review of the literature on immigrant women and violence, Raj and Silverman (2002) kept returning to the notion that rates of intimate partner violence may be higher among women who are immigrants because of factors such as cultural traditions, especially as these relate to women's status. This seems curious given that the main impetus of their argument seems to rest on structural considerations such as immigrant status, language, and social context.

Although a so-called culturalist perspective may have some validity, "Culture talk," as Razack (1994) has suggested, "is a double-edged sword" (p. 896). It can reify cultures as static entities, obscure relations of power within and outside the cultural group, and fail to consider the relational aspects of cultural identity (Abraham, 1995) as emergent from a migrant, diasporic existence (Dossa, 1999). Add to this the contextual backdrop of systemic and everyday racism (Essed, 1990), and the focus on culture quickly becomes one of implicitly or explicitly comparing a seemingly backward, traditional, and oppressive cultural system to the modern, progressive, and egalitarian culture of the West (Burns, 1986; Lai, 1986; Said, 1979). Such an approach can result in the production of cultural prescriptions that further entrench stereotypic representations of particular ethnic groups (Razack, 1998).

Singling out particular cultural communities and suggesting they have a proclivity to violence is thus part of the overall process of racialization. It stigmatizes these communities as others, and this results in further marginalization (Narayan, 1997). Furthermore, the fear that their communities will be criminalized can inhibit the women who are part of them from disclosing the violence (Flynn & Crawford, 1998; MacLeod & Shin, 1990; Raj & Silverman, 2002; Razack, 1998). The end result is a vicious circle wherein these young women and their older counterparts are caught walking a tightrope. As Burns (1986) noted,

> Our abuse has been hidden in our communities' refusal to acknowledge the pervasiveness of violence in our lives. This refusal is not maliciousness but a protective measure born of the legitimate fear that such information would be used as a weapon by the dominant culture. Our abuse has been hidden behind bravado and denials. The result is the creation of a climate of tolerance. (p. 4)

Rather than engage once again in so-called culture talk, the attempt within this article, then, is to present a more balanced structural analysis by situating the experiences of, and vulnerability to, violence among young women from racialized immigrant communities to their social and structural location within society at large. In particular, the aim is to explicate the ways in which they define violence and to highlight the connections between processes of racialization and the violence of racism.

An analysis of how racism interlocks with other systems of domination to influence the life chances and reality of girls who are racialized requires acknowledging racism as a form of violence that is endemic and pervasive. Nevertheless, although it has become increasingly common to accept the structured inequality produced and reproduced by sexism in Canada, the same does not hold true for racism. This means that rather than accepting racism as a structure of domination, similar to sexism, and as arising from a legacy of colonialism, the reality of racism in this country has to be "proven" continually (Bannerji, 1987, 1993).

In contrast to the Canadian context, American and British studies on violence tend to underscore the structural impact of racism and outline the differential rates of violence against African American girls and women (Kenny, Reinholtz, & Angelini, 1997; Mama, 1989; O'Keefe, 1994; Urquiza & Goodlin-Jones, 1994; Wyatt & Riederle, 1994), as well as Hispanic and Asian girls who are at risk and/or who come from a variety of different cultural backgrounds (e.g., Joe & Chesney-Lind, 1995; Musick & Barker, 1994). Many of these studies succeed in demonstrating the differential rates of victimization and, in some cases, offer a detailed analysis of the ways in which systemic forms of violence, such as racism, intersect with sexism, ageism, poverty, and marginalization to contribute to a heightened vulnerability among specific groups of young and adult women. In a similar vein, Hampton, Oliver, and Magarian's (2003) study of male anger and violence in the African American community offers useful insights into how structural and institutionalized forms of racism influence the production and reproduction of specific kinds of Black masculinities, which in turn escalate the conditions for and prevalence of gender-based violence. This example is highly cogent given the salience and recognition of racism against African Americans in contemporary U.S. society.

In contrast, and despite documented evidence of the presence of institutional and gendered racism in Canadian society (Fleras & Elliot, 1996; Ng, 1993; Thobani, 1998), the tendency here—as suggested earlier—has been to favor culturalist and interpersonal interpretations of violence. In other words, and as Davis (2000) has suggested, a major challenge facing us is how to "develop analyses and organizing strategies against violence against women that acknowledges the race of gender and the gender of race" (p. 2).

THE INS AND OUTS OF PARTICIPATORY RESEARCH

In examining the intersections of racism and sexism within the context of gender-based violence, it is clear that the kinds of violence that immigrant and refugee women and girls who are racialized encounter are mediated by their particular status as girls and women, as "raced" subjects and as individuals defined by their official status in terms of nationality and citizenship. It is apparent that a significant aspect of the lives of girls who are immigrants and girls of color who are refugees is their own intersectionality—at the junctures of race, gender, class, and age. Given that the issue of violence is itself stigmatized because of its connotations with deviance and criminality and its location in the private sphere, and to minimize any barriers to discussing violence within the focus groups and interviews, the current research was conducted with the assistance of community organizations and partners in the social services sector. Many of these facilitators had conducted interviews prior to their involvement in the current research, and many were aware of the code of silence extant within immigrant communities with regard to issues of gender-based violence. Furthermore, the facilitators were chosen because of their involvement in organizing and working with youth and, in some cases, being youths themselves. To ensure interviewees' and focus group participants' comfort and identification with the facilitators, the latter were also members of immigrant racialized communities. In addition, the initial open-ended questions drafted by the researcher were vetted by a group of young women of color from immigrant communities who were convened as an advisory group to the project, as well as by another advisory group consisting of policy makers, social service personnel, and other researchers.

The desire to conduct the current research in a participatory fashion was based on several key assumptions. The first revolved around the issue of a power differential and its links to racial identity. By using interviewers and focus group facilitators who were themselves from the various communities of color and/or of immigrant background, it was thought that the power differential that generally exists between the researched and the researchers could be diminished (Lather, 1991; Ristock & Pennell, 1996). Second, it was felt that in embracing a postcolonial framework, an overt acknowledgment was being made of how the categories of race, class, and gender have traditionally been used to "other" those who are different and, most important, to discount their experiences (hooks, 1990, 1995). Finally, it was felt that in engaging researchers who shared experiences and came from the same structural group as the researched, we would be harnessing a grounded expertise based on the knowledge of being marginalized and serving a marginalized population (Smith, 1999).[2]

That said, the current research did not deliberately seek to match the race and/or ethnic backgrounds of the facilitators with the young women being interviewed or those who participated in the focus groups. For one, there were few researchers available who were representative of the ethnic and racial backgrounds of the particular focus groups being conducted. Nevertheless, where possible, a representative from a similar community group conducted the focus group, as, for example, in the case of the African Caribbean focus groups where a young African woman facilitated the discussions. In cases involving focus groups and interviews in rural areas, however, it was difficult to locate a suitable facilitator. In these cases, the facilitator chosen was always of a racialized, immigrant background even if of a different ethnocultural heritage. I would suggest that the latter situation did not have a negative impact on data collection. On the contrary, in some cases the difference in background actually favored access to girls and fostered their participation in the focus groups. If by keeping immigrant status constant we were able to create a base of empathy and commonality that enabled focus group participation, the retaining of an element of difference enabled us to ensure that the girls and young women from within a particular community did not feel that their confidences would be violated by a facilitator who was an insider to their community.[3]

METHOD

In total, five focus groups were convened. Three were ethno-specific focus groups consisting of a Persian (Iranian) group of girls, an African Caribbean group of girls, and a Latina group of girls. The other two consisted of mixed groups of girls of color, one of which was held at the conclusion of a 2-day participatory theater workshop. In addition, individual interviews were conducted with a total of 14 girls located in rural and urban areas.

Through partnerships with community organizations and community researchers, a total of 52 girls and/or young women were recruited to participate in the project. The youngest was 13 years old, and the oldest participant was 22. The majority of the girls were between ages 15 and 16 years. Their or their parents' countries of origin included Antigua, Barbados, China, Congo, Ethiopia, Fiji, India, Iran, Jamaica, Mexico, Pakistan, the Philippines, St. Kitts, Taiwan, Thailand, Trinidad, and Zaire.

The focus group and individual interview questions were drawn up in collaboration with an advisory group of girls convened through various community organizations. Many of these girls had participated in an earlier experiential-based 2-day workshop using various tools of popular education. The types of questions asked varied from those dealing specifically with their experiences as girls and young women of color, to those dealing with their encounters with racism and sexism. In addition, we asked questions pertaining to their use of media, their friends and support networks, the kinds of things they did in their leisure time, and how they would define themselves vis-à-vis the larger society. Questions about violence were framed in an exploratory way, beginning with general questions about how they defined violence, the kinds of experiences of violence they had encountered, the sites in which these incidents took place, and where they turned for help or support. Data from the interviews were transcribed and coded. Coding was based on the categories that emerged from the data rather than categories imposed on the data. All personal identifiers were removed. The only identifying characteristics retained dealt with the racial identity of the young woman speaking. However, the coding was not done on an ethno-specific basis but rather in terms of the wider issues emergent from the data, such as definitions of violence, experiences of violence, self-definitions, and access to support services.

For the purposes of the current analysis, data collated around the themes of violence and racism are included and presented through selected quotes. The following discussion is based on a thematic analysis of the data.

RESULTS AND REALITIES

In talking to the young women who participated in the focus groups and individual interviews, it was apparent that they negotiated multiple realities. To highlight the element of negotiation, I use the term *Walking the Hyphen* from Batth's (1998) illuminating thesis on South Asian girls in Vancouver, Canada. The notion of negotiation implies multiple subject positions and the fluidity of identity as mediated by structural location and systemic factors. However, what is of particular interest is that in negotiating identity and assuming multiple subject positions, the language used to define this condition of walking the hyphen tends to collapse various kinds of experiences, so that they merge based on the individual's subject position. The following exchange between the group facilitator and the African Caribbean focus group participants demonstrates this phenomenon in action, with the experience of violence and the experience of racism becoming interconnected at the level of the feelings that both engender in the young women concerned:

> Interviewer: How would you define violence? If I said, what's the definition of violence, what would you say?
> Girl: Hitting people.
> Girl: Abuse.
> Girl: That would be a verbal.
> Girl: Verbal, physical, mental, [visual?].
> Girl: Anything that makes you feel bad.
> Interviewer: So it's not just hitting?

Girl: No, it doesn't have to be physical. It can be . . . like if someone
  calls someone a Black bitch or something, that's still violent
  because obviously that pissed you off because you went and
  busted the girl in the head. So obviously anything that breaks
  someone down, that doesn't make them feel good.
Interviewer: Do you think racism is violence?
Girl: Yeah.
Girl: Very. That's to the top of the list.

RACISM

The majority of the girls and young women identified racism as
the dominant and most pervasive form of violence they encounter in their daily lives. On one hand, they defined racism in interpersonal and systemic terms—from discriminatory treatment by
teachers in schools, to the dismissal of their participation, the
silencing of their voices, and the erasure of their histories and cultural realities in the school curriculum. On the other hand, they
identified racism as acts of verbal and physical abuse that cause
pain and that result in their othering, inferiorization, and exclusion. Many noted that they had witnessed an increase in violence,
gender- and race-related, in their schools. The following examples provide a sense of how the participants defined racism in
terms of a continuum from subtle forms of harassment and name-
calling to outright exclusion. In the words of one,

> I have a Caucasian friend, she is very intelligent, the best one at
> school. She always tells me that White people are the best and
> when I say that I would like to do this or what I am going to do, she
> goes, "Oh no." She says that GAP is for White people. Because I
> had something from GAP and she asked me, "Where did you buy
> it?" "In GAP." [She said], "Don't you know that that place is for
> White people?" (Latina focus group)

Another participant stated,

> This White guy was bullying some little Persian guy, and I'm like,
> "What the hell are you doing? Stop it. He can't stand up to you."
> And he's like, "Yeah, you go back to your own country, too. All of
> you FOBs." But I got pissed off. I'm really totally mad. I'm like,
> "Watch what you're saying. You don't even know me. You can't
> just call everybody names when you don't know anybody." I got
> really angry. (Iranian focus group)

GENDERED RACISM AND GENDERED VIOLENCE

When asked if they or anyone they knew had experienced violence, none disclosed experiences of intimate violence. However, a few alluded to the experiences of friends and family members. This may have been because interviewers explained to the girls that they would be obliged to report abuse if it was disclosed in the interviews. The fear of involving police, and the stigma attached to drawing any kind of public attention to the matter, reinforces the code of silence that shrouds intimate forms of violence. As this young Iranian woman reported

> Yeah. I know a person, she gets beaten up by her parents. And she [. . .] with bruises on her body a couple of times. And it's gotten worse. Sometimes she cries and she hits herself. She blames herself, "Maybe I am doing this to my parents," so she hits herself. But she told me that her dad has hit her, smacked her, pulled her hair, beaten up, physically been abusive. . . . There's nothing that I can do. Just to calm her down and say, "Don't burn yourself, this is not your problem. They're just having some kind of problem. It's not your problem. Don't blame yourself. It's not what you've done wrong. They're just having this problem and they're kind of getting you involved." . . . I've told her. Like I told her, "Hey, why don't you go call the police or call organizations that help people, would help you with this problem." But she's like, "They might take away my dad." So she's kind of scared of telling anybody except me and a bunch of her other friends. So she would never go to the police because she was afraid that [they'd] take her dad away or something. And they don't want that.

Another young Iranian woman recounted the experience of her friend:

> One of my friends, she is actually Romanian . . . was physically abused. Her parents would hit her if she didn't do what they wanted. But she couldn't tell anybody, and sometimes she'd be crying in the school for us. But we weren't allowed to tell anybody, and she wouldn't want to get help because she knew it would get worse. She thought it would be worse. She didn't want us to tell anybody. We [swore] to her that we wouldn't tell anybody.

Many of the young women interviewed also identified incidents of violence within the schools. As this young African Canadian woman commented,

Actually I had a friend who was experiencing violence and I told her to tell her parents, and she told her parents first, and then her parents told her to tell the counselor. She was going to her locker, and this boy was there and then he started touching her, she doesn't know him, he's like in Grade 10 and she's in Grade 9, and then he starts touching her and she told him stop it, and she yelled it so loud in the hall and then she talked to parents, and the parents told her to tell the counselor. The counselor didn't really do anything, she just said if he keeps on doing that just tell her and then she will talk to him about it.

SEXUALIZATION

Immigrant and refugee girls are uniquely sexualized by the dominant culture. Although none of the girls in our focus groups discussed trafficking and sexual exploitation explicitly, many spoke about the simultaneous construction of their culture as exotic and as devalued. In this construction, the "exotic Other" is sexually available to the dominant culture. One young woman described being mistaken for a prostitute:

> I was on the street. My cousins were here. And we were waiting for the bus, and the police walked by, and we started showing off. And they stopped and they walked around the block and they looked at us. And they walked around the block and they came back and they walked around again. And I'm like, "We're not prostitutes. We're waiting for the bus." (African Caribbean focus group)

Another from the same group spoke about the exoticization of difference:

> They always ask us about our hair, and they always feel our hair, and it really bothers us. "Oh, is that your real hair or is that extensions?" They come up to you on the bus and start feeling your hair without asking if they can touch your hair.

An inverse side to this sexualization or exoticization is the tendency of the girls themselves to see White males in a positive light because of their ability to provide access to resources. However, the contradictions inherent in this perception are clearly communicated in the following comment by a young woman participant in the mixed girls' theater workshop:

I would think too, with girls coming from different countries—I don't know—some, they're more trusting than other people. I've seen people from Canada, an Asian person would be more trusting to a White guy because he's White and he's supposedly knowing—how can I explain this? He's the one to offer you things. We're so more trusting to him thinking that, "Oh, he's going to give me an education" or something and that leads to violence and rape or something like that. Like there's a situation where a whole bunch of Filipino nannies were being brought to Canada but then being raped and killed afterwards just because they're women, and they're weaker than others. Like we're more dependent on the White people, I guess. So they're supposed to be like giving us opportunities and stuff, but yet they're taking advantage of us. I've noticed that.

HIERARCHICAL AND HORIZONTAL VIOLENCE

Many of the young women we interviewed and those who participated in the focus groups alluded to horizontal though hierarchical forms of violence, in other words, violence between girls of different racial backgrounds. Sometimes, this took place between White girls and girls who were racialized:

One of my friends, she's Persian, she got into a fight with a White girl because—what was the reason? Just because the White girl was kind of like popular in school or whatever and she was giving the Persian girl bad looks. And she didn't take it. She like started a fight. (Individual interview, Iranian girl)

Sometimes the conflict began with girls from different racialized groups and escalated:

There was a fight between a Persian girl and a Chinese girl. And then these White girls were behind the Chinese girl so they were calling my friend FOB loud, all the White girls. I heard that. I wasn't there but I heard it. And that's the only thing. (Individual interview, Iranian girl)

A lot of the horizontal violence seemed to revolve around boyfriends. As this young Iranian woman recalled in an interview,

Last year me and my group of friends were just sitting, and this girl came up to us and she told me that, "I just wanted to let you know that you guys should stop looking at those two guys," or "You guys should stop that." And I'm like, what the hell, what is she talking about? Why would we even . . . we don't even know those two guys. We'd be in Grade 9. Those two guys were in Grade 12. We don't even know them. And then the next day—I wasn't there in school—my friends came and told me that this girl, her name is [xxxx] and she's White, too. She came up to us and she told us and I got so mad because I felt that it was kind of bringing me down because they're telling me that I'm looking at her guy or something. I felt so low. I went up to her and I'm like, "What are you talking about? What did you say?" And she's like, "You're giving me attitude now." And I'm like, "What the hell are you talking about?" And she's like, "Fuck, you're giving me attitude." And I'm, "No. I'm asking you why you came up and said that. Why did you say that?" And then she said, "I'm telling you, I just sent a message to you not to look at those two guys." And I'm like, "What the hell. Who would even look at your guy?" And I said, "What a bitch." And I came back and she came and she grabbed my neck and she's holding my neck and she's like, "What did you just say?" I'm like, "Your group is fucked up. . . . You guys are all fucked up. What the hell is your problem?" And there was a teacher passing and she was grabbing my neck, right? She let me go and then I went upstairs and I was sitting with my friend beside my locker and she came up to me and she was with her boyfriend and another guy. And her boyfriend was Persian, too. That's the thing, that her boyfriend was Persian and the girl was White. And she came up to us and she said, "Get your butt up." And I'm like, "I don't want to." She's like, "I told you. Get your butt up." I'm like, "Are you going to make me?" And she came and she grabbed my jacket and the locker was a bit behind me and I stood up and I think she pushed me. Oh she was holding my hand so I couldn't really do anything with my hands, right? So she had really, really long hair and she had curly hair and I went like that to her.

What this quote reveals is the influence of patriarchal values in terms of possessing a boyfriend, but more particularly, having possession over boys, regardless of their race. This is where racism comes in—as a vehicle by which to translate and transmit violence, but also to communicate territoriality in a psychological and a physical sense—in other words, through the expression of attitude as well as physical aggression. The narrative used to recount this incident is indicative of the anger, resentment, and immediacy of these kinds of experiences of violence. The potency of these experiences comes through when we realize that there are few places that these young women can turn for support or intervention. Within this unsafe space of the school, White girls were often seen as privileged and favored, able to escape punitive mea-sures by teachers and granted special dispensations. As one Iranian girl commented,

> I don't know what it is but my teacher, when we come in late, she starts yelling at us, she starts saying, "Why are you late again? La, la, la, la." But some White girl comes in, she goes, "Oh, where have you been?" She goes, "I was out with my friends, I'm so sorry," and she starts laughing. I would be like, "What the hell is going on?" Why is she yelling at us and not her and she's not saying anything. Or assignments. You hand them in one day late, "Oh that's a zero for you." But then Canadian people, I don't know what they do, suck up to them or whatever, and they can get the marks. (Individual interview)

Despite being aware of the ranking and differential privileges accorded to different groups—and the obvious anger that they feel about this situation—the girls and young women who partic-ipated in the current study did not perceive this as a systemic issue. On the contrary, many attributed the interracial violence and hostility to the innate characteristics of different groups and to a violent school environment.

PARENTAL CONFLICTS

The interviews and focus group discussions revealed a sophis-ticated understanding of parental conflict that went beyond it being seen simply as a so-called culture clash or a case of conflict-ing cultures. Rather, participants talked of how their position as girls and young women meant that they were subject to patriar-chal codes that appeared to be more pronounced in their families than in the dominant and/or host society. I would venture that this gendered awareness gains its salience from their position as minorities in a dominant culture. Often it is rooted in a binary dis-tinction of "our" culture versus "Canadian," though as the fol-lowing quote suggests, the notion of just what Canadian is remains a somewhat hazy concept:

> When I speak to my dad, I don't talk too loud because I respect my dad, I'm almost scared of him because I respect him. But he wants me to be innocent and not act like boys or whatever. Say if I'm hug-ging a guy friend, he'd like, "Maybe you shouldn't do that." And I

tell my dad, "This is Canada. It's not Iran any more. I'm a grown woman. I know what I'm doing. It's just a hug." (Individual interview, Iranian girl)

Despite these kinds of conflicts over values, most young women identified their families as sites of support. Many young women acknowledged the fact that their parents would rather return to their country of origin but were making sacrifices by remaining in Canada so as to improve opportunities for their children.

FITTING IN

Many girls spoke poignantly about the difficulty of fitting into the dominant culture. Studies have shown how girls who are differently located because of race, sexual orientation, disability, or class are vulnerable to taunts and violent acts because the dominant society does not value those who do not conform to White, middle-class ideals (Jiwani, 1998), and certainly the girls in the current study reinforced these findings. The most vulnerable girls who were immigrants and refugees are those who have just arrived in Canada. In schools, recent immigrants are called FOBs, an acronym for "fresh off the boat." One young woman defined FOB:

FOB is like "fresh off the boat." It means that you're really . . . geeky and you don't know how to speak and stuff. You dress stupidly or whatever, right? (Individual interview, Iranian girl)

Her definition encapsulates the racism and classism that are rarely named and spoken about in Canadian society. Given the derision that new immigrants face in schools, the most effective strategy for immigrant and refugee girls is to learn how to fit in. Distancing oneself and one's peer group from those who have just immigrated is one way to do this. One Iranian girl spoke of the self-policing that accompanies the internalization of dominant norms and perceptions precipitated by this form of racism:

Persians are loud people. . . . People would be looking and staring at us, White people. And I'd be like, "Shut up. Don't speak so loud. Everybody's looking at us." Because I don't like that kind of stuff. Like we should balance out. We don't like everybody to stare at us.

We don't want everybody to say, "Oh, those people are so loud."
(Individual interview)

Another young Iranian girl expressed resentment over the double standards inherent in this process of fitting in. She said,

> Well they make fun of my name . . . White people. Well my name is [xxx]. It looks like gonads. It's close to that. They make fun of it or they say that, "Your name is stupid." Sometimes they say that [wrong]. Like I want my name to be what it is. I don't have to shorten it for people to make it easier for them. I mean I have to learn their way to fit in but they can't say my name properly, spell my name properly, or pronounce it properly. Like if I don't say it right, they would make fun of me. They'd like, "Oh, you're an FOB." (Individual interview)

The ultimate form of violence within the lives of these young women, and perhaps the most profound and harmful manifestation of the desire to fit in, was the negation of self. This process can occur as a result of assimilation, internalized racism, and sexism. As Kelly (1998) poignantly described in her analysis of young Black youth in Canada, the ultimate insulting question they get asked is, "Where are you from?" Although the young women in the focus groups and individual interviews did not refer specifically to being asked this question, they did address the kind of self-denial that they experienced with regard to their identity. As one African Caribbean focus group participant said, "Sometimes I feel like I have to lose my true identity to fit in." Another young woman of South Asian background described her identity in more relational terms:

> I don't think being a Canadian means that you're not something else. Like if someone was to ask me where I was from, I'm still from Pakistan. I'm always going to be from Pakistan and ultimately, somewhere deep down inside, that's my baseline foundation. But I have a Canadian flag on my backpack and if I were to backpack for a year . . . I'd be Canadian.

What this young woman's words illustrate is the contextual nature of Canadian identity—here in Canada, she is a Pakistani, whereas elsewhere (backpacking in Europe, say), she'd be a Canadian. In part, this split sense of belonging is connected to these young women's own hybridity: emerging from their diasporic location on one hand, and their rejection from the dominant society on the other.

INSTITUTIONALLY SANCTIONED VIOLENCE

Services for girls who are immigrants in the schools are typically limited to English as a second language (ESL) courses. These services are concentrated in urban centers. One Thai girl, who lives in a small town in a rural area, reported that she attended school for 2 weeks before her father informed the school that she did not understand English. Because there were no ESL courses available in her school, she was placed in remedial classes. The isolation and ostracism experienced by girls who are immigrants and refugees living in rural communities are compounded by the fact that they do not have peers who share their cultural background. A service provider from the same town described the experience of two sisters with whom she worked:

> At home, they were loved by their parents, and the parents wanted them to learn and go to work and do everything like anybody else does. But at school, these two young girls felt very isolated. People would look at them, stare at them, and call them names. . . . People wouldn't sit beside them because they felt East Indian girls were smelly. So their experience at school was very, very difficult. All they wanted to do was learn, but they didn't look forward to going to school.

Given that isolation is a key risk factor for violence (Jiwani, 2001a, 2001b; Raj & Silverman, 2002; Websdale, 1998), the situation of girls who are immigrants and refugees in rural areas is in this one sense worse than their urban counterparts. The lack of variety or alternatives often forces these girls and young women to internalize the violence and rejection they are experiencing and to attempt to fit in to peer groups that are not always accepting of their difference.

Although less isolated than their rural counterparts, girls and young women in urban communities still face a hostile school environment. The problem is exacerbated by the fact that many principals and teachers refuse to acknowledge racism in the schools. Many girls described their frustration with teachers who discriminate against girls who are immigrants and principals who dismiss them when they describe racist acts. In the words of one of them,

> I wouldn't go to a principal because they would go against me, too. It has happened a couple of times that they would say, "Oh, this is not about race." Somebody in our school got suspended because she said she felt one of her teachers was really racist. She got suspended even though she didn't say who it was. (Individual interview, Iranian girl)

This quote highlights the denial and dismissal of racism by White school authorities. More than that, it demonstrates the fear that girls experience in calling attention to such racism, largely because of the retaliation they might experience as a result. Another interviewee, while outlining the potentially dangerous consequences for girls who remain silent about racist acts and incidents also alluded to the possible dangers in telling just anyone about them:

> From what I've seen, the kids fear it so they won't go and tell people about it. They'll just keep it inside. And I think that sooner or later, it's just going to make them explode. So if I could give them advice, I'd tell them, number one, go to a person who you know you can trust. I wouldn't say first to go to somebody at school. (Individual interview, South Asian girl)

In other words, school, though a primary system within which these girls are inculcated, is not seen as a safe place. Rather, as a microcosm of the larger society, it mirrors and reproduces the very relations of power that make violence systemic.

DISCUSSION

Despite the fact that none of the young women or girls interviewed disclosed any personal experiences of intimate or gender-based violence, they all reported on the systemic and pervasive forms of violence that they encountered on a daily basis. Everyday racism (Essed, 1990) permeated their lives and resulted in their othering through inferiorization, trivialization, exoticization, and erasure. In part, and as mentioned earlier, the reluctance to discuss personal experiences of violence could stem from the ethical requirements involved in doing this kind of research. On one hand, interviewers are legally bound to report all disclosures of abuse to the police. On the other hand, the interviewees' own fear of involving authorities such as the police reinforces the code of silence that exists around violence in these marginalized and stigmatized communities.

Grewal's (Grewal & Kaplan, 1994) notion of "scattered hegemonies" is particularly relevant here in terms of highlighting the ways in which patriarchal structures within transnational communities become allied with those of the dominant society. In this case, the patriarchal structure within immigrant communities allies itself with the patriarchal structures outside to contain and, more important, draw a veil of silence over all forms of gender-based violence. That said, attempts on the part of the dominant society to culturalize violence and culturalize racism through the attribution of gender-based violence to inherent cultural traits suggests that the alliance between scattered hegemonies is tenuous at best. In other words, when the chips are down this so-called alliance is more likely to be shattered in the interests of maintaining a White patriarchal dominant order.

The hierarchical nature of racism as violence is also apparent in the categories used by these racialized young women to distinguish one group from another. The distinction they draw between those who are assimilated and those who are fresh off the boat, for instance, suggests that the dominant hegemonic order works in an insidious manner, privileging conformity over difference and valuing assimilation over plurality.

The violence of racism also comes through in the form of the pressure to fit in, to conform to the codes and values of the dominant society. The negation of self that is implied in the very act of fitting in (i.e., fitting in through erasure of difference) is the ultimate form of violence. Assimilation through fitting in not only erases identity but also erodes identification with one's community, especially when the latter is continually inferiorized.

Generally, the interviews and group discussions revealed that girls who are immigrants and refugees felt unable to access school counseling services. Echoing the findings of other studies, this feeling came as a result of experiences of racism: racism that was communicated through acts of cultural insensitivity and language barriers, as well as threat that their disclosures would not be held in confidence (Handa, 1997; Kunz & Hanvey, 2000). Studies show that this same unwillingness to access certain services and distrust in using them is shared by parents of immigrant and refugee children (Janovicek, 2000; National Association of Women and the Law, 1999).

It is apparent that service providers need to be cognizant of the ways in which systemic racism and everyday racism affect and influence the lives of these young women and girls. It is the continuum of the violence of racism that requires consideration, not just those instances of overt racism that are marked by physical violence. Furthermore, it seems that the best strategies for service provision need to be grounded in the lived realities of girls and young women from immigrant and refugee communities. This needs to be combined with an awareness of the ways in which national policies around immigration and refugee status impose constraints that further render them vulnerable to victimization through poverty, isolation, othering, and exclusion.

LIMITATIONS

These research findings are limited in terms of generalizability as a result of two interconnected factors. The first concerns issues of methodology. Given the social context, the priorities of the facilitators and interviewers often overwhelmed the research agenda. Because of significant cut-backs in existing social services as well as a pronounced lack of services targeted to immigrant and refugee groups, many of the interviewers ended up making this a focal point of their interviews with young women and other service providers. The second drawback was generational. Those interviewers who were younger (younger than age 25 years) identified with the young women and consequently failed to probe them at particular times. They accepted these young women's overt definitions of their realities without probing deeper into the various structural and social forces that contribute to their heightened vulnerability to violence. In some cases, the interviewers accepted a so-called culturalized explanation of violence without interrogating what was in fact meant by *culture* in the interview context. That said, the findings that were generated from the interviews and focus groups were highly revealing.

They point to the necessity of doing participatory and empowering research, while reducing the kinds of shortcomings that might accrue from involving marginalized communities who may not necessarily have expertise in doing such research.

Another factor has to do with the particular geographic location of the research. Different countries and different regions within them have marked and distinctive patterns of racialization. Thus, each region has its own set of defined out-groups and in-groups. While race in terms of skin color carries certain connotations within the Western industrialized world, there is also a hierarchy of races, whereby some are more privileged than others. Hence, within Canadian society, those groups that tend to be the most devalued are Aboriginal peoples. Immigrants of various backgrounds are located above them, whereas the White groups tend to be situated at the top and hold the reins of power. Porter (1965) described this society as a vertical mosaic.

Within this research, there was no attempt to differentiate between the positioning of the various groups (e.g., Iranian as opposed to Latina). Rather, the aim was to delineate the common experiences of violence that were shared by young women who are racialized as others.

CONCLUSION

These interviews and focus group discussions reveal the extent to which racism as a form of systemic violence influences and shapes the lives of young women and girls from racialized immigrant communities. In addition, what the data reveal is a situation whereby young women and girls are caught on a tightrope between the demands of fitting in as imposed by the dominant society, and the often-conflicting demands imposed by the sites of support available to them through their homes and families. The racism inherent in the school system forces many of these girls to remain silent about any abuse and to become reliant on the family for a sense of self and identity. Alternatively, it can result in young women and girls becoming more isolated from their peer groups and their families and attempting to fit in, with often disastrous consequences. As the existing literature demonstrates, isolation and dependency are the two major risk factors contributing to an increased vulnerability to violence (Duffy & Momirov, 1997; Jiwani, 2001b; Johnson, 1996). Clearly, much more needs to be done to ameliorate the situation of young women who are marginalized. Secure and confidential gender-specific services are an utmost necessity if society is not to reproduce the long-term sequelae of childhood and/or youth victimization. Identifying the structural underpinnings of a hyphenated social reality is an essential first step. Given that schools are major sites in which girls and young women spend time, develop a sense of self, and mature into adults, it is imperative that measures are implemented within these sites to recognize and reduce the impact of racism as a major form of violence.

NOTES

1. This is reminiscent of the use of women's bodies to communicate national boundaries and safeguard cultural identity (Anthias & Yuval Davis, 1992; McClintock, 1995; Yegenoglu, 1998).

2. *Marginalization* in this context refers to immigrant status and racialization.

3. Given the small size of many of these communities, it is likely that individuals know each other and/or know each other's families. In the case of girls belonging to the Persian and/or Iranian community, for instance, we had a young Iranian woman conduct the individual interviews while a young South Asian researcher facilitated the Iranian girls' focus group.

REFERENCES

Abraham, M. (1995). Ethnicity, gender, and marital violence: South Asian women's organizations in the United States. *Gender & Society, 9*, 450-468.

Anthias, F., & Yuval-Davis, N. (1992). *Racialized boundaries: Race, nation, gender, color and class and the anti-racist struggle.* London: Routledge.

Bannerji, H. (1987). Introducing racism: Towards an anti-racist feminism. *Resources for Feminist Research, 16*, 10-12.

Bannerji, H. (1993). Returning the gaze: An introduction. In H. Bannerji (Ed.), *Returning the gaze: Essays on racism, feminism and politics* (pp. ix-xxix). Toronto, Canada: Sister Vision Press.

Basit, T. N. (1997). *Eastern values, Western milieu: Identities and aspirations of adolescent British Muslim girls.* Aldershot, UK: Ashgate.

Batth, I. (1998). *Centering voices from the margins: Indo-Canadian girls' sport and physical activity experiences in private and public schools.* Unpublished master's thesis, University of British Columbia, Vancouver, Canada.

Beijing declaration and platform for action. (1995, September 15). Fourth World Conference on Women: Action for Equality, Development and Peace, Beijing, China.

Beiser, M. (1998). Towards a research framework for immigrant health. *Metropolis Health Domain Seminar, Final report* (pp. 23-32). Ottawa: Minister of Public Works and Government Services Canada.

Berman, H., & Jiwani, Y. (Eds.). (2002). *In the best interests of the girl child: Phase II report.* London, Canada: Alliance of the Five Research Centres on Violence.

Bourne, P., McCoy, L., & Smith, D. (1998, spring). Girls and schooling: Their own critique. *Resources for Feminist Research, 261,* 55-68.

Burns, M. C. (Ed.). (1986). *The speaking profits us: Violence in the lives of women of color.* Seattle, WA: Center for the Prevention of Sexual and Domestic Violence.

Canadian Centre for Justice Statistics. (1994). *Statistics Canada report: Family violence in Canada, current national data.* Ottawa, Canada: Department of Justice.

Carraway, C. G. (1991). Violence against women of color. *Stanford Law Review, 43,* 1301-1309.

Champion, J. D. (1996). Woman abuse, assimilation, and self-concept in a rural Mexican American community. *Hispanic Journal of Behavioral Science, 18,* 508-521.

Choi, G. (1997). Acculturative stress, social support, and depression in Korean American families. *Journal of Family Social Work, 2,* 82-97.

Dasgupta, D. S., & Warrier, S. (1996). In the footsteps of "Arundhati": Asian Indian women's experience of domestic violence in the United States. *Violence Against Women, 2,* 238-259.

Davis, A. (2000). The color of violence against women. *ColorLines, 3*(3). Retrieved February 20, 2001, from www.arc.org/C_Lines/CLArchive/story3_3_02.html

Dossa, P. (1999). *The narrative representation of mental health: Iranian women in Canada* (Working Paper Series, #99-18). Vancouver, Canada: Vancouver Centre for Excellence, Research on Immigration and Integration in the Metropolis (RIIM).

Drury, B. (1991). Sikh girls and the maintenance of an ethnic culture. *New Community, 17,* 387-399.

Duffy, A., & Momirov, J. (1997). *Family violence in Canada: A Canadian introduction.* Toronto, Canada: James Lorimer & Co.

Essed, P. (1990). *Everyday racism: Reports from women of two cultures* (C. Jaffe, Trans.). Claremont, CA: Hunter House.

Faith, K., & Jiwani, Y. (2002). The social construction of "dangerous girls" and women. In B. Schissel & C. Brooks (Eds.), *Marginality and condemnation: An introduction to critical criminology* (pp. 83-107). Halifax, Canada: Fernwood.

Fleras, A., & Elliot, J. L. (1996). *Unequal relations: An introduction to race, ethnic and Aboriginal dynamics in Canada* (2nd ed.). Scarborough, Canada: Prentice Hall.

Flynn, K., & Crawford, C. (1998). Committing "race treason": Battered women and mandatory arrest in Toronto's Caribbean community. In K. D. Bonnycastle & G. S. Rigakos (Eds.), *Unsettling truths: Battered women, policy, politics, and contemporary research in Canada* (pp. 91-102). Vancouver, Canada: Collective Press.

Friedman, S., with Cook, C. (1995). *Girls: A presence at Beijing.* New York: NGO Working Group on Girls.

Geertz, C. (1973) *The interpretation of cultures.* New York: Basic Books.

Gilroy, P. (1987). *There ain't no black in the Union Jack: The cultural politics of race and nation.* Chicago: University of Chicago Press.

Grewal, I., & Kaplan, C. (Eds.). (1994). *Scattered hegemonies, postmodernity and transnational feminist practices.* Minneapolis: University of Minnesota Press.

Hall, S. (1990). The whites of their eyes: Racist ideologies and the media. In M. Alvarado & J. O. Thompson (Eds.), *The media reader* (pp. 7-23). London: British Film Institute.

Hampton, R., Oliver, W., & Magarian, L. (2003). Domestic violence in the African American community: An analysis of social and structural factors. *Violence Against Women, 9,* 533-557.

Handa, A. (1997). *Caught between omissions: Exploring "culture conflict" among second generation South Asian women in Canada*. Unpublished doctoral dissertation, University of Toronto, Canada.

hooks, b. (1990). *Yearning: Race, gender, and cultural politics*. Toronto, Canada: Between the Lines.

hooks, b. (1995). *Killing rage, ending racism*. New York: Henry Holt.

Huisman, K. (1996). Wife battering in Asian American communities. *Violence Against Women, 2*, 260-283.

Hutnik, N. (1986). Patterns of ethnic minority identification and modes of adaptation. *Ethnic and Racial Studies, 9*, 150-167.

Isaacs, H. (1975). *Idols of the tribe: Group identity and political change*. New York: Harper & Row.

Jabbra, N. (1983). Assimilation and acculturation of Lebanese extended families in Nova Scotia. *Canadian Ethnic Studies, 15*, 54-72.

Janovicek, N. (2000). *On the margins of a fraying safety net: Aboriginal and immigrant women's access to welfare*. Vancouver, Canada: Feminist Research, Education, Development, and Action Centre.

Jiwani, Y. (1992, August). Canadian media and racism, to be and not to be: South Asians as victims and oppressors in *The Vancouver Sun*. *Sanvad, 5*(45), 13-15.

Jiwani, Y. (1998). *Violence against marginalized girls: A review of the current literature*. Vancouver, Canada: Feminist Research, Education, Development, and Action Centre.

Jiwani, Y. (1999). Erasing race: The story of Reena Virk. *Canadian Woman Studies, 19*, 178-184.

Jiwani, Y. (2001a). *Intersecting inequalities: Immigrant women of color who have experienced violence and their encounters with the health care system*. Vancouver, Canada: Feminist Research, Education, Development, and Action Centre.

Jiwani, Y. (2001b). *Mapping violence: A work in progress*. Vancouver, Canada: Feminist Research, Education, Development, and Action Centre. Retrieved April 22, 2004, from www.harbour.sfu.ca/freda/articles/fvpi.htm

Joe, K., & Chesney-Lind, M. (1995). "Just every mother's angel": An analysis of gender and ethnic variations in youth gang membership. *Gender & Society, 9*, 408-431.

Johnson, H. (1996). *Dangerous domains: Violence against women in Canada*. Scarborough: Nelson Canada.

Kelly, J. (1998). *Under the gaze: Learning to be Black in White society*. Halifax, Canada: Fernwood.

Kenny, J. W., Reinholtz, C., & Angelini, P. (1997). Ethnic differences in childhood and adolescent sexual abuse and teenage pregnancy. *Journal of Adolescent Health, 21*, 3-10.

Keyes, C. F. (1981) The dialectics of ethnic change. In C. F. Keyes (Ed.), *Ethnic change* (pp. 4-30). Seattle: University of Washington Press.

Kim, J. K. (1980). Explaining acculturation in a communication framework: An empirical test. *Communication Monographs, 47*, 155-179.

Kobayashi, A., Moore, E., & Rosenberg, M. (1998). *Healthy immigrant children: A demographic and geographic analysis* (Publ. No. W-98-20E). Retrieved June 12, 2000, from www.hrdc-drhc.gc.ca/sp-ps/arb-dgra/publications/research/abw-98-20e.shtml

Kunz, J., & Hanvey, L. (2000). *Immigrant youth in Canada*. Ottawa, Canada: Canadian Council on Social Development. Retrieved October 8, 2000, from www.ccsd.ca/subsites/cd/docs/iy/hl.htm

Lai, T. A. (1986). Asian women: Resisting the violence. In M. C. Burns (Ed.), *The speaking profits us: Violence in the lives of women of color* (pp. 8-11). Seattle, WA: Center for the Prevention of Sexual and Domestic Violence.

Lather, P. (1991). *Getting smart: Feminist research and pedagogy within/in the postmodern*. New York: Routledge.

Lyman, S. M., & Douglas, W. A. (1973). Ethnicity: Strategies on collective and individual collection management. *Social Research, 40*, 5-18.

MacLeod, L., & Shin, M. (1990). *Isolated, afraid and forgotten: The service delivery needs and realities of immigrant and refugee women who are battered.* Ottawa: National Clearinghouse on Family Violence, Health and Welfare Canada.

Mama, A. (1989). *The hidden struggle: Statutory and voluntary sector responses to violence against Black women in the home.* London: London Race and Housing Research Unit.

Matthews, J. M. (1997). A Vietnamese flag and a bowl of Australian flowers: Recomposing racism and sexism. *Gender, Place, and Culture, 4*, 5-18.

McClintock, A. (1995). *Imperial leather: Race, gender and sexuality in the colonial context.* New York: Routledge.

Meleis, A. I. (1991). Between two cultures: Identity roles and health. *Health Care for Women International, 12*, 365-377.

Miles, R. (1989). *Racism.* London: Routledge.

Miller, B. D. (1995). Precepts and practices: Researching identity formation among Indian Hindu adolescents in the United States. *New Directions for Child Development, 67*, 71-85.

Mogg, J. (1991). *The experience of bicultural conflict by Vietnamese adolescent girls in Greater Vancouver.* Unpublished master's thesis, Vancouver, Canada: Simon Fraser University.

Musick, J. S., & Barker, G. (1994). Rebuilding nests of survival: A comparative analysis of the needs of at-risk adolescent women and adolescent mothers in the U.S., Latin America, Asia and Africa. *Childhood, 2*, 152-163.

Narayan, U. (1997). *Dislocating cultures: Identities, traditions, and third-world feminism.* New York: Routledge.

National Association of Women and the Law. (1999). *Gender analysis of immigration and refugee protection legislation and policy* [Submission to Citizenship and Immigration Canada]. Ottawa, Canada: NAWL Ad Hoc Committee on Gender Analysis of the Immigration Act.

Ng, R. (1993). Racism, sexism, and immigrant women. In S. Burt, L. Code, & L. Dorney (Eds.), *Changing patterns: Women in Canada* (pp. 279-301). Toronto, Canada: McClelland & Stewart.

O'Keefe, M. (1994). Racial/ethnic differences among battered women and their children. *Journal of Child and Family Studies, 3*, 283-305.

Onder, Z. (1996). Muslim-Turkish children in Germany: Socio-cultural problems. *Migration World Magazine, 24*, 18–24.

Perilla, J. L., Bakeman, R., & Norris, F. H. (1994). Culture and domestic violence: The ecology of abused Latinas. *Violence and Victims, 9*, 325-339.

Porter, J. (1965). *The vertical mosaic: An analysis of social class and power in Canada.* Toronto, Canada: University of Toronto Press.

Raj, A., & Silverman, J. (2002). Violence against immigrant women: The roles of culture, context, and legal immigrant status on intimate partner violence. *Violence Against Women, 8*, 367-398.

Razack, S. H. (1994). What is to be gained by looking White people in the eye? Culture, race, and gender in cases of sexual violence. *Signs, 19*, 894-923.

Razack, S. H. (1998). *Looking White people in the eye: Gender, race, and culture in courtrooms and classrooms.* Toronto, Canada: University of Toronto Press.

Razack, S. H. (Ed.). (2002). *Race, space and the law: Unmapping a White settler society.* Toronto, Canada: Between the Lines.

Rhee, S. (1997). Domestic violence in the Korean immigrant family. *Journal of Sociology and Social Welfare, 24*, 63-77.

Ristock, J. L., & Pennell, J. (1996). *Community research as empowerment: Feminist links, postmodern interruptions.* Toronto, Canada: Oxford University Press.

Rosenthal, D., Ranieri, N., & Klimidis, S. (1996). Vietnamese adolescents in Australia: Rela-
    tionships between perceptions of self and parental values, intergenerational conflict,
    and gender dissatisfaction. *International Journal of Psychology, 31,* 81-91.
Russell, S. (1996) *The girl child.* Ottawa: Canadian Beijing Facilitating Committee.
Said, E. W. (1979). *Orientalism.* New York: Vintage.
Schissel, B. (1997). *Blaming children: Youth crime, moral panics and the politics of hate.* Halifax,
    Canada: Fernwood.
Smith, L. T. (1999). *Decolonizing methodologies: Research and indigenous peoples.* London: Zed
    Books.
Thobani, S. (1998). *Nationalizing citizens, bordering immigrant women: Globalization and the
    racialization of women's citizenship in late 20th-century Canada.* Unpublished doctoral dis-
    sertation, Simon Fraser University, Vancouver, Canada.
Thomlinson, B., Stephens, M., Cunes, J. W., Grinnell, R. M., & Krysik, J. (1991). Characteris-
    tics of Canadian male and female child sexual abuse victims. *Journal of Child and Youth
    Care,* (Special Issue), 65-76.
Urquiza, A., & Goodlin-Jones, B. L. (1994). Child sexual abuse and adult revictimization
    with women of color. *Violence and Victims, 9,* 223-231.
Websdale, N. (1998). *Rural woman battering and the justice system: An ethnography.* Thousand
    Oaks, CA: Sage.
Wideen, M., & Bernard, K. (1999). *Impacts of immigration on education in British Columbia: An
    analysis of efforts to implement policies of multiculturalism in schools.* Vancouver, Canada:
    Vancouver Centre of Excellence, Research on Immigration and Integration in the
    Metropolis Working Paper Series.
Wyatt, G. E., & Riederle, M. (1994). Sexual harassment and prior sexual trauma among
    African American and White American women. *Violence and Victims, 9,* 233-247.
Yegenoglu, M. (1998). *Colonial fantasies: Towards a feminist reading of orientalism.* Cambridge,
    UK: Cambridge University Press.

*Yasmin Jiwani, Ph.D., is an assistant professor in communication studies at Con-
cordia University, Montreal, Canada, and a research associate with the London
Centre for Research on Violence Against Women and Children, as well as the
FREDA Centre for Research on Violence Against Women and Children. She is the
author and coauthor of various policy research monographs dealing with rural
women and violence, race, gender and violence, and more recently, racialized girls
and violence. Her major research interests focus on the intersecting and interlocking sites linking interpersonal and systemic forms of violence.*

[14]

Intersections of Immigration and Domestic Violence

Voices of Battered Immigrant Women

Edna Erez
University of Illinois at Chicago
Madelaine Adelman
Arizona State University, Tempe
Carol Gregory
Baldwin-Wallace College, Berea, Ohio

Feminist criminologists have helped to criminalize domestic violence in the United States and elsewhere. With this significant accomplishment, scholars also have critiqued the intended and unintended consequences of such reliance on the state for women's safety. One such critique reveals the intersectionality of social inequalities, social identities, and domestic violence. Here, the authors analyze the relationship between immigration and domestic violence based on interviews with 137 immigrant women in the United States from 35 countries. They find that immigration shapes how women understand domestic violence, their access to resources, and responses to domestic violence. This project documents observed dynamics of structural intersectionality for immigrant women as national origin and citizenship status are considered as another layer of identity politics and marginalization in relation to domestic violence.

Keywords: *immigration; domestic violence; intersectionality; intimate partner violence; national origin; citizen status*

Over the past 30 years, feminist academics and practitioners have revealed the extent and variety of gender violence, ranging from street-level sexual harassment (Stanko, 1985) to woman battering (Dobash & Dobash, 1979). According to Chesney-Lind (2006), "naming of the types and dimensions of female victimization had a significant impact on public policy, and it is arguably the most tangible accomplishment of both feminist criminology and grassroots feminists concerned about gender, crime, and justice" (p. 7). Indeed, feminist criminological research was part of the battered woman's movement's hard-won efforts to criminalize domestic violence (Adelman & Morgan, 2006). Feminist criminologists, their cross-disciplinary

Authors' Note: This research was conducted with the support of Grant #98-WT-VX-0030 from the National Institute of Justice. Views expressed in this article are those of the authors and not of the funding agency.

associates, and others also have been part of the growing critique of the limits or unintended effects of the criminalization of domestic violence (Britton, 2000; Chesney-Lind, 2006; Coker, 2001; Snider, 1998). Together, scholars and activists have identified harms induced by the criminal justice system not only on battered women, and poor battered women of color in particular, but also on men who batter, and in particular poor men of color who batter (Merry, 2000).

Noting the interconnection between racist violence, violence against women, and the institutionalization of the battered woman's movement within U.S. social service and criminal justice systems, feminist criminologists and others have called for antiracist, multicultural feminist analyses of gender violence and other forms of crime (Burgess-Proctor, 2006; Potter, 2006; see Baca Zinn & Thornton Dill, 1996, and Crenshaw, 1991, for foundational elaborations on intersectionality). Much of this analysis has looked at immigrant status as part of one's racial location in the social hierarchy (e.g., Crenshaw, 1991; Scales-Trent, 1999). Here, we build on the history of feminist criminology with an integrated feminist analysis of immigration and domestic violence. Rather than consider immigration as a variable or static category within race, we consider immigration as part of the multiple grounds of identity shaping the domestic violence experience. It is part of the interactive dynamic processes that, along with race, gender, sexual orientation, and class, inform women's experiences of and responses to domestic violence. We do so by analyzing one-on-one interviews with immigrant battered women from a variety of countries, revealing common experiences among immigrants in an effort to highlight *immigrant* as a separate and multiplicative aspect of identity, violence, and oppression.

We situate our study within the literature on gender, immigration, and domestic violence, noting the scholarly focus on discrete groups of immigrants (e.g., by ethnicity or national origin) rather than the commonalities experienced by various immigrant groups. We then outline our research methods and sample, followed by an analysis of the data that focus on commonalities across immigrant battered women's experiences. Specifically, we suggest that although significant investment has been made by federal and state governments, and local community-based organizations, to improve the criminal justice system response to immigrant battered women in terms of legal reform, law enforcement training, and increased services, immigrant battered women continue to face considerable structural barriers to safety. These barriers exist prior to immigration (e.g., social pressure to marry) and as a result of immigration (e.g., economic disadvantage that has gendered consequences). In turn, immigration law and women's perceptions of law enforcement inform their attitudes toward reporting intimate partner violence. We conclude with a discussion of our research findings and their implications for theory and practice, expressing concern with the level of awareness of existing legal options for battered immigrant women and the growing anti-immigrant trend across the United States to devolve enforcement of federal immigration law to local authorities.

Feminist Theory of Intersectionality

Feminist discourse on intersectionality has developed over the past two decades. Although there are some differences in interpretation and application, intersectionality theory considers the ways that hierarchies of power exist along multiple socially defined categories such as race, class, and gender. These categories mutually construct each other via structural inequalities and social interaction, creating a matrix of intersecting hierarchies that is not merely additive but multiplicative in terms of unearned privilege, domination, and oppression (Baca Zinn & Thornton Dill, 1996; Collins, 1991/2000; Crenshaw, 1991; Higginbotham, 1997; Steinbugler, Press, & Johnson Dias, 2006). In this way, both opportunities (including social and material benefit) and oppressions may be simultaneously created by intersecting forms of domination (Baca Zinn & Thornton Dill, 1996; Steinbugler et al., 2006). Thus, for instance, "a gay Black man may experience privilege vis-à-vis his maleness but be marginalized for his race and sexuality" (p. 808). Angela Harris (1990), along with other critical race feminism legal scholars, refers to this notion of intersecting, indivisible identities as "multiple consciousness." Theories of intersectionality have inspired scholars across many disciplines to notice how various forms of privilege and oppression operate simultaneously as well as to reveal those forms of social identities that go unnoticed.

Writings on intersectionality use country of origin as an example of how racial and ethnic identities result in domination or oppression. Crenshaw (1991) specifically refers to immigrant status as an example of how race affects violent victimization in the United States. In this article, we show how the experiences of legal and undocumented immigrants are different from those of U.S. citizens and yet similar to one another, regardless of country of origin. Notwithstanding the racialized politics associated with immigration in the United States, and recognizing the racism that many immigrants face, our effort here is to build on the substantial literature on intersectionality to reveal the intersection of immigration and domestic violence. We do so to highlight the salience of immigration for battered women in terms of how immigration affects the level and types of intimate partner violence women experience and shapes marital dynamics and women's helpseeking opportunities. We also examine how immigration and the policing of immigration may compromise women's safety. Thus, although we attend to the racialized category of immigration and the racist anti-immigrant sentiment aimed at immigrants, analytically, we have separated immigrant status from race/ethnicity as a category of intersectionality.

Immigration

Twenty-first century migration across international borders is a significant global phenomenon (Sassen, 1998). Motivated by a combination of push and pull factors such as impoverishment and economic opportunities, political instability and the opening of previously closed borders, and the loss or gain of family ties, large numbers of people enter key receiving countries such as the United States each year. The United States is considered "a nation of immigrants." Nevertheless, who is allowed to legally immigrate has varied over time. U.S. immigration and naturalization laws have shaped the resulting immigrant pool in terms of gender, race or nationality, sexual orientation, and marital status. These social identities have been central to U.S. immigration law, ranging from the exclusion of Chinese prostitutes in the 1870s to the men-only Bracero Program instituted in 1942 (Calavita, 1992). Subsequent changes in immigration policy, including an amnesty initiative in the mid-1980s, led to heterosexual family reunification and an increase in the numbers of women and children who migrated to the United States. Such gendered, racialized, and sexualized patterns reflect how immigration and naturalization law serves to police the purported moral as well as political boundaries of the nation (Gardner, 2005). These immigration laws affect why, when, how, and with whom women immigrate and their experiences of domestic violence subsequent to arrival in the United States.

One factor among many that motivates emigration from Southern toward Northern tier states is immigration policies that focus on family reunification. Other factors include the intensification of economic globalization under neo-liberal policies and relative ease of movement between political borders. Together, these factors are responsible for women making up an ever-increasing proportion of immigrants to the United States. Indeed, by the turn of the century, "close to 60 percent of immigrants from Mexico, China, the Philippines and Vietnam were female"; a similar percentage of female immigrants were between ages 15 and 44, significantly younger than their native-born counterparts (Zhou, 2002, p. 26). This young age cohort requires of female immigrants a long-term commitment to domestic and workplace labor in their new country of residence. In addition to their unpaid domestic and paid workplace labor, female immigrants also frequently contribute financially to the economy of their countries of origin via remittances home. In areas other than age and labor, however, female immigrants, as a whole, are a diverse group: migrating alone or with children and family; undocumented and/or dependent on male kin who sponsor their immigration. Some women arrive as highly skilled workers and successfully secure well-paid jobs. Other women, regardless of their skill sets, become among the lowest paid in the U.S. workforce. Still, female immigrants share the gendered effects of their border crossing.

As research on the gendered nature of immigration has emerged in terms of changing patterns over time of migration, identity formation and transformation, education, fertility, health care, and employment (Gabaccia, 1992; Hondagneu-Sotelo, 2003; Pessar, 1999; Strum & Tarantolo, 2002), so too has insight into the so-called domestic lives of immigrants. Ethnographers, for example, have analyzed how the meaning of marriage, along with women's and men's expectations of intimate relationships, may change as a result of migration patterns, access to education, and women's economic opportunities (Hirsch, 2003). These studies of immigrant domestic life help trace continuities and disruptions of the construction of gender across the migration process. For our purposes, one of the most critical links lies between the transformation of gender across the migration process and domestic violence.

Immigration and Domestic Violence

Violence against women is one of the most common victimizations experienced by immigrants (Davis & Erez, 1998; see also Erez, 2000, 2002; Raj & Silverman, 2002). Working together, battered immigrant women, activists, and scholars have documented how immigration intensifies domestic violence and creates vulnerabilities that impair immigrant women's management of domestic violence, preventing them from successfully challenging men's violence, from securing decreases in rates or types of men's violence, or from leaving their intimate partners. According to domestic violence scholars, "immigrant women arrive with disadvantages in social status and basic human capital resources relative to immigrant men" (Bui & Morash, 1999 p. 774) or cannot participate as actively in networks as male counterparts do (Abraham, 2000). As a result, barriers to safety for immigrant women include a lack of resources for battered women, social isolation or lack of local natal kin, economic instability, and perceptions that disclosure of battering to outsiders sullies community status. Criminal justice agencies that lack translation services and/or knowledge of immigration law, lack of trust in law enforcement and/or government authorities, and immigration law that dictates legal and sometimes economic dependency on the batterer, who may be undocumented or lacking legal immigrant status, also pose significant barriers (Bui, 2004; Dasgupta, 2000; Wachholz & Miedema, 2000).[1]

U.S. immigration law endangers battered immigrant women by giving near total control over the women's legal status to the sponsoring spouses, replicating the doctrine of coverture, under which "a wife could not make a contract with her husband or with others" (Calvo, 1997, p. 381). Coverture, in effect, identifies the married couple as a single legal entity, within which the husband has control over the property and body of the wife and their children. Similarly, women who immigrate as wives of U.S. citizens, legal permanent residents, diplomats, students, or workers are legally dependent on others to sponsor, pursue, and complete their visa petitions. This legal dependency intensifies gendered inequality, creates new ways for men to abuse and control their intimate partners, and entraps battered women (Erez, 2002; Salcido & Adelman, 2004). As part of the Violence Against Women Act (VAWA), legal reforms have been instituted to relieve some of the legal and economic dependencies imposed on battered immigrant women. These reforms include self-petition, which lets an abused spouse apply for a green card on his or her own; cancellation of removal, which lets an abused spouse who has already been subjected to removal proceedings request to remain in the United States; the U-visa, which lets a victim of crime (including domestic violence) who has been helpful to its investigation or prosecution apply for a nonimmigrant visa and work permit; and access to public benefits such as food stamps (Orloff, 2002; see also Wood, 2004). Obstacles to these well-intentioned legal reforms for immigrant battered women remain, in particular due to the complex nature of legal qualifications, including who is eligible to apply for which form of legal relief, and meeting the threshold required to demonstrate having been subjected to battery or extreme cruelty. The rise in anti-immigrant public sentiment has resulted both in the exclusion of some immigrants from access to education and medical care and in increased local law enforcement of federal immigration law. When coupled with post-9/11 delays in processing visa applications, the consequences of anti-immigrant sentiment further complicate the implementation of legal reforms for immigrant battered women.

Knowledge of immigrants' experiences with domestic violence is largely culled from case studies of discrete communities. Due in large part to the depth of social and cultural capital required to conduct sensitive research with members of marginalized immigrant communities, researchers tend to focus on small, local samples of battered women from specific immigrant communities (but see Menjivar & Salcido, 2002). Thus, we have insightful contributions based on the experiences of domestic violence by immigrant women to the United States from, for example, Bosnia (Muftic & Bouffard, 2008), Cambodia (Bhuyan, Mell, Senturia, Sullivan, & Shiu-Thornton, 2005), Mexico (Salcido & Adelman, 2004), Russia (Crandall, Senturia, Sullivan, & Shiu-Thornton, 2005), South Asia (Abraham, 2000), and Vietnam (Bui & Morash, 1999). These studies generate critical albeit partial knowledge with regard to immigration and domestic violence. In addition, until now, much of the holistic knowledge on immigrant battered women has been (rightly) directed toward services and policy-based interventions.

In this study, we take a different approach. We offer a detailed analysis situated within a theoretical framework of intersectionality, using *immigrant* as a positioned identity within the social structure as well as within interactions. This approach highlights the commonalities experienced by battered immigrant women, regardless of their ethnic or national group membership or countries of origin. Aware of the specific and unique contextual elements affecting domestic violence in each immigrant group, and the heterogeneity of domestic violence experiences that immigrant women from different cultures or ethnic groups endure, in focusing on the commonalities experienced rather than the unique elements of violence against immigrant women, we expect to highlight the theoretical value of the findings as well as draw public policy implications.

Research Methods

As previously noted, extant case studies of immigrant battered women typically consist of small, local samples derived from within one discrete community group. Our goal was to create a relatively large sample of diverse participants to be interviewed about their experiences with immigration and domestic violence. Diversity of participants in this study is based on each participant's language, ethnicity, nationality, cultural groupings, and country of origin. The sampling frame originated in states with large numbers of recent immigrants, with diverse immigrant communities, and with communities residing in both urban and rural areas: California, New York, Florida, Texas, Michigan, Wisconsin, and Iowa were selected as research sites.

Major immigration legal assistance organizations in these states helped to identify relevant social service agencies that provide direct services to immigrants. The directors of the social service agencies were contacted by phone about possible participation. In addition, members of social service agencies from other parts of the country who attended various regional and national meetings related to training or discussions about battered immigrant women and other issues concerning domestic violence and immigration were also approached for possible participation. Representatives from several agencies in New Jersey, Ohio, and Washington who expressed interest in participation were added to the list of participating agencies. Altogether, 17 agencies participated in the study, conducting interviews.

The interviews also addressed contacts with the criminal justice system, which some immigrant women may be unwilling to discuss with strangers. In light of the sensitive nature of the interview content and common reluctance among immigrant battered women to disclose detailed accounts of victimization and criminal justice experiences to outsiders, each participating agency instructed its bilingual social service provider to initiate contact with battered immigrant women with whom the provider had previously established rapport and a helping relationship of trust. As with much feminist research, one considers the positionality of the research subject in devising the methodology and conducting the research. The providers' relationship with the immigrant women was an integral component of the data collection phase because the providers were not only familiar with interviewees' strengths, concerns, and needs but also shared their language and, commonly, their culture. Therefore, the provider asked each woman if she was willing to be interviewed, explained the purpose of the research project, and, once the woman gave her consent, conducted the interview.

We recognize that where a power differential existed between the social service agency staff and the helpseeking interviewees, it may have compromised the validity of those data pertaining directly to access to or quality of social services. However, as noted below, many of the social service agents were battered immigrant women turned advocates, where the power differential was minimal. Furthermore, given the logistical barriers (e.g., training and sending interviewers to agencies in multiple states) and skill-based challenges (e.g., language competency) involved in collecting sensitive data from such a diverse sample, on balance we determined that access to a range of immigrant battered women, secured in large part due to the relationship of trust they had established with the agency staff and the linguistic comfort afforded to participants, overrode this limited, albeit important, methodological concern.

The bilingual social service providers who conducted the interviews ($N = 20$), were employees or volunteers who either had training in social services or, in some cases, were themselves survivors of domestic violence who had become battered women advocates. Each was given sets of questionnaires and instructions concerning the interviews (e.g., ethical standards such as confidentiality and interview techniques such as probing questions). The questionnaires, originally written in English, were sent ahead of time to the agencies so that the interviewers could become familiar with their content and be prepared, if necessary, to conduct simultaneous translations.[2] The social service providers/interviewers most often conducted interviews in the immigrant women's native language (i.e., in about two thirds of the cases).

The interviewees ($n = 137$) were immigrant women who sought help related to their immigration and/or domestic violence problems. As such, they are not necessarily representative of all battered immigrant women but represent a subsample of this population: those who have overcome barriers to reveal abuse or seek help, and those whose battering came to the attention of social services, often due to the gravity of their victimization. Furthermore, they are not representative of the subgroup of immigrant women seeking help, as they have been recruited through requests for interviews by agencies that agreed to participate in the study. There were several organizations that for practical or resource reasons did not elect to participate ($N = 8$). Some could not afford the time to conduct lengthy interviews; others were not successful in identifying battered immigrant women who were willing to participate. The sample, therefore, is not a random representation of the universe of battered immigrant women in the United States. The value of the data reported in this study, however, lies in providing accounts of the dynamics of the interaction between domestic violence and immigration from a diverse sample of women who vary by language, ethnicity, nationality, and country of origin.

Most interviews were conducted in the first (non-English) language of the interviewees, as reported by the interviewers.[3] English also was used in some interviews in part or throughout the interview, if the woman being interviewed was well versed and expressed comfort in speaking English. The interviews lasted between 45 minutes and 2½ hours and included closed- and open-ended questions about the women's demographic characteristics, circumstances of their arrival in this country, experiences with abuse and violence in their home countries and in the United States, and their attempts to seek criminal justice and/or social services to ameliorate their situations.

Interviewees were offered a modest stipend ($20) for their time, regardless of whether they completed the interview. Interviews were completed most commonly in one session, but a few were completed during a second session. Any requests to skip a certain question because an interviewee was uncomfortable about describing issues she considered private were honored. Despite an extensive list of interview questions, most women responded to our questions in great detail. Translation problems invalidated some of the responses or resulted in partial responses.[4] For these reasons, the results for a small number of items in the interview schedule present only the range of responses rather than a quantified version of the responses.

Quantitative data were calibrated and the open-ended questions transcripts were analyzed through coding techniques described by Glaser (1992). As we read each response, we searched for and identified patterns and variations in participants' experiences and we reached a set of conceptual categories or propositions. The analysis was conducted by applying the logic of analytic induction, which entails the search for "negative cases" and progressively refining empirically based conditional statements (Katz, 1983). When negative cases were encountered, we revised our propositions until the data were saturated, making the patterns identified and the propositions offered consistent throughout the data. Once no new conceptual categories could be added, or propositions had to be reformulated, it was assumed that saturation had been reached.

Research Sample Profile

Female immigrants to the United States in the final research sample (*n* = 137) came from 35 countries.[5] They self-identified with a variety of religions: Christian (58%, of which 36% identified as Catholic),[6] Muslim (22%), Hindu (5%), and Jewish (1%). The age of the women ranged from 19 to 56 years, with a mean age of 32.5 and median age of 31.

In terms of marital status, approximately the same percentage of women were married in their home countries (45%) or were never married (i.e., single and/or living apart from an intimate partner) before coming to the United States (43%). The rest of the sample were either divorced (4%), separated (2%), or living with someone (2%) in their home countries prior to immigrating to the United States. At some point after immigrating to the United States, most single women got involved with an intimate partner. The percentage of "never married" decreased from 43% to 6% and those living with someone increased from 2% to 18%. Although the percentage of women in the sample who were married during the interview was the same as those who were married in their home countries prior to the move to the United States (45%), the percentage of women who stated their marital status was "divorced" at the time of the interview increased from 4% to 18%, and the percentage of women who were separated from their spouses rose from 2% to 23% of the sample.

Table 1
English Proficiency

English Language Literacy	Fluent	Some Ability	No Ability	Total
Reading	27%	46%	27%	100%
Writing	25%	37%	38%	100%
Speaking	26%	48%	25%	99%

The range of years the women have lived in the United States was from 1 to 30 years, with a mean of 8.7 years and a median of 6. The length of time they lived with the abuser was between 1 and 30 years, with a mean of 7.6 and median of 6 years.

In terms of family size, the overwhelming majority of interviewees had children (86%). The mean number of children was 2.4, and the median was 2. The educational level of the interviewees ranged from 5 to 16 years of education, with a mean of 11.6 and a median of 11 years of education (where 12 refers to high school graduate), excluding one woman who stated she had no education at all.

A quarter (25%) of the women in this sample had no ability to speak English, whereas 48% had some ability and another 26% were fluent English speakers. Thus, the use of interviewers skilled in the participants' native language was imperative. Only 27% were fluent readers of the English language, whereas 25% were fluent writers. The vast majority of women sampled had only some or no ability to read (46% some ability; 27% no ability) or write (37% some ability; 38% no ability) in English. The English proficiency of the sample as reported by interviewees is detailed in Table 1.

Immigration status varied among interviewees and between interviewees and their intimate partners at the time of the interview (see Table 2). Immigration status was divided into the following categories: U.S.-born citizens, naturalized citizens, lawful permanent residents (LPRs), VAWA self-petition, work visa, undocumented, and temporary visa. Consistent with the definition of immigrant, none of the women in this sample were U.S.-born citizens, whereas 11% of partners were natural-born citizens. Two categories described the largest percentage of female participants: LPR and undocumented. Thirty-four percent of participants were LPRs whereas 36% of their partners were LPRs, and 24% of participants were undocumented immigrants whereas only 15% of partners were undocumented. Naturalized citizens were 19% of our sample of women and 34% of partners. Nine percent of participants and 4% of partners had temporary visas, 9% were VAWA self-petitions, and 5% had work visas. No partners in this study had work visas or were VAWA self-petitions. In general, male partners occupied a citizenship status with greater rights and privileges than did the female victims in this study.

More than half of the women (58%) were employed at the time of the interview. Most often, employment involved unskilled work, and domestic labor was the most

Table 2
Immigration Status

Immigration Status	Female Immigrants	Intimate Partners
U.S.-born citizen	—	11%
Naturalized citizen	19%	34%
Lawful permanent resident (LPR)	34%	32%
		4% amnesty LPR[a]
VAWA self-petition	9%	—
Work visa	5%	0%
Undocumented	24%	15%
Temporary visa[b]	9%	4%
Total	100%	100%

NOTE: VAWA = Violence Against Women Act.
[a]Previously undocumented, but secured LPR as part of 1986 Immigration Reform and Control Act.
[b]Temporary visas included tourist, student, and work visas.

common type of work reported (15%) by those employed. Almost half of the women (42%) had no gainful employment. More than three quarters of the husbands or partners (78%) were employed, most often in menial, service, unskilled, or skilled labor. About one quarter of both men (27%) and women (26%) sent money remittances to family in their home countries. More than one third of the women (39%) either used or planned to use public benefits.

Women reported being subjected to a lengthy period of abuse, ranging from 6 months to 25 years, with a mean of 5.5 years and median of 4 years of mistreatment, which included physical, mental, and sexual abuse, as well as verbal assaults. Women were also subjected to threats of being reported to Immigration and Naturalization Services (INS, now referred to as Immigration and Customs Enforcement [ICE]), being deported, or having their children taken away. The abuse also included tactics of isolating the woman to perpetuate her dependency on the abuser (e.g., she was not allowed to go to English classes, to go to school, to have employment, to be in touch with friends or family members, etc.).

Getting Married

All the women in the study had been married at one time. These marriages may have originated outside or inside the United States. Regardless of its place of origin, women indicated a lack of choice or a feeling that their resistance to the marriage was ignored. One third of the women in our study experienced arranged marriages,[7] typically through parents or relatives, often meeting the spouse days or weeks before the marriage. Women reported futile resistance to such arrangements. One woman explained, "I refused to marry him. . . . Nobody heard my refusal." Another echoed this sense of entrapment:

Yes, in five days, between knowing/hearing about him and setting the date of the wedding, we were married. I had not seen him before the wedding day. My father told me that he has drinking problems but God willing he will change after marriage. I did not want to marry him, but I had no choice.

Two thirds self-selected their spouses, having met in the country of origin through family, friends, work, or another connection such as shared neighborhood or religion. Those who met their spouses in the United States did so through immigrant community resource organizations. The impetus to marry was generally instigated by forces from without, primarily from family and peers, and even by those who married for love. Women who married for love highlighted the salient effect of familial and communal pressure to marry. Of the women who stated that they chose to marry their mates (two thirds of the sample), more than one quarter (27%) felt pressured to get married. Pressure to marry derived from financial instability, being too young to effectively resist, or, in a few cases, pregnancy. One woman who was married at age 15 explained, "We had no opinion or choice. Whatever our parents would say, we had to do." Others who were perceived of as too old also felt pressure to marry:

> I was the oldest girl in my family, and my younger sister already received a proposal, and my family felt that I was holding the marriage up since no one who had seen me in the past had wanted to marry me. There were 15 other men who had seen me and rejected me, so there was a lot of pressure to marry.

Women also stated how they wed to escape ongoing abuse they were suffering at home.

> I was abused by [my] father physically. The day I left the house, and was proposed by [my soon-to-be] husband, my father beat me so badly I accepted the marriage proposal, in attempt to get out of the violence I was living in at home.

In this way, for the young as well as those perceived to be too old to remain unmarried, marriage was an escape route from economic instability, surveillance and constant pressures by peers and family, victimization, or unplanned pregnancy. However, in the long term, marriage became yet another site of entrapment for newly immigrant women.

Becoming an Immigrant Battered Woman

Women reported various reasons for coming to the United States. One third (34%) followed their spouses, and one eighth (13%) married U.S. citizens, most of whom ($n = 10$) were military men.[8] About one fifth (16%) came for family reunification. A substantial proportion of the women immigrated for economic reasons: 29% came to improve their economic status and 12% to work. Another significant proportion fled violence in the home country (18%) or political repression (10%).

In the United States,[9] most of the women (87%) reported that the gendered division of labor was clear-cut; women focused on being a wife and mother and were solely responsible for housework and child care. In a minority of cases (17%), women were responsible for grocery or child-related shopping. Most often, they did not have access to a car or did not have a driver's license (60%). Men were responsible for gainful employment and money transactions related to the family, and only in a minority of cases (13%), the women stated that their men helped with work around the house.

According to female interviewees, the abuse resulted in severe mental and physical harm, including depression, withdrawal, numbness, and anxiety. About one third of the women (34%) required hospitalization to treat the injuries that resulted from the battering. Almost half of the women (46%) reported being battered while they were pregnant, with the abuser often trying to hit, kick, or otherwise interfere with the pregnancy. This abuse took place in all parts of the house, in particular in the bedroom or kitchen. Contrary to popular myths concerning domestic violence, it also occurred in public areas such as medical clinics, cars, and various social service offices, in front of family, children, neighbors, and other community members. Members of the husband's family often participated in the abuse.[10] Victimization in the presence of others is indicative of a perception that the abuse is justified or that it will garner no consequence to the perpetrator. The former suggests that the offender's actions are condoned by friends, family, and the community. The latter raises questions about institutional responses to publicly displayed abuse and how the immigrant status of the victim affects the perceptions and reactions of medical and social service workers.

Immigrant women have an added risk of victimization due to relocation. For women who immigrated with a spouse or partner, the move seemed to have an adverse effect on men's level of violence and control tactics. Following their arrival to the United States, for half of these women, the level of violence increased, and almost one quarter (22%) stated that the violence began after arrival: "It has gotten worse. Now he takes out all the frustration on me." For one fifth (20%) of the women, the level of violence stayed the same, for 6% it decreased, and for 2% it stopped. The escalation of abuse was particularly difficult for immigrant women who had left their natal families behind: "I don't have family here, so he tells me that I don't have another choice but to stay with him." Another woman argued that "if he were in Syria, he would take into consideration my parents and would not act abusively as in U.S." Lacking natal family and an extended kin network led to a high rate of social isolation and a deep sense of vulnerability for immigrant women.

Immigration affected husbands and wives differently. For example, some women reported that immigration removed what they understood as constraints against domestic violence, which were rooted in their home countries. "If I want to compare it to Iraq and the U.S., of course the move has affected us. In Iraq we have family, parents, relatives. Here there is drinking and open society, especially for men."

Women explained that men acquired new interests, such as alcohol, drugs, gambling, and women, which often accompanied the abusive behaviors of the spouse.

In addition to marital arguments to which men who batter often respond with abuse (e.g., jealousy, infidelity, drinking, money issues, child discipline, or education issues), there also were distinct issues created by the move to the United States that caused tension in the marriage and exacerbated the abuse. For example, many of the women reported that remittances they or their husbands made (i.e., sending money to family members in country of origin) often precipitated arguments or fights. Other issues included the husband's inability to provide for the family in the new country or his insistence that the wife, although now in the United States, continue to be a "traditional woman and never ask him about anything" or that she remain "a very traditional Latina wife, waiting on him hand and foot and never raising my voice on him." Women often explained the reasons for their battering as "my being a bad wife and mother" or "I needed to do what he told me to do, when he told me to do it."

According to women who took advantage of economic opportunities opened for them in the new country, this change provoked their spouses and led to abuse: "In the U.S. he suffered jealousy attacks and saw me prosper—he did not like that."

Economic Challenges

Economic challenges are not unique to immigrant families, but finding suitable employment or any job at all presents major difficulties for most immigrant families. The difficulty of securing employment that matches one's skills is a significant source of conflict between husbands and wives (e.g., being an engineer but working at a gas station). One woman attributed domestic violence to her husband's unemployment and resultant idleness: "He did not work, stayed home, which made him crazy." Another suggested that unemployment, per se, was not the problem. Rather,

> the dissatisfaction, failure, disappointment, not being able to meet one's economic expectations in life switches the burden on the wife. She becomes the reason of his failures. She is blamed all the time. She consistently tries to please him; it doesn't work. She gets all the frustration and all kinds of abuses.

At the same time, battered immigrant women also are deprived of supportive community, extended family, or a social network that could help them during such difficulties.

> If a spouse did not have work in home country, family or relatives would extend him money and help him. Here in U.S., there are many bills to pay; there is no one to give you a hand. One gets embarrassed.

On the other hand, for women working outside the home, their absence is often seen by men as a threat to the gender hierarchy. Women reported that although they worked outside the home, they controlled little to none of the money they earned and were subject to abuse and domination by their husbands.

> It was really good in the beginning, and then he lost his first job and things started getting really bad. It has not been very happy at work, and that is why he would take things out on me. We used to be happy. He would always keep the money and occasionally would demand a lot of sex, but then after a few years, he really started beating me up . . . [in particular] when I had to file his immigration papers.

Immigrant Status

Some women reported that the increase in emotional, sexual, and physical abuse coincided with immigration-specific activities such as entering the country, filing immigration papers, or accessing social welfare systems. The majority of women who came with their spouses reported that the transition and move to the United States altered the dynamics of the relationship: "He has had more power to manipulate in the U.S. because I am illegal and depended on him and I didn't have any rights here". An immigrant woman's dependency on her male partner elevates his position of dominance over her. At the same time, legal dependency represents a macrostructural vulnerability that systematically marginalizes immigrant women by limiting their access to goods and resources, such as work, social services, protection under the law, and so on. Although law is not intentionally gender biased, one that creates a status-marriage dependency, such as immigration law, makes immigrant women more vulnerable to the domestic violence power dynamic (Erez, 2000; Menjivar & Salcido, 2002).

Husbands became increasingly abusive, and the physical and emotional battering became more conspicuous and severe. One woman explained that "the relationship had gotten bad in Mexico and continued the same in the U.S. The abuse changed from verbal to physical." Another woman agreed that the violence worsened after immigration: "I believe when I came to the U.S. my husband treated me more like a kid. I do not have control over my life." Still another woman explained how "he has become more abusive. He knows the system; I don't. He speaks English; I don't. I don't have family support or someone living with me, so he can lie about me." Even one woman who had divorced her husband still was being threatened by him with regard to her immigration status: "He's going to call INS, because I lied that I was single instead of divorced. [From California] he stalks me, contacts me at home, at work in Michigan."

The overwhelming majority of women (75%) described how men used immigrant status to force them into compliance. "He used my immigration status against me. He would tell me that without him, I was nothing in this country." Men threatened women in a number of ways with regard to immigration including that they would call ICE officials and report their immigration status (40%); get them deported (15%); withdraw their petition to immigrate or otherwise interfere with the naturalization process (10%); take away the children or deny their custodial rights (5%); and, more generally, use immigration status to humiliate or degrade them (5%). One undocumented woman succinctly stated, "He makes threats to report me to the INS if I don't do what he wants."

Women also illustrated the connection between immigration and domestic violence being particularly painful for mothers. "He would tell me I did not have any rights in this country. He threatened to take our children—and he finally did!" In another instance, a woman was forced to trade custody of her children for an adjustment of her immigration status. In addition, mothers feared that their children would be deprived of opportunities for a brighter future that, in the minds of the women, the United States can provide. One woman was concerned about "employment for my older children and their immigration status. [My] son wants to be a U.S. citizen, to attend school and work here." Women did not want to jeopardize their children's immigration status and thought that divorce or leaving the United States would have negative consequences for their children.

Many battered immigrant women who do not have lawful permanent residency believe that divorce means losing their right to work or stay in this country. "If ever I challenge him to stay here, he will divorce me; I will lose my green card and will not be able to financially survive." This translates to jeopardizing her ability to sustain herself financially. Although the VAWA (1994) and its subsequent reauthorization (2000) Public Law 103-322, Violence Crime Control and Law Enforcement Act of 1994 Public Law 106-386, Victims of Trafficking and Violence Protection Act of 2000 provided battered immigrant women a self-petition option, most immigrant women are not aware of it. A husband uses the woman's lack of knowledge, dependency, and immigration status as a weapon to threaten and demand compliance. A man can easily manipulate his control over the relationship and the family because of an immigrant woman's actual or perceived legal dependency: "What prevents me from leaving is the immigration status. I need my green card." Abusers commonly convinced immigrant women that they have no rights (or that they are not entitled to any rights in this country) or that the abusers have the power to cancel their status at any time. Some threatened to withdraw the petitions already filed on the women's behalf or to tell ICE officials that the women married for the sole purpose of legal residency. Most of the women reported enduring abuse for long periods of time because of their desire to remain in the United States, in hopes that their husbands would change their immigration status to legal.

Culture and Community

The majority of the women (65%) reported abuse-tolerant perspectives in their home countries where, they explained, domestic violence is not considered a crime.

On one end of the abuse tolerant–intolerant continuum, a woman stated that "my national community doesn't believe that domestic violence exists." Another woman described another position along the continuum: "In Armenian culture, it is okay for a husband to hit his wife, and she should accept it. In America, it is considered a crime." Other women also drew a sharp contrast between their home countries, where domestic violence is a normal part of the marriage, and the United States: "There's a difference because here it's a crime. In Nicaragua if the couple makes up, then it's okay." Overall, women reported being raised in households where fathers and husbands were considered authoritarian decision makers with the right to wield violence as needed to secure women's compliance and that their communities expected them to reproduce such marital arrangements.

> The man is the center of authority. He is the supreme decision maker. He is the bread-winner; without him, in general, it is very hard to survive financially, especially if you are unskilled or uneducated.

> I was raised in a Hindu household . . . to be obedient and considerate of your elders.

> Tradition [says] that you stay with the person you married no matter what he does. Women stay home, to be housewife and put up with domestic violence. Here divorce is acceptable more so domestic violence not accepted.

> Women in Latin America and Mexico are supposed to suffer a lot with their husbands.

> We have to listen to men more than the American women. We have to stay home most of the time when we get married. We have to be more responsible for children and husbands.

These general comments were reinforced by more individualized lessons:

> My mother and father told me to go back and be a better wife. Otherwise I would be shaming them.

> My mother told me to bear it, since it was my decision to marry him.

> At first they were sad, told me to be patient. God will solve it.

Family members warned that divorce would negatively affect their children's welfare or chances for a good marriage or would decrease their younger sisters' prospects to marry. They used fear of shame, gossip, and guilt to convince their daughters to stay with their abusive husbands. In addition, some women also expressed fears, based on their respective husbands' threats, that leaving would lead to serious injury or even death. Despite their fear and familial admonitions to "put up with domestic violence" and "listen to men," the majority (85%) of women made one or more attempts to leave the abusers. Many of the women tried from 1 to 15 times to extricate themselves from the violence. Some women stated that they attempted to leave hundreds of times.

Reporting Abuse

Women reflected on the expectation that "everything stays in family. Sometimes we don't even tell our families, only after many years of problems." According to their immigrant communities, marital strife was to be kept private and should not be disclosed:

> A man can do anything; he is the head of the family, and a woman should always sacrifice to make things work. The expectations for men and women are different. Our culture does not welcome outside intervention. We don't involve outsiders in family issues. We do not consider domestic violence as a crime; police do not get involved. We don't go to shelters. Legal system does not get involved.

> They don't like [public intervention], because they want to have the liberty of committing family violence at will.

> In this town, it will label the woman. It will make it harder on the woman. [Public intervention is] not a good idea.

In the face of abuse-tolerant and privacy-affirmative perspectives, more than half (54%) of the women stated that they did not report the abuse because of their culture or religion. Nearly half the women did end up dealing with the criminal justice system as a result of the abuse (46%); however, in one third of these cases (35%), it was because someone other than the victim called the police (neighbor, family member, friend, or hospital staff).

Given the public pressure to keep domestic violence private, women struggled to maintain their social identity and status within their immigrant communities as they struggled to obtain safety for their children and themselves. "I will be ostracized and then where will I go?" Women reflected on distinctions between "home" and "here" attitudes toward criminal justice and other public interventions into domestic violence: "Here the police will help you. In El Salvador, they won't." Unaccustomed to involving outsiders or reporting domestic violence to the police at home ("I'm from Haiti; there is no such law to protect women against domestic violence"), women discussed the tension here in immigrant communities about disclosing abuse to family members and law enforcement.

Female interviewees "became aware of domestic violence in this country, because we know that many people can help us with our problem," including law enforcement, who "are very responsive here and very helpful." Immigrant women "now . . . think [domestic violence] is a crime here," and "Americans treat it like a crime, because that's what it is." Moreover, "here in U.S., a woman demands her rights. The Arab woman does not have a say in Arab countries." As a whole, women identified that "in the U.S. there is more support and protection for the victims, more services" and that "a woman in U.S. has her say, can make her own decisions. The government helps her to have the kids. In our country, no welfare benefits." One woman was impressed that "the clergy here in U.S. encourage you to report [domestic violence] to authorities."

Overall, women felt empowered by having at least the option to mobilize the justice system for help. It provided them a "big relief," or they found it "positive" or "helpful." In some cases, individual women's growing awareness was matched by communal acceptance of domestic violence as a behavior that deserves intervention, in particular when abuse resulted in serious injury. Women distinguished between those who shared ethnic or national identities in the home country and those in the United States.

> The Armenians from Armenia think police intervention is bad but Armenians in the U.S. generally do not think police intervention is a bad thing.

> In Mexico, they do not interfere until the woman is sent to the hospital; in the U.S. they interfere at an early stage, before there is need to send women to hospital.

Women also distinguished between known cases of domestic violence and those that remain hidden from sight, due to either literally or figuratively closed doors:

> It depends. When cases are really bad, like publicly seen abuse, the community 100% supports. When cases happen behind closed doors, the community is hesitant.

> It depends from case to case. If you or your family has a social standing.

However, they were well aware that their communities, or segments thereof, did not view favorably intervention by outsiders, in particular law enforcement.

> The community is accepting the outside intervention, except the religious leaders. Still even if the spouse is very abusive, they do not give religious divorce to victims. The batterer immediately remarries while the victim is helpless. Also, the community is not very supportive to a divorced woman.

In light of these mixed messages, "it makes you hesitate. Even if you know it is the right thing to do, you postpone the outside intervention."

Some immigrant women had negative experiences (either in the home country or here) with the justice system. Ambiguous messages about and ambivalent attitudes toward law enforcement when coupled with a persistent lack of material resources made many battered women reluctant to seek such intervention. These immigrant community views affected women's responses to the abuse, prolonged their marriages, or prevented them from seeking outside help. Still, individual women prevailed with assistance from immigrant community organizations to secure a semblance of physical security, social standing, and legal stability: "My children and the family unit is what keeps me in the relationship. However, he has promised to stop hitting me. I used to fear deportation, not anymore—I filed my own papers. I also wanted to protect my children."

Conclusion

Battered women in general face a number of interrelated and intricate barriers that complicate their pursuit of safety. Women struggle with, among other factors, embarrassment and shame about disclosing abuse and seeking help from social service or criminal justice agencies; emotional connection to and economic dependency on batterers; reluctance to break up families; and fear of myriad forms of violence, control, and retaliation by abusers and their communities. Although heterosexual men who batter are found in all social groups and at all economic levels, regardless of ethnicity, religion, national origin, cultural affiliation, or immigration status (Volpp, 2001), we have demonstrated that men who batter immigrant women, the majority of whom are immigrants themselves, have access to unique forms of domination and control, some of which are facilitated or even sanctioned by federal immigration law.

In our analysis of 137 battered women who had immigrated to the United States from 35 countries across the globe, we found that the general difficulties that battered women face coexist with challenges they experience as immigrants. Battered immigrant women face a range of legal, economic, and social challenges to safety. Legal challenges include lack of familiarity with or access to social service or criminal justice systems that possess limited immigrant-related cultural and linguistic competencies; legal dependency on batterers; and lack of legal knowledge. In terms of economic barriers, immigrant battered women report that their communities' economic marginalization combined with the continued responsibility for sending remittances home figures large in batterers' justification for abuse. The social implications of battering are no less central to immigrant battered women than legal and economic barriers. Internal to the community, individual women are limited by a deep fear of losing social status in and the support of their immigrant communities— often the only communities they know—and a fear of various forms of violence, control, and retaliation by the husband and his family, often the only kin they have in the new country. Among other social complications external to the community, immigrant battered women face racist anti-immigrant public sentiment that exacerbates their desire to keep violence private in order to transmit an untarnished and positive image of immigrant community. These patterns persist, despite any differences among the sample.

The interaction of domestic violence and immigration informs not only the level and type of abuse men perpetrate but also individual and community-based responses to the abuse. We found that, over time, immigration shaped the meaning that battered women gave to the controlling behaviors and violence perpetrated against them by their intimate partners. For the most part, women distinguished between attitudes and practices related to domestic violence "here" and "there." That is, they labeled their home countries as abuse tolerant and their adopted country as abuse intolerant. Moreover, despite existing antiracist critiques of the institutionalization of the criminalization of domestic violence, and mixed messages from their own communities as to the appropriateness of reporting domestic violence to the authorities, immigrant battered women seemed to appreciate that domestic violence was considered a crime in the United States and perceived that law enforcement officers were willing to assist as they sought safety for themselves and their children.

However, although at least some immigrant battered women feel empowered to mobilize the criminal justice system, few seem to be familiar with new policies promulgated to protect battered immigrant woman, such as the VAWA self-petition option. And even for those who obtain relevant information and meet legal criteria, pursuit of such remedies may be limited by lack of access to legal assistance or fear of turning to legal authorities, including the criminal justice system. Undocumented immigrants, as well as those in the midst of applying for legal status, or even legal immigrants may avoid engagement with the criminal justice system, in particular if they are part of a "mixed-status" immigrant family or in order to prevent law enforcement from entering an immigrant-majority neighborhood.

The commonalities among immigrants from across such a wide range of countries of origin raise two additional concerns related to immigrant battered women and the criminal justice system. First, over the past decade, the criminalization of immigrants has escalated in the United States, where immigrants are perceived of as criminals-in-the-making who make "real" Americans vulnerable to uninsured drivers, lower wages, unemployment, and property crimes as well as drug, gang, and trafficking-related violent crime. It is "immigrant" on "American" visible forms of crime that populate public discourse. Rarely mentioned is the less visible crime of intimate partner violence. When referenced, intimate partner violence among immigrants is either naturalized (i.e., that's just the way they are) or culturalized (i.e., that's how they treat their women). Naturalization and culturalization of immigrant domestic violence blame intimate partner violence on membership within the group, minimize the effect of intimate partner violence on its victims, and dismiss victims' claims for justice. Moreover, it erases intimate partner violence among so-called "assimilated" and/or native-born members of U.S. society. As such, although we acknowledge that meanings and patterns of domestic violence vary across cultures, we write against the tendency to stereotype domestic violence as an inherent part of "other" cultures (Razack, 1998; Volpp, 1996, 2001). Such views reinforce the notion that gender-based violence does not warrant state intervention because it is part of the "way of life" (Ferraro, 1989), is the "mentality," or is "part of the culture" (Adelman, Erez, & Shalhoub-Kevorkian, 2003) of certain religious, ethnic, or national groups. This perception also precludes examinations of how structural inequalities and systemic responses (e.g., criminal justice system) may sometimes diminish the material conditions and safety options for individual immigrant women and their families. Dismissing domestic violence as an immigrant or cultural problem also precludes serious considerations of how to ameliorate commonly experienced structural inequalities or how to work with battered immigrant women to identify helpful systemic responses.

Second, in the post-9/11 era, the trend in cities, counties, and states is to enter "287(g) agreements" with the federal government to enforce immigration law as proxies for ICE (Versanyi, 2008). This means that local law enforcement officers, those charged with protecting battered women, are now responsible for enforcing the civil matters of federal immigration law as well. Undocumented immigrants, as well as legal immigrants who face criminal charges, are at risk for deportation, with or without their children. As a result, immigrants, in general, and immigrant women, in particular, regardless of legal status, may go further underground with their need for domestic violence services, thereby rejecting the investment made into the criminal justice system for victims of domestic violence. Further complicating immigrant battered women's pursuit of safety is the recent move by local governments to bar undocumented immigrants from education and social services. These developments make ambiguous which government agencies, including the criminal justice system and members of law enforcement, immigrants and their families have the right to approach—and whom to trust. Individual immigrant women, who commonly shoulder the responsibility for their children's welfare, face the structurally produced hardship of choosing between their safety and a stable, brighter future for their children. Designing social and legal policies that do not further entrap battered immigrant women will continue to challenge feminist criminologists.

Notes

1. Collaborative efforts among battered immigrant women, activists, and researchers also have resulted in the identification of strategies productively used by immigrant women. For examples of barriers and safety strategies, see online materials available at www.immigrantwomennetwork.org, produced by the National Network to End Violence Against Immigrant Women. Many of these issues shaped the legislation addressing the plight of battered immigrant women in the Violence Against Women Act of 1994 and its subsequent revisions.

2. Due to confidentiality requirements, it was not possible to conduct quality control of the translation. However, agencies did not report translation of the questions as a problem.

3. Primary languages included Arabic, Armenian, Bengali, Farsi, French, Haitian, Hindi, Japanese, Malaysian, Portuguese, Russian, Spanish, and Turkish.

4. Most questions invalidated due to translation pertained to criminal justice procedural issues associated with the events described during the interviews.

5. These countries are Armenia, Bahrain, Bangladesh, Brazil, Colombia, Costa Rica, Egypt, El Salvador, Former Yugoslavia, Albania, Germany, Great Britain, Guatemala, Guyana, Haiti, Honduras, India, Iran, Iraq, Israel, Palestine, Japan, Latvia, Lebanon, Mexico, Morocco, New Zealand, Nicaragua, Peru, Syria, Trinidad, Turkey, Venezuela, Vietnam (South), and Yemen.

6. Christians described themselves as Adventist, Armenian Apostolic, Assyrian Christian, Baptist, Jehovah's Witness, Lutheran, Mormon, Pentecostal, Protestant, or Roman Catholic.

7. This applied to the marriages they reported, whether in their countries of origin or in the United States.

8. The circumstances and experiences of these "military brides" are described in Erez and Bach (2003).

9. This clear-cut division of labor was also the case in the home country. We focus on the U.S. responses to examine whether division of labor changed as a result of immigration to the United States.

10. Those who have family members in the United States can immigrate due to family unification laws. Thus, men who immigrate have family members in the United States whereas women who follow their husbands leave their own families behind.

References

Abraham, M. (2000). *Speaking the unspeakable: Marital violence among South Asian immigrants in the United States*. New Brunswick, NJ: Rutgers University Press.

Adelman, M., Erez, E., & Shalhoub-Kevorkian, N. (2003). Policing violence against women in a multi-cultural society: Gender, minority status and the politics of exclusion. *Police and Society, 7*, 103-131.

Adelman, M., & Morgan, P. (2006). Law enforcement versus battered women. *Afflia: Journal of Women and Social Work, 21*(1), 28-45.

Baca Zinn, M., & Thornton Dill, B. (1996). Theorizing difference from multiracial feminism. *Feminist Studies, 22*(2), 321-331.

Bhuyan, R., Mell, M., Senturia, K., Sullivan, M., & Shiu-Thornton, S. (2005). "Women must endure according to their karma": Cambodian immigrant women talk about domestic violence. *Journal of Interpersonal Violence, 20*(8), 902-921.

Britton, D. M. (2000). Feminism in criminology: Engendering the outlaw. *Annals of the American Academy of Political and Social Science, 571*(1), 57-76.

Bui, H. (2004). *In the adopted land: Abused immigrant women and the criminal justice system*. Westport, CT: Praeger.

Bui, H., & Morash, M. (1999). Domestic violence in the Vietnamese community: An exploratory study. *Violence Against Women, 5*, 769-795.

Burgess-Proctor, A. (2006). Intersections of race, class, gender and crime: Future directions for feminist criminology. *Feminist Criminology, 1*(1), 27-47.

Calavita, K. (1992). *Inside the state: The Bracero Program, immigration and the INS*. New York: Routledge.

Calvo, J. (1997). Spouse-based immigration law: The legacy of coverture. In A. Wing (Ed.), *Critical race feminism: A reader* (pp. 380-386). New York: New York University Press.

Chesney-Lind, M. (2006). Patriarchy, crime and justice: Feminist criminology in an age of backlash. *Feminist Criminology, 1*(1), 6-26.

Coker, D. (2001). Crime control and feminist law reform in domestic violence law: A critical review. *Buffalo Criminal Law Review, 4*(2), 801-860.

Collins, P. H. (2000). *Black feminist thought: Knowledge, consciousness and the politics of empowerment*. New York: Routledge. (Original work published 1991)

Crandall, M., Senturia, K., Sullivan, M., & Shiu-Thornton, S. (2005). "No way out": Russian-speaking women's experiences with domestic violence. *Journal of Interpersonal Violence, 20*(8), 941-958.

Crenshaw, K. (1991). Mapping the margins: Intersectionality, identity politics and violence against women. *Stanford Law Review, 41*, 1241-1298.

Dasgupta, S. (2000). Charting the course: An overview of domestic violence in the South Asian community in the United States. *Journal of Social Distress and the Homeless, 9*(3), 173-185.

Davis, R. C., & Erez, E. (1998). *Immigrant population as victims: Toward a multicultural criminal justice system* [Research in brief]. Washington, DC: National Institute of Justice.

Dobash, R. E., & Dobash, R. (1979). *Violence against wives: A case against the patriarchy*. New York: Free Press.

Erez, E. (2000). Immigration, culture conflict and domestic violence/woman battering. *Crime Prevention and Community Safety: An International Journal, 2*, 27-36.

Erez, E. (2002). Migration/immigration, domestic violence and the justice system. *International Journal of Comparative and Applied Criminal Justice, 26*(2), 277-299.

Erez, E., & Bach, S. (2003). Immigration, domestic violence and the military: The case of "military brides." *Violence Against Women, 9*(9), 1093-1117.

Ferraro, K. J. (1989). Policing woman battering. *Social Problems, 36*(1), 61-74.

Gabaccia, D. (Ed.). (1992). *Seeking common ground: Multidisciplinary studies of immigrant women in the U.S.* Westport, CT: Greenwood Press.

Gardner, M. (2005). *The qualities of a citizen: Women, immigration and citizenship, 1870-1965.* Princeton, NJ: Princeton University Press.

Glaser, B. G. (1992). *Basics of grounded theory analysis.* Mill Valley, CA: Sociology Press.

Harris, A. (1990). Race and essentialism in feminist legal theory. *Stanford Law Review, 42*, 581-616.

Higginbotham, E. (1997). Introduction. In E. Higginbotham & M. Romero (Eds.), *Women and work: Exploring race, ethnicity, and class* (xv-xxxii). Thousand Oaks, CA: Sage.

Hirsch, J. S. (2003). *A courtship after marriage: Sexuality and love in Mexican transnational families.* Berkeley: University of California Press.

Hondagneu-Sotelo, P. (Ed.). (2003). *Gender and U.S. immigration: Contemporary trends.* Berkeley: University of California Press.

Katz, J. (1983). A theory of qualitative methodology. In R. Emerson (Ed.), *Contemporary field research* (pp. 127-148). Boston: Little, Brown.

Menjivar, C., & Salcido, O. (2002). Immigrant women and domestic violence: Common experiences in different countries. *Gender & Society, 6*(6), 898-920.

Merry, S. (2000). *Colonizing Hawai'i: The cultural power of law.* Princeton, NJ: Princeton University Press.

Muftic, L. R., & Bouffard, L. A. (2008). Bosnian women and intimate partner violence: Differences in experiences and attitudes for refugee and nonrefugee women. *Feminist Criminology, 3*, 173-190.

Orloff, L. (2002). Women immigrants and domestic violence. In P. Strum & D. Tarantolo (Eds.), *Women immigrants in the United States* (pp. 49-57). Washington, DC: Woodrow Wilson International Center for Scholars and the Migration Policy Institute.

Pessar, P. (1999). Engendering migration studies: The case of new immigrants in the United States. *American Behavioral Sciences, 42*, 577-600.

Potter, H. (2006). An argument for Black feminist criminology: Understanding African American women's experiences of intimate partner violence using an integrated approach. *Feminist Criminology, 1*(2), 106-124.

Raj, A., & Silverman, J. (2002). Violence against immigrant women: The roles of culture, context, and legal immigrant status on intimate partner violence. *Violence Against Women, 8*, 367-398.

Razack, S. (1998). *Looking White people in the eye: Gender, race, and culture in courtrooms and class-rooms.* Toronto, CA: University of Toronto Press.

Salcido, O., & Adelman, M. (2004). "He has me tied with the blessed and damned papers": Undocumented-immigrant battered women in Phoenix, Arizona. *Human Organization, 63*(2), 162-173.

Sassen, S. (1998). *Globalization and its discontents.* New York: New Press.

Scales-Trent, J. (1999). African women in France: Immigration, family and work. *Brooklyn Journal of International Law, 24*, 705-737.

Snider, L. (1998). Toward safer societies: Punishment, masculinities and violence against women. *British Journal of Criminology, 38*(1), 1-39.

Stanko, E. (1985). *Intimate intrusions.* New York: HarperCollins.

Steinbugler, A. C., Press, J. E., & Johnson Dias, J. (2006). Gender, race and affirmative action operationalizing intersectionality in survey research. *Gender & Society, 20*(6), 805-825.

Strum, P., & Tarantolo, D. (Eds.). (2002). *Women immigrants in the United States.* Washington, DC: Woodrow Wilson International Center for Scholars and the Migration Policy Institute.

56   Feminist Criminology

Versanyi, M. (2008, April 20). Should cops be la migra? *Los Angeles Times*. Available April 22, 2008, from www.latimes.com

Volpp, L. (1996). Talking "culture": Gender, race, nation, and the politics of multiculturalism. *Columbia Law Review, 96*(6), 1573-1617.

Volpp, L. (2001). Feminism versus multiculturalism. *Columbia Law Review, 101*(5), 1181-1218.

Wachholz, S., & Miedema, B. (2000). Risk, fear, harm: Immigrant women's perceptions of the "policing" solution to women abuse. *Crime, Law and Social Change, 34*(3), 301-317.

Wood, S. (2004). VAWA's unfinished business: The immigrant women who fall through the cracks. *Duke Journal of Gender, Law & Policy, 11*, 141-155.

Zhou, M. (2002). Contemporary female immigration to the United States: A demographic profile. In P. Strum & D. Tarantolo (Eds.), *Women immigrants in the United States* (pp. 23-34). Washington, DC: Woodrow Wilson International Center for Scholars and the Migration Policy Institute.

Edna Erez is a professor and the head of the Department of Criminology, Law, and Justice at the University of Illinois at Chicago. She has a law degree from Hebrew University of Jerusalem and a PhD in sociology/criminology from the University of Pennsylvania. Her research areas include victims in the justice system, violence against women (especially immigrant women), and women in terrorism. Her publications have appeared in professional journals such as *Criminology, The British Journal of Criminology, Justice Quarterly, Crime & Delinquency, Criminal Law Review, Studies in Conflict and Terrorism*, and others. Her current federally funded research focuses on terrorism, crime and the Internet, and electronic monitoring of domestic violence cases.

Madelaine Adelman is an associate professor in the School of Justice & Social Inquiry at Arizona State University and a faculty affiliate in women and gender studies. She has a PhD in cultural anthropology from Duke University. She has guest edited a special issue of the *Journal of Poverty: Innovations on Social, Political & Economic Inequalities* and is currently writing a book on the politics of domestic violence in Israel and coediting a volume (with Miriam Elman) entitled *Jerusalem Across the Disciplines*. She has published numerous articles in both disciplinary and interdisciplinary journals such as *American Ethnologist, Political and Legal Anthropology Review*, and *Violence Against Women* and edited volumes on gender violence, youth conflict, law, and culture in the Middle East and the United States.

Carol Gregory is an assistant professor of sociology at Baldwin-Wallace College. She has a PhD in sociology from the University of Delaware (2004). Her areas of expertise include victims and violence, gender and justice, and evaluation research. Her publications address various facets of batterer intervention programs and violence against women issues.

Part V
Feminist Assessments of the Criminal Justice Enterprise

[15]

Gender Bias and Juvenile Justice Revisited: A Multiyear Analysis

John M. MacDonald
Meda Chesney-Lind

This study presents a multiyear empirical examination of gender bias in the handling of juvenile court cases in Hawaii. Based on prior qualitative and quantitative data, it is hypothesized that once female juvenile offenders are found delinquent, they will be sanctioned more severely than male offenders by the juvenile court, holding other factors constant. Results from a series of analyses indicate significant differences between male and female juvenile justice outcomes, particularly for youth of color. Female offenders are more likely than male offenders to be handled informally at the early stages of the system, but the court's benevolence declines as girls move into the disposition stage. The implications of these findings for resolving inconsistencies in prior research are discussed. Also considered are policy implications with regard to congressional initiatives to de-emphasize the deinstitutionalization of status offenses and reduce concerns about minority overrepresentation in the juvenile justice system.

The ways in which societies have dealt with youths' problems have varied tremendously over the past few centuries and have had a distinct impact on the lives of girls. Although girls account for one in four arrests of juveniles (Federal Bureau of Investigation, 1999), discussions of delinquency and juvenile justice policy have generally ignored young women and their problems. A review of the juvenile justice system's long-documented bias against girls suggests that careful consideration of girls' issues would shed considerable light on the shortcomings of the system as a whole. Historically, the offenses that have brought girls into the juvenile justice system reflect its dual concerns with adolescent criminality and moral conduct. These concerns have also reflected a unique and intense preoccupation with girls' sexuality and their obedience to parental authority, particularly in the early years of the system. As the juvenile justice system enters its next century, and as the national debate on its future rages (Feld, 1999), there is confusion about whether such concerns still dominate the system's treatment of girls or whether more contemporary concerns about serious juvenile offending have eclipsed earlier court practices.

JOHN M. MACDONALD: College of Criminal Justice, University of South Carolina. **MEDA CHESNEY-LIND**: Women's Studies Program, University of Hawaii at Manoa.

PRIOR LITERATURE

Studies of early family court activity reveal that almost all of the girls who appeared in family courts were charged with immorality or waywardness (Chesney-Lind, 1971; Schlossman & Wallach, 1978; Shelden, 1981). The sanctions for such misbehavior were extremely severe. For example, between 1899 and 1909, the Chicago family court sent half the female juvenile delinquents—but only a fifth of the male juvenile delinquents—to reformatories. In Milwaukee, twice as many girls as boys were committed to training schools (Schlossman & Wallach, 1978). In Memphis, girls were twice as likely as boys to be committed to training schools (Shelden, 1981). In Honolulu during 1929 and 1930, more than half of the girls referred to the juvenile court were charged with immorality, which meant there was evidence of sexual intercourse, and 30% were charged with waywardness. Girls were twice as likely as boys to be detained for their offenses and spent 5 times as long in detention as their male counterparts. They were also nearly 3 times as likely to be sent to a training school (Chesney-Lind, 1971). Additionally, Odem and Schlossman's (1991) research on the Los Angeles juvenile court in 1920 and 1950 showed that girls were overwhelmingly referred for status offenses in both time periods. In 1950, for example, 31% of the girls were charged with running away from home, truancy, curfew violations, or "general unruliness at home." Nearly half of the status offenders were charged with sexual misconduct, although again, this was "usually with a single partner; few had engaged in prostitution" (Odem & Schlossman, 1991, p. 200).

Vedder and Somerville's (1970) analysis during the 1960s revealed that although girls were incarcerated in training schools for the "big five" (running away from home, incorrigibility, sexual offenses, probation violations, and truancy), "the underlying vein in many of these cases is sexual misconduct by the girl delinquent" (p. 147). Such attitudes were also present in other parts of the world. Naffine (1987) wrote that in Australia, official reports noted that "most of those charged (with status offenses) were girls who had acquired habits of immorality and freely admitted sexual intercourse with a number of boys" (p. 13). Overall, these studies indicate the juvenile court's preoccupation with girls' sexuality and immorality, a concern that was not equally exhibited for boys.

The empirical studies of the processing of girls' and boys' cases between the 1950s and early 1970s documented the impact of judicial attitudes toward girls. These studies found that girls charged with status offenses were more harshly treated than boys and girls charged with criminal offenses (Chesney-Lind, 1973; Cohn, 1970; Datesman & Scarpitti, 1980; Gibbons & Griswold, 1957; Hancock, 1981; Odem, 1995; Odem & Schlossman, 1991; Pope &

Feyerherm, 1982; Schlossman & Wallach, 1978; Shelden, 1981). Together, the studies of the juvenile courts during the decades predating the early 1970s suggest that court personnel participated directly in the judicial enforcement of the sexual double standard. Such activity was most pronounced in the system's early years, but there is some evidence that the pattern continues, in part because status offenses can still serve as buffer charges for sexual misconduct. Some of the problems with status offenses, although discriminatory, are understandable. They are not like criminal cases, where judges have relatively clear guidelines. In status offense cases, judges have few legal guidelines. Many judges apparently fall back on one of the orientations built into the juvenile justice system: the puritan stance, whereby judges support parental demands more or less without question, or the progressive stance, whereby they take on parental roles. These orientations were severely tested during the 1970s, when critics mounted a major drive to deinstitutionalize status offenders and divert them from formal court jurisdiction.

Challenges to the Double Standard

Correctional reformers concerned about the abuse of the status offense category by juvenile courts (although not necessarily about girls) were instrumental in urging Congress to pass the Juvenile Justice and Delinquency Prevention Act of 1974 (JJDP). The JJDP Act required that states receiving federal delinquency prevention money begin to divert and deinstitutionalize status offenders. Despite erratic enforcement of the provision and considerable resistance from juvenile court judges, girls were the beneficiaries of the reform effort. Incarceration of young women in training schools and detention centers across the country fell dramatically. Also encouraging is the fact that studies of court decision making found less clear evidence of discrimination against girls in parts of the country where serious diversion efforts were occurring (Teilmann & Landry, 1981).

Despite the intentions of the JJDP Act, there is considerable evidence that status offenders, particularly girls, are still being harshly sanctioned years after its passage (see Chesney-Lind & Shelden, 1997). Even more disturbing are recent efforts to roll back the modest gains made in promoting more equitable and appropriate treatment of status offenders or, even worse, to repeal the whole initiative. For example, juvenile justice officials have successfully narrowed the contemporary definition of a status offender so that any child who violates a "valid court order" will not be covered under the deinstitutionalization provisions (U.S. House of Representatives, Sub-Committee on Human Resources of the Committee on Education and Labor, 1980). This means that a young woman who runs away from a court-ordered placement (a halfway house, foster home, or the like) can be relabeled as a delinquent and locked up. More recent studies of the impact of these contempt proceedings suggest that they have been particularly disadvantageous for female status offenders. Frazier and Bishop's (1990) analysis of contempt proceedings in Florida, for example, indicates that girls are far more likely to be treated severely by the courts than boys charged with similar contempt offenses. From their results, Frazier and Bishop (1990) conclude that "neither the cultural changes associated with the feminist movement nor the legal changes illustrated in the JJDP Act's mandate to deinstitutionalize status offenders have brought about equality under the law for young men and women" (p. 22). These findings, coupled with recent policy shifts in the reauthorization of the JJDP Act, underscore the importance of examining gender disparity in the juvenile justice system.

The Treatment of Girls and Policy Shifts in the Reauthorization of the JJDP Act

Related to the issue of gender disparity in the juvenile justice system is the concern with gender equity in the area of services. Indeed, it could well be that the gender disparity observed in recent years may in part be a product of the limited options that the juvenile courts have to deal with female offenders. Hearings held in 1992 in conjunction with the reauthorization of the JJDP Act provided a first step in addressing this issue on a national level. For the first time, Congress addressed the "provision of services to girls within the juvenile justice system" (*Hearings on the Reauthorization*, 1992). During this hearing, the double standard of juvenile justice, as well as the paucity of services for girls, was discussed. Representative Matthew Martinez (D-California) ended the hearing by asking, "I wonder why, why are there no other alternatives than youth jail for her?" (*Hearings on the Reauthorization*, 1992, p. 2). As a result of this hearing, the 1992 reauthorization of the JJDP Act included specific provisions requiring each state that received federal funds to include "an analysis of gender-specific services for the prevention and treatment of juvenile delinquency . . . and a plan for providing needed gender-specific services for the prevention and treatment of juvenile delinquency" (Juvenile Justice and Delinquency Prevention Amendments, 1992). Additional funds were set aside as part of the JJDP Act's challenge grant program for states to develop policies to prohibit gender bias in placement and programs to assure girls equal access to services. As a result, 23 states embarked on such programs (Girls Inc., 1996).

   The most recent review of state-based activities in the area of girls' programming in the juvenile justice system comes from the data on challenge grant funds applied for from the Office of Juvenile Justice and Delinquency Prevention (Chesney-Lind, Kato, Koo, & Fujiwara-Clark, 1998). This review indicated that most states were still in the very early stages of understanding the needs of girls in their juvenile justice systems and that virtually all states that applied for challenge grant funds were using the money to gather data on the basic needs of the girls in their systems. Only 38% of these states (eight states) had funded specific new programs for girls or expanded existing programs that appeared to be successful. Furthermore, only two states indicated that their juvenile justice committees were involved in crafting specific legislation and/or systematic policy changes to address female delinquents (Chesney-Lind et al., 1998).

However, the optimism one could have gained from the policies set forth under the reauthorization of the JJDP Act in 1992 and the initial implementation of challenge grants may no longer be well founded. In the past few years, Congress has repeatedly attempted to overhaul the JJDP Act and virtually all of the provisions that could have benefited girls and increased the gender equality of the juvenile justice system. During several recent sessions of Congress, major overhauls of the JJDP Act were sought, and virtually all of the initiatives considered were ominous for girls. The bills that were introduced generally attempted to refocus national attention on the "violent and repeat juvenile offender" (read boys) while granting states "flexibility" in implementing some if not all of the four core mandates of the original JJDP Act. Key among these mandates is the deinstitutionalization of status offenders, although conservative lawmakers are also taking aim at efforts to separate youth from adults in correctional facilities, efforts to reduce minority overrepresentation in juvenile detention and training schools, and efforts to remove juveniles from adult jails (Schiraldi & Soler, 1998).

In a debate that featured discussion of "guns, the Ten Commandments, the Internet, video games and the movies," there was considerable emphasis on punishment (such as allowing the prosecution of 13-year-olds as adults; Boyle, 1999). Most ominous for girls are efforts to loosen restrictions on the detention of status offenders. Here, conservative legislators were clearly influenced by juvenile court judges, who pushed for a recriminalization of status offenses. Judge David Grossman, who testified before Congress representing the National Council of Juvenile and Family Court Judges, contended that the deinstitutionalization was a "movement" whose time had passed: "All too often, it left the intended young beneficiaries of its advocacy adrift on the streets, fallen between the cracks" (Alexander, 1998, p. 46). He advocated that instead, status offenders be returned to the court's jurisdiction.

Perhaps as a result of testimony of this sort, Senate Bill 254 (1999) called for the National Institute of Justice to conduct a study on the effect of detention on status offenders compared to similarly situated individuals who are not placed in secure detention in terms of continuation of their inappropriate or illegal conduct, delinquency or future criminal behavior, and evaluation of the safety of status offenders placed in secure detention.

At present, both the House and Senate versions are in conference committees (Alexander, 2000; Boyle, 1999). These efforts clearly indicate that solid information is needed on the problems girls currently encounter in the juvenile justice system. Otherwise, the modest gains of the JJDP Act may be completely eroded.

Recent Empirical Studies

These potential policy shifts toward a more discretionary juvenile justice system call for further investigation into the issues of gender equity in the administration of justice for juveniles. There is still considerable debate about whether bias against girls exists in the juvenile justice system in the post–JJDP Act era. Not all of the more recent research confirms the existence of bias against girls in the juvenile justice system. Several studies of gender disparity find no evidence of gender bias or bias that shows a preference for girls. Some researchers argue that the evidence suggests that throughout the juvenile justice system, girls are treated more leniently than boys (Poe-Yamagata & Butts, 1996). Johnson and Scheuble (1991), for instance, examined all dispositions in one state over a 9-year period and found evidence of bias in favor of girls (with the exception of repeat offenders committing more serious offenses).

Other studies suggest that that there is no clear evidence of bias in favor of either gender. Teilmann and Landry (1981), for example, examined court dispositions of youthful offenders in several locations, relying heavily on data from a five-state study of services to status offenders. By controlling for "offense type" and prior record, they found that "status offenders are consistently given harsher treatment than delinquent offenders" but "this is true for boys as it is for girls" (Teilmann & Landry, 1981, p. 47). From this, they concluded that treatment within the court was "relatively even-handed" (Teilmann & Landry, 1981, p. 47). In an analysis of serious delinquents in Miami, Horowitz and Pottieger (1991) also found little evidence of gender disparity, with the exception of prostitution cases. There are several other studies that report little evidence that female status offenders were more harshly sanctioned than their male counterparts once the impact of a variety of extralegal variables were statistically controlled (Carter, 1979; Clarke & Koch, 1980; Cohen & Kluegel, 1979; Dannefer & Schutt, 1982; Datesman & Scarpitti, 1980; Fenwick, 1982; Phillips & Dinitz, 1982).

Some of the research findings from the past decade that indicate little evidence of differential treatment for female offenders could also reflect actual changes resulting from the deinstitutionalization movement. But, that is not the only possible explanation. The bias against girls may be less overt. From courtroom observations, Mahoney and Fenster (1982) found that many of the girls being taken into custody for crimes had actually exhibited behavior that could have been classified as status offenses. For example, girls who broke into their parents' homes to take food and clothing to prolong their runaway status were being charged with burglary.

More recently, additional evidence has emerged suggesting that girls and boys charged with similar offenses are treated unequally. Shelden and Horvath (1986) found that girls referred to court for status offenses were more likely than boys referred for the same offenses to receive formal processing (i.e., a court hearing). Girls were also more likely than boys to be detained for status offenses (although the differences were not statistically significant). Mann's (1979) research on runaway youth in the Midwest also showed that girls were more likely than boys to be detained and to receive harsher sentences.

Differences in the labels given to the noncriminal behavior of boys and girls may play a major role in producing differential treatment for girls. Girls are far more likely than boys to appear before a court for status offenses, especially running away from home and incorrigibility (Chesney-Lind & Shelden, 1997; Stahl, 1998). As might be expected, predominantly female-related status offenses bring on the greatest use of detention, even though research suggests that male status offenders are more likely to have committed other criminal violations (e.g., violent and serious property offenses; Boisvert & Wells, 1980; Stahl, 1998).

Together, evidence of changes following the passage of the JJDP Act in official responses to girls who appear in the juvenile courts is mixed. Some studies have found more evenhanded treatment in recent years (Snyder & Sickmund, 1999), whereas others have not. Some of these differences may be due to differences in geographic location or time period. Many studies, for example, are limited to examining these issues with a single year of data. Also, different studies analyze different decision-making points in the juvenile justice system. As a result, evidence of bias in favor of girls at the entry point into the juvenile court, for example, may mask bias that favors boys at later decision-making points (e.g., assignment to formal supervision). It is also possible that discrepancies about gender bias are a result of the differences in the types of status offenses that girls and boys commit. Girls typically appear for running away and other offenses that signal that they are beyond parental control, and boys appear for curfew and liquor law violations. These differences could account for some of the juvenile court's apparent differential responses to male and female youthful offenders. The historical literature suggests that the juvenile justice system has a lengthy history of treating female juveniles differently from their male counterparts (Poulin, 1996).

The exploration of how the juvenile court responds to these forms of status offenses as well as other forms of delinquency requires further examination. This issue is particularly salient in the post–JJDP Act era, when legislative changes should have minimized the differences between how boys and girls are handled in the juvenile justice system. Additionally, the recent juvenile justice focus during the reauthorization of the JJDP Act, which would return more discretion to the juvenile courts, necessitates a further examination of the influence of gender in the juvenile justice system. If the system is to return to pre–JJDP Act practices, policy makers should have a better understanding of the issue of gender equity in the system prior to the implementation of any broad-based changes. This issue is important for practical (e.g., having adequate facilities and services) and constitutional (e.g., equal protection under the 14th Amendment) reasons.

Issues of Race and Ethnicity

Issues of race and ethnicity are also closely tied to issues of gender equity in both the administration of justice and the equity of services in the juvenile justice system. The issue of disproportionate minority confinement, for example, has received extensive investigation over the past decade as a result of congressional mandates (see Kempf-Leonard & Sample, 2000). However, rarely has disproportionate minority confinement research examined this issue as it relates to girls. This is an unfortunate oversight. After all, the data indicate that girls of color are disproportionately represented in the juvenile justice system (Snyder & Sickmund, 1999). If the juvenile justice system is to truly provide for the "best interests" of girls, it must respond to issues of gender equity as well as those of race, ethnicity, and culture.

THE PRESENT STUDY

The present study draws on data from Hawaii's juvenile court system. Hawaii provides an ideal comparative framework from which to examine issues of gender equity in the administration of justice outcomes for juveniles while paying close attention to issues of race and ethnicity. Because of the diversity of its population, Hawaii is currently confronting issues that many other states will confront in the not too distant future, as America's population becomes increasingly more ethnically diverse. Hawaii is probably the most ethnically diverse state in the nation. The largest population groups are East Asians, Caucasians, and those of Hawaiian or partly Hawaiian ancestry (Kassebaum et al., 1995).

Although Hawaii is ethnically diverse, it has its share of racial and ethnic tensions. Class and ethnic divisions tend to reflect the economic and political power struggles of the state's past as a plantation-based economy and its current dependence on mass tourism. Recent immigrants as well as the descendants of the islands' original inhabitants (Hawaiians) are among the most dispossessed. Consequently, both male and female youth actively involved in gangs are drawn disproportionately from groups that have recently immigrated to Hawaii (Samoans and Filipinos) or from the marginalized native Hawaiian population. Youth from these economically marginalized groups in Hawaii face unique challenges in its socioeconomic order. Filipino and Samoan youth tend to share the stresses of immigration, which include language difficulties, crowded inner-city living, and economic marginality. Native Hawaiians have much in common with other Native American groups in that their culture was severely challenged by the death and disease that resulted from contact with the Western world (Daws, 1968). These groups, like urbanized Native Americans and low-income African Americans, have accommodated the strains of poverty and social isolation by occasionally normalizing behaviors such as early motherhood, high rates of school dropout, welfare dependency, and high rates of crime and delinquency (see Joe & Chesney-Lind, 1995).

The goal of the present study is to examine the degree to which gender differences affect the treatment of juveniles in Hawaii's juvenile court. Particular focus is placed on the role that gender plays in the administration of court processing, taking into consideration issues of ethnicity and geographic location. Given contemporary debates about policy reforms in the juvenile justice system and the growing diversity of the juvenile population, it is important to gain a better understanding of how gender affects the administration of juvenile justice. Based on prior qualitative and quantitative studies that found evidence of gender bias, it is hypothesized that once female juvenile offenders are found delinquent, they will be sanctioned more severely than male offenders by the juvenile court, holding other factors constant. The diversity of the study population also permits the exploration of these issues among a diverse group of boys and girls of color.

182   CRIME & DELINQUENCY / APRIL 2001

METHOD

Data

The data used for this study were collected by the Hawaii State Judiciary and provided to the National Juvenile Court Data Archive.[1] The data consist of all family court case records in the state of Hawaii from 1980 to 1991. The primary collection of the data was done with the aid of court clerks at the time of case referral, and the courts subsequently followed these cases through the various processing stages. Hawaii consists of four county family courts located in the counties of Hawaii, Honolulu, Kauai, and Maui. For the purposes of this study, both delinquency and status offenses will be analyzed.[2] The sample consists of 85,692 cases referred to the Hawaii Family Court during this period. The advantages to these data are that they are longitudinal and that they represent the entire state of Hawaii instead of a single juvenile court. In addition, a large percentage of cases referred to the court concern female adolescents.

Geographic identifiers were also available in the family court records that indicated the ZIP codes where juveniles lived. These geographic identifiers were merged with census ZIP code data for the censuses of 1980 (U.S. Bureau of the Census, 1985) and 1990 (U.S. Bureau of the Census, 1990).[3] These data sources provided detailed estimates of the sociodemographic characteristics of the areas in which these youth resided. These data were used to create specific social class variables used in the analyses.[4]

Dependent Variables

The dependent variables used in this study to measure gender differences in juvenile court outcomes were three binary measures of juvenile court outcomes, reflecting the petition, adjudication, and disposition stages of the court. In an effort to capture the outcome of cases at the three different stages of the juvenile court process, a series of dummy variable measures were computed. These outcome measures included (a) whether a case was officially petitioned (0 = no, 1 = yes); (b) whether a case resulted in a finding of delinquency at the adjudication hearing (0 = no, 1 = yes); and (c) whether a case resulted in a formal (confinement or probation) disposition (0 = no, 1 = yes).

Independent Variables

The independent variables used in this study include both demographic factors as well as the seriousness of the current offense. In terms of demographic information, the control variables included the sex, age, ethnicity (Hawaiian, White, East Asian, Pacific/South East Asian, and other), and composite measures of the poverty and wealth of the area where each youth resides.[5] Theses variables were constructed similarly to those used by Sampson and Laub (1993) in their study of structural variations in juvenile court processing. In addition, a dummy variable for the court location was created to control for potential differences between urban and rural courts. Prior studies suggest that there are potential differences between urban and rural courts in the handling of juvenile court cases (Feld, 1991).[6] In terms of legally relevant variables, a measure of the seriousness of each juvenile's current offense was included. The current offense variable was created as a revised version of Wolfgang's Crime Severity Index (Wolfgang, Figlio, Tracy, & Singer, 1985).[7] A dummy variable, census year, was also included to control for changes that could occur in the poverty and wealth measures over time.[8]

Description of Participants

For the 12-year period analyzed in this study (1980 to 1991), 30% ($n = 25,902$) of the cases concerned female juvenile offenders. Consistent with the literature on gender differences in offending, these data indicate that girls are more likely than boys to be referred to the court for running away from home (32% of girls vs. 9% of boys). In contrast, boys were more likely than girls to be referred for property (32% of boys vs. 20% of girls) and violent (2% of boys vs. 0.2% of girls) offenses.[9] In terms of court location, 40% of the cases were handled in rural courts. In terms of ethnicity, 35% of those referred were of Hawaiian ancestry, 25% were Caucasian, 9% were East Asian, 23% were Samoan or Filipino (Pacific), and 7% were of other ethnicities (see Table 1). To examine whether gender affected the outcome of juvenile court cases, multivariate models were employed.[10]

Model Design

Because the dependent variables in this study were binary and represent three separate stages of the juvenile justice system, logistic regression was used to estimate the decision making of the Hawaii Family Court. In the first model, in which the petition stage was estimated, a standard logistic regression model was used. For the subsequent stages of the juvenile justice system (adjudication and disposition), conditional logistic regression was used because these cases were a group selected from the larger sample of juveniles referred to the court (Liao, 1994).

TABLE 1: Summary Measures

Variable	M (SD)
White	0.25
East Asian	0.09
Pacific	0.23
Other	0.07
Hawaiian	0.35
Gender (0 = male, 1 = female)	0.30
Age (0 = 13, 1 = 14-16, 2 = 17+)	1.26 (0.73)
Court (0 = urban, 1 = rural)	0.40
Poverty[a] (% below poverty + % female head household with children under 18 years below poverty + % persons living on public assistance)	3.92 (0.46)
Wealth[a](% households > $50,000 + per capita income)	9.26 (0.40)
Seriousness Scale[a]	3.67 (0.55)
Census year (0 = 1980-1985, 1 = 1986-1991)	0.57

a. Natural logarithmic transformation.

ANALYSIS AND FINDINGS

Examining Boys and Girls Separately

In an effort to determine if the effects of gender are invariant with regard to the juvenile justice process in Hawaii, the male and female populations were modeled separately. To provide statistical justification for separating the data into two groups, a chi-square ratio test comparison was conducted to compare the full model (boys and girls) to the separate gender-distinct models.[11] Across all three decision-making stages (petition, adjudication, and disposition), there was a statistically significant difference, indicating that specifying two gender-distinct models was a preferable method to examine in more detail how juvenile court processing in Hawaii differs by gender.[12]

From a comparison of the coefficients in the gender-distinct models at the petition, adjudication, and disposition stages, one can determine how court decision making is the same or different across gender. An examination of the direction and odds ratios of the coefficients across models allows for an examination of similarities and differences across gender. Table 2 shows the male and female models for the petition stage. The largest ethnic difference for girls and boys exists between White youth and Hawaiian youth. For White boys and girls, the probability of being petitioned was statistically significantly less likely compared with Hawaiian youth of the same gender. In terms of odds ratios, the odds decreased for White boys and girls by 37% and 43% respectively. The seriousness of the current offense and court location also

TABLE 2: Male and Female Logistic Regression Equations for Petition

Variable	(β_{male})	SE	Odds	(β_{female})	SE	Odds
White	−.45*	.02	.63	−.54*	.03	.57
East Asian	−.22*	.03	.79	−.16*	.05	.84
Pacific	−.14*	.02	.86	−.08*	.03	.91
Other	−.29*	.03	.74	−.33*	.05	.71
Age	.15*	.01	1.16	−.01	.01	.98
Court	−1.58*	.02	.20	−1.14*	.03	.31
Poverty[a]	.10*	.02	1.11	.09*	.03	1.09
Wealth[a]	−.14*	.05	.86	−.03	.07	.96
Seriousness Scale[a]	1.35*	.01	.25	1.19*	.03	.30
Census year	.41*	.03	1.50	.28*	.05	1.33
Constant	6.29*			4.30*		
−2log likelihood	69900.70*			30122.03*		

NOTE: Hawaiian is the reference group.
a. Natural logarithmic transformation.
*$p < .01$.

exhibited similar directions and effects across both male and female models. In other words, both boys and girls charged with more serious offenses and tried in urban courts (Honolulu) were significantly more likely to be petitioned. Controlling for other variables, both boys and girls from areas of poverty were also statistically significantly more likely to be petitioned. The relative influence of being from an area of poverty was minimal for both groups. Being from an area of poverty increased the odds of a referral being petitioned by only 11% for boys and only 9% for girls. Age and the wealth of a youth's residence, however, had a significant impact (although small in terms of odds ratio) for only male offenders.

Table 3 shows the conditional logistic regression models for boys and girls at the adjudication stage. Examination of gender differences at the adjudication stage indicates more similarities than differences between the correlates of a delinquent finding. For instance, White boys and girls were less likely than Hawaiians to be found delinquent, with decreases in odds of 34% and 43% respectively. Age had a similar effect across gender in the adjudication stage. A one-unit increase in age increased the odds of a delinquent finding by roughly 20% for both boys and girls. Boys and girls tried in urban courts were also significantly more likely to have their cases result in delinquent findings.

Analysis of differences in the gender-specific models at the disposition stage also indicates differences and similarities across gender (see Table 4). In terms of ethnicity, both White boys and girls were significantly less likely than Hawaiians of the same gender to be formally disposed. For the male

TABLE 3: Male and Female Logistic Regression Equations for Adjudication

Variable	(β_{male})	SE	Odds	(β_{female})	SE	Odds
White	−.41*	.02	.66	−.56*	.05	.57
East Asian	−.15*	.03	.85	−.29*	.07	.74
Pacific	−.14*	.02	.86	−.22*	.05	.79
Other	−.22*	.04	.79	−.43*	.08	.64
Age	.18*	.01	1.19	.18*	.02	1.20
Court	−1.16*	.02	.31	−1.08*	.04	.33
Poverty[a]	.01	.02	1.01	−.02	.05	.97
Wealth[a]	.02	.05	1.02	−.06	.10	.93
Seriousness Scale[a]	1.46*	.01	.23	2.09*	.04	.12
Census year	.00	.03	1.00	−.01	.07	.98
Constant	4.28*			6.96*		
−2log likelihood	62176.25*			17019.77*		

NOTE: Hawaiian is the reference group.
a. Natural logarithmic transformation.
*$p < .01$.

model, however, East Asians (all else equal) were the least likely ethnic group to receive a formal disposition (probation/confinement). In terms of odds, being an East Asian boy decreased the odds of the formal disposition by 45%. For the female model, however, being a White girl reduced the odds of receiving a formal disposition the most. However, the direction of the effect was similar across other variables. The poverty and wealth variables, for example, increased the odds of an official disposition in both boys and girls. Seriousness of offense had the opposite effect than expected in both the male and female statistical models.[13] Less serious offenses were more likely to result in an official disposition (all else equal). Court location also had similar effects across gender. Contrary to the earlier decision-making points, both male and female youth tried in rural courts were more likely than those tried in urban courts to receive official sanctions. In terms of odds, being disposed of in a rural court increased the odds of an official sanction for boys and girls by 689% and 372% respectively. This suggests that for both boys and girls, judges in rural jurisdictions, once they find a juvenile delinquent, are more likely to give him or her a restrictive sanction than similarly situated juveniles in Honolulu's urban court.

However, there are limitations to using the direction and odds ratio as a method of comparison. It is quite possible that there are gender differences that are not revealed by this simple comparison. To more accurately examine the gender differences across decision-making points, a difference of coefficients test was employed (Paternoster, Brame, Mazerolle, & Piquero, 1998).[14] The resulting test statistic provides the probability that the difference

TABLE 4: Male and Female Logistic Regression Equations for Disposition

Variable	(β_{male})	SE	Odds	(β_{female})	SE	Odds
White	−.46*	.05	.62	−.33*	.11	.71
East Asian	−.58*	.06	.55	−.25*	.13	.77
Pacific	−.22*	.04	.79	−.24*	.09	.78
Other	−.27*	.06	.76	−.37*	.15	.69
Age	−.14*	.02	.86	−.12*	.05	.88
Court	2.06*	.05	7.89	1.55*	.11	4.72
Poverty[a]	.27*	.04	1.32	.08*	.10	1.08
Wealth[a]	.97*	.09	2.64	.53*	.21	1.71
Seriousness Scale[a]	−.27*	.03	1.32	−.88*	.08	2.43
Census year	−.56*	.06	.56	−.61*	.15	.54
Constant	−9.90*			−7.24*		
−2log likelihood	19899.70*			3966.82*		

NOTE: Hawaiian is the reference group.
a. Natural logarithmic transformation.
*$p < .01$.

between the two regression coefficients is equal to 0. In other words, the resulting value tells one the probability that there is no difference between the coefficient effects of the male and female models. A difference of coefficients test for charge seriousness (Seriousness Scale) at the petition stage, for example, indicates no statistically significant difference ($Z = .28$). Therefore, the effect of charge seriousness on the court's decision to petition a case is similar for both boys and girls. At the adjudication stage, however, the effect of charge seriousness is not equal across both male and female samples (see Table 3). The difference of coefficients test is statistically significant at the $p < .01$ level ($Z = 15.75$). From these findings, we concluded that charge seriousness was more important for girls in the decision to adjudicate a female delinquent than it was for similarly situated boys.

Interestingly, when one moves to the disposition decision stage, the influence of charge seriousness between boys and girls is reversed (see Table 4). A comparison of coefficient differences between boys and girls reveals a statistically significant difference ($Z = −7.62$; $p < .01$) in the opposite direction of the adjudication stage. This suggests that for boys and girls entering the disposition stage of the juvenile justice process, the impact of charge seriousness is not equal across gender. The offense seriousness had a stronger predictive influence on the decision to formally dispose (probation/confinement) boys compared with girls. In other words, once girls were found delinquent, they were more likely than boys to be given a restrictive sanction for less serious offenses. This is not a surprising fact when one examines the charges for which female juvenile offenders in Hawaii receive

188   CRIME & DELINQUENCY / APRIL 2001

formal dispositions. For example, 6% of girls given formal dispositions were referred to the court for running away from home, compared with only 0.8% of boys. In terms of more violent offenses, 1% of girls were given formal dispositions for robbery-related offenses compared with 3% of male delinquents. In terms of property offenses, 10% of girls were given formal dispositions for burglary offenses compared with 24% of boys. Theft was the most common property offense to result in a formal disposition for girls (37%) and boys (28%), but its proportion of formally disposed cases was significantly higher for girls. Overall, from an examination of the breakdown of offenses, it is clear that girls are more likely to be disposed of formally for offenses that are seemingly trivial compared with the male juvenile offenders given restrictive sanctions.

The analysis across three decision-making stages in the Hawaii juvenile justice system suggests that charge seriousness does have a differential impact on court processing across gender. It appears that in the early stages of the decision-making process, charge seriousness affects the decision to petition boys and girls equally. Specifically, both boys and girls are significantly more likely to be officially petitioned if they are charged with a more serious offense. At the adjudication stage, charge seriousness also affects both boys and girls in the predicted direction. Its influence, however, is not equal across gender. Instead, charge seriousness appears to have a greater impact for girls compared with boys. However, the influence of charge seriousness at the disposition stage suggests the opposite effect. Girls are more likely to be formally disposed for less serious offenses compared with boys. This implies that once a female adolescent is found guilty, the seriousness of the charge has less of an influence on determining the court's disposition compared with a similarly situated boy. Overall, these findings suggest that gender plays an important role in Hawaii's juvenile court processing. Consistent with prior literature that found evidence of gender bias at specific decision-making points (see, e.g., Bishop & Frazier, 1992), girls in the Hawaii Family Court are more likely than boys to be informally handled at the early stages of the system, but the court's benevolence declines as girls enter the disposition stage.

These results also suggest that the effects are not equal across ethnic groups. White boys and girls are the least likely to have their cases result in official petitions. Having entered the adjudication stage, White boys and girls are also the least likely to be found delinquent. In terms of dispositions, the findings also indicate that White boys and girls are significantly less likely than Hawaiians to be given formal dispositions. These findings highlight the fact that ethnicity also plays an important role in Hawaii's juvenile court process. From these analyses, it appears that girls of marginalized ethnic groups (e.g., Hawaiians) are dually disadvantaged in Hawaii's juvenile court process.

CONCLUSION AND DISCUSSION

Debates about the extent of gender bias as well as related concerns about the role of race in juvenile justice processing have recently benefited from the development of more sophisticated methodologies for assessing bias at various points in the system (see Pope & Feyerherm, 1995).

The present study allowed for a statewide review of the dimensions of gender bias across a long period of time (1980 to 1991), years after one would expect to see the effects of the national deinstitutionalization initiative. Clearly, the results explain much of the inconsistency in prior research. At early points of court handling, it appears that gender has no effect on decision making once all relevant legal factors are held constant. At arguably the most important point of decision making, however, gender does matter and in the most significant ways. Specifically, the data suggest that if a girl gets past earlier stages of the filter, she is likely to be more harshly sanctioned than her male counterparts. Thus, it appears that there may be some support for girls receiving equal treatment at earlier stages of the process (petitioning and adjudication), but at disposition, girls are more likely to receive harsh dispositions for relatively minor offenses, particularly for running away from home. This study suggests that girls who come into the juvenile justice system in Hawaii often experience "partial justice" (Rafter, 1990).

In essence, these data suggest that court officials are ultimately unable to completely shed the gender bias that has haunted the system since its inception, particularly with chronic offenders. Similar to the conclusions reached by Bishop and Frazier (1992), these research results suggest that the court has particular difficulty with persistent female defiance, particularly defiance involving running away from home. Such a concern for running away among girls reaches back to the court's earliest history and reflects the continued presence of a commitment to what might be called a double standard of juvenile justice. Moreover, the fact that these findings occur years after the passage of the JJDP Act, which was supposed to cause systematic changes, highlights the difficulty of having an institution with such a long history of paternalism reform itself (see Kempf-Leonard & Sample, 2000).

Providing Equal Protection

Even if the juvenile justice systems in Hawaii and other states are able to reform themselves and provide equity in processing and treatment, such reforms as gender-specific programming should not be a justification for returning to the "good old days" when lower-class girls were trained in the "womanly arts." Rather, such services should be devoted to the promotion of

190   CRIME & DELINQUENCY / APRIL 2001

empowerment and building self-esteem so that the juvenile justice system does not simply revictimize this vulnerable population. Programming for girls in the juvenile justice system must take into consideration girls' unique situations and their special problems in a gendered society. Traditional delinquency treatment strategies, employed in both prevention and intervention programs, have been shaped largely by commonsense assumptions about what boys need. Sometimes, girls can benefit from these assumptions, but often, they cannot. As Marian Daniel, director of the Baltimore Female Intervention Team, stated, "for years people have assumed that all you have to do to make a program designed for boys work for girls is to paint the walls pink and take out the urinals" (quoted in Girls Inc., 1996, p. 34). Research to date, however, does not provide strong evidence on innovative and effective programs for female delinquents. Today, the knowledge base is essentially the same as in the late 1980s, when Bergsmann (1989) noted in her national review of programming for female offenders in the juvenile justice system that girls remain the "forgotten few."

In addition, results from this research provide further evidence relating to the issue of disproportionate minority confinement across gender and the diversity of the population that the juvenile justice system must serve. These findings highlight the need for programs to be culturally specific as well as gender specific because girls' lives are shaped by both their cultures and their gender. In Hawaii, as in other locations, an increasing number of girls of color are drawn into the juvenile justice system, whereas their White counterparts are diverted. There is a need for programs to be rooted in specific cultures. Because girls of color have different experiences with the dominant societal institutions (Amaro, 1995; Amaro & Agular, 1994; LaFromboise & Howard-Pitney, 1995; Leadbeater & Way, 1996), programs designed to divert and deinstitutionalize must be shaped by the unique developmental issues confronting minority girls and must build on the specific cultural resources available in ethnic communities.

The Future of Gender in Juvenile Justice

The judicial commitment to punishing "unruly" girls and women reaches back in time to the court's earliest concerns for the "moral" behavior of youth. Findings of gender disparity in the post–JJDP Act era also shed important light on a curious theme in the current congressional debates about the future of the JJDP Act. Currently stalled in Congress (Alexander, 1998, 2000), various versions of the reauthorization of this landmark legislation have sought to weaken its commitment to deinstitutionalization, particularly in the case of runaway youth. In fact, some versions would allow status offenders to again be jailed with adults for 24 hours and to be held longer in juvenile facilities (Schiraldi & Soler, 1998). Clearly, the court's long tradition of concern with youthful morality remains a theme in the contemporary juvenile justice system, and this bodes ill for girls, especially if juvenile justice policies shift back to the "good old days."

There is no shortage of work to be done to understand how to better serve girls who find themselves in the juvenile justice system. Research on girls' problems and experiences in the juvenile justice system suggests that gender has long played a role in juvenile justice, whether officially recognized or not. The challenge that confronts academics and policy makers in the juvenile justice arena is to take what is known about girls' development, the influence of culture, and the ways in which girls' problems evolve into delinquent behavior to craft appropriate policies that address gender equity in processing and programming.

NOTES

1. The data utilized in this research were housed in and made available by the National Juvenile Court Data Archive, which is maintained by the National Center for Juvenile Justice in Pittsburgh, Pennsylvania, and supported by a grant from the Office of Juvenile Justice and Delinquency Prevention of the U.S. Department of Justice. The data were originally collected by the Hawaii State Judiciary. Neither the Hawaii State Judiciary nor the National Center for Juvenile Justice bear any responsibility for the analyses or interpretations presented herein.

2. After 1991, the data collection for the county of Honolulu changed, and thus, the integrated statewide data were no longer available.

3. The census data utilized in this study were made available in part by the Inter-university Consortium for Political Science and Social Research. The data for the Census of Population and Housing, 1980 Mater Area Reference File and Tiger File, were collected by the U.S. Department of Commerce, Bureau of the Census. Neither the collector of the original data or the Inter-university Consortium for Political Science and Social Research bear any responsibility for the analyses or interpretations presented herein.

4. Although ZIP codes indicators are often criticized for not corresponding to readily identifiable neighborhood boundaries, this problem is not a serious concern in the state of Hawaii. Although not perfect measures of neighborhoods, ZIP codes in Hawaii are informative because a majority of them do correspond to identifiable areas. These conclusions were reached through consultation with ZIP code maps located in Hawaiian telephone directories, the postal ZIP code data dictionary, and conversations with Mark Goodman, vice president of marketing for E.A. Buck Co., Honolulu, Hawaii.

5. Due to the highly skewed nature of these variables, they were transformed into their natural logs for the multivariate analyses.

6. To protect judicial anonymity, no distinctions were made in the analysis between the specific rural islands in Hawaii. Basic descriptive information has also suggested that there may be differences in how urban and rural juvenile courts handle cases in Hawaii (see Kassebaum et al., 1995).

192   CRIME & DELINQUENCY / APRIL 2001

7. Specifically, the scale comprises 77 different measures of offense seriousness, with 1 representing the most serious offense (i.e., murder) and 77 representing the least serious offense. The coefficient from this variable was subsequently multiplied by −1 in the analyses to ease the interpretation of the findings.

8. Specifically, for 1980 to 1985, the 1980 census data were used, and for 1986 to 1991, the 1990 census data were used.

9. The numbers were rounded to the nearest integer. These statistics were also consistent on a yearly level. Therefore, for the reader's ease, only the aggregate 12-year numbers are reported.

10. Multicollinearity diagnostics using both the auxiliary R^2 test and bivariate correlations indicated that there were no collinearity problems with the independent variables.

11. The following equation was used to compare the fit of the main-effects model to the models separated by gender: $\chi^2 = (-2\log \text{likelihood}_{\text{Main}} - (-2\log \text{likelihood}_{\text{males}} + -2\log \text{likelihood}_{\text{females}})$.

12. For the full petition model and the gender-stratified models, the difference was a chi-square of 186.32 with 9 degrees of freedom ($p = .000$). In the adjudication models, there was a chi-square difference of 260.20 with 9 degrees of freedom ($p = .000$). The disposition model's difference was a chi-square of 91.29 with 9 degrees of freedom ($p = .000$).

13. An analysis of gender-distinct models for the period from 1980 to 1987 that included a control variable for the number of prior offenses indicated that the effect of charge seriousness was eliminated for boys but not for girls. This suggests that prior record is a more important factor in whether male offenders are officially sanctioned than for female offenders. However, there is an issue with sample stratification that is partially responsible for these results. Specifically, few female juveniles are adjudicated as delinquent for offenses that rank high on the seriousness scale. As a result, this measure may not capture the complete context of the charge importance in female cases.

14. The equation used to compare the regression coefficient differences between male and female samples is equally applicable to all regression-based analyses that yield maximum likelihood estimates. The following equation was used: $Z = (\beta_1 - \beta_2 / \text{SQRT } \text{SE}\beta^2_1 + \text{SE}\beta^2_2)$.

REFERENCES

Alexander, B. (1998, October). Hatch quarterbacks sneak play for youth crime bill. *Youth Today*, 46-47.

Alexander, B. (2000, December/January). Gun-loaded juvenile crime bill a no-show. *Youth Today*, 46-47.

Amaro, H. (1995). Love, sex, and power: Considering women's realities in HIV prevention. *American Psychologist, 50*, 437-447.

Amaro, H., & Agular, M. (1994). Programa mama: Mom's project. In *A Hispanic/Latino Family Approach to Substance Abuse Prevention*. Washington, DC: The Substance Abuse and Mental Health Services Administration, Center for Substance Abuse Prevention.

Bergsmann, I. R. (1989). The forgotten few: Juvenile female offenders. *Federal Probation, 53*, 73-78.

Bishop, D., & Frazier, C. (1992). Gender bias in the juvenile justice system: Implications of the JJDP Act. *The Journal of Criminal Law and Criminology, 82*, 1162-1186.

Boisvert, M. J., & Wells, R. (1980). Toward a rational policy on status offenders. *Social Work, 25*, 230-234.

Boyle, P. (1999, July/August). Youth advocates gear up to fight over the fine points. *Youth Today*, 46-47.

Carter, T. (1979). Juvenile court dispositions: A comparison of status and non-status offenders. *Criminology, 17*, 341-359.

Chesney-Lind, M. (1971). *Female juvenile delinquency in Hawaii*. Unpublished master's thesis, University of Hawaii at Manoa.

Chesney-Lind, M. (1973). Judicial enforcement of the female sex role. *Issues in Criminology, 8*, 51-71.

Chesney-Lind, M., Kato, D., Koo, J., & Fujiwara-Clark, K. (1998). *Girls at risk: An overview of gender-specific programming issues and initiatives*. Honolulu, HI: Social Science Research Institute.

Chesney-Lind, M., & Shelden, R. G. (1997). *Girls, delinquency, and juvenile justice* (2nd ed.). Pacific Grove, CA: Brooks/Cole.

Clarke, S. H., & Koch, G. C. (1980). Juvenile court: Therapy and crime control, and do lawyers make a difference? *Law and Society Review, 14*, 263-308.

Cohen, L. E., & Kluegel, J. R. (1979). Selecting delinquents for adjudication. *Journal of Research on Crime and Delinquency, 16*, 143-163.

Cohn, Y. (1970). Criteria for the probation officer's recommendation to the juvenile court. In P. G. Garbedian & D. C. Gibbons (Eds.), *Becoming delinquent* (pp. 190-206). Chicago: Aldine.

Dannefer, D., & Schutt, R. K. (1982). Race and juvenile justice processing in court and police agencies. *American Journal of Sociology, 87*, 1113-1132.

Datesman, S., & Scarpitti, F. (1980). Unequal protection for males and females in the juvenile court. In S. K. Datesman & F. R. Scarpitti (Eds.), *Women, crime and justice* (pp. 300-318). New York: Oxford University Press.

Daws, G. (1968). *The shoal of time*. Honolulu: University of Hawaii Press.

Federal Bureau of Investigation. (1999). *Crime in the United States 1998*. Washington, DC: U.S. Department of Justice.

Feld, B. (1991). Justice by geography: Urban, suburban, and rural variations in juvenile justice administration. *Journal of Criminal Law and Criminology, 82*, 156-210.

Feld, B. (1999). *Bad kids: Race and the transformation of the juvenile court*. New York: Oxford University Press.

Fenwick, C. R. (1982). Juvenile court intake decision making: The importance of family affiliation. *Journal of Criminal Justice, 10*, 443-453.

Frazier, C., & Bishop, D. (1990, March). *Gender bias in the juvenile justice system: Implications of the JJDP Act*. Paper presented at the annual meeting of the Academy of Criminal Justice Sciences.

Gibbons, D. C., & Griswold, M. G. (1957). Sex differences among juvenile court referrals. *Sociology and Social Research, 42*, 106-110.

Girls Inc. (1996). *Prevention and parity: Girls in juvenile justice*. Indianapolis, IN: Author.

Hancock, L. (1981). The myth that females are treated more leniently than males in the juvenile justice system. *Australian and New Zealand Journal of Sociology, 16*, 4-14.

Hearings on the reauthorization of the Juvenile Justice and Delinquency Prevention Act of 1974: Hearings before the Subcommittee on Human Resources of the Committee on Education and Labor. 102d Cong., 1st Sess. (1992).

Horowitz, R., & Pottieger, A. E. (1991). Gender bias in juvenile justice handling of serious crime-involved youth. *Journal of Research in Crime and Delinquency, 28*, 75-100.

Joe, K., & Chesney-Lind, M. (1995). "Just every mother's angel": An analysis of gender and ethnic variations in youth gang membership. *Gender & Society, 9*, 408-431.

194   CRIME & DELINQUENCY / APRIL 2001

Johnson, D. R., & Scheuble, L. K. (1991). Gender bias in the disposition of juvenile court refer-
    rals: The effects of time and location. *Criminology, 29,* 677-699.
Juvenile Justice and Delinquency Prevention Amendments, Pub. L. No. 102-586, 106 Stat. 5035
    (1992).
Kassebaum, G., Marker, N., Lau, C.W.S., Kwack, D., Shera, W., Leverette, J., Niimoto, G.,
    Allingham, E., & Kato, D. (1995). *Assessing disproportionate representation of ethnic
    groups in Hawaii's juvenile justice system: Phase two.* Honolulu, HI: The Center for Youth
    Research.
Kempf-Leonard, K., & Sample, L. L. (2000). Disparity based on sex: Is gender specific treat-
    ment warranted? *Justice Quarterly, 17,* 89-128.
LaFromboise, T. D., & Howard-Pitney, B. (1995). Suicidal behavior in American Indian female
    adolescents. In S. Canetto & D. Lester (Eds.), *Woman and suicidal behavior* (pp. 157-173).
    New York: Springer.
Leadbeater, B., & Way, N. (1996). *Urban girls: Resisting stereotypes, creating identities.* New
    York: New York University Press.
Liao, T. F. (1994). *Interpreting probability models: Logit, probit, and other generalized linear
    models.* Thousand Oaks, CA: Sage.
Mahoney, A. R., & Fenster, C. (1982). Female delinquents in a suburban court. In N. Rafter &
    E. Stanko (Eds.), *Judge, lawyer, victim, thief* (pp. 221-236). Boston: Northeastern University
    Press.
Mann, C. (1979). The differential treatment between runaway boys and girls in juvenile court.
    Juvenile and Family Court Journal, 30, 37-48.
Naffine, N. (1987). *Female crime: The construction of women in criminology.* Sydney, Australia:
    Allen and Unwin.
Odem, M. E. (1995). *Delinquent daughters: Protecting and policing adolescent female sexuality
    in the United States, 1885-1920.* Chapel Hill: University of North Carolina Press.
Odem, M. E., & Schlossman, S. (1991). Guardians of virtue: The juvenile court and female
    delinquency in early 20th century Los Angeles. *Crime & Delinquency, 37,* 186-203.
Paternoster, R., Brame, R., Mazerolle, P., & Piquero, A. (1998). Using the correct statistical test
    for the equality of regression coefficients. *Criminology, 36,* 859-866.
Phillips, C. D., & Dinitz, S. (1982). Labelling and juvenile court dispositions: Official responses
    to a cohort of violent juveniles. *Sociological Quarterly, 23,* 267-278.
Poe-Yamagata, E., & Butts, J. A. (1996). *Female offenders in the juvenile justice system.* Pitts-
    burgh, PA: National Center for Juvenile Justice.
Pope, C., & Feyerherm, W. H. (1982). Gender bias in juvenile court dispositions. *Social Service
    Research, 6,* 1-17.
Pope, C., & Feyerherm, W. H. (1995). *Minorities and the juvenile justice system: Research sum-
    mary.* Washington, DC: Office of Juvenile Justice and Delinquency Prevention.
Poulin, A. B. (1996). Female delinquents: Defining their place in the justice system. *Wisconsin
    Law Review, 3,* 541-575.
Rafter, N. H. (1990). The social construction of crime and crime control. *Journal of Research in
    Crime and Delinquency, 27,* 376-389.
S. 254, 106th Cong., 1st Sess. (1999).
Sampson, R., & Laub, J. (1993). Structural variations in juvenile court processing: Inequality,
    the underclass, and social control. *Law and Society Review, 27,* 285-311.
Schiraldi, V., & Soler, M. (1998). *The will of the people? Public opinion of the Violent and
    Repeat Juvenile Offender Act of 1997.* Washington, DC: Justice Policy Institute and the
    Youth Law Center.

Schlossman, S., & Wallach, S. (1978). The crime of precocious sexuality: Female juvenile delinquency in the progressive era. *Harvard Educational Review, 48*, 65-94.

Shelden, R. (1981). Sex discrimination in the juvenile justice system: Memphis, Tennessee, 1900-1971. In M. Q. Warren (Ed.), *Comparing male and female offenders* (pp. 52-72). Beverly Hills, CA: Sage.

Shelden, R., & Horvath, J. (1986, September). *Processing offenders in a juvenile court: A comparison of males and females.* Paper presented at the annual meeting of the Western Society of Criminology, Newport Beach, CA.

Snyder, H., & Sickmund, M. (1999). *Juvenile offenders and victims 1999 national report.* Washington, DC: U.S. Department of Justice, Office of Juvenile Justice and Delinquency Prevention.

Stahl, A. L. (1998). *Offenders in juvenile court, 1996.* Washington, DC: U.S. Department of Justice, Office of Juvenile Justice and Delinquency Prevention.

Teilmann, K. S., & Landry, P. H. (1981). Gender bias in juvenile justice. *Journal of Research in Crime and Delinquency, 18*, 47-80.

U.S. Bureau of the Census. (1985). *Characteristics of the population and housing 1980: 1979 county and MCD by ZIP code, ICPSR 8051.* Washington, DC: U.S. Government Printing Office.

U.S. Bureau of the Census. (1990). *Characteristics of the population and housing 1990: Tiger file.* Washington, DC: U.S. Government Printing Office.

U.S. House of Representatives, Subcommittee on Human Resources of the Committee on Education and Labor. (1980). *Juvenile Justice Amendments of 1980.* Washington, DC: U.S. Government Printing Office.

Vedder, C. B., & Somerville, D. B. (1970). *The delinquent girl.* Springfield, IL: Charles C Thomas.

Wolfgang, M., Figlio, R. M., Tracy, P. E., & Singer, S. I. (1985). *The national survey of crime severity.* Washington, DC: U.S. Department of Justice, Bureau of Justice Statistics.

[16]

CRIERS, LIARS, AND MANIPULATORS: PROBATION OFFICERS' VIEWS OF GIRLS˙

EMILY GAARDER˙˙
Arizona State University

NANCY RODRIGUEZ˙˙˙
Arizona State University West

MARJORIE S. ZATZ˙˙˙˙
Arizona State University

This study examines the perceptions of girls held by juvenile probation officers, psychologists, and others involved in juvenile court decision making. Through qualitative analysis of girls' probation case files and in-depth interviews with juvenile probation officers, we discuss the social construction of gender, race, culture, and class. Our findings suggest that in an environment marked by scarce resources, gender and racial/ethnic stereotypes leave girls few options for treatment and services in the juvenile court. Some probation officers expressed distaste for working with girls and had little understanding of culturally or gender-specific programming. Others were frustrated by the lack of programming options for girls in the state. Based on our findings, we question whether the current ideology or structure of juvenile probation can nurture a holistic approach to justice for girls.

˙ We would like to thank Donna M. Bishop and the anonymous reviewers for their valuable comments on an earlier draft of this article.

˙˙ Emily Gaarder is a Ph.D. candidate in Justice Studies at Arizona State University. She earned her M.A. in Women's Studies from the University of Cincinnati. She has worked extensively with at-risk and imprisoned youth in a variety of settings. Her research and advocacy focus on restorative justice, environmental justice, and girls in the criminal justice system.

˙˙˙ Nancy Rodriguez is an associate professor in the Criminal Justice and Criminology Department at Arizona State University West. Her research interests include sentencing policies, juvenile court processes, and substance abuse. She has various publications on three strikes law, juvenile drug courts, and restorative justice. Please direct all correspondence to: Nancy Rodriguez, Ph.D., Criminal Justice and Criminology, Arizona State University West, 4701 W. Thunderbird Rd., Glendale, AZ 85306-4908, Phone: 602/543-6601, Fax: 602/543-6658; e-mail: Nancy.Rodriguez@asu.edu.

˙˙˙˙ Marjorie S. Zatz is a professor in the School of Justice Studies at Arizona State University. Her research interests address the ways in which race, ethnicity, and gender impact juvenile and criminal court processing and sanctioning; social constructions of race and gender; Chicano/a gangs; Latin American legal systems; and comparative justice. She has published articles in scholarly journals including *Criminology, Journal of Quantitative Criminology, Social Problems,* and *Law and Society Review*.

Feminist scholars and practitioners who work with girls in the juvenile justice system have long been searching for ways to raise awareness about girls' experiences and how their needs and issues might differ from boys' (Alexander, 1995; Belknap & Holsinger, 1998; Chesney-Lind, 1997; Chesney-Lind & Shelden, 2004; Kunzel, 1993; Odem, 1995; MacDonald & Chesney-Lind, 2001). A number of contemporary works by academics and practitioners alike call for an emphasis on gender, race, and class to fully understand girls' social and economic realities, and to provide programming appropriate to that context (Acoca, 1998b; Bloom, Owen, Deschenes, & Rosenbaum, 2002a; MacDonald & Chesney-Lind, 2001). Accordingly, we reviewed juvenile probation case files and interviewed juvenile probation officers in one metropolitan county in Arizona to better understand how girls are perceived, how their unique histories of abuse and related problems are interpreted, and how juvenile courts respond to these perceptions and interpretations in prescribing treatments for girls.

Drawing from theories and research on the social construction of gender, race, culture, and class, we observe how such constructions influence perceptions juvenile court personnel hold and how such perceptions sustain the "disconnect" between girls' images and their realities. How are ideas about "acceptable" behaviors and lifestyles embedded in notions of gender, culture, and class? To the extent that girls are seen as manipulative or "harder to work with," we ask: What are the repercussions of this image? Last, we address whether and how probation officers understand gender and culturally specific needs and programming, and the availability of such programming. One of the conundrums faced in this court, as elsewhere, is that these constructions are nested within an environment characterized by scarce resources. We end by discussing how attitudes of probation officers interact with the structure and priorities of juvenile probation, including especially treatment options (given scarce resources), and implications for girls in the system.

REVIEW OF THE LITERATURE

The Construction of Girls' Lives: Gender, Race, and Class

The "intersectionalities" of gender, race, and class have been identified as central to studies of gender construction (see Chesney-Lind, 1999; Crenshaw, 1989; Daly & Maher, 1998; Kempf-Leonard & Sample, 2000; Martin & Jurik, 1996; Messerschmidt, 1997; Miller, 1998; Morrison, 1992; West & Zimmerman, 1987). We know it is essential to connect racial and ethnic oppression, patriarchal domination, and culture if we are to expand current research in criminology (Mann & Zatz, 2002; Zatz, 2000). Moreover, those few studies that have explicitly addressed gender construction within marginalized communities add a distinct dimension to our understanding of girls' delinquency (see Arnold, 1990; Chesney-Lind, 1997, 1999; Joe & Chesney-Lind, 1995; Hunt, MacKenzie, & Joe-Laidler, 2000; Portillos, 1999).

The vast majority of research on girls and the juvenile court addresses the influences of gender on juvenile court processing (e.g., Beger & Hoffman, 1998; Bishop & Frazier, 1992; Horowitz & Pottieger, 1991; Johnson & Scheuble, 1991; Chesney-Lind, 1989; McDonald & Chesney-Lind, 2001; Miller, 1996; Triplett & Myers, 1995). Gender differences have been most consistently observed in cases involving status offenses. While self-report data show that girls and boys commit status offenses in roughly the same numbers, the proportion of girls arrested and referred to juvenile court for status offenses is higher (Alder, 1998; Chesney-Lind & Shelden, 2004; Kempf-Leonard & Sample, 2000). To build upon these findings, we suggest that hypotheses addressing the treatment of girls by police, probation officers, and the courts must also consider the impact of social factors such as race and class.

Much research documents how Black women and girls are more likely to be targeted for arrest and processed more harshly than their White counterparts (e.g., Chesney-Lind, 1998; Gilbert, 1999; Mauer & Huling, 1995; Miller, 1996). The different gender role expectations of women according to race have contributed to differential treatment of both victims of crime and offenders (Young, 1986). Gilbert (1999, p. 234) attributes African American women's sentencing to prison more to "their racial status, sex role, and life circumstances ... than [to] their law violations."

Other research has delved into how depictions of youth are constructed according to gender and race. For example, Rosenbaum and Chesney-Lind (1994) found that case files routinely included notes about girls' physical appearance and sexuality, but not about boys'. Kempf-Leonard and Sample's (2000) survey of juvenile and family court judges discovered that "manipulative or deceitful actions" influenced case processing for girls but not boys.

Bridges and Steen (1998) conducted the most comprehensive analysis to date of how race plays into perceptions held by juvenile court staff. Their study examined probation officers' official court records, finding that court staff perceive and judge minority juveniles differently than they do White juveniles. Specifically, probation officers tend to explain delinquent acts committed by Black juveniles in terms of negative internal attributes (e.g., personality characteristics and attitudes) while Whites' delinquency is more frequently attributed to external characteristics (e.g., family structure, substance abuse). Although the authors used a sample of boys and girls, they did not address the convergence of gender and race in probation officers' thinking about the youths, their offenses, future potential, or how those constructions influence gender appropriate treatment.

Although prior work has documented the role of class and gender on delinquency (Chesney-Lind & Sheldon, 2004; Rubin, 1976; Orenstein, 1994), relatively few studies have examined how gender, race, and class interact to influence juvenile justice decision making processes. Among those that have (see Miller, 1996; Sarri, 1983), findings reveal that White middle-class juvenile offenders are far more likely to be processed informally than their Black lower-class counterparts. Miller's (1996) work on delinquent girls, which relied on a content analysis of investigation reports of girls on probation, found that juvenile court officials use class-based standards (specifically, middle-class) to make disposition recommendations.[1] Among adults, Visher (1983) and Chiricos and Bales (1991) point to the interaction of race, gender, and indicators of class (e.g., unemployment), finding that the influence of gender on police and court decisions differs depending upon the person's race and class.

We still lack adequate knowledge of how probation officers and other court officials view girls' pathways to crime, personal attributes, and future possibilities (Miller, 1996). Such descriptions can tell us a great deal about how girls are perceived and socially constructed according to race, gender, and class. They also allow us to compare these perceptions with the reality of girls' lives, helping to discover whether common stereotypes permeate probation officers' analyses of girls and influence treatment or confinement decisions.

The Disconnect Between Girls' Lives and Treatment Programs

The depiction of girls in the juvenile court system as documented in prior studies has brought to light many unique dimensions of girls' lives (Chesney-Lind & Shelden, 2004). One of the most recognized and well-documented realities of girls in the justice system is a prior history of abuse and neglect (Belknap &

---

[1] Unfortunately, this study included the review of only 30 investigation reports.

Holsinger, 1998; Chesney-Lind & Shelden, 2004; Wyatt, Newcomb, & Riederle, 1993). In a study of girl offenders, Acoca (1998a) found that 40% reported being victims of sexual abuse. Furthermore, substance abuse among girls has been linked to multiple incidents of sexual abuse. The interaction between prior victimization and lack of appropriate treatment confounds efforts to address girls' delinquency and health-related problems (e.g., pregnancy, miscarriage, drug and alcohol addiction, eating disorders, and sexually transmitted diseases) (Holsinger, 2000).

Properly assessing the risk factors associated with girls' delinquency and recidivism is extremely difficult given the relatively few programs designed to serve girls' needs (Bloom, Owen, Deschenes, & Rosenbaum, 2002b; Hoyt & Scherer, 1998). Programs for young women have received low funding priority. As Chesney-Lind (1997) notes, only 5% of federal, local, and private funds for juvenile justice are designated for girls.

Belknap, Holsinger, and Dunn (1997) attribute the differential treatment of girls to stereotypes held by professionals. Studies have found that youth workers perceive girls as "difficult to work with" given their problems and available treatment options (Baines & Alder, 1996; Belknap et al., 1997; Bond-Maupin, Maupin, & Leisenring, 2002). The perceived difficulty in working with girls may be attributed to the lack of training in identifying girls' needs and the lack of appropriate programs to meet these needs. For example, Gaarder and Belknap's (2004) study of girls incarcerated in a women's prison found that officers received little to no special training on how to work with juvenile girls, and expressed frustration when assigned to work in the under-21 unit. The prison offered no groups on sexual abuse for the girls, and limited recreational, educational, and work opportunities. Cultural and linguistic barriers can exacerbate these programming problems. Indeed, Acoca (1998b) found that 20% of incarcerated women interviewed reported having difficulty receiving the services they needed because of language difficulties, specifically their own struggles speaking English.

We draw on the literature on the social construction of gender, race, and class to develop a more informed approach to effective programming for delinquent girls (e.g., Bloom et al., 2002b; Hoyt & Scherer, 1998; Miller, 1998; Messerschmidt, 1997; Chesney-Lind, 1999). Unfortunately, institutions and programs that house girls have often reinforced stereotypic gender norms such as femininity and passivity. These programs and institutions usually lack a more holistic approach to treatment, such as family involvement,

552   CRIERS, LIARS, AND MANIPULATORS

drug/alcohol treatment, sexual/physical abuse counseling, and community involvement (Chesney-Lind, 1997).

What Do Gender- and Culturally Responsive Programming Mean?

Given the importance that feminist scholars and practitioners place on the intersection of gender, class, race, and culture, the second part of our study explores how knowledgeable probation officers are with regard to gender- and culturally specific needs and programming. Defining gender and culturally appropriate programming is extremely important given the relatively few programs that address such needs. A national report by Girls Incorporated (1997, p. v) recommends that any program for juvenile female offenders "be gender specific, designed to meet the needs of young women as individuals, to take female development into account, and to avoid perpetuating limiting stereotypes based on gender, race, class, language, sexual orientation, disability, and other personal and cultural factors."

Lindgren's (1996) survey of members of the Minnesota Adolescent Female Subcommittee of the Advisory Task Force on the Female Offender in Corrections elicited a wide range of responses to the question, "What is your definition of gender-specific programming for adolescent females?" The most important themes that emerged were a safe and nurturing environment, the importance of relationships and connections, and comprehensive programming. Based on the comments derived from this study, Lindgren defines gender-specific programming as "comprehensive programming that addresses and supports the psychosocial developmental process of female adolescents, while fostering connections in the context of a safe and nurturing environment" (1996, p. iv).

In 1992, Congress listened to the concerns of practitioners serving youth, who related the need for more attention and services addressing the needs of girls. Subsequently, the reauthorization of the 1974 Juvenile Justice and Delinquency Prevention Act highlighted the need for designing "gender-specific" programs for delinquent girls. A number of studies on gender-specific programming for girls followed, some aided by this new federal attention and funding. Keys to the girls' success in these programs were staff recruitment and training, skills training for the girls, and family and community involvement (Greene, Peters, & Associates, 1997).

Other research has emphasized the importance of a continuum of care that includes both front-end prevention and back-end aftercare programs (American Bar Association, 2001; Belknap et al., 1997; Owen & Bloom, 1998). Counseling support and education around issues of sexual abuse, domestic violence, sexuality, and pregnancy are crucial for girls. Attention to cultural background, language barriers, and immigration concerns are essential elements. Economic needs, housing, jobs, and medical services were also identified.

While there are few existing templates that demonstrate the above characteristics, some programs do exist that can help us identify and measure what kinds of programming work for girls. Nationally based organizations such as Girls Incorporated, and local programs such as P.A.C.E. Center for Girls can serve as examples of successful programming (Girls Incorporated, 1996). Such programs provide comprehensive evaluations of girls based on gender-specific education and therapeutic services in educational-based settings. In Canada, Toronto's Earlscourt Child and Family Centre has developed promising early interventions. Their Girls' Connection program is the first-known attempt in Canada to offer girls and their families a gender-specific, holistic intervention that provides long-term services and follow-up care (see Chesney-Lind, Artz, & Nicholson, 2001; Levene, 1997).

DATA AND METHODS

To address whether and how gender, race/ethnicity, and class influence perceptions of girls held by juvenile court personnel and how such perceptions may contribute to the already limited treatment options for girls, we use two primary data sources. The first are official case file narratives from court records for a random sample of 174 girls referred to juvenile probation in Maricopa County, Arizona during 1999. These files include juvenile court petition information, disposition reports, progress reports, and psychological evaluations normally maintained by the juvenile court, both from the 1999 case and from any earlier referrals of these girls to juvenile probation.[2]

Our intent with the girls' case files was threefold. First, we retrieved narrative statements about the girls and about juvenile court officials' presentations of their cases (i.e., perceptions of girls' behavior and situations). The majority of our data are these narratives written by probation officers, but we also include psychological reports. Although the latter are not written by

---

[2] In Maricopa County, the county attorney files a petition (i.e., referral) against a juvenile who has allegedly committed a delinquent and/or incorrigible act. The adjudication process begins with a hearing to determine whether or not a juvenile is delinquent or whether or not a juvenile is a status offender. A disposition occurs when a juvenile offender is assigned treatment and/or placement.

probation officers, they contribute to the overall "image" of a girl that is created in a probation file. These psychological reports are used by probation and other court officers to assess a girl's background, behavior, and delinquency issues, and can influence the type of treatment or programming she receives. Second, in an effort to better assess girls' lives, we collected narrative information on the girls' parents/guardians, siblings, and extended family members. Third, given the well-documented need for gender appropriate treatment, we examined the treatment recommendations made by juvenile court staff and relate them to the experiences of girls (i.e., substance abuse, sexual abuse, pregnancy).

We supplemented the case file narratives with 14 semi-structured interviews conducted with juvenile probation officers.[3] The women we interviewed included five Whites, two African Americans, one Asian American, one Hispanic, and one Middle Eastern. Of the four male probation officers, two were African American, one White, and one Hispanic. The probation officers averaged 11.2 years of experience, with a range from 1 to 24 years. Probation officers represented various units including standard probation, intensive probation, detention, a school safety program, treatment services, community services, a sex offender program, drug court, transfers, and program services. The semi-structured interviews lasted 45 to 90 minutes. All interviews were taped and transcribed by the interviewer.

The 174 girls in the sample were racially and ethnically diverse: 58% were White, 24% were Hispanic, 13% Black, 4% American Indian, and fewer than 1% Asian Pacific Islander.[4] All were between 12 and 17 years old and had been referred to juvenile court for person, property, drug, and status offenses and for probation violations. To capture information on the structural dimensions of the girls in our sample, we linked their residential zip codes with 2000 census data (U.S. Bureau of the Census, 2000). While these data are aggregate, they provide insights into the demographic characteristics of the geographic areas where the girls lived. The median family income for census respondents

---

[3] The names and contact information for these officers was supplied by the director of Juvenile Court Services. We requested a diverse list with respect to gender, race/ethnicity, years of experience, and probation jurisdiction. After completing 14 interviews, we felt we had reached a point of saturation and were ready to begin review of the case files.

[4] The girls in our study are a random sample of girls referred to juvenile probation in 1999. Compared to all girls on probation, though, our sample underrepresented Hispanic girls and overrepresented White and African American girls. In 2001, the Maricopa County Juvenile Probation Department reported that 51% of girls referred to juvenile court were White, 35% were Hispanic, 8% were Black, 3.7% were American Indian, and fewer than 1% were Asian Pacific Islander (data supplied by the Maricopa County Juvenile Probation Department).

within the girls' zip codes was $42,258 a year. Twenty-two percent reported having less than a high school education, 6% reported being unemployed, and 10% lived below the poverty level. The majority of the communities were occupied by Whites (61%) and Hispanics (28%). Twenty-two percent identified Spanish as their primary language.

Thematic content analyses of the interview and case file data were conducted to explore major themes in the data, which are described in later sections (Lofland & Lofland, 1995). A coding scheme was created to quantitatively analyze these themes. We report both the prevalence of the themes and excerpts from case files. Following each excerpt, we provide a case number and the ethnicity of the girl. We do not provide the gender and ethnicity of probation officers because they could too readily be identified given the demographics of our interview sample.

FINDINGS

Three dominant themes emerge from the case file narratives and interviews with probation officers. The first of these is the gap between probation officers' and other court officials' perceptions of the girls as whiny and manipulative and the realities of the girls' lives, including sexual abuse and teen motherhood. The second is the disconnect between official perceptions of the girls' families as "trashy" and irresponsible and the realities of the girls' family circumstances, including such structural dimensions as poverty as well as individual histories of abuse. The third is the lack of knowledge and understanding on the part of probation officers regarding culturally and gender appropriate treatments, as well as the reality of limited programming services for girls.

It is important to note that prevalence speaks not to how often girls in the sample were abused or how many mothers fit negative stereotypes, for example. Rather, prevalence refers to how often a juvenile court official noted a particular issue in the girls' files. Thus, the percentages that we present are underestimates if the court officials, for whatever reason, did not explore and/or comment on a particular theme (e.g., abuse that was part of the girls' family history and circumstances).

While the realities of girls' lives were consistently emphasized in case file narratives and interviews, we found that stereotypical images of girls outweighed any realities. We also found that girls were often referred to treatment services that did not appear to match their needs. Moreover, the juvenile court lacked the insight and capacity to meet their needs. That is, we found that probation officers, like other criminal justice officials, seem to inadvertently "blunder" when attempting to be sensitive to race, gender, and class (Zatz, 2000, p. 519). They also had little training and few resources at their disposal to match the gender and culturally specific needs of girls on their caseloads.

Perceptions of Girls: Criers, Liars, and Manipulators

Consistent with findings of Baines and Alder (1996), Belknap et al. (1997), and Bond-Maupin et al. (2002), common images in girls' probation files included fabricating reports of abuse, acting promiscuously, whining too much, and attempting to manipulate the court system. In our sample, about 20% of girls were depicted by probation officers and other court officials as sexually promiscuous and 16.5% as liars and manipulators. For example, girls were described in case files as: very manipulative, whining, pouting (#126—African American girl); not inhibited in any way... possesses loose morals (#39—Hispanic girl); and manipulative, unpredictable personality (#12—Hispanic girl).

Interviews with probation officers revealed similar images. Several probation officers used words like promiscuous, manipulative, liars, and criers in their descriptions. Girls were "harder to work with," "had too many issues," and were "too needy." The following responses convey these messages.

> They play the system real well. Girls play the system better than the boys do. They're manipulative. They, you know: "Pity poor me. I'm the innocent bystander and nobody's listening to me." They play the role as if they're so helpless... and the majority of the judges are male and they fall into that trap every single time.

> You just don't see a lot of girls in here [intensive probation]. And to be honest with you we groan when we have one... you know, the issues. I don't know why you groan—maybe because they're definitely a lot needier.

> It's very important to be clear with the girls... because they're more manipulative.

> They're more like criers. Girls will do that. They'll break down and you'll be in the sympathy thing for awhile you know, but then you realize what they're doing.

Two female probation officers, however, commented on some of the reasons why girls might lie or complain.

> They always say when you get girls on your caseload—oh, they're so whiny and they're so needy. I mean, that's true, but sometimes they just need to vent, they just need to bitch a little bit... they have a lot of problems.

Another officer who worked in the detention unit offered a different perspective.

Oh yes, that's their survival sometimes... getting what
they need by going around the back door, not giving the
truth, or just flat out lying.

She recalled a recent incident where a girl had reported being
raped at her residential treatment center. The girl wanted to speak
to a counselor about it. The probation officer later discovered that
the incident did happen, but more than 2 years ago. The girl had
reported it as though it had just happened.

What she wanted was some one-on-one attention with an
adult staff. Girls get their needs met through attention,
through their relationships with people.

When attempting to explain the cause of girls' delinquent
behavior, Baines and Alder (1996) found that youth workers often
relied on the abuse histories of girls to contextualize their path into
delinquency. Consistent with their findings, 11 of the 14 probation
officers we interviewed felt that most of the girls on their caseload
had histories of sexual and/or physical abuse, emotional abuse, and
neglect. Most made connections between the offending behaviors
and past victimization. One remarked, "I hardly ever get a girl who
hasn't been raped, sexually abused, or physically abused," noting
an apparent direct correlation. Another indicated that girls have
usually been victims and that "involvement in sexual activity,
criminal activity, is increased after that."

Some probation officers also identified poverty and lack of
opportunity as directly related to girls' delinquency.

American Indian girls... some of them come from
reservations and a lot of poverty. The connection in
talking with them has been a lot of abuse and drinking.
They don't see a lot of future. Education does not appear
to be valued in their families, because there's no future
whether you have an education or not.

Although most officers were sympathetic to the girls' histories,
a few believed that the abuse stories that girls told were untrue or
exaggerated, or that girls were partially responsible for being
abused.

They feel like they're the victim. They try from, "Mom
kicked me out" to "Mom's boyfriend molested me" to "My
brother was sexually assaulting me." They'll find all kinds
of excuses to justify their actions. Because they feel if I say
I was victimized at home that justifies me being out on the
streets... Or while they were out there they got raped. Or,
they were mistreated. Personally, I think 98% is false...
98% of the girls say the exact same story, so it's as if they
just get together on the units and think up these things.

[The interviewer asked about victimization/offending
connections.] I think there is a connection but it starts

before that. It started with their behavior, being out there on the streets, being out there with those people. You know, they end up in these situations. One of them—she was already incorrigible before this—took off with her boyfriend. She was raped and she refused to give his name because he was in a gang and she was afraid. She came home and did detention for a little while because she had run away, so yeah, because I don't think she's dealt with these issues, she runs away from them. So they do have a correlation, but I don't know which one comes first. The behavior came first because she, you know, got in that situation.

One psychological evaluation echoes these sentiments.

She has walked extensively on the wild side, committing many misdeeds, making many bad choices, and now... she is already haunted by a lot of ghosts. Her past is catching up to her, and it is spoiling her present and future. Her depression is a part of her own doing. She has used practically every street drug, she has been promiscuous, and in general, she has committed many unforgivable misdeeds. The problem here is that she is unable to forgive herself for all the bad choices that she has made... Perhaps she should be referred to a psychiatrist and prescribed antidepressant medication, for this might relieve her depressive symptoms some. However, to completely rid herself of the depression, she must reach a stage of innocence again, which is unlikely (from psychological evaluation #123—Hispanic girl).

As these probation officers and court psychologists indicate, girls are seen as being very difficult to work with. Whether the officers blame or sympathize, they perceive the girls as being troubled and troublesome. We turn next to the realities of the girls' lives, with particular attention to their histories of sexual abuse, substance abuse, and teen motherhood.

Reality of Girls' Lives: Sexual Abuse and Teen Motherhood

The direct and indirect relationships between girls' emotional, sexual, and physical abuse and delinquency have been substantially documented in prior work (Alexander, 1995; Belknap & Holsinger, 1998; Chesney-Lind & Shelden, 2004; McCormack, Janus, & Burgess, 1986; Rhodes & Fischer, 1993). Given the prevalence of sexual abuse histories reported in previous studies (e.g., Acoca, 1998a; Belknap & Holsinger, 1998), we were surprised to find that a relatively low percentage of girls in this study (18.8%) were identified as victims of sexual abuse. However, as previously noted, these data represent instances where a court official was informed of such abuse and actually reported it in the girl's file.

Pregnancy is also a distinct reality for girls in the juvenile justice system (Acoca, 1998a). Although we found that 12.5% of girls were teen mothers and 7.8% became pregnant while on probation, probation officers document the problems teen mothers face but rarely recommend treatment options or services. Two cases illustrate this problem.

> (Girl's name) was stressed due to overwhelming responsibility with school and her infant. This officer set up counseling to remedy the problem. The juvenile wanted to hang out with friends rather than stay home caring for her baby. The family decided that it would be a good idea to have her live with her father in (city omitted), California and attend school there after her probation was up on (date omitted). Her mom would care for the baby to relieve some of the stress (#114—African American girl)

> It appears that (Girl's name) has tremendous concern for her unborn child. She is concerned about being a teenage mother, and not married at this time. Due to (Girl's name) not getting along with her stepmother, it appears she runs away from home instead of dealing with the circumstances in the home. (#113—White girl)

In the first case, counseling was recommended given the girl's stress. No concrete support system, however, was made accessible to her. In the second, the juvenile was placed in parenting classes and given community work hours. Again, parenting classes are the best the probation officer can recommend for a girl in this situation of needing a safe place to stay because she runs way from home.

The depiction of girls' sexuality as "dirty" or inappropriate has led to an assumption that girls need to be protected from the dangers associated with their sexuality. Interestingly, we found minimal effort to protect or assist these girls. Girls' sexual activity, while documented in case files, was not dealt with in conjunction with other risk factors such as sexual abuse or mental health problems. In fact, even when these two girls had suffered extensive sexual abuse, they were still perceived as manipulators.

> (Girl's name) also claims a history of rape on two occasions, but according to her mother, she did not report it to anyone and did not mention it to anyone for over a year after it supposedly happened. She also was pregnant in (date omitted) and attempted suicide. The letter in the record is suggestive of a long and somewhat chronic history of mental health issues and it would appear that she has been somewhat manipulative in her behavior. There are indications to suggest that she has superficial lacerations on her forearms, suggestive of cutting herself

subsequent to an argument with the parents. In the past, (Girl's name) was raped four different times. The first occurred when she was 7 years old; twice at age 13 (once by three boys) and another time at a party. She would not talk about the most recent incident, the fourth rape (#82—White girl)

She reports being sexually active and also reports having an abortion two months ago. She states that the father of her child is actually a 35-year-old man who has his own business. She reports being sexually active, as she prostituted herself on and off since she was 13. (Girl's name) reports for her evaluation in a very candid manner, yet she does appear to be somewhat manipulative. She likely, in fact, sexualizes many of her relationships when communicating with males. She states that she tried to commit suicide recently while in detention, reporting trying to tie a sheet around her neck (#165—White girl)

We found these depictions of girls as manipulative thought provoking. On the one hand, it is not surprising that girls with a history of abuse might be seen as manipulative. For example, the mental health literature tells us that victims of incest might try to control or manipulate individuals (e.g., an abusive father) or situations to reduce the likelihood of further abuse. Manipulating others thus becomes a survival tactic.

Yet our reading of the case files and our reflections on the interviews with probation officers suggest that rather than simply describing a behavior as manipulative, the probation officers take the further step of ascribing a personality trait. There is a difference, we argue, between a recognition that girls may be manipulative in specific situations to achieve a desired end (e.g., not being abused) and the construction of the girl herself, and of all girls by extension, as manipulative by nature and therefore difficult to work with.

The key, we suggest, is whether the probation officers reflect on the girls' contexts and the underlying problems to which manipulative behaviors may be a reasonable response. If they do, we should expect to see them searching for appropriate programs that can adequately respond to the girls' problems and needs. Unfortunately, we do not find that to be the typical response. Rather, some probation officers simply assume that the girls are making up stories. Too many others recognize that girls have problems due to their histories of victimization but do not respond in sympathetic ways, instead writing the girls off through gendered stereotypes and treating the victimization and manipulative behaviors as independent realities.

Perceptions of Girls' Families: Trashy, Manipulative, and Sexually Irresponsible

Perceptions of girls' families were also examined. The majority of the probation officers interviewed felt that the family was crucial to the juvenile's success. In particular, they commented on how important it is that parents take responsibility for their children, seek help for their parenting problems, and be willing to work with probation officers.

Yet some of the same probation officers spoke of the girls' mothers in terms similar to those used to describe the girls themselves—"promiscuous" and "sluts." Indeed, in 6.1% of the case files, the probation officers made such notes. Again, we emphasize the particular language used to describe girls' mothers, and not on using such statements as an indicator of mothers' behavior.

> The girl was accompanied to the intake interview by her mother who was dressed in black Bermuda shorts and a white, sleeveless crop top (#24—Hispanic girl)

> [From an interview] Her background is the classic. Her sister uses drugs. The other sister has a baby, has had two or three kids. Mom—she's a slut. Mom—she's on her third marriage.

> [From an interview] The daughters and sons are going through life with no supervision, no rules. All of the sudden the girl is 14, comes home with hickeys and dressed like a slut and Mom wants to give her rules. And Mom comes home at 3 a.m. with five different guys.

Interestingly, not a single probation officer commented on the fathers' marital status, physical attire, or sexual activities in the case files. We also found that 7.9% of mothers described in case files were presented as liars, or as manipulating the juvenile court system.

Class was an important factor in assessments of the girls' families, though this seemed to operate in several, perhaps contradictory, ways. The most extreme examples of economic disadvantage were cases where families were homeless. Three case files noted that girls living in homeless families were being punished for not attending treatment sessions regularly or missing appointments with their probation officers, both of which are considered probation violations. Probation officers sometimes noted that girls were being labeled delinquent simply because they were homeless. Some probation officers expressed sympathy for girls and families with economic challenges. One derogatory comment, however, targets the economic situation of a low-income, single-parent household.

> This officer has tried to work with this family in order for
> (Girl's name) to be successful on probation, since much of
> her problems appear to be related to the lifestyle which
> they choose to live. This officer was not raised in an
> environment where people chose to live around discarded
> items, even having disabled vehicles permanently placed
> in the driveway, but it is still this officer's opinion that it
> is a choice of lifestyle that (Girl's mother) chooses for
> herself and her family (#6—White girl).

During interviews, some officers said that lower-income
parents were easier to work with because they were uneducated,
intimidated by the court, and not knowledgeable of court services.
Another probation officer, however, identified these as barriers
that poorer families face in seeking help for their children.

> Basic communication skills and having the confidence to
> interact with government and community agencies. A lot
> of lower-class/working-class parents are afraid to get the
> phone book out or go to the police station or their
> community center and start asking what they think are
> maybe awkward or silly questions.... Middle- and upper-
> class parents are more confident through their jobs and
> education and everything. They're more confident to
> interact with the bigger system.

This officer also noted that very poor and middle-class families
receive more services than working poor families, because they
either qualify for free services (in the case of poor families) or can
afford to pay for treatment (in the case of middle-class families).

> The lower middle-class or working poor make $20,000 and
> don't qualify for welfare or have medical benefits. They
> can't pay $50 per hour for a counselor.

As a result, these girls are left with few options. If their families
are working but do not qualify for federal assistance they do not
receive services.

> An African American probation officer noted that because his
> caseload was predominantly Hispanic and African American, it
> limited the types of services he was able to provide. He saw a
> relationship between race/ethnicity and class. Some services were
> located in geographic areas at a considerable distance from
> neighborhoods where economically disadvantaged minority
> families tended to live. Girls were frequently unable to travel to
> the locations where they could receive treatments. In essence,
> services were simply not an option for all.

Realities of Girls' Families: Abuse, Poverty, and Racism

Culture and class are central to the social construction of
gender, including both what girls see as their available options and

what others see as appropriate behaviors for girls. Portillos (1999) has shown how Chicanas and Mexicanas, in search of independence from the expectations of the family, may turn to gangs to alleviate experiences as marginalized women. Others have identified the traditional household duties of Hispanic girls (see Burgos-Ocasio, 2000) and the development of values such as strength and independence among African American girls to deal with the challenges of labor markets (Rice, 1990). We found that 12.3% of Hispanic women in our sample dealt with language barriers, poverty, discrimination, and familial and economic expectations associated with living close to the Mexican border.

> It is believed that this family is somewhat economically disadvantaged, which may influence the family, on occasions, to change their address. (Girl's name) parents are Spanish speaking only, but the juvenile seems to have a fairly good grasp of the English language (#75—Hispanic girl).

> (Girl's name) was indicating that if her parents divorced, that she and her mom would move out. (Girl's name) stated that her mom plans on going back to Mexico to live. (Girl's name) stated that if this happens, she will most likely live with her 22-year-old sister, O. However, (Girl's name) stated if the divorce does not happen before she is 18, once she is 18 in February, she may go live with a friend "up north" (#17—Hispanic girl).

Interestingly, and consistent with Bridges and Steen's (1998) findings regarding court officials' perceptions of intrinsic causes of African American delinquency and extrinsic causes of White delinquency, when Hispanics and/or their families contradict some of these cultural dimensions, their involvement in delinquent acts are viewed as mishaps. For example, a Hispanic girl's family is described as cooperative and functional because they speak English and are in the country legally.

Substance abuse plays a significant role in these girls' lives. Case file narrative data showed that 43% of girls were current drug users or had a history of drug use. For some, language barriers made treatment or assessment difficult given the probation officer's inability to communicate effectively with parents.

> There was no response from the family regarding my initial letter to them and the request to contact me. I was able to finally get a hold of the father at his work number. (Father's name) speaks mostly Spanish and therefore conversation with him was limited. He speaks some English but may not have fully understood some of my questions. Parents are divorced but are still living together. They both work long hours and [are] rarely home

564   CRIERS, LIARS, AND MANIPULATORS

in the day. Both parents admitted that lack of supervision
is contributing to the behaviors of their daughter. It was
very clear that the parents know their children are using
drugs but that there is little that they feel they can do to
stop the behavior. This officer found their complacency
about the activities in their home disturbing (#59—
Hispanic girl).

In 18.8% of cases, we found that extended family members
served as guardians when biological parents were unable to raise
their children.

There are eight other children also living with
grandparents. The grandparents are in their 70s and both
are still working; they seem to be very responsible caring
people. Both natural parents have histories of problems
with the law. Mom has problems with alcohol and "rock"
and dad also has alcohol problems (#105—Hispanic girl).

(Girl's name) family life has been far from ordinary. She
lost her mother in 1995 due to excessive alcoholism, drug
use, and a blood clot in her brain. (Girl's name) also lost
her older brother in a gang-related shooting in (date
omitted), and her youngest brother died at 2 months of age
approximately 2 years ago. (Girl's name) was passed
around from her maternal aunt to her grandmother. In
the process, she has been in 13 different schools (#137—
Hispanic girl).

Research has found that girls are much more influenced by
family expectations and family conflict than boys (Hoyt & Scherer,
1998). These experiences vary by race/ethnicity. For example,
Taylor, Biafora, Warheit, and Gail (1997) found that Hispanics are
significantly influenced by family substance abuse, and African
American youths by the levels of family communication. For some
girls, substance abuse in combination with other family problems,
including financial stability, domestic violence, and sexual abuse,
compound their situations. Two narratives illustrate this clearly.

(Girl's name) is currently a ward of the state and is living
in a group home. She was brought to the interview by her
CPS caseworker B. (Girl's name) mother is living
somewhere on the streets in (city omitted) and reportedly
is dying of AIDS while her father is incarcerated in Mexico
for murder. The caseworker reported that (Girl's name)
has had a lot of problems with anger but seems to be
making some progress recently. She was kicked out of her
grandmother's house for assaulting her and then kicked
out of her foster mother's house for assaulting her also.
She has run away, attempted suicide, been assaulted and
abused, been involved with gangs, drugs, and marijuana
and has been on probation previously. However, as I
stated, it appears that there has been progress and (Girl's
name) seems to have mellowed out some. According to her

grandmother, (Girl's name) was sexually abused at 6 years of age (#48—Hispanic girl)

(Girl's name) is a 17-year-old American Indian youth who, at the present time, is doing quite well with her counseling and doing well at (school name). She has had a very sad and rocky childhood, she had to watch her mother die in front of her eyes from drug and alcohol abuse and has been from foster home to youth home and in hospitals and numerous counseling sessions to deal with her depression, her anger, and some of the violent and abusive situations that she has been exposed to (#58—American Indian girl)

Bond-Maupin et al. (2002) found that probation officers were often sympathetic to the conflicts Hispanic girls faced (i.e., having "traditional" parents and living as an "Americanized" girl). During our interviews with probation officers, we found they also identified with the struggles faced by Hispanics and commented on the valuable support system that extended families provide:

Personally I think some of the girls, especially Hispanic girls, are brought up to believe that their purpose in life is to stay home and have kids and do nothing. But they're growing up in the 90s.... I think a lot of them feel really torn—well, am I supposed to go out and have kids or am I supposed to have a career?

(The interviewer asked if she used different techniques with juveniles/families of color.) A Hispanic family or African American family for example, with a family intact—that becomes a real resource. Usually with extended families, you can include them as a support system, because they have been historically used as a support system. You have grandparents raising grandkids. You have uncles and aunts coming in and that has been a source of support.

Regarding family conflict, many probation officers expressed concern about domestic violence and noted that children were often punished for fights started by parents.

Politically, there was a change roughly 10 years ago... the legislature decided if the police go into a home and there's a domestic violence incident, somebody has to leave. And starting at that point the kids were the obvious ones to take out of the home. If you arrest the parents, than you have to shelter the kids.... So the police just make the kids go away and the numbers of kids being referred to the juvenile court for assaulting their parents or for disorderly conduct or punching walls or doors... the numbers have just been increasing tremendously because of that political change.

The whole thing just burns a hole in me.... Say the police respond to a case of domestic violence. You have a 3-year-old girl, a 16-year-old girl, and the mother fighting. Say the mother grabbed that girl and started pounding her face into cement. They're not going to take Mom to jail when there is a 3-year-old daughter there. But they need to separate the two of them. So a lot of times it really is the parent's fault but the kid gets hauled away to jail for protection and they're not going to take Mom who has to support the 3-year-old and go to work the next morning.

Although some probation officers identified the conflicts at home, economic instability, and substance abuse as the root of the problems the girls faced, they were unable to provide the needed services. The lack of appropriate treatment options and services for girls is our third theme.

Gender-Specific Needs

Many scholars and practitioners recognize the need for more appropriate treatment for girls but the small number of girls relative to boys makes it difficult for court officials to justify specialized, often expensive, treatments that are culturally and gender appropriate (Alder, 1998; Bloom et al., 2002a; Freitas & Chesney-Lind, 2001; McDonald & Chesney-Lind, 2001).

In our interviews, we asked probation officers whether they believed girls had different problems or needs than boys. We also asked if they worked differently with the girls on their caseloads. The majority of probation officers noted immediately that girls were more likely to be referred for incorrigibility or domestic violence offenses. Other likely offenses included probation violations (usually running away), truancy, drugs, and prostitution. Half of the probation officers reported that girls were more likely to be arrested for status offenses. These officers said that parents tend to "keep a closer eye" on girls, or try to "over control" them.[5] They also noted that boys were more likely to be rewarded for sexual behavior and girls punished. As one probation officer noted, "Girls get picked up for stuff that males don't." Another said, "Girls are involved with the court process more for their best interests, not necessarily because she is a danger to the community, but for her own safety." Yet not all officers saw this as positive. One commented, "Domestic violence and incorrigibility needs to be directed away from the courtroom and into specialized programs. We're turning a lot of these girls into criminals."

---

[5] To contrast this point of view, we also note that one officer said, "I can't take any example of any kid... where the parent was excessive or punitive in discipline. I see just the opposite. I see an incredible permissiveness in parents allowing kids freedoms and privileges that shouldn't have been extended to the kid."

However, four of the 14 probation officers asserted that juveniles all had similar needs and should not be treated or approached any differently based on gender. They rejected the need for gender-specific programming, preferring to decide on treatment options based on individual characteristics or circumstances. When asked about the kinds of programs in which girls were successful, another officer replied,

> I don't feel like you can just say that this program works for girls or whatever—they're children. Some of them are ready and some of them aren't. Whether they be boys or girls.

Some of these officers believed that treating girls "differently" would be assuming that all girls had the same issues and problems. Three alluded to the fact that some girls were not in fact acting normally.

> These days you can't do that. I have some young ladies on my caseload that are kind of like—they have a macho side, I guess.

> [There are] girls on our caseload who are kind of macho girls. They're not the normal, everyday girl that you deal with.

> They're not your typical girls... you know, the fingernails, the make-up, the Ms. Prissy. They're just like the boys. They're worse than some of the boys. They go out and they prove themselves like they're not feminine. You know they don't want anybody to think... well, I'm helpless. I can take care of myself, so they play the role as portraying to be something that they're not.

When girls did not adhere to "feminine" behaviors or attitudes, there was often an assumption that they were "becoming more like boys," and should be treated as boys would be. Probation officers also relied on gender stereotypes to define specific issues facing girls. Several of the probation officers believed that the girls were promiscuous and needed sexual education programming. Early sexual activity, pregnancy, and sexually transmitted diseases were seen as feminine issues. As one officer commented,

> It would be good to have gender specific—all girls—for feminine problems or feminine-related issues—we have a lot of STDs transmitted.

Another suggested that sex education was needed, "definitely for the females because they ... they produce the seed." Interestingly, one probation officer who earlier had called promiscuity a "girl problem," began to question herself after prompting from the interviewer.

> Probation officer: You know what? (long pause) I think there is ... umm ... you know I think there is, but maybe

> with the girls it's more noticeable. They're always getting STD's—but they must be getting them from the guys, so ... (trails off)

In addition to labeling girls' sexuality as specifically problematic (as opposed to boys), two probation officers also made reference to the "hormonal" issues underlying girls' tendency to be "difficult."

> Girls are much more difficult to case manage. Their affect is different—they will push you away when really they want to come closer. They will make your life miserable— whereas boys will just sort of go along with the program.... A lot of it, I think, in my opinion, is hormones. In fact, when I had a lot of girls on a caseload, you could almost watch the ebb and tide. When their hormones are on the move and they're ovulating, you couldn't stand to be around them.

> Males and females—I mean male delinquent teenagers go through different things than females. You know females ... get to that certain age—they, you know, got different hormones ... psychological issues they might have to deal with also.

Despite gender stereotyping, or conversely, the denial that any differences existed, nearly all the officers admitted that they "talked to girls more." Girls were more open than boys to sharing details about their lives and relationships. This was in spite of the fact that many of the probation officers felt uncomfortable "acting like counselors."

It is important to note here that only one probation officer had ever attended training that focused on gender or culturally specific needs. This is a particularly disappointing finding given the federal resources (e.g., challenge grants) allocated to make juvenile court practitioners more attentive and responsive to gender. In fact, we found no evidence in case files noting a need for gender or culturally specific programming. However, there were a few probation officers who spoke at great length concerning the specific needs of girls in the system, and their style of working with girls.

> For me it's very respectful.... I try very hard not to be judgmental, because I don't always know where they're coming from. So I try to find out who they are, and what their backgrounds are before I say anything... but at the same time setting boundaries on what is acceptable behavior here.

Research suggests that one of the most important factors in working with girls is establishing relationships (see Alder, 1998; Chesney-Lind & Sheldon, 1998; Taylor et al., 1995; Lindgren, 1996). For example, Belknap et al.'s (1997) data from focus groups with incarcerated girls outlined the importance of respectful and caring relationships between girls and adult staff. In general, girls did not feel respected by the staff in their agencies and institutions. They wanted to be listened to by caring adults, and desired one-on-one relationships in which they could discuss their feelings. In step with this, when asked what kind of problems the girls on her caseload faced, one officer had this to say:

> Girls face relationships. Their number one problem in my opinion is self-esteem issues, and how to relate to the world around them.... Girls are more interested in whether the relationship—you know, if they like you as a P.O. or whatever. You have to get through that barrier first.

Despite a few exceptions, which we have noted, most of the probation officers understood gender-specific needs and programming for girls as sex education (especially STD and pregnancy prevention), good parenting skills, and building self-esteem. Their interpretations are not surprising, given the attention to issues such as sexual activity, pregnancy, and victimization in case file narratives. When it came to dealing with these issues, however, the only resources that the probation officers offered the girls were Planned Parenthood and Parents Anonymous.

Gender-Specific Programming

Both the interviews and our review of case files revealed a severe lack of programming for girls. The majority of probation officers in our study could not name a single program designed specifically for girls. A persistent theme regarding treatment services for girls was the disconnect between the realities of the girls' lives and appropriate treatment options. As mentioned, a girl whose family was homeless and living on the streets had probation violations for not attending her drug treatment and for not staying in contact with her probation officer. Sadly, the only option the probation officer could suggest was counseling. In another case, a pregnant teen received sex education as part of her terms of probation.

> (Girl's name) is currently pregnant. She reports that she has used marijuana since being pregnant. She denies any other usage. (Girl's name) and her grandmother are hopeful that they can find an adoptive family for the baby. At her doctor's appointment on (date omitted), (Girl's name) admitted to having an abortion in (date omitted). She is in need of life skills training and sex education (#5—White girl).

570   CRIERS, LIARS, AND MANIPULATORS

Case file narrative data reveal that nearly 16% of girls were referred to detention or a state institution for treatment. Unfortunately, a lack of available and appropriate treatment programs made confinement the only option for some.

In some cases where girls were sexually active and suffered from histories of abuse, probation officers openly admitted to being "confused as to what is best for the child." For others, institutionalization was the only alternative given the "difficult" nature of girls' cases—often meaning that girls frequently ran away or did not succeed in existing programs. Many probation officers expressed frustration with the lack of funding for programming in general and for girls specifically. This attitude is consistent with Kempf-Leonard and Sample's (2000) survey of juvenile and family court judges and officers. The majority of those surveyed noted that females did not have adequate access to treatment, especially for mental health problems, status offending, chemical dependency, and sexual victimization.

Half the officers believed that gender-specific programming was a good idea. "Maybe it would be good to have a gender-specific program for girls—just to see how they'd react," one officer said, adding, "I don't know if any are available." Different reasons were given, however, for why gender-specific programming might be needed. Some reasoned that girls and boys become distracted by each other when they are together. Others recognized that girls may be reluctant to talk about their situations when boys are present.

Attempts to address girls' needs all too often result in ill-fitting programs and frustration regarding the limited options available. Most programs that were all girl were in locked institutions. There were even fewer options for early intervention programming or chemical dependency issues. Once a psychological evaluation was conducted and mental health issues were identified, girls were usually placed on medication and sent to counseling.

Culturally Specific Needs

The cultural differences identified in prior works have stressed the importance of addressing the cultural dimensions of girls' lives (e.g., Fishman, 1998; Miller, 1998; Chesney-Lind, 1999). Recognizing the relationship between gender, culture, and class is a first step toward providing girls with the services they need. Some officers spoke at length about cultural differences and needs of the girls on their caseloads. One response was particularly representative.

Girls of color have a double whammy pretty much. They are minorities from ethnic standing. They are female from gender standing. There are different psychodynamics when you talk about different ethnic females. If you have Hispanic females—the males the machismo. If you have African American—African American females tend to be the backbone of the Black culture. It's just different. It's different all the way down the line.

Other officers tried to incorporate culturally sensitive methods in their work, but lacked training and resources. Racial stereotypes and misunderstandings regarding cultural differences can persist if probation officers are not adequately trained. False assumptions about cultures can lead to inappropriate assessments of girls' needs. For example, a probation officer told the story of a Hispanic boy molesting a cousin, and of their therapist not being aware that cousins do marry in some Hispanic cultures. The officer suggested that therapists should better understand the cultures of those they work with.

Culturally Specific Programming

When asked about culturally sensitive programs we found that, again, probation officers could not name even one program that was culturally aware. Many officers reported that they referred kids to programs based on the gender and race of the counselor, not on what the program itself offered. The growing and varying racial/ethnic make-up of juveniles on probation seems to only compound the problems associated with providing proper programs for juveniles. Two probation officers mentioned that there were no culturally appropriate resources available to deal with the growing Asian American population.

We don't have anything within the probation department that focuses on Asian American issues. Right now, I'm seeing more kids of Asian parents... the parents may be first or second generation in the U.S. They don't know the language. They're more easily manipulated by their kids. And the kids are more quickly sucked into the drugs and alcohol and partying and rebellious stuff... that's happening a lot with Asian American families. I got a bunch of Filipino families... They do not know how to be a parent in the U.S. with all these problems. They're just desperate. They're begging for help. [But] they're not real receptive once we start making suggestions, because it is totally foreign to them.

There are a lot more Southeast Asians here now. It's a trend from California—Vietnamese, Laotian, Cambodian ... there are no resources for them, no interpreters, no communities, there's really nothing.

When asked if there were differences in terms of race/ethnicity that needed to be considered in programs or counseling, one probation officer remarked:

> The only time I'll typically look for ethnicity is when I have a Spanish-only speaking kid and I need a counselor who speaks Spanish.... I don't like making big issues about that. I have major issues with people saying a lot of rights are broken because of the color they are, when a lot of rights for White people are as well. My perspective is, if they're a good counselor, they can work with any of them. It's only an issue if it's a language barrier or an ethnic issue in it. Like Indians—they do their sweat lodges and they do all that. I can't do one of those. So in essence, they need to have an Indian do that.

On the other hand, another probation officer saw her race/ethnicity (Asian American) as a helpful attribute in working with girls of color:

> I went with another probation officer to see the girls on our caseload. She had an American Indian girl on her caseload and the girl would not talk to her. She made some kind of comment about 'just another White agency person coming to see me.' But she would talk to me.

DISCUSSION OF THE FINDINGS

The social construction of gender, race/ethnicity, and class has a profound impact on girls in the juvenile justice system. In this study, we found that juvenile court staff often act based more on the perceptions they have of girls and their families than on the realities the girls face, including both individual and societal factors. Our findings suggest that gender and racial/ethnic stereotypes leave girls few options for treatment and services in juvenile courts.

Some probation officers we interviewed believe that the ideology of the juvenile court means they should do what they see as best for the juvenile while at the same time providing equitable treatment for all. In doing so, they struggle between providing the best services available to girls and dealing with the possibility of stereotyping or providing preferential treatment. As in other studies (Bloom et al., 2002a), staff acknowledge that they need training in dealing with girls. For example, most probation officers identify the need for gender and culturally responsive programming. It is important to recognize that girls have different issues and different histories than boys, and that the most effective styles for girls may differ significantly from those for boys. These probation officers, however, often find that existing programs and institutions did not have the resources to provide such programming. The inevitable outcome is either that needs are not met, or that officers must recommend that girls be committed to residential or institutional confinement as the sole locale in which the girls' needs can be addressed. It is noteworthy that a handful of probation officers expressed a prevailing disbelief in the need for gender- or culture-specific services.

Whether probation officers are sympathetic to girls' needs or not, they generally seek to maintain a certain emotional distance from them, both because they do not think they should act as counselors and because they see the girls' needs as so overwhelming. One consequence of this emotional distance is that the girls may not trust the officers. A second and related consequence is that officers may not understand the extent to which gender enters into many of the girls' problems and efforts— some of which get them into serious problems with the law—to solve those problems. Both of these points also speak to research on the gender-specific needs of girls. As stated, a number of studies highlight the fact that girls seem to respond best to court interventions and programming when they have positive, trusting relationships with adults. To effectively communicate with a female probationer, a probation officer must first build a connection with her.

The lack of available funding for gender-specific programming and the paucity of information available to court workers on programs has a destructive impact on girls within both juvenile and criminal courts. A few officers in this study commented that gender-specific programming is present in detention, but not before that point. We know that detention and other forms of institutionalization are used in place of programs because either there are no services available or there is a lack of spaces in the programs that do exist (Bond-Maupin et al. 2002). Gaarder and Belknap's (2002) research on girls sentenced to adult prison found that of the 22 studied, five had no prior record, and 10 had never been placed in foster care, residential treatment, or a long-term correctional program before being sentenced to prison. "Essentially," the study concludes, "many of these girls had never been given a chance to succeed in the juvenile justice system before being sentenced to adult prison" (Gaarder & Belknap, 2002, p. 509).[6] Remand decisions assume transferred youths have failed in

---

6 Unfortunately, this has not yet resonated with some court personnel. One probation officer we interviewed admitted that "placements overall are being dismantled and being noncontracted.... we don't have enough resources across the board." However, when asked whether adult prison was appropriate for girls or did them any good, the officer replied, "It's not a matter of doing them good or not. It's a

the juvenile court and choose not to make use of treatment (Bortner, Zatz, & Hawkins, 2000). In reality, girls may be transferred to the adult system without ever receiving appropriate treatment within the juvenile justice system. The unaddressed issues of girls were exacerbated within the walls of an adult prison that offered little therapeutic programming and was ill-equipped to meet even the most basic needs of the girls imprisoned there (Gaarder & Belknap, 2004).

These issues demand the serious attention of both researchers and practitioners. One important move is to step up our research on gender and culturally specific needs/programming. There is a certain amount of confusion over what gender or culturally specific programming looks like and why it works. For instance, Kempf-Leonard and Sample's (2000, p. 118) review of current gender-specific recommendations found it "difficult to understand how good female-specific services differ from good youth services." There is also disagreement about whether and when "gender-specific" programming means separate programming (all girls).

Furthermore, Kempf-Leonard and Sample (2000) caution that advocates of gender-specific programming be aware of how such language can actually be used to perpetuate "separate but equal" juvenile justice interventions, such as the overmedication of girls, "bootstrapping," and other forms of gender bias. If more resources are allocated to programming for girls, we must be careful that these programs fulfill existing needs, rather than simply contributing to the widening net of social control.

There is still much discussion and debate around the meaning of "gender-specific" needs and programming. Not surprisingly, the lack of clarity regarding the concept of gender or cultural needs/programming (along with the relative "newness" of the terminology) leads to confusion among practitioners about how to implement such ideas. In step with our findings, Belknap et al. (1997) found that practitioner awareness of gender differences and appropriate services varied widely. One of their recommendations includes the coordination of "regional gender-specific sensitivity training and information sharing sessions for juvenile justice and youth serving professionals" (1997, p. 33). They also note that "few individuals have developed the ability to identify appropriate and effective programs for delinquent girls" (1997, p. 33). They urge the development of assessment tools to measure the effectiveness of

matter of consequence, because they've had all their chances and there is nothing else you can do for them. My opinion is that once they've gone all the way to the adult court, then it's a consequence issue, not 'Can we turn them around?' anymore."

girls' programs, as well as periodic program evaluations. While we recognize that additional resources are needed to better serve all juvenile offenders in the juvenile court system, risk/needs tools that focus on mental health (e.g., depression, which is more often internalized by girls than boys) and victimization would more appropriately address female delinquency than current efforts. Programming that highlights relationship building and incorporates an understanding of how culture directly influences girls' delinquent and nondelinquent behavior is also needed. Last, family-based treatment can provide girls with an important support system, one that is often lacking in girls' lives.

CONCLUSION

The juvenile justice system has long been criticized for inadequate attention to the situations and needs of girls. We suggest that framing the problem theoretically as the social construction of gender, race, and class in juvenile probation helps us to better understand the disjunctures between court actors' perceptions of girls and what they see as culturally appropriate gendered behaviors. Probation officers expect one set of behaviors and attitudes from the girls and their families, but due to economic and social forces (e.g., homelessness, immigration restrictions, histories of sexual abuse) as well as individual factors (e.g., mental health problems), the girls do not manifest these hegemonic expectations. This results in disappointment on both parts—girls are not treated according to the reality of their lives, and probation officers continue to express frustration and even hostility towards girls who are not responding favorably to the programming being offered.

As Chesney-Lind and Shelden (2004, p. 6) remind us, "An appreciation of a young women's experience of girlhood, particularly one that attends to the special problems of girls at the margins, is long overdue." We urge the continued development and implementation of gender and culturally responsive approaches and programming that can help confront the social and economic realities of girls. More detailed information and rigorous evaluation of programming for girls is needed. Without these analyses, probation officers and other court officials will continue to rely on stereotypical images of "proper girl behavior" and psychological assessments of their conduct, while discounting the power that oppressive structures and institutions hold over people. As contemporary feminist research begins to solidify its definition and understanding of "what works for girls," we face the equally enormous task of communicating this information to practitioners, administrators, and other decision makers. It is apparent from this study that the message has not yet been heard.

REFERENCES

Acoca, L. (1998a). Outside/inside: The violation of American girls at home, on the street, and in the juvenile justice system. *Crime & Delinquency, 44,* 561–589.

Acoca, L. (1998b). Defusing the time bomb: Understanding and meeting the growing health care need of incarcerated women in America. *Crime & Delinquency, 44,* 49–69.

Alexander, R. (1995). *The "girl problem": Female sexual delinquency in New York, 1900–1930.* London: Cornell University Press.

Alder, C. M. (1998). "Passionate and willful" girls: Confronting practices. *Women and Criminal Justice, 9,* 81–101.

American Bar Association and National Bar Association. (2001). *Justice by gender: The lack of appropriate prevention, diversion, and treatment alternatives for girls in the justice system.* Washington, DC: American Bar Association Juvenile Justice Center.

Arnold, R. A. (1990). Women of color: Processes of victimization and criminalization of black women. *Social Justice, 17,* 153–166.

Bains, M., & Alder, C. (1996). Are girls more difficult to work with?: Youth workers' perspectives in juvenile justice related areas. *Crime & Delinquency, 42,* 467–485.

Beger, R., & Hoffman, H. (1998). The role of gender in detention dispositioning of juvenile probation violators. *Journal of Crime and Justice, 21,* 173–188.

Belknap, J., & Holsinger, K. (1998). An overview of delinquent girls: How theory and practice have failed and the need for innovative changes. In R. Zaplin (Ed.), *Female crime and delinquency: Critical perspectives and effective interventions* (pp. 13–64). Gaithersburg, MD: Aspen.

Belknap, J., Holsinger K., & Dunn, M. (1997). Understanding incarcerated girls: The results of a focus group study. *The Prison Journal, 77,* 381–404.

Bishop, D. M., & Frazier, C.E. (1992). Gender bias in juvenile justice processing: Implications of the JJDP Act. *Journal of Criminal Law and Criminology, 82,* 1162–1186.

Bloom, B., Owen, B., Deschenes, E., & Rosenbaum, J. (2002a). Moving toward justice for female juvenile offenders in the new millennium: Modeling gender specific policies and programs. *Journal of Contemporary Criminal Justice, 18,* 37–56.

Bloom, B., Owen, B., Deschenes, E., & Rosenbaum, J. (2002b). Improving juvenile justice for females: A statewide assessment in California. *Crime & Delinquency, 48,* 526–552.

Bond–Maupin, L., Maupin, J., & Leisenring, A. (2002). Girls' delinquency and the justice implications of intake workers' perspectives. *Women and Criminal Justice, 13,* 51–77.

Bridge, G. S., & Steen, S. (1998). Racial disparities in official assessments of juvenile offenders: Attributional stereotypes as mediating mechanisms. *American Sociological Review, 63,* 554–570.

Bortner, M. A., Zatz, M. S., & Hawkins, D. F. (2000). Race and transfer: Empirical research and social context. In J. Fagan and F. Zimring (Eds.), *The changing borders of juvenile justice* (pp. 277–320). Chicago: University of Chicago Press.

Burgos-Ocasio, H. (2000). Hispanic women. In M. Julia (Ed.), *Constructing gender: Multicultural perspectives in working with women* (pp. 109–137). Belmont, CA: Brooks/Cole.

Chesney-Lind, M. (1989). Girls' crime and woman's place: Toward a feminist model of female delinquency. *Crime & Delinquency, 35,* 5–29.

Chesney-Lind, M. (1997). *The female offender: Girls, women, and crime.* Thousand Oaks, CA: Sage Publications.

Chesney-Lind, M. (1999). Girls, gangs, and violence: Reinventing the liberated female crook. In M. Chesney-Lind and J. M. Hagedorn (Eds.), *Female gangs in America: Essays on girls, gangs and gender* (pp. 295–310). Chicago: Lake View Press.

Chesney-Lind, M., Artz, S., & Nicholson, D. (2001). *Making the case for gender-responsive programming.* Paper presented at the Annual Meeting of the American Society of Criminology, Atlanta.

Chesney-Lind, M., & Shelden, R. G. (2004). *Girls, delinquency, and juvenile justice.* Los Angeles, CA: West/Wadsworth.

Chiricos, T. G., & Bales, W. D. (1991). Unemployment and punishment: An empirical assessment. *Criminology, 29,* 701–724.

Crenshaw, K. (1989). Demarginalizing the intersection of race and sex: A black feminist critique of antidiscrimination doctrine, feminist theory, and anti–racist politics. *University of Chicago Legal Forum, 4,* 139–167.

Daly, K., & Maher, L. (1998). Introduction. In K. Daly and L. Maher (Eds.), *Criminology at the crossroads: Feminist readings in crime and justice* (pp. 1–17). New York: Oxford University Press.

Fishman, L. (1998). Images of crime and punishment: The black bogeyman and white self-righteousness. In C. R. Mann and M. S. Zatz (Eds.), *Images of Color, Images of Crime* (pp. 109–125). Los Angeles: Roxbury.

Freitas, K., & Chesney-Lind, M. (2001). Difference doesn't mean difficult: Practitioners talk about working with girls. *Women, Girls and Criminal Justice, 2,* 65–79.

Gaarder, E., & Belknap, J. (2002). Tenuous borders: Girls transferred to adult court. *Criminology, 40,* 481–517.

Gaarder, E., & Belknap, J. (2004). Little women: Girls in adult prison. *Women and Criminal Justice, 15,* 51–80.

Girls Incorporated. (1996). *Prevention and parity: Girls in juvenile justice.* Washington, DC: Office of Juvenile Justice and Delinquency Prevention.

Gilbert, E. (1999). Crime, sex, and justice: African American women in U.S. prisons. In S. Cook and S. Davies (Eds.), *Harsh Punishment: International Experiences of Women's Imprisonment* (pp. 230–249). Boston, MA: Northeastern University Press.

Greene, Peters, & Associates. (1997). *Guiding principles for promising female programming: An Inventory of best practices.* Nashville, TN: Office of Juvenile Justice and Delinquency Prevention.

Holsinger, K. (2000). Feminist perspectives on female offending: Examining real girls' lives. *Women and Criminal Justice, 12,* 23–51.

Horowitz, R., & Pottieger, A. E. (1991). Gender bias in juvenile justice handling of seriously crime involved youths. *Journal of Research in Crime and Delinquency, 28,* 75–100.

Hoyt, S., & Scherer, D. (1998). Female juvenile delinquency: Misunderstood by juvenile justice system, neglected by social science. *Law and Human Behavior, 22,* 81–107.

Hunt, G., MacKenzie, K., & Joe-Laidler, K. (2000). "I'm calling my mom": The meaning of family and kinship among homegirls. *Justice Quarterly, 17,* 1–31.

Joe, K. A., & Chesney-Lind, M. (1995). "Just every mother's angel": An analysis of gender and ethnic variations in youth gang membership. *Gender & Society, 9,* 408–430.

Johnson, D. R., & Scheuble, L. K. (1991). Gender bias in the disposition of juvenile court referrals: The effect of time and location. *Criminology, 29,* 677–699.

Kempf-Leonard, K., & Sample, L. (2000). Disparity based on sex: Is gender-specific treatment warranted? *Justice Quarterly, 7,* 89–128.

Kunzel, R. (1993). *Fallen woman, problem girls: Unmarried mothers and the professionalization of social work.* London: Yale University Press.

Lindgren, S. J. (1996). Gender specific programming for female adolescents. Unpublished Master's Thesis. Minneapolis, MN: Augsburg College.

Levene, K. (1997). The Earlcourt girls connection: A model intervention. *Canada's Children, 4,* 14–17.

Lofland, J., & Lofland, L. (1995). *Analyzing social settings: A guide to qualitative observations and analysis.* Belmont, CA: Wadsworth.

MacDonald, J., & Chesney-Lind, M. (2001). Gender bias and juvenile justice revisited: A multiyear analysis. *Crime & Delinquency, 47,* 173–195.

Mann, C. R., & Zatz, M. S. (Eds.). (2002). *Images of color, images of crime.* Los Angeles: Roxbury Publishing.

Martin, S., & Jurik, N. S. (1996). *Doing justice, doing gender.* Thousand Oaks, CA: Sage Publications.

Mauer, M., & Huling, T. (1995). *Young black Americans and the criminal justice system.* Washington, DC: The Sentencing Project.

McCormack, A., Janus, M., & Burgess, A. W. (1986). Runaway youth and sexual victimization: Gender differences in an adolescent runaway population. *Child Abuse and Neglect, 10,* 387–395.

Messerschmidt, J. W. (1997). *Crime as structured action: Gender, race, class, and crime in the making.* Thousand Oaks, CA: Sage Publications.

Miller, J. (1996). An examination of disposition decision making for delinquent girls. In M. D. Schwartz and D. Milovanovic (Eds.), *Race, gender, and class in criminology: The intersection* (pp. 219–245). New York: Garland Publishing.

578   CRIERS, LIARS, AND MANIPULATORS

Miller, J. (1998). Up it up: Gender and the accomplishment of street robbery. *Criminology, 36,* 37–65.

Morrison, T. (Ed.). (1992). *Race-ing justice, en-gendering power: Essays on Anita Hill, Clarence Thomas, and the construction of social reality.* New York: Pantheon Books.

Odem, M. E. (1995). *Delinquent daughters: Protecting and policing adolescent female sexuality in United States.* Chapel Hill: University of North Carolina Press.

Orenstein, P. (1994). *Schoolgirls.* New York: Doubleday.

Owen, B., & Bloom, B. (1998). *Modeling gender specific services in juvenile justice: Policy and program recommendations.* Final Report submitted to the Office of Criminal Justice Planning of the State of California.

Portillos, E. L. (1999). Women, men and gangs: The social construction of gender in the barrio. In M. Chesney-Lind and J. Hagedorn (Eds.), *Female gangs in America: Essays on girls, gangs, and gender* (pp. 232–244). Chicago: Lake View Press.

Rhodes, J. E., & Fischer, K. (1993). Spanning the gender gap: Gender differences in delinquency among inner city adolescents. *Adolescence, 28,* 879–889.

Rosenbaum, J., & Chesney-Lind, M. (1994). Appearance and delinquency: A research note. *Crime & Delinquency, 40,* 250–61.

Rice, M. (1990). Challenging orthodoxies in feminist theory: a black feminist critique. In L. Gelsthorpe and A. Morris (Eds.), *Feminist Perspectives in Criminology* (pp. 57–69) Bristol, PA: Open University Press.

Rubin, L. (1976). *Worlds of pain: Life in the working class family.* New York: Basic Books.

Sarri, R. (1983). Gender issues in juvenile justice. *Crime & Delinquency, 29,* 381–397.

Taylor, D. L., Biafora, F. A., Warheit, G., & Gail, E. (1997). Family factors, theft, vandalism, and major deviance among a multiracial multiethnic sample of adolescent girls. *Journal of Social Distress and the Homeless, 6,* 71–87.

Taylor, J., Gilligan, C., & Sullivan, A. (1995). *Between voice and silence: Women and girls, race and relationship.* Cambridge, MA: Harvard University Press.

Triplett, R., & Myers, L. B. (1995). Evaluating contextual patterns of delinquency: Gender-based differences. *Justice Quarterly, 12,* 58–84.

United States Census Bureau. (2000). Summary File 3. [Online]. Available: http://www2.census.gov/census_2000/datasets/Summary_File_3/Arizona/

Visher, C. (1983). Gender, police arrest decisions, and notions of chivalry. *Criminology, 21,* 5–28.

West, C., & Zimmerman, D. (1987). Doing gender. *Gender and Society, 9,* 8–37.

Wyatt, G. E., Newcomb, M. D., & Riederle, M. H. (1993). *Sexual abuse and consensual sex: Women's developmental patterns and outcomes.* Newbury Park, CA: Sage Publications.

Young, V. D. (1986). Gender expectations and their impact on black female offenders and victims. *Justice Quarterly, 3,* 305–326.

Zatz, M. S. (2000). Convergence of race, ethnicity, gender, and class on court decision making: Looking toward the 21st century. In J. Horney (Ed.), *Policies processes, and decisions of the criminal justice system* (pp. 503–552). Washington, DC: U.S. Department of Justice, Office of Justice Programs, National Institute of Justice.

[17]

The Words Change,
But the Melody Lingers

The Persistence of the Battered Woman Syndrome
in Criminal Cases Involving Battered Women

KATHLEEN J. FERRARO

Arizona State University

Acceptance of expert testimony on the battered woman syndrome in criminal and civil cases has established expectations about "real" battered women that reinforce conventional notions of femininity. Despite well-documented and publicized analyses of the status of the syndrome as no longer reflecting the range of knowledge relevant to battered women in legal settings, the expectations of helplessness promoted by the syndrome persist. In this article, specific cases are discussed in which the characteristics described in the syndrome are contrasted with the assertiveness, strength, and strategic decision making expressed by female defendants who had been battered. The negative consequences of the persistence of the battered woman syndrome in court are also described.

Is it so difficult to understand why battered women fear for their lives without relying on a dubious psychological malady? Apparently it is. Despite the clarity of arguments rejecting the use of the term "battered woman syndrome" in favor of testimony describing the full range of social, institutional, relational, and psychological impacts of battering, judges, attorneys, and juries continue to rely on a mythical stereotype that constricts perceptions of what "real" battered women look like. The persistence of the battered woman syndrome construct is consistent with dominant paradigms for viewing violence against women as individualistic pathology. The comfortable conviction that severe battering is committed by "sick" men against women who are psycho-

AUTHOR'S NOTE: The author wishes to acknowledge the helpful comments of the anonymous reviewers of *Violence Against Women*, the women who shared their stories, and the defense attorneys who assisted in these cases.

logically impaired ignores the pervasive normalized violence against women and the institutionalized barriers to escaping intimate violence. The use of expert testimony to educate judges and juries about the effects of battering must continually work against this paradigm to be effective and to promote social change rather than stasis.

I have assisted in 72 criminal and civil cases as an expert witness on the effects of battering, beginning in 1983. I have conducted training on the effects of battering for probation officers, law enforcement, the Arizona Bar Association, the Arizona Association of Criminal Attorneys, and the Arizona Board of Executive Clemency. This article draws on my experiences, as well as my observation of four clemency hearings in Arizona, and interaction with legislators. Although I originally used the language of syndrome in my own testimony in accordance with the literature of the time, since 1995 I have described my testimony and expertise as being about "the effects of battering," as suggested in the literature and by the National Clearinghouse for the Defense of Battered Women.[1] I have not been very successful in getting defense attorneys, prosecutors, judges, and legislators to move away from the battered woman syndrome construct. Many of these people continue to hold a very narrow view of "real" battered women due to their continued reliance on this construct. As a result, battered women who fail to meet the standard of "the syndrome" have ended up serving long prison sentences, have been unable to receive compensation for injuries they sustained, and have lost custody of their children.

BACKGROUND OF
THE BATTERED WOMAN SYNDROME

The introduction of expert testimony on the battered woman syndrome in the early 1980s was an important intervention in masculinist legal culture. Laws on homicide and assault reflect the experiences of men and have been written and interpreted to respond to male experiences (MacKinnon, 1982; Smart, 1989). Laws defining justifiable homicide, or self-defense, are premised on the "reasonable man" standard; that is, homicide is justifiable if in the same circumstances a reasonable man would fear imminent death (Browne, 1987; Schneider, 2000). Expert testimony has been introduced to explain battered women's perceptions of danger that may, without explanation, seem very different from those of a reasonable man facing an assailant. First articulated by Lenore E. Walker (1979), the battered woman syndrome provided a mechanism for educating attorneys, judges, and juries about the ways in which the experience of battering impacts women's perceptions, reactions, and decisions. Originally, the syndrome was used in homicide cases in which women killed their abusers to expand on the reasonable man standard implicit in self-defense statutes and case law. It later was introduced by prosecutors to assist in prosecuting abusers and men who killed their partners and was offered in civil and domestic relations cases. It also was introduced by the defense in support of women who had committed crimes other than homicide that, like the homicide cases, were related to their battering. Testimony about battering and its effects was also introduced in various stages of the postconviction process, including in incarcerated battered women's clemency hearings. Over time, the battered woman syndrome gained both psychological and legal recognition as a scientifically valid basis for expert testimony and thus opened the doors for courts to become educated about the nature of battering and its relevance to civil and criminal decisions (see Dutton, 1996, for a review).

Although recognizing the potential benefits of expert testimony on the battered woman syndrome, a number of scholars and activists raised concerns about the broader implications of adopting "syndrome" language. Most important, the syndrome contributed to an image of battered women as psychologically defective or pathological and diverted attention from the rational and deliberate strategies of survival that women employ when they are in violent situations. Although meeting the legal standards for admissible expert testimony, the syndrome is not composed of specific psychological traits that are either unique to a battered woman or present in all battered women. Walker's ideas and research on the topic are contained in *The Battered Woman Syndrome* (1984) and developed in later articles by herself and others (Dutton, 1992; Walker, 1988, 1996). Walker has described the battered woman syndrome as including the following components: learned helplessness, effects of trauma, and self-destructive coping mechanisms. It is also related to Walker's three-phase cycle theory of violence that includes tension building, an acute battering incident, and a honeymoon phase. The cycle is described to explain why women do not have an unequivocal negative perception of their abusers because the so-called "honeymoon phase" contributes to a perception that violence is an aberration and the abuser is truly in love and deserves another chance.

The concept of learned helplessness, which is the most prominent component of the syndrome, was adapted from Seligman's experimental work with animals (Walker, 1984). It describes the results of repeated experiences of noncontingency that condition women to perceive that their actions have no relationship to their partner's violence. The theory proposes that because women's behavior is unrelated to their partner's battering, women learn to be helpless and thus do not perceive opportunities for escape in the same ways that a person who has not experienced this trauma might. The emphasis on learned helplessness in the battered woman syndrome model created a stereotype of passivity that obscures the reality of women's active strategies of help seeking and survival. Furthermore, because one of the uses of testimony about the syndrome in court is to explain women's behavior—including their criminal actions—it is often difficult to reconcile helplessness with women's actions, especially violent ones.

The characterization of battered women as helpless reinforces conventional notions of femininity. These notions have historically defined working women, lesbians, and women of color as "less feminine" (Collins, 1998, 2000; Moraga & Anzaldúa, 1983). The race and class distinctions that defined White, middle-class women as physically and emotionally fragile and dependent, and women of color as sturdy and capable, became entrenched in public policy during industrialization and continue to influence social policy (Mink, 1998). These distinctions are prominent within legal decision making in terms of responses to women's offending and victimization (Arnold, 1995). The stigma attached to women of color within the criminal justice system is demonstrated in the disparity in incarceration rates between African American and European American women, with African American women having a six times greater chance of incarceration (Richie, 1996, 2001). The historical exclusion of women of color, working women, and lesbians from Eurocentric images of femininity as passive and helpless makes application of the battered woman syndrome (which reinforces notions of passivity and helplessness) less likely for marginalized women (Ammons, 1995). In the 19 years I have served as an expert witness on battering, only two African American women have been referred to me by their defense counsel. Although I have not conducted research on this question, it seems possible that attorneys are less likely to view African American women clients as battered women than women from other racial and ethnic groups.

In addition to concerns about the exclusionary and pathologizing impact of the syndrome, by 1995, serious evaluation indicated "the term 'battered woman syndrome' is no longer useful or appropriate" (Dutton, 1996, p. 4). The U.S. Department of Justice (DOJ) and U.S. Department of Health and Human Services (USDHHS) issued a three-part report in 1996 as part of the mandate of the 1994 Violence Against Women Act (DOJ, National Institute of Justice [NIJ], USDHHS, & National Institute of Mental Health [NIMH], 1996). Experts on the psychological and legal aspects of battering evaluated the scientific evidence and legal history of the battered woman syndrome in terms of medical and psychological testimony, as well as state, tribal, and federal court cases, and conducted an assessment of the effects of evidence of battered woman syndrome. The report affirmed the scientific validity of research outlining the effects of battering on women: "Expert testimony on battering and its effects can be based on and supported by an extensive body of scientific and clinical knowledge on the dynamics of domestic violence and traumatic stress reactions" (Dutton, 1996, p. 4). At the same time, the authors reject the use of "the battered woman syndrome" and suggest the substitution of "battering and its effects" to refer to proffered expert testimony. The contributors to the report argued that the notion of a "syndrome" focuses on psychological deficits rather than the full "range of issues on the nature and dynamics of battering, the effects of violence, battered women's responses to violence, and the social and psychological context in which domestic violence occurs" (Dutton, 1996, p. 13). The report is clear and articulate about the many problems associated with the use of the term "battered woman syndrome," and it is available on the Internet and through the DOJ.[2]

Despite the clarity of the report's recommendations, the prevailing imagery of the battered woman syndrome has proved resistant to change, both in terms of explicit language and the expectations of women who are victims of battering. Moving the discourse forward to embrace the full range of information included in testimony or discussion about "battering and its effects" has been difficult due in part to the persistence—and occasional utility—of the imagery of the passive, helpless, "good" battered woman elicited by the use of "battered woman syndrome." For those few battered women who do fit the syndrome stereotype, testimony about battered woman syndrome can be very helpful to support their claim or action. However, because most battered women are not passive or helpless and may have done things that make them appear less than "good," information about these stereotypes is most frequently used against them, instead of in support of them. Syndrome-based testimony is often introduced to show what a "real" battered woman is like and then it is used to show how this particular woman differs (often dramatically) from this mythic "real" battered woman. Syndrome testimony is often used by the other side in a case to help "prove" that the particular woman could not be a battered woman. Below, I will examine cases in which evidence of battering was introduced for defense, prosecution, and clemency purposes. Through these examples, I will identify the basis for the persistence of the syndrome imagery as well as the damage to women it has wrought.

"SHE CAN STAND UP FOR HERSELF"

The concept of learned helplessness was intended to describe the perceptions of abused women specifically with regard to their abusive situations. It was never intended as a global descriptor of women's complete helplessness to take care of themselves and their children. Nevertheless, the incorporation of learned helplessness as part of the battered woman syndrome did establish a perception that assertiveness, strength, and an outgoing personality were inconsistent with being a battered woman. In the cases in Arizona in which evidence of the effects of battering have been introduced as part of a woman's legal defense, the prosecution has routinely invoked testimony regarding women's strength as counter-evidence of battering.

In a case in Yavapai County, Arizona, I provided expert testimony on battering to assist the defense in establishing a self-defense claim by a woman who had killed her abusive husband. The prosecutor in the case tried to portray Dianne (pseudonym), a White, working-class woman with no children, as a tough woman who could defend herself physically and as an "outrageous flirt," who did not fit the so-called typical image of a battered woman.[3] In the depositions she conducted with me and other witnesses, the prosecutor tried to elicit testimony that would counter the "syndrome" image of battered women as always being meek and outwardly passive. For example, one witness who had known both Dianne and her deceased husband, James, described how James berated Dianne for her clothing and called her a whore. The prosecutor tried to direct the witness, but he would not agree with her view.

> **Prosecutor:** Can I ask you something? When he would do that with her and be verbally abusive with her, what would she do?
> **Witness:** [She would say] "Oh, James, you're full of shit, you don't know what you're talking about." You know, Dianne was really calm. You know, Dianne would be calm until he smacked her and then she'd smack him back. I never seen her do anything to him, you know, it was always him doing it to her, and then she would fight back.
> **Prosecutor:** She could probably hold her own, though.
> **Witness:** Well, she tried. No, not, well, I don't think she could hold her own, but she was pretty tough, she's a pretty tough girl, you know.
> **Prosecutor:** Strong, physically strong.
> **Witness:** Yeah, well, she's got courage. She's got a heart, you know, she would try ... up to a point, you know, and then he'd overpower her. Was all you could see, you know, was two black eyes and a bloody lip, you know, her arms out of whack or, you know, she's got gravel up her back. (Unpublished deposition, 1994, p. 7, on file with author)

The witness acknowledged that Dianne had "courage" and "heart" and that she was "tough," and the prosecutor tried to use these characteristics as evidence that she was a woman who could defend herself and could not possibly be battered. Prosecutorial interviews with witnesses are often quite intimidating, especially for people who have no prior experience with the legal system. This witness, however, refused to construct Dianne's violence as equal to her husband's or to acquiesce to the prosecutor's view of

Dianne as able to "hold her own." His firsthand knowledge of the relationship allowed him to recognize that Dianne was simultaneously tough and battered, but the prosecutor worked to portray these two qualities as incompatible.

In the prosecutor's deposition of me, she built a hypothetical scenario and asked me if women whose husbands were pathologically jealous typically engaged in flirtatious conduct.

> Let me ask you this: Built into that scenario, is it also typical for the woman knowing that her husband, her mate, tends to be jealous, to go out and flirt absolutely outrageously with everyone in sight when they're in a social situation? Cause we have a lot of testimony that she did that, too. (Unpublished deposition, 1994, p. 16, on file with author)

The prosecution used statements from the victim's family that she was an "outrageous flirt" and from friends that she was "friendly and outgoing" to argue that Dianne could not have been a battered woman. Dianne took a plea of manslaughter and evidence on the effects of battering was introduced at sentencing for mitigation purposes. Dianne was sentenced to the few months she had already spent in jail and intensive probation. Given that Dianne was facing second-degree murder charges, it appears that the testimony about battering was helpful to the judge in his decision about Dianne's sentence. However, I believe this woman had an excellent self-defense claim. I believe that with proper evaluation and assessment, these charges against her could have even been dismissed. However, in this case, the prosecution was eager to exploit myths and misconceptions about battered women to help "prove" that this defendant was not a battered woman and therefore did not act in self-defense. These techniques of trying to show during a trial that the defendant is tough and assertive as "proof" that she is not battered are often very effective in eroding the defendant's overall credibility and lessening jurors' willingness to even try to understand the defendant's behavior and state of mind (fear) based on her experiences of being battered.

Another woman, Leah, was similarly portrayed by the prosecution as being too tough to be a real battered woman. Leah is an American Indian (Tohono O'odham), low-income woman with four children, who was battered for 10 years by her husband. The prosecution portrayed her as a violent woman because she carried a knife in her boot and admitted to once slapping her friend when she learned she was having an affair with her husband and had given birth to his child. Numerous witnesses, including police officers, testified to the extreme levels of physical violence committed against Leah by her husband over a period of many years. Leah had medical records of her injuries, and her husband had been incarcerated for his abuse.

On the day of his death, Leah's husband ran at her with outstretched arms. Leah believed he was going to attack her, picked up a gun to try to ward off his attack, and shot him. The prosecution argued that the shooting was committed out of jealousy and that Leah was a tough and violent woman who would not be intimidated by her abuser. A psychologist who never met her testified at the trial that Leah did not fit the profile of a battered woman. Although evaluating a person without speaking to her is an unethical practice in itself, the psychologist relied on reports of Leah's jealousy and minor acts of violence to argue that she could not have been battered. Leah was convicted in 1992 of second-degree murder in the shooting death of her husband and sentenced to 9 years in a federal prison. In handing down his sentence, the judge said he saw no evidence of fear, only anger and jealousy.

Danielle is a middle-class, White woman with three children. Her case was not a traditional self-defense case, as her estranged husband was robbed and killed by a third party at a separate residence. The state's theory was that Danielle hired the person to kill her husband. As indicated by Parrish (1996, p. 14), use of expert testimony on battering for third-party homicide cases has been accepted in 20% of states, and only four states have refused testimony in murder for hire cases. Considerable evidence validated Danielle's claims of battering, including hospital records and a marriage counselor who witnessed bruises and her husband's admission of battering. Despite this evidence, the prosecution drew on evidence that Danielle was assertive and independent to undermine testimony on battering and its effects.

Danielle's husband was a person who enjoyed giving the appearance of wealth. He was renting a very expensive home, drove a luxury car, and wore designer clothing and jewelry. After his death, Danielle discovered that he was massively in debt and owned none of his property. He was killed by an acquaintance of

Danielle's who boasted to several girlfriends that he was about to come into a large amount of money. He stole a Rolex watch from Danielle's husband after he killed him, which was not only the evidence that connected him with the homicide but also the basis for charges of armed robbery and burglary. There was no evidence that Danielle offered him anything in exchange for the killing of her husband, but tapes made of conversations she had with an undercover police officer suggested she had colluded with the killer.

As the expert witness in this case, I did not use "syndrome" language at any point. I emphasized Danielle's fear of physical and sexual abuse as well as her husband's threats to take their three children out of the country. I also emphasized the economic constraints she faced as a high school dropout working at a minimum wage job and the bond she felt to her husband that inhibited her from testifying about his abuse even as she was on trial for her life. Her coworkers and her supervisor were called on to testify that Danielle "stood up" to aggressive customers and did not allow rude people to walk all over her. This, the prosecution argued, was evidence that she was not a battered woman. Those familiar with the effects of battering understand that fear of a batterer does not translate into a global inability to assert one's rights and opinions in any situation. The syndrome's emphasis on "learned helplessness" establishes an expectation of total docility, which is inconsistent with most women's efforts to maintain employment and maternal roles that require assertive decision making and action.

Evidence of Danielle's assertiveness combined with an affair she had while married were used to convince the jury that she was not battered but was a wily manipulator who was feigning battering to avoid the death penalty that the county attorney originally sought. After one hung jury, Danielle was convicted of first-degree armed robbery, burglary, and conspiracy to commit murder in the first degree and sentenced to 25 years in prison. Again, although the effects of battering were taken into consideration, that was not sufficient to argue successfully for self-defense.

Evidence of "standing up for herself" has also been used to discredit evidence of battering in cases in which women have been murdered and their abusers stand trial. In the case of State of Arizona v. Dale Dozier (*State v. Dozier*, 1996), the defense argued that the victim, Heidi Dozier, could not have been a battered woman because she publicly stood up to a group of miners.[4] The small, rural community of Clifton-Morenci depends primarily on copper mining, and Dozier worked in one of the mines. He was an alcoholic and drug addict who obtained drugs from coworkers. His violence escalated when he was using drugs, so Heidi went to the mine one morning and threatened the coworkers who supplied them. This assertive act was used as evidence by Dozier's defense attorney that she could not be a battered woman, as battered women are incapable of standing up for themselves. Dozier shot Heidi in the face as she crawled through the window of their home to retrieve her belongings. He was sitting, waiting for her, with a loaded gun. At his trial, Dale Dozier argued self-defense saying that he didn't recognize his wife and thought someone was breaking into his house. He was convicted of manslaughter and sentenced to 12 years.

WOMEN'S SEXUALITY AND
THE BATTERED WOMAN SYNDROME

The conception of femininity promoted by the battered woman syndrome not only excludes assertive, outgoing, strong, competent women, it also reinforces a notion of female sexual passivity and the conventional sexual double standard that accepts male sexual infidelity as natural and female extramarital sex as evidence of aggression. Sexual abuse accompanies physical battering in at least 40% of abusive relationships, and many women lose sexual attraction to their partners as the sexual, physical, and emotional battering progresses (Campbell, 1989; Shields & Hanneke, 1983). It is not unusual, therefore, to turn to other people for the emotional support and physical gratification that a positive sexual relationship can provide. Women who kill their abusive partners, however, are often held to a standard of sexual conduct that condemns extramarital relationships or nonexclusive sexual relationships. The battered woman syndrome's emphasis on helplessness counters the agency implied in establishing a sexual relationship with another person. From the prosecutor's perspective, such relationships demonstrate that the woman was not truly afraid of her partner's violence or she would not risk the rage such a relationship would engender. In these types of cases, even if not directly argued, I have seen prosecutors insinuate that not only was the killing not done in self-defense, but it was planned in order to "eliminate a barrier" to a new relationship. Even when a woman's deceased, abusive partner was involved in multiple sexual affairs or when the allegations of infidelity rely on unverified sources, the invocation of a woman's sexual infidelity usually raises doubts about the veracity of her claims of being battered.

In Danielle's case discussed previously, the prosecutor focused on her sexual affair with a young man and her coworkers' perceptions of her assertiveness as counter-evidence of the effects of battering. When the prosecution questioned me concerning my knowledge of the affair, he projected a photograph of an 18-year-old African American man to emphasize both the age and racial difference between Danielle and her lover. There was no apparent reason for me or the jury to know what this young man looked like, and no photographs of her deceased husband or the man who killed him were presented. The photograph appeared to be employed to incite a negative reaction toward Danielle from the jury. Although her husband had multiple sexual affairs with young women and was alleged to have been engaged in the business of prostitution and exotic dance clubs, Danielle's brief and passionate affair with a young African American man was repeatedly invoked as evidence of her immorality and lack of fear of her husband. The prosecutor wanted the jury to wonder why Danielle would engage in this affair if she were truly afraid of her husband. The affair was also used to try to establish a motive other than fear for the homicide. The prosecution argued that Danielle and her boyfriend wanted her husband out of the way so they could pursue their relationship. This was the only affair Danielle had in 18 years of an abusive marriage to a man she met at 16, and it caused her to feel enormous shame. It was the first time a man had treated her with respect and kindness, and the emotional support she obtained from him helped her to realize that relationships could be better than the one she shared with her husband. This relationship, as well as her feelings and realizations, did not change the fact that she was battered and intensely fearful of her husband, who she believed would never agree to a divorce and who had threatened to leave the country with their children. Yet I believe that information about this affair helped make the jury less willing to believe that Danielle acted in self-defense and helped to convince them that she was guilty of first-degree murder.

Eve, a low-income White woman with two children, was charged with conspiracy to commit first-degree murder when her husband's friend killed him with an ax and left him in the bathtub for 3 days before burying him. Even though Eve did not know about the killing until after the fact, she was charged with conspiring to commit the murder due in part to her failure to call the police immediately after the homicide. The man who committed the homicide, Andrew, reported the crime when he became concerned that Eve had informed a neighbor. In his account, Eve had asked him to commit the murder. Eve had urged her husband to end his friendship with Andrew, as he was a heavy drug user and Eve was trying to help her husband stay away from drugs. She also felt uncomfortable around Andrew because he stared at her and followed her around the apartment complex. A few days before the homicide, Andrew raped Eve while her husband slept in another room. The newspapers and the prosecutor defined the rape as an "affair" and refused to believe Eve's account and her fear. Andrew killed her husband while Eve was at the park with her children. When she returned, he pulled her into the bathroom, slammed her against the wall, and showed her the body in the bathtub. He told her that if she let anyone know what happened, he would kill her and her children and bury them in the desert where they would never be found. She believed him, and as he never let her out of his sight, she did not try to call the police. She did try to ask a male neighbor for help and that is when Andrew went to the police. Andrew and the police accused Eve of having sex with the neighbor, which she denies. No one believed that she had been battered by her husband, but they did believe that she had an affair with the man who killed her husband with an ax. Andrew was released when the prosecutor found a lack of evidence to support a case against him. Eve was arrested, accepted a plea to manslaughter, and was sentenced to 11 years.

Terry, a White, middle-class woman with two children, left her nonviolent husband to live with a very violent man, Tom, who shared her addiction to crystal methamphetamine. Tom was charged with the murder of two men on two separate occasions. Terry was present during both murders and did not report them to the police, and she was also charged with two counts of first-degree murder. Although the state originally asked for the death penalty for both Terry and Tom, they eventually offered Terry a plea bargain for second-degree murder based on the mitigating factor of battering. After 6 years in jail waiting for her codefendant to go to trial, she was sentenced to 22 years, with credit for the 6 years she had served. Tom has been sentenced to death.

Terry was sexually abused by a series of male relatives from the time she was about 3 years old. Her older sister confirmed Terry's stories of multiple abusers within their family. Although Terry managed to attend college, marry, have children, and hold down a good job, she became addicted to crystal as an adult and was caught shoplifting. Her drug usage and shoplifting were her only crimes prior to the homicides. Tom was an extremely violent person who controlled a small group of people who spent time at their remote ranch. He shot at Terry, killed her cat with a knife, and promised he would rip her heart out if she told police about his first homicide. Once Terry was charged, however, two witnesses reported that she was sexually gratified by watching violence, although one later recanted this statement in writing. One young man reported that Tom had beaten him while Terry watched and laughed and appeared to be "having an orgasm." Terry denies any erotic arousal from violence and explains this testimony as a misperception of her tendency to laugh when she is under extreme stress. Although both witnesses are known addicts and one recanted her statement, their comments about Terry's sadistic pleasures contributed to the prosecutor's view of her participation in the second homicide.

The second homicide, committed 1 month after the first, was of a man who propositioned Terry at a gas station. When she told Tom what had happened, believing he would find out she was talking to another man and punish her, he ordered her to page the man and invite him to her home to "party." Terry did as she was told, and after he arrived, Tom beat him to death over a period of hours while keeping him locked in an oven-like car trunk between beatings. After the death, Tom, acting alone, took the body to the desert, where it was decapitated and the teeth removed. Although Terry did not actively participate in either crime, her presence, failure to report, and "enticement" of the second victim to the scene of his gruesome death established the foundation for felony murder, kidnapping, and burglary charges. The judge and prosecutor believed she was battered but also argued that her sexual conduct showed evidence of complicity and enjoyment of the violence committed in her presence. In handing down her sentence, the judge stated that battering had been considered in dropping the death penalty, but she did not impose the minimum sentence due to the gravity of the offenses and Terry's failure to act to protect an innocent man from what she knew was Tom's lethal potential.

Although evidence of battering assisted in obtaining mitigated sentences in these cases, the ways in which women's character traits and actions were used to contrast with so-called "typical" battered women reflects the ways in which the helplessness and passivity associated with the syndrome continue to influence court decision making and prosecutorial and defense approaches to cases involving battered women.

THE IMPORTANCE OF LANGUAGE

In discussions with attorneys and policy makers, my critique of syndrome language is usually met with irritated comments about "semantics." My personal experience in Arizona has been that many of the people who want to assist battered women charged with crimes are unimpressed with arguments about the problems associated with using the term "battered woman syndrome." This has been the case particularly with legislators and attorneys working on clemency for incarcerated battered women who argue it is impossible for people to understand the effects of battering without reference to a syndrome. It is possible that the responses to the women's crimes described above would have occurred regardless of the language used to describe battering and its effects over the past 20-plus years. It is also true that in a small number of cases, expert testimony that a woman is suffering from the battered woman syndrome has benefited that individual woman in the level of charges brought, type of sentencing, or in clemency decisions. However, a social action should not be evaluated only by its immediate impact but also by the larger effect it has on social relations and perceptions of social issues.

For many years, mainstream social science relied on a transparent view of language as simply describing a phenomenon that existed external to the observer and prior to investigation. From this perspective, there was a clear, objective social reality that could be defined, measured, and explained through rigorous application of the scientific method. The knowledge produced through scientific research accurately described social conditions and provided a basis for sound social policy. Although there was never unanimous acceptance of this view of social science in the United States, it dominated a great deal of federally funded research through the 1960s and was particularly influential in psychology, the field in which the battered woman syndrome was "discovered."

By the turn of the millennium, however, there were few social scientists who maintained that language is a mere tool for describing the social reality that awaits discovery. The influence of many schools of social thought (e.g., phenomenology, symbolic interactionism, critical theory, feminism, and poststructuralism) has forced recognition of the constitutive role of language in creating, maintaining, and changing social relations. It is widely recognized that language does not merely reflect "reality" but is the primary mechanism through which social realities are constructed.

Development of the discourse describing various forms of violence against women over the past 20 years has advanced theoretical and empirical understanding and formed the basis for laws and social policies. "Sexual harassment," for example, does not just describe a phenomenon. It allows women to construct meaning of the routine, demeaning behaviors they previously endured at work and school as disgusting but inevitable aspects of living in a sexist culture. It provides a tool for laws and policies and generates a specific, negative moral evaluation of a range of conduct, from hostile environments to quid pro quo sex. The language has changed the way people understand and respond to behaviors that have existed for a very long time.

The battered woman syndrome does not just describe a set of behaviors that develop in response to battering by an intimate partner. It creates a social understanding of the effects of battering that influences responses and establishes expectations. Because it is compatible with conventional notions of heterosexual femininity, it endorses those notions and establishes boundaries between "real" battered women and others who may be battered but are viewed unsympathetically by courts and juries because they violate these boundaries. Women who are strong, competent, aggressive, and sexually active do not correspond to the imagery connoted by "learned helplessness."

The language used to describe battering and its effects constructs social images of women and a general understanding of what happens to women who live with intimate violence. Scholars have documented the many ways in which women act rationally, with strength and courage, to survive intimate violence and protect their children and other family members. Yet the expectations in courtrooms when battered women kill or are charged with other crimes remain anchored to a pathological image of a passive, helpless victim who cannot hold a job, "stand up for herself," or enjoy sex. The persistence of the battered woman syndrome is not only a result of misrepresentations by scholars, activists, and expert witnesses but also of the ease with which a pathological view of battered victims coexists with dominant views of crime and family relationships. Its resilience reflects its consistency with these views and cannot easily be undermined through repudiation by individuals.

CONCLUSION

The analysis in this article represents my perspective as a scholar-activist within Arizona, a conservative state that is somewhat insulated from theoretical and policy advances emanating from more progressive environments. I have not participated as an expert witness on battering in other states or other countries, so I can make no claim to the generalizability of my account. For those for whom this experience with the battered woman syndrome is familiar, it is important to continue to educate our communities about the strength of women who endure violence within intimate relationships and the overwhelming barriers they experience in responding to violence. For many women, the perception that there is no escape from an abuser or no possibility of refusing his commands is not a psychological maladjustment but a realistic assessment. The advocacy and education we perform in our communities must continue to resist pressures to define battered women as sick, deviant, or deficient without discounting the impact of intimate violence. This is as true for work in shelters and other service programs as in the criminal justice system.

The persistence of the battered woman syndrome as a construct is connected to social processes that are not easily altered through the issuance of reports or the conduct of training sessions. The refusal to acknowledge the widespread prevalence of terrorism within families, the double-binds faced by women trying to maintain economic security for themselves and their families while escaping violent partners, and an increased emphasis on marriage preservation in federal legislation and welfare regulations create enormous barriers for women in violent relationships. At the same time, acceptance of an individual pathology model of battering, for both perpetrators and victims, is deeply ingrained in U.S. cultural processes. Individual behavior is considered the source of success and failure, and social change efforts have most often been aimed at the transformation of individuals rather than of social systems. These structural and cultural dynamics contribute to the persistence of the battered woman syndrome. Academic and advocacy work to change perceptions of the effects of battering must occur in tandem with efforts to transform the social, cultural, and economic processes that support the rampant violence against women.

NOTES

1. The National Clearinghouse for the Defense of Battered Women is a resource and advocacy center that provides information and support to battered women charged with crimes and to their defense teams (e.g., attorneys, battered women's advocates, expert witnesses). They can be reached at National Clearinghouse for the Defense of Battered Women, 125 S. 9th Street, Suite 302, Philadelphia, PA 19107; phone: 215-351-0010, fax: 215-351-0779.

2. Plain text versions of the report are available from http://www.ncjrs.org/txtfiles/batter.txt, and a PDF version is available from http://www.ncjrs.org/pdffiles/batter.pdf. Bound copies of the report can be ordered from the National Criminal Justice Reference Service at 1-800-851-3420 for $23 (request document no. NCJ160972).

3. Although the cases discussed are concluded and are a matter of public record, I have used pseudonyms for women and their partners to protect them from unnecessary publicity. In some cases, women have completed their sentences and are trying to build new lives, so publishing their names could have a negative impact on them and their families.

4. I have not disguised the name of this offender, an abuser who killed his wife when she tried to leave the marriage.

REFERENCES

Ammons, L. L. (1995). Mules, Madonnas, babies, bathwater, racial imagery and stereotypes: The African American woman and the battered woman syndrome. *Wisconsin Law Review, 5*, 1004-1080.

Arnold, R. A. (1995). Processes of victimization and criminalization of Black women. In B. R. Price & N. J. Sokoloff (Eds.), *The criminal justice system and women: Offenders, victims, and workers* (pp. 136-166). New York: McGraw-Hill.

Browne, A. (1987). *When battered women kill.* New York: Free Press.

Campbell, J. C. (1989). Women's responses to sexual abuse in intimate relationships. *Health Care for Women International, 8*, 335-347.

Collins, P. H. (1998). *Fighting words: Black women and the search for justice.* Minneapolis: University of Minnesota Press.

Collins, P. H. (2000). *Black feminist thought: Knowledge, consciousness, and the politics of empowerment* (2nd ed.). New York: Routledge.

DOJ, NIJ, USDHHS, & NIMH. (1996, May). *The validity and use of evidence concerning battering and its effects in criminal trials.* Washington, DC: Authors.

Dutton, M. A. (1992). *Empowering and healing the battered woman.* New York: Springer.

Dutton, M. A. (1996). Impact of evidence concerning battering and its effects in criminal trials involving battered women. In *The validity and use of evidence concerning battering and its effects in criminal trials* (section 1). Washington, DC: DOJ, NIJ, USDHHS, and NIMH. Retrieved from www.ncjrs.org/pdffiles/batter.pdf

MacKinnon, C. A. (1982). Feminism, Marxism, method, and the state: An agenda for theory. *Signs, 7*, 514-544.

Mink, G. (1998). *Welfare's end.* Ithaca, NY: Cornell University Press.

Moraga, C., & Anzaldúa, G. (Eds.). (1983). *This bridge called my back.* New York: Kitchen Table/Women of Color Press.

Parrish, J. (1996). Trend analysis: Expert testimony on battering and its effects in criminal cases. In *The validity and use of evidence concerning battering and its effects in criminal trials* (section 2). Washington, DC: DOJ, NIJ, USDHHS, and NIMH. Retrieved from www.ncjrs.org/pdffiles/batter.pdf

Richie, B. E. (1996). *Compelled to crime: The gender entrapment of battered Black women.* New York: Routledge.

Richie, B. E. (2001). Challenges incarcerated women face as they return to their communities: Findings from life history interviews. *Crime and Delinquency, 47*, 368-389.

Schneider, E. M. (2000). *Battered women and feminist lawmaking.* New Haven, CT: Yale University Press.

Shields, N. M., & Hanneke, C. R. (1983). Battered wives' reactions to marital rape. In D. Finkelhor, R. J. Gelles, G. T. Hotaling, & M. A. Straus (Eds.), *The dark side of families: Current family violence research* (pp. 131-148). Beverly Hills, CA: Sage.

Smart, C. (1989). *Feminism and the power of law.* London: Routledge.

State v. Dozier, CR-2913-A, Superior Court of Arizona, (Greenlee County 1996).

Walker, L. E. (1979). *The battered woman.* New York: Harper and Row.

Walker, L. E. (1984). *The battered woman syndrome.* New York: Springer.

Walker, L. E. (1988). The battered woman syndrome. In G. T. Hotaling & D. Finkelhor (Eds.), *Family abuse and its consequences: New directions in research* (pp. 139-148). Newbury Park, CA: Sage.

Walker, L. E. (1996). Assessment of abusive spousal relationships. In F. W. Kaslow (Ed.), *Handbook of relational diagnosis and dysfunctional family patterns* (pp. 338-356). New York: John Wiley.

Kathleen J. Ferraro is director and associate professor of women's studies at Arizona State University. She is the current coordinator of the board of directors of the Arizona Coalition Against Domestic Violence. She is writing a book on the relationship between intimate terrorism and women's criminality to be published by Northeastern University Press.

[18]

Moral agent or actuarial subject:

Risk and Canadian women's imprisonment

KELLY HANNAH-MOFFAT
Brock University, Ontario, Canada

Abstract _____

Few have examined the moral and political aspects of categories of risk, or the differential impact of actuarial risk claims on different populations. This analysis is intended to complement the growing body of literature analysing the implementation of actuarial or risk-based assessments of behaviours and situations in a variety of contexts. It examines wider claims of risk theorists in light of recent developments in Canadian women's imprisonment. Based on an analysis of a proposed model of risk assessment for Canadian women prisoners, I argue: that in practical instances of governing the concept of 'risk' is ambiguous, fractured and flexible; that actuarial techniques of assessing women prisoners' risks tend to redefine needs as risk factors; and that subjective disciplinary techniques of governing co-exist and interrelate with actuarial techniques of risk management.

Key Words _____

Canada • governmentality • prison • risk • theory • women

Morality is embedded in risk technologies and in systems of risk management. (Ericson and Haggerty, 1997: 123)

Neo-liberal rationalities and technologies which profess to measure and precisely define risk are quite obviously present in western penality. The manifestation of risk techniques is one of several characteristics of an increasingly technocratic and calculated system of governing. During the past five years a theoretical and practical debate about risk and risk management has surfaced in the governmentality and criminology literatures. The largely theoretical risk literature argues that a risk-based society is emerging and that the governance of individuals and populations increasingly relies on actuarial techniques of risk management (Simon, 1987, 1988; Castel, 1991; Defert, 1991; Ewald, 1991; Feeley and Simon, 1992, 1994; O'Malley, 1992; Simon and Feeley, 1995; Parton, 1996; Ericson and Haggerty, 1997; Pratt, 1997). The self described 'new penology literature' (Feeley and Simon, 1992, 1994; Simon and Feeley, 1995) addresses the specific issue of actuarial forms of power and risk-based technologies in correctional settings. The new penology framework of Feeley and Simon (1992, 1994) expands on the claims of earlier attempts by Bottoms (1983) and others (Peters, 1988; Tuck, 1991) to describe changes in the penal system by examining the growth of what Bottoms (1983) describes as 'managerialism' (Garland, 1995). These analyses argue that the evolution of a 'risk society' is reflected in penality. Crime and its management are presented as a problem of actuarial management (Simon and Feeley, 1995: 147–8). The new task of penology is managerial, not disciplinary and transformative (Cohen, 1985).

While several theoretically focused risk scholars have studied the dynamics of risk-oriented institutions and new management techniques (Simon, 1987, 1988, 1993, 1994; Castel, 1991; Defert, 1991; Ewald, 1991; O'Malley, 1992; Ericson and Haggerty, 1997), few have examined the moral and political aspects of categories of risk, or the differential impact of actuarial risk claims on different populations. The discussion of the emergent risk society has offered some valuable insights, but there are four areas in which further research is required. We need to examine: the moral and/or political components of actuarial techniques; the claim that actuarial techniques are more efficient and objective; the somewhat unquestioned assumption that in most settings actuarial forms of power have displaced or replaced alternative regimes; and finally, the presumption that risk governance acts uniformly across whole populations rather than differently according to gender, race and other variables. In short, in the literature describing this transformation there is, at best, limited recognition and acknowledgement of the subjective, moralistic and disciplinary capacity of actuarial techniques. Although a few researchers (Ericson and Haggerty, 1997) are beginning to investigate these concerns, further empirical studies are needed.

This article examines these issues in light of recent developments in Canadian women's imprisonment. Based on an analysis of a proposed model of risk assessment for Canadian women prisoners, it argues: that in practical instances of governing, the concept of 'risk' is gendered, ambiguous and flexible; that subjective disciplinary techniques of governing co-exist and interrelate with actuarial techniques of risk management; and that actuarial techniques of assessing women prisoners' risks tend to redefine needs as risk factors.

The Canadian correctional context

Over the past eight years, Canadian correctional officials have restructured federal women's imprisonment and created a new 'woman-centred model of punishment'.[1] The origin of this reform initiative can be traced to the 1990 report of the Task Force on Federally Sentenced Women *Creating Choices* (TFFSW, 1990). The context of this reform document is shaped by a long history of struggle and survival. Tragic conditions and overt discrimination in the Prison for Women (P4W), Canada's only federal institution for women serving a sentence of more than two years, has been a source of frustration for feminists, researchers, bureaucrats and advocates since P4W opened in 1934 (Berzins and Cooper, 1982; Adelberg and Currie, 1987, 1993; [Hannah-] Moffat, 1991; Shaw, 1991; Cooper, 1993). In March of 1989, the Government responded to these concerns by setting up a joint government and community (including advocates, academics, federally sentenced women, Aboriginal women's organizations and others) task force. Despite numerous reservations (Shaw, 1993; Hannah-Moffat, 1995, 1997), the Government and the community worked together to design a prototype for a woman-centred model of corrections. The recommendations of the Task Force on Federally Sentenced Women led to the opening of five new regional prisons for women across Canada[2] reportedly committed to the development and implementation of the woman-centred philosophy outlined in their report *Creating Choices*.

Creating Choices stressed the need for reform strategies that recognize the differences between male and female offenders, reflect the social realities of women and respond to the individual needs of each woman. Correctional policy documents extended this principle of woman-centredness beyond programming to characterize the general approach to institutional planning for female offenders. Corrections Canada has (in theory) replaced the traditional male, static security-based approach to correctional programming and management with a more individualized, dynamic model of punishment that responds to the needs and risks represented by women (TFFSW, 1990: 91). However, the implementation of this model has been marred by exclusion, and by redefinitions of the meaning of woman-centred corrections and of the experiences and realities of the female offender (as outlined in *Creating Choices* and by feminist researchers and advocates). Some of the most significant of these changes include the definition, assessment and management of women's risk and needs in the new regional prisons.

Gendering risk: the female prisoner

The following analysis explores the claims made by risk theorists in light of proposed woman-centred methods of identifying and managing risk in Canadian women's prisons. As Simon (1987, 1988, 1994) acknowledges, our definitions and interpretations of what constitutes risk are contingent upon specific cultural, political and moral evaluations of behaviours and events. Criminology, and feminist criminology in particular, fails to examine the shifts in the governance of women prisoners from 20th-century welfare-based models of punishment and treatment to neo-liberal risk-based technologies. While risk theorists have quite accurately observed a wider shift in rationalities and technologies of government, in particular the emergence of actuarialism, they have not yet examined the micro-politics of government. Like Feeley and Simon (1992), I argue that actuarial, risk-based technologies are pervasive in contemporary penal discourses. What is less certain, however, is how this new focus on risk has influenced the patterns of penal governance in specific situations and how seemingly neutral actuarial categories like risk are shaped by wide factors like gender.

I argue that risk is gendered. When feminist criminologists discuss the issue of 'risk' in relation to the female offender they tend either to use 'anti-risk' language or to locate the source of risk exclusively in male behaviour. In the first instance, feminists argue that women prisoners are generally convicted of relatively minor, non-violent offences, and that when women are perpetrators of violence their victims are often abusive partners. Reformers and state officials have actually lobbied for improved prison conditions and additional community programming on the basis that women in prison *do not* represent a substantial risk to the safety of the public. In the second instance, feminist researchers and Task Force members argued that rather than presenting a risk to society in the traditional sense, women in prison are *at risk* of being victimized by men or of harming themselves through self-mutilation or self-abusive behaviours. Women in prison are portrayed as very similar to women in the community: it is argued that women in general often find themselves in 'risky situations' with few structural supports. Unlike the male prisoner, the woman prisoner is rarely constructed as a risk to the community: but like women in the community, she is often portrayed as being at risk of being victimized by men. Feminist criminologists and advocates emphasize the common links between the struggle for penal change and societal change without questioning the concept of risk. These themes are clearly outlined in the 1990 report of the Task Force *Creating Choices* (TFFSW, 1990).

When risk is discussed in women's corrections by feminist researchers, it is in the context of a critique of traditional gender neutral classification systems and methods of risk management which usually assumes that women prisoners are risky by virtue of their 'offender' status. In this instance, feminist researchers are mainly concerned about the use of classification criteria originally based on male correctional populations with female prisoners. Canadian women offenders, because of their small numbers and administrative convenience, have generally been managed with the same technologies used to govern incarcerated male populations.[3] Apart from a concern with the construction of women prisoners as a risk to the community, and a criticism of male-based classification systems as overstating the risk to the public presented by women prisoners, feminists have not yet analysed the concept of risk as it applies to women's penal regimes; nor have they provided a detailed critique of existing techniques for measuring risk, except to suggest that these measures do not adequately reflect the context of women's experiences and behaviours. Feminist critiques of the inadequacies of these measures for women offenders mean that claims about more efficient government need to be qualified. Past practices of governing women prisoners have not strictly relied on actuarial techniques of risk assessment and risk management and sophisticated risk calculations are *not* used with women prisoners. In fact, the assessment and management of women prisoners' risk is quite subjective and fluid. For example one feminist researcher states:

> risk classification is generally a very simple undertaking for female offenders: you can generally tell as soon as you get to know the inmate, and therefore [it] does not require a highly sophisticated classification system (which usually have poor predictive capacities in any case). (Axon, 1989: 72)

However, in keeping with the trends identified by Feeley and Simon (1992, 1994) in the new penology literature, Canadian correctional administrators are trying to create a more sophisticated woman-centred model of risk classification. Correctional researchers are engaged in the technocratic managerial practice of testing the reliability and validity of risk criteria for female offenders (see Hann and Harman, 1989; Coulson, 1993; Loucks and Zamble, 1994; Blanchette and Motiuk, 1995; Bonta et al., 1995; FSWP, 1995; Blanchette, 1996).

Woman-centred classification and the new federally sentenced women's facilities

On a practical level, there is a qualified acknowledgement of the gendered aspect of risk assessment and risk management. Over the past 10 years, the Correctional Service of Canada (CSC) has made several innovative changes in the management of federally sentenced women that have received a great deal of favourable international attention. These reforms, suggested in the report of the Task Force on Federally Sentenced Women (TFFSW, 1990), have attempted to restructure women's corrections by integrating a feminist analysis of the experiences and needs of federally sentenced women, while fulfilling the legal requirements of custodial facilities. One of the primary objectives of this initiative was to identify and respond to the gender-specific causes of women's crime. The technique of risk assessment plays a critical role in defining the correctional needs and experiences of federally sentenced women, and actuarial techniques have penetrated the managerial and operational realities of corrections. Canadian correctional researchers are still attempting to test traditional classification criteria and techniques for their validity on women prisoners (Hoffman, 1982; Coulson, 1993; Bonta et al., 1995). Reformers continue to favour the development of 'gender sensitive' assessment tools which they believe more adequately reflect the experiences of women and, in particular, violence in women's lives.

Taking into consideration the limitations of traditional risk classification systems and consistent with the emergent rhetoric of managerialism, the new regional facilities for federally sentenced women have developed a unique *security management model*. The risk classification system relied upon in the new prisons is based on the system used at Shakopee Woman's facility in Minnesota, the only purportedly woman-centred risk classification in operation. The Shakopee classification system is a behaviour-based system which outlines clearly articulated performance expectations and consequences. The system was designed to assign a security/risk classification (medium, minimum or maximum) to federally sentenced women (CSC, 1995: 3). This model differs from the established security classification levels which currently exist in federal institutions. Unlike the new women-centred *security management model*, past practices of classification did not incorporate a gender-specific understanding of women's risks and needs, and how their risks and needs are different from men's. The *security management system* uses a numeric management level in conjunction with conventional security levels. The prisoner is given a number between one (minimum) and five (maximum) which corresponds with a certain set of privileges and level of supervision. In the new security management model, levels four and five are maximum security, level three is medium security and levels one and two are minimum security. When a new prisoner arrives at the prison unclassified she is given an 'admission level status' which does not correspond to any particular security/risk classification (FSWP, 1995: 7). The initial process for designating a prisoner's management level occurs after 'all relevant information received upon the admission date is summarized and analysed by the team leader, the case management officer and the primary (correctional) worker' (p. 6). The reports and documents relied on include the results of the case management interview with the federally sentenced women, the security classification assessment, the observation reports on daily life in the housing unit, scholastic equivalency results and other information including any disciplinary reports (p. 6).

The security classification process is quite significant because it is 'used to record the analysis of all information leading to the recommendation for security classification and management level assignment' (FSWP, 1995: 9). The primary criteria used in the classification process are *institutional adjustment*, *escape risk* and *public safety* (figure 16).

The factors used to rate *institutional adjustment* include violent incidents, disciplinary convictions, continuation of criminal activity, administrative interventions, behaviour and programme participation. The category 'violent incidents' is operationalized according to the following criteria: degree of violence, personal life situation, victimization, role as a follower or a leader in incidents, the harm caused and the use of a weapon. The 'disciplinary conviction' is relatively straightforward: it refers to the pattern, nature and circumstances surrounding convictions for violations of institutional rules. The determination of continued criminal activity while in custody is dependent upon preventative security information which relies on the use of institutional informants, surveillance of mail, telephone calls and visits, as well as police information suggesting that the prisoner continues to be involved in criminal activity. 'Administrative intervention' refers to previous transfers, incompatibilities with other prisoners which may lead to a need for protection and patterns of disruptive behaviour. The institutional adjustment criteria refer to behaviour and programme participation. This section addresses:

> the ability [of the offender] to adapt to open living situations; effect on the good order of the institution; level of cooperation in addressing the criminogenic factors addressed in her correctional plan; consider positive results of current or previous programming; ability to deal with anger; level of participation in institutional work or personal development programs; consider mental health concerns, are they causing adjustment problems (e.g. non-compliance with medication etc.); physical health concerns causing adjustment problems; cultural identity indicating a requirement for special intervention on an ongoing basis; and any other special needs that should be considered (such as protection, suicidal tendencies, self-mutilation etc.). (p. 11)

Research has repeatedly indicated that many of the 'risk factors commonly used in classification can not be validated for female offenders because of the limited amount of cases which prevent sound statistical study' (p. 16). Nonetheless, the Correctional Service of Canada continues to use measures such as *offence history,* and *escape risk* in the 'woman sensitive' model of *security management* (FSWP, 1995).

The second set of criteria used to evaluate a woman prisoner's security classification is *escape risk*. Escape risk is measured through an evaluation of previous escapes or attempts to escape, sentence status and 'other concerns'. The measure for escape or attempted escape is evidence of an actual escape or attempt or of other 'breaches of trust', such as failure to respect a curfew at a community correctional centre, failure or late return from an unescorted temporary absence and failure to report to a parole officer or the police while on parole or statutory release. The sentence status is another variable believed to be indicative of escape risk: here the length of sentence, outstanding charges, possibility of deportation, pending appeals and time remaining prior to release are considered relevant to whether or not a prisoner will attempt an escape. The final category 'other concerns' is a residual category which is used to classify:

> any unusual circumstances having the potential to increase the FSW [federally sentenced woman's] escape risk (e.g. is she involved in a custody battle, is she concerned about the placement of her children, outstanding problems with spouse, gambling or drug debts, 'incompatibles' within the facility and her ability to adjust to open security). (p. 13)

The vagueness of this category permits criteria such as woman's concern for her children, which in most instances is a highly regarded and often encouraged maternal quality, to be construed as a potential escape risk factor. In some cases, a woman's concern about these areas, if she were a free citizen, would make her a responsible parent or partner. However, in this instance a woman's overt display of moral and parental responsibility can be used to her disadvantage.

The final criterion in the security classification schema is *public safety*, which is subdivided into four sections: violent incidents; programme participation; mental illness or disorder; and other public safety concerns. The first refers to the prisoner's involvement in violent incidents in the community, triggers of these events, the use of a weapon, degree of violence and harm caused and the offender's role. Second, programme participation considers the level and benefit derived from programme involvement, and the likelihood of the correctional plan having an effect on recidivism. Interestingly, these two criteria: violent incidents and programme participation, which are used as measures of institutional adjustment, reappear as measures of public safety. Even though the emphasis here is on the community context, there is a duplication, and consequently an over-emphasis on previous violence and/or non-compliance with institutional requirements. The section of the evaluation which considers mental illness or disorder considers all information relating to the therapeutic intervention, psychological and psychiatric assessments and compliance with therapeutic requirements, such as taking medication as required. The final residual category of 'other' incorporates the following information: third-party information about whether a prisoner will reoffend and the prisoner's level of need in 'primary need areas' (such as employment, family, social integration, associates, substance abuse, community functioning, attitude or personal emotional stability, *notoriety*—likely to evoke a negative public image, victim or police reaction).

Within each of these categories it is necessary to evaluate the seriousness, frequency and recency of each factor as well as any progress that the prisoner may have made to mitigate the concerns identified in each category. Once this evaluation has occurred a cumulative rating for each of the three areas is given: high, medium or low.

The proposed[4] woman-centred security management system is organized around several guiding principles. The primary aim of this technology is 'to enable FSW [federally sentenced women] to serve their sentence within the least restrictive possible environment [which reflects] their needs and the risks they present, while preparing them for release at the time considered most appropriate' (p. 4). In order to satisfy this requirement, the security management system 'recognizes the ability of FSW to accept responsibility for their actions, make informed choices on the basis of their needs, and thus, assume all consequences thereof' (p. 4). The principles outlined also suggest that the proposed technology is more than a process for the designation of a security classification. This new model is an essential component of a 'holistic' and personalized approach to women's corrections. At the heart of this model is the belief that 'participation in the programs aimed at meeting offenders' needs significantly reduces the risk they present', and that this technology be used to 'encourage and reinforce appropriate behaviour, as well as regular participation in programs, on the part of FSW by increasing their privileges as they progress' (p. 4). Another premise of the security management model is the expectation that staff will consistently and constantly revise the management level/security classification based on their perception of a prisoner's progress (or lack thereof).

Besides pointing to the responsibility of the offender to be accountable for her actions and make choices, this model, not surprisingly, suggests that there will be consequences for a woman prisoner's failure to meet institutional standards and take responsibility for minimizing her risk through the realization of her needs. Her progress is monitored and evaluated by correctional staff. Perhaps the most astonishing illusion is that the prisoner will accept her role in this regulatory process as 'an informed and committed participant' (p. 4).

In his 1994 article, Simon claims that one of the recent phenomena of modern forms of government is a shift in emphasis from 'choice and the responsibility for choice' to an emphasis 'on creating the condition for responsible choices'. There is some validity to this later construction of choice within the realm of women's corrections. Making choices, however, is as much a process of government as a practice of freedom. O'Malley claims that actuarial governing does not necessarily leave individuals free: it also includes strategies for the responsibilization of citizens. Risk management is, in many regards, the responsibility of the individual as well as of the authorities. O'Malley (1992: 261) labels this realignment of responsibility *prudentialism*, which he describes as 'a construct of governance which removes the key conception of regulating individuals by collective risk management, and throws back upon the individual the responsibility for managing risk'. Under a prudential mode of governing an individual is governed through the expectation that he/she will engage in activities of self-governance and avoid situations, behaviours and populations deemed 'risky'. Within this framework, prisoners are treated 'as if' they were free, rational and responsible individuals responsive to rewards and benefits (Garland, 1995).

The remainder of my analysis here uses the above risk assessment model to elaborate on some of the ambiguities of 'actuarial penality'.

Some ambiguities of risk technologies

> Determinations of risk straddle the distinction between objective and value
> dimensions. Moral standards are not asserted openly but in quantitative,
> theoretical, and causal forms. (Parton, 1996: 105)

The persistence of discipline and the return of subjectivity

The actuarial language of risk gives the impression of being objective,
calculable and scientific. Parton (1996: 105), drawing on Douglas (1986,
1992), argues that 'as notions of risk have become more central to politics
and public policy, its connection with technical calculations of probability
has weakened'. Contrary to the myth of actuarial penality, there does not
appear to be a sophisticated calculation used to generate determinations of
risk. The designation of a security/risk classification, which simply adds
ratings in three distinct categories, presents an interesting management
dilemma. Given that the implications for management are clearly different
for an offender with a high risk of escape versus an offender who is unable
to adjust to institutional living, the combination of these individual concerns into a singular classification raises questions about the usefulness of
these ratings in the management of individual problems. While there is an
attempt to adopt a 'personalized and holistic approach', the techniques
used to achieve this goal do not appear to satisfy this objective. Within this
new model there seems to be much confusion about the aim of the
classification process. This risk classification scheme is unable to differentiate between different types of risks and the severity of risk. The
cumulative risk score (management level) is based on the sum of several
independent assessments. The all-important details of these assessments are
obscured in this cumulative process. The management level assigned to an
inmate is therefore meaningless and the generic management of risk is not
particularly useful or efficient as an actuarial technique.

    In addition to this confusion, concerns about the accuracy, validity and
reliability of the categories and tools used to assess and predict risk remain.
For example, despite popular beliefs, some researchers argue that there is
little relationship between behaviour in prison and that outside (Shaw,
1991; Loucks, 1995). Margaret Shaw notes:

> there would appear to be no direct relationship between offending back-
> ground and risk of institutional disruption or violence. In fact, such
> disruption or violence may tell us more about the characteristics of the
> institution concerned than about the risk posed by the individuals involved
> in the disruption. (1991: 81)

Yet, risk classifications are generally contingent upon a prisoner's offence,
and her subsequent release is often predicated on her behaviour while
incarcerated. This inconsistency is overlooked by woman-centred classification models. The assumption that these behaviours are linked often ob-

scures other significant issues such as the relationship of the prison environment to the production and provocation of 'risky behaviours'.

Contrary to the claims of risk theorists (e.g. Castel, 1991), and to Feeley and Simon's (1992, 1994) new penology thesis, practical uses of risk technologies are not:

> depersonalised or concerned primarily about independent, abstract statistical categories and populations. One of the practices that demonstrates the limits of the 'new penology' is the fact that when actuarial tools are used, correctional officials frequently use 'overrides' to adjust risk assessment scores to what *they feel* is most appropriate. The use of overrides means that 'exceptions can be made to the initial classification instrument *when warranted*, both to increase and decrease the security classification. (FSWP, 1994a: 11, emphasis added)

The use of overrides poses a serious threat to objective classification systems and signals an unwillingness of staff fully to embrace actuarial systems. In the case of women prisoners, overrides are commonly used to compensate for the perceived deficiencies of many traditional methods of classification.[5] Clinicians using these tools for women from specific cultural groups (i.e. Aboriginal) frequently include disclaimers that indicate the results of risk assessments should be interpreted with caution because of the tool's cultural limitations.

As Kim Pate, Executive Director of the Canadian Elizabeth Fry Societies, noted:

> the systems that are set up to look as though they are objective tests of certain behaviours aren't taking into account, in our opinion, the subjective opinion that staff have in terms of incredible leeway to interpret behaviour as certain things. So, for instance, someone singing or calling out which may be seen from one person's perspective as objectively innocuous, may, from another person's perspective be seen as threatening. (Arbour Commission, Public Hearings, 1995: 696)

Another example of the limits of actuarialism and the persistence of subjective judgements is that one of the components of a criminal risk assessment is the case manager's 'own judgement of criminal history risk based on a thorough review of the offender's criminal record' (Motiuk, 1996: 22). The items typically used for an assessment of 'criminal history risk' are: offence severity; sexual offence history; number of convictions; previous offences; length of sentence; placement in institutional segregation; institutional misconduct; and mild, moderate or serious 'psychological harm'. But an offender's criminal record, police reports, pre-sentence reports and sentences are not objective representations of an offender: they are often the outcome of a series of legal and normative processes which are arguably quite subjective (Ericson and Baranek, 1982). The previously discussed woman-centred classification scheme includes categories such as institutional adjustment and programme participation, which have similar limitations. These practices do not appear to be closely aligned with the objective statistical technologies supposedly used in actuarial approaches to correctional management identified earlier by risk theorists.

Old-fashioned personal judgement by a correctional officer is by no means eliminated by actuarialism. We can also see that contrary to 'the new penology' thesis, moral regulation and disciplinary powers also persist. For example a correctional researcher claims that:

> the higher stability of the inmate's street life, the more likely she will abide by the prison rules and not escape. Thus, the inmate who has completed high school, held a fulltime job and been married is a better risk (Alexander, 1988 in FSWP, 1994a: 6).

This quotation illustrates the amalgamation of moral evaluations of behaviour and actuarial assessments of risk. The new regime at the Federally Sentenced Women's Facilities (prisons) makes two pivotal assumptions which result in what I call a hybrid moral/actuarial penality. First, implicit in the new *holistic* approach to women's corrections is developing techniques to manage an individual's moral character. This holistic emphasis is contrary to an actuarial management technique which is inclined to be concerned not with the whole person but instead with a specific category of risky behaviour. Second, there is also a tacit assumption that prisoners, in particular women, require a therapeutic intervention, and that these interventions will ultimately reduce recidivism. The managerial techniques used to reinforce these assumptions include processes for the identification of women's 'criminogenic needs' and risks, which involve the participation of the prisoner, but tend to rely on the opinions of correctional staff; the use of ongoing institutional monitoring and assessments of the prisoner's emotional stability, behaviour, adjustment to the institution and progress in programmes; and an institutional requirement to participate in therapeutic programmes.

Disciplinary elements are also evident in the four core programme areas outlined for the new Federally Sentenced Women's Facilities (prisons): *abuse and trauma*; *substance abuse*; *parenting skills*; and *vocational and educational training*. These programme areas are expected to address the needs of most women prisoners, thereby reducing their risk. Participation in these programmes and co-operation with therapeutic interventions can lower a person's security classification/management level, while a refusal to co-operate with this regime could result in an increased or at best unaltered security classification/management level. For example, in the *Program Strategy* for federally sentenced women, the Correctional Service of Canada notes: 'An offender's progress towards addressing specific needs and in reducing the level of risk serves as a major factor in the decision-making process, and its assessment is central to the management of the offender throughout the sentence' (CSC, 1996: 5). Programmes endeavour to teach the prisoner how to fit into categories associated with lower risk. Vocational and educational training in the *Literacy and Continuous Learning* programme encourages women to acquire the skills deemed 'essential to reintegrating FSW [federally sentenced women] as law-abiding citizens' (FSWP, 1994a: 17). But a woman who chooses to support herself through prostitution, exotic dancing, shoplifting or selling drugs is not likely to be supported or regarded as having made meaningful or responsible career choices.

Overall, these programmes make a series of moral assumptions about women's characters, responsibilities and abilities. For example leisure training assumes that women do not engage in socially legitimate activities during their leisure time and that they need to be taught about health, wellness and nutrition and to be apprised of recreational alternatives which do not include the use of alcohol, drugs or, in some cases, tobacco. Some programmes outline criteria and rules for participation that are quite regulatory. These programmes are making clear moral assessments of past, present and future conduct and choices. While all of these programmes serve an important material and moral purpose—to discourage future criminality and to offer women options—this does not eliminate their capacity to regulate prisoners morally for both therapeutic *and* risk management purposes.

The link between these forms of moral regulation and actuarialism occurs when programmes and moral categories are used as criteria and data in managerial risk assessment tools, such as the *security management system* described earlier, and through institutional discipline. Women prisoners are often penalized for lack of deference or resistance to an institutional regime which tries to produce 'healed', 'productive' and moral citizens who no longer engage in 'criminal', 'deviant', 'immoral' or 'risky' activities. Resistance often results in higher security classifications. In short, a designation of 'high risk', by this new managerial technology, is linked to a moral interpretation of a prisoner's character and to arbitrary prediction of future risks.

When needs become risks

Here, my concern is with one of the unobserved byproducts of actuarial technologies of government, and with the flexibility of the term 'risk'. In struggling to understand the qualitative differences between men's and women's risk factors, the Correctional Service has focused on the 'needs' of women prisoners. What has emerged from this practice is an interesting slippage between the concepts of need and risk. It seems that where there is an unsatisfied need there is a potential risk factor. In some cases, these two categories are indistinguishable.

Historically, correctional systems have been denounced for their unresponsiveness to women's needs (Hannah-Moffat, 1991, 1995, 1997; Shaw, 1991, 1993; Shaw et al., 1992; Kendall, 1993, 1994), and only recently have there been serious attempts to redress this neglect (TFFSW, 1990; FSWP, 1994b). While discussions about women prisoners' needs and the lack of response to these needs have traditionally operated as a critique of existing institutions of government and, more specifically, women's corrections, it is now an accepted technique through which women can be governed. Recent bureaucratic interpretations of women prisoners' needs were heavily influenced by feminist (and therapeutic) analyses of the experiences of criminal women and of women more generally. The emphasis on needs in the new *security management system* (FSWP, 1995) arises out of two assumptions in women's corrections literature: first, because the woman prisoner is not a risk to society, her correctional management should not stress risk; second, the woman prisoner has a multiplicity of needs which must be addressed holistically during her incarceration (TFFSW, 1990: 89–90). These two assumptions resulted in members of the Task Force on Federally Sentenced Women (TFFSW, 1990) posing the following question: what are the security needs of women?

The term *security needs* presents an interesting paradox. It combines two quite different elements: traditional security concerns, which are generally associated with danger and the prevention of harm to others, and a more recent emphasis on needs, which by contrast implies being without something and entitled to resources.

While the members of the Task Force initially supported the concept of 'woman-based criteria for classification', they ultimately concluded that 'assessments to gain better understanding of a woman's needs and experiences are more appropriate than classification' (p. 92). This conclusion relies on the perception that classification is based on security risks, whereas *needs assessment* 'looks at the whole spectrum of women's needs from a holistic perspective, including the needs relating to programming, spirituality, mental and physical health, family, culture and release plans' (p. 92). It is argued that this type of assessment allows staff to respond to 'the constellation of needs by appropriate support and intervention strategies which also consider the protection of society and the reduction of risk' (p. 92). However, an unintentional byproduct emerging in the correctional logic of the new women's prisons is that the concept of 'need' shifts from a vindication of a claim for resources (the feminist view) to a calculation of criminal potential (or risk of recidivism). Thus, correctional strategies and programmes now 'govern at a distance' by regulating women through their needs. Unlike past feminist narratives on women's needs that stress women's entitlement, the Correctional Service uses a language of needs to facilitate responsibilization. The prisoner is expected to 'cure' herself and manage her own risk by satisfying her criminogenic needs.

The legislation (Corrections and Conditional Release Act and Regulations) and policy guidelines (TFFSW, 1990; FSWP, 1994b; CSC, 1996) governing the management of federally sentenced women and principles of woman-centred corrections emphasize a specific legal and moral requirement to address the needs of federally sentenced women. Corrections Canada has acknowledged that women offenders have a 'different range and types of problems that contribute to their criminal behaviour than do men', that 'environmental, situational, political, cultural and social factors experienced by women offenders, as well as physiological and psychological factors, are not the same as those experienced by men', that 'women's criminal behaviour is largely associated with their backgrounds and life circumstances', and that 'a holistic approach to correctional programming for women should be adopted' (FSWP, 1994a: 5).

Several interrelated problems and characteristics have been identified as *criminogenic female needs*. According to Blanchette (1997a: 40) 'criminogenic needs reflect *risk* factors of the offender that are changeable and, when modified, reflect changes in the likelihood of recidivism'. Some of these criminogenic needs include: dependency; low self-esteem; poor educational and vocational achievement; parental death at an early age; foster care placement; constant changes in the location of foster care; residential placement; living on the streets; prostitution; suicide attempts; self-injury; substance abuse; and parental responsibilities (FSWP, 1994a: 5). Besides these characteristics, awareness and acknowledgement of women prisoners' survival of abuse and trauma play a key role in the management of their sentence and programme planning. While some policy literature suggests that survival of abuse or trauma does not constitute a criminogenic factor because 'there has been no statistical link between surviving violence/abuse/ trauma and criminal behaviour' (p. 5), correctional researchers are linking an adult history of abuse to violent recidivism (Bonta et al., 1995). Furthermore, while feminist researchers (e.g. Heney, 1990) have clearly argued that women's self-injury is often a 'coping mechanism' and that it should be treated as a mental health concern and not a security issue, correctional researchers are correlating self-injury with violent recidivism and arguing that a history of self-injury is a risk factor (Bonta et al., 1995; Blanchette, 1997a, 1997b).

Present policy discussions about the 'needs' of women prisoners are dominated by correctional researchers and technicians, who tend to emphasize the criminogenic characteristics of women's needs. In this instance, 'criminogenic' refers to characteristics or factors that are thought to be linked to an individual's involvement in criminal activities. The recent redefinition of needs as risks in the correctional sphere emerges from a desire to improve predictive capacities for both male and female prisoners. Researchers argue that there are two critical elements to classification and assessment. The first is distinguishing between, on the one hand, the characteristics of offenders and their circumstances which are subject to change over the course of an offender's sentence and, on the other, the factors which will remain constant. The second is identifying which of these factors indicate an increased or reduced chance of recidivism (Andrews, 1989: 13). Accordingly, correctional researchers encourage practitioners to look beyond static risk factors such as criminal history, history of substance abuse and poor adjustment to prison life early in the prisoner's sentence when doing risk management. Andrews suggests that in order to detect shifts in the chances of recidivism, 'risk factors which are dynamic must be assessed'; 'these dynamic risk factors are often called *criminogenic need* factors' (p. 13, emphasis in original). According to Andrews (p. 15), the *needs principle* asserts that 'if correctional treatment services are to reduce criminal recidivism, the criminogenic needs of offenders must be targeted'. This interpretation of needs as *criminogenic* neatly locates them within a realm of correctional managerialism and justifies normative interventions aimed at reducing the effect of criminogenic needs/risks.

Andrews' (1989) research is based primarily on the larger male correctional population, but, it illustrates the slippage between risk and need that is replicated in current research and policy on the federal female offender. Andrews' suggestion to 'look beyond static risk factors' (p. 13) has prompted several comparative studies of the characteristics and needs of different types of women offenders (Loucks and Zamble, 1994; Blanchette and Motiuk, 1995, 1997; Bonta et al., 1995; Blanchette, 1996, 1997a, 1997b, 1997c; Dickie and Ward, 1997; Lavinge et al., 1997). Much of the recent policy literature on the female offender uses the hybrid term 'risk/need', and correctional research tends to identify certain offender characteristics as both risk and needs. Characteristics of the female offender that were previously considered needs (i.e. history of abuse, history of self-injury, single motherhood, mental health concerns and dependency on financial aid/welfare) are now also defined as 'criminogenic factors' or risk factors that can predict recidivism. The danger here is that as hybrid risk/need factors, characteristics like self-injury, history of abuse and incidences of mental health problems can be used by correctional officials to justify various interventions, increase security and to hold the offender accountable for her actions and life circumstances.

In current correctional policy, risk minimization and needs satisfaction are often linked to therapeutic intervention. Unsatisfied needs are seen as both risk factors and as a mental health concern. For example a 1995 report on the mental health of federally sentenced women that recommended the development of an 'intensive healing programme' for high-need women notes that some women have 'special needs which make them a management problem' (Whitehall, 1995; Laishes and Lyth, 1996). It is also argued that 'needy women' require more intensive supervision and that a woman prisoner's resistance to therapeutic intervention is a risk factor. To accommodate these high-need women the Correctional Service proposed the development of an 'intensive healing programme', which is to occur in an 'enhanced unit'. The enhanced unit is to be used for both high-need and high-risk women.

> The enhanced unit is contained within the main building; it is a closed unit and has its own enclosed exercise yard. The unit consists of four cells and program areas, with two levels of supervision (Segregation—23 hour restriction; or Maximum with access to program participation). The unit has 24 hour supervision by staff. *It provides housing for inmates who: exhibit*

violent behaviour and/or have special needs, and/or serve disciplinary sentences. (Whitehall, 1995: 22, emphasis added)

From this description, there is no difference between the management of women who are considered 'high risk' due to violence and women who are 'high need' because of 'mental health' problems. Similarly, the classification of maximum security does not appear to differentiate between the management of a woman designated 'high need and low risk' and a woman who is 'high risk and low need'.

There is now great distance between certain feminist interpretations of women's needs as they are identified and outlined by researchers and in the report of the Task Force on Federally Sentenced Women (*Creating Choices*) as opposed to recent operational interpretations of needs within a broader context of actuarial penality. Unlike the present tendency to speak of risks and needs as if they were indistinguishable, the Task Force clearly outlined what it perceived to be a set of distinct cultural and gender-specific needs shared by most female offenders. The Task Force was critical of available methods of assessing and managing women's needs of the traditional models of security classification and risk management used in women's prisons. The Task Force, like many feminist researchers, argued that traditional techniques of classification tend to overclassify female offenders and fail to contextualize their offences, especially violent offences (Axon, 1989; TFFSW, 1990; Shaw and Dubois, 1995). Many reformers and researchers continue to believe that the category 'risk' is not highly relevant in the case of female offenders (TFFSW, 1990; Arbour Commission, Public Hearings, 1995).

Nancy Fraser (1989: 159) argues that 'needs-talk functions as a medium for making and contesting political claims', that it is an 'idiom in which political conflict is played out and through which inequalities are symbolically elaborated and challenged', and finally that 'in welfare state societies, needs-talk has been institutionalized as a major vocabulary of political discourse'. Rather than adopting a more conventional approach to the analysis of needs that would examine and identify the needs of a given population, and assessing the ability of certain organizational structures to satisfy these needs, Fraser (1989) focuses her inquiry on discourses about needs and the politics of needs interpretation. This approach is a useful method of illustrating 'the contextual and contested character of needs claims' (p. 160). Most criminological needs analyses have concentrated on the necessary tasks of identifying prisoners' needs, and the more controversial project of determining whether or not predefined needs have been met. Less common are critical discussions about the ways in which these needs are interpreted, who interprets prisoners' needs, from what perspective and in light of what interests. In correctional settings, there are indeed multiple discourses of need. There are therapeutic, administrative, feminist and actuarial vocabularies for the discussion of women prisoners' needs. These vocabularies are interwoven into a complex needs-talk which is mobilized to accommodate a variety of contradictory political ends.

To understand the dynamics of women's penal governance, it is important to acknowledge the plurality of vocabularies about needs/risks. These vocabularies are linked to feminist, psychiatric and actuarial modes of governing. And there is even a hybrid, 'feminist-psychiatric-actuarial governance', a normative strategy with very real disciplinary implications. The blurring of needs with risks has an important consequence for risk theory. Typically, risk theorists have suggested that in the shift towards a society governed through technologies of risk there has been less emphasis on earlier individualized and therapeutic technologies (Castel, 1991; Feeley and Simon, 1992). By collapsing need and risk categories, hybrid management techniques emerge. The emergent needs-talk which informs women's correctional management does not rely on feminist interpretations of women's needs or their claims to entitlement; rather, it depends on correctional interpretations of women's needs as potential or modified risk factors that are central to the efficient management of incarcerated women. The Correctional Service of Canada's adoption of the premise that federally sentenced women are generally 'high need' and not 'high risk', their claims that these prisoners do not require the same level and type of security measures as are required for male offenders (TFFSW, 1990) and the subsequent development of a unique security management model to address these qualities illustrates an organizational commitment to serving women's needs as they define them. Thus far, this tactic has co-opted and distorted the feminist critique of correctional risk assessment and risk management practices. The fact that women are now constructed as 'high need' as opposed to 'high risk', makes little substantive difference in their correctional management. Increasingly, needs are being treated in the same manner as risks in terms of defining carceral responses to women. Women prisoners are responsible for the management of their own risk and needs.

Conclusion

This article has outlined some of the main arguments of risk theory and the new penology thesis. It has also highlighted some of the limitations of these theories through an empirical evaluation of a new system of risk management in women's prisons. My analysis demonstrates that correctional research and policy models developed to describe and analyse women's risk (in particular risk in corrections) need to be modified. I have argued that risk technologies are part of a wider programme of neo-liberal governance that seeks to discipline and responsiblize the female offender. I have shown that risk is a normative concept able to mobilize culturally specific constructions of gender, and that its use in women's corrections is not representative of more efficient and objective actuarial technologies of governing; that the moral agent has not been replaced by an actuarial subject; and finally, that a language of risk is intimately linked to and dependent on a corresponding discussion of women's needs. Several strategies of government are mobilized by the process of being identified as 'a risk' or 'in need' and the development of managerial strategies to minimize them.

Risk is a fractured, fluid and flexible category that can be linked to a wide range of strategies and techniques aimed at governing offenders as well as the wider law-abiding population. The impact and meaning of risk is often contingent upon the objective of governing. Although 'risk technologies' exhibit this fluidity, they often appear stable. Within penality, ideas of risk assessment and risk management are equated with seemingly objective, and neutral categories that often use actuarial or statistical data as a form of legitimation. While there are in fact complicated and sophisticated managerial strategies in place for risk assessment and risk management, these techniques are gendered, culturally specific and subjective. New forms of actuarial penality have not displaced past disciplinary strategies of penal governance. Instead, they are bound to co-exist in a highly unstable and unpredictable network of penal powers. Assessments of risk and the application of technologies for the management of risk are integrally linked to, and enabled through, the exercise of non-actuarial forms of power.

I suggest that rather than using risk to understand changes in women's corrections and penality more generally, we can use these sites further to theorize the concept of risk and certain techniques of neo-liberal governance. In doing this, it is necessary to reflect on how actuarial techniques of governance are used with, and in some cases, dependent upon alternative and pre-existing conditions and technologies of governing. Recent new penology theories, which could be reframed as theories about actuarial penality, are indeed applicable to women's corrections to some extent. However, there are some important qualitative differences in the understanding of risk when applied to the respective governance of women and men. The types of offences committed by women, the context in which those offences occur and the past histories and experiences of female offenders differ from those of men. Our understanding, assessment and management of risk in women's correctional settings should account for these differences. Further studies will likely demonstrate that these differences are not peculiar to gender, and that actuarial governing is affected by race, class and other variables depending on the social, political, cultural and historical conditions of governing. For example in Canada there have been similar challenges to the inadequacy and discriminatory nature of white classification systems which are being used to govern Aboriginal prisoners. Recently there have been similar attempts to modify our understanding of risk in order to reflect the reality of Aboriginal prisoners' experiences.

To a large extent, we are left with the project of determining how the new actuarial knowledges and techniques of risk are used by practitioners to govern correctional populations. Questions which remain unanswered for risk theorists include: to what extent, and how, are actuarial forms of power more efficient or less coercive than other forms of power? To what degree, and under what conditions, have old disciplinary technologies of power been replaced/displaced by a new actuarialism? Have these shifts remained at the level of discourse or have they affected material practices in particular settings? In the case of new forms of governing such as actuarialism, it is evident that different forms of power enable and reinforce other forms. We are often too quick to assume that one form of power (such as disciplinary powers in the prison) is omnipresent, and that all technologies are thereby ascribed a disciplinary significance. It is much more useful to think of social settings such as the prison as locations for the simultaneous exercise of several technologies that are often guided by quite divergent rationalities.

Notes

I would like to thank Pat O'Malley, Jonathon Simon, Margaret Shaw, Anne-Marie Singh, Carolyn Strange, Mariana Valverde, Lorna Weir and the anonymous reviewers for their helpful suggestions on earlier drafts of this article. I also thank the many individuals at the Centre of Criminology, University of Toronto who commented on this article, and my research assistants Marie Crouch, Kelly Lamorie and Dawn Moore.

1. For a more detailed discussion and critique of this model see: Hannah-Moffat (1991, 1995, 1997); Shaw (1993, 1996).
2. The new regional prisons are located in Truro, Nova Scotia; Joliette, Quebec; Kitchener, Ontario; Edmonton, Alberta; Maple Creek Saskatchewan (Aboriginal Healing Lodge).
3. The feminist critique of women and classification has, for the most part, emphasized three general questions: are women overclassified or inadequately classified when processed through the same system as male offenders? Should practitioners use different criteria to assess the security risks and programme needs of women prisoners? Should needs be stressed more than security risks?
4. This article was written when a version of this security management was in use to evaluate the 'risk level' of federally sentenced women being transferred to the new regional facilities for women that opened in 1996.
5. Interview with prison psychologists, October 1995.

References

Adelberg, E. and C. Currie (1987) *Too Few to Count: Women and the Canadian Justice System*. Vancouver: Press Gang Publishers.

Adelberg, E. and C. Currie (1993) *In Conflict with the Law.* Vancouver: Press Gang Publishers.

Alexander, Jack (1988) *Security Classification Guidelines for Females.* New York: Department of Correctional Services.

Andrews, D.A. (1989) 'Recidivism is Predictable and Can Be Influenced: Using Risk Assessments to Reduce Recidivism', *Forum on Corrections Research.* Ottawa: Correctional Service of Canada.

Arbour Commission, Public Hearings (1995) *Transcript of Proceedings: Commission of Inquiry into Certain Events at the Prison for Women in Kingston.* (Phase II-P.C. 1995–608; volume 4).

Axon, Lee (1989) *Model and Exemplary Programs Available to Federally Sentenced Women.* Ottawa: Correctional Service of Canada.

Berzins, Lorraine and S. Cooper (1982) 'Political Economy of Correctional Planning for Women', *Canadian Journal of Criminology* 24: 399–416.

Blanchette, K. (1996) 'The Relationship Between Criminal History, Mental Disorder, and Recidivism Among Federally Sentenced Female Offenders'. Unpublished Master's thesis. Ottawa: Carleton University.

Blanchette, K. (1997a) 'Classifying Female Offenders for Correctional Interventions', *Forum on Corrections Research* 9(1): 36–41.

Blanchette, K. (1997b) 'Comparing Violent and Non-Violent Offenders on Risk and Need', *Forum on Corrections Research* 9(2): 14–18.

Blanchette, K. (1997c) *An Examination of Medium and Maximum Security Federally Sentenced Female Offenders.* Ottawa: Correctional Service of Canada, Corrections Research and Development.

Blanchette, K. and L. Motiuk (1995) 'Female Offender Risk Assessment: The Case Management Strategies Approach'. Paper presented at the Annual Convention of the Canadian Psychological Association, Charlottetown.

Blanchette, K. and L. Motiuk (1997) *Maximum Security Female and Male Federal Offenders: a Comparison.* Ottawa: Correctional Service of Canada, Correctional Research and Development.

Bonta, J., B. Pang and S. Wallace-Capretta (1995) 'Predictors of Recidivism Among Incarcerated Female Offenders', *Prison Journal* 75(2):135–64.

Bottoms, Anthony (1983) 'Neglected Trends in Contemporary Punishment', in D. Garland and P. Young (eds) *The Power to Punish*, pp. 166–202. London: Heinemann.

Castel, Robert (1991) 'From Dangerousness to Risk', in G. Burchell, C. Gordon and P. Miller (eds) *The Foucault Effect: Studies in Governmentality*, pp. 281–98. Chicago, IL: University of Chicago Press.

Cohen, Stanley (1985) *Visions of Social Control.* Cambridge, MA: Polity Press.

Cooper, S. (1993) 'The Evolution of the Federal Woman's Prison', in E. Adelberg and C. Currie (eds) *Too Few to Count: Women and the Canadian Justice System*, pp. 127–46. Vancouver: Press Gang Publishers.

Correctional Service of Canada (CSC) (1996) *The Correctional Strategy.* Ottawa: Correctional Service of Canada, Federally Sentenced Women Program.

Coulson, Grant (1993) 'Using, the Level of Supervision Inventory in Placing Female Offenders in Rehabilitation Programs', *IARCA Journal* 5:12–13.

Defert, Daniel (1991) 'Popular Life and Insurance Technology', in G. Burchell, C. Gordon and P. Miller (eds) *The Foucault Effect: Studies in Governmentality*, pp. 211–34. Chicago, IL: University of Chicago Press.

Dickie, I. and L. Ward (1997) 'Women Offenders Convicted of Robbery and Assault', *Forum on Corrections Research* 9(2): 29–32.

Douglas, Mary (1986) *Risk Acceptability According to the Social Sciences*. London: Routledge & Kegan Paul.

Douglas, Mary (1992) *Risk and Blame: Essays in Cultural Theory*. London: Routledge.

Ericson, R. and P. Baranek (1982) *The Ordering of Justice: The Accused as Dependent in the Criminal Justice Process*. Toronto: University of Toronto Press.

Ericson, R. and K. Haggerty (1997) *Policing the Risk Society*. Toronto: University of Toronto Press.

Ewald, F. (1991) 'Risk and Insurance', in G. Burchell, C. Gordon and P. Miller (eds) *The Foucault Effect: Studies in Governmentality*, pp. 197–210. Chicago, IL: University of Chicago Press.

Federally Sentenced Women Program (FSWP) (1994a) *Literature Review*. Ottawa: Correctional Service of Canada, Federally Sentenced Women Program.

Federally Sentenced Women Program (FSWP) (1994b) *Correctional Program Strategy for Federally Sentenced Women*. Ottawa: Correctional Service of Canada, Federally Sentenced Women Program.

Federally Sentenced Women Program (FSWP) (1995) *Security Management System*. Ottawa: Correctional Service of Canada, Federally Sentenced Women Program.

Feeley, Malcolm and Jonathon Simon (1992) 'The New Penology: Notes on the Emerging Strategy for Corrections and Its Implications', *Criminology* 30(4): 49–74.

Feeley, Malcolm and Jonathon Simon (1994) 'Actuarial Justice: The Emerging New Criminal Law', in David Nelken (ed.) *The Futures of Criminology*, pp. 173–201. New Delhi: Sage.

Fraser, Nancy (1989) 'Talking About Needs: Interpretive Contests as Political Conflicts in Welfare State Societies', *Ethics* 99 (January): 150–81.

Garland, David (1995) 'Penal Modernism and Post Modernism', in T. Blomberg and S. Cohen (eds) *Punishment and Social Control*, pp. 181–210. New York: Aldine de Gruyter.

Hann, Robert and William Harman (1989) *Release Risk Prediction: Testing the Nuffield Scoring System For Native and Female Inmates*. Ottawa: Correctional Service of Canada.

Hannah-Moffat, Kelly (1991) 'Creating Choices or Repeating History: Canadian Female Offenders and Correctional Reform', *Social Justice* 18(3): 184–203.

Hannah-Moffat, Kelly (1995) 'Feminine Fortresses: Women-Centred Prisons?', *The Prison Journal* 75(2): 135–64.

Hannah-Moffat, Kelly (1997) 'From Christian Maternalism to Risk Technologies: Penal Powers and Women's Knowledges in the Governance of Female Prisons'. Unpublished PhD thesis. Toronto: University of Toronto, Centre of Criminology.

Heney, J. (1990) *Report on Self Injurious Behaviour in the Kingston Prison For Women*. Ottawa: Correctional Service of Canada.

Hoffman, P.B. (1982) 'Females, Recidivism, and Salient Factor Score: A Research Note', *Criminal Justice and Behaviour* 9(2): 121–5.

Kendall, Kathleen (1993) *Literature Review of Therapeutic Services for Women in the Prison for Women, volumes 1–3*. Ottawa: Correctional Service of Canada.

Kendall, Kathleen (1994) 'Creating Real Choices: A Program Evaluation of Therapeutic Services at the Prison for Women', *Forum on Corrections Research*. Ottawa: Correctional Services of Canada.

Laishes, Jane and Sandra Lyth (1996) *Intensive Healing (Mental Health) Program*. Ottawa: Correctional Service of Canada, Federally Sentenced Women Program.

Lavinge, B., L. Hoffman and I. Dickie (1997) 'Women Who Have Committed Homicide', *Forum on Corrections Research* 9(2): 25–9.

Loucks, A. (1995) 'Criminal and Violent Behaviour in Adult Female Offenders'. Unpublished PhD thesis. Kingston: Queen's University, Department of Psychology.

Loucks, A. and E. Zamble (1994) 'Some Comparisons of Female and Male Serious Offenders', *Forum on Corrections Research* 6(1): 22–5.

Motiuk, L. (1993) 'Where Are We In Our Ability to Assess Risk?', *Forum on Corrections Research* 5(2): 12–13.

Motiuk, L. (1996) 'Targeting Employment Patterns to Reduce Offender Risk and Need', *Forum on Corrections Research* 8(1): 22–4.

O'Malley, Pat (1992) 'Risk, Power and Crime Prevention', *Economy and Society* 21(3): 252–75.

Parton, N. (1996) 'Social Work, Risk and the Blaming System', in N. Parton (ed.) *Social Theory, Social Change and Social Work*. New York: Routledge.

Peters, A. (1988) 'Main Currents in Criminal Law Theory', in J.J.M. van Dijk (ed.) *Criminal Law in Action*, pp. 19–36. Deventer: Kluwer.

Pratt, John (1997) *Governing the Dangerous*. Sydney: The Federation Press.

Shaw, Margaret (1991) *The Female Offender: Report on a Preliminary Study*. Ottawa: Ministry of the Solicitor General.

Shaw, Margaret (1993) 'Reforming Federal Women's Imprisonment', in E. Adelberg and C. Currie (eds) *In Conflict with the Law*, pp. 50–75. Vancouver: Press Gang Publishing.

Shaw, Margaret (1996) 'Is There a Feminist Future for Women's Prisons?', in R. Matthews and Peter Francis (eds) *Prisons 2000: An International Perspective* on the Current State and Future of Imprisonment, pp. 179–200. Hampshire: Macmillan.

Shaw, Margaret and Sheryl Dubois (1995) *Understanding Violence by Women: A Review of the Literature.* Ottawa: Correctional Service of Canada.

Shaw, Margaret with K. Rodgers, J. Blanchette, T. Hattem, L.S. Thomas and L. Tamarack (1992) *Paying the Price: Federally Sentenced Women in Context.* Ottawa: Ministry of the Solicitor General.

Simon, Jonathon (1987) 'The Emergence of a Risk Society: Insurance, Law and the State', *Socialist Review* 95(1): 93–108.

Simon, Jonathon (1988) 'The Ideological Effects of Actuarial Practices', *Law and Society Review* 22(4): 771–800.

Simon, Jonathon (1993) *Poor Discipline: Parole and the Social Control of the Underclass, 1890–1990.* Chicago, IL: University of Chicago Press.

Simon, Jonathon (1994) 'In the Place of the Parent: Risk Management and the Government of Campus Life', *Social and Legal Studies* 3(3): 15–45.

Simon, Jonathon and M. Feeley (1995) 'True Crime: The New Penology and Public Discourse on Crime', in T. Blomberg and S. Cohen (eds) *Punishment and Social Control*, pp. 147–80. New York: Aldine de Gruyter.

Task Force on Federally Sentenced Women (TFFSW) (1990) *Report of the Task Force on Federally Sentenced Women: Creating Choices.* Ottawa: Ministry of the Solicitor General.

Tuck, M. (1991) 'Community and the Criminal Justice System', *Policy Studies* 12(3): 22–37.

Whitehall, G.C. (1995) *Mental Health Profile and Intervention Strategy for Atlantic Region Federally Sentenced Women.* Correctional Service of Canada, Federally Sentenced Women Program.

KELLY HANNAH-MOFFAT is an assistant professor in the Department of Sociology at Brock University. She recently completed her PhD in Criminology at the Centre of Criminology at University of Toronto. She also worked as a researcher and policy advisor for the *Commission of Inquiry into Certain Events at the Prison for Women in Kingston.* She is the Past-president of the Toronto Elizabeth Fry Society, a halfway house and organization that works for and on behalf of all women in conflict with the law. Her publications and research focus on sociology of punishment, governmentality, feminist criminology, parole and social policy.

[19]

" Rather than signaling the decline of the gendered organization, the equality with a vengeance era marks a shift in how gender is conceived and elaborated within the criminal justice system. "

EMBODIED SURVEILLANCE AND THE GENDERING OF PUNISHMENT

JILL A. MCCORKEL
Northern Illinois University

JILL A. MCCORKEL is an assistant professor in the Sociology Department at Northern Illinois University. Her articles on drug policy, social control, and resistance in women's prisons have appeared in a number of journals, including Symbolic Interaction, Journal of Offender Rehabilitation, Drugs & Society, *and* Qualitative Sociology. *Her current research examines the conditions women face following their release from prison and documents their strategies for survival in the wake of changes in welfare policy and social service provision.*

This ethnography explores the enactment of "get tough" politics in a state prison for women and considers whether the implementation of seemingly gender-neutral programs and policies implies that women's prisons are no longer operating as "gendered organizations." The author will demonstrate that even when women's prisons attempt to mimic the disciplinary policies associated with men's facilities, they modify disciplinary practices in response to perceived differences in offending between men and women. A crucial modification is the use of an "embodied surveillance" that sharply differs from Foucault's analysis of penal surveillance mechanisms. The article concludes with an analysis of how the practice of an embodied surveillance is embedded within a larger structure of gendered punishment.

Keywords: *prisons, gendered organizations, surveillance, drug treatment, Foucault*

R esearch on punishment and prison is dominated almost exclusively by explorations and accounts of men's institutions. Some of the earliest studies of women's prisons were comparative, examining sex role socialization and different styles of adaptation to prison life between men and women (Giallombardo 1966; Heffernan 1972). Later studies contrasted resources, deprivations, and programming in men's and women's prisons (Baskin et al. 1989; Ross and Fabiano 1986; Morash, Haarr, and Rucker 1994; Leonard 1983). This research was crucial because it challenged criminology's exclusive focus on male prisoners and problematized conditions in women's prisons. Furthermore, these studies of women's prisons raise important questions regarding how gender organizes the structure and practice of punishment.

This ethnography builds on earlier feminist scholarship by examining the prison as a "gendered organization" (Acker 1990). Acker's concept suggests that organizations are not gender neutral entities through which gendered bodies pass. Instead, she argued that organizational structure is fundamentally gendered. This concept has been elaborated in research studies of work organizations to demonstrate that gender-based wage differentials and the glass ceiling are not necessarily the by-

AUTHOR'S NOTE: An earlier version of this article was presented at the ninety-fifth annual meeting of the American Sociological Association, August 12-16, 2000, Washington, D.C. I am grateful to Jody Miller, Kristen Myers, Kirk Miller, and anonymous JCE *reviewers for their insightful comments.*

products of bad (male) managers encoding their sexism into decisions that otherwise violate the rationality of the organization (Cook and Waters 1998; England et al. 1994; Ridgeway 1997). Instead, these studies suggest that gender inequality is produced at the level of organizational structure—organizational conceptions of jobs, workers, and hierarchies are premised on a substructure of gender difference in which men's (hetero)sexuality, bodies, and relation to paid and unpaid labor serve as the ideal, a normative and material baseline for the universal worker. Acker (1992) contended that gender is "present in [the organization's] processes, practices, images, and ideologies, and distributions of power" (p. 567).

The implications of Acker's theory extend beyond studies of gender inequality in work organizations. Indeed, studies ranging from an examination of instrument selection in alternative rock bands (Clawson 1999) to an analysis of harassment in public places (Gardner 1995) suggest that Acker's theory of gendered organizations is a useful tool for grasping gender inequality in other forums. Britton (1999, 2000) has recently applied Acker's theory to prison organizations. Her research explores inmate supervision as a form of work and considers how the job of guarding female inmates became feminized over the course of the twentieth century. The present study builds on this literature but shifts from an examination of the gender politics of work in the paid labor market to the gender politics of punishment in the criminal justice system. Subsequently, my focus is on supervision and surveillance as aspects of punishment rather than as forms of work per se. As Foucault (1977) has demonstrated, the practice of punishment and surveillance is organized within a wider field of social relations. A number of prison scholars have used Foucault's history of the prison to consider the link between penal practices and the political economy. What is missing from this work is a consideration of women's prisons and the experiences of female inmates. Indeed, Foucault's work assumes that crucial concepts such as surveillance, discipline, and punishment are universal in their application. Recent feminist scholarship, however, would suggest that this may not be the case.

The present study analyzes qualitative data gathered during a four-year ethnographic investigation of a state prison for women. The intent of this research is to explore how gender is implicated in the mechanisms of surveillance and punishment and to examine why it figures so prominently in how punishment is conceived at the organizational

44   JOURNAL OF CONTEMPORARY ETHNOGRAPHY / FEBRUARY 2003

level. Building on the work of both Foucault and Acker, I will argue that punishment and surveillance are gendered concepts in the sense that they are enacted differently in men's and women's institutions and that differences in penal practice are legitimated within the prison organization by conceptualizing female inmates as both "gender deviants" and "deviant criminals."

FOUCAULT, PRISON, AND GENDER

The history of prison is almost exclusively the history of men's institutions. While Rafter (1995) and Freedman (1981) have made notable contributions through their analyses of the emergence of sex-segregated punishment and the birth of women's reformatories, discursive constructions of punishment, surveillance, resistance, and control within mainstream criminology remain premised on studies of men in male-dominated prisons, jails, and penitentiaries. The failure to include analyses of the practices, policies, and politics within women's prisons suggests that prominent theories and conceptualizations of punishment are partial, incomplete, and occlusive.

The omission of gender is particularly troubling in the case of Foucault, whose historical analyses of a variety of eighteenth-century disciplinary institutions have earned a prominent place in contemporary discussions of punishment and modern power. For Foucault (1977), the objective of modern disciplinary institutions and the surveillance mechanisms they employ is to produce "docile and useful bodies" (p. 138). Within the wider body of prison literature, the making of docile bodies is associated with the class politics of the paid labor market and men's access to factory work (for example, see Rusche and Kirchheimer 1939; Reiman 1998). Though Foucault's bodies masquerade as genderless in *Discipline and Punish*, the examples he used to elaborate his analysis suggest that these are in fact male bodies. Indeed, he explicitly used the example of soldiers' relations to their weapons and students' relations to their desks as indicative of the "body-object articulations" that form a "coercive link with the apparatus of production" (p. 153). As Bartky (1988) noted, "Foucault treats the body throughout as if it were one, as if the bodily experiences of men and women did not differ and as if men and women bore the same relationship to the characteristic institutions of modern life" (p. 63).

Bartky's (1988) criticism of Foucault centers on the observation that while men and women are herded through similar disciplinary institutions (e.g., public school), Foucault's analysis overlooks those disciplines that "produce a modality of embodiment that is explicitly feminine" (p. 64). Subsequently, Bartky called for an analysis of disciplinary practices and institutions such as the cosmetics and fashion industries whose explicit mission is to gender bodies. This is a valuable direction for future analyses to take, but it is possible to go another step forward. Bodies are not only gendered by specific practices and regimes intended to code them as masculine or feminine. Bodies are actively gendered within institutions whose stated mission is directed to other goals. For example, in Thorne's (1994) study of public elementary schools, she found that teachers and students have intricate mechanisms for gendering space and patterns of activity in the course of pursuing broader institutional goals such as discipline and literacy. In the act of organizing lines of students according to gender divisions (e.g., "girls in front, boys in back"), the school participates in the gendering of bodies. Thorne's observations are consistent with Acker's (1990) argument that precisely because organizations are not gender neutral, their policies and practices will both activate and sustain differentiation on the basis of gender. Subsequently, it is not necessarily the case that similar institutions will enact the same disciplinary practices for men and women. Given a gendered regime, we can expect that the nature and purpose of control and discipline will, in important instances, vary across gender.

Historical studies of women's reformatories make precisely this point. The purpose of disciplining the bodies of women in the reformatory system was not for work in the paid labor market but for reproductive labor in the domestic sphere (Rafter 1995; Freedman 1981; Feinman 1984). However, it was not only the case that institutions prepared men and women for different kinds of labor and, therefore, set them up to have different relations to the political economy. Studies of women's correctional facilities suggest the gendering of bodies also occurred through the act of discipline itself. In Rafter's (1995) work, it is clear that rape and sexual assault of women inmates by male guards serve as mechanisms for maintaining institutional order, as well as reinforcing men's dominance over women. In a study of intake procedures at the California Youth Authority during the 1960s, Rosenbaum and Chesney-Lind (1994) discovered that girls' case files routinely included discussions of physical attractiveness as well as the results of gynecological determinations of virginity. The ability of female delinquents to successfully "do gender" was a crucial element in the logic and application of punishment and surveillance in this particular institution. Punishment, in other words, did not merely produce docile bodies. It produced docile girls.

Current research on women's prisons reveals two major sets of trends that distinguish contemporary facilities from their reformatory predecessors. First, criminal justice policies are increasingly punitive in nature. For example, Bloom, Chesney-Lind, and Owen (1994) reported that dramatic increases in the number of women incarcerated in California between 1982 and 1992 are not caused by a "worsening" of the types of crimes women commit; rather, the system has become more punitive toward women, particularly women convicted of drug-related offenses. Similar findings have been reported in Rhode Island, Massachusetts, New York, Connecticut, and Hawaii (for a review, see Chesney-Lind and Pollock 1995). Second, women's prisons have begun to resemble the architecture of men's. Facilities built in the 1980s and 1990s are no longer patterned after the cottage model with its manicured gardens and domestic amenities (Chesney-Lind and Pollock 1995; Owen 1998). Instead, institutions such as the Central California Women's Facility (CCWF) and Baylor Women's Correctional Institution in Delaware have razor wire, steel doors, security housing units (SHUs), and administrative segregation. In Illinois, even older institutions such as Dwight Women's Correctional Facility have transitioned former "dorms" into SHUs. Owen (1998) reported that in CCWF, the central concern among administrators is overcrowding, and they devote much of the facility's resources to security and population management. There is little emphasis on treatment and rehabilitation.

Notably, one characteristic of women's prisons that remains essentially unchanged is the limited availability of meaningful treatment, educational, and vocational programming. Vocational training continues to be mainly in feminized, low-wage occupations such as cosmetology, data entry, food services, and clerical work (Pollock 1990; Morash, Haarr, and Rucker 1994). Treatment, vocational, and educational programs have increased in number since the late 1980s following a series of successful 14th Amendment lawsuits challenging unequal treatment and denial of due process in women's facilities (Chesney-Lind and Pollock 1995; Pollock 1998). Unfortunately, many of the rehabilitative programs mimic treatment modalities like boot camps and therapeutic communities (TCs) developed for and by men (see Lockwood, McCorkel, and Inciardi 1998; Pollock 1998). Such programs are often unable to deal with the complexity of women's criminality—particularly the ways in which offending is linked to women's experiences with physical and sexual victimization, poverty, and racism. So great is the mismatch between institutional programming and the needs of women prisoners that prominent criminologists such as Chesney-Lind and Pollock (1995) referred to this era in women's corrections as "equality with a vengeance."

The "equality" principle that characterizes this new era demands careful and thorough investigations into the structure and practice of social control in women's prisons. Historical studies suggest that discipline and control were organized according to highly gendered sets of expectations regarding the cult of "true" womanhood and women's place in society. Current research reveals a new twist in the gender politics animating women's prisons—women prisoners continue to suffer from unequal conditions, while, concomitantly, institutional policies and procedures appear to be gender neutral. This begs the question— has the salience of gender in women's prisons diminished over time? Feminist research on work organizations has documented how policies and procedures that masquerade as gender neutral actually serve to advantage men and disadvantage women while exacerbating conditions of gender inequality (see Acker 1990; Lorber 1994). Recent ethnographies such as Owen's (1998) suggest that gender has not disappeared from women's prisons; it has been reconstituted. Understanding the gender politics of the "equality with a vengeance" era requires detailed investigations into the practices, relationships, and policies within women's institutions. The present study contributes to this effort by examining the practices that constitute punishment and surveillance in a state prison for women. It is the goal of this analysis to delineate how and to what extent gender persists as a salient and urgent component of punishment.

RESEARCH SETTING AND METHOD

The present study is based on an ethnography conducted from 1994 through 1998 in East State, a medium-security state prison for women

48   JOURNAL OF CONTEMPORARY ETHNOGRAPHY / FEBRUARY 2003

located on the East Coast.[1] This was a particularly chaotic time in the prison's history. Unprecedented levels of overcrowding, spurred on in large part by the state's war on drugs, resulted in a series of inmate law-suits that forced the state to build a new facility that would accommo-date the steady tide of women sentenced to prison for drug offenses. The new prison was completed in 1992, and by the first half of 1993, the inmate population exceeded the new prison's rated capacity of two hun-dred. East State's administrators were in a bind. The construction of the new prison exacerbated budgetary dilemmas, and moreover, the depart-ment of corrections denied East State additional funds to expand the facility.[2] At the same time, projected increases in the inmate population over a five-year period meant that administrators could quickly find themselves facing another round of inmate-initiated lawsuits. In the midst of it all, state politicians continued to publicly express enthusi-asm for the "get tough" platform and the war on drugs—characterized by massive arrests of low-level street dealers and lengthy, mandatory sentences. In short, administrators had no reason to believe that the overcrowding problem was going to disappear any time in the near future.

I arrived on the scene in the midst of the crisis. Desperate to find solu-tions to the overcrowding problem, officials at East State began a series of talks with researchers at the local university, social service providers, local judges, and private companies selling drug treatment services. For administrators at East State, the only apparent solution to the problem seemed to be a radical revisioning of their punishment regime. Recidi-vists constituted more than 40 percent of those sentenced to the institu-tion, and the vast majority of recidivists (85 percent according to the warden) had persistent problems with illegal drugs (either as users, sell-ers, or both). After a series of conferences and some preliminary research on the extent to which drugs were implicated in the commis-sion offenses of the inmate population, administrators concluded that the best strategy for dealing with the overcrowding problem was to host an experimental drug treatment program in the prison and to make con-ditions in the main facility more rigid or, in the words of the deputy war-den, "more hard core."

The drug treatment program was a three-year demonstration project funded by a grant from a federal agency. At the conclusion of the three-year period, funding was to revert back to the state department of cor-rections pending the conclusions reached by an external evaluation team and by administrators within the prison. I gained official access to the prison as a member of the evaluation team. In that role, I was provided with a high-level security clearance that allowed me to visit the institution at any time of day. For the most part, I was able to walk freely throughout the prison and talk to virtually anyone I came across. In addition, I was regularly invited to attend the warden's weekly conferences with top-level administrative staff, as well as classification meetings and various meetings with treatment providers. I was provided with copies of internal memos, prison newsletters, various sets of population statistics, and reports. When the evaluation was completed in 1997, I received permission from the warden and the director of the drug treatment program to remain in the prison and continue an independent ethnography that I had initiated in the summer of 1994. Throughout the four-year period, I conducted semistructured interviews with seventy-four inmates who, at one point during their time in East State, participated in the drug treatment program. In addition, I formally interviewed a total of thirteen administrators and influential decision makers within East State and the state department of corrections, ten correctional officers, and six counselors from the drug treatment program regarding their views on punishment, rehabilitation, and women offenders. This study is based on these interviews, as well as participant observation and thousands of informal conversations with inmates, former inmates, correctional officers, social workers, administrators, activists, family members, and counselors at East State.

In many ways, East State and the drug treatment program it hosted are particularly well suited for an analysis of how gender is implicated in the ideologies and mechanics of punishment. Overcrowding generated a legitimation crisis of sorts (see Habermas 1975). Administrators, correctional officers, and inmates began to question the politics, functions, and consequences of punishment as it was practiced in the institution. Central to this dialogue were assumptions about gender and questions about whether and to what extent women offenders were different from men and the implications of gender difference for social control in the institution. Subsequently, during this particular moment in the institution's history, gender was frequently in the foreground of discussions about punishment and was often a subject of considerable disagreement and debate. My participation in the setting offers a unique opportunity to glimpse how assumptions about gender are translated (and contested) at the level of institutional control policies and interpersonal practices.

Furthermore, Project Rehabilitate Women (PRW), the drug treatment program that the institution agreed to play host to, represents the height of what Foucault (1977, 1980) defined as the nature of modern power. The structure of control in PRW and the program's philosophy of addiction are based on the TC model.[3] Practitioners believe that addiction is caused by a "disordered" or "diseased" personality that is attributable to a complex of biological, psychological, and social factors (Pan et al. 1993). The primary stated mission is to "habilitate" rather than "rehabilitate" inmates since the nature of their addictive disorders handicaps them in their ability to think, feel, and act in accordance with social norms (DeLeon 1997). Habilitation is accomplished, in part, by an emphasis on casual authority, visibility, surveillance, and public confrontation and humiliation.

PRW was among the first prison-based TCs for women in the country. Like other treatment modalities developed exclusively for men, PRW struggled with how much modification was necessary to accommodate the gender-specific needs of women inmates. It was the "sister" program to an in-prison TC for men that boasted better-than-average results with respect to recidivism, reoffending, and drug use. Prison Industries Inc. (PII), the company that had a contract with the state to develop and manage both TCs, did not want to tamper with success. In the end, very little modification was made to the structure of PRW, and the changes that were made could be considered little more than cosmetic. The program added a weekly session on parenting (e.g., how to discipline children, how to relieve stress, how to help with homework, etc.) but did not hold seminars or training sessions on other things that affected the women such as domestic violence, abuse, rape, loss of loved ones, racism, and poverty. Staff were never trained on "women's issues" (though this was initially promised by PII), nor were counselors hired who specialized in domestic violence and/or sexual abuse, despite the recommendations of evaluators. PRW staff and the management team of PII argued that addiction and abuse were separate and discrete issues. Their job was to treat addiction rather than abuse. Dr. Richardson, the vice president in charge of treatment services, explained in an interview that modifications to the structure and content of the TC were unnecessary because victimization was not just a "women's issue":

The men in [prison TC] have been victimized too but they don't focus on it. Women in [PRW] are really weak in this regard. They won't focus on what they need to be focusing on [addiction]. Instead, they wallow in victimization.

Subsequently, there is little that distinguishes PRW's structure from that of the men's program. It houses a total of forty-six inmates for the six- to eighteen-month period prior to their release and is organized according to a rational authority model in which staff serve as a fixed set of leaders in the community. Beneath them, authority positions are graded with residents occupying positions of power according to their seniority and their ability to follow a strict set of rules. Staff are rarely visible as leaders—it is the residents who are responsible for organizing the day-to-day affairs of life in the community. Residents are expected to police themselves and one another. The failure to do so often results in punishments more severe than those received by the actual offender(s).

It is important to note that many of the characteristics of control in the program mirror those of the disciplinary institutions Foucault studied. For example, power is capillary, in that it is everywhere and not located merely with a particular individual or vested position. Furthermore, since the aim of control is "habilitation" rather than repression per se, the nature of power in the program becomes self-amplifying. For Foucault (1977), self-amplification refers to the fact that modern power does not simply act as a counterweight to an oppositional force; rather, modern power is enhanced through the course of its own exercise. In the case of PRW, discipline is accomplished through public rituals in which offenders are confronted by staff and residents regarding their misdeeds and are then subject to lengthy and often painful analyses regarding the nature of their "real" selves (see McCorkel 1998). The confrontations reinforce the program's philosophy (deviant behavior reflects the state of the diseased self) and the vulnerability of all residents to the iron grip of the collective gaze. A third parallel between PRW and Foucault's penitentiary is that the visibility afforded by both the architecture of the program unit and the pervasiveness of surveillance mechanisms[4] contributes to the production of "cases" in which control over the subject is linked to intimate knowledge of her habits, desires, history, perversities, and fears.

PRW exerted considerable influence over the wider dynamic of punishment and control in East State. The differences between the prison and PRW were a matter of degree. By the end of the 1990s, the paternalism that had previously characterized the institution's approach to inmates had given way to the "hard core" disciplinary practices of PRW. The prison even underwent a series of cosmetic changes (from the blacking out of windows in the central control room to the installation of metal detectors in the front lobby) to symbolize the administration's commitment to surveillance and security. Though the relationship between PRW and the prison was often rocky, they shared a common problem (overcrowding), promoted a common solution (drug treatment), and held similar beliefs regarding gender and punishment. For these reasons, a sizable portion of the analysis that follows is devoted to an examination of practices and interactions occurring within PRW.

Furthermore, the analysis itself is organized around the detailed examination of a single event—a therapy session known as the encounter group (EG)—and the incident that precipitated it. Although the analysis is supplemented with interview and participant observation data gathered over the course of the four-year period, I made the decision to focus on this event rather than countless others for three reasons. First, the interactions and control strategies that ensue in the course of the EG are representative of the internal dynamics within the facility. The EG is what distinguishes the TC from other treatment modalities, and "pinball" (a version of the EG used in PRW) is what distinguishes PRW's tactics as hard core. Second, pinball and EG sessions are central to mythology and ritual within East State prison. Both staff and inmates reconstruct, re-create, and reinterpret the interactions that unfold during the sessions. Often, dramatic retellings of a single episode pass throughout the prison for weeks. Third, the decision to develop the analysis across thick description rather than bundling it in neat typologies is based on the subject matter itself. Prison is not a familiar place for most readers. Moreover, the internal dynamics of prison programs have long been referred to as a "black box" given the paucity of data that exists regarding the actual practices and interactions that occur therein (see Pan et al. 1993; Pollock 1998). Since this is a study of how discipline and surveillance can be understood as gendered concepts, it is necessary to spend some time scrutinizing how they were enacted. Subsequently, to cast some light on a black box, I have chosen to provide an in-depth account of the type of confrontation that character-izes the hard core approach to disciplining women inmates.

DISCIPLINE THROUGH CONFRONTATION

EGs were popular among both residents and staff of the PRW pro-gram. Indeed, clinicians from PII and counselors in the program regarded these groups as the quintessential characteristic that distin-guished the TC from other forms of therapy. The appeal for residents was that the group provided them with a forum for expressing their anger, outrage, and pain in response to the words or misdeeds of other residents in the program. As one resident put it, "EG lets us blow off steam and get everything out in the open." In most cases, the appeal of "blowing off steam" outweighed residents' fears that they would be among those who were selected for confrontation and, when they were, the humiliation associated with being the target of such a confronta-tion.[5] According to the program director, the therapeutic purpose of EGs was twofold. First, by mobilizing peer pressure against the target, the groups were intended to challenge the way the target conceptualized her "real" self and to make her aware of how her actions affected others around her. Second, EGs were intended to teach women how to control their emotions, something PRW staff did not believe their clients were particularly well equipped to do. Indeed, by preventing targets from responding to the accusations leveled against them, PRW staff believed that the groups forced residents to come to grips with the powerful emo-tions that arose during the sessions. Beyond therapeutic goals, however, EGs were popular with counselors because they provided a wealth of information about residents (e.g., how often rules are violated, the sub-stance of rule violations, relations among residents in the program, etc.).

EGs groups took a variety of forms, depending on the number of resi-dents available for the session, the substance and frequency of rule infractions, and the intensity of the tensions running between and among residents and staff. When tensions were high, residents were considerably more likely to disobey program rules and challenge the authority of staff. To regain control, staff and high-ranking residents modified the traditional EG into a game referred to as pinball. In a

54   JOURNAL OF CONTEMPORARY ETHNOGRAPHY / FEBRUARY 2003

pinball session, the target sits alone in the middle of a circle of residents and is confronted in rapid-fire style by staff, as well as by other residents whom the staff hand selects to participate in the confrontation.[6] Pinball differs from the traditional EG mainly in terms of how much pressure is brought to bear on the target. In the traditional group, the target is not physically singled out and placed in the center of the group but instead remains seated among her peers. Also, only residents who actually reported the target to the staff for engaging in a rule violation were allowed to participate in the confrontation, and the confrontations themselves were limited to a total of five minutes. In pinball, staff could designate anyone to participate in the confrontation, and there was no limit on the duration of the session. Furthermore, pinball sessions did not function as a forum for residents to critique one another but for the staff and supervisory residents to strongly condemn the behaviors and attitudes of residents deemed "troublemakers." Residents who were selected by the staff to participate in the confrontation generally echoed the sentiments of the staff members rather than expressing their own feelings about the target's actions. In all, this type of game allowed staff to bring considerable social pressure to bear on selected targets.

EGs were scheduled to be held twice a week, but over the course of my participation in the program, they only occurred once a week or once every other week. Although the groups themselves were considered the cornerstone of therapy in the TC modality, paperwork demands and staffing problems frequently prevented the counselors from holding the groups on a biweekly basis. The failure to hold groups, particularly groups that served as an outlet for relieving the frustrations residents experienced toward one another and the program, caused considerable control problems for the staff. For example, during one such period after the group had not been held for two weeks, Sarah walked off the floor and into her room while one of the counselors was admonishing her for passing a note to another woman in the program. Such blatant disrespect for the authority of a counselor was infrequent and signaled, according to staff, the potential for widespread disruption. Counselor Tynice explained,

> You can't let them be up in your face because they'll keep pushing it and pushing it until they've got control. That's how they do it on the street and with their families. They take and they push, till they get what they want—drugs, money, whatever. You let one of them do it without answering back and you've put whatever you've accomplished with the

rest of them in jeopardy. Deep inside they're still addicts, no matter what they look like on the surface, and they'll take advantage if they can. Part of our job is knowing when it's [rule violations] going on and putting a stop to it.

At exactly ten o'clock in the morning after Sarah's act of insubordination, Counselor Tynice convened the residents in the center of the unit and instructed them to set up the chairs in a circle for a game of pinball. Several women broke into a trot toward the storage area and emerged with dozens of plastic chairs, murmuring to each other all the while. Newer residents asked the more experienced what pinball was, since many had never seen or heard of this particular version of the EG, while other residents speculated about who among them was "gonna get it" from the counselors. In minutes, all of the women in the program were seated and comported in the "ready for treatment" posture (feet on the floor, backs straight, chins set and lifted, faces expressionless, and hands placed palms down on the knees). Standing in the doorway to the staff office with two other counselors, Counselor Tynice looked sternly around the room, taking a moment to look directly into the eyes of the women who faced her. After whispering for a moment or two with the other staff members, Tynice strode into the center of the circle wheeling behind her an office desk chair. Before taking a seat beside one of the residents in the circle, she took great care to place the desk chair in the precise center of the circle, aligned almost directly underneath a glass skylight in the unit's ceiling.

As she moved to take her seat, Tynice called, "Sarah, you can take the seat in the middle. Put your hands on your knees and spin toward me." Sarah did as she was told, though breaking with program etiquette by glancing at two other residents in the circle and rolling her eyes. She swiveled the office chair so that she was facing Counselor Tynice and, with chin held high, stared directly at the counselor.

Family,[7] I put you in this circle today to give you some information which you so desperately need about yourself and your emotions. You see, you're not in control like you think you are. You ain't got no control at all. Know how I know that?

At the beginning of the confrontation, Counselor Tynice's voice was low, barely audible. By the time she spoke of Sarah's lack of control, however, her voice was booming so that the question came out as a

56   JOURNAL OF CONTEMPORARY ETHNOGRAPHY / FEBRUARY 2003

controlled scream. The other residents, who were leaning forward in their chairs to hear her, jumped back almost in tandem as she began yelling.

"Sarah, I asked you a question. Do you know how I know that you're not in control? Dialogue."[8] Sarah, her faced flushed, shook her head negatively.

> Sarah, I instructed you to dialogue, not gesture. I'm going to ask again and this time I want an answer. You're not going to control me or this session. You can't, you don't have the control you think you do. Now, I asked you twice, and I'm asking you again, and unless you're truly so dumb or so confused as to not know the answer, I want to know why I know, but you don't seem to, that you're not in control.

With her jaw set firmly Sarah responded, "I control what I think and how I behave, not you. Isn't that what this program is telling us? That we're responsible for our behaviors. . . ."

> *Counselor Tynice:* Family, that's enough. That's it, I've had it with your atti-tude. If you were truly in control, if you had all this power, would you be in here? What kind of woman, what kind of mother, would choose—if she had control—would choose to be in prison? Come on, family, you're talking shit now and we all know it. Responsibility and control are two different matters. I know you don't got no learning disabilities or other serious mental impairments, so you better believe that you're responsi-ble for what you do. I'm holding you responsible right now for your neg-ative behavior the other day.

The onlookers remained riveted on Sarah throughout Counselor Tynice's discussion. A bead of sweat slid down Sarah's forehead.

> *Sarah:* You're saying that I don't have any control, and you're asking me how you know that? Well, I guess you know that 'cause you got all them bitches in here monitoring everyone's behavior all the time, and we can't make a move without one of them ass kissers all up in your office saying, "Oh, Sarah did this and that to this one and said these nontherapeutical things and all that." I guess you know about me 'cause you is watching me and you think you know me.

As Sarah spoke, she glared at one of the women in the room whose assigned job as "expediter" required that she "act as the eyes and ears of the community." In terms of the program's social hierarchy, the expediter was responsible for ensuring that residents reported one another for rule violations and forwarding these reports directly to staff members.

> *Counselor Tynice:* Sarah, I know you're not in control of yourself because I understand the disease of addiction. I know what an addict looks like, feels like, thinks like. I can read the signs, and sister, they're written all over you. Does this sound like you? You can't deal with your emotions and you try to control them by taking your drugs. What was yours? Oh yeah, you was a whore for your crack, I remember. And when you whored around with all those men, you was manipulating all right. But not just them, no, no. You were repressing those emotions, but as you did you let crack rule you. You let those men rule you; you manipulated yourself. A whore is helpless, and that is you.

As Counselor Tynice spoke, Sarah's shoulders rolled in toward her chest and she began to cry. Her eyes were cast downward, and she appeared to be gazing at the leg of Tynice's chair. Around the room, other residents fidgeted in their seats, some looked at Counselor Tynice, and others looked blankly at one another. No one, with the exception of Counselor Tynice and the two counselors who stood in the corner of the facility, looked at Sarah. The scene was strangely ethereal as a ray of sun streaming into the room from the skylight above cast itself directly onto Sarah, who sat slumped on the office chair. Indeed, the setting, the participants, and the image of a lone figure humbled before the sun's rays were eerily reminiscent of Eastern State Penitentiary, the American archetype of Jeremy Bentham's *Panopticon*, an eighteenth-century blueprint for the optimization of social control in total institutions.

Like Jeremy Bentham's design of the Panopticon and early American penitentiaries such as Philadelphia's Eastern State, PRW sought to maximize control of inmate behavior through an architecture that allowed for continuous surveillance (Foucault 1977; Beaumont and de Tocqueville [1833] 1964). In PRW, this was realized by the arrangement of inmate cells in a two-tiered semicircle along the outside wall of the unit. All of the rooms faced the guard station and staff offices, and each had a window that was eight inches wide and ran the length of the door, allowing anyone within a few feet of the cell to see the activities taking place inside. Supervision was further enhanced by the requirement that residents oversee one another and report rule violations,

58   JOURNAL OF CONTEMPORARY ETHNOGRAPHY / FEBRUARY 2003

which created a system of interpersonal surveillance networks. The surveillance networks contributed to the arrangement of an interaction order in which any and all thoughts, feelings, or behaviors were potentially knowable to everyone within the community.

The program's fixation with control through surveillance is rooted in its quest to reform the "flawed" characters of the women. Eighteenth- and nineteenth-century penal reformers did so by designing the "separate system" that sought to ritualistically purify the prison environment by housing inmates in individual, separate cells (thereby eliminating the possibilities for moral contagion that were theorized to arise when prisoners interacted with one another) (Rothman 1971; Beaumont and de Tocqueville [1833] 1964). Purity was also sought through promoting the prisoners' spiritual connectedness with god, and to that end, the ceiling of each cell housed a small window that allowed a single shaft of light to penetrate the room. Inmates were told that the ray of light was the "hand of god" and that during those hours in which the sun shone in their cells, they were to kneel before the light and engage in intense and solemn deliberations about their character and the possibilities of reform while in the "spiritual presence of the Maker" (Barnes 1926, 162).

It is doubtful, of course, that Counselor Tynice's effort to place the pinball chair in the direct path of the sunlight was a deliberate reference to eighteenth-century penology. Nor was it intended to symbolize an omniscient god.[9] On the other hand, the act of placing the intended receiver of one of these confrontations in the direct path of the sun was not unintentional. The counselors did so with too great a frequency and too deliberate a method for it to be merely coincidence. Indeed, the term *hot seat* as a moniker for the center chair was coined by residents to dually refer to the emotional discomfort associated with being the target of a confrontation as well as the physical discomfort of being forced to sit directly in the sun throughout the duration of the confrontational episode.

In PRW, the emphasis on purity and the ritualistic cleansing of moral contamination from the residents is just as intense as it was for the early penal reformers; however, it is not the eyes of god that symbolize the totality of institutional control, nor is it the souls of inmates that mark the target of social control efforts. In fact, it is the self, rather than the soul, that is regarded as befouled, and it is the diagnostic powers of the professional therapist that are celebrated as the higher power from which moral salvation is to be achieved. But at the heart of diagnostic power is premised an overwhelming concern for, and reliance on, surveillance. This, then, is what is represented with the placing of the desk chair in the sun—the awesome heat and intense brightness of the sun's rays as they shine through the single skylight in the unit's ceiling are at once symbolic of the counselors' omniscience and the denudation of the residents' selves.

THERAPY AND SURVEILLANCE

The importance of Bentham's *Panopticon* and the early penitentiary system for the present study is that this period in history represents not only the birth of the modern prison but the emergence of a system of social control premised on surveillance. In Foucault's (1977) analysis of the eighteenth-century penitentiary system, he argued that through incarceration and surveillance, the institution of the prison is quite literally inserted into the mind of the prisoner. Consider the architectural design of early American penitentiaries modeled after the Panopticon. Several tiers of cells were arranged in a circular pattern, all of which surrounded a central guard tower. The activities occurring at any moment, in any corner of each of the cells, were entirely visible to guards stationed in the tower. The activities of guards within the central tower, however, were invisible and unknown to the prisoners watching from their cells. The Panopticon represented a style of surveillance that was continuous, visible, and yet unverifiable (p. 201). The surveillance was visible and continuous because the inmates were aware of the omnipresence of the guard tower and knew that during any given moment, they were being watched from the tower. The act of observation was itself unverifiable because, ultimately, the inmates never knew exactly when the guards were watching them. With a system of visible, continuous, and yet unverifiable surveillance, the act of social control becomes one of self-control. Inmates organize their behaviors on the assumption that they are being observed and not only conform with institutional rules but internalize them as well. And while the institution continues to control bodies in the sense that they regulate movement to and from the cells, the body is no longer the target of institutional control as it is in the case of corporal punishment. The target is the mind, as the pervasiveness of surveillance forces the prisoner to adopt the role of

60   JOURNAL OF CONTEMPORARY ETHNOGRAPHY / FEBRUARY 2003

the other (in this case the prison) and view himself or herself from the perspective of the institution. It is a system of social control that influences not simply the behavior but the perception of inmates.

Therapy, itself a system of social control, also endeavors to alter perception (Horwitz 1984; Szasz 1963). In particular, the work of therapy involves challenging the client's perceptions about the self by providing him or her with a reinterpretation of the behavior, attitudes, feelings, and events occurring throughout his or her life course (Bloor, McKeganey, and Fonkert 1988; Hardesty 1986). Sociological analyses of therapy have often focused on the extent to which therapists actively construct an alternate reality about the lives and selves of their patients, particularly women, but such analyses have downplayed the importance of surveillance (see Russell 1995; Gill and Maynard 1995; Warren 1991; Bloor, McKeganey, and Fonkert 1988; Goffman 1961).

The connection between therapy and surveillance is not a new one. The early penal reformers, interested in rehabilitation rather than vengeful punishment, regarded penitentiaries as a therapeutic rather than a punitive environment (Hirsch 1992). What qualified the penitentiary as a rehabilitative institution was the requirement that inmates develop a spiritual connectedness with god and, more important, that totalizing surveillance (embodied by the symbolic eye of god and the literal eyes of guards) produced total conformity. Penal reformers of the day argued that inmates, in fear of being labeled deviants, would align their behavior with institutional and social conventions since they knew that doing otherwise would undoubtedly be discovered by either their god or their keepers. As Foucault (1980) noted of penal reformers, "They thought people would become virtuous by the simple fact of being observed" (p. 161).[10]

A similar assumption undergirds the structure of punishment within East State. I have indicated how architecture and the formal structuring of relationships among residents combine to produce a surveillance mechanism that is virtually impenetrable. But surveillance is not only embedded in the structure of the program, it is celebrated in the program's culture. For example, throughout the unit there are handmade posters designed by residents and commissioned by the staff that are composed in the center by a large, blue eye. Beneath the eye are the words (sometimes stenciled, sometimes handwritten), "EVERYWHERE YOU GO, EVERYTHING YOU DO, KNOW THAT SOMEONE IS WATCHING YOU." More recently, the phrase was modified to read, "EVERYWHERE YOU GO, EVERYTHING YOU DO, THE EYES ARE ALWAYS WATCHING YOU." There are also signs rewarding residents whose surveillance performance is deemed to be excellent by the staff. These posters depict the same blue eye with the words "MOST AWARE" written underneath it. Each week, a new name is Velcroed to the bottom of the poster, and a "MOST AWARE" sticker is placed on the door of the week's most celebrated resident. All of these signs appear almost everywhere in the facility, on resident doors, inside resident cells, and on the front and back walls of the large group room. The only place where the signs do not appear is within the environs of staff offices.

The signs first began to appear around the unit during the program's tenth month of operation. The program's first months in the prison were difficult ones. Counselors had a hard time recruiting inmates into the program and were barely able to fill half of the forty-six program beds. Furthermore, the rate at which residents prematurely left the program ranged from 65 percent to 80 percent during that period. The program was under considerable pressure from the prison administration, the state government, and grant administrators to fill the beds. They made arrangements with drug court judges to sentence women directly into the program and stipulated that dropouts would receive lengthier prison terms. In addition, instead of using the knowledge of program residents to improve recruitment and retention efforts by asking for their suggestions, the program opted to crack down on "immature" behavior in the unit (which consisted of smuggling forbidden candy into the unit, hair styling, and writing love letters) by placing more stringent demands on behavior, limiting various privileges, and increasing the amount of surveillance directed at residents' behavior. Counselors instructed residents to make the signs to remind themselves that they were always being watched.[11] During a meeting with evaluators, PRW's director explained that the crackdown was necessary because the women lacked "structure" in their lives. Rules and guidelines for even the most minute behaviors (e.g., when, where, and how to brush one's teeth and proper cleaning procedure and storage space for the brush) were necessary, she explained, because the women were poorly socialized. Indeed, one of her most frequently repeated statements to public officials, evaluators, prison administrators, and other program outsiders was that PRW "has to do habilitation with these women before we ever even think about *RE-habilitation!*" (emphasis hers).

62   JOURNAL OF CONTEMPORARY ETHNOGRAPHY / FEBRUARY 2003

Regardless of the reasons behind the increase in surveillance and program rules, the shift was felt by the residents. Latasha, a resident who had been in the program from its inception, experienced the evolution firsthand:

> In the beginning there was a lot of confusion and not much control, er, control in terms of them [staff] just watching and waiting for us to do somethin' bad, you know? But I didn't mind it in the beginning; it wasn't bad like it sounds. I mean the confusion, that wasn't so bad 'cause it was like we was *all* trying to set up this therapeutical community. Like we all had a part in it. Now, they's just telling us we're sick and we need some structure. Well, yeah, you know, I'm in here to get some help for my sickness, but I didn't think help would be no prison. Yeah, that's it! They watch us more than the COs [correctional officers] did in general pop. And all that watching, it gets to you. . . . It's not like you're necessarily doing something bad; it's just you don't want everything about yourself to be known by everyone. You want to keep some stuff private, even if it ain't stuff that's embarrassing and believe me they know all about the embarrassing stuff [laughs and discusses how staff and residents discussed her bout with diarrhea for several moments at a house meeting]. . . . You want to keep stuff private because it's private. It's that part of you that is yours, that you know.

A fundamental part of punishment within PRW and the prison more generally is behavioral control, and most frequently this control is achieved through complete surveillance. Like the eighteenth-century reformers, counselors believed that the awareness of a pervasive system of surveillance would inhibit residents from engaging in deviant acts. In response to a question about why residents were given very little privacy in the program, Counselor Elizabeth answered,

> Well, they're addicts. What do you expect? The problem with addicts is if you give them enough rope, they'll hang themselves. It's in their nature. The thing about addiction is that it's a disease of the whole person—that means what they do in every part of their life. I don't care if it's pissing. You let them piss alone and they'll find a way to fuck everything up. That's who they are. It's the nature of the beast.

In this sense, the rhetoric of program staff is quite similar to that of the early penal reformers—constant vigilance is required to prevent deviant persons from engaging in deviant behavior. And while the continuity and visibility of surveillance are not embodied in the form of a guard tower erected in the center of the unit, they are symbolized by the images of eyes that are hung throughout the unit and ritualized in confrontation ceremonies where behaviors thought to be hidden from scrutiny are made the subject of public discussion.

Such was the case during the initial confrontation between Counselor Tynice and Sarah that had later given rise to the pinball session. Sarah had written two letters to Joyce indicating that she was having romantic feelings toward her. The counselors officially learned of the letters when Joyce, after receiving the second letter, reported it to the expediter who, in turn, told the staff.[12] After reading the letters and passing them to other staff members, Counselor Tynice waited only a few minutes to call all the residents into the center of the unit. "Family, one of you—maybe more—sure has been up to some sneaky things. Some things you thought maybe you could hide; maybe you thought that something taking place behind closed doors was a secret. FAMILY," and at this point Tynice was yelling, "DO WE HAVE SECRETS IN THIS HOUSE?" The residents collectively shook their heads in the negative, and some murmured "no."

"Sarah, get up to the center of the floor." Sarah looked at Counselor Tynice and pointed to herself while mouthing the word, "Me?" When Tynice nodded, Sarah rose from where she was sitting and walked to the center of the room. A resident who had never been in any kind of significant trouble before, Sarah seemed shocked as did several members of the audience.

"What have you been up to behind our backs, Sarah? What secrets have you been keeping?" Tynice looked disgusted. At first Sarah denied keeping any secrets, but after being questioned several more times by Tynice, she divulged that she had smuggled a candy bar into the unit that she had shared with two other residents in the program.

"Well, you're right about that, but it ain't no candy bar that I'm concerned with right now. It's that other sweet tooth you got is what I'm concerned with." Tynice waved the letters in the air. "Do you know what these are, Sarah?" Sarah shook her head negatively. "These are letters from you to another woman." Sarah stared stonily at Tynice, but her shaking hands belied her surprise.

"These are letters from you to another woman in here, indicating your romantic interest in this woman." Tynice read from part of the letter and asked, "Did you write these letters, Sarah?"

"No, no," Sarah managed to stammer. Tynice called Joyce to stand beside Sarah on the floor and asked, "Joyce, did you receive these letters?" Sarah glanced at Joyce just long enough to see Joyce nod. Tynice repeated the question, "Sarah, did you write these letters?"

"No, I didn't. I ain't no lesbian; everyone in here knows that." Tynice looked at Joyce and asked, "Who gave you these letters?"

"Sarah did, ma'am." Joyce's head was lowered. Several of the women in the audience gasped.

> *Sarah:* That's a lie; I'm not homosexual and I didn't write no romantic letters to another woman—
>
> *Counselor Tynice:* Come on, Sarah. You know we were gonna find out sooner or later. I got Joyce saying you did it, and not only that, but several people in this house including your roommate remember seeing you write notes during your free time, and I got a person that says she saw you pass the note to Joyce.

Sarah glared at Joyce who was still standing beside her. "What does that sign behind you say, Sarah?" Sarah turned to look at one of the posters of the blue eye. She mumbled, "Everywhere you go, everything you do, someone is always watching you."

"We're watching you, Sarah. Got it? Now admit this so we can move on and those things the addict keeps hidden can come out into the light." Sarah shook her head at Tynice and ran off the floor into her cell, slamming the door on the way in.

EMBODIED SURVEILLANCE

Confrontation ceremonies such as the one recounted above remind residents of both the continuity of surveillance (that it is ever present) and the intrusiveness of surveillance (that it has access to behavior that is put on for public display as well as private thoughts and feelings). But the ceremonies do something more. They emphasize to residents that this is an embodied surveillance, wherein the observer and the observed are known to one another. It is, in fact, a verifiable form of surveillance, although verification may occur after the fact. This is a significant difference from the disembodied method of observation that Foucault (1977, 1980) discussed in his analysis of the penitentiary. Unable to discern whether or by whom they were being watched, inmates in the

Panopticon were arguably prevented from even the thought of revolt. As Foucault (1977) explained,

> He is the object of information, never a subject in communication. . . . And this invisibility is a guarantee of social order. [Among convicts] there is no danger or a plot, an attempt at collective escape . . . that this architectural apparatus should be a machine for creating and sustaining a power relation independent of the person who exercises it; in short, that the inmates should be caught up in a power situation of which they are themselves the bearers. (pp. 200-201)

In PRW, there was no effort to hide the identities of witnesses from those who stood accused of wrongdoing or an attempt to render surveillance as anything less than a universal responsibility demanded of every resident in the program. For Foucault, the ability of the observed to identify their observers creates the potential for disruptions in the social order and thereby threatens to erode the institution's control over inmate behavior. To be sure, verifiability creates problems of order in PRW, but it does so in a way that solidifies the power of the counseling staff over their charges. The situation between Sarah and Joyce is an important one in this regard. Staff sought to prevent residents from becoming friends with one another (one of the most frequent phrases uttered by staff members to residents was, "There are no friends in treatment") because they regarded the friendship dyad as having the potential to usurp therapeutic control. Close relations with peers (be they romantically motivated or otherwise) jeopardize surveillance since friends will be less likely to report one another for subversive thoughts and behaviors. To prevent the formation of friendships and other types of intimate relations, staff went to great lengths to force friends to confront one another for misdeeds. This appeared to be largely successful as the majority of residents reported that they "trusted no one" in the program. With such confrontations, disruptions in order occurred, but order was only destabilized at the bottom, not the top. In the case of Sarah and Joyce in the weeks following the confrontation, Sarah stopped talking to Joyce altogether and took an active role in trying to get her in trouble with staff. Indeed, the challenge Sarah's defiance posed for the authority of the counseling staff was not only neutralized but was used to reify surveillance and increase the legitimacy of the staff's diagnostic abilities.

66   JOURNAL OF CONTEMPORARY ETHNOGRAPHY / FEBRUARY 2003

In fact, surveillance need not be anonymous as it was in men's penitentiaries because surveillance is intimately related to the process of diagnosis, rather than existing simply to prevent the occurrence of behaviors that deviate from institutional guidelines. Indeed, an embodied surveillance where the observer and the observed are known to one another was preferred in this setting because it lent greater validity to the therapeutic diagnosis. This was the case in the scenario depicted at the beginning of the analysis section. Sarah, initially confident enough in her own knowledge of self to act defiantly in front of Counselor Tynice (first by terminating a confrontation and later by challenging Counselor Tynice's assessment of her as "not in control"), suffered a virtual mental and physical collapse toward the conclusion of the pinball confrontation. Sarah's final statement while still on the hot seat in the center of the group indicates a newfound insecurity with respect to her ability to understand herself and her relations with others:

> What you said hurts, it does. . . . But it's true. It's all true. I did those things; I am those things. I guess I just needed someone else to see it— what I couldn't see myself, about myself. The control is something I want, that I wanted, which I thought I could get at . . . could achieve it [begins to cry]. Today, now, feeling helpless, I know that you've helped me to get in touch with my real feelings. I am helpless against this disease [addiction].

In sum, the purpose of surveillance for punishment in PRW and East State more generally is threefold. First, as was the case in the early penitentiaries, surveillance is a repressive device in that it is used as a mechanism of control designed to prevent the occurrence of rule-breaking behavior. Given the severity of the penalties associated with violating program rules, staff believed residents were unlikely to engage in rule-breaking behavior if they knew they were being watched. Counselors justified repressive measures by referencing the "manipulative" and "criminogenic" selves of addicts. Staff's claims about the self were alluded to earlier in the quotation from Counselor Elizabeth regarding the necessity of eliminating zones of privacy to prevent "poorly socialized" women from "fucking everything up." It is not possible within the perimeters of this particular article to examine the organizational construction of residents' identities in great detail, but it is important to emphasize here that beliefs about the women's lack of "socialization" and "structure" were the primary discursive mechanism used to justify the program's extensive use of repression and surveillance.

The second characteristic of surveillance is that it is productive. By this I mean to suggest that surveillance yields information about the women that is central to the interpretive process and thus the diagnostics of therapy. The discussion of Sarah's rule breaking illustrates this point well. Counselor Tynice interpreted available information about Sarah (e.g., the romantic content of a note, claims to heterosexuality, and walking off the floor in the middle of a confrontation) as intentional defiance of the program norms and diagnosed her as being "out of control." Furthermore, information that is garnered through confrontation operates to further enhance control structures as aggrieved residents like Sarah vow to report others who engage in rule violations. Diagnosis and discipline are ultimately extensions of the surveillance mechanism.

Third, the embodied nature of the surveillance mechanism functions to legitimate therapeutic diagnoses. Again, using Sarah as an example, the veracity of Counselor Tynice's claim was established not through reference to her own professional competence (e.g., I've been a drug and alcohol counselor for ten years) but through the observations of Sarah's behavior by Tynice and the others. It did not occur to Sarah to contest the observation, only the initial claim that she was out of control.

THE GENDERING OF PUNISHMENT

It is clear that surveillance operates differently in PRW and East State than it does in men's institutions. The reason that it does is because surveillance in women's prisons is intimately related to the process of diagnosis, rather than simply existing to prevent the occurrence of behaviors that threaten institutional security, however broadly conceived. Emphasis within men's institutions across the state was on repression, deprivation, and warehousing—a trend that was replicated in men's prisons across the country throughout the 1980s and 1990s (Irwin and Austin 1997). Ironically, PRW's "brother" program was marginalized within the men's prison. Despite the success of outcome data and the increasing proportion of drug offenders among the inmate population, prison administrators were unwilling and uninterested in

68   JOURNAL OF CONTEMPORARY ETHNOGRAPHY / FEBRUARY 2003

working with the TC either to increase its size or to expand outreach services to inmates in the general population.[13]

The women's facility was also influenced by "get tough" politics, though not in quite the same way. The popularity of the get tough philosophy was evident in the early meetings administrators held with criminal justice professionals regarding the overcrowding problem. Administrators theorized if they were not so "soft," women would "think twice" before committing another crime upon their release. PRW's appeal (beyond the fact that it was a federally funded program for the first three years of operation) was that it offered, in the words of the warden, "a more rigorous form of therapy." PRW was considered "hard core." Nonetheless, the reason that PRW survived and prospered within the institution had as much to do with its appearance as a get tough program that emphasized personal responsibility for one's crimes as it did with the fact that PRW promised to habilitate the diseased selves of women drug offenders.

This begs the question—why are therapy and diagnosis so tightly bound up with punishment in East State? The answer can be found in the contradictory ways administrators, counselors, and prison staff conceptualize criminality in general and women's criminality in particular. The get tough philosophy is premised, in part, on the belief that the criminal's actions are based on rational, self-interested calculations. Masculinity is implicit in this construction of the criminal—the "typical" criminal is a masculine subject. Criminals are motivated by power and economics; they are dissuaded by harsh penalties and the likelihood of capture. East State's transition to hard core punishment was legitimated by referring to this popular discursive construction of the criminal. Administrators did not attribute the upward surge in the prison population to the increased surveillance and mandatory sentencing policies of the drug war; rather, they saw increases as an outcome of the decisions and actions of individual offenders.

At the same time, constructions of the "typical" criminal competed with what prison staff understood as the "reality" of women's crime. In interviews, staff and administrators would frequently contrast the economic aspect of men's crimes with the baseness and "sickness" of women's. During an interview, the warden explained,

> Yeah, poverty plays a role. You don't see a lot of college students or rich divorcees in here. At the same time, there is something else going on.

> Poor men stick somebody up or sell drugs. To me, as strange as this may
> sound coming from a warden, that is understandable. I can see how you
> would make that choice. Women degrade themselves. Selling them-
> selves, you should hear some of the stuff they do. There is no sense of
> self-respect, of dignity. . . . There is something wrong on the inside that
> makes an individual take up those kind of behaviors and choices.

Women are considered "deviant criminals" in the sense that their choice
of crimes is seemingly inexplicable. Their crimes are not seen as rational responses to structural conditions in the way that men's crimes are.
Ironically, the fact that women do participate in crime categories such
as robbery and drug sales is overshadowed by their participation in certain types of crime, particularly drug use and prostitution, which is considered evidence of women's deviance as offenders.

Administrators, staff, and decision makers use psychological rather
than structural explanations to account for women's criminality and
justify this by reporting, in great detail, inmates' departures from appropriate gender displays. As in the above quotation from the warden and
the confrontation described between Counselor Tynice and Sarah, sexuality took center stage in this discussion. Promiscuity, prostitution,
and lesbianism signaled that something was "wrong." Notably, respondents rarely thematized inmates' past sexual victimization in their discussions of sexuality and offending, and only a few (a nurse, a PRW
counselor, and several correctional officers) suggested that sexual victimization played a key role in what was "wrong." In addition to
problematizing women's sexuality, administrators and staff at East
State also questioned their performance as mothers. One correctional
officer who had worked in East State for four years commented,

> I'm a mother of two and I know what that impulse, that instinct, that
> mothering instinct feels like. It just takes over, like, you would never put
> your kids in harm's way. . . . Women in here lack that. Something in their
> nature is not right, you know? They run out and leave their kids alone,
> babies, while they score drugs or go over to their boyfriend's house, you
> know? They neglect them, leave them with strangers or get high in front
> of them. And I know a lot of them feel really bad about it when they get in
> here and stop and think about it. But it's like they don't think of it out
> there, in the moment. That's a sign something is wrong, some kind of
> psychological problem or something.

Administrators and staff reconcile the self-interested criminal of the get tough platform with the disparate reality of women's offending by pointing to women's gender deviance, which, in turn, they use to legitimate psychological explanations and therapeutic interventions. The fact that hard core punishment comes by way of "rigorous" therapy is premised on the belief that women offenders have "something wrong on the inside." This is the significance of PRW's emphasis on habilitation rather than rehabilitation. Institutional beliefs regarding women's deviance extend beyond the sense that inmates have failed to internalize norms regarding substance use and unlawful behavior; it goes to their very embodiment of gender. The continual references to inmates' incomplete "socialization" and "lack of structure" refer to their failure to competently "do" gender (West and Zimmerman 1987). Women, according to institutional ideology, are (among other things), monogamous and heterosexual, diligent caretakers of children and the elderly, responsible, clean, and self-restrained. Indeed, the focal points of concern in PRW involve women's patterns of food consumption and weight, hygiene, romantic relations with other women, and relations with one's family, particularly children. These focal points of concern were mirrored within the prison more generally.

Prison staff were similarly concerned with "habilitating" their charges. The deputy warden noted during a 1996 interview,

> The problem before was that we tried to rehabilitate them, to show them where they went wrong. We didn't understand that they lack even the basics on which to build from. [PRW] showed us that. Now we hold them responsible for their behavior and we're tougher on them than we used to be, but we also want to make them better people when they get out of here.

Even the use of surveillance reflected the institution's interest in habilitating the gender deviant. For example, while the prison drug economy thrived in East State during the 1990s, correctional officers regularly used new surveillance technologies (cameras, listening devices, etc.) to confiscate "romantic" notes sent between inmates. The notes, more frequently than drugs or other serious rule violations, were a prominent topic of discussion in classification meetings. Classification personnel routinely used women's relations with family members and other inmates—information garnered primarily through surveillance tactics—as an assessment tool to determine whether an inmate was "willing to change" and what kinds of programs and work opportunities would be suitable. Indeed, many of the diagnostic patterns that characterized interaction in PRW were replicated in the general prison facility. Surveillance techniques differed between the general prison facility and PRW (mounted cameras replaced graphic depictions of blue eyes), but the practice of surveillance operated in much the same way for similar ends.

Ironically, although "habilitation" was the stated goal, neither PRW nor the prison was equipped to restore inmates to the institution's idealized conception of femininity. The masculine subtext of the get tough philosophy made this an impossibility. East State opted to replicate the hard core characteristics of men's prisons in the hopes that such disciplinary practices would improve recidivism rates. They upgraded surveillance equipment, installed razor wire, and most important, brought in PRW. PRW's philosophy of the addict, like the get tough philosophy of criminality, presumed a masculine subject. The program's goal was the creation of an autonomous, self-interested self. From this perspective, women responded poorly indeed. The vice president of PII complained that women, unlike men in treatment, "wallow in their victimization." Their failure was not attributed to the program structure; it was attributed to the "feminine" self. Consider how Sarah's identity is constructed by Counselor Tynice in the pinball session—Sarah is characterized as weak, emotional, out of control, codependent, and hypersexual. Habilitation is accomplished not by teaching Sarah how to be an empowered, responsible woman—it is accomplished by alienating Sarah from qualities associated with a feminine self (e.g., displaying emotion and relational qualities are serious rule violations, and residents are reminded, "there are no friends in treatment").

PRW and the get tough platform of which it was a part were developed for men based exclusively on men's subject positions and their experiences with drugs and crime. In a model in which masculinity serves as the normative baseline, women's unique experiences and needs are rendered either invisible or deviant. There is no register for acknowledging that women occupy distinct positions in the social structure and that these distinct positions make the application of "universal" (read masculine) strategies to deal with criminality and drug use erroneous. Although prison staff informally acknowledged that women's criminality was different from men's, they attributed this to psychological rather than structural conditions. Subsequently, women's "difference" became the target of institutional control efforts.

The disciplinary hybrid that emerged, embodied surveillance, represented the institution's effort to fit a square peg (women's criminality) in a round hole (hard core control).

CONCLUSION: GENDER IN THE "EQUALITY WITH A VENGEANCE" ERA

On the surface, the "equality with a vengeance" era in women's corrections would appear to suggest that prisons have achieved a sort of gender neutrality, in which policies and programs that once would have been considered unthinkable in women's facilities are now implemented with widespread support. This study demonstrates that rather than signaling the decline of the gendered organization, the equality with a vengeance era marks a shift in how gender is conceived and elaborated within the criminal justice system. Sex role stereotypes are no longer the primary discursive vehicle through which new policies and programs are justified and implemented. Instead, get tough policies and hard core disciplinary practices are legitimated according to theories and characterizations of the "typical" criminal. This is similar to recent shifts in the gender politics of the welfare state. The 1996 passage of the Personal Responsibility Work Opportunity Reconciliation Act transferred what remained of state support for stay-at-home mothering to an exclusive focus on work in the paid labor market and work-related activities. The normative baseline for this model of welfare reform is the citizen worker—characterized by independence from the state, detachment from familial demands, and self-interest (Korteweg 2001; Fraser 1997). And just as the citizen worker is based on a masculine subject, so too is the typical criminal.

While current get tough policies occlude women's subjectivity, it is not the case that prison organizations treat women and men the same way. There is widespread acknowledgment within the system that women are different, but the source of the difference is attributed to psychological rather than structural elements. In this way, high rates of offending and recidivism are not seen as a failure of the system but as a failure of the women themselves. This necessitates a modification in the seemingly gender-neutral structure of control. Instead of preoccupying themselves with breaches in security and the potentiality of inmate revolt, administrators in East State were concerned with displays of gender deviance. To simultaneously fix the feminine self and punish the criminal, administrators modified the hard core structure to include an embodied form of surveillance, one in which the observed and the observer are known to one another. This is in contrast to Foucault's (1977, 1980) discussion of the unverifiable character of surveillance mechanisms and therefore represents a crucial distinction between men's and women's prisons in the equality with a vengeance era. The gendered character of punishment results in a distinct system of social control within women's prisons that merges key features of punishment (in the form of surveillance) and therapy (in the form of diagnosis) to advance institutional claims about the deviant self and to engineer a shift in behavior. Notably, what is being inserted into the minds of inmates are not only institutional norms guiding conduct and behavior but institutional claims about gender and subjectivity.

NOTES

1. Pseudonyms are used in place of actual names to ensure confidentiality. In addition, the use of identifying information is avoided.

2. Women's prisons are economies of scale. Women typically constitute less than 10 percent of a state's inmate population, and subsequently, institutions and services for women receive a considerably smaller slice of the corrections budget than do services and facilities that cater to men (McCorkel 1996; Fletcher, Shaver, and Moon 1993; Ross and Fabiano 1986).

3. For a detailed discussion of therapeutic communities, see Bloor, McKeganey, and Fonkert (1988); DeLeon (1997); and Lockwood, McCorkel, and Inciardi (1998).

4. The Project Rehabilitate Women (PRW) program is housed in a separate wing of the prison facility in which inmate cells are arranged in a semicircular fashion around the perimeter of the unit. The interior of the cells is visible from virtually any central location in the unit since the doors are constructed of wood with a lengthy panel of glass running down the center of the door.

5. Given the myriad rules regulating conduct and expression in the program, all residents were selected to be the targets of confrontation at one point or another. The vast majority of residents were regularly confronted because staff believed the confrontations were a necessary and critical component of therapy.

6. According to the PRW orientation manual, pinball is a

> unique and dynamic encounter group where no one is safe from being addressed or allowed to respond to the confrontations. The energy created by this rapid-fire type of encounter commits residents to confront each other in a manner that is both uncensored, and at times verbally hostile. . . . The effect is two-fold. First, the resident is not able to respond and is forced to contain her

feelings until she is able to deal with them at a latter [*sic*] time. Secondly, the random confrontations provoke residents into exposing and breaking negative relationships.

7. In keeping with therapeutic community traditions established during the 1970s in treatment centers such as Synanon and Daytop Village, staff and residents of the program referred to one another as "family."

8. "Dialogue" is a command issued by counselors that gives residents permission to speak during periods such as encounter group when they are not otherwise permitted to do so.

9. In contrast to the prison facility within which it is a part, PRW is essentially secular. Residents are not required to participate in religious services, although the program does make an effort to accommodate the "spiritual needs" of residents by allowing them to observe religious holidays and participate in Sunday services held in the general prison. References to a "higher power" are made by staff during Alcoholics Anonymous and Narcotics Anonymous groups when they are reading from Alcoholics Anonymous/Narcotics Anonymous literature, but in general, spirituality is considered a private matter in which staff rarely interfere.

10. The term *penitentiary* derives its meaning from Greek for "everything" and "a place of sight."

11. Although the depiction of an eye and the poster's phrase were supplied by the counselors, the color of the eye was selected by residents. That the eye was blue and not brown appears to be a comment on the racial character of institutional power. One of the residents who was in the program when the signs were first commissioned commented, "Yeah, it's pretty much brown eyes watching in here, but some of us are down; you know, it's the big blue eye in the sky! The white man, you know?"

12. "Sexual acting out" (as all nonheterosexual behaviors are deemed by the staff) was strictly forbidden in the program and served as grounds for immediate expulsion even if the behavior was consensual.

13. A number of research studies have reported that treatment and rehabilitative programs are often marginalized within men's prisons (see Pan et al. 1993; Irwin and Austin 1997; Inciardi and Lockwood 1994).

REFERENCES

Acker, Joan. 1990. Hierarchies, jobs, bodies: A theory of gendered organizations. *Gender & Society* 4 (2): 139-58.
———. 1992. From sex roles to gendered institutions. *Contemporary Sociology* 21:565-69.
Barnes, Henry Elmer. 1926. *The repression of crime*. New York: George H. Doran.
Bartky, Sandra Lee. 1988. Foucault, femininity, and the modernization of patriarchal power. In *Feminism and Foucault*, edited by Irene Diamond and Lee Quinby, 61-86. Boston: Northeastern University Press.

Baskin, Deborah, Ira Sommers, Richard Tessler, and Henry Steadman. 1989. Role incongruence and gender variation in the provision of prison mental health services. *Journal of Health and Social Behavior* 30:305-14.

Beaumont, Gustave, and Alexis de Tocqueville. [1833] 1964. *On the penitentiary system in the United States and its application to France.* Carbondale: Southern Illinois University Press.

Bloom, Barbara, Meda Chesney-Lind, and Barbara Owen. 1994. *Women in California prisons.* San Francisco: Center on Juvenile and Criminal Justice.

Bloor, Michael, Neil McKeganey, and Dick Fonkert. 1988. *One foot in Eden.* New York: Routledge.

Britton, Dana. 1999. Cat fights and gang fights. *Sociological Quarterly* 40 (3): 455-74.

―――. 2000. The epistemology of the gendered organization. *Gender & Society* 14 (3): 418-34.

Chesney-Lind, Meda, and Joycelyn Pollock. 1995. Women's prisons: Equality with a vengeance. In *Women, law & social control*, edited by Alida Merlo and Joycelyn Pollock, 155-76. Boston: Allyn & Bacon.

Clawson, Mary Ann. 1999. When women play the bass: Instrument specialization and gender interpretation in alternative rock music. *Gender & Society* 13 (2): 193-210.

Cook, Clarissa, and Malcolm Waters. 1998. The impact of organizational form on gendered labor markets in engineering and law. *Sociological Review* 46 (2): 314-39.

DeLeon, George. 1997. *Community as method.* Wesport, CT: Praeger.

England, Paula, Melissa Herbert, Barbara Kilbourne, Lori Reid, and Lori Megdal. 1994. The gendered valuation of occupations and skills. *Social Forces* 73:65-99.

Feinman, Clarice. 1984. An historical overview of the treatment of incarcerated women. *The Prison Journal* 63 (2): 12-26.

Fletcher, Beverly, Lynda Dixon Shaver, and Dreama Moon. 1993. *Women prisoners: A forgotten population.* Westport, CT: Praeger.

Foucault, Michel. 1977. *Discipline and punish.* New York: Random House.

―――. 1980. *Power/knowledge.* New York: Pantheon.

Fraser, Nancy. 1997. *Justice interruptus.* New York: Routledge.

Freedman, Estelle. 1981. *Their sister's keepers.* Ann Arbor: University of Michigan Press.

Gardner, Carol Brooks. 1995. *Passing by: Gender and public harassment.* Berkeley: University of California Press.

Giallombardo, Rose. 1966. *Society of women.* New York: John Wiley.

Gill, Virginia Teas, and Douglas Maynard. 1995. On "labeling" in actual interaction. *Social Problems* 42 (1): 11-37.

Goffman, Erving. 1961. *Asylums.* New York: Doubleday.

Habermas, Jurgen. 1975. *Legitimation crisis.* Boston: Beacon.

Hardesty, Monica. 1986. Plans and mood: A study in therapeutic relationships. In *Studies in symbolic interaction: Supplement 2 the Iowa school*, edited by Norman K. Denzin, 209-30. Greenwich, CT: JAI.

Heffernan, Ester. 1972. *Making it in prison.* New York: John Wiley.

Hirsch, Adam Jay. 1992. *The rise of the penitentiary in America.* New Haven, CT: Yale University Press.

Horwitz, Allan. 1984. Therapy and social solidarity. In *Toward a general theory of social control: Vol. 1*, edited by Donald Black, 211-50. New York: Academic Press.

Inciardi, James, and Dorothy Lockwood. 1994. When worlds collide. In *Drug abuse treatment*, edited by Frank Tims, Bennett Fletcher, James Inciardi, and Arthur Horton, 63-78. Wesport, CT: Greenwood.

Irwin, John, and James Austin. 1997. *It's about time.* Boston: Wadsworth.

Korteweg, Anna. 2001. What a difference a job makes: Welfare reform and the subject of the working mother. Presentation at the annual meeting of the American Sociological Association, 18-21 August, Anaheim, CA.

Leonard, Eileen. 1983. Judicial decisions and prison reform: The impact of litigation on women prisoners. *Social Forces* 31:45-58.

Lockwood, Dorothy, Jill McCorkel, and James Inciardi. 1998. Developing comprehensive prison-based therapeutic community treatment for women. *Drugs & Society* 13 (1/2): 193-212.

Lorber, Judith. 1994. *Paradoxes of gender.* New Haven, CT: Yale University Press.

McCorkel, Jill. 1996. Justice, gender, and incarceration: An analysis of the leniency and severity debate. In *Examining the justice process*, edited by James Inciardi, 157-76. New York: Harcourt Brace.

———. 1998. Going to the crackhouse. *Symbolic Interaction* 21 (3): 227-52.

Morash, Merry, Robin Haarr, and Lila Rucker. 1994. A comparison of programming for women and men in US prisons since the 1980s. *Crime & Delinquency* 40:197-221.

Owen, Barbara. 1998. *In the mix.* Albany: State University of New York Press.

Pan, Hao, Frank Scarpitti, James Inciardi, and Dorothy Lockwood. 1993. Some considerations on therapeutic communities in corrections. In *Drug treatment and criminal justice*, edited by James Inciardi, 30-43. Newbury Park, CA: Sage.

Pollock, Joycelyn. 1990. *Women, prison, & crime.* Belmont, CA: Wadsworth.

———. 1998. *Counseling women in prison.* London: Sage.

Rafter, Nicole Hahn. 1995. *Partial justice: Women, prisons, and social control.* New Brunswick, NJ: Transaction Publishers.

Reiman, Jeffrey. 1998. *The rich get richer and the poor get prison.* Boston: Allyn & Bacon.

Ridgeway, Cecelia. 1997. Interaction and the conservation of gender inequality. *American Sociological Review* 62:218-35.

Rosenbaum, Jill, and Meda Chesney-Lind. 1994. Appearance and delinquency: A research note. *Crime & Delinquency* 40 (2): 250-61.

Ross, Robert, and Elizabeth Fabiano. 1986. *Female offenders: Correctional afterthoughts.* Jefferson, NC: McFarland.

Rothman, David. 1971. *The discovery of the asylum.* Boston: Little, Brown.

Rusche, Georg, and Otto Kirchheimer. 1939. *Punishment and social structure.* New York: Columbia University Press.

Russell, Denise. 1995. *Women, madness, and medicine.* Cambridge, UK: Polity.

Szasz, Thomas. 1963. *Law, liberty, and psychiatry.* New York: Collier Books.

Thorne, Barrie. 1994. *Gender play.* New Brunswick, NJ: Rutgers University Press.

Warren, Carol. 1991. *Madwives: Schizophrenic women in the 1950s.* New Brunswick, NJ: Rutgers University Press.

West, Candace, and Don Zimmerman. 1987. Doing gender. *Gender & Society* 1:125-51.

[20]

celling black bodies:
black women in the global
prison industrial complex

Julia Sudbury

abstract

The 1980s and 1990s have witnessed an explosion in the population of women prisoners in Europe, North America and Australasia, accompanied by a boom in prison construction. This article argues that this new pattern of women's incarceration has been forged by three overlapping phenomena. The first is the fundamental shift in the role of the state that has occurred as a result of neo-liberal globalization. The second and related phenomenon is the emergence and subsequent global expansion of what has been labelled a 'prison industrial complex' made up of an intricate web of relations between state penal institutions, politicians and profit-driven prison corporations. The third is the emergence of a US-led global war on drugs which is symbiotically related and mutually constituted by the transnational trade in criminalized drugs. These new regimes of accumulation and discipline, I argue, build on older systems of racist and patriarchal exploitation to ensure the super-exploitation of black women within the global prison industrial complex. The article calls for a new anti-racist feminist analysis that explores how the complex matrix of race, class, gender and nationality meshes with contemporary globalized geo-political and economic realities. The prison industrial complex plays a critical role in sustaining the viability of the new global economy and black women are increasingly becoming the raw material that fuels its expansion and profitability. The article seeks to reveal the profitable synergies between drug enforcement, the prison industry, international financial institutions, media and politicians that are sending women to prison in ever increasing numbers.

keywords

war on drugs; globalization; prison industrial complex

introduction

> My mother got twelve years. She's in Foston Hall. They can give people those long sentences
> just for knowing drugs are in the house. He sentenced her to 12 years for knowing. She
> wasn't even involved and he knew that. But he said she knew it was in the country and if
> had got through, she would have benefited from it, from any money. He said one only has to
> read the papers every day to know the trouble it causes once it gets in the pubs and clubs,
> what it does to people... There was a recorder in the cage and she was saying: 'Why did you
> do it?' They convicted her on that (Janet, HMP Holloway).

Janet[1] is an African—Caribbean woman in her mid-twenties serving a seven-year
sentence for importation of Class A drugs. She was six months pregnant when she
was arrested at Heathrow airport and brought to HMP Holloway, England's oldest
and most notorious women's prison. After having her son, she was transferred to
the Mother and Baby Unit where I interviewed her. In this 'compassionate' penal
environment, designed to punish the mother but not her innocent child, Janet and
son are confined to a 6 by 8 foot cell with a bed, toilet and closet from 8pm to
8am. During the day, they have intermittent access to a creche, playroom and roof
garden where the baby can breathe fresh air under wire mesh designed to prevent
escape attempts. When her son reaches nine months, Janet will be transferred to
another unit where she can keep him for a further nine months, at that stage, they
will be separated while she serves the remainder of her sentence. While Janet was
sentenced to a 'lenient' seven years because of her guilty plea, her mother, who
was not involved in the drug trade, was sentenced to 12 years because of her
failure to report her daughter to the police.

Janet, her mother and her son represent three generations caught up in an ever
expanding network of penal repression and profit that increasingly defies national
borders. The past two decades have witnessed dramatic increases in women's
incarceration accompanied by expansive prison building programme in Britain as
well as the rest of western Europe, North America and Australasia. At the same
time, there has been a shift in the nature of confinement as the private prison
industry has been embraced by New Labour and Conservatives alike, and the
deprivation of liberty has become an extremely profitable enterprise. This article
will argue that the explosion in women's incarceration is the hidden face of neo-
liberal or 'corporate' globalization and cannot be understood without reference to
three overlapping phenomena. The first is the fundamental restructuring of
national economies and social welfare provision that has occurred as a result of
the globalization of capital. The second and related phenomenon is the emergence
and subsequent global expansion of what has been labelled a 'prison industrial
complex' made up of an intricate web of relations between state penal
institutions, politicians and profit-driven prison corporations. The third is the
emergence of a US-led global war on drugs, which is symbiotically related and
mutually constituted by the transnational trade in criminalized drugs.[2] These new
regimes of accumulation and discipline, I will argue, build on older systems of

1 Between 1999 and
2001 I interviewed 50
women in prisons in
England, Canada and
the US. All names of
women prisoners are
pseudonyms.

2 The 'threat' of
drugs can be seen to
be socially
constructed insofar
as some drugs with

addictive properties and damaging social consequences including violence and theft (tobacco, alcohol) are sold to the public legally under government license, and others (heroin, cannabis, cocaine) are criminalized. In addition, substances that are illegal in one context (alcohol during Prohibition), may be enjoyed legally in another. Others may be simultaneously legal and illegal (medical marijuana in California). Referring to 'criminalized' rather than 'illegal' drugs reminds us that 'the criminal', like 'the crime' she commits are products of penal regimes that shift over time.

3 Writing about gender and race transnationally generates problems of naming, since racial terms have different meanings depending on location. In this article, I use 'black' as the common term for women of African, Caribbean and Asian origins in Britain only; since 'black' in the US and Canada refers only to women of African descent, I use 'women of colour' to refer to women of African, Asian, Latin American and indigenous communities transnationally. I also use the term 'women of the global south' since this is now widely used by activists to refer to women in what is often, and problematically called 'the Third World'.

racist and patriarchal exploitation to ensure the super-exploitation of black women and women of colour[3] within the global prison industrial complex.

the global boom in women's imprisonment

Since the early 1990s, increases in the prison population in England and Wales have sparked a boom in prison construction, leading commentators to comment on 'the largest prison building program since the middle of the 19th century' (Morgan, 1999: 110). While women make up a small proportion of those incarcerated, their rates of imprisonment have multiplied faster than men's, causing feminist activists to call for drastic measures to counter 'the crisis in women's prisons'.[4] Between 1985 and 1998, for example, the number of women in prison more than doubled, from 1532 to 3260 (Prison Reform Trust, 2000). The prison service has responded by contracting with private corporations to build and operate new prisons, and by re-rolling men's prisons for women. Recent government initiatives designed to slow the increase in the use of incarceration, such as Home Detention Curfews, have had little impact on the number of women sentenced to prison, which continued to grow during the year to April 2001 by 9%, compared to 2% for men.

The British pattern is mirrored elsewhere. In the US, where the prison and jail population reached two million in the year 2000, women's incarceration is also spiralling upwards at a greater pace than that of men. While the number of men in US prisons and jails doubled between 1985 and 1995, women's imprisonment during the same period tripled (Department of Justice, 1998). In 1970, there were 5600 women in federal and state prisons, by 1996, there were 75 000 (Currie, 1998). In Australia, a surging women's prison population, accompanied by pressure from activist organizations, forced the Parliament of New South Wales to commission a Select Committee on the Increase in Prisoner Population (Bacon and Pillemer, 2000). The Select Committee was instructed to investigate a 20% increase in men's and 40% increase in women's incarceration (Parliament of New South Wales, 2001). In Canada, the increase in federally sentenced women prisoners, accompanied by pressure from penal reform organizations, has led to the construction of five new federal prisons for women (Hannah-Moffatt and Shaw, 2000). In Ontario, spiralling numbers of prisoners have fueled the construction of three 1600-bed superjails where a growing women's population will be warehoused within US-style, austere co-ed facilities.

Aggregate rates of increase in prison populations under-represent the impact of the prison boom on black women, women of colour and indigenous women. In all the countries mentioned above, oppressed racialized groups are disproportionately represented. For example, in New South Wales, while all women's imprisonment increased by 40% in five years, aboriginal women's incarceration increased by 70% in only two years. In Canada, aboriginal people comprise 3% of the general population and 12% of federal prisoners, a figure that increases to over 60% in provinces like Saskatchewan and Alberta (Canadian Criminal Justice Association, 2000). African Canadians are also disproportionately policed, prosecuted and incarcerated (Commission on Systemic Racism in the Ontario Criminal Justice System, 1994). In the US, Latinas and African-American women make up 60% of the female prison population. And despite their small numbers in the population, Native Americans are ten times more likely than whites to be imprisoned (Rojas, 1998). Finally, 12% of women prisoners in England and Wales are African–Caribbean British passport holders[5] compared to 1% of the general population (Elkins *et al.*, 2001). In addition, British prisons hold numerous women from West Africa, the Caribbean and Latin America, either as immigration detainees, or serving sentences for drug importation. The crisis of women's prisons can therefore be read as a crisis for black women and women of colour worldwide.

the emergence of the prison industrial complex

Activist-intellectuals in the US have traced the emergence of what has been labelled the 'prison industrial complex' to the economic transformations of the 1970s (Davis, 1998; Goldberg and Evans, 1998). As advances in technology enabled corporations to transport information and capital between distant geographic locations in fractions of a second, new forms of globalized capital began to appear. US-based corporations downsized their unionized Western workforces and relocated manufacturing operations to locations in the global south where labour was cheap and labour and environmental protections minimal. Multinational trade agreements such as NAFTA and GATT and the establishment of Free Trade Zones hastened the process, opening the doors to the unhindered super-exploitation of predominantly young women of colour from Tijuana to Manila. The impact of massive downsizing in the US on urban African-American and Latino communities was catastrophic. Redlining and racist violence had kept African-Americans and Latinos out of the 1950s suburbanization drive that had allowed many working class white families to move out of the inner cities, restricting the former to urban ghettos where they were warehoused with few opportunities for mobility (Oliver and Shapiro, 1995). As job cuts hit these communities, they were devastated by pandemic rates of unemployment, a declining tax base and resultant cuts in social, welfare, educational and medical provision. The result: spiralling rates of poverty, drug addiction, violence and social dislocation. These conditions were not met passively. The Black Liberation Army, Black Panthers, Young Lords, Chicano Power and American Indian movement were the organized voice of the resistance that sprung from these oppressive conditions. However, these movements encountered brutal repression and criminalization. The FBI's Counter Intelligence Program (COINTELPRO) identified the Black Panthers as THE number one threat to the security of the US and targeted activists such as Assata Shakur, Pam Africa

4 'The Crisis in Women's Prisons', Press Release, Leeds Metropolitan University, April 7, 1999 http// www.lmu.ac.uk/ news/press/archive/ apr99/prisons.htm.

5 British officials have changed the way in which they report ethnic origin in order to downplay the number of black women and men in prison. By excluding non-British passport-holders, the Home Office Research Development Statistics unit has 'reduced' the proportion of African Caribbean women prisoners by 51% to 12% of prisoners, compared to 1% of the general population (Elkins *et al.*, 2001). However, this is revealed to be a sleight of hand if one considers the large number of black British residents who hold 'commonwealth' passports.

and Angela Y. Davis for neutralization via trumped up charges, massively publicized manhunts and incarceration in maximum security institutions (Churchill, 1990). The scene had therefore been set for the mass criminalization of African-Americans, Native Americans and Latinos. In the white imagination, black protest was synonymous with lawlessness and violence. While overt Jim Crow racism had waning public acceptance in this post-Civil Rights era of Martin Luther Kingesque integrationist policies, criminalization provided a new camouflaged racist language in which code words such as 'criminal', 'drug dealer' and 'welfare queen' could be used to refer obliquely to the racialized 'enemy within' (Davis, 1998: 66). *Criminalization therefore became the weapon of choice in dealing with the social problems caused by the globalization of capital and the protest it engendered.*

Joel Dyer argues that three components make up the 'perpetual prisoner machine' that transforms criminalized populations in the US into fodder for the prison system and has caused the prison population in the US to increase ten-fold in 20 years (Dyer, 2000). The first is the consolidation of large media corporations that rely on violent and crime-oriented content to grab ratings and that have created a dramatic rise in the fear of crime in the US population at large. The second is the increasing use of polling and market research by politicians to align their platforms with 'popular' views about policy areas, leading to 'tough on crime' rhetoric on both sides of the electoral spectrum. This rhetoric is translated into policies such as mandatory minimums, truth-in-sentencing and three strikes that cause more people to serve prison sentences, for longer terms, and leads to spiralling prison populations. The third is the intervention of private prison corporations such as Wackenhut Corporation and Corrections Corporation of America, which provide a way for governments to expand their prison estate without having to spend the initial capital cost of prison construction. The mutually profitable relationship between private corporations and public criminal justice systems enables politicians to mask the enormous cost of their tough-on-crime policies by sidestepping the usual process of asking the electorate to vote for 'prison bonds' to raise funds to build publicly operated prisons. Instead, they can simply reallocate revenue funds from welfare, health or education into contracts with privately run-for-profit prisons. Since the 1980s, the private sector has allowed prison building to continue, even where public coffers have been exhausted by the prison construction boom. It has been rewarded with cheap land, tax breaks and discounts in sewage and utilities charges, making prison companies a major beneficiary of corporate welfare. These three components constitute the 'political and economic chain reaction' that we have come to know as the prison industrial complex: *a symbiotic and profitable relationship between politicians, corporations, the media and state correctional institutions that generates the racialized use of incarceration as a response to social problems rooted in the globalization of capital.*

the PIC goes global

Although the prison industrial complex (PIC) emerged in the US, the past 15 years have witnessed its transformation into a global phenomenon. Multinational prison corporations have fueled this expansion through an aggressive strategy of pursuing foreign markets through sophisticated marketing techniques. Targeting British politicians has proven particularly fruitful. During the 1980s, Labour and Conservative politicians were invited to the US for tours of flagship private prisons where the new steel and glass buildings and latest technological advances in surveillance appeared to offer a striking advance over Britain's decaying penal estate. The glossy rhetoric of the 'new corrections' where prisoners were called 'residents', prison guards 'supervisors' and cells 'rooms' was favourably compared to the brutal and dehumanizing prison culture in Britain that had long proved resistant to reform. Prior to this time, both sides of the House of Commons were opposed to prison privatization. Politicians tended to view the denial of freedom as too serious an undertaking to be entrusted to private interests and subjected to the vagaries of the profit motive. However, these carefully orchestrated visits led to a sea-change. As Sir Edward Gardner, Chair of the all-party penal affairs group commented after a visit to the US in 1986: 'We thought it was stunning. These places didn't feel like prisons and didn't smell like prisons. There was nothing we could find to criticize.' (Young, 1987: 3).

In 1987, a Home Affairs Select Committee visited four adult and juvenile jails run by the Corrections Corporation of America and the Radio Corporation of America. The Select Committee subsequently recommended that corporations should be invited to bid for contracts to build and manage custodial institutions, initially as an experiment. A key to the recommendation was that privatization would *dramatically accelerate* the prison-building program, which was hindered by lack of public funds (Speller, 1996). Gradually, key British politicians and administrators were won over to the possibilities for cost cutting, modernization and prison expansion offered by the corporate agenda. Privatization was presented as a panacea to the problems facing the prison service: overcrowding, old buildings, high annual costs, resistance to reform and a rigid prison guard culture reinforced by the powerful Prison Officers Association. Between 1991 and 1994 the mutually profitable relationship between Conservative politicians and the prison industry culminated in a series of Acts which allowed for corporations to design, construct, manage and finance new prisons and to bid to operate existing prisons. By 1997, when New Labour came to power, Britain had become a profitable location for multinational prison corporations, producing revenues of over £95 million for the five leading private incarcerators, Premier Prison Services (a joint venture of Wackenhut and Sodexho), Wackenhut (UK) Ltd., UK Detention Services (a joint venture of Corrections Corporation of America and Sodexho), Securicor, and Group 4 (Prison Privatisation Report International, 1998a; Sudbury, 2000). Although Labour had condemned the Conservative privatization programme, pre-election promises to return prisons to the public sector were short lived (Prison

Privatisation Report International, 1996). Within a year of election, Home Secretary Jack Straw announced that privately run prisons would only return to the public sector if the latter could outbid their private competitors, and that new prisons would be built under the Private Finance Initiative (Prison Privatisation Report International, 1998b).

While Wackenhut Corporation, Corrections Corporation of America and others have reaped enormous profits in the US since the 1980s, their profits have recently been compromised. A radical popular prison movement, and a series of high profile legal cases have pushed the US prison industry into a period of crisis as shares go into freefall.[6] Critical Resistance, the Prison Moratorium Project and the Black Radical Congress' 'Education not Incarceration' campaign have mobilized popular support and media coverage in questioning the logic of ever increasing incarceration. At the same time, private prisons corporations have proven vulnerable to the 'Jena' effect, whereby a case of malpractice turns the tide of popular and political sentiment and corporations are left with legal costs and empty facilities due to cancelled contracts.[7] Potentially damaging incidents of prisoner abuse, sexual assault, violence and protests are generated by the very conditions that make prisons profitable: low paid non-unionized staff, low staffing ratios and sparse provision of activities for prisoners (Yeoman, 2000). Although corporations engage in a process of damage limitation, whereby they seek to suppress public knowledge about such incidents, close scrutiny by prison activists has severely limited their ability to do so. As domestic profits come under threat, foreign operations play a key role in maintaining corporate viability. New prisons in Marchington, Olney and Peterborough therefore play an important role in maintaining the viability of the multinational prison industry as it seeks new markets in South Africa and further afield (Martin, 2001). Women and men serving time in British prisons thus fuel stock market profits from London to New York, reinforcing the logic of incarceration with the logic of capitalist accumulation.

6 Between 1998 and 2000, Corrections Corporation of America (aka Prison Realty) shares fell from $40 to $2, Wackenhut shares fell from $30 to $9 (Martin, 2001).

7 In September 2000, the State of Louisiana agreed in federal court to cease contracting with privately run juvenile facilities after an investigation found that boys in Wackenhut's Jena facility had been abused with pepper spray and tear gas and denied basic needs from underwear to food (Martin, 2001).

the war on drugs wages war on women

> With the entering of the New Year, I want to give you the gift of vision, to see this system of Modern Day Slavery for what it is. The government gets paid $25,000 a year by you (taxpayers) to house me (us). The more of us that they incarcerate, the more money they get from you to build more prisons. The building of more prisons create more jobs. The federal prison system is comprised of 61% drug offenders, so basically this war on drugs is the reason why the Prison Industrial Complex is a skyrocketing enterprise.
>
> (Smith, 1999)

In 2000, two African-American women were among the prisoners granted clemency by outgoing President Clinton. Dorothy Gaines and Kemba Smith's cases had been highlighted by organizations including Families Against Mandatory Minimums, the

Kemba Smith Justice Project and the Million Woman March as evidence of the egregious injustices occurring as a result of the 'war on drugs' and the particular impact on women. Kemba Smith's case in particular attained national attention and was widely reported in the mainstream press.[8] Kemba was a student at Hampton College, a traditionally black college in Virginia. She became involved with a young man, Khalif Hall, who, unknown to her, was a key figure in a large drug operation. Kemba stayed with Hall despite abuse and threats to kill her because she was afraid for her family and herself and because she had become pregnant. Shortly before the drug ring was apprehended, Hall was shot and killed. Kemba pleaded guilty to conspiracy to distribute crack cocaine, but hoped Hall's abusive behaviour would be taken into account. Instead, she was held responsible for the full 255 kilos involved in the offense, although she personally was not found to have handled the drugs, and was sentenced to 24.5 years in prison. Kemba, like Janet and her mother (above) have been targeted by a transnational war on drugs that emerged in the mid 1980s in the United States and has since been aggressively exported around the globe. While the shadowy figure of the drug dealer or trafficker tends to be envisioned in the popular media as male, increasingly women are the low level 'footsoldiers' within the transnational drug trade who are most vulnerable to arrest and punishment.

The current war on drugs was announced by Ronald Reagan in the early 1980s and formalized in the 1986 Anti Drug Abuse Act. The Act made a critical break with the concept of drug users as a medical population in need of treatment, and instead targeted them as a criminal population. It also utilized the erroneous assumption that users would be deterred from their habit and dealers and traffickers incapacitated by punitive and extensive use of penal sanctions. By removing those involved in the criminalized drug trade from the streets for long periods of time, it was assumed, syndicates would be severely damaged in their ability to get drugs to the streets.[9] Since 'liberal' judges could not be trusted to hand down sufficient sentences to deter and incapacitate those involved in the drug trade, the Act removed discretion and imposed mandatory minimum sentences. Thus treatment programmes and community service were effectively barred in cases involving drugs, and sentence length related not to the role of the defendant in the offense, but to the weight and purity of drugs involved. In the US, African-American women and Latinas are disproportionately affected by mandatory minimums. Since the only way a lesser sentence can be given is in cases where the defendant provides 'substantial assistance' in the prosecution of another person, women, who tend to be in subordinate positions within drug syndicates and thus have little access to information are usually unable to make such an agreement. The crack-cocaine disparity also feeds the disproportionate impact on women of colour. The mandatory minimum sentence for crack cocaine is one hundred times harsher for crack than for powder cocaine. Since crack is cheaper, and has flooded poor inner city neighbourhoods, African-Americans and Latinos receive disproportionate

8 Kemba Smith's case is a composite of factors which make her both representative of and different from the majority of women incarcerated as a result of the war on drugs. As an African-American woman, young mother and victim of domestic violence, she is typical enough to become a symbol of the anti-war on drugs campaign. As a middle-class, articulate student, she is clearly untypical, yet her class status strengthens the message to 'middle America', that this could happen to 'your daughter'.

9 This has not been the case, instead, criminalization and targeting by law enforcement artificially inflate the price of drugs, so that manufacturing, trafficking and selling them become immensely profitable and increasingly associated with violence. This mutually profitable relationship between law enforcement and the drug trade has been labelled the 'international drug complex' (Van Der Veen, 2000).

sentences when compared with white powder cocaine users and dealers (Waters, 1998).

While the war on drugs has had a dramatic impact on US communities of colour, it has reached far beyond US borders.[10] From the mid-1980s, the war on drugs increasingly played a key role in US foreign policy decisions as the Reagan and Bush administrations pushed a US drug agenda on the global community. Initial efforts focused on the G7 countries as the Reagan administration used US economic clout to push for international compliance with US drug policy. In 1988, the Toronto Summit endorsed a US-proposed taskforce, which in turn led to the 1988 United Nations Convention Against Illicit Traffic in Narcotic Drugs and Psychotropic Substances (Friman, 1996). The Convention contained a number of controversial conditions that ran counter to the policies of other member states. By requiring states to criminalize drug cultivation, possession and purchase for personal use, maximize the use of criminal sanctions and deterrence and limit early release and parole in drug-related cases, the Vienna Convention represented the transnational spread of the US punitive 'law and order' agenda (Albrecht, 2001). By signing the Convention, member states signed onto the logic of incarceration, pledging to use criminal justice sanctions in place of medical or social solutions and turning decisively away from legalization.[11] By the mid-1990s, Canada, Australia, New Zealand, Taiwan, South and Central America, the Caribbean and African countries including Nigeria and South Africa were fully fledged partners in the US-driven transnational war on drugs.

The Americanization of drug policy is evident in the British approach to criminalized drug use, trafficking and retail. While the 'British System' of prescribing heroin or methadone to addicts, dating to the 1920s, indicates a medical approach to drug use, it exists uneasily alongside recent developments that draw on the US model of criminalization and incarceration. UN conventions are not the only way in which US drug policy is exported abroad. Indeed, British politicians on both sides of the house have 'gratefully accepted and sometimes sought' the 'benevolence, advice, influence and leadership' of the US on drug matters (Bean, 2001: 90). US–British synergy on drug policy comes about as a result of exchanges of research findings, fact-finding missions to the US by politicians and administrators, international conferences and visits by 'specialists' to Britain. An infamous case involves Drug Enforcement agent Robert Stutman's 1988 visit to Britain. Addressing the Assistant Chief Police Officers Conference, Stutman 'scared the hell' out of the participants with his apocalyptic visions of the crack epidemic in the US and its inevitable migration to Europe as the US market became saturated. Stutman's account was based on an unpublished report and anecdotal evidence. Nevertheless, a 1989 Home Affairs Committee Report echoed Stutman's unsubstantiated argument that there is 'no such person as a fully recovered crack addict' and that crack, by its very nature, called for a penal, rather than a medical response (Bean, 2001). Stutman's presentation had

10 In Latin America, the war on drugs has been a military war. Since 1989, Colombia has seen deployment of US military personnel, financial assistance for policing, provision of attack helicopters and weaponry to assist in the fight against 'narcoterrorists'. This fight has been closely associated with counter-insurgency measures against left wing guerillas such as the FARC and ELN and has thus fuelled a bitter civil war. US counter-drug measures have also included spraying of crops with herbicides including Agent Green, which indigenous groups claim has destroyed the rainforest and polluted the water table. For the impact of the war on drugs on Colombian women, see Sudbury (2001).

11 Although Dutch coffee shops selling cannabis and the British practice of prescribing to heroin addicts have gone largely unaffected by the 1988 Convention, they are in opposition to and theoretically threatened by its provisions.

immediate and racialized effects. From the late 1980s, the press ran reports of crack infiltrating British cities. Crack became a foreign threat, an enemy brought into Britain by Yardies, with African–Caribbean communities as the Trojan Horse enabling the foreign infiltration. As a result, resources were pumped into law enforcement activities such as Operation Dalehouse and the Crack Intelligence Coordinating Unit, specifically to increase the surveillance and policing of black communities. Coinciding with the entrenchment of 'Fortress Europe', the crack threat was also a justification for a heightened suspicion of black British women and men entering Britain after vacations abroad, as well as Caribbean nationals entering to visit family and friends. With such targeted policing and customs attention, the numbers of African–Caribbean women and men apprehended for possession, sales and importation of both class A and lesser drugs increased dramatically. In some instances, retail of crack was largely inspired by police operations and protection of informants, as is the case in a northern city where a senior police officer admitted that undercover police buyers stimulated demand that disappeared once the police operation was over (Joyce 1998). While the belief that Britain was on the verge of a US-style 'crack epidemic' was found by the mid-1990s to be a 'media inspired panic' (Joyce, 1998: 181), the pattern of targeted surveillance has continued unabated. As public funds are poured into the high-tech policing of black suspects, a self-fulfilling cycle is generated whereby increased arrests in the black community reinforce the public fear of African–Caribbean drug dealers and traffickers, legitimate the continuation of racially discrepant policing practices and generate additional resources for the police.[12] The impact on black women has been devastating. While in 1980, 4.4% of women serving time in prisons in England and Wales were incarcerated on drug-related offenses, by 2001 that figure had risen to 39% (HMSO, 1982; Elkins *et al.*, 2001). Between April 2000 and April 2001 alone, the number of women sentenced to prison as a result of the war on drugs grew by 20% (Elkins *et al.*, 2001).

As the risk of apprehension at Heathrow, Toronto or New York increases, drug syndicates find it increasingly profitable to use black women and women of colour as low level 'mules' to carry drugs through customs. Women are seldom involved in the planning and organization of drug trafficking, nor are they party to the large profits involved (Harper and Murphy, 1999). Male dealers may believe that women will be less likely to come under suspicion of carrying drugs and more likely to receive lenient sentencing if they are apprehended. However, black women are not the recipients of such chivalrous behaviour, since they do not fall under the benevolent patriarchal protection of the white men who judge them. Nicole, a 29-year-old black British woman incarcerated with her daughter at HMP Holloway explained:

> The judge when he sentenced me said he's going to use me as an example. Because he knows I've been set up, but he has to give a message the world: 'Don't bring drugs'. He used me as an example because he knew I was pregnant. I was set up by a friend of mine, if you

12 In winter 2000, the Metropolitan Police received £800,000 to carry out Operation Crackdown, targeting low level dealers of crack and class A drugs on council estates in boroughs with large black populations. The operation led to surveillance of 700 private properties, over 80 raids and 1000 arrests ('1000 arrested in London Class A drugs offensive', Press release, Metropolitan Police 01/03/2001). An evaluation of the operation found that it had 'little discernible impact' on London's crack trade, which quickly adapted to meet continuing demand (Rose 2001).

can call him that. And they knew that. But still he said that's why they're using women to bring drugs to the country because they think that the system is not going to be as hard on women as on male prisoners. He said that's not the case.

The women I interviewed became involved in the transnational drug trade through three paths: economic need, threats and coercion, and deception. Faced with poverty and often without a second income to support the family, many women make the choice to risk carrying drugs, sometimes believing it will be a one-off. Interviewees often had specific financial goals, such as an emergency medical bill, or school fees for a son or daughter. Marta, a Jamaican mother of four serving a five-year sentence at HMP Winchester explained:

> They do it mainly for the kids, to support the kids. You have a mother who has four or five kids, two is very sickly, every time she visit the hospital or the doctor, you have to pay to register, you have to pay for medicine, you have to pay for an X-ray. Everything costs money. So anything comes up they're going to jump at it, the easiest way to make money.

Marta is typical of women who import out of economic necessity. Knowing little about the punitive criminal justice system that awaited her in Britain, she took a calculated risk based on the limited options available for her to ensure the survival of herself and her children:

> I was self employed doing a bit of selling. I was married but my husband wasn't supportive after sending the kids to school and the money kept going down. I never knew nothing much about drugs, the only form of drugs I know is ganja, we call it weed. That's the only hard drugs I've known of in my life until I come here. And I was just asked by somebody to carry some baggage for $100 000 Jamaican dollars and I just jump at it, thought it could really help out. They said there is no risk involved, they make it look so easy, just carry the drugs and collect your money and that's it and come back. They didn't show me the possibility that I could get caught, just do it.

While Marta was not told explicitly that she was importing drugs, the fee involved made it evident to her that the package was illegal. In contrast, Maureen, a middle class North Londoner of Jamaican ancestry and mother of six was unaware of the contents of her luggage. While on a visit to her father in Jamaica, she was approached by an acquaintance who asked her to carry coconuts, rum and cans of coconut cream to England. She was apprehended at customs and cocaine was found in the cans:

> I'm so embarrassed. I haven't told no-one. I keep going over in my head, what have I done wrong? What happened? Was I set up? Was I being duped? I don't know what happened to me. I told them the truth and they didn't believe me. I know so many people who lie to them and they get off, they get a few years. Its not fair. And then again the jury was all white and it was a verdict of 10 to 2.

Maureen's case, she believes, was exacerbated by a customs officer who mistook her for another detainee and stated that she was carrying £9500, rather than the few hundred pounds she actually had with her. In the face of racialized stereotypes of African–Caribbean drug traffickers, Maureen's class status is erased. She is processed through the criminal justice system as 'just another' courier, found guilty by a predominantly white jury and given a mandatory minimum sentence.

While it may be tempting to draw a bold line between guilt and innocence in these two cases, the reality of women's involvement in importation is far more blurred. In many instances, importing was part of a complex emotional relationship between a male dealer or trafficker, often himself a minor player in the drug trade, and a lover/partner/'mule'. Diane, a biracial Canadian 25-year-old, is serving the second half of a five-year sentence for importation at the Elizabeth Fry halfway house in Toronto. As a young woman, Diane left home and moved into a women's shelter because of her abusive relationship with her father. While she was there, she entered into a relationship with a Grenadan man who was subsequently arrested for drug dealing. While he was incarcerated, Diane visited him regularly and he discussed marriage with her. Shortly after his release, she gave up her job and started importing drugs for him, not knowing at the time that his previous courier had been arrested and incarcerated. She was not paid in cash for the trips she made, but occasionally, he would buy her expensive gifts such as jewelry and a computer:

> He looked at it this way, he was paying the rent, he was paying for the food, he was paying the bills, if I needed anything I'd ask him for it. If I needed a new pair of shoes. But it was hard for me to ask him for anything because I don't like asking anybody for anything. I never got any money.

Diane and her partner were married before she was finally arrested and incarcerated at Grand Valley State, Kitchener. During the first few days of her sentence, she met the first courier and also learned that her husband had already moved in with another girlfriend. Nevertheless, she refused to trade information for a shorter sentence out of loyalty and respect for his paternal role:

> I had been told don't implicate him because he's still on parole, so he'd do more time than I would, because he'd go back to jail to finish the remainder of his sentence, plus a new charge. So I figure I can't do that to him because I'd be taking the kids away from their father. And altogether I was with him for $7\frac{1}{2}$ years.

Diane's case illustrates the complex web of emotion, economics and abuse that often draw women into criminalized activities. In her study of battered African American women, Beth Richie argues that 'gender entrapment' best describes the way in which black women are incarcerated due to their involvement with a coercive and violent male (Richie, 1996). While Diane was not subjected to physical violence, her partner's controlling behaviour in relation to the money that she generated through importation, the deception with regard to his other girlfriends, and his apparently cynical use of marriage as a means of controlling her labour form a web of abuse and exploitation. By controlling the labour of his 'stable of mules' through promises of love and commitment, Diane's partner generates wealth for himself without either taking the personal risk of importation, or paying the going rate of several thousand dollars per trip. This web of economic/emotional exploitation was a factor in the stories of many of the women I interviewed. As Marta explained:

> Men do it [import], but they tend to prey on the women more. Because they know that the woman in Jamaica, they care for their family, especially their kids. They would do anything to make-sure their kids is looked after. So they mainly prey on the woman, especially single woman. You have men do it, but the number isn't as large as the woman.

Women's subordinate role in heterosexual relationships and their role as the primary and often sole carers of children combine to devalue their labour in the drug trade. The low value of women's labour in the drug trade is demonstrated by the women I interviewed who reported being 'set up' as decoys so that their arrest would distract customs officials from a larger shipment coming through. Paid anywhere from zero to a few thousand pounds for carrying a shipment worth upwards of £100 000, women form a cheap and replaceable army of labourers. As one is incarcerated, another, like Diane, quickly fills her place.

the global feminization and racialization of poverty

While transnational drug policies play an important role in channelling women of colour into prisons from Cape Town to Toronto, women are not without agency and do, of course, make choices within the options available to them. As the global economy has been transformed, however, these options have become increasingly limited. In the global south, this economic transformation has driven a shift in the role of the state. Firstly, governments have been formed to scale down their role as providers of a social-welfare fabric as international financial institutions have driven neo-liberal economic reform. In Jamaica, policies introduced since the mid-1980s by the Jamaican Labour Party working closely with the US, IMF and World Bank, have led to cutbacks in public sector employment, the scaling back of local government services, health and education, increases in the cost of public utilities as state-owned companies are sold to the private sector and a dramatic decline in real wages. Such cuts hit women particularly hard as they carry the burden of caring for children and sick or elderly relatives (Harrison, 1991). Marta's experience exemplifies the increasing economic pressures facing women:

> Things in Jamaica is very expensive. Its hard for a single woman with kids, especially anywhere over three kids, to get by without a good support or a steady job. It doesn't mean that I didn't have an income. I did have an income, but having four kids and an ex-husband who doesn't really care much. I had to keep paying school fees and the money kept going down. I did need some kind of support. That's why I did what I did. We don't get child

support in Jamaica, three-quarters of the things that this country offers for mothers here we don't have it. This country gives you a house, they give you benefits, we get nothing in Jamaica. We have to pay for hospital, not even education is free. Primary school used to be free under one government hand, but under another government it has been taken away. You're talking about high school, you're talking about fifteen up to twenty thousand dollars a term, for one kid to go to high school. Its difficult in Jamaica.

Secondly, while the state has cut back its role in social welfare, it has stepped up its role in subsidizing foreign and domestic capital. Free Trade Zones established in Kingston, Montego Bay and elsewhere offer foreign garment, electronic and communications companies equipped factory space, tax exemptions, a cheap female workforce and, for the busy executive, weekends of sun, sea and sand.[13] Foreign-owned agribusiness and mining companies have also been encouraged, displacing traditional subsistence farming and causing migration from rural areas to the cities, which now account for 50% of the Jamaican population. As the economy has shifted, women working in the informal economy as farmers and 'higglers' find themselves unable to keep up with the rising costs of survival. While younger women may find employment in the tourist industry as maids, entertainers or prostitutes, or within the Free Trade Zones assembling clothes or computers for Western markets, working class women in their thirties and older have fewer options. Even where these women do find employment, low wages, driven down by multinational corporations in search of ever greater profit margins and kept low by governments unwilling to set a living minimum wage for fear of losing foreign investment, mean that they cannot earn a sufficient income to support their families. The failure of the legal economy to provide adequate means for women's survival is the key incentive for those who chose to enter the drug trade as couriers.

13 'Jamaica: Island of Opportunity' www.vega-media.com/jamaica/Jamaica.html

The feminization of poverty in the global south is mirrored by conditions among black people and communities of colour in the West. As Naomi Klein argues, the flight of manufacturing jobs from the West to the global south has led to the Macdonaldization of jobs in North America and Europe, with part-time, casual, low-wage jobs the norm in the new service and 'homeworker' economies (Klein, 2001). At the same time, successive governments, whether espousing compassionate conservativism or the 'third way', have pursued market-led economic reforms which have dramatically reduced public services, introduced widespread privatization and raised the cost of living. The result is the disenfranchisement of working class and black communities and black women in particular as the state sheds its social welfare responsibilities. In Britain, as in the US and Canada, this has entailed a dramatic reform of welfare, and the targeting of single mothers in particular as a drain on the public purse. It is this impoverishment that acts as the motor to women's involvement within the retail end of the drug trade and their subsequent targeting by the criminal justice systems of these countries. Working class women, and in particular women of colour therefore bear the brunt of both the punitive and economic regimes of neo-liberal globalization. The devaluation of their labour within the criminalized economy of the international drug trade is closely interrelated to their superexploitation within the formal sectors of the global economy (the Free Trade Zones and minimum wage tourism and service sectors). Both are made possible by the radical feminization and racialization of poverty that is an essential part, rather than an unfortunate offshoot, of the corporate maximization of profits in the global arena.

conclusion: towards resistance

As the new millennium ushers in an era of unchecked capital accumulation and massive and widening divides between information-rich elites and disenfranchised majorities, feminists and anti-racists need to respond by infusing our praxis with the new politics. The new social movements of the 21st century are more likely to be found shutting down Niketown in San Francisco or battling the WTO in Seattle than at a take back the night rally or consultative meeting on institutional racism. While women of the global south and disenfranchised communities of the north have been active in vibrant anti-globalization protests, feminist scholars have been slower to identify corporate globalization as central to their concerns. Gradually, a body of knowledge is being developed that can serve as a valuable resource for feminist and anti-racist organizers as well as anti-globalization activists. Research into sex tourism, the trafficking of women, women as workers in the Free Trade Zones and homeworkers in the garment industry and women in the global food chain have all demonstrated the centrality of black women and women of colour to the new global regimes of accumulation (Kempadoo, 1999; Phizacklea, 1990; Shiva, 2001; Ching Yoon Louie, 2001). Less attention has been paid to the repressive penal regimes that underpin these processes. The prison-like conditions under which women labour in the Free Trade Zones, with restricted access to restrooms, forced overtime and punitive sanctions for union activities and pregnancy, have generated considerable outrage among researchers and activists alike (Klein, 2001). The confinement of increasing numbers of women in the prisons and jails of the global north, where they are subject to separation, sometimes permanent, from children, sexual abuse, medical neglect and forced labour has, however, been muted.

Perhaps the explanation for this muted response lies in a failure to connect women's incarceration to the social, economic and environmental concerns generated by the new global economy. The prison has traditionally served the purpose of separating those who have 'offended' from the social body politic. Prisoners are therefore seen as 'criminals' whose behaviour is qualitatively different from that of 'normal' people and must therefore be analysed using different tools, hence the existence of criminology as a distinct discipline. Yet if the complex web that has led to the massive increases in women's (and men's) imprisonment documented in this article is to be understood and challenged, prisons must be liberated from the criminologists and criminal justice professionals, and brought under the scrutiny of anti-globalization, feminist and anti-racist scholars and activists. Prisons serve a vital role in suppressing dissent and invisibilizing disenfranchised populations. They therefore maintain the viability of corporate globalization and mask its devastating effects on global majority communities. Prisons also play a direct role in capital accumulation since their operation generates profit for corporations engaged in building, equipping and operating them as well as those employing prisoners as cheap labour. Increasingly, black women and women of colour are the raw material that fuel the prison industrial complex: as scapegoats of tough-on-crime rhetoric, targets of drug busting operations that generate millions for police, customs and military budgets, or workers sewing and assembling electronics in prison workshops. There is a need for a new anti-racist feminism that will explore how the complex matrix of race, class, gender and nationality meshes with contemporary globalized geo-political and economic realities. It must be transnational in scope and womanist in its integrated analysis of gender—race—class and in locating black women and women of colour at the centre. As the gendered and racialized bodies that turn prison cells into profit margins, women of colour play a vital role in the global prison industrial complex. As activists, inside and outside of the prison walls, we are a critical part of the forces that are challenging its parasitic existence. The challenge for scholars and activists alike is to make visible the women hidden behind prison walls and to dismantle the profitable synergies between drug enforcement, the prison industry, international financial institutions, media and politicians that are celling black women in ever increasing numbers.

author biography

Julia Sudbury is Associate Professor of Ethnic Studies at Mills College, Oakland, USA, and author of *Other Kinds of Dreams: Black Women's Organizations and the Politics of Transformation* (Routledge 1998). She was formerly director of Sia, a national development agency for the black voluntary sector based in London and coordinator of Osaba Women's Center in Coventry.

references

Albrecht, H.J. (2001) 'The international system of drug control: developments and trends' in J. Gerber, and E. Hensen (2001) editors, *Drug War, American Style: The Internationalization of Failed Policy and Its Alternatives*, New York and London: Garland Publishing.

Bacon, W. and Pillemer, T. (2000) 'Violence blamed as women fill prison', *Sydney Morning Herald*, www.smh.com.au/news/001/08/national/national1.html, January 8, 2000.

Bean, P. (2001) 'American influence on British drug policy' in J. Gerber, and E. Hensen (2001) editors, *Drug War, American Style: The Internationalization of Failed Policy and Its Alternatives*, New York and London: Garland Publishing.

Canadian Criminal Justice Association (2000) *Aboriginal Peoples and the Criminal Justice System*, Ottawa.

Ching Yoon Louie, M. (2001) *Sweatshop Warriors: Immigrant Women Workers Take on the Global Factory*, Cambridge, MA: Southend Press.

Churchill, W. (1990) *Cointelpro Papers: Documents from the FBIs Secret Wars Against Domestic Dissent*, Boston: South End Press.

Commission on System Racism in the Ontario Criminal Justice System (1994) *Racism Behind Bars*, Toronto: Queens Printers.

Currie, E. (1998) *Crime and Punishment* in America, New York: Henry Holt and Co.

Davis, A.Y. (1998) 'Race and criminalization: black Americans and the punishment industry' in J. James (1998) editor, *The Angela Y. Davis Reader*, Malden, MA: Blackwell Publishers.

Dyer, J. (2000) *The Perpetual Prisoner Machine: How America Profits from Crime*, Boulder, CO: Westview Press.

Department of Justice (1998) Women in Criminal Justice: A Twenty Year Update, http://www.usdoj.gov/reports/98Guide/wcjc98/execsumm.htm, accessed July 13, 2001.

Elkins, M., Gray, C., and Rogers, K. (2001) *Prison Population Brief England and Wales April 2001*, London: Home Office Research Development Statistics.

Friman, H.R. (1996) *Narcodiplomacy: Exporting the US War on Drugs*, Ithaca and London: Cornell University Press.

Goldberg, E., Evans, L. (1998) *The Prison Industrial Complex and the Global Economy*, Berkeley, CA: Agit Press.

Hannah-Moffatt, K. Shaw, M. (2000) *An Ideal Prison?: Critical Essays on Women's Imprisonment in Canada*, Halifax: Fernwood Publishing.

Harper, R., Murphy, R. (1999) *Drug Smuggling: an analysis of the traffickers 1991–1997*, London: Middlesex Probation Service.

Harrison, F.V. (1991) 'Women in Jamaica's urban informal economy' in C.T. Mohanty, R. Ann and T. Lourdes (1991) editors, *Third World Women and the Politics of Feminism*, IN, USA: Indiana University Press.

HMSO (1982) *Prison Statistics England and Wales 1980*, London: HMSO.

Joyce, E. (1998) 'Cocaine trafficking and British foreign policy' in E. Joyce and M. Carlos (1998) editors, *Latin America and the Multinational Drug Trade*, Basingstoke: MacMillan Press.

Kempadoo, K. (1999) editor, *Sun, Sex and Gold*, New York: Rowman and Littlefield Publishing.

Klein, N. (2001) *No Logo: Taking Aim at the Brand Bullies*, Toronto: Vintage Canada.

Martin, W. (2001) 'Privatizing prisons from the USA to SA: controlling dangerous Africans across the Atlantic' *ACAS Bulletin*, Winter, No. 59, http://acas.prairienet.org/Wackenhutv5.htm.

Morgan, R. (1999) 'New Labour "law and order" politics and the House of Commons Home Affairs Committee Report on alternatives to prison sentences' *Punishment and Society*, July 1, No. 1.

Oliver, M., Shapiro, T. (1995) *Black Wealth, White Wealth: a New Perspective on Racial Inequality*, London and New York: Routledge.

Parliament of New South Wales (2001) Select Committee on the Increase in Prisoner Population, www.parliament.nsw.gov.au, accessed July 4.

Phizacklea, A. (1990) *Unpacking the Fashion Industry: Gender, Racism and Class in Production*, London and New York: Routledge.

Prison Privatisation Report International (1996) '*Labour to Halt New Private Prisons*', London: Prison Reform Trust. June.

Prison Privatisation Report International (1998a) *'UK profits'*, Nov/Dec.

Prison Privatisation Report International (1998b) *'Labour's prison U-turn complete'*, June.

Prison R.T. (2000). *Justice For Women: The Need for Reform*, London: Prison Reform Trust.

Richie, B. (1996) *Compelled To Crime: The Gender Entrapment of Battered Black Women*, London and New York: Routledge.

Rojas, P.M. (1998) 'Complex facts', *Colorlines*, Vol. 1, No. 2, pp.13.

Rose, D. (2001) 'Opium of the People', *The Observer*, www.observer.co.uk/focus/story/ 0,6903,518495,00.html.

Shiva, V. (2001) *Yoked to Death: Globalization and Corporate Control of Agriculture*, New Delhi: RFSTE.

Speller, A. (1996) *Private Sector Involvement in Prisons*, London: Church House Publishing.

Smith, K. (1999) 'From the Desk of Kemba Smith', www.geocities.com/CapitolHill/Lobby/8899/pen. html, December 13, 1999.

Sudbury, J. (2000) 'Transatlantic visions: resisting the globalization of mass incarceration' *Social Justice*, Vol. 27, No. 3: pp.133–149.

Sudbury, J. (2001) 'Globalisation, Incarcerated Black Women/Women of Colour and the Challenge to Feminist Scholarship' *Women's Studies Network: (ed) 2001 Millenial Visions Issues for feminism*, Cardiff University Press.

Waters, M. (1998) 'Congressional black Caucus blasts president's crack/powder cocaine sentencing recommendations', Press Release, www.house.gov/waters/Pi_980722_cocaine.html, July 22. 1998.

Yeoman, B. (2000) 'Steeltown Lockdown', *Mother Jones*, May/June.

Young, P. (1987) *The Prison Cell*, London: Adam Smith Institute.

Van Der Veen, H. (2000) *The International Drug Complex*, Amsterdam: Center for Drug Research, University of Amsterdam.

Part VI
Feminist Perspectives on the Law and on Justice

[21]

Predators:
The Social Construction
of "Stranger-Danger"
in Washington State
as a Form of Patriarchal Ideology

Neil S. Websdale

ABSTRACT. The article critically examines Washington State's Predator Law (1990). The most controversial part of the law provides for the indefinite civil commitment of "sexually violent predators." Under the legislation, husbands who victimize their wives and children cannot be defined as predators. I argue that the social construction of predators as sick strangers is an ideological construct. This non-conspiratorial construct diverts attention from the fact that male intrafamilial violence is by far the greatest threat to the safety of women and children. These diversionary tendencies in the predator discourse constitute a hitherto scarcely publicized backlash against feminist arguments about the need for criminal laws that work in the interests of all women and children. *[Article copies available from The Haworth Document Delivery Service: 1-800-342-9678.]*

INTRODUCTION:
SEXUAL PSYCHOPATHY, HEINOUS ACTS
AND DRACONIAN LEGISLATION

Sexual Psychopathy

Edwin Sutherland (1950) argued that the emergence of sexual psychopathy laws from the late 1930s was heavily influenced by the media

Neil S. Websdale, Department of Criminal Justice, Northern Arizona University, Flagstaff, AZ 86011.
The author wishes to thank Ray Michalowski, Stanley Cohen, David Rudy, Ed Reeves, Byron Johnson, Rick Northrup, John Lafond and the anonymous reviewers for their helpful contributions to the earlier drafts of this article.

and the psychiatric community. The media manipulated public opinion and sensationalized sex offenses. This manipulation created an overreaction on the part of the public which was further seized upon by the media and whipped up into hysteria. The psychiatric community sought to colonize the problem of sex offenses and thereby bolster its own professional standing and influence. For Sutherland, the sexual psychopathy laws represented a shift from punishment to medical treatment of sex offenders. In 1937, Michigan became the first state to enact a sexual psychopathy law. By the mid-1980s over half of the states had followed suit. However, these statutes fell into disuse with the growing realization that sex offenders did not suffer from any mental illness and were not therefore amenable to treatment. This left treatment programs open to the possibility of legal attack. According to Brakel, Perry and Weiner, this possibility was one of the reasons states shied away from using these laws (1985:739-43). By 1990, only a handful of states had sexual psychopathy laws on their books and few made regular use of them.

Heinous Acts

Prior to 1990, the State of Washington incarcerated all its sex offenders with the general prison population. However, after a spate of heinous sex crimes, there were increasing calls for a more drastic solution to the threat posed by serious recidivist sex offenders. There were two main triggering offenses. First, Gene Raymond Kane, a work release prisoner who had two previous convictions for sexual assault, raped and murdered Diane Ballasiotes in Seattle in September 1988. Second and most significantly, Earl Shriner was found guilty of raping, assaulting and attempting to kill a seven-year-old boy. Prior to these offenses the infamous serial killer, Ted Bundy, murdered a number of women in Washington State during the 1970s and early 1980s. The Green River Killer, one of the most infamous of all modern day American serial killers, performed most of his fifty or more killings in Washington State. More recently, the predatory acts of murderer Wesley Alan Dodd made national headlines and did much to publicize the phenomenon of sexually violent predation in Washington State. Dodd, who was executed in January 1993 for the murder of three children, admitted molesting more than one hundred children over a period of fifteen years.

Draconian Legislation

On July 1, 1990, Washington State's Community Protection Act went into effect (Washington Laws, 1990, Chapter 3, hereafter referred to as

CPA). This law, commonly known as the Predator Law, was passed in order to better manage the state's sexual offenders. The constitutionality of this law was upheld in August 1993 by a vote of six to three by the Washington State Supreme Court in the case of *State of Washington v. Andre Brigham Young*. Under the terms of the Act, sex offenders were to receive longer sentences and stricter monitoring both in and out of prison. Three strategies stand out. The first, and by far the most controversial strategy was the indefinite civil commitment clause (CPA, Part X, Civil Commitment, Washington Laws, 1990:97-102). Upon committing the necessary heinous sex crimes or after serving a full prison term for such an offense, the sex offender could be subject to indefinite civil commitment to a mental health facility for control, care and treatment. This neatly sidesteps the problem posed by offenders such as Shriner who authorities "knew" would re-offend, but who authorities could no longer detain. The predator law was primarily designed to cope with those offenders who had served their full term and who still posed a threat, while the CPA also sought longer prison terms for new sex offenders (CPA, Part VII, Criminal Sentencing, Washington Laws, 1990:70-91). The two other strategies required the registration of sex offenders in the communities in which they lived (CPA, Part IV, Registration of Sex Offenders, Washington Laws, 1990:49-54) and the notification of the community that a sex offender had moved into the area (CPA, Part I, Community Notification, Washington Laws, 1990:13-36).

The legislation defines a sexually violent predator as: "any person who has been convicted of or charged with a crime of sexual violence and who suffers from a mental abnormality or personality disorder which makes the person likely to engage in predatory acts of sexual violence" (CPA Part X, Sec. 1002{1}, Washington Laws, 1990:97-98). Predation refers to acts: "directed toward strangers or individuals with whom a relationship has been established or promoted for the primary purpose of victimization" (Section 1002{2}, Washington Laws, 1990:98). The intent of the Governor's Task Force which drafted the legislation was to make it extremely difficult to define an offender as a sexually violent predator. This intent is evident in the law itself: "The legislature finds that a small but extremely dangerous group of sexually violent predators exists" (CPA, Section 1001, Washington Laws, 1990:97).

Under the Act, it may be possible to prove that an acquaintance rapist is a sexually violent predator. However, intrafamilial sexual violence and abuse are not covered. In the majority of cases, the sexually violent predator will be a rapist (almost always unknown to the victim), or an extra-familial child molester (CPA, Section 1002{4}, Washington Laws, 1990:

98). In all twenty or so cases to date, the predator has been male. Therefore it is not the act of rape, molestation, mutilation, murder, etc., that is of central concern. Rather, it is the political context within which the act occurs. Under Washington's Community Protection Act, predators are primarily strangers. Husbands cannot be predators. If the victim is known to the perpetrator in any way other than in a relationship that has been established or promoted for the primary purpose of victimization, then that perpetrator cannot be convicted as a predator. The legislature did not intend that the law be applied to sexually violent husbands.

It was not the intent of the Washington State legislature to sweep marital rape and intrafamilial child abuse under the carpet by not making husbands subject to indefinite civil commitment. Rather, legislators felt that to make husbands subject to indefinite civil commitment for intrafamilial abuse would have had the effect of discouraging victims within families from reporting his abuse. The legislature reasoned that wives would not report husbands because, for example, they feared the loss of a husband's economic support if he were to be subject to indefinite civil commitment.

The main objections to the predator law were summarized in a Brief of Amicus Curiae written for the American Civil Liberties Union by University of Puget Sound Professor of Law, John Lafond. This brief was in support of appellants Andre Brigham Young and Vance Cunningham who had been detained as sexual predators. In Lafond's opinion, the predator law is unconstitutional because it: (1) authorizes lifetime preventive detention; (2) does not meet constitutional requirements for involuntary civil commitment; (3) does not require constitutionally adequate proof of dangerousness; and, (4) is too vague and does not specify constitutionally adequate commitment criteria (see Brief of Amicus Curiae in Support of Appellants Andre Brigham Young and Vance Cunningham, Supreme Court of Washington, No. 57837-1:11).

It is important to bear in mind that the legal debate about predation has remained firmly fixed on the issues of constitutionality. The protagonists did not raise the issue of systemic intrafamilial male sexual abuse of women and children, nor the perils of a predator law which focused solely on "stranger danger."

THE GENDERED NATURE OF THE PREDATOR LAW

The legislative and media embellishment of the threat posed by predators produces a skewed analysis of sexual violence against women who, in reality, face far greater danger from the men they know (Russell 1990,

Finkelhor and Yllo 1985, Radford and Russell 1992, Dobash and Dobash 1979, Hanmer and Saunders 1984, Stanko 1990). This obfuscation effect also counteracts feminist progress in the area of passing legislation that does have some beneficial effect in the lives of women (e.g., marital rape, sexual harassment and mandatory arrest laws). The article returns to these counteracting effects in the final section.

Diana Russell's rigorous survey conducted by women interviewers with a random sample of 930 women in San Francisco revealed that among 2,588 reports of rape and attempted rape, 38% were committed by the husband or ex-husband, and 13% by a lover or ex-lover. Only 6% were committed by strangers. This suggests that roughly half of all rapes or attempted rapes are committed by men who are in, or have been in, an intimate relationship with the victim (1990:67). In general, she found that sexual assaults by husbands were twice as common as those committed by strangers. Finkelhor and Yllo (1985) surveyed 323 Boston area women. They found that 10% of the women had been raped by their husbands or ex-husbands, compared with 3% who had been the victims of stranger-rape (1985:6-7).

The prevalence of wife rape is compounded by the fact that wives may be raped more than once. Russell found that 70-80% of the victims of wife rape were raped more than once. In a related vein, Finkelhor and Yllo (1985:23) found that half the victims of wife rape had experienced sexual assault on twenty or more occasions.

Finkelhor (1984) reports a 600 percent rise in child sexual abuse between 1976 and 1982. Undoubtedly, this increase reflects a dramatic increase in reporting rather than a significant escalation of abuse. The recent recognition of child sexual abuse as a major social problem should not obscure the historically enduring presence of this form of child exploitation. As Linda Gordon observes, the recent "discovery" of child sexual abuse merely highlights a problem well known to the Progressive Era and nineteenth century social workers (1988:7). Following Gordon and other feminist arguments on child sexual abuse and incest, I argue these phenomena are best understood as part of the power relations of gender. Gordon puts it succinctly:

> One of the most striking things about incest, that most extraordinary and heinous of transgressions, is its capacity to be ordinary. . . . In the family violence case records it is a behavior of very ordinary people. . . . incest participants made sense of their behavior precisely in terms of their family positions. Men referred to their paternal

rights, girls to their filial duty. Men spoke of men's sexual 'needs' and their prerogative to 'have' women. (1988:204)

In discussing the history of child sexual abuse in Great Britain, Carol Smart points to a discourse characterized by both consternation and complacency, with concern about child/stranger abuse:

> oddly nourishing the complacency over abuse by fathers. . . the more concern is expressed about the threat of strangers, the less close relatives could be brought into the frame. The more child sexual abuse was depicted as a horrible pathology, the less could 'ordinary' fathers be seen as enacting such deeds. (1989:52)

This displacement effect highlighted by Smart can also be seen in the definitional imperatives of Washington State's predator law. The focus on aberrance serves to distance child sexual abuse from its authentic locus, namely the patriarchal family. As feminists have noted, the problem of child sexual abuse is the problem of male sexuality (see Herman with Hirschman, 1981). Child sexual abuse is a widespread phenomenon that occurs most frequently within families. Men are overwhelmingly the perpetrators of this abuse. In Russell's survey mentioned above, she found that 16 percent of her sample of women reported incest occurring before the age of eighteen. Nearly all of the perpetrators in Russell's study were reported by incest victims to be men.

The link between intrafamilial sexual violence toward women and children is that both are an expression of male power within a patriarchal system of families. To argue, as the Washington State legislature did, that wives would not report intrafamilial sexual violence under a predator law, because they feared the loss of a husbands' economic support, is profoundly ironic. Here we see wives' and children's economic dependence on husbands and fathers being used as a rationale for disqualifying large numbers of sexually violent men from being predators. This rationale, embedded in the predator law, constitutes patriarchal ideology par excellence.

It is not the argument of this article that the victims of predators, the victims' families, politicians and criminal justice system personnel who contributed to the media construction and sensationalization of predation, deliberately set out to divert attention away from everyday sexual violence against women and children. Neither did the media, as claims-makers, conspire to marginalize everyday sexual violence against women and children. Rather, the media presentation of predation is best seen as an integral part of a patriarchal ideology, the power of which is most insidious when its operation is silent and largely unobserved. Nevertheless, because of the definitional imperatives of the predator law and the media sensationalization of rare one-on-one stranger violence, everyday sexual violence against women and children remains marginalized.

Before proceeding to discuss the ways in which a moral panic developed around sexually violent predators, it is important to situate my argument within the broader context of feminist theories of the law and the state. While these theories remain to be developed, some important headway has been made. According to Catherine MacKinnon: "the state is male in the feminist sense. The law sees and treats women the way men see and treat women" (1987:140). Likewise "the state, in part through law, institutionalizes male power" (1987:141). While MacKinnon's work has been criticized as both essentialist and deterministic (see Smart, 1989:66-89), she nevertheless deconstructs the objectivist posturing of liberal theories of the law, which fail to recognize the historical significance of the public/private divide. Liberal legal discourse denies the life experiences of women and subsumes them under an empiricist and allegedly gender neutral code. The failure of the state to encroach upon the domain of domestic relations is justified under liberal law by an appeal to rights of privacy and the sanctity of the family from state interference. The hierarchical relationship between the modern liberal state and its citizenry is rooted in and based upon the nature of the patriarchal family and the historic rights of a husband over his wife and children (see Dobash and Dobash, 1979; MacKinnon, 1987; Hall, 1984; Aries, 1962).

Carol Smart criticizes MacKinnon for seeing male power as omnipotent. According to Smart, MacKinnon's approach leaves insufficient room to theorize the resistance of women. Smart sees the law as more of a contested arena and less of a monolithic tool than MacKinnon. Although Smart acknowledges that law is androcentric, it is nevertheless possible at times for women to use the state and the law for their own benefit. At one point Smart argues: "Yet law remains a site of struggle. While it is the case that law does not hold the key to unlock patriarchy, it provides the forum for articulating alternative visions and accounts" (1989:88). Smart's approach is consistent with the work of other feminists who have acknowledged the way the state has changed its response to the plight of women. Patriarchy is not an unchanging trans-historical phenomenon. As the machinery of the modern patriarchal state developed, divorce became easier to obtain, certain forms of legal (not de facto) discrimination have been confronted, laws were passed against wife battering and in some cases marital rape. In short, there is an ebb and flow in the area of gender legislation, which usually but not always favors the patriarchal interests of men.

It is the argument of this article that the predator law constitutes andro-centric legislation which, under the guise of protecting women and children, effectively upholds the historic separation of public and private spheres. The predator law works against the feminist claim that the private is political and that the private constitutes the central locus of women's oppression. Nevertheless, following Smart rather than MacKinnon, I also suggest that this law is part of the historical ebb and flow of gender legislation. After examining the media sensationalization of sexually violent predation, this article concludes with a discussion of the possible reasons why the predator law can be seen as part of the ebb and flow of patriarchal legal discourse.

EXAMINING THE PREDATOR LAW, ITS ENFORCEMENT AND THE EMERGING MEDIA DISCOURSE

The central question of my analysis is: "What ideological positions benefitted from the particular orientation of the predator law?" Another related question was: "How did the various excerpts from discursive themes in the media support the orientation of the law and further feed into the ideology that "stranger-danger" posed an awesome threat to women and children?"

I reviewed various sources to access the political themes of the predator discourse. Information for my analysis of sexually violent predation was obtained primarily through: (1) analysis of legislation, newspaper articles, hard and soft news shows and the true crime literature; (2) interviews with legal scholars and criminal justice personnel responsible for implementing the predator law; and, (3) taping and transcription of the legal debates.

The analysis of newspaper articles began with the *Seattle Times (ST)* and the *Tacoma News Tribune (TNT)*. My impressions of the ideological slant of the predator discourse were formed as a member of the public and as a working scholar living in Tacoma in the late 1980s/early 1990s. The term "predator" was first coined in 1989 by the Governor's Task Force on community protection. The *Seattle Times* picked up on the term from the Task Force. An initial computer search of a data base covering 150 news-papers revealed that about ninety percent of all articles on sexual predators came from the *Seattle Times*. The remaining articles took their lead from the early pieces in the *Seattle Times*. In this article I use those quotes which most succinctly and powerfully summarize a discursive theme. No articles or other media presentations even remotely contextualized the act of predation against the wider structure of patriarchy.

Transcripts from television shows provide the substrate for the analysis of hard and soft news stories. My content analysis of these news shows seeks to deconstruct some of the messages and explore some of the nuances and meanings of the spoken and unspoken word.

I conducted unstructured interviews with key informants. Interviewees were point-people in their respective fields (policing, law, corrections) who worked with predators and the operationalization of the predator law. Eight key informant telephone interviews were conducted with police officers (one chief, one lieutenant, three sergeants and three detectives) from the following departments in Washington state: Seattle, Tacoma, Olympia and Puyallup. These interviews provided insights into the per-spectives of police officers and the way they contextualized predation within their wider world view. Discussions about the predator law were held with two prosecutors from the King County (Seattle) Prosecutor's Office, two attorneys from the Attorney General's Office and a public defender in Tacoma. One of the key legal players in the predator discourse is University of Puget Sound Professor of Law, John Lafond. Lafond appeared on news shows such as ABC Nightline and drafted the American Civil Liberties Union brief against the predator law. I discussed the preda-tor law at length with Lafond. Finally, three telephone interviews were conducted with Washington State Department of Corrections staff.

PANICKING ABOUT SEXUALLY VIOLENT PREDATORS

Stanley Cohen (1980) used the term moral panic to refer to a stylized societal overreaction to vandalism and the general "disorderly" behavior of youth during the 1960s in England. Cohen identifies the importance of the media and other claims-makers in the construction of "folk devils." Moral panics serve as a form of social control since they produce an overreaction on the part of authorities and ultimately some kind of crack-down. There are a number of parallels between the panic over vandalism studied by Cohen and the "discovery" of sexually violent predation in Washington state. In many ways the construction of the sexually violent predator as a fiendishly dangerous individual could be seen in terms of a moral panic. The predator resembles Cohen's folk devil. However, the sociology of deviance and the anomie tradition which Cohen draws upon have not readily accommodated issues of gender. Consequently, this ar-ticle employs an analytical scheme which is informed by Cohen's work, but linked much more closely to the politics of gender. Excerpts from the legal and media discourses on sexually violent predators are presented in the next section in order to expand upon the main theoretical argument that the predator law constitutes patriarchal ideology. This section begins by examining the initial construction of predation and goes on to analyze the rise of what I call the "decontextualized predator." These two subsections preface a discussion of the way predators made it onto prime time soft news shows.

The Initial Construction of Sexually Violent Predators

Three interrelated themes permeated the early construction of the predator discourse. First, the danger posed by predators was frequently magnified for all to see. Second, predictions were made about the potential future dangerousness of predators. Third, a symbolic code of language emerged to describe predators.

The Magnification of Danger

The initial reporting of the Shriner incident took the form of what Bromley, Shupe and Ventimiglia (1979) have called an "atrocity tale." We hear of the physical mutilation alongside statements concerning the innocence of children and the ineffectiveness of the criminal justice system. The *TNT* reported that the seven-year-old son of Helen Harlow had been found in a wooded area at around 9:00 p.m. on May 20, 1989. He had been raped and his penis had been cut off. The *TNT* reported the boy: "was too traumatized to speak or cry" (*TNT*, May 22, 1989:A7, "Past sex offender suspect in attack: Boy too traumatized to cry by mutilation"). Two days later, an editorial in the *TNT* stated that this was: "a crime of unfathomable depravity. . . . How could anyone inflict such an atrocity upon a child? Why couldn't the system stop such a monster?" (May 24, 1989: Editorial, "An Offense that Calls for Outrage"). Using the language of predation, the *TNT* then went on to note that Shriner had been: "preying upon children for the last 24 years" (May 24, 1989: Editorial, "An Offense that Calls for Outrage").

This was an inflammatory statement given that Shriner (only a suspect at the time of the newspaper article) had been incarcerated for the majority of those 24 years. The impression was conveyed that there were large numbers of innocent children under threat from the omnipresence of predators. One of the newspaper reports introduced the group called SAVUS (Stop All Violent Unnecessary Suffering). This group asked that the public: "barrage Governor Gardner with 10,000 sneakers, each representing a child who needs protection" (*TNT*, June 21, 1989:B1-2, "Stay Angry, Crowd Told: Violent Crime Can Be Halted, Speakers Say").

The aim of this barrage was to seek legislative changes that would guard against sex offenders like Shriner being released if they presented a "danger" to the community. The reference to 10,000 children in need of protection was a gross exaggeration in the context of the discussion about offenders such as Shriner. Using the acronym SAVUS was profoundly ironic, because the SAVUS group, which made initial headway in its claims-making activities by publicizing the rape and murder of Diane Ballasiotes and the mutilation of Helen Harlow's son, failed entirely to contextualize these rare acts of stranger violence against the wider back-drop of intrafamilial violence. "Stop all unnecessary suffering" might have been more aptly named "stop all unnecessary extra-familial suffer-ing."

The most important point about the early media analysis of predation was that it constructed the threat posed by sexual predators such as Shriner to be more pervasive than it was. One columnist warned: "over the past 10 days, we have learned that there is no place to hide" (*TNT*, 30 May 1989:B1, "Fury over mutilation must be converted into solutions").

No one is safe from the marauding predator and no one can hide. There is an unspoken exception here. Adult men are safer because predators go for the relatively defenseless, especially women and children. Raymond Kane had murdered a woman and Earl Shriner had mutilated a small boy. All of the twenty or so "predators" confined in the Monroe Sex Offender Program victimized women and children.

Predicting Future Acts of Predation

According to Stanley Cohen, moral panics assume that deviant acts and/or atrocities will recur. Perhaps the most explicit statement of predic-tion in the predator discourse came from Pierce County Prosecutor John Ladenburg. He was critical of a criminal justice system that let recidivist sex offenders out after serving their time. Ladenburg was quoted as say-ing: "We've got to wait for the guy to commit a major offense when everybody knows he's going to re-offend" (*TNT*, 24 May 1989: "An Offense that Calls for Outrage," Editorial). The word "everybody" im-plies readers agree Shriner will re-offend and simultaneously constructs the predator as "*outsider.*" *The exclusivity of the predator derives from* his depraved sexuality vis-à-vis the "normal" sexuality of the family man. The alternative opinion appeared as Dr. James Reardon, a spokesperson for the Washington State Psychiatric Association said: "There is absolutely no credible evidence that we can predict dangerousness" (*ST*, 25 October 1990:A1, "Mental health experts criticize sex-predator law").

Assumptions of the eventual recidivism of newly released sex offenders underpinned the early calls for changes in the sex offender legislation. If these men were a menace, then a law was needed that informed communities of their whereabouts. Washington State's Attorney General called for a law: "that strips offenders of confidentiality so that they are known to their neighborhoods" (*TNT*, 21 June 1989:B2).

Symbolic Language and Sexually Violent Predation

Perhaps the most powerful imagery was that of the sex predator or fiend who stalked innocent children. The predator was projected into the dark unknown beyond the bounds of existing criminality. One columnist noted: "This case is different because it gives us the opportunity to face the darkness" (*TNT*, 30 May 1989:B1). In the predator, the media had discovered someone that the criminal justice system could not cope with. The *TNT* reported Tacoma School Board Vice President Cathy Pearsall speaking at a "rally" attended by 175 people: 'Our young children walk this way but once,' Pearsall told the audience, which had its share of young children gazing at the balloons, the clowns and candy they had been given" (*TNT*, 21 June 1989:B1). The reporting of the danger posed to children is imbued with a sense of legitimacy because it comes from the mouth of a school board vice president. When this danger is set alongside the carefree activities of childhood, predation assumes an even more sinister presence.

The hanging of sneakers on trees around the state capitol was a dramatic way of capturing press attention. The sneaker, as a symbol of the freedom of the child to roam, emotively evoked memories of how that same freedom can bring the child into the clutches of the predator. Helen Harlow's son had been attacked in a wooded area in South Tacoma. One resident, Linda Land, heard screams about 15 minutes before the seven-year-old boy was found. She said that she: "never allows her children to play in the wooded area where she said she found mattresses and pornographic magazines" (*TNT*, 22 May 1989:A7). However, other residents were less eager to restrict the movements of their children. Local resident Mike Inske said that: "many neighborhood children including my eight-year-old son often ride bicycles by themselves in the woods" (*TNT*, 22 May 1989:A7).

The polarization is dramatically laid out here. The carefree play of childhood which apparently exposes the child to the dangers of the wooded areas where Helen Harlow's son was "stalked," is contrasted with a restricted childhood which undermines the spirit of play. One observation missing here is that freedom and adventure in childhood have always been more readily available to boys than girls. Another hidden implication is the presumption of safety in the patriarchal home, which, as I argued earlier, is the site of much child sexual abuse.

What we begin to see through this imagery is the condensation of what Goffman (1963) called stigma. By stigma, Goffman is referring to an attribute that is "deeply discrediting." The stigmatized person is seen to be less than human. Long before Shriner was found guilty, his past record had been resurrected and he had been labeled as a sexual deviant. Bearing these observations in mind, it is easier to understand the initial reception of Shriner by local police: "The only sound during the 30 seconds Earl Shriner spent in the police station hallway after his arrest . . . came from an officer near a sergeant's desk who said, 'Get him out of here' " (*TNT*, 22 May 1989:A1).

The Rise of the Decontextualized Predator

The construction of sexually violent predators proceeded in a manner which disconnected predators from the patriarchal culture of predation. This process of further construction took its lead from the patriarchal ideology embedded in the predator law. The silence of the media on issues germane to the interests of women, helped further facilitate the decontextualization of the predator.

The article now examines the way initial ideological positions were consolidated and discusses the way atrocities were autopsied.

Refining and Consolidating Initial Ideological Positions

The intensity of Shriner's stigma was continually reinforced by the dark presence of his act of castration. It is possible that the act of castration touched one of the deepest nerves in the phallocentric social body. We cannot easily discount the fact that Shriner's act of castration may have been a major contributing factor in the passage of the predator law. The atrocity tale was restated by Judge Sauriol who handed down Shriner's sentence. Reflecting on his original signing of the search warrant in the case in May 1989, Sauriol said: "I read about the third paragraph and stopped and said this is incredible. I don't think in 37 years in the field of law I've heard of, been part of, seen a criminal offense that borders on extreme cruelty more than this one" (*ST*, 26 March 1990:A1, A5, "Shriner gets 131 years"). Sauriol re-articulated the theme of the vulnerability of children when he observed that Shriner constituted: "A danger to the defenseless" (*ST,* 26 March 1990:A1). The defenselessness theme was repeated on numerous occasions in the press and on local TV. In one article, a journalist summarized the central questions: "How could the abuser do this to a helpless child? How can society allow predators to be free?" (*ST,* 19 June 1989:E1, "Healing the hurt"). This is a thinly disguised reference to the fact that sex offenders, like all other offenders, are released after they have served their sentence. According to the journalist, society (mistakenly) allows "predators" to be released upon completion of their term in prison. What this quote fails to acknowledge is that the "freedom" of men to "prey" on women underpins patriarchal relations. In a rape trial under current criminal law, juries in judging the intent of the rapist still have to overcome a common belief that it is men who initiate sex. It is not a question of freeing predators, but rather a question of asking (critically) why men are free to prey on women and why this predatory behavior has not been systematically challenged by the criminal justice system.

The castration of Helen Harlow's son was revisited in the media on a number of occasions. In fact the mutilation of this seven-year-old boy received by far the widest coverage of any of the acts of the predators. Roughly half a million dollars was raised for the boy. In stark contrast in March 1990, little less than a year after the Shriner atrocity, a three-year-old girl was mutilated by an alleged predator (see *State of Washington v. Randy Russell Smith,* Case Number 14532-4). The girl suffered internal and external tearing of the vagina. Her injuries, like those of Helen Harlow's son, required reconstructive surgery. The press coverage of her case was relatively low key compared to the Shriner case and only $10,000 was raised on her behalf. The differential press coverage and the much greater sum raised for the boy, may have reflected the fact that the boy's case was the first act of predation to make the headlines. It may have reflected the fact that the Seattle-Tacoma area is far more heavily populated and has a wider readership than the Olympia area. However, the differential treatment of the boy and girl may also reflect the publicly perceived values of the penis and vagina in a patriarchal society. More recently in the case of Lorena Bobbit, we have seen how the act of castration generates enormous media attention and electrifies the already inflamed discourse on crime. We had already been informed that Shriner was a "defective delinquent" who was "mildly retarded" (*TNT,* 21 June 1989:A7, "Stay angry crowd told"). The *TNT* informed its readers that as a child, Shriner attended a school for developmentally disabled children. His mother had said that doctors had told her that Shriner had some damage to the lower brain

(*TNT*, 21 June 1989:B1, B2, "Shriner attorney details plans"). When the verdict was read at his trial, we were told that Shriner was "emotionless." This observation appeared beneath a two-inch by one-inch drawing of Shriner which depicted him in the likeness of a Neanderthal Man (*ST*, 7 February, 1990:A1, A2, "Shriner guilty"). The point is that the reporter had no way of knowing Shriner's emotions. A more accurate statement might have been that there were no visible signs as to what Shriner was feeling. The use of the word "emotionless" underneath the drawing, strongly implied that Shriner was sub-human. This implication was compounded by other statements. We learn that the only public utterance made by Shriner during his trial was "Uh-huh" (*ST*, 7 February, 1990:A2, "Shriner guilty").

Autopsying Atrocities: The Road to the Predator Law

The "atrocious actions" of predators were explained in terms of individual defects and the softness of the criminal justice system. These explanations sensitized the public, politicians, criminal justice personnel and social services to the "need" for a predator law. This sensitization process enabled the predator law to be passed without a dissenting vote in the state legislature. Following a discussion of these themes in the sensitization process, the article addresses the way the enforcement of the new predator law amplified the phenomenon of stranger-danger and helped make the topic newsworthy at a national level.

The Defective Individual

Shriner's possible brain damage, his developmental disabilities and his alleged emotionless posture all implied that he was biologically defective. Other explanations were more psychological. The treatment professionals pushed counseling and group therapy as a potential form of rehabilitation. In one report, we learn that some therapists: "use aversion techniques, such as having the offender follow his deviant fantasy with a whiff of a noxious odor such as ammonia or rotting placenta" (*ST*, 18 June 1989:A1, A8, "Treating sexual deviants"). Such treatment techniques imply that sexually violent predatory behavior can be modified or eliminated through conditioning. The sexual deviant would then return to the ranks of the "sexually normal." Even if it is possible to deter this form of sexually violent predation, the conditioning approach assumes that an absence of predation results in the adoption of "normal" rather than patriarchally constructed sexuality.

Predation and the Failure of the Criminal Justice System

Diane Ballasiotes was raped and murdered by a work release prisoner, Gene Kane, who had been previously imprisoned for two different sexual assaults. Had he not been on work release, the Ballasiotes murder might never have happened. Her mother, Ida Ballasiotes, who obtained access to extensive press coverage after the Shriner incident, argued that violent sexual offenders should be banned from work release programs.

Others attacked Washington State's inadequate sentencing laws that did not "protect" the public. For example, attempts had been made by the Department of Social and Health Services and the Department of Corrections to commit Shriner to Western State Hospital rather than permit his release. However, a Pierce County court commissioner, for reasons not stated, declined to do this (*TNT*, 21 June 1989:B1, "Shriner attorney details plans"). The point was that Shriner had served his full term and the state had no legal provision to further detain him. The SAVUS group, among others, sought to change this.

Another cause of the predation problem, it was argued, was that the public was not well informed of the whereabouts of released sex offenders. There was no requirement under existing law for ex-sex offenders to register in the communities in which they lived. Privacy laws meant that law enforcement agencies could not inform the public about the location of ex-offenders.

News surfaced that Shriner had served only 67 days in the county jail in December 1988 for an unlawful imprisonment charge (*TNT*, May 22, 1989:A7, "Past sex offender suspect in attack"). This stemmed from an attack on a 10-year-old boy who Shriner had tied to a post and beaten. The boy later escaped. In this case, Shriner was originally charged with attempted statutory rape and unlawful imprisonment. However, these two charges were plea bargained down to unlawful imprisonment. Here the plea bargain appeared to be yet another symptom of a criminal justice system gone soft.

Sensitization, Social Control and the Passage of the Predator Law

The atrocity tales associated with predators such as Kane, Shriner, Dodd, Bundy and the Green River Killer, sensitized the public, the police, the courts, social services and the state legislature to the dangerousness of these sexually violent marauders. Police in the State of Washington received many more calls from the public concerning "suspicious" or potentially "predatory" individuals.

Persistent calls for the passage of tougher legislation to protect Washington State's citizens from sex offenders emerged during the immediate aftermath of the Shriner incident. These calls came from a number of sources and were directed at the legislature. At a local rally publicizing the threat posed to children by predators, Attorney General Ken Eikenberry urged Governor Booth Gardner to call a special session of the legislature to effect a number of changes in the laws related to sex offenders. Suggesting that these changes may be slow to materialize, Eikenberry told the crowd: "You people stay mad, stay committed and keep talking" (*TNT*, 21 June 1989:B1, "Shriner attorney details plans").

Earlier that day, the newly formed group, SAVUS, issued its demands. The mothers of the victims of Kane and Shriner spoke in support of the SAVUS agenda. The confluence of interests between state prosecutors and SAVUS attracted considerable press attention. Helen Harlow, the mother of Shriner's much publicized victim revealed: "This isn't something that just started with my son's victimization. . . . People have been working for changes for many years. That's one of the most disheartening discoveries I've made" (*TNT*, 21 June 1989:B2, "Shriner attorney details plans").

In the ensuing months, a Task Force on Community Protection was established. This Task Force produced a number of recommendations including the indefinite civil commitment of sexually violent predators. As noted, the ensuing legislation provided a variety of strategies for dealing with sex offenders.

Enforcing the Predator Law

Police officers in Seattle, Tacoma and Olympia, were adamant that public awareness of predators had been dramatically increased from the late 1980s. One officer, who trains law enforcement personnel on sex offender issues, stated that calls were coming in over incidents that previously were not seen to be suspicious. For example, unknown cars parked near schools became the subjects of reports to police (Telephone interview with Mark Mann, Tacoma Police Department, 17 March 1992).

Within police departments, we see a gearing up to deal with the new threat from predators. One police chief noted that sexual predators were the "new thing" in law enforcement (Police Chief Lockie Reeder, Puyallup Police Department, Washington, 9 April 1991). In-service training increased dramatically. In Tacoma, the police began to use counselors from the Mary Bridge Hospital's sex abuse program to interview victims. At the Olympia Police Department, Detective Nancy Gatchett reported that an additional detective had been hired to deal with sex offenses. Gatchett noted that detectives in Olympia were now much better prepared to interview victims (Telephone interview, 16 March 1992).

The police were also required to register offenders and notify communities of their presence. Just over 4,000 sex offenders are registered in the State of Washington. The state police oversee the registry of addresses. City and county police authorities have developed a classification system based on the future dangerousness of newly released sex offenders. A level one sex offender has the lowest likelihood to re-offend. He is a minimal offender. At this level, police agencies would notify each other by circulating a photograph and history of the offender. At level two, police also notify the community by informing neighborhood watches and schools that a particular offender is at large. It is at level three that the word sexual predator comes into use. Once a level three classification has been made, news media are informed. Photographs of offenders can be released to the press and the offenders' whereabouts made known.

In spite of the objections to the constitutionality of the law, the Washington courts proceeded to process would-be sexually violent predators. As of September 1993, there were twenty one "residents" (all men) in the Monroe facility either detained for treatment or awaiting a civil commitment trial. Earlier information on the profiles of fourteen Monroe Reformatory residents shows that nearly all of them were detained because of offenses against women and children they did not know. The offenses ranged from statutory rape, rape, attempted rape, indecent liberties, indecent exposure, child molestation, sexual assault and communicating with a minor for indecent purposes. Only one of the residents had victimized acquaintances, although those acquaintance victimizations were not the reason that he was detained as a sexual predator.

The autopsying of the atrocities in terms of the defectiveness of offenders and the softness of the criminal justice system, coupled with the passage and subsequent enforcement of the predator law, all made the topic of sexually violent predation highly newsworthy. It is in this direction that the analysis now turns.

Predators and Prime Time: The Dispersion of Danger

Thousands of press articles have appeared both locally and nationally about sexual predators. Hard news stories on this phenomenon are commonplace in Washington. A detailed media analysis lies beyond the scope of this article. I will work from Joel Best's (1990) distinction between primary and secondary claims-makers in order to classify the media involvement. Primary claims-makers use a certain style and rhetoric in order to attract the attention of the public. This was the case, for example, with the SAVUS group's symbolic hanging of sneakers on trees. Secondary claims-makers translate and transform the messages of the primary claims-makers (Best 1990:19). As Best argues, the public's perception of a social problem comes largely from the secondary claims-makers. These secondary claims-makers include the makers of hard news (report daily developments in ongoing cases), soft news (feature stories) and popular true crime literature (in the case of predators, see for example, Olsen 1989, 1991; Rule 1989; Smith and Guillen 1991).

In a complex manner and through a variety of media sources, the predator discourse has spread far beyond the families of the initial victims. This article briefly focuses on ABC's Nightline "Washington State's Sexual Predator Law" (April 26, 1991), CBS' 48 Hours "Predators" (November 20, 1991) and a Frontline Special "Monsters Among Us" (November 10, 1992). These shows reached a wide audience and were characterized by the same sensationalism. The focus was upon the stigma of the predator, his twisted biography and the ways in which predation might be managed.

ABC's Nightline started by introducing Andre Brigham Young who had been convicted of six rapes. An ABC news person was then shown talking with a prisoner:

> News person: "You have molested how many children?"
>
> Prisoner: "Oh, not a whole lot. About 30 or so."

Having set the scene emotionally and tapped into the anger reflex of the nation, the show proceeded to discuss the constitutionality of indefinite civil commitment, the dangerousness of the "predator" and how we might measure it and predict it, and finally, the possibility of treating predators, or at least warehousing them. Nightline failed to note the systemic nature of sexual violence within families.

Like Nightline, the CBS 48 Hours special entitled "Predators" also failed to contextualize the "stranger-danger" phenomenon against the incidence of known-offender sexual violence. CBS correspondent Bernard Goldberg pointed out: "There is a frustration in much of America. Too often criminals seem to be winning the war on crime" (Transcript, Predators, 1991:14). Goldberg made this point as he introduced the Tennis Shoe Brigade (SAVUS). Helen Harlow appeared and questioned the indefinite civil commitment clause. She stated a preference for life imprisonment: "Let's just lock them up, and if we could kill a few of them that would be cool" (Transcript, Predators, 1991:16).

The longest media presentation to date was a Frontline special entitled, "Monsters Among Us," which aired on November 10, 1992. This show captured the public imagination for a number of reasons. A central character in the show was Wesley Alan Dodd. Dodd made headlines nationally by requesting that he be put to death for the murder of three children. He had chastised the criminal justice system for not locking him up for a sufficient period of time. This attack on the softness of the system fed into the rhetoric of law and order advocates, who complained about lax sentencing, plea bargaining and the seemingly endless appeals involved in executing an offender. Although Dodd was never defined by the courts as a sexually violent predator, he fit the bill perfectly. Had he not been eligible for the death penalty, Dodd could eventually have qualified as a predator and been confined at Monroe. As noted earlier, Dodd was another reason Washington State needed a predator law. Had such a law been in place, Dodd may never have had the opportunity to kill three children.

"Monsters Among Us," also captured imaginations by presenting a retinue of predators who informed viewers in graphic detail of the atrocities they had committed. Dodd was introduced against the backdrop of the town of Richland, Washington, where he grew up. Correspondent Al Austin told viewers that Richland was seen as a "good place to grow up in" and an "ordinary town." He noted: "But people here, like people in other peaceful places, have learned to fear their parks and playgrounds and parking lots and homes because something happened in Richland that happens in many good places to grow up in. A monster grew up here" (Transcript, Monsters Among Us, 1992:1)

Out of this dichotomy of the "good and peaceful place" and the spawning of the "monster," Austin poses important questions: "How was this monster created? How could we have stopped him? How can we stop any of them?" (Transcript, Monsters Among Us, 1992:1).

Frontline, in concert with the other prime time shows, never stopped to frame the presence of these "monsters" against the systemic sexual violence against women and children by known offenders. The show proceeded to expand upon the distinctiveness of the pathology of the predators. Viewers learned in great detail of Dodd's fifteen year career as a child molester and child killer. Austin confronted what he called the startling thing about Dodd. That is: "how ordinary he seems—small and harmless looking. The handcuffs seem unnecessary. He speaks in a matter of fact voice about unspeakable things" (Transcript, Monsters Among Us, 1992:1). Other predators appeared on the show. Mike, for example, shared that he has been involved in three gang rapes. Correspondent Austin informed viewers that Mike: "looks like anything but a rapist . . . " he was "an ordinary looking young man like Wesley Dodd" (Transcript, Monsters Among Us, 1992:3).

Viewers may have assumed that rapists possess horns. Had Frontline presented the research showing that rapists are much more likely to be known to the victim rather than to be predatory strangers, the powerful political schism between "sexually violent predation" and "everyday sexual violence" would have disappeared. It is in the direction of the continuities between predators and patriarchy that draws this article to a close.

PREDATORS AND PATRIARCHY: SOME CONCLUDING REMARKS

I have argued that the ideological thrust of the predator law reproduces the power relations of gender by obfuscating systemic social problems such as woman battering, marital rape and the gendered nature of child sexual abuse. This ideological thrust inherent in the predator law has been reinforced by the sensationalist media treatment of predation. The social construction of sexually violent predators does not confront the very threatening realization that sexually violent predation is but one form of patriarchal violence.

There has not been a conspiracy to divert attention away from patriarchal violence. It is not the argument of this article that predators like Shriner should be ignored or their violence be seen as insignificant. Rather, it is a question of primary claims-makers, resorting to individualistic explanations that secondary claims-makers such as the news media, fail to contextualize against the systemic sexual violence that characterizes patriarchal relations. This failure on the part of the media, whether conscious or not, reflects and contributes to a patriarchal discourse that reproduces the domination of men over women. My argument about predation resembles other approaches to patriarchal ideology and the media (see Tuchman, Daniels and Benet, 1978; Spender, 1980, 1983; Soothill and Walby, 1991) and capitalism, racism and the media (see Hall et al., 1978). Likewise it parallels recent work by Philip Jenkins on the social construction of serial homicide. Jenkins (1994) argues that the threat posed by serial killers has been blown out of proportion and served the vested interests of certain claims-makers. Interestingly, Jenkins points out that feminist claims that serial killing is an almost exclusively male activity are based on suspect empirical evidence and much rhetorical posturing (see Jenkins, 1994, chapter seven, "Women as Serial Killers"). As I have noted above, those defined as "predators" in Washington State have all been men.

One theme to emerge from the predator discourse was that predators prey upon multiple victims. The construction of the serial rapist and/or sexually violent predator as the most threatening rapist to women is consistent with the criminal justice system's emphasis on "forcible rape." By focusing upon "forcible rape," the criminal justice system concentrates upon sexual intercourse which occurs through the use, or threatened use, of violence. This feeds the ideological construct that sexual intercourse otherwise occurs between "consenting" partners in a manner that is ostensibly free from coercion. As noted, Russell (1990) has shown that women are much more likely to experience rape or attempted rape at the hands of husbands or ex-husbands, than they are from strangers. If the word "serial" did not refer to a perpetrator who attacked more than one victim in distinctive episodes, we might make the case that husbands, lovers, etc., would be the most likely candidates for serial rapists. Modern social science has yet to invent a catchword for the husband/non-stranger who rapes the same woman on many occasions. Without wishing to impute any blame to the victims of marital/date/acquaintance rape, the paradoxical term "companionate rapist" might suffice.

The media hype about monstrous sexual violence ignores the fact that if you take the violence away, women still do not have control of their sexuality. Catherine MacKinnon puts it as follows:

> Calling rape violence, not sex, thus evades . . . the issue of who controls women's sexuality and the dominance/submission dynamic that has defined it. When sex is violent, women may have lost control over what is done to us, but absence of force does not ensure the presence of that control. (1987: 144)

This type of logic begins to trace links between sexual intercourse within marriage, rape, and sex between a prostitute and a john. All encounters tend to involve varying degrees of "non-consent" that reflect the operation of patriarchal social structures. The offenses of the sexually violent predator can be situated at a point along this continuum, rather than being seen as so aberrant and marginal vis-à-vis "everyday" interactions between men and women.

With these empirical and theoretical observations in mind, feminists have called for a number of reforms including the more stringent policing and prosecution of rape and domestic violence. Others have been keen to point out the limitations of legal change (Smart, 1989; Ferraro, 1993). They have also sought to explode the myth that offenders such as sexually violent predators warrant a heightening of awareness on the part of potential victims. As Betsy Stanko points out, precaution is a normal part of women's existence in a patriarchal society (1990:173-83). Crime prevention strategies advise women about "safe" living at the expense of systematically spelling out that the violence is mostly meted out by "known" others, not strangers.

Neil S. Websdale 65

Soothill and Walby's (1991) analysis of 5,000 newspapers from a 40 year period in Great Britain indicates that the reporting of sex crimes has become increasingly sensationalist. These authors note recent feminist demands vis-à-vis the criminal justice system. However, Soothill and Walby stress that the feminist demands have been resisted and an alternative perspective has arisen. From this alternative perspective: "sex crimes are dreadful, but rare, and are best dealt with by an increased law and order effort, rather than wider social reform" (1991:145).

The findings of Soothill and Walby raise a crucial question. Has the recent increase in the sensational reporting of sex crimes, been a part of the backlash directed at feminist arguments about the systemic nature of patriarchal violence? This question is directly relevant to the predator law in Washington. It is possible that this draconian law first appeared in Washington because of the presence of a relatively high number of nationally celebrated serial killers and predators. Doubtless, the primary claims-making of victims' rights groups such as SAVUS and the Governor's Task Force contributed greatly to the uniqueness of the Washington situation. However, I want to argue that the predator law developed in part as a conservative response to the growing publicity over phenomena such as spouse abuse during the 1980s. Like police across the United States, police in Washington State were directed to be more sensitive to domestic calls. In Washington, marital rape became a crime in 1988 and new measures were introduced to address intrafamilial child abuse. As Dobash and Dobash have recently noted, the State of Washington has a strong commitment to altering the criminal justice response to violence against women (1992:200). For example, they observe that: "with the introduction of mandatory arrest . . . there was a fourfold increase in the number of arrests (of batterers) and a 300 percent increase in successful prosecutions" (1992:200).

These reforms were encouraged by feminist pressure. However, feminists have also pointed out that unless the structure of patriarchy is changed, reforming the criminal justice system will be nothing more than window dressing. In conclusion, I suggest the predator law and the gendered coverage of sexually violent predators has had the effect of counteracting the feminist push for deeper seated reform over gender issues, by suggesting the real dangers to women and children come from freakish strangers rather than intimates or companions. It must be restated that this backlash against feminism is not something that the Washington State legislature or the media conspired to contribute to. The contribution to the backlash is more of an unforeseen twist in the ebb and flow of the predator discourse which ends up reproducing patriarchal relations. The reason the

Washington State legislature did not go after intrafamilial "predation" is that legislators feared that such an approach would reduce the reporting of intrafamilial abuse. I have noted how this rationale was underscored by patriarchal assumptions about the relationship between husbands, wives and children.

Finally, if the predator law is not seen as part of the ebb and flow of gender legislation, then its possible adoption in other states will be challenged only on the grounds that it offends constitutional guarantees. Such a challenge takes for granted the way in which liberal law upholds the sanctity of the public/private divide, a divide which continues to work against the interests of women.

REFERENCES

"An offense that calls for outrage." (Editorial). *Tacoma News Tribune.* May 24, 1989.

Aries, Phillipe. 1962. *Centuries of childhood: A social history of family life.* New York: Random House.

Best, Joel. 1990. *Threatened children.* Chicago: University of Chicago Press.

Bromley, David G., Anson D. Shupe, J.D. Ventimiglia. 1979. "Atrocity tales: The Unification Church and the social construction of evil." *Journal of Communication.* 29:45-53.

Brakel, S.J., J. Perry, B. Weiner. 1985. *The mentally disabled and the law.* American Bar Association (Third Edition).

Cohen, Stanley. 1980. *Folk devils and moral panics.* Second Edition. New York: St. Martins.

Dobash, R. Emerson and Russell Dobash. 1979. *Violence against wives.* New York: Free Press.

Dobash, R. Emerson and Russell Dobash. 1992. *Women, violence and social change.* London and New York: Routledge.

Ferraro, Kathleen J. 1993. "Cops, courts and women battering" in Pauline Bart and Eileen Geil Moran (Eds.), *Violence against women: The bloody footprints* (pp. 165-176). Sage: London.

Finkelhor, David. 1984. *Child sexual abuse: New theory and research.* New York: Free Press.

Finkelhor, David, Kersti Yllo. 1985. *License to rape: Sexual abuse of wives.* New York: Holt, Rinehart and Winston.

"Fury over mutilation must be converted into solutions." *Tacoma News Tribune.* May 30, 1989: B1.

Goffman, Erving. 1963. *Stigma: Notes on the management of spoiled identity.* Englewood Cliffs, NJ: Prentice Hall.

Gordon, Linda. 1988. *Heroes of their own lives: The politics and history of family violence.* New York: Penguin.

Hall, Stuart. 1984. "The state in question," in G. McLennan, D. Held and S. Hall (Eds.) *The idea of the modern state*. Milton Keynes: Open University Press.

Hall, Stuart, Chas Critcher, Tony Jefferson, John Clarke, and Brian Roberts. 1978. *Policing the crisis: Mugging, The state and law and order.* London: MacMillan.

Hanmer, Jalna, and Sheila Saunders. 1984. *Well founded fear.* London: Hutchinson.

"Healing the hurt." *Seattle Times.* June 19, 1989: E1, E2.

Herman, Judith with Lisa Hirschman. 1981. *Father-daughter incest.* Cambridge, MA: Harvard University Press.

Jenkins, Philip. 1984. *Using murder: The social construction of serial homicide.* New York: Aldine De Gruyter.

Journal Graphics Transcripts. ABC Nightline. Washington State's Sexual Predator Law, Show no. 2590 (26 April 1991); 48 Hours. Predators. Show no. 173 (20 November 1991); Frontline. Monsters among us. show no. 1105 (10 November 1992).

LaFond, John. 1991. Brief of Amicus Curiae in support of appellants Young and Cunningham in the Supreme Court of the State of Washington. No. 57837-1.

MacKinnon, Catherine. 1987. "Feminism, marxism, method and the state: Toward a feminist jurisprudence." In *Feminism and Methodology.* (ed.) S. Harding, (pp. 135-156). Indianapolis: Indiana University Press

"Mental health experts criticize sex-predator law." *Seattle Times.* October 25, 1990: A1.

Olsen, Jack. 1989. *Doc: The rape of the town of Lovell.* New York: Anthenum.

Olsen, Jack. 1991. *Predator: Rape, madness and injustice in Seattle.* New York: Delacorte.

"Past sex offender suspect in attack: boy too traumatized to cry by mutilation." *Tacoma News Tribune.* May 22, 1989: A1, A7.

Radford, Jill and Diana Russell. (Eds.) 1992. *Femicide.* New York: Twayne Publishers.

Rule, Ann. 1989. *The stranger beside me: Ted Bundy his shocking true story.* New York: Penguin.

Russell, Diana, E.H. 1990. *Rape in marriage.* Bloomington and Indianapolis, IN: University Press.

"Shriner attorney details plans." *Tacoma News Tribune.* June 21, 1989: B1, B2.

"Shriner gets 131 years." *Seattle Times.* March 26, 1990: A2, A5.

"Shriner guilty." *Seattle Times.* February 7, 1990: A1, A2.

Smart, Carol. 1989. *Feminism and the power of law.* London: Routledge.

Smith, C. and T. Guillen. 1991. *The search for the green river killer.* New York: Penguin.

Soothill, Keith and Sylvia Walby. 1991. *Sex crimes in the news.* London and New York: Routledge.

Spender, Dale. 1980. *Man made language.* London: Routledge.

Spender, Dale. 1983. *Women of ideas (and what men have done to them).* London: Ark.

Stanko, Elizabeth. 1990. "When precaution is normal: A feminist critique of crime prevention," Chapter 13 in *Feminist Perspectives in Criminology.* (Eds.) Lorraine Geisthrope and Alison Morris. Open University Press. Milton Keynes: (pp. 78-83).

State of Washington v. Andre Brigham Young. 1993. Washington State Supreme Court.

State of Washington v. Randy Russell Smith. Case Number 14532-4.

"Stay angry, crowd told: Violent crime can be halted, speakers say." *Tacoma News Tribune.* June 21, 1989: B12.

Sutherland, Edwin. 1950. "The diffusion of sexual psychopath laws." *American Journal of Sociology.* 55 (pp. 142-148).

"Treating sexual deviants." *Seattle Times.* June 18, 1989: A1, A8.

Tuchman, Gaye, Arlene Kaplan Daniels, James Benet (Eds.). 1978. *Hearth and home: Images of women in the mass media.* New York: Oxford University Press.

[22]

Feminist engagement with restorative justice

KATHLEEN DALY AND JULIE STUBBS

Griffith University, Australia and University of Sydney, Australia

Abstract

We analyse five areas of feminist engagement with restorative justice (RJ): theories of justice; the role of retribution in criminal justice; studies of gender (and other social relations) in RJ processes; the appropriateness of RJ for partner, sexual or family violence; and the politics of race and gender in making justice claims. Feminist engagement has focused almost exclusively on the appropriateness of RJ for sexual, partner or family violence, but there is a need to broaden the focus. We identify a wider spectrum of theoretical, political and empirical problems for future feminist analysis of RJ.

Key Words

anti-racist theories • feminism • race and gender politics
• restorative justice • violence against women

Feminist engagement with restorative justice (RJ) takes several forms, and this article maps five areas of theory, research and politics. They are theories of justice; the role of retribution in criminal justice; studies of gender (and other social relations) in RJ processes; the appropriateness of RJ for partner, sexual or family violence; and the politics of race and gender in making justice claims. There is overlap among the five, and some analysts or arguments may work across them. However, each has a particular set of concerns and a different kind of engagement with RJ.

The most developed area of feminist scholarship concerns the appropriateness of RJ for partner, sexual or family violence. It is not surprising that feminist analysts have focused on this area: it is a common context in which women come into contact with the justice system, and the significance of gender is readily apparent. It is also an area in which RJ advocates are poorly informed. At the same time, it is important to recognize other domains of feminist engagement with RJ.

Theories of justice

A sketch of feminist theorizing about justice, even a highly selective one, is daunting because the term 'justice' has many referents. We limit our discussion to the response to crime, but we recognize that some believe that criminal justice is not possible without social justice or that RJ can promote social justice. However, social justice includes a far broader set of aspirations that are beyond the reach of this article.

Early feminist thought (1970s and 1980s)

Feminist engagement with alternative justice pre-dated the emergence of RJ, which occurred around 1990 (see Daly and Immarigeon, 1998). The introduction of a range of informal justice practices, including alternative dispute resolution and the 'different voice' construct of Carol Gilligan (1982) have had a large impact on feminist theory and activism.

Different voices

Gilligan (1982) argued that girls' (or women's) moral reasoning was not inferior, as might be inferred from Kohlberg's stage theory, but was guided by an ethic of care centred on moral concepts of responsibility and relationship; it was a concrete and active morality. By contrast, the ethic of justice privileged by Kohlberg centred on moral concepts of rights and rules; it was a formal, universalizing and abstract morality. Gilligan argued that both the male and female voice should have equal importance in moral reasoning, but that women's voices were misheard or judged as inferior to men's.[1] The different voice construct was popular for many reasons; among them, it seemed to respect and honour 'women's ways of knowing' and was adopted by many feminists.

Frances Heidensohn (1986) and Kay Harris (1987) applied the care/justice dichotomy to the criminal justice system. Heidensohn compared a 'Portia' model of justice, which values rationality and individualism, and is centred on law, equality and procedure, with a more women-centred 'Persephone' model, which values caring and personal relations, and is centred on responsibility and cooperation. Heidensohn urged that greater attention be given to the values and concepts of justice associated with a Persephone model. Harris argued 'for a massive infusion of the values associated with the care/response model of reasoning' (1987: 32), although she also believed that it would be mistaken to substitute a justice/rights orientation with a care/response orientation. Harris's comment demonstrates a feminist unease with alternative justice forms. Although individualist and rights-based approaches ignored women's caring relationships and embeddedness in a 'community', there were concerns with 'forced community' (Olsen, 1984: 393–4), that is, women would not be able to enjoy individual freedoms in communities that were male-normed or dominated by men, or they would not be able to leave harmful social relationships.

Daly (1989) challenged the association of justice and care reasoning with male/masculine and female/feminine voices, arguing that this gender-linked association was not accurate empirically, and that it would be misleading to think that an alternative to men's forms of criminal law and justice practices could be found by adding women's voice or reconstituting the system along the lines of an ethic of care. Interpreting and applying law often involves relational and concrete reasoning, and thus the problem was not the absence of such forms or reasoning, but that certain gender or other hierarchical relations were presupposed, maintained and reproduced.

Although some feminist scholars continue to emphasize the need to bring women's experiences and 'voices' into the criminological and legal frame, Gilligan's different voice construct has been superseded by more complex and contingent analyses of ethics and moral reasoning. However, some RJ advocates have not kept up with these developments. For instance, Masters and Smith (1998) invoke Gilligan's work in their attempt to compare retributive justice and RJ, and they argue that RJ offers a more caring response to crime (see Daly's critique, 2002a: 64–6).

Informal justice

Research and theory on the possibilities of informal justice (Abel, 1982; Matthews, 1988), and experimentation with victim–offender mediation and community conflict resolution during the 1970s and 1980s provided an impetus towards RJ. These and other alternative justice practices gave concrete expression to the aspirations of social movement and community development activists, but they also attracted feminist critique.

Although some feminist analysts saw mediation as compatible with feminist values, it continues to be controversial in some contexts. For example, it has been criticized for defining battering (or other offences) as 'disputes', for 'pushing reconciliation', 'erasing victimization' and 'limiting [formal] justice options' (Lerman, 1984; Presser and Gaarder, 2000: 180–1). Critiques of mediation have been influential in curbing feminist interest in RJ, but mediation and RJ practices are not the same (Presser and Gaarder, 2000: 181). For example, in their ideal form, RJ practices recognize crime victims and offenders, there is no push to reconcile, nor is victimization erased. Additional support people are present beyond the victim–offender dyad, and a normative stance against partner violence can be articulated by community members, including feminist groups (Braithwaite and Daly, 1994).

Later feminist thought (1990s to the present)

Psychoanalytical, postmodern and critical race theories have had a significant impact on theorizing gender differences and differences among women. For example, in characterizing gender difference, some feminists argue that it may not be possible to construct 'woman' except as a lack, an absence or as 'not man'. Thus, the question arises, is the subject of law (or justice) ultimately always masculine, such that woman is 'always and only the Other' (Hudson, 2003: 133)? If the answer is yes, then 'there can be no possibility of different but symmetrical (male and female) subjectivities' (Hudson, 2003: 133), as Gilligan had posited. In characterizing differences among women, critical race theorists have emphasized power differences among women and a racial/ethnic inflection of 'woman' (Wing, 1997).

Major debate exists among feminist philosophers concerning the term *woman*: is it a stable unified category, or a fluid and contingent one? As characterized by Barbara Hudson (2003: 136–7), scholars such as Iris Marion Young and Seyla Benhabib argue that specific identities, such as black woman or lesbian, are formed in advance of encounters with others, and are invoked in 'staking claims to justice'. Others, such as Drucilla Cornell and Judith Butler, argue that specific identities are fluid and contingent, based on what occurs in interactions with others. Thus, for Young and Benhabib it would be possible to construct a 'procedural basis for deliberating issues of justice' (Hudson, 2003: 136), whereas for Cornell and Butler this would not be possible, except at a local level. What unites these theorists, along with critical race feminists, is that the category woman is not stable and unified, but inflected by other elements of difference among women. If this is so, then the idea of a 'woman's justice' or a 'feminist justice' is not possible because the subject woman (or category women) is too differentiated or contains hierarchies of difference, which cannot be smoothed over or blended without excluding and oppressing some groups of women. Thus, major challenges exist for imagining alternative ways of 'doing justice' in a socio-legal order that assumes different subjectivities and positionalities.

Hudson (2003) builds on feminist and other social theorists to conceptualize a post-liberal and post-communitarian justice, which must satisfy certain conditions (see also Hudson, this issue). Among the conditions, she endorses the 'liberal ideas of rights and equal respect and equal liberty' of Habermas and 'his proposals of a communicative ethics', which provide for a 'discursive justice', where multiple views are heard (Hudson, 2003: 175). However, she identifies weaknesses in his position (or other liberal and communitarian perspectives on justice): they lack an 'openness to Otherness' to 'alterity' (2003: 175) and have overlooked key insights from recent feminist thought. Within criminal justice, a lack of openness to Otherness may lead to repression and expulsion of those members 'who cannot or will not be assimilated into a homogeneous community identity' (2003: 205). Thus, criminal justice should be 'predicated on difference rather than identity' and the major principle of justice should be 'equal respect' (2003: 206).

Hudson argues that justice must be 'relational, discursive, plurivocal, rights regarding, and reflective' (2003: 206). She believes that RJ 'could meet these requirements of justice', but she has reservations about how RJ ideals are implemented in practice. Notwithstanding a stated interest in balancing the interests of offenders, victims and the community in RJ practices, she argues that there is 'insufficient regard for offenders' interests and moral status' (2003: 207); and despite the promise of a more discursive justice, the potential remains for victims, offenders or both to be dominated by others in RJ encounters. She advocates adopting a '"deep" relationalism', in which 'the situated self' and his or her relationship to a community or the wider society is more fully examined, but she finds instead that in RJ practices, the only relationship considered is between victim and offender (2003: 210–1).

Hudson sees RJ's major strength as its discursive potential, but this is also where RJ may reach its limits: it assumes that different perspectives can be reconciled, that community members share values and beliefs, and that others are 'like us'. But what of harms that are incomprehensible, that are alleged to have been committed by those 'we do not recognize as our fellows' (Hudson, 2003: 213)? For these crimes and alleged lawbreakers, a group of 'ultra-Others', Hudson argues that we require a 'strong commitment to universal, inalienable, human rights . . . All persons, not just members of one's own community, not just members in good standing in any community, have rights that each of us is morally obliged to uphold' (2003: 213).

Hudson's analysis is a singularly important contribution to the field. Rather than asking, does RJ satisfy the justice claims of feminist, critical race or other groups, she outlines a set of justice principles and asks, to what degree does RJ meet these principles? At the same time, she gives passing reference to particular kinds of criminal justice policies and practices, including RJ, and their implications for gender difference and women's situation, or for feminist debates in these areas. It is to these areas that we now turn.

The role of retribution in criminal justice

Feminist engagement with RJ cannot avoid considering the role of criminal law and the aims of punishment in achieving justice. Whereas some believe that 'law can never bring justice into being' (Hudson, 2003: 191), others are more hopeful that better laws can achieve a more responsive criminal justice system. We focus on retribution because it is often used, wrongly in our view, to typify established criminal justice and to make comparisons with RJ.

Feminist debates about retribution are difficult to characterize because commentators presuppose an opposition of retributive and restorative justice (for a critique see Daly and Immarigeon, 1998; Daly, 2000, 2002a).

Moreover, retribution is used in varied ways: often it is used negatively to refer to responses that are punitive, degrading and/or involve incarceration; but it can also be used neutrally to refer to censuring harms (e.g. Hampton, 1998; Daly, 2000; Duff, 2001) or deserved punishment in proportion to a harm (von Hirsch, 1993). Finally, commentators mistakenly refer to established criminal justice practices as retributive justice, when it is widely accepted that a variety of theories of punishment have been and are used.

Some feminists have criticized a feminist over-reliance on the criminal law to control men's violence against women (Martin, 1998; Snider, 1998).[2] They challenge feminist uses of 'punitive criminalization strategies', which rest on naïve beliefs that criminal law has the capacity to bring about social change and that deterrence promotes safety (Martin, 1998: 155, 184),[3] and they raise concerns that feminist reforms have not empowered women and may have been detrimental to racial and ethnic minority group women (Snider, 1998: 3, 10).

Jean Hampton has a more positive reading of the 'retributive ethic' in criminal justice. She distinguishes vengeance—a '[wish] to degrade and destroy the wrongdoer'—from retribution—a '[wish] to vindicate the value of the victim' (Hampton, 1998: 39). She also asks if it is possible to 'add something to this retributive response in order to express a kind of compassion for the [wrongdoer] in ways that might do him good, and if he has been the victim of injustice, acknowledge and address that injustice' (1998: 43).[4] Hampton desires a 'more sophisticated way of thinking about the nature and goals of a punitive response, one that incorporates both compassion and condemnation . . .' (1998: 37). She anticipates that a 'well-crafted' retributive response should be cognitive, to 'provok[e] thought' in the mind of the wrongdoer (1998: 43; see also Duff, 2001). But what form and amount of retributive punishment are appropriate or necessary to vindicate victims? In considering the relationship between RJ and the expressive functions of punishment, Hudson (1998) proposes that censure for an act should be decoupled from the quantum of punishment, and this activity should occur in a context of penal deflation overall.

Annalise Acorn (2004) makes a different case for retribution in her critique of RJ. She believes that expecting compassion from victims in face-to-face RJ encounters is wrong. Acorn conceives of justice as 'some kind of counterbalancing pain for the wrongdoer' (2004: 47), and she is critical of RJ advocates who 'see these connections between justice and the infliction of pain on the offender as arbitrary . . .' (2004: 47). She argues that 'our institutions of retributive punishment put forward measured, state-administered punishment *precisely as a token* in order to prevent outraged victims and communities from going for what they *really* want' (2004: 51, emphasis in original). RJ meetings may 'provide an opportunity for the victim to vent or blow off steam' towards an offender, but they do not 'validate or legitimate the victim's desire to see the perpetrator suffer' (2004: 53). She thinks that the 'lived experience of relational justice' (defined as 'the personal achievement of relations of repair, accountability, healing, respect and equality'), which RJ promises, is unlikely to be achieved. Nor does she think that RJ's sense of justice is desirable, even as a utopian vision (2004: 162). Acorn contends that in an RJ encounter, 'the compassion we feel for the offender . . . often upstages the compassion we feel for the victim. [And] the victim's compassion for the offender overshadows their desire to receive compassion for their own loss' (2004: 150).

Acorn is primarily concerned with how victims can be 'used' in an RJ process and how their suffering is too quickly ignored, whereas Hudson is primarily concerned that offenders' interests are not given sufficient weight. Their different views reveal a fault line in feminist engagement with RJ: is it possible to balance both victims' and offenders' interests?

In the context of genocide and collective violence, Martha Minow (1998) considers a spectrum of responses from vengeance to forgiveness. She argues that no one path is the right one, and much depends on the contexts of the violence (1998: 133–5); moreover, survivors vary in 'their desires for revenge [and] for granting forgiveness' (1998: 135). She distinguishes vengeance from retribution and views retribution as important and necessary to vindicate victims (although it may not be the right path for some nations following a mass atrocity); but at the same time, 'retribution needs constraints' (1998: 135). While she sees a role for bounded retribution in the aftermath of collective violence, she distinguishes this path from RJ, which she equates with reparation.

That RJ is posed as an 'alternative' to established criminal justice can create confusion in debates on the role of retribution (see also Duff, 2003: 48). By de-coupling retribution from vengeance and vindictiveness, and by not engaging in dichotomous and oppositional thinking about justice practices, it may be possible to deploy the positive and constructive elements of retribution in a restorative process.

Gender (and other social relations) in RJ processes

There are few empirical studies of how gender and other social relations (such as class, race and age) are evinced in RJ practices. Major projects on conferencing, such as the Re-Integrative Shaming Experiments (RISE) in Australia and associated research on victims' experiences (Strang, 2002), have little to say about gender. Gender is not mentioned in key studies of youth justice conferences in New Zealand (Maxwell and Morris, 1993; but see Maxwell et al., 2004 below), the Thames Valley police restorative cautions (Hoyle et al., 2002) or referral orders and RJ in England (Crawford and Newburn, 2003).

Daly (1996) examined class, race, age and gender dynamics within youth justice conferences in the ACT and South Australia. Based on observations of 24 conferences, she found that they were highly gendered events: few offenders were female (15 per cent), but women were over half of the offender's (52 per cent) or victim's (58 per cent) supporters, and more mothers than fathers were present. She observed that 25 per cent of the victims present were treated with disrespect or were re-victimized in the conferences; all but one were female. A New Zealand study (Maxwell and Morris, 1993: 119) also found that 25 per cent of victims felt worse after attending a conference, but they did not indicate the victim's gender.

A second study by Daly of 89 conferences in South Australia found that the experiences of victims and offenders were conditioned by the gendered contexts of offending and victimization in the larger society (Daly, 2002c). Female victims of female assaults were distressed and frightened by the offence and the offender, and female victims of certain property offences perceived a threat of violence, more so than the male victims. Thus, a feminist lens should extend beyond assaults against girls or women. Moreover, any claimed benefits of conferences, especially reductions in victims' fear or the degree to which victims have recovered from offences, need to be qualified by reference to the gender composition and other features of the offence. As for female offenders, they were as self-assured as their male counterparts; and they were more defiant and less apologetic for their behaviour.[5]

Maxwell et al.'s (2004) study of youth justice conferences in New Zealand shows similar patterns in the gender composition of conferences to Daly's (1996) earlier study. From interviews with 520 youth, the study found that higher proportions of girls (58 per cent) than boys (41 per cent) had problems growing up (such as moving around a lot, experiencing violence and abuse and running away from home) or were reported for care and protection (2004: 73). Girls were less likely to say that the police treated them fairly during the police interview (26 per cent) or the conference (51 per cent) than the boys (44 per cent and 64 per cent, respectively) (2004: 151). Although most youth had generally positive experiences of the conference process, the girls were less positive (2004: 150–1). As in Daly's later study (2002b), the girls appear to be less compliant and more challenging of the conference process than the boys. Maxwell et al. found that a lower share of girls (21 per cent) than boys (37 per cent) said that going to the conference helped them to reduce their offending (2004: 151–2), although the girls were less likely to have re-offended (two-thirds) than the boys (80 per cent) (2004: 196–7). The study did not analyse gender and victimization.

The findings reported thus far fall within a realist epistemology in that the research has sought to determine whether, by observational or interview data, the experiences of RJ differ for males and females or for members of dominant and minority racial-ethnic groups. Such information is crucial and not easily obtained or interpreted. None the less, realist approaches need to be supplemented by phenomenological and discursive approaches that, although rarely used in RJ research, offer the potential to deepen our understanding of gender (and other social relations) in RJ processes. For instance, research could take a social constructionist approach to gender and RJ (see Cook, this issue); or it could analyse RJ as a gendering strategy (Smart, 1992) or through the lens of 'sexed bodies' (Daly, 1997; Collier, 1998).

The appropriateness of RJ for partner, sexual and family violence

Feminist analysts face dilemmas in addressing the appropriateness of RJ for partner, sexual and family violence. Many desire a less stigmatizing and less punitive response to crime in general, but we are not sure that RJ, as currently practised, is capable of responding effectively to these offences (see, for example, contributors to Strang and Braithwaite, 2002).[6] The potential problems and benefits of RJ for such offences are highlighted below; bear in mind that some problems may be more acute for some offences, and potential benefits, more likely for others.

Potential problems with RJ

These potential problems have been identified by Stubbs (1997, 2002, 2004), Coker (1999, 2002), Goel (2000), Presser and Gaarder (2000), Shapland (2000), Lewis et al. (2001), Busch (2002), Acorn (2004) and Hopkins et al. (2004).

- *Victim safety.* As an informal process, RJ may put victims at risk of continued violence; it may permit power imbalances to go unchecked and reinforce abusive behaviour.
- *Manipulation of the process by offenders.* Offenders may use an informal process to diminish guilt, trivialize the violence or shift the blame to the victim.
- *Pressure on victims.* Some victims may not be able to advocate effectively on their own behalf. A process based on building group consensus may minimize or overshadow a victim's interests. Victims may be pressured to accept certain outcomes, such as an apology, even if they feel it is inappropriate or insincere. Some victims may want the state to intervene on their behalf and do not want the burdens of RJ.
- *Role of the 'community'.* Community norms may reinforce, not undermine male dominance and victim blaming. Communities may not be sufficiently resourced to take on these cases.
- *Mixed loyalties.* Friends and family may support victims, but may also have divided loyalties and collude with the violence, especially in intra-familial cases.
- *Impact on offenders.* The process may do little to change an offender's behaviour.
- *Symbolic implications.* Offenders (or potential offenders) may view RJ processes as too easy, reinforcing their belief that their behaviour is not wrong or can be justified. Penalties may be too lenient to respond to serious crimes like sexual assault.

Critics typically emphasize victim safety, power imbalances and the potential for re-victimization in an informal process. However, the symbolic implications are also important. Critics are concerned that in not treating serious offences seriously, the wrong messages are conveyed to offenders. They also believe that as an informal process, RJ may 're-privatize' male intimate violence after decades of feminist activism to make it a public issue.

Potential benefits of RJ

These potential benefits have been identified by Braithwaite and Daly (1994), Hudson (1998, 2002), Martin (1998), Morris and Gelsthorpe (2000), Presser and Gaarder (2000), Daly (2002b), Morris (2002), Pennell and Burford (2002), Koss et al. (2003), Hopkins et al. (2004) and Daly and Curtis-Fawley (2005).

- *Victim voice and participation.* Victims have the opportunity to voice their story and to be heard. They can be empowered by confronting the offender, and by participating in decision making on the appropriate penalty.
- *Victim validation and offender responsibility.* A victim's account of what happened can be validated, acknowledging that she is not to blame. Offenders are required to take responsibility for their behaviour, and their offending is censured. In the process, the victim is vindicated.
- *Communicative and flexible environment.* The process can be tailored to child and adolescent victims' needs and capacities. Because it is flexible and less formal, it may be less threatening and more responsive to the individual needs of victims.
- *Relationship repair (if this is a goal).* The process can address violence between those who want to continue the relationship. It can create opportunities for relationships to be repaired, if that is what is desired.

Although there is considerable debate on the appropriateness of RJ for partner, sexual or family violence, empirical evidence is sparse. There have been few studies of RJ for these offences (they include Braithwaite and Daly, 1994; Lajeunesse, 1996; Daly, 2002b, 2005; Pennell and Burford, 2002; Daly and Curtis-Fawley, 2005; see also the discussion of circle sentencing later), but insufficient attention has been paid to the great variation in the contexts and seriousness of these offences.

With the exception of circle sentencing, RJ has largely been kept off the agenda for partner and sexual violence, in part due to feminist or victim advocacy. New Zealand and South Australia are the only two jurisdictions in which RJ is used routinely in youth justice cases of sexual assault. In the New Zealand pilot of RJ as pre-sentence advice for adult cases, partner and sexual violence cases are currently ineligible. The US project RESTORE appears to be the first pilot to test RJ in adult cases of sexual violence (Koss et al., 2003).

After reviewing 18 conference cases of youth sexual violence, Daly (2002b: 81–6) concluded that the question of the appropriateness of RJ for these offences may be impossible to address in the abstract. In a more recent study of nearly 400 sexual violence cases finalized in court, by conference or formal caution, Daly (2005) concluded that conferences were a better option for victims, if only that there was an admission to the offence and an outcome. More of the youth at conferences than in court were required to attend an adolescent sex offender counselling programme, and this, in turn, was associated with reductions in re-offending. While the court process may vindicate some victims, nearly half of court cases were dismissed or withdrawn.[7]

Evaluations of RJ must recognize the different kinds of violence experienced by victims in these cases, and whether it is ongoing, as is more likely in partner violence and some family violence cases. Feminist critiques of RJ focus mainly on partner violence and have raised well-founded concerns with RJ in these cases. Zehr, a major RJ advocate, now suggests that 'domestic violence is probably the most problematic area of application, and here great caution is advised' (2003: 11, 39). The central place of apology in RJ practices is suspect for partner violence, since 'the skill of contrite apology is routinely practiced by abusers in violent intimate relationships' (Acorn, 2004: 73). Acorn also argues that in emphasizing forgiveness and reconciliation, RJ would be inappropriate in cases of sexual violence and is antithetical to vindicating a victim's suffering. While some RJ advocates emphasize forgiveness and reconciliation, and Zehr (2003: 8) suggests that 'this may occur more often' in RJ, he also insists that there is 'no pressure to choose to forgive or to seek reconciliation' and that these are not primary goals of RJ (see also Minow, 1998). However, some analysts question the assertion that the power to forgive is necessarily a choice freely open to victims; for example, Goel (2000: 326–7) suggests there are pressures on women to forgive in circle sentencing.

Debate continues over whether RJ may be more constructive than formal court processes in cases such as historical child sexual abuse (see Jülich, this issue), sexual violence or certain family violence cases. The use of RJ to divert admitted offenders from court remains controversial for many feminist activists, and specific consideration needs to be given to what is proposed by diversion. For instance, project RESTORE involves post-charge diversion, but requires sex offender treatment and ongoing monitoring of offenders (Koss et al., 2003). Much depends on the model used in carrying out RJ. For example, Joan Pennell and Gale Burford (2002) use a 'feminist praxis framework' in conceptualizing RJ responses to family violence; their approach is tailored to the dynamics of partner and family violence in ways that the standard RJ package is not.

Race and gender politics: different justice claims

One of the legacies of the 1960's and 1970's social movement activity is that justice claims for offenders and victims are overlaid by race and gender politics, respectively. Specifically, racial and ethnic minority groups' claims commonly centre on the treatment of suspects and offenders, while feminist claims more likely centre on the treatment of victims. This can create problems in finding common ground.

Indigenous communities often show a willingness to engage with alternative forms of justice, born in part from a critique of the damage wrought by conventional criminal justice, and many are keen to adopt RJ. However, Indigenous aspirations for justice are commonly holistic and associated with calls for self-determination; and these elements are not often acknowledged in considerations of alternative modes of justice, nor are Indigenous women's perspectives typically addressed. As Chris Cunneen (2003) argues, little attention is paid to whether alternatives such as RJ are consonant with Indigenous aspirations for justice. Claims that RJ is derived from Indigenous practices and/or is particularly appropriate for Indigenous communities have been challenged for denying the diversity among Indigenous peoples (Cunneen, 2003: 188) and for re-engaging a white-centred view of the world (Daly, 2002a: 61–4). Critics also say that RJ has been imposed on Indigenous communities, is neo-colonialist, not community driven and is an adjunct rather than an alternative to conventional criminal justice (Tauri, 1998).

Circle sentencing is one form of RJ (and Indigenous justice practice) that has been used widely in Canada and adopted more recently in Australia. In Canada, women's experiences with sentencing circles are mixed. Concerns have been raised that the subordination of women in some Canadian First Nations communities means that they do not enter the circle on an equal basis (Goel, 2000; Stewart et al., 2001) and that women have sometimes been excluded, silenced or harmed because power relations were not recognized or gendered violence not taken seriously. Whether in the context of circles or conventional criminal justice, Razack argues that 'culture, community, and colonialization can be used to compete with and ultimately prevail over gender-based harm' (1994: 907). Thus 'cultural' arguments (such as that sexual violence occurs because the community is coming to terms with the effects of colonialization) may be accepted while 'women's realities at the intersection of racism and sexism' (1994: 913) are ignored. Hampton (1998: 43) underscores this point for disadvantaged and racialized men more generally:

> If, say, poverty and a history of discrimination played a part in a young man turning to violence, our failing to punish him, or our punishing him lightly, ends up further hurting the people who were already hurt by his violence.
>
> (1998: 42)

In the Australian context, Melissa Lucashenko suggests that state 'forms of violence against Aboriginal people have been relatively easy for academics and Black spokespeople to see' and 'to point a finger at' than 'the individual men doing the bashing and raping and child molesting' (1997: 155–6). She shows the difficult situation in which Indigenous women are placed: 'Black women have been torn between the self-evident oppression they share with Indigenous men—oppression that fits uneasily . . . into the frameworks of White feminism—and the unacceptability of those men's violent, sexist behaviours toward their families' (1997: 155–6).

How, then, do these race and gender politics relate to RJ? First, there is considerable debate, and no one position. For instance, in Australia, there is support for RJ principles by many Indigenous people and organizations (*Aboriginal and Torres Strait Islander Women's Task Force on Violence Report*, 2000; Behrendt, 2003: 188–9). However, the use of RJ to divert men, who have been involved in family violence, from the criminal justice system is accepted by some communities (Blagg, 2002: 200), but strongly resisted by others. Indigenous communities vary culturally, politically and in their access to resources.

Second, violence is experienced differently in Indigenous and non-Indigenous communities. 'Family violence' is the commonly preferred term for Australian Indigenous women and encapsulates a broader range of 'harmful, exploitative, violent, and aggressive practices that form around . . . intimate relations' (Blagg, 2002: 193) than what is typically contemplated in feminist approaches to partner or domestic violence. Thus, if RJ-like responses are introduced, they will require significant reconceptualization of what is, ultimately, a white justice model. RJ cannot be prescribed, nor adopted formulaically. Rather it needs to be explored and transformed with due regard to Indigenous principles of self-determination, with reference to existing Indigenous initiatives, and with explicit recognition of Indigenous women's interests (Blagg, 2002: 199; see also Stewart et al., 2001: 57; Behrendt, 2003; Cameron, this issue; Coker, this issue).

Third, Indigenous and non-Indigenous women may differ in their conceptualization of, and responses to, RJ. For instance, Heather Nancarrow (this issue) found greater support by Queensland Indigenous women than non-Indigenous women for RJ in domestic and family violence cases. Whereas the Indigenous women viewed it as a means of potentially empowering Indigenous people, the non-Indigenous women equated RJ with mediation. She found that non-Indigenous women had greater trust in the criminal justice system, whereas Indigenous women's support for RJ lay, in part, with their distrust of established criminal justice.

Finally, race and gender politics have a particular signature, depending on the country and context examined; and there is considerable debate among and between Indigenous and non-Indigenous women. For example, in contrast to Nancarrow's findings cited above, research by Anne McGillivray and Brenda Comaskey (1999) found that among the Canadian Indigenous women they interviewed, who had been long-term victims of partner violence, there was 'overwhelming support for punishment [jail]', although 'they also supported effective treatment programs' (1999: 117). The women 'saw jail as real and symbolic punishment, as a guarantee of some period of immediate safety', and that treatment without jail would be ineffective (1999: 125). They had more mixed views of diversion: 'most thought diversion [was] worth a try' (1999: 127), but they wanted to see conditions met such as 'guarantee[ing] treatment and victims' safety, and be[ing] immune to manipulation by abusers' (1999: 133). McGillivray and Comaskey noted the women's options were limited because of 'reserve politics' and a lack of resources (1999: 133), factors suggesting that the women's personal security was a more pressing concern than an abstract sense of justice. Other Canadian studies have not reported a strong preference for criminal justice, and some note disillusionment with, but not necessarily a rejection of, some models of alternative justice. For instance, Goel (2000) argues that problems with circle sentencing could be addressed by empowering women within their communities to ensure that they enter a circle on a more equal footing.

Conclusion

Feminist engagement with the idea of RJ is recent and evolving. Although there is scepticism about what RJ can do to advance women's, including racialized women's, justice claims, there is some degree of openness to experimenting with a new set of justice practices. Feminist debate on the merits of RJ revolves around those who believe that justice alternatives can offer more options for victims, offenders (or suspects) and communities than established criminal justice; and those who see more dangers than opportunities with informal justice, who are concerned with the symbolic significance of RJ as appearing to be 'too lenient', and who are critical of RJ's overly positive and sentimental assumptions of human nature for victims and victimizers. There are differences between and among white and racialized women in the degree to which the state and the criminal justice system are viewed as trustworthy and effective sites for responding to violence against women. We know that because of historical and contemporary experiences of racism in established criminal justice practices, racialized women are more open to experimenting with alternative justice practices. For Indigenous women, such practices need to be tied to principles of self-determination.

   We have identified a wide spectrum of theoretical, political and empirical problems for future feminist engagement with RJ. More attention needs to be given to ideal justice principles and to whether RJ measures up to those principles. For instance, greater reflection is required on the roles of retribution and punishment in RJ and mainstream criminal justice, and the potential for RJ across a wider range of offences and in handling broader forms of community conflict. This largely uncharted empirical ground should use the tools of realist, social constructionist and discursive analyses. We require comparative analyses of feminist debates about RJ in different countries and for different communities, necessitating greater sophistication in comparative work. The different political contexts of feminist debates must be recognized. Whereas Cameron (this issue) calls for a moratorium on new RJ or Indigenous justice initiatives for intimate violence cases in Canada, Coker (this issue) argues that this position would be 'disastrous' in the USA because it would mean greater federal inter-vention in the lives of American Indian women, using inappropriate crime control measures. A fundamental problem for comparative analysis is that the meanings and practices of RJ vary greatly. Among the more contentious areas is the optimal relationship between RJ and established criminal justice, especially for racialized women. The relationship of RJ to other new justice forms such as Indigenous justice, transitional justice and international criminal justice is a rich, but untapped area.

Since the late 1980s, feminist analyses of justice have shifted from notions that criminal justice could be reformed by adding 'women's voice' or an 'ethic of care' to a more sobering appraisal of what, in fact, criminal law and justice system practices can do to achieve women's and feminist goals (Smart, 1989). During this period, several new justice forms have emerged, among them RJ; as a consequence, we face a far more complex justice field than a decade ago. It is clear that feminist and anti-racist theories and politics must engage with these new developments, at the national and international levels, and with state and community political actors. At the same time, we should expect modest gains and seek additional paths to social change.

Notes

We would like to acknowledge Brigitte Bouhours and Jocelyn Luff for their research assistance.

1. Gilligan later re-formulated her argument: she recognized that 'care' re-sponses made within a 'justice' framework left 'the basic assumptions of a justice framework intact . . . and that as a moral perspective, care [was] less well elaborated' (Gilligan, 1987: 24).

2. This work has offered a welcome challenge to any naïve reliance on criminalization strategies, but some analysts have failed to acknowledge the diversity of responses to violence against women, which include hybrid models that engage advocacy groups, community groups and criminal justice agents (see Stubbs, 2004).

3. Martin considers established criminal justice to have an 'individualistic retribution ethic at its core' (1998: 155); she equates retribution with punishment, and punishment with imprisonment. Retributivists such as von Hirsch (1993) would not equate retribution with general or specific deter-rence, but rather with censure and punishment that is proportional to the seriousness of a crime.

4. The masculine pronoun is used because Hampton is discussing a case that involved male prisoners' rights to vote.

5. This result is partly a consequence of a high proportion of 'punch-ups' in the female offence distribution.

6. Family violence (the commonly preferred term among Australian Indigen-ous women) refers to a broader array of offences than partner violence (e.g.

child sexual abuse and family fights; Blagg, 2002) and in youth justice cases, would include sibling assaults and assaults on parents by children.
7. In South Australia, RJ is set in motion only after a youth admits the offence to the police (or in court). More research is needed to determine whether RJ, as diversion from court, may offer incentives for those who have offended to make admissions.

References

Abel, Rick (1982) *The Politics of Informal Justice* (2 vols). New York: Academic Press.
Aboriginal and Torres Strait Islander Women's Task Force on Violence Report (2000) Brisbane: Department of Aboriginal and Torres Strait Islander Policy and Development.
Acorn, Annalise (2004) *Compulsory Compassion: A Critique of Restorative Justice*. Vancouver: UBC Press.
Behrendt, Larissa (2003) *Achieving Social Justice: Indigenous Rights and Australia's Future*. Annandale: Federation Press.
Blagg, Harry (2002) 'Restorative Justice and Aboriginal Family Violence: Opening a Space for Healing', in Heather Strang and John Braithwaite (eds) *Restorative Justice and Family Violence*, pp. 191–205. Cambridge: Cambridge University Press.
Braithwaite, John and Kathleen Daly (1994) 'Masculinities, Violence and Communitarian Control', in Tim Newburn and Elizabeth A. Stanko (eds) *Just Boys Doing Business? Men, Masculinities, and Crime*, pp. 189–213. London: Routledge.
Busch, Ruth (2002) 'Domestic Violence and Restorative Justice Initiatives: Who Pays if We Get it Wrong?', in Heather Strang and John Braithwaite (eds) *Restorative Justice and Family Violence*, pp. 223–48. Cambridge: Cambridge University Press.
Cameron, Angela (2006) 'Stopping the Violence: Canadian Feminist Debates on Restorative Justice and Intimate Violence', *Theoretical Criminology* 10(1): 49–66.
Coker, Donna (1999) 'Enhancing Autonomy for Battered Women: Lessons from Navajo Peacemaking', *UCLA Law Review* 47(1): 1–111.
Coker, Donna (2002) 'Transformative Justice: Anti-Subordination Processes in Cases of Domestic Violence', in Heather Strang and John Braithwaite (eds) *Restorative Justice and Family Violence*, pp. 128–52. Cambridge: Cambridge University Press.
Coker, Donna (2006) 'Restorative Justice, Navajo Peacemaking and Domestic Violence', *Theoretical Criminology* 10(1): 67–85.
Collier, Richard (1998) *Masculinities, Crime and Criminology: Men, Heterosexuality and the Criminal(ised) Other*. London: Sage Publications.
Cook, Kimberly J. (2006) 'Doing Difference and Accountability in Restorative Justice Conferences', *Theoretical Criminology* 10(1): 107–24.

Crawford, Adam and Tim Newburn (2003) *Youth Offending and Restorative Justice: Implementing Reform in Youth Justice.* Cullompton: Willan Publishing.

Cunneen, Chris (2003) 'Thinking Critically about Restorative Justice', in Eugene McLaughlin, Ross Fergusson, Gordon Hughes and Louise Westmarland (eds) *Restorative Justice Critical Issues*, pp. 182–94. London: Sage Publications.

Daly, Kathleen (1989) 'Criminal Justice Ideologies and Practices in Different Voices: Some Feminist Questions about Justice', *International Journal of the Sociology of Law* 17(1): 1–18.

Daly, Kathleen (1996) 'Diversionary Conferencing in Australia: A Reply to the Optimists and Skeptics', paper presented at the American Society of Criminology Annual Meeting, Chicago, November.

Daly, Kathleen (1997) 'Different Ways of Conceptualizing Sex/Gender in Feminist Theory and Their Implications for Criminology', *Theoretical Criminology* 1(1): 25–51.

Daly, Kathleen (2000) 'Revisiting the Relationship between Retributive and Restorative Justice', in Heather Strang and John Braithwaite (eds) *Restorative Justice: Philosophy to Practice*, pp. 33–54. Aldershot: Dartmouth/Ashgate.

Daly, Kathleen (2002a) 'Restorative Justice: The Real Story', *Punishment & Society* 4(1): 55–79.

Daly, Kathleen (2002b) 'Sexual Assault and Restorative Justice', in Heather Strang and John Braithwaite (eds) *Restorative Justice and Family Violence*, pp. 62–88. Cambridge: Cambridge University Press.

Daly, Kathleen (2002c) 'Widening the Feminist Lens on Restorative Justice', paper presented at the American Society of Criminology Annual Meeting, Chicago, November.

Daly, Kathleen (2005) 'Restorative Justice and Sexual Assault: An Archival Study of Court and Conference Cases', *British Journal of Criminology*, Advance Access Publication Paper available at: http://bjc.oxfordjournals.org/cgi/rapidpdf/azi07v1

Daly, Kathleen and Sarah Curtis-Fawley (2005) 'Restorative Justice for Victims of Sexual Assault', in Karen Heimer and Candace Kruttschnitt (eds) *Gender and Crime: Patterns of Victimization and Offending*, pp. 230–65. New York: New York University Press.

Daly, Kathleen and Russ Immarigeon (1998) 'The Past, Present, and Future of Restorative Justice: Some Critical Reflections', *Contemporary Justice Review* 1(1): 21–45.

Duff, R. Antony (2001) *Punishment, Communication, and Community.* New York: Oxford University Press.

Duff, R. Antony (2003) 'Restoration and Retribution', in Andrew von Hirsch, Julian Roberts, Anthony Bottoms, Kent Roach and Mara Schiff (eds) *Restorative Justice and Criminal Justice: Competing or Reconcilable Paradigms?*, pp. 43–59. Oxford: Hart Publishing.

Gilligan, Carol (1982) *In a Different Voice*. Cambridge: Harvard University Press.

Gilligan, Carol (1987) 'Moral Orientation and Moral Development', in Eva Kittay and Diana Meyers (eds) *Women and Moral Theory*, pp. 19–33. Totowa: Rowman & Littlefield.

Goel, Rashmi (2000) 'No Women at the Centre: The Use of Canadian Sentencing Circles in Domestic Violence Cases', *Wisconsin Women's Law Journal* 15(2): 293–334.

Hampton, Jean (1998) 'Punishment, Feminism, and Political Identity: A Case Study in the Expressive Meaning of the Law', *Canadian Journal of Law and Jurisprudence* 11(1): 23–45.

Harris, M. Kay (1987) 'Moving into the New Millennium: Toward a Feminist Vision of Justice', *Prison Journal* 67(2): 27–38.

Heidensohn, Frances (1986) 'Models of Justice: Portia or Persephone? Some Thoughts on Equality, Fairness and Gender in the Field of Criminal Justice', *International Journal of the Sociology of Law* 14(3–4): 287–98.

Hopkins, C. Quince, Mary Koss and Karen Bachar (2004) 'Applying Restorative Justice to Ongoing Intimate Violence: Problems and Possibilities', *Saint Louis University Public Law Review* 23(1): 289–311.

Hoyle, Carolyn, Richard Young and Roderick Hill (2002) *Proceed with Caution: An Evaluation of the Thames Valley Police Initiative in Restorative Cautioning*. York: Joseph Rowntree Foundation.

Hudson, Barbara (1998) 'Restorative Justice: The Challenge of Sexual and Racial Violence', *Journal of Law and Society* 25(2): 237–56.

Hudson, Barbara (2002) 'Restorative Justice and Gendered Violence: Diversion or Effective Justice?', *British Journal of Criminology* 42(3): 616–34.

Hudson, Barbara (2003) *Justice in the Risk Society*. London: Sage Publications.

Hudson, Barbara (2006) 'Beyond White Man's Justice: Race, Gender and Justice in Late Modernity', *Theoretical Criminology* 10(1): 29–47.

Jülich, Shirley (2006) 'Views of Justice Among Survivors of Historical Child Sexual Abuse: Implications for Restorative Justice in New Zealand', *Theoretical Criminology* 10(1): 125–38.

Koss, Mary, Karen Bachar and C. Quince Hopkins (2003) 'Restorative Justice for Sexual Violence: Repairing Victims, Building Community and Holding Offenders Accountable', *Annals of the New York Academy of Science* 989: 384–96.

Lajeunesse, Therese (1996) *Community Holistic Circle Healing in Hollow Water, Manitoba: An Evaluation*. Ottawa: Solicitor General of Canada.

Lerman, Lisa (1984) 'Mediation of Wife Abuse Cases: The Adverse Impact of Informal Dispute Resolution on Women', *Harvard Women's Law Journal* 7(1): 57–113.

Lewis, Ruth, Rebecca Dobash, Russell Dobash and Kate Cavanagh (2001) 'Law's Progressive Potential: The Value of Engagement for the Law for Domestic Violence', *Social and Legal Studies* 10(1): 105–30.

Lucashenko, Melissa (1997) 'Violence against Indigenous Women: Public and

Private Dimensions', in Sandy Cook and Judith Bessant (eds) *Women's Encounters with Violence: Australian Experiences*, pp. 147–58. London: Sage Publications.

McGillivray, Anne and Brenda Comaskey (1999) *Black Eyes All of the Time.* Toronto: University of Toronto Press.

Martin, Dianne L. (1998) 'Retribution Revisited: A Reconsideration of Feminist Criminal Law Reform Strategies', *Osgoode Hall Law Journal* 36(1): 151–88.

Masters, Guy and David Smith (1998) 'Portia and Persephone Revisited: Thinking about Feeling in Criminal Justice', *Theoretical Criminology* 2(1): 5–27.

Matthews, Roger (1988) 'Reassessing Informal Justice', in Roger Matthews (ed.) *Informal Justice?*, pp. 1–24. Newbury Park: Sage Publications.

Maxwell, Gabrielle and Allison Morris (1993) *Family, Victims and Culture: Youth Justice in New Zealand.* Wellington: Institute of Criminology, Victoria University of New Zealand.

Maxwell, Gabrielle, Venezia Kingi, Jeremy Robertson, Allison Morris and Chris Cunningham (2004) *Achieving Effective Outcomes in Youth Justice: Final Report.* Wellington: Ministry of Social Development.

Minow, Martha (1998) *Between Vengeance and Forgiveness: Facing History after Genocide and Mass Violence.* Boston, MA: Beacon Press.

Morris, Allison (2002) 'Critiquing the Critics: A Brief Response to Critics of Restorative Justice', *British Journal of Criminology* 42(3): 596–615.

Morris, Allison and Loraine Gelsthorpe (2000) 'Re-Visioning Men's Violence against Female Partners', *Howard Journal of Criminal Justice* 39(4): 412–28.

Nancarrow, Heather (2006) 'In Search of Justice for Domestic and Family Violence: Indigenous and Non-Indigenous Australian Women's Perspectives', *Theoretical Criminology* 10(1): 87–106.

Olsen, Frances (1984) 'Statutory Rape: A Feminist Critique of Rights Analysis', *Texas Law Review* 63(3): 387–432.

Pennell, Joan and Gale Burford (2002) 'Feminist Praxis: Making Family Group Conferencing Work', in Heather Strang and John Braithwaite (eds) *Restorative Justice and Family Violence*, pp. 108–27. Cambridge: Cambridge University Press.

Presser, Lois and Emily Gaarder (2000) 'Can Restorative Justice Reduce Battering? Some Preliminary Considerations', *Social Justice* 27(1): 175–95.

Razack, Sherene (1994) 'What Is to be Gained by Looking White People in the Eye? Culture, Race, and Gender in Cases of Sexual Violence', *Signs* 19(4): 894–923.

Shapland, Joanna (2000) 'Victims and Criminal Justice: Creating Responsible Criminal Justice Agencies', in Adam Crawford and Jo Goodey (eds) *Integrating a Victim Perspective within Criminal Justice: International Debates*, pp. 147–64. Aldershot: Ashgate.

Smart, Carol (1989) *Feminism and the Power of Law.* London: Routledge.

28   *Theoretical Criminology 10(1)*

Smart, Carol (1992) 'The Woman of Legal Discourse', *Social and Legal Studies* 1(1): 29–44.

Snider, Laureen (1998) 'Toward Safer Societies: Punishment, Masculinities and Violence against Women', *British Journal of Criminology* 38(1): 1–39.

Stewart, Wendy, Audrey Huntley and Fay Blaney (2001) *The Implications of Restorative Justice for Aboriginal Women and Children Survivors of Violence: A Comparative Overview of Five Communities in British Columbia.* Ottawa: Law Commission of Canada. Available at http://www.lcc.gc.ca/en/themes/sr/rj/awan/awan_toc.asp

Strang, Heather (2002) *Repair or Revenge: Victims and Restorative Justice.* Oxford: Clarendon Press.

Strang, Heather and John Braithwaite (eds) (2002) *Restorative Justice and Family Violence.* Cambridge: Cambridge University Press.

Stubbs, Julie (1997) 'Shame, Defiance, and Violence against Women: A Critical Analysis of "Communitarian" Conferencing', in Sandy Cook and Judith Bessant (eds) *Women's Encounters with Violence: Australian Experiences,* pp. 109–26. London: Sage Publications.

Stubbs, Julie (2002) 'Domestic Violence and Women's Safety: Feminist Challenges to Restorative Justice', in Heather Strang and John Braithwaite (eds) *Restorative Justice and Family Violence,* pp. 42–61. Cambridge: Cambridge University Press.

Stubbs, Julie (2004) *Restorative Justice, Domestic Violence and Family Violence.* Issues Paper 9. Sydney: Australian Domestic and Family Violence Clearinghouse. Available at http://www.austdvclearinghouse.unsw.edu.au/PDF%20files/Issues_Paper_9.pdf

Tauri, Juan (1998) 'Family Group Conferencing: A Case Study of the Indigenisation of New Zealand's Justice System', *Current Issues in Criminal Justice* 10(2): 168–82.

Von Hirsch, Andrew (1993) *Censure and Sanctions.* New York: Oxford University Press.

Wing, Adrien (ed.) (1997) *Critical Race Feminism: A Reader.* New York: New York University Press.

Zehr, Howard (2003) *The Little Book of Restorative Justice.* Intercourse, PA: Good Books.

KATHLEEN DALY is Professor of Criminology and Criminal Justice at Griffith University, Brisbane. Since 1995, she has directed a programme of research on restorative justice and the race and gender politics of new justice practices in Australia, New Zealand and Canada.

JULIE STUBBS is Associate Professor and Deputy Director of the Institute of Criminology, University of Sydney. Her research and publications deal primarily with violence against women (including homicide, self-defence, battered woman syndrome and child contact in the context of post-separation domestic violence) and restorative justice.

[23]

Gendered War and Gendered Peace: Truth Commissions and Postconflict Gender Violence: Lessons From South Africa

Tristan Anne Borer[1]

Abstract

That war is profoundly gendered has long been recognized by feminist international relations scholars. What is less recognized is that the postwar period is equally gendered. Currently undertheorized is how truth-seeking exercises in the aftermath of conflict should respond to this fact. What happens to women victims of war violence? The difficulties of foregrounding gendered wartime violence in truth telling are illustrated by the South African Truth and Reconciliation Commission. The article explores some consequences of the failure to uncover gendered truth, including its impact on the government's reparations policy, and continued "peacetime" violence perpetrated against women in South Africa.

Keywords

gender, reparations, sexual violence, South Africa, truth commissions

That war is profoundly gendered has long been recognized by feminist international relations scholars (Enloe, 2000; Jacobs, Jacobson, & Marchbank, 2000; Turshen & Twagiramariya, 1998). In World War I, 80% of war casualties were soldiers, which meant men. In World War II, only 50% of casualties were soldiers; by the Vietnam War, this number had fallen to 20%. By the 1990s, a full 90% of casualties were civilians, mainly women and children (Pettman, 1996). For those who survive, many are forcibly displaced, becoming refugees and internally displaced persons, 80% of whom are again women and children. Civil conflicts—the type which most often fuels calls for truth telling after transitions to democracy—have specific forms of violence, including state terror enacted by agents or by

[1]Connecticut College

Corresponding Author:
Tristan Anne Borer, Box 5316, 270 Mohegan Avenue, New London, CT 06320
Email: tabor@conncoll.edu

vigilante groups or paramilitaries with state complicity directed primarily against innocent civilians; much of this violence is again gender specific, with women being targeted through gender-based humiliation and torture. In general, most feminist scholars argue that sexual violence against women specifically is a constitutive aspect of war.[1] Although it is clear that war is gendered, less recognized are the ways in which the postwar period is equally gendered. What happens to women victims of war violence? What role does righting gender inequities play in postwar reconstruction? Although the gendered dimension of violent conflict has received much theoretical attention, what has not been adequately theorized is how truth-seeking exercises in the aftermath of conflict should respond to this fact. The difficulties of foregrounding gender in truth telling are illustrated by examining the South African Truth and Reconciliation Commission (TRC). In this article, I argue that the TRC was not terribly successful at uncovering the truth about women's experiences, specifically of sexual violence, under apartheid. I offer several explanations for this, including the definition of human rights violations that governed the work of the commission, the primacy given to civil and political over economic and social rights violations, the adoption of a gender-neutral approach to truth gathering, and the criteria used for qualifying for amnesty. The article then explores some consequences of the failure to uncover the truth about sexual violence, including its impact on the government's reparations policy, and continued "peacetime" violence perpetrated against women in South Africa.

War Is Gendered. So Is Peace

Richard Rayner (1997) argued that military training involves socialization into an extreme kind of masculinity, in which a young soldier must prove he is a good soldier—that is, that he is neither a "girl" nor gay. This militarized masculinity, which results from breaking men down and reconstructing them as soldiers, Pettman (1996) argued, "regularly includes the vilification of women and consciously plays on young men's sexual insecurities and identities" (p. 93). Rayner (1997) argued that in this warrior culture militarism, masculinity and sexualized violence are connected: "There is a set of attitudes, including hypermasculinity, adversarial sexual beliefs, sexual promiscuity, acceptance of violence against women, hostility toward women and sex-role stereotyping, that is correlated with rape and a proclivity for it" (p. 29). And while Rayner questions whether rape is a necessary corollary to the bottom line of an army's function—killing—others believe that sexual harassment and violence are not only inevitable but indeed a necessary part of the military. He quotes Reagan Administration Undersecretary of Defense for Policy Fred C. Iklé, for example, who argues that "military life may correctly foster the attitudes that tend toward rape, such as aggression and single-minded self-assertion" (Rayner, 1997, p. 29).

In light of Rayner's "warrior culture," it is not surprising that in all types of violent conflicts, women are targeted specifically as women by sexual violence. As a result, rape as a tool of war has become endemic. Diken and Lausten (2005) argued that rape can, in fact, be viewed as a prime strategy of asymmetric warfare, as soldiers attack civilian women rather than male combatants, and have only the indirect aim of taking a territory. The Women's Rights Project of Human Rights Watch has detailed the variety of ways in which rape has been used as a war weapon and as a tool of political repression; it is clear that sexual violence is a worldwide and pan-cultural phenomenon (Human Rights Watch, 1995a, pp. 1-3).[2] Although it has become increasingly evident that women are vulnerable to rape by soldiers from the "other" side as a way of getting at "their" men, demonstrating the failure of their men as protectors, recent events have revealed that rape is not a tool reserved only for emasculating and humiliating the enemy. Women, it is now clear, face the prospect of being raped both by soldiers from their own countries and by peacekeepers; in both cases, women are being raped by soldiers who are supposedly their protectors.[3]

While overwhelmingly the case, women are not only victims in war. Despite widespread assumptions and popular images associating men with violence and war and women with peace, many women also join war efforts, in a variety of roles. They join voluntary state militaries and take up arms as combatants in liberation wars. What happens to these women— both victims/survivors and warriors—after war? Can truth telling bring gender relations to the fore as a concern for long-term sustainable peace? Pettman (1996, p. 126) argued that whatever women's participation in armed struggles, they are routinely pushed back into the private sphere when the fighting is over, their contributions erased. She is particularly interested in what happens to women and to gender relations after liberation movements have prevailed and the state has been captured, as was the case in many countries that subsequently instituted truth commissions, from El Salvador to South Africa. Repeatedly, she argues, after liberation women are relegated to roles of being protected and are made invisible in debates about how to build new, representative, and legitimate state institutions, including the military. Moreover, she notes a widespread pattern of regression in terms of women's claims and participation after the state is won, arguing that there is a near universal tendency for women to lose out in state consolidation politics. It appears to be difficult for women to translate their activism in wars and nationalist struggles into rights and effective participation when the fighting is done. Even in cases where large numbers of women bore arms, "'peace' seems to see enormous pressure on those women to return 'home,' to give up both jobs and political representation in favour of men" (Pettman, 1996, p. 137). Why might the trends prevail, and how might postwar truth telling prevent or ameliorate these problems? Pettman offers several hypotheses for why traditional gender roles are so often strongly reasserted, even within those states where women played important roles in antistate militaries and where gender interests were incorporated into revolutionary rhetoric.

One possible reason is that the transfer of state power is not always accompanied by effective control over territory and population. This was true during the cold war, when new governments almost immediately faced foreign-backed counterrevolutionary forces, such as South African–funded antistate forces in both Angola and Mozambique. More recently, power transfers in areas such as Afghanistan and Iraq support the notion that state capture and state consolidation are not necessarily synonymous. Faced with immediate legitimacy crises, Pettman argues, states tend to quickly prioritize state survival and defense, which often translates into intensified militarization. When this occurs, gender transformation policies are either postponed or abandoned altogether. Gender issues are also quickly set aside as well when the state immediately faces an economic crisis, such as reconstruction. When the state becomes the main source of rewards, competition for positions within it is fierce, with men being rewarded more handsomely than women. Moreover, it serves the state's interests to revert to traditional notions of "women's work," so women's labor is exploited cheaply. Third, new governments frequently need to absorb a large number of demobilized soldiers. And even though many women fought as soldiers, "soldier" comes to mean male, and "governments seek to 'disarm' soldier men as a potential threat to state power, and might reward them with 'returned' power over women, rather than risk further discontent through social policies that undermine men's roles and 'the' (patriarchal) family" (Pettman, 1996, p. 140). Underlying Pettman's three hypotheses of state consolidation, political economy, and male elite power interests is the reality that during wars, gender roles are often suspended; however, demobilization into a postwar context often means a return to prewar gender relations, a return to "normalcy."

In terms of sexual violence, similar dynamics appear to be at play. Because violence was considered a legitimate means for waging and ending conflict, men use violence against women in the aftermath of conflict to reestablish and retain control over family resources and over women's productive and reproductive rights. Across contexts, domestic violence incidents increase as women are revictimized by returning husbands and sons (Duggan & Abusharaf, 2006). Whatever the combination of reasons for a reversion to old gendered dynamics accompanied by continuing (and sometimes increased) violence against women, the implications for long-term sustainable peace are clear: failure to address gendered power relations both before and during conflicts means that they are unlikely to be addressed, much less transformed, in its aftermath (Pettman, 1996). It is precisely during this aftermath that the potential for truth telling to grapple with both the history and the future of gender power relations is at its highest.

Truth Telling and Gendered Peace

If women are specifically targeted with violence during war, will those responsible for such violence be held accountable at war's end? If not, what does this say about the government's commitment to the rule of law and human rights? Moreover, can truth-telling mechanisms help avert the problem of women's contributions to overthrowing authoritarian governments subsequently being erased? If not, then Pettman's (1996) statement that "even in postrevolutionary situations where women are declared legally equal, profound inattention to or defence of unequal gender relations ensures that national liberation will not mean women's liberation" (p. 140) is disturbing indeed in terms of prospects for lasting peace. Christine Bell and Catherine O'Rourke (2007), however, provide insight into just how difficult a postwar gendered focus might prove to be, pointing to the visible exclusion of women in all aspects of transitional justice processes, beginning with their near absence from the fora that decide which type of transitional justice mechanisms, if any, will be adopted. Because transitional justice mechanisms, including truth commissions, are generally products of peace negotiations, and because negotiation processes themselves are deeply gendered (with negotiators from both state and nonstate parties to the conflict as well as international negotiators being overwhelmingly men), conceptualizations of how accountability, justice, and human rights will be approached cannot help but be gendered.[4] Echoing Pettman's concerns, they conclude that "for women in transitions an emphasis on postconflict restoration without challenging uneven gender power relations can mean giving up the perverse equality gains of war and returning to the home and perhaps other forms of abuse" (Bell & O'Rourke, 2007, p. 41). And indeed, this proved to be generally true in the South African case.

The South African TRC and Gendered Violence

In any truth commission, "the process of defining the terms of a commission's mandate, the 'truth' that it is aiming toward, is a high-stakes political terrain" (Nesiah, 2006, p. 6). In South Africa, the commissioners—seven of whom were women— had to determine how they would fulfill their given mandate, in terms of granting amnesties (deciding who the perpetrators were) and certifying those eligible for reparations (deciding who the victims were). The commissioners were guided by the Promotion of National Unity and Reconciliation Act of 1995, which stated that persons would be eligible for amnesty if they made "full disclosure of all the relevant facts relating to acts associated with a political objective" (ch. 2, sec. 3[1][b]). "Victims" were defined as those who had suffered physical or mental injury, emotional suffering, pecuniary loss, or a substantial impairment of human rights as a result of a gross violation of human rights (GVHR), along with (sometimes) their relatives and dependents (ch. 1, sec. 1[xix]). In determining whether a person had suffered a GVHR, the TRC again looked to the Act for guidance. Four things constituted gross violations of human rights: killing, abduction, torture, or severe ill-treatment (ch. 1, sec. 1[ix]), although severe ill-treatment was not clearly defined in the Act. While undoubtedly unintentional, these definitions (of victims, violations, and those eligible for amnesty) had profound implications for the TRC's ability to address both gendered violence of the past and gender justice in the future.

The Human Rights Violations Committee of the TRC collected more than 21,000 victim statements describing 37,672 human rights violations. An interesting gendered phenomenon emerged almost immediately during the period of statement giving: more African women—most middle aged or elderly—came to the Commission than any other category of people. Even more striking, however, was the fact that although most people who told the Commission about violations were women, they overwhelmingly testified about violations against men (South African Truth and Reconciliation Commission, 1998a, pp. 165-171). Women, it appeared, were unwilling to talk about their own experiences of human rights violations under apartheid. This held true especially in terms of reporting sexual violence that they had experienced. Indeed, of the over 21,000 testimonies given, only 140 explicitly mentioned rape (South African Truth and Reconciliation Commission, 1998b, p. 296), although given the prevalence of rape during wartime, the number was very likely much higher. In terms of the first charge in the TRC's mandate, "establishing as complete a picture as possible of the causes, nature and extent of the gross violations of human rights which were committed" (South African Truth and Reconciliation Commission, 1998a, p. 55), the TRC thus faced a rather large obstacle: the "truth" about women's experiences as women (as opposed to as wives and mothers) never fully emerged. Why did women refuse to discuss their own histories of apartheid-era violations, finding it more comfortable to tell the stories of their male relatives? At least two explanations are possible, both of which hold policy implications for future truth-telling exercises.

The first explanation is that the definition of GVHR that governed the work of the TRC—that is, that only killing, abduction, torture, or severe ill-treatment would count as a violation—affected women's testimonies. Fiona Ross (2003) argued that the Act's definitions of violence and violation were excessively narrow. With its focus on what are known as bodily integrity rights (South African Truth and Reconciliation Commission, 1998b, p. 64), other types of violence were not the focus of the Commission. Women, however, are more likely than men to suffer from structural violence, which arises from social, economic, and political structures that increase the vulnerability of particular groups—for example, poor women who experience higher infant mortality rates due to limited access to health care systems (Peterson & Runyon, 1999). Indeed, socioeconomic vulnerability may well increase during violence with the economic burden of caring for and supporting the family being further shifted onto women who often find themselves as single heads of households due to high mortality and/or disappearance rates of men (Duggan & Abusharaf, 2006).

Heightened vulnerability was especially the case for women under the apartheid system, which was more than just a system of racism; it was also a highly developed system of economic segregation. The economic consequences of apartheid policies were profound indeed, and African women were the population group that suffered the most. The integrated systems of migrant labor, forced removals, inadequate or no education, neglect of traditional agriculture, and lack of basic health care combined to create a system of extreme poverty, with tremendously high unemployment rates, severely skewed income distributions, and tragic health differentials. Rural homeland areas were especially poverty-stricken, and this affected women more than men as men migrated to urban areas in search of employment, leaving women, children, elderly, and infirm behind. Beth Goldblatt and Sheila Meintjes (1998), in a submission on gender to the TRC, argued that the history of apartheid was not only one of racial domination. Less emphasized was "the way in which patriarchal power relations were integrated and used to bolster the power of the oppressors within indigenous communities" (p. 29). These power relations, while long predating apartheid, were exacerbated by it.[5]

Thus the primacy given to violations of civil and political rights by the Act creating the TRC had implications for how much truth the Commission would eventually be able to uncover. Feminist human rights scholars have long argued that the dichotomy between—and primacy given to—civil and political rights, which are seen as operating primarily in the public sphere of the state, and economic rights, which are seen as pertaining primarily to the private sphere, obscures and downplays the violations from which women most suffer (Charlesworth, 1995). To be clear: it is not that women do not suffer direct violence perpetrated by the state; they do. However, they are much more likely than men to suffer from violations of indirect or structural violence. It is precisely these social and economic rights which fell outside of the purview of the TRC. The consequences for women, Ross (2003) argued, were profound:

Permitting the expression of pain of a particular kind, [the Commission] empha-
sised bodily violation at the expense of a broader understanding of apartheid and
its consequences. Foregrounding certain forms of violence in the public record,
it rendered some kinds of pain more visible while displacing other forms of experience and its expression. Its work points to the ease with which women's
experiences are homogenised and the range of expressions to give voice to experience restricted. (p. 162)

The TRC was not unaware of the narrow interpretation of its mandate. It addressed,
somewhat defensively, the issue of types of violations it investigated twice in its
report: once, in a general overview of the difficulty of defining gross violations of human
rights, and once specifically in relation to the gendered implications of this difficulty.
In its general comment on interpreting the Act's definition of GVHR, the Commission
reported:

This definition limited the attention of the Commission to events which emanated
from the conflicts of the past, rather than from the policies of apartheid. There had
been an expectation that the Commission would investigate many of the human
rights violations which were caused, for example, by the denial of freedom of movement through the pass laws, by forced removals of people from their land, by the
denial of franchise to citizens, by the treatment of farm workers and other labour
disputes, and by discrimination in such areas as education and work opportunities.
Many organizations lobbied the Commission to insist that these issues should form
part of its investigations. Commission members, too, felt that these were important
areas that could not be ignored. Nevertheless, they could not be interpreted as falling
directly within the Commission's mandate. (South African Truth and Reconciliation
Commission, 1998c, p. 12)

The Commission reiterated its stance that its hands were tied by its enabling Act, in its
defense of not having adopted a wider interpretation of violations in terms of gender:

The Commission's relative neglect of the effects of the "ordinary" workings of
apartheid has a gender bias. . . . A large number of statistics can be produced to substantiate the fact that women were subject to more restrictions and suffered more in
economic terms than did men during the apartheid years. The most direct measure of
disadvantage is poverty, and there is a clear link between the distribution of poverty
and apartheid policies. Black women, in particular, are disadvantaged, and black
women living in former homeland areas remain the most disadvantaged of all. . . .
To integrate gender fully, however, would have required the Commission to amend
its understanding of its mandate and how it defined gross human rights violations.
(South African Truth and Reconciliation Commission, 1998b, pp. 287-288)

Despite this defensiveness, however, the Commission honestly acknowledged its shortcomings in this area in its final report, noting that "the definition of gross violation of human

rights adopted by the Commission resulted in a blindness to the types of abuse predominantly experienced by women" (South African Truth and Reconciliation Commission, 1998b, p. 316).

South African women did not tell their stories for a second reason: Women, in general, find it difficult to discuss their experiences of rape and other forms of sexual violence; this is true in private, if not more so in public. And indeed, as the statistic above of only 140 reported rapes testifies, women were reluctant to discuss this part of their personal history during apartheid; many refused outright to do so. There are undoubtedly many reasons why this was the case, some of which are generalizable across cultures, others of which are South Africa–specific. Some women chose not to testify out of a sense of shame, or fear of rejection by family members. Still others felt that bringing up old memories of sexual assault was too painful, certainly in terms of answering questions in a public forum about it. Some felt that they simply did not have the language to express what they had endured. Some women were aware that their rape was a symbolic act meant to humiliate men for not being able to protect them, and for that reason felt that testifying would only further humiliate men. Some women feared that they would no longer be marriageable, while others feared retaliation. Some were loath to make statements that their children might one day read (Ross, 2003).

Some reasons given for their silence were South Africa–specific. Especially in relation to having been raped by men in the liberation movement, some women did not want their testimony to be used to equate individual human rights violations by some ANC members with the systematic violations of apartheid (Goldblatt & Meintjes, 1998). Some women feared that recounting their rapes would be seen as selling out or outing their comrades. Others were afraid of jeopardizing their own careers, as noted by South African clinical psychologist Numfundo Walaza: "Another deterrent is that some of the rapists hold high political positions today—so if you spoke out you would not only undermine the new government you fought for, but destroy your own possibilities of a future" (quoted in Krog, 1998, p. 240). Other, already-prominent women feared a future loss of status. Goldblatt and Meintjes (1998) quoted one woman who said, "Some of these women are now in high-powered positions—in government or as executives. How will it impact on them now in the positions that they hold, given the gender bias that people have about sexually abused women and the concept that women always ask for it anyway?" (p. 53). Walaza testified that these women's fears were not unfounded: "If you knew that a particular Minister had been raped—what would go through your mind when you saw her on television?" (quoted in Krog, 1998, pp. 239-240). In addition to some of the rape victims being public figures, another reason for not testifying was the fact that some of the rapists were also public figures. In a game of "he said/she said," women were undoubtedly aware of whose story was likely to be believed and were unwilling to be publicly discredited. Antjie Krog (1998) relates the story of Rita Mazibuko, who recounted to the Commission that she had been raped by members of the ANC in exile and had received aid from other ANC members, including Mathews Phosa and Jacob Zuma (South Africa's deputy president from June 1999 through June 2005). However, she reported to the Commission, she was warned by Phosa, who was by then a provincial premier in the new government, not to testify because he would be obliged to defend ANC members against her claim. Krog concluded that Mazibuko left the witness table a defeated woman, "as if she knows no one will stand up for her." Not even the truth commission: "The Truth Commission does not utter a single word in Mazibuko's defense. Not one of the commissioners, not one of the feminists agitating for women's rights, stands up and says: 'we respect the right of Rita Mazibuko to tell the truth as she sees it, just as we respect the right of Mathews Phosa to tell the truth as he sees it. But we expect him to do the same'" (Krog, 1998, p. 242). However, whereas Mazibuko opened herself to public criticism, ridicule, and charges of lying, Phosa didn't even bother to testify. In such an atmosphere, it was simply not in their interest for women to testify about sexual violence suffered at the hands of "allies."

For a variety of reasons, therefore, women were unwilling or unable to speak publicly about their experiences of sexual violence. Ross (2003) warned, however, against an over-emphasis on the lack of testimony about sexual violence, and pointed out that women were not only unwilling to testify about their experiences as victims and survivors of this type of violence but also unwilling to testify about their experiences in other ways as well. She noted that little was revealed about women in roles other than victim. Moreover, because women's testimony was dominated by their accounting of what had happened to others, mostly their husbands and sons, the commission added little knowledge about women as activists and resisters. Women were also perpetrators, and very little is known about the circumstances surrounding their entry into these roles. Indeed, the one-dimensional focus on women solely as passive recipients of action translated into the unfortunate reference, by both the commission and the media, to women as secondary victims, as opposed to primary victims.[6]

Almost immediately after it began its public hearings in April 1996, the TRC became aware that women were not testifying about their own experiences and tried to rectify the situation. In doing so, it tried to follow the advice given to it in a submission by Goldblatt and Meintjes, both South African feminist academics.[7] They argued that the hearing format already in place was not conducive to women testifying, in that the context of public hearings made it difficult for women to overcome the stigma attached to sexual violence. To rectify this, they made a series of recommendations regarding how women's testimony should be handled by both statement takers and in public hearings.[8] These included, among others, a provision that statements could be made confidentially, assuring that women need not testify publicly, allowing women deponents to request that their statements be taken by women, and that women be allowed to testify in closed hearings before only women commissioners. Another recommendation was for the Commission to organize a series of women's hearings, arranged in conjunction with women's organizations, attended by women commissioners only, and assisted by psychologists and social workers (Goldblatt & Meintjes, 1998). The TRC, for the most part, adopted these suggestions for making the Commission more gender sensitive and held three all-women public hearings in August and October of 1996 and July of 1997. In the course of these hearings, some women were willing to discuss their experiences as victims and activists under apartheid.[9] Through the several dozen women who testified, most of whom were political leaders or leaders in the activism movement, the TRC was able to ascertain that women did indeed suffer gross violations of human rights themselves including rape, other forms of sexual violence, physical and psychological abuse and torture in and out of detention, and even death. What the TRC did manage to uncover therefore confirms patterns of violence against women seen world-wide: South African women were subjected to rape and other sexual violence by parties from all sides of the political conflict, including the South African Defence Force and opposition groups including the African National Congress, the Inkatha Freedom Party (IFP), and the United Democratic Front (UDF) as well as by men in refugee centers. Despite service as soldiers on the battlefield and activists in civil society, women could not count on not being raped by their fellow liberationists.

In its final report, the Commission concluded that "women too suffered direct gross violations of human rights, many of which were gender specific in their exploitative and humiliating nature" (South African Truth and Reconciliation Commission, 1998c, p. 256). More specifically, it found that the state was responsible for the severe ill-treatment of women in custody; that women were abused in ways which specifically exploited their vulnerabilities as women; and that women in exile were also subjected to various forms of sexual abuse, including rape. It is worth noting, perhaps, that these findings on women, which amounted to little more than a few sentences, were the penultimate findings in a 62-page chapter devoted to findings and that no mention was made of women's suffering from socioeconomic violations under apartheid.

Despite its attempts to break out of the gender-neutral approach to truth gathering, the TRC was not terribly successful at doing so—at least not in a way that elicited a full understanding of the myriad ways in which women suffered under apartheid, in terms of civil/political and socioeconomic rights violations, in terms of sexual and nonsexual violence, and in terms of women in their full repertoire of roles, not simply as victims.[10] The TRC itself acknowledged this, noting that the pattern of women refusing to speak of themselves "persisted over the full period of the hearings" (South African Truth and Reconciliation Commission, 1998b, p. 283).

If one reason the TRC was unable to establish more truth about human rights violations under apartheid was because women were unwilling to tell their stories, men were also unwilling to come forward and tell the truth about their involvement in these abuses—specifically in terms of rape and other forms of sexual violence. And again, one reason for this relates to the legal mandate handed to the Commission by its enabling act, in this case the criteria for qualifying for amnesty. To qualify, the Act stated that the "act, omission or offence" for which an applicant was seeking amnesty had to be "associated with a political objective" (Promotion of National Unity and Reconciliation Act of 1995, ch. 4, sec. 18). Whether an objective was political or not was determined by a long set of criteria enumerated in the act, two of which were that it had to be proportional to the objective pursued and that it could not have been committed out of malice (ch. 4, sec. 20[3][f][ii]). The Commission determined that rape could be categorized as either torture or severe ill-treatment and that a person could therefore be granted amnesty, if all criteria were met (B. Goldblatt, personal communication, June 4, 2007). The Amnesty Committee, however, never had the opportunity to wrestle with the questions of whether rape could ever be justified as being politically motivated, or could ever be committed without malice, or whether the means of rape could ever be deemed to be proportional to any ends, because no person applied for amnesty for the crime of rape or for any other sexual violations. The reasons for this are not clear, but one could surmise that several explanations were likely in play. One is that any potential amnesty applicants likely knew that proving the presence of the above criteria (political motivation, proportionality, absence of malice) would be extremely difficult.[11] Another is that raping women was simply not deemed a serious enough crime to warrant opening oneself up to public exposure. Finally, some potential applicants may have wagered on the fact that so few women would publicly testify about their rapes, and would likely not be willing to name names, for all of the reasons already noted.

That men did not apply for amnesty is unfortunate for several reasons, all of which have serious consequences for the human rights of women in the postapartheid and posttruth commission period. First, as Goldblatt and Meintjes (1998) noted, the process of examining the act of rape, even though very few perpetrators would have likely been granted amnesty for its perpetration in their opinion, would have allowed the Commission to highlight the deeply political function of rape during wartime.[12] That sexual violence is a tool of all conflicts, apartheid included, could have been confirmed by the TRC. As it is, however, the TRC's final report is almost silent on the issue. Although it does note that women were victims of sexual violence, no analysis is provided of how such violence functioned politically. Second, because no men applied for amnesty for rape, no one was held accountable for these crimes; if granted amnesty, which would likely have been rare, then amnesty would have served as a form of accountability, as the very fact of having been granted amnesty certified a person as a perpetrator. If denied amnesty, perpetrators would have at least been publicly unveiled as such, which one could argue was a form of accountability, more so than the silence that prevailed as a result of the absence of amnesty applications. The ability to apportion blame and hold perpetrators accountable is deemed a hallmark of a society based on the rule of law. The lack of accountability may well contribute to a climate of impunity—which is the antithesis of a human-rights-respecting culture based on respect for the rule of law. Third, applications for amnesty for rape and other forms of sexual violence would have helped to expose just how widespread the use of rape was during the period under TRC investigation. Only 140 women testified about rape before the commission; no men admitted to it. One could surmise from this that rape was not a serious problem for South African women; in doing so, one would be wrong. Rather, what existed in South Africa was a profound silence about women's violent experiences during apartheid—neither victims nor perpetrators were willing to reveal the truth about these experiences. What former TRC Commissioner Yasmin Sooka (2004) called a "conspiracy of silence" between victims and perpetrators (n.p.), Antjie Krog (1998) called a "bizarre collusion":

Then again, few women have testified about rape, and fewer, if any, have named the rapists. So why would a rapist apply for amnesty at all? There seems to be a bizarre collusion between the rapist and the raped. Although rumors abound about rape, all these mutterings are trapped behind closed doors. Apparently high-profile women, among them Cabinet ministers, parliamentarians, and businesswomen, were raped and sexually abused under the previous dispensation—and not only by the regime, but by their own comrades in the townships and liberation camps, but no one will utter an audible word about it (p. 239).

The South African case, then, offers a cautionary tale about the difficulties associated with the ability of truth-telling mechanisms to serve the cause of fostering a truly gendered human rights culture. Its overemphasis on bodily integrity rights at the expense of second-generation social and economic rights had the effect, Ross (2003) argues, of sanitizing apartheid and limiting the ability to recognize the duration of its effects. Indeed, although the TRC was able to uncover some part of the picture of women's experiences—revealing that women did indeed suffer gross violations of human rights under apartheid—this picture remained incomplete. What was not recorded by the Commission, and thus not open to the sort of analysis that the rest of the report invited, was the history of patriarchy that accompanied and supported the race-based discrimination of the apartheid system. This limitation has consequences for South African women in the postapartheid era, where patriarchy remains largely intact, despite the legal elimination of race-based discrimination. Although a full overview of the status of women in postapartheid South Africa is not possible here, it is clear that there continues to be widespread economic, social, and legal discrimination against women, along with high levels of violence, including sexual violence against them. In 2003, there were 52,425 officially reported rapes, a third of the estimated actual number. Forty percent of the victims were 18 years old or younger. At the moment, one might argue that rather than a culture of rights, there is a culture of sexual violence in South Africa. One study concluded that women in South Africa view violence and sexual coercion as a "normal" part of everyday life (Human Rights Watch, 2004, pp. 10-11).[13]

Lessons Learned? Policy Implications

In its final report, the TRC, in a section akin to a self-evaluation (although no such evaluation was mandated by its enabling act), listed several of the Commission's shortcomings (South African Truth and Reconciliation Commission, 1998c, pp. 206-208). Its ability to uncover more truth about women's experiences or to hold perpetrators of gross violations of women's human rights accountable for their actions was not among them. The above analysis of the TRC's inability to provide more dignity to apartheid's women victims, to deliver a measure of gender justice in terms of at least apportioning blame for those responsible for gender-based crimes, and the reality of a postapartheid human rights culture in which women are still victimized because of their gender and still suffer as second-class citizens, indicate that a deeper evaluation was perhaps warranted. Although the TRC was not willing to offer some lessons learned for future truth-telling undertakings, some policy implications can nevertheless be derived from the South African experience.

One set of policy recommendations revolves around getting more truth, both from victims and perpetrators. In terms of getting more women to be forthcoming about their own experiences—as opposed to their experiences as women who lost sons, daughters, husbands, and fathers—the TRC did heed advice and hold women-only hearings. Other truth commissions have already adopted (and are likely to continue doing so) similar approaches to enabling gender-sensitive testimony to emerge, including allowing women to testify only before women commissioners, allowing them to testify in camera, and allowing them to remain anonymous. Other attempts to increase gender sensitivities could be added. Sooka (2004) suggested that at least half of all commissioners should be women and that data-bases, constructed to collect and analyze specific acts of violence to issue findings and recommendations, should be designed to allow for the specific collection of data appropri-ate to the experiences of women and girls and to allow for the disaggregation of data along gendered lines.[14] Although these policies may help elicit more information from women, they are not without controversy. Disagreement always arises when women are treated sep-arately from men, and the TRC was no exception. Although the TRC did adopt recommendations provided by them in terms of separate women's hearings, Beth Goldblatt and Sheila Meintjes (1999) were nevertheless unimpressed, accusing the TRC of failing to adopt a gendered analytical framework to guide its work, noting that women were treated separately in the final chapter of Volume 4 of the report, which only served to create "a ghet-toised female subjectivity," in which women were relegated to a category of essentialized difference, at the same time as differences between women were homogenized.

Even if truth-telling mechanisms come to include more effective ways of getting women to discuss their own histories of violations, the second half of the equation—getting men to talk about their histories as perpetrators of these violations—remains unchanged. And if eliciting more truth from victims is difficult, doing so from perpetrators is undoubtedly even more so, if the TRC is an indication of the unwillingness of men to admit to rape as a tactic of conflict. Getting women to talk without simultaneously getting men to do the same does little more than maintain the culture of impunity, with little to no accountability, a situation hardly conducive to strengthening the rule of law. One recommendation is to hold the threat of prosecution over those who refused to testify and then to actually prosecute where evi-dence of wrongdoing exists. However, this recommendation is also not unproblematic. First, such a step would require other changes, such as reforms of national legal systems. Sooka (2004) argued that in most national legal systems, it is almost impossible to prosecute rape and crimes of sexual violence given the legal requirements, the evidentiary burden, and the culture and attitude of those who serve in the criminal justice systems. A second problem is that the recommendation presupposes the political will to prosecute violent sexual crimes. In South Africa there appears to be little will to carry out post-TRC prosecutions of any sort, let alone of rape and other forms of sexual violence (Amnesty International and Human Rights Watch, 2003). Moreover, in South Africa, only a small fraction of rapes are reported to police, only about a third of those reported are prosecuted, and only about half of those prosecuted result in convictions (Human Rights Watch, 1995b, p. 90). It thus appears that both problems with the legal system and a lack of political will may indeed be unfortunate realities in the South African context. A third, and perhaps the most significant, problem is in gaining the cooperation of women in trials. If it is difficult for women to testify in the relatively friendly atmosphere of women-only hearings, it is significantly more difficult for them to do so in the hostile environment of a trial.[15] All in all, in terms of the ability of truth-telling mechanisms to elicit the full truth about gendered violations from either victims or perpetrators, there is little reason to express much optimism. Sadly, in this instance, some skepticism may be justified.

Other policy implications for future truth-telling exercises emerge from the South African experience. It is clear, for example, that the ability of a truth-telling mechanism to adopt a truly gendered approach is determined early on, embedded in the enabling legislation and the mandate handed to it.[16] Sooka (2004) noted, for example, that the South African TRC's enabling act made no reference to gender-based violations and did not mention women as a special target group. In contrast, the Sierra Leone TRC's enabling act stated that the Commission should pay special attention to the "subject of sexual abuses and to the experiences of children within armed conflict." In addition to the mandate itself, the way in which concepts are interpreted also affects the ability of truth-telling mechanisms to address gender issues. In South Africa, for example, the definition of gross violations of human rights did not specifically address gendered violence, specifically sexual violence. According to Sooka (2004), it was left to the "gender lobby," including women commissioners, to make the argument that torture and severe ill-treatment should be utilized to address sexual violence (p. 7). This had implications for the types of reparations recommended by the TRC. Sexual violence in South Africa was only included as a subcategory in a long list of harms considered as torture or severe ill-treatment rather than being categorized as a separate violation. According to Goldblatt (2006), "sexual violence would have been more centrally placed on the national agenda had it been mentioned in the founding legislation of the TRC" (p. 80)[17] In contrast, in Sierra Leone, the TRC was mandated to record "violations and abuses of human rights and international humanitarian law related to armed conflict." Sooka (2004) argues that, when read together with the mandate to pay attention to sexual abuse, the TRC was able to apply a much wider, more comprehensive, definition of gross violations of human rights there, one which specifically included gender-based violations. As a result, Sooka notes that, unlike in South Africa, women and girls came out in large numbers to speak to the Sierra Leone commission.[18] In sum, if gender-based violence is to be taken seriously in truth telling, the enabling legislation for truth-telling mechanisms should include those forms of violence in definitions of concepts like victims and violations.

Gendered Peace? Reparations

If any lesson emerges from the South African case, it is that silence has consequences. It would be unfair to say that the TRC discovered no truth at all about gendered violence. Some truth did indeed emerge about gross violations of human rights suffered by women. However, three major elements were absent in the final work of the TRC. What did not emerge from the TRC's work, or in its final report, is an overarching picture of patriarchy resulting in the second-class citizenship of women. Nor did the reality that women suffered immeasurably more from violations of socioeconomic rights rather than civil and political ones. Finally, the TRC failed to apportion blame for those responsible for the violations suffered by women, leaving perpetrators unaccountable for their actions. Why are these absences consequential? Perhaps the most lasting impact a truth commission can have is the implementation of its recommendations. A truth commission cannot in and of itself bring about reforms needed to improve the status of women. It can, however, make recommendations to the state and to civil society groups regarding actions that could be taken, for example, to ensure accountability of perpetrators of such violence, or for improving the economic status of women, or for making it easier for women to escape violent relationships, or to receive medical treatment for HIV/AIDS. Of course, if recommendations do not exist, they can hardly be implemented. Perhaps the most serious consequence of the lack of a gendered lens was that the 45-page chapter on recommendations compiled by the TRC was silent on the issue of women. Despite a promising sentence in the chapter's introduction that states, "It is important to state explicitly that there is a need for sensitivity to the particular issues pertaining to women and children" (South African Truth and Reconciliation Commission, 1998c, p. 305), not one of the over 100 recommendations is explicitly aimed at improving the human rights of women.[19] The lack of a gendered lens resulted in another absence, notably the absence of a gendered reparations policy.

It would seem obvious that if women and a concern for gender are primarily absent in the input stage of designing transitional justice mechanisms,[20] the outputs of these mechanisms—such as reparations policies—will reflect this. And indeed, a comparative study conducted by International Center for Transitional Justice (ICTJ) on gender and reparations found that across contexts reparations programs have shared a number of features: they exclude women from policy design, they show a lack of deep knowledge of gender-based violence in defining violations to be repaired (although rape is generally included), the criteria used for defining beneficiaries tends to adversely affect women, the benefits given are not as women-friendly as could be, and the implementation of reparations programs can hurt women (by requiring a bank account, for example—something many women do not have; Bell & O'Rourke, 2007). In addition, Duggan and Abusharaf (2006) detailed various obstacles impeding women's abilities to exercise their right to reparation, including a lack of legal autonomy (women are often not treated as equal citizens), legal pluralism (in many societies gender-based social and legal practices such as requiring a wife to obtain her husband's consent before approaching the legal system impede women's access to justice), and social and cultural attitudes and mores (the stigma attached to rape or social norms limiting women's ability to travel to collect reparations). Beyond this, gender biases can often be inadvertently reproduced or incorporated into a reparations policy whose designers believed was gender appropriate. Rubio-Marín (2006) noted, for example, that employment disability insurance schemes that are sometimes relied on to assess loss of income generation may be ill suited to assess the material destitution of women victims of sexual abuse who are abandoned by their partners, rendered unmarriageable, and then ostracized by their communities.

It is especially important, Duggan and Abusharaf (2006) argued, that reparations programs are designed with a commitment to repairing sexual violence. Not only is sexual violence perhaps the most egregious form of gender-based violence, its socioeconomic impact on women can undermine their chances for recovery and for reintegration into the family, the community, and the state. At the same time, judicial recourse through the courts is often unlikely for women victims of sexual violence, as laws for criminal and civil prosecution and redress of sexual crimes are often weak, discriminatory, or nonexistent, often most ill equipped to deal with complex crimes during times of transition.

Transformation of norms and institutions is generally a slow process; reparations in the interim can not only lay the social and political groundwork for this transformation but also help temporarily offset some of the consequences of gendered violence (Duggan & Abusharaf, 2006). For all these reasons, then, it is important for governments to get their reparations programs right vis-à-vis women. Unfortunately, most evidence suggests that this has yet to be the norm.[21]

Not surprisingly, given the lack of attention paid to women in the TRC final report's chapter on recommendations, the chapter on reparations fails to mention women at all. This neglect, according to Goldblatt (2006), was not from a lack of effort on the part of civil society organizations, several of whom tried to make gender-sensitive suggestions throughout the TRC process.[22] In the end, however, the efforts of NGOs and activists amounted to little, with few of their suggested recommendations being adopted by the TRC. The result is that the reparations program recommended by the Commission, and the eventual program adopted by the government, remained in Goldblatt's (2006) words, "largely 'ungendered'" (p. 58). The gender neutrality of the reparations program was evident in the financial payout given to victims.[23] Although the TRC proposed a sum of approximately US$2,713 per victim per year for 6 years, with the amount varying according to location (urban or rural) and according to the number of dependents, the government agreed only to a onetime payment of US$3,750 (R30,000) to each victim with no variance for location or number of dependents. Both the TRC and the state were silent on the issue of harms suffered by women as a category. So, for example, women who lost breadwinners and thus faced a lifetime of impoverishment were given no more compensation than a person who suffered no material disadvantage at all (Goldblatt, 2006).[24]

However, while the reparations program may have been gender neutral in terms of input (i.e., the policy recommendations), it certainly was not so in terms of outcomes (i.e., its impact on women). To receive reparations, applicants had to have a bank account. Around the world, South Africa being no exception, many poor people do not have such accounts. As women are the poorest members of society, this requirement disproportionately affected them. In several cases, women with no bank accounts had to sign the money over to their husband's accounts, where they undoubtedly had less control over it (Goldblatt, 2006). Moreover, until 1998, women married under customary law were considered minors for the purpose of some commercial transactions and thus lost control over their grants to their husbands in that way (Goldblatt, 2006). Another gendered implication of the program was that reparation was tied to truth telling; in other words, one could only be considered a victim—and thus eligible for reparations—if one came forward to tell one's story to the commission.[25] Many women victims of sexual violence undoubtedly felt unable to approach the TRC for reasons already noted. Women's resistance to being forthcoming about their own experiences meant they faced an excruciating choice: to risk estrangement from their families and social exclusion on one hand, and making themselves ineligible for reparations on the other (Anderlini, Conaway, & Kays, 2004). Rubio-Marín (2006) concluded that "forcing women to 'come out' as victims to qualify for reparations may have a largely inhibiting effect, especially for victims of sexual violence who hold back because of shame or fear" (p. 34). For this reason, Goldblatt (2006) recommended that future truth commissions delink the granting of reparations from truth telling.

Conclusion

The ICTJ concludes its report by stating that "many truth commissions have failed women—the crimes they have suffered are underreported, their voices are rendered inaudible, their depiction in commission reports is one-dimensional, and their needs and goals are deprioritized in recommendations for reparations, reform and prosecutions" (Nesiah, 2006, p. 41). This article, too, has provided a somewhat pessimistic overview of gender and truth telling in the South African context. Two final points are worth mentioning. First, it is of course not fair to blame the TRC for the realities that many South African women face daily: lives of poverty, violent relationships, and an overwhelming vulnerability to HIV/AIDS. The TRC was but one postapartheid institution, and societal changes—either positive or negative—are always multivariate. In addition, the TRC existed for a short period of time—less than half a decade. The work of undoing generations of patriarchal attitudes and their consequent effects on women will surely take much longer. Moreover, what happens after a truth commission has shut down is not the responsibility of that commission. Although a commission can lay the foundation for a culture based on human rights, it is the responsibility of the state, civil society, and individuals to build on the foundation. Still, the fact that the TRC did not employ a gender-sensitive approach to the past could not have helped South African women overcome the reality that Pettman (1996) noted: that women's lives rarely improve much, if at all, in all too many postconflict societies.

Second, whatever contributions the TRC and South Africa as a whole have made toward improving the lives of women, one thing remains clear: the legal provision of rights means little if they are not translated into a culture of rights. The TRC, throughout its work, highlighted the concept of human rights repeatedly over a period of time. Its commitment has been backed up by government policies. In terms of gender, South Africa has done rather well in the public sphere. By 1998, it ranked seventh in the world in governmental representation, with women constituting 25% of national-level representatives, and third in the world when ranked with other developing countries. The government also established a national Commission on Gender Equality. Furthermore, South Africa's active and independent Constitutional Court has handed down several judgments in support of women's rights, and parliament has passed several pieces of legislation prohibiting discrimination on the basis of race and gender. Such institutions and policies are clearly important; government actions send messages to its citizens about what is acceptable and what is valued. However, good institutions and processes are necessary but not sufficient underpinnings of a human rights culture. The question becomes how and whether the positive, human rights culture-promoting elements of the South African TRC and government are being translated into culture, in terms of attitudes, beliefs, and South Africans' shared understanding about being a people who embrace human rights. Although the TRC itself attempted to foster a human rights-respecting culture, it could not ensure that this culture would become firmly entrenched. As Sooka (2004) stated, "We do not suffer from a lack of law and policy but we suffer from a deficit of implementation" (p. 4). Formal commitments to gender equality must result in policies that mean real changes in women's lives. The possibility of these changes being wrought is immeasurably more difficult when one key institution devoted to raising awareness about the culture of human rights—such as a truth commission—turns a blind eye, no matter how unintentional, to the plight of women.

Acknowledgments

The author thanks the anonymous reviewers for their helpful comments and suggestions for improving the manuscript. She also thanks John D. Nugent for his editing assistance.

Declaration of Conflicting Interests

The author(s) declared no potential conflicts of interest with respect to the authorship and/or publication of this article.

Funding

The author disclosed receipt of the following financial support for the research and/or authorship of this article: The United States Institute of Peace and the R. F. Johnson Fund at Connecticut College.

Notes

1. Feminist scholars are not alone in their analysis of the gendered dimension of war. In 2000, the UN Security Council unanimously passed Resolution 1325, which expresses "concern that civilians, particularly women and children, account for the vast majority of those adversely affected by armed conflict, including as refugees and internally displaced persons, and increasingly are targeted by combatants and armed elements" (UN Security Council, 2000).

2. Although the ubiquity of rape during war has long been known, the issue received added scholarly attention with the revelation of the widespread use of rape in the various wars resulting in the breakup of the former Yugoslavia in the 1990s. Indeed, Diken and Lausten (2005) viewed rape as "a crucial signifier" in the Bosnian war (p. 114). The United Nations General Assembly concurred in GA Resolution 49/205 of 2005, which asserted that the "heinous practice [rape and abuse of women] constitutes a deliberate weapon of war in fulfilling the policy of ethnic cleansing carried out by Serbian forces in Bosnia and Herzegovina" (Diken & Lausen, 2005, p. 113). The breakup of Yugoslavia proved to be an illustrative, albeit tragic—one rough estimate is that between 20,000 and 50,000 Bosnian war rape survivors exist—case study for advancing an understanding of various aspects of war rape including how rape fosters nationalism, rape as a tool of ethnic cleansing, rape as a tool of community punishment, and the relationship between wartime rape and "peace" time domestic violence. The literature of wartime rape in Yugoslavia is vast; see, for example, Bracewell (2000), Diken and Lausten (2005), Jones (1994), Nikolic-Ristanovic (1996), Salzman (1998), and Stigelmayer (1994). Although there seems to be little disagreement that mass rape and war are correlated, less agreement exists on why this correlation exists. For an overview of various explanations for the root cause of rape during war, see Gottschall (2004).

3. In the first instance, recent scandals have highlighted both the scope and severity of sexual crimes against U.S. female soldiers by U.S. male soldiers. Over the past decade, for example,

over 140 female cadets have reported rapes or assaults at the U.S. Air Force Academy in Colorado Springs. Moreover, since August 2002, at least 273 sexual assaults against U.S. female soldiers by their fellow soldiers have been reported in Afghanistan, Kuwait, and Iraq (National Public Radio, 2005). In terms of the second instance—which some might argue falls more in line with sexual exploitation than with rape and sexual assault—a March 2005 UN report revealed that in 2004 UN peacekeeping soldiers were faced with 1,221 allegations of sexual exploitation and abuse of women under their protection in missions around the world, including Bosnia, Kosovo, Cambodia, Timor-Leste, West Africa, and the Democratic Republic of the Congo (DRC). This issue received widespread attention in early 2005 with the revelation that peacekeepers in DRC had sex with Congolese women and girls in exchange for food or small sums of money (Al-Hussein, 2005).

4. Given this gendered nature of peace negotiations, it should come as no surprise that other postconflict peacebuilding initiatives enshrined in peace agreements (besides transitional justice) are equally gendered. For example, attention is increasingly being drawn to the fact that the design of postconflict disarmament, demobilization, and reintegration (DDR) programs have paid insufficient attention to gender. Disarmament involves the collection and disposal of both heavy and light arms of ex-combatants on all sides of conflict; demobilization is a short-term process of downsizing or disbanding armed forces and reintegration is a complex long-term process in which ex-combatants are assisted in resettling in communities. Reintegration initiatives can vary and can include the provision of civilian clothing, cash payments, housing, land, job training, school fees, credit counseling, and psychological and health support (Dzinesa, 2007). Women combatants, of course, face special reintegration challenges, especially in terms of rape-related posttraumatic stress symptoms, access to land, and the legal ability to gain control over monetary resources and credit. Any DDR programs that do not take these special needs into account will necessarily have adverse effects on female ex-combatants. Such was the situation in Namibia, for example, where "bereft of gender-specific reintegration assistance, women former fighters, including single mothers encountered significant difficulties" (Dzinesa, 2007 p. 86). For this reason, the World Bank recommends the provision of female-friendly demobilization centers, equal assistance packages with male compatriots, and gender-focused health, medical, and developmental training (cited in Dzinesa, 2007, p. 75). Likewise, noting that DDR is not only a part of a broader postconflict reconstruction and development framework, but indeed—in the words of Kofi Annan—"the single most important factor determining the success of peace operations," a United Nations-sponsored conference on DDR and stability in Africa offered as one of its core recommendations that "reintegration programmes must be more gender-sensitive than in the past" (United Nations, 2005, pp. 2-5). In the case of South Africa, one can undoubtedly safely assume that DDR initiatives inadequately met the needs of female ex-combatants as most scholars agree that DDR in general was "poorly planned, badly executed, and wholly inadequate in meeting the needs of ex-combatants," both men and women (Dzinesa, 2007, p. 81).

5. Goldblatt and Meintjes (1998) traced the consequences of these unequal power relations for African women in all spheres of life. For example, although intended to determine the movement of African men, the pass laws regulating migrant labor were even harsher in their effects on women. At the same time that women were left to care for children and the

elderly, they were disadvantaged by custom in their access to land and to the labor market. As Marjorie Jobson, the Chairperson of the Board of the Khulumani Support Group—a victims' rights NGO—noted, "it was women who carried a significant proportion of the suffering caused by the uprooting and dumping of three million South Africans in inhospitable environments without adequate infrastructure" (Jobson, 2005).

6. The Promotion of National Unity and Reconciliation Act of 1995, the TRC's enabling legislation, defined victims not only as those who had directly suffered gross violations of human rights, but in certain circumstances as their relatives and dependents, as well. Hence when women testified about the harms suffered by their husbands and sons, they were deemed to be victims in the second sense noted in the legislation. As relatives of victims, the Commission and media took to referring to them as secondary victims, a term that does not appear anywhere in the Act or in the TRC's mandate. However, although the Act did not distinguish between primary and secondary victims, the Reparations and Rehabilitation Committee did make this distinction, defining secondary victims as relatives or dependents of primary victims who were only entitled to monetary reparations when the primary victim died (Goldblatt, 2006).

7. Their submission emerged from a workshop titled, "Gender and the Truth and Reconciliation Commission," hosted by the Centre for Applied Legal Studies at the University of Witwatersrand in Johannesburg in March 1996. Goldblatt and Meintjes were two of several women's activists lobbying the TRC, especially its women commissioners, to put gender issues on the agenda. Goldblatt (2006) stated that women had to "bargain" for gender issues and felt that they were "humored" (p. 56).

8. Before individuals gave testimony at public hearings, they first gave statements to statement takers. Individuals were then chosen from among the many statements given to present their stories publicly in hearings organized by the Human Rights Violations Committee, one of three Committees of the Commission (the other two being the Amnesty Committee and the Reparations and Rehabilitation Committee). About 10% of those who gave statements subsequently testified at these victims hearings. In total, 76 public hearings were held across the country between April 1996 and June 1997. For a detailed overview of the process of selecting testifiers as well as the rituals surrounding public hearings, see Ross (2003).

9. The TRC adopted other measures as well to encourage women to tell their own stories. By April 1997, the protocol preparing women deponents was modified to include a note which read: "IMPORTANT: Some women testify about violations of human rights that happened to family members or friends, but they have also suffered abuses. Don't forget to tell us what happened to you yourself if you were the victim of a gross human rights abuse" (Ross, 2003, p. 23).

10. Not all analysts take such a negative view of the TRC in terms of gender. Pumla Gobodo-Madikizela (2005), a former member of the TRC's Human Rights Violations Committee, has argued that the TRC was "progressive and gender-sensitive" in terms of its approach to women. Her claim is that women's unwillingness to testify about their own experiences was a deliberate strategy on the part of women to generate empathy for those who had suffered and that women were thereby taking on a special responsibility for the collective sense of national healing (pp. v-vii; see also World Bank, 2006).

11. Could any applicant have proved that her rape was motivated by politics? Although the answer will always remain unknown, and although Goldblatt and Meintjes (1998) predicted that the Commission would have had a difficult time separating political from personal motives, some evidence did surface before the TRC that hinted at the political nature of at least some rapes. Krog (1998) reported on a study about the use of rape in townships during the 1980s, the period of highest political violence. In one township, Sebokeng, a group of youth formed the South African Rapist Association (SARA), whose goal was to provide senior comrades with women to rape, as a way to keep them busy. Had these youths applied for amnesty, the TRC would have had to establish whether the raping of nonpolitical women to keep the comrades busy could qualify as a political act.

12. That rape serves a political function during times of conflict is clear. However, it sometimes also serves an almost economic function, as was revealed in a chilling testimony before the TRC by a former ANC general, Andrew Masondo. The ANC made two separate submissions to the TRC, which were accompanied by testimonies. During one such submission, the ANC acknowledged the sexual abuse of women, which it euphemistically called "gender-specific offences." As explanation, Masondo revealed that women soldiers in the ANC army Umkhonto we Sizwe (MK) were viewed almost as economic commodities in MK camps in exile in Zambia, Angola, and Tanzania. He testified to the TRC that the ratio of female-to-male MK soldiers in these camps was roughly 22 to 1,000, and that the law of supply and demand simply took over (South African Truth and Reconciliation Commission, 1998b, p. 307; see also Graybill, 2001, pp. 263-264). The ANC submission omitted the names of perpetrators, none of whom subsequently applied for amnesty.

13. A particularly low point for women in South Africa was the rape trial of Jacob Zuma, the former Deputy President of South Africa, who was charged with raping a woman in December 2005 and acquitted in May 2006. Women's rights advocates were disheartened by the trial, where the judge allowed the accuser's sexual history to be brought up in cross-examination (which revealed, among other things, that she had been raped during exile while an antiapartheid activist). The trial, women's organizations assert, proved the continuing obstacles facing rape survivors in the postapartheid era.

14. These suggestions are consistent with those outlined in the International Center for Transitional Justice (ICTJ) report, *Truth Commissions and Gender: Principles, Policies, and Procedures*, highlighting the notion of "a technology of truth," which includes the organizing, classifying, and filtering of information. For example, those who take testimonies can be properly trained in a range of interview techniques and the breadth of human rights experiences to recognize cues to patterns of abuse, thereby cutting down on the underreporting of women's experiences. In addition, the statement-taking form can be structured so that victim testimony is not overdetermined by rigid categories of standardized legal boxes (Nesiah, 2006, pp. 8, 19-22).

15. Some feminist scholars have questioned the ability of a courtroom approach to deliver justice for gender-based violence, noting a disillusionment of survivors of sexual violence with adversarial processes. Bell and O'Rourke (2007) cited Mertus who contends that "adversarial legal forums subject witnesses to repeated attempts to undermine their credibility, prevent the complete expression of their individual accounts and reify their position as women victims lacking agency" (p. 33).

16. An even earlier necessary step, of course, although not the focus of this article, is the inclusion of women in all stages of the peace processes, including negotiations, so that women can influence the identification of reconstruction priorities. Many feminists, however, note that simply including women is not sufficient if no opportunities are provided for them to reshape end goals, where women are asked to operate along already set (gendered) assumptions about conflict, peace, and security. As Bell and O'Rourke (2007) noted, "The increased participation of women does not equate in any simple way with a feminist reshaping of either peace processes or transitional justice mechanisms" (p. 34).

17. She notes that one reason for a lack of gendered input into the enabling legislation is that women's organizations themselves showed little interest in the TRC at first. The commission was not seen as a priority for women activists, who focused their energies on more forward-looking tasks and on the immediate challenges facing women, giving the "backward-looking project" of transitional justice a lower priority (p. 53).

18. Bell and O'Rourke (2007) cite other advances in this regard, noting that "analysis of more general developments in the mandates of TCs indicates a positive trend, whereby the 'gender-neutral' stance of the early Latin American commissions of Argentina and Chile can be contrasted with the comprehensive understanding of harms demonstrated by the recent East Timor/Timor Leste commission" (p. 28). For a more in-depth overview of the Sierra Leone commission, as well as an overview of the gendered advances of the Peruvian commission, see World Bank (2006) and Nesiah (2006). Indeed, the World Bank (2006) credits the South African TRC's decision to hold gender hearings specifically for beginning slow but steady incremental improvement in attempts to secure accountability for gender-based violence through truth commissions. For a discussion of the gendered approach of the Ghana National Reconciliation Commission (NCR), see Nesiah (2006).

19. Under a section titled, "Prevention of Gross Human Rights Violations in the Future," the TRC does state that "the recognition and protection of socio-economic rights are crucial to the development and sustaining of a culture of respect for human rights" (South African Truth and Reconciliation Commission, 1998c, p. 308). However, this sentence is never fleshed out, nor are the economic rights of women in particular mentioned.

20. Christopher Colvin (2006) argued that an even earlier problem existed: Not only were women and gender absent from a discussion of reparations from the beginning but also was the entire issue of reparations itself neglected, both during the negotiations phase to end apartheid and the interim constitution and subsequent permanent constitution that these negotiations produced.

21. They do state, however, that incremental improvement has occurred. They note that progression toward a more gender-sensitive approach to justice can be tracked by comparing the processes of truth telling and reparation in the decade from 1993 (the El Salvador truth commission) to 2003 (the Peruvian truth commission). They conclude that "reparations for sexual violence may be moving away from being an afterthought by policymakers, often tacked onto State programs in the wake of political pressure and lobbying especially from external groups, to becoming a more fundamental issue which appears more centrally on the agenda of transitional governments" (Duggan & Abusharaf, 2006, p. 636).

22. Examples of these interventions include a request to parliament by the Center for the Study of Violence and Reconciliation (CSVR) that women be recognized in all symbolic reparations projects, the suggestion by a group of academics and NGOs to provide some mechanism for women to make statements (thus making them potentially eligible for reparations) after the official close of the commission in recognition of the difficulty some women feel in speaking about their experiences, and a series of additional recommendations by the CSVR. These included, among others, that research be conducted into gender biases inherent in quantifying reparations according to the approach used in civil damages claims.

23. In addition to recommending individual financial reparations, the TRC also made recommendations for symbolic reparations, community rehabilitation, and institutional reform.

24. An even more fundamental question besides whether women's harms were more egregious than those suffered by men is that of quantifying harm. Whether any amount of monetary compensation can ever suffice for human rights violations is a question much debated, with many maintaining that monetary measures can never remedy nonmonetary harms. Martha Minow, for example, argues that "no market measure exists for the value of living an ordinary life, without nightmares or survivor guilt" (quoted in Duggan & Abusharaf, 2006, p. 640). In relation to women and sexual violence, however, the question of quantifying harm is arguably even more complicated, when such intangible assets as purity and social standing have been taken and where in some cultures accepting money for sexual abuse makes matters worse (Duggan & Abusharaf, 2006).

25. In addition, one could be certified as a victim as a result of truth uncovered during an amnesty hearing. In either case, eligibility for reparations in South Africa was predicated on individual truth telling.

References

Al-Hussein, Z. R. Z. (2005). *A comprehensive strategy to eliminate future sexual exploitation and abuse in United Nations peacekeeping* (Report A/59/710). New York: United Nations.

Amnesty International and Human Rights Watch. (2003). *Truth and justice: Unfinished business in South Africa.* Retrieved July 24, 2009, from http://web.amnesty.org/library/Index/ENGAFR530012003

Anderlini, S. N., Conaway, C. P., & Kays, L. (2004). Transitional justice and reconciliation. In Women Waging Peace Network (Ed.), *Inclusive security, sustainable peace: A toolkit for advocacy and action* (pp. 1-15). Retrieved July 24, 2009, from http://www.womenwaging-peace.net/content/toolkit/chapters/Transitional_Justice.pdf

Bell, C., & O'Rourke, C. (2007). Does feminism need a theory of transitional justice? An introductory essay. *International Journal of Transitional Justice, 1,* 23-44.

Bracewell, W. (2000). Rape in Kosovo: Masculinity and Serbian nationalism. *Nations and Nationalism, 6,* 563-590.

Charlesworth, H. (1995). Human rights as men's rights. In J. Peters & A. Wolper (Eds.), *Women's rights, human rights: International feminist perspectives* (pp. 103-113). New York: Routledge.

Colvin, C. (2006). Overview of the reparations program in South Africa. In P. de Greiff (Ed.), *The handbook of reparations* (pp. 176-213). New York: Oxford University Press.

Diken, B., & Lausten, C. B. (2005). Becoming abject: Rape as a weapon of war. *Body & Society, 11*, 111-128.

Duggan, C., & Abusharaf, A. M. (2006). Reparation of sexual violence in democratic transitions: The search for gender justice. In P. de Greiff (Ed.), *The handbook of reparations* (pp. 623-649). New York: Oxford University Press.

Dzinesa, G. A. (2007). Postconflict disarmament, demobilization, and reintegration of former combatants in Southern Africa. *International Studies Perspectives, 8*, 73-89.

Enloe, C. (2000). *Maneuvers: The international politics of militarizing women's lives.* Berkeley: University of California Press.

Gobodo-Madikizela, P. (2005). *Women's contributions to South Africa's Truth and Reconciliation Commission.* Washington, DC: Hunt Alternatives.

Goldblatt, B. (2006). Evaluating the gender content of reparations: Lessons from South Africa. In R. Rubio-Marín (Ed.), *What happened to the women: Gender and reparations for human rights violations* (pp. 48-91). New York: Social Science Research Council.

Goldblatt, B., & Meintjes, S. (1998). South African women demand the truth. In M. Turshen & C. Twagiramariya (Eds.), *What women do in wartime: Gender and conflict in Africa* (pp. 27-61). New York: Zed Books.

Goldblatt, B., & Meintjes, S. (1999, June). *Women: One chapter in the history of South Africa? A critique of the Truth and Reconciliation Report.* Paper presented at The TRC: Commissioning the Past conference.

Gottschall, J. (2004). Explaining wartime rape. *Journal of Sex Research, 41*, 129-136.

Graybill, L. (2001). Gender and post-conflict resolution in South Africa and Rwanda. *Mind and Human Interaction, 12*, 261-277.

Human Rights Watch. (1995a). *The Human Rights Watch global report on women's human rights.* New York: Author.

Human Rights Watch. (1995b). *Violence against women in South Africa: The state response to domestic violence and rape.* New York: Author.

Human Rights Watch. (2004). *Deadly delay: South Africa's efforts to prevent HIV in survivors of sexual violence.* New York: Author. Retrieved July 24, 2009, from http://www.hrw.org/reports/2004/southafrica0304/southafrica0304.pdf

Jacobs, S., Jacobson, R., & Marchbank, J. (Eds.). (2000). *State of conflict: Gender, violence and resistance.* New York: Zed Books.

Jobson, M. (2005). *Women and the TRC: A perspective from Khulumani Support Group.* Retrieved July 24, 2009, from http://www.khulumani.net/

Jones, A. (1994). Gender and ethnic conflict in ex-Yugoslavia. *Ethnic and Racial Studies, 17*, 115-134.

Krog, A. (1998). *Country of my skull: Guilt, sorrow, and the limits of forgiveness in the new South Africa.* New York: Random House.

National Public Radio. (2005, January 7). *David Chu and Debby Tucker discuss the Pentagon's new sexual assault policies. All things considered.* Washington, DC: Author.

Nesiah, V. (2006). *Truth commissions and gender: Principles, policies, and procedures.* New York: International Center for Transitional Justice.

Nikolic-Ristanovic, V. (1996). War and violence against women. In J. Turpin & L. A. Lorentzen (Eds.), *The gendered new world order* (pp. 195-210). New York: Routledge.

Peterson, V. S., & Runyon, A. S. (1999). *Global gender issues* (2nd ed.). Boulder, CO: Westview Press.

Pettman, J. J. (1996). *Worlding women: A feminist international politics.* New York: Routledge Press.

Rayner, R. (1997, June 22). The warrior besieged. *New York Times Magazine,* p. 55.

Ross, F. (2003). *Bearing witness: Women and the Truth and Reconciliation Commission in South Africa.* London: Pluto Press.

Rubio-Marín, R. (2006). The gender of reparations: Setting the agenda. In R. Rubio-Marín (Ed.), *What happened to the women? Gender and reparations for human rights violations* (pp. 20-47). New York: Social Science Research Council.

Salzman, T. A. (1998). Rape camps as a means of ethnic cleansing: Religious, cultural, and ethical responses to rape victims in the former Yugoslavia. *Human Rights Quarterly, 20,* 348-378.

Sooka, Y. (2004, September). *Building peace through accountability: A comparative experience between South Africa and Sierra Leone.* Paper presented at Peace Needs Women and Women Need Justice: A Conference on Gender Justice in Post-Conflict Situations, New York. Retrieved from http://www.womenwarpeace.org/webfm_send/1506

South African Truth and Reconciliation Commission. (1998a). *Truth and Reconciliation Commission of South Africa report, Vol. 1.* Cape Town, South Africa: Juta Press.

South African Truth and Reconciliation Commission. (1998b.) *Truth and Reconciliation Commission of South Africa report, Vol. 4.* Cape Town, South Africa: Juta Press.

South African Truth and Reconciliation Commission. (1998c.) *Truth and Reconciliation Commission of South Africa report, Vol. 5.* Cape Town, South Africa: Juta Press.

Stiglemeyer, A. (1994). The rapes in Bosnia-Herzegovina. In A. Stiglemeyer (Ed.), *Mass rape: The war against women in Bosnia-Herzegovina* (pp. 82-169). Lincoln: University of Nebraska Press.

Turshen, M., & Twagiramariya, C. (Eds.). (1998). *What women do in wartime: Gender and conflict in Africa.* New York: Zed Books.

United Nations. (2005). *Disarmament, demobilization, reintegration (DDR) and stability in Africa.* (Conference Report). Retrieved July 24, 2009, from http://www.un.org/africa/osaa/reports/DDR%20Sierra%20Leone%20March%202006.pdf

U.N. Security Council. (2000). *United Nations Security Council Resolution 1325 on Women, Peace and Security* (S/REs/1325). New York: United Nations. Retrieved July 25, 2009, from http://www.peacewomen.org/un/sc/1325.html

World Bank. (2006). *Gender, justice, and truth commissions.* Washington, DC: Author.

Bio

Tristan Anne Borer is professor of government at Connecticut College, New London, Connecticut.

Name Index